Notable
Twentieth-Century
Pianists

Notable Twentieth-Century Pianists

A Bio-Critical Sourcebook
Volume 2, K–Z

John Gillespie
and Anna Gillespie

Bio-Critical Sourcebooks on Musical Performance

Greenwood Press
Westport, Connecticut • London

Library of Congress Cataloging-in-Publication Data

Gillespie, John.
    Notable twentieth-century pianists : a bio-critical sourcebook /
John Gillespie and Anna Gillespie.
       p.   cm.—(Bio-critical sourcebooks on musical performance,
ISSN 1069–5230)
    Includes bibliographical references and index.
    ISBN 0–313–25660–8 (set : alk. paper).—ISBN 0–313–29695–2 (vol.
1 : alk. paper).—ISBN 0–313–29696–0 (vol. 2 : alk. paper)
    1. Pianists—Biography. I. Gillespie, Anna. II. Title.
III. Series.
ML397.G45   1995
786.2′092′2—dc20
  [B]   95–9757

British Library Cataloguing in Publication Data is available.

Library of Congress Catalog Card Number: 95–9757
ISBN: 0–313–25660–8(set); 0–313–29695–2(v.1); 0–313–29696–0(v.2)
ISSN: 1069–5230

First published in 1995

Greenwood Press, 88 Post Road West, Westport, CT 06881
An imprint of Greenwood Publishing Group, Inc.

Printed in the United States of America

The paper used in this book complies with the
Permanent Paper Standard issued by the National
Information Standards Organization (Z39.48–1984).

10 9 8 7 6 5 4 3 2 1

Copyright Acknowledgment

Every reasonable effort has been made to trace the owners of copyright
materials in this book, but in some instances this has proven impossible.
The author and publisher will be glad to receive information leading to
more complete acknowledgments in subsequent printings of the book
and in the meantime extend their apologies for any omissions.

For our children . . .

And their children . . .

Contents

Photo Essay follows General Bibliography

Preface_____

This source book of notable pianists contains biographical data; style analyses (culled from reviews, recordings, articles, essays); pedagogical history and methods, when applicable; lists of selected references and reviews; and a representative discography.

Recordings, or lack of recordings, basically set the perimeters of the study. With few exceptions, some recordings are available by which to evaluate each pianist's performance; and, with careful, sensible listening, even the early acoustic discs, many of which have been reissued in CD format, will reveal characteristics of a pianist's style.

How were the pianists selected? A preliminary list was compiled from a questionnaire sent in 1986 to pianists and pedagogues in music conservatories and colleges throughout the United States. Each respondent supplied names of pianists that he or she would include among the 100 most significant pianists who have performed and recorded in the 20th century. We tabulated the results, including our own choices, then throughout eight years of library research and reams of correspondence, we added and deleted names.

We have tried to be as impartial and as "scientific" (if that word may be used in this context) as possible, but of course the final list of 100 pianists will not, could not possibly, please everyone. We excuse the omission of names from the current crop of impressive young pianists on the grounds that they have not been around long enough to acquire "notable" status.

Listening (recordings, recitals, concerts) has been a major part of the study from the very beginning, and we concentrated on trying to listen objectively. But it soon became evident that if we were to give a fair, objective appraisal of each pianist, we had to study reviews of performances throughout all the stages of a career and from as many diverse sources and as many different critics as possible. The process of first finding reviews, interviews and articles for each pianist, then weighing the contents (an ongoing project all through the study) was absolutely fascinating—and addictive! The diverse, highly individual, often eccentric personalities among these 100 pianists make for interesting reading. But the fascinating part has been discovering and comparing individual musical styles, musical approaches, practice methods, repertoire choices and attitudes toward the piano itself. Some pianists first work on technique and technical problems; others prefer to study the qualities of the music first. One will practice eight hours or more at a time, another only one or two hours. Some never practice on the day of a performance; others practice in the dressing room right up to the moment of walking onstage.

There are pianists who will play only works they feel very strongly about; others try to acquire as large a repertoire as possible. Some try to develop a personal "sound" that audiences will recognize as theirs every time they play; others avoid a recognizable sound. Some performers obviously have a wonderful time onstage; others are terrified. Some pianists refuse to play if the piano is not exactly right; other pianists take in stride whatever piano comes along on a tour.

Perhaps most fascinating of all was realizing that digesting so many reviews spread across a century inevitably created a naturally evolving critical process based on the critic's subjectivity (personal likes and dislikes, expectations, comments on past performances); the critic's qualifications (education, experience, writing skill); and how his or her critique compares with others of the same performance.

Working with so much material uncovered a multitude of conflicting facts. One example: In *Gramophone* of January 1991 we read that "the Chopin Etudes were not part of Bolet's repertoire." But in the May 1991 issue of *Gramophone* another writer says that Bolet played the Etudes regularly and programmed the complete Opus 25 set on a number of occasions. That discrepancy is but one of hundreds encountered during this project. By checking, rechecking, sifting and comparing data, we have done our best to uncover true facts and correct dates (nearly impossible) among all the myths and flowery prose surrounding many pianists, especially those from the past. All told, the results, we believe, are fair.

We have carefully noted sources and dates for all quoted reviews and have for the most part omitted the names of the critics. One reason for this omission was to avoid having the fame of the critic influence the reader. Another reason was that in such a large book there would be just too much namedropping. (Sometimes, however, an important concert or record review will appear in the Selected Reference section to each entry.) Selected reviews and sources for quoted reviews are identified by abbreviations explained in the Periodical and Newspaper Abbreviations list at the front of the book. Text references to items in the General Bibliography are likewise identified by abbreviations given for each bibliographical item. Orchestras in the discographies are frequently abbreviated: i. e., SO (Symphony Orchestra), PO (Philadelphia Orchestra), CO (Chamber Orchestra); FO (Festival Orchestra), RAI (Italian Radio Orchestra).

Compiling discographies has been difficult and frustrating. Record labels appear and disappear, seemingly almost from one month to another. Discs can change from one label to another. For example, Rosalyn Tureck's Bach

CDs, originally issued under the Albany label, are now distributed under the VAIA label. Since many companies will issue only a restricted number of a certain CD, it may be out of print by the time the next record catalogue appears.

By the time this work is published, many listed recordings may no longer be available through regular record outlets. However, often they can be obtained through stores specializing in hard-to-find items. To locate such items and also foreign releases not distributed in the United States, try the following sources:

USA releases:
Parnassus Records (914) 246-3332
56 Parnassus Lane
Saugerties, NY 12477

H & B Records Direct (800) 222-6872
2186 Jackson Keller-Dept. F
San Antonio, TX 78213

Rose Records (800) 955-7673
214 South Wabash Avenue
Chicago, IL 60604

Europe/Great Britain:
Harold Moores Records & Video
2 Great Marlborough St.
London W1V 1DE, Great Britain

MDT Mail Order
6 Old Blacksmiths Yard, Sadler Gate
Derby DE1 3PD, Great Britain

Tandy's Records, Ltd.
24 Islington Row, Birmingham
B15 1LJ, Great Britain

Another possibility is to locate an out-of-print item at libraries or at special archives such as:

Historical Sound Recordings Program
226 Sterling Morton Library
1603A Yale Station
New Haven, CT 06520

Phonograph Record Library
Woolworth Center of Musical Studies
Princeton University
Princeton, NJ 08540

International Piano Archives at Maryland
Music Library, Hornbake 3210
University of Maryland
College Park, MD 20740

Library of Congress
Recorded Sound Division
Music Division, Library of Congress
Washington, D. C., 20540

Rodgers and Hammerstein
Archives of Recorded Sound
The New York Public Library
111 Amsterdam Avenue
New York, NY 10023

Stanford Archive of Recorded Sound
Stanford University, The Knoll
Stanford, CA 94305

Discography listings and numbers come primarily from the Schwann Opus catalogue, Musical Heritage Society (a private record label with recordings not listed in Schwann) and the Gustafson Piano Library. Cassettes from the latter may be obtained on loan. Write to:

> Gustafson Piano Library
> Interlibrary Loans Officer
> John Bassett Memorial Library
> Bishop's University
> Lennoxville, Quebec, Canada J1M 1Z7

We have used principally the following record guides: *Fanfare*, *Gramophone*, *American Record Guide*, plus selected reviews from other sources. Most listings are CDs, identified by the number 2 appended to the record number (i.e., 6257-2) or the use of the letters CD. When a significant performance is available only in cassette or LP format, we have included it in our discography.

We have restricted most of our reference materials and reviews to articles in English, and have used hundreds of sources, principally *The New York Times* and *The Times* (London) and the periodical *Performing Arts* (1978–present, see Bibliog.), available in many libraries.

Some pianists have had societies established in their names:

Fondation Cziffra, 1 Place Saint-Pierre, 60300 Senlis, France
Emil Gilels Society, P. O. Box 22124, Carmel, CA 93922
The Glenn Gould Society, c/o Moesstraat 9f, 9717 JT Groningen, The Netherlands
International Percy Grainger Society, 7 Cromwell Place, White Plains, NY 10601
Association Clara Haskil, Case postale 234, CH-1800 Vevey 1, Switzerland
Société Paderewski, Centre Culturel, Place du Casino 1, CH-1110 Morges, Switzerland
Friends of Sviatoslav Richter, Low Warden Barns, Hexham NE46 4SN, Great Britain
Rachmaninoff Society, 5215 West 64th Terrace, Prairie Village, KS 66208

We did the research, writing and "word-processing" ourselves, none of which would have been nearly as complete without the efficient help of the many librarians who kindly responded to inquiries, pianists' agents who generously supplied information, and others who assisted in so many ways. We are very grateful to the pianists who graciously responded to our inquiries and to Mr. James Methuen-Campbell, whose books and articles have proven invaluable to our research. Also, special thanks must be given to the following:

Edwin Alan (Appian Publications
  & Recordings)
John Berrie (Friends of Sviatoslav
  Richter)

Bryan Crimp
Mrs. Gwendolyn Cutner
Michael Rolland Davis (Chesky
  Recordings)

Allan Evans   Fred Maroth (Music & Arts
Richard Fisher   Programs of America)
Shirley Freeman   Mrs. Fergus Pope
Mrs. Bice Horszowski   Pro Arte Productions
Mrs. Griselda Kentner   Dr. Raymond Warner
Wynfred Lyddane   Lou Waryncia

And, finally, we are grateful to *all* of the reviewers and critics, past and present, for their keen observations and analyses. In particular, we have greatly enjoyed reading and comparing the writings of Paula Adamick, Mark Adamo, Richard Aldrich, John Amis, Carl Apone, John Ardoin, Joseph Banowetz, Melinda Bargreen, Greta Beigel, Byron Belt, Gregor Benko, Karen Berger, Martin Bernheimer, Louis Biancolli, Alan Blyth, Hugh Canning, Scott Cantrell, Neville Cardus, Daniel Cariaga, Claudia Cassidy, Peter Catalano, Abram Chasins, Olin Chism, Joan Chissell, Robert Commanday, James Francis Cooke, Bryan Crimp, Will Crutchfield, Peter G. Davis, Wynne Delacoma, Olin Downes, David Dubal, Bob Doerschuk, Paul Driver, Jessica Duchen, Richard Dyer, Thor Eckert, Jr., Dean Elder, Susan Elliott, Raymond Ericson, Allan Evans, Hilary Finch, Henry Finck, Robert Finn, Josiah Fisk, Shirley Fleming, Alfred Frankenstein, Richard Freed, Rena Fruchter, Leslie Gerber, Harris Goldsmith, Noel Goodwin, Channing Gray, Albert Goldberg, Peter Goodman, Edward Greenfield, Paul Griffiths, John Gruen, Philip Hale, Max Harrison, A. M. Henderson, Donal Henehan, Derrick Henry, Paul Hertelendy, Maurice Hinson, Jan Holcman, Bernard Holland, Joseph Horowitz, Paul Hume, James Huneker, Stuart Isacoff, Speight Jenkins, Barbara Jepson, Rafael Kammerer, Nicholas Kenyon, Michael Kimmelmann, Irving Kolodin, Allan Kozinn, Herbert Kupferberg, Theodore W. Libbey, Jr., Joseph McLellan, Nancy Malitz, Donald Manildi, Robert C. Marsh, Lisa Marum, Robert Matthew-Walker, James Methuen-Campbell, Karen Monson, Carol Montparker, Bryce Morrison, James R. Oestreich, Robert Offergeld, Ates Orga, Richard Osborne, Tim Page, Malince Peris, Donna Perlmutter, Stephen Pettitt, Andrew L. Pincus, Andrew Porter, Michael Redmond, Howard Reich, John von Rhein, Alan Rich, Trevor Richardson, Kate Rivers, John Rockwell, John Rosenfield, Edward Rothstein, Peter Runkel, Harvey Sachs, Harold C. Schonberg, Marc Shulgold, Robert J. Silverman, Larry Sitsky, David Patrick Stearns, Mark Swed, Howard Taubman, Virgil Thomson, Anthony Tommasini, Marilyn Tucker, Lesley Valdes, Michael Walsh, Daniel Webster and Stephen Wigler.

Periodical and Newspaper Abbreviations_____

AA	Adelaide (Australia) Advertiser	ARSC	Association for Recorded Sound Collections Journal
ABJ	Akron (OH) Beacon Journal	AT	Anchorage (AK) Times
AC	Ashville (NC) Citizen		
ADN	Anchorage (AK) Daily News	BaS	Baltimore (MD) Sun
AEE	Aberdeen (Scotland) Evening Express	BDG	Berkeley (CA) Daily Gazette
AG	Arkansas Gazette (Little Rock)	BDN	Bangor (ME) Daily News
AJ	Atlanta (GA) Journal (-Constitution)	BE	Berkshire Eagle (Pittsfield, MA)
AJL	American Jewish Ledger	BEE	Bournemouth Evening Echo (England)
ALJ	Albuquerque (NM) Journal	BEN	Buffalo (Evening) News (NY)
AM	Asia Magazine	BET	Boston (MA) Evening Transcript
AMICA	Automatic Musical Instrument Collectors' Assn.	BG	Boston (MA) Globe
		BH	Boston (MA) Herald
AmM	American Music	BJ	Beacon Journal (Cleveland, OH)
APP	Asbury Park Press (Neptune, NJ)	BP	Boston (MA) Post
AR	Arizona Republic (Phoenix)	BPh	The Bulletin (Philadelphia)
ARG	American Record Guide	BS	Boston (MA) Sentinal
		BT	Belfast Telegraph (Ireland)

CA	Commercial Appeal (Memphis, TN)	CT	Chicago (IL) Tribune
CaT	Capitol Times (Madison, WI)	DC	Daily Camera (Boulder, CO)
CCC-T	Corpus Christi (TX) Caller-Times	DDN	Dayton (OH) Daily News
CD	Columbus (OH) Dispatch	DeDN	Detroit (MI) Daily News
		DeT	Detroit (MI) Times
CDJ	Chicago (IL) Daily Journal	DFP	Detroit (MI) Free Press
CDM	Charleston (SC) Daily Mail	DMN	Dallas (TX) Morning News
CDN	Chicago (IL) Daily News	DMR	Des Moines (IA) Register
CDR	CD Review	DN	Deseret News (Salt Lake City, UT)
CE	Cincinnati (OH) Enquirer	DNH	Daily News (Halifax, Nova Scotia)
CEA	Chicago (IL) Evening American	DNL	Daily News (Lebanon, PA)
CED	Columbus (Ohio) Evening Dispatch	DNLA	Daily News (Los Angeles)
CEP	Chicago (IL) Evening Post	DO	(Daily) Oklahoman (Oklahoma City)
CG	Charleston (SC) Gazette	DP	Denver (CO) Post
CH	Chronicle Herald (Halifax, Nova Scotia)	DT	Daily Telegraph (London)
CHE	Chicago (IL) Herald Examiner	DTH	Dallas (TX) Times Herald
CiP	Cincinnati Post		
C-J	Courier-Journal (Louisville, KY)	EP	Evening Post (Charleston, SC)
CL	Clavier	EPNZ	Evening Post (New Zealand)
C-L	Clarion-Ledger (Jackson, MS)	ES	Evening Sun (Baltimore, MD)
CLA	Classic (CD)	ESQ	Esquire
CNC	Charleston (SC) News & Courier	ET	Evening Times (Glasgow, Scotland)
CO	Charlotte (NC) Observer	Etude	Etude
CoP	Connecticut Post (Bridgeport)		
CP	Classical Pulse	Fan	Fanfare
CPD	Cleveland (OH) Plain Dealer	FB	Fresno (CA) Bee
		FJ	Flint (MI) Journal
CS	Columbia (SC) State	FLSS	Fort Lauderdale (FL) Sun/Sentinel
CSM	Christian Science Monitor	FT	Financial Times (London)
CST	Chicago (IL) Sun-Times		

FTU	Florida Times-Union (Jacksonville)		KCT	Kansas City (MO) Times
FWJG	(Fort Wayne) Journal-Gazette (IN)		KeCl	Keyboard Classics
			KeM	Keyboard Magazine
GBPG	Green Bay (WI) Press-Gazette		Key	Keynote (Magazine for the Musical Arts Including the Program Guide for WNCN 104 FM)
GH	Glasgow Herald (Scotland)		KJ	Knoxville (TN) Journal
GloM	The Globe and Mail (Toronto, Canada)		LADN	Los Angeles (CA) Daily News
GM	Guardian (Manchester, England)		LAHE	Los Angeles (CA) Herald Examiner
G-M	Gazette (Montreal)		LAM	L.A. Magazine
Gram	Gramophone		LAT	Los Angeles (CA) Times
GRP	Grand Rapids (MI) Press		LDN	London Daily News
GT	Gazette Telegraph (Colorado Springs, CO)		LF	*Le Figaro* (Paris)
GWN	Garnett Westchester Newspapers		LI	The Listener
			LIN	Long Island (NY) Newsday
HA	Herald American (Boston, MA)		LM	*Le Monde* (Paris)
HaC	Hartford (CT) Courant		LMP	London Morning Post
HB	Honolulu (Star-) Bulletin (HI)		MA	Musical America
HC	Houston (TX) Chronicle		MABR	Morning Advocate (Baton Rouge, LA)
HF	High Fidelity		MC	Musical Courier
HF-MA	Hi Fi/Musical America		MD	Michigan Daily
HKS	Hong Kong Stardard		MG	Montreal Gazette (Canada)
HP	Houston (TX) Post		MH	Miami (FL) Herald
HR	Hudson Revue		MiT	Minneapolis (Star and) Tribune (MN)
IHT	International Herald Tribune		MJ	Milwaukee (WI) Journal
IN	Indianapolis (IN) News		MJA	Montgomery (Journal &) Advertiser (AL)
IND	The Independent (London)		MM	Music and Musicians
IrT	Irish Times (Belfast)		MO	Musical Opinion
IS	Indianapolis (IN) Star		MoC	Morning Call (Allentown, PA)
IT	Indianapolis (IN) Times		MoT	Montclair (NJ) Times
JS	Journal & Star (Lincoln, NE)		MQ	Musical Quarterly
			MS	Milwaukee (WI) Sentinel
KCS	Kansas City (MO) Star		M-SH	Mail-Star (Halifax)

MT	Musical Times	OT	Oakland (CA) Tribune
MuJ	Music Journal	OV	Ovation
MuM	Music Magazine	OWH	Omaha (NE) World Herald
NAO	News and Observer (Raleigh NC)	PEB	Philadelphia (PA) Evening Bulletin
Nat	The Nation		
ND	Newsday (New York, NY)	PI	Philadelphia (PA) Inquirer
NDN	Newport (RI) Daily News	PJ	Providence (RI) Journal (-Bulletin)
NewY	New York	PL	Patriot Ledger (Pittsburgh, PA)
NHR	New Haven (CT) Register	PM	People Magazine
NM	New Mexican	PoJ	Poughkeepsie (NY) Journal
NO	National Observer		
NR	New Republic	PP	Pittsburgh (PA) Press
NW	Newsweek	PPG	(Pittsburgh) Post-Gazette (PA)
NY	New Yorker		
NYA	New York American	PPH	Portland (ME) Press Herald
NYCT	New York City Tribune		
NYDN	New York Daily News	PQ	Piano Quarterly
NYEM	New York Evening Mail	PS	Press-Scimitar (Memphis)
NYEP	New York Evening Post		
NYHT	New York Herald Tribune	P-S	Post-Standard (Syracuse, NY)
NYJA	New York Journal American	RDC	(Rochester) Democrat & Chronicle (NY)
NYP	New York Post		
NYS	New York Sun	RE	Reading (PA) Eagle/Times
NYT	New York Times		
NYTr	New York Tribune	RIR	Records in Review
NYW	New York World	RMN	Rocky Mountain News (Denver, CO)
NYWT	New York World-Telegram and Sun	RNL	Richmond (VA) News Leader
NZZ	*Neue Züriche Zeitung*		
		RR	Records and Recordings
OaR	Oak Ridger (TN)	R-S	Register-Star (Rockford, IL)
OC	Ottowa Citizen (Canada)		
OCR	Orange County Register (Santa Ana, CA)	RT	Richmond (VA) Times (Dispatch)
OP	Opus	RTU	(Rochester) Times-Union (NY)
ORE	The Oregonian (Portland)		
OrS	Orlando (FL) Sentinel	RTW-N	Roanoke (VA) Times & World-News
OS	Oregon Statesman (Salem)		

SBNP	Santa Barbara (CA) News-Press		TC	Tucson (AZ) Citizen
SCMP	South China Morning Post		TEN	Tennessean (Nashville)
			TET	Toronto Evening Telegram (Canada)
SDU	San Diego (CA) Union		Time	Time
S-E	Star-Eagle (Newark, NJ)		TL	The Times (London)
SFC	San Francisco (CA) Chronicle		TP	Times Picayune (New Orleans, LA)
SFE	San Francisco (CA) Examiner		TS	Toronto Star (Canada)
			TT	Toronto Telegram (Canada)
SFR	Santa Fe (NM) Reporter			
SH-J	Syracuse (NY) Herald-Journal		TU	Times Union (Rochester, NY)
SJM	San Jose (CA) Mercury		TUA	Times-Union (Albany, NY)
SJS	San Juan Star (Puerto Rico)		TWaI	The World and I
SL	Standard (London)			
S-L	Star-Ledger (Newark, NJ)		USA	USA Today
SLGD	St. Louis (MO) Globe-Democrat		V-P	Virginian-Pilot (Norfolk)
SLPD	St Louis (MO) Post Dispach		VV	Village Voice (New York, NY)
SLT	(Salt Lake) Tribune (UT)		WDT	Worcester (MA) Daily Telegram (and Gazette)
SM	Scotsman (Edinburgh)			
SMH	Sydney Morning Herald		WE	Wichita (KS) Eagle (-Beacon)
SMU	Springfield (MA) Morning Union		WEJ	Wilmington (DE) Evening Journal
SN	Sunday News (New York, NY))		WEP	Worcester (MA) Evening Post
SP	Spectator (Raleigh, NC)			
SPI	Seattle (OR) Post Intelligencer		WG	Westminister Gazette
			WP	Washington (DC) Post
SPPP	Saint Paul (MN) Pioneer Press Dispatch		WS	Washington (DC) Star
			WSJ	Wall Street Journal (New York, NY)
SPT	St. Petersburg (FL) Times		W-SJ	Winston-Salem Journal (NC)
SR	Saturday Review			
ST	Seattle (WA) Times		WS-N	Washington Star-News
STL	Sunday Times (London)		WT	Washington (DC) Times
StR	Stereo Review		W-T	World Telegram
SU	Sacramento (CA) Union		WWD	Women's Wear Daily
T-A	Times-Argus (Montpellier, VT)		YO	Yorkshire Observer (England)
TB	Toledo (OH) Blade			

General Bibliography———————

A. BOOKS

Abd/Bla   Abdul, Raoul. *Blacks In Classical Music*. New York: Dodd, Mead and Company, 1977.

Ald/Con   Aldrich, Richard. *Concert Life in New York 1902–1923*. Freeport, New York: Books for Libraries Press, 1971(1941).

Ali/Pia   Alink, Gustav A. *Piano Competitions: A Comprehensive Directory of National and International Piano Competitions*. Den Haag: CIP-Gegevens Koninklijke Bibliotheek, 1990.

Bac/Pia   Bacon, Ernst. "Pianists Then and Now." *Clavier*, Nov 1981, pp. 22–25. Brief recollections of Paderewski, Carreño, d'Albert, Grainger, Gabrilowitsch, Bauer, Hofmann, de Pachmann, Godowsky, Lhévinne, Backhaus, Rachmaninoff.

Bak/Bio   *Baker's Biographical Dictionary of Musicians*. Seventh Edition, rev. Nicolas Slonimsky. New York: Schirmer Books. 1984.

Ben/For   Bennett, Joseph. *Forty Years of Music*. London: Methuen and Co., 1908.

Bie/His   Bie, Oscar. *A History of the Pianoforte and Pianoforte Players*, trans. E. E. Kellett and E. W. Naylor. New York: Da Capo Press, 1966 (1899).

Bla/Gra   Blaukopf, Kurt. *Les Grands Virtuoses*, traduit de l'Allemand par Jean–Claude Salel. Paris: Editions Corrêa, 1955.

Bro/Mas   Brook, Donald. *Masters of the Keyboard*. London: Rockliff, 1947.

Bro/Mod   Brower, Harriette. *Modern Masters of the Keyboard*. New York: Books for Libraries Press, 1969 (1926).

Bro/Par   Brody, Elaine. *Paris: The Musical Kaleidoscope 1870–1925*. New York: George Braziller, 1987.

Bro/Pia   Brower, Harriette. *Piano Mastery*. New York: Frederick A. Stokes Company, 1915.

Bro/PiS   Brower, Harriette. *Piano Mastery*. Second Series. New York:
             Frederick A. Stokes Company, 1917.
Bül/Br   Bülow, Hans von. *Briefe*. Leipzig: Druck und Verlag von
             Breitkopf und Härtel, 1908, 7 volumes.
Bül/Let   Bülow, Hans von. *Letters*, New York: Vienna House, 1972.
Cal/MG   Calvocoressi, M. D. *Musicians Gallery*. London: Faber and Faber
             Limited, 1933.
Cal/Mus   Calvocoressi, M. D. *Music and Ballet*. London: Faber and Faber,
             1934.
Car/Del   Cardus, Neville. *The Delights of Music*. London: Victor Gollancz
             Ltd., 1966.
Car/Ful   Cardus, Neville. *Full Score*. London: Cassell, 1970.
Car/Tal   Cardus, Neville. *Talking Of Music*. London: Collins, 1957.
Cat/Mus   *Catalog of Music-Rolls for the Duo-Art Reproducing Piano*. New
             York: The Aeolian Company, 1924.
Cen/Lib   *Century Library of Music*, ed. Ignace Jan Paderewski. New York:
             The Century Co., 1900. 20 vols.
Cha/Gia   Chapin, Victor. *Giants of the Keyboard*. Philadelphia: J. G.
             Lippincott Co., 1967.
Cha/Spe   Chasins, Abram. *Speaking of Pianists*. New York: Alfred A.
             Knopf, 1958.
Coh/Rec   Cohn, Arthur. *Recorded Classical Music*. New York: Schirmer
             Books, 1982.
Con/Bak   *The Concise Baker's Biographical Dictionary of Musicians*. Eighth
             Edition. New York: Schirmer Books, 1994.
Coo/Gre   Cooke, James Francis. *Great Men and Famous Musicians on The
             Art of Music*. Philadelphia: Theo. Presser Co., 1925.
Coo/GrP   Cooke, James Francis. *Great Pianists on Piano Playing*. New
             York: AMS Press, Inc., 1976 (1917).
Cur/Bio   *Current Biography*. New York: H. W. Wilson, 1940–.
Dan/Con   Daniels, Robin. *Conversations With Cardus*. Foreword by Yehudi
             Menuhin. London: Victor Gollancz Ltd., 1976.
Dic/Am   *Dictionary of American Biography*. New York: Charles Scribner's
             Sons, 1928–1936. 20 volumes, 2 supplementary volumes.
Doe/Tra   Doerschuk, Bob. "Tradition & Innovation in Bach Keyboard
             Performance." *Keyboard*, March 1985, pp. 13–16, 78–84.
Dow/Oli   Downes, Olin. *Olin Downes on Music*. New York: Simon &
             Schuster, 1957.
Dub/Eve   Dubal, David. *Evenings with Horowitz*. New York: Birch Lane
             Press, 1991.
Dub/Ref   Dubal, David. *Reflections from the Keyboard*. New York:
             Summit Books, 1984.
Eld/Pia   Elder, Dean. *Pianists at Play*. Evanston: The Instrumentalist
             Company, 1982.
Ewe/Li   Ewen, David. *Living Musicians*. New York: The H. W. Wilson
             Co., 1940.

Ewe/Li2   Ewen, David. *Living Musicians*, First Supplement. New York: The H. W. Wilson Co., 1957.

Ewe/Me   Ewen, David. *Men and Women Who Make Music.* New York: Merlin Press, 1949.

Ewe/Mu   Ewen, David. *Musicians Since 1900.* New York: The H. W. Wilson Co., 1978.

Ffr/Mus   Ffrench, Florence. *Music and Musicians in Chicago.* New York: Da Capo Press, 1979 (c. 1899).

Fin/My   Finck, Henry T. *My Adventures in the Golden Age of Music.* New York: Funk and Wagnalls Company, 1926.

Fin/Suc   Finck, Henry T. *Success in Music and How it is Won.* New York: Charles Scribners's Sons, 1909.

Ful/Doo   Fuller-Maitland, J. A. *A Door-Keeper of Music.* London: John Murray, 1929.

Gai/Liv   Gaines, James R. *The Lives of the Piano.* New York: Harper Colophon, 1983.

Gai/Mus   Gaisberg, F. W. *The Music Goes Round.* New York: The Macmillan Company, 1942.

Gav/Vin   Gavoty, Bernard. *Vingt Grands Interprètes.* Lausanne: Les Editions Rencontre, 1966.

Gel/Mus   Gelatt, Roland. *Music-Makers.* New York: Alfred A. Knopf, 1953.

Ger/Fam   Gerig, Reginald. *Famous Pianists and Their Technique.* Washington, New York: Robert B. Luce, Inc., 1974.

Gil/Boo   Gill, Dominic, ed. *The Book of the Piano.* Ithaca, New York: Cornell University Press, 1981.

Gol/Jou   Gollancz, Victor. *Journey Towards Music.* New York: E. P. Dutton and Company, Inc., 1965.

Gra/Bib   Gray, Michael and Gerald D. Gibson. *Bibliography of Discographies*, Vol. 1. New York: R. R. Bowker Company, 1977.

Gra/Cla   Gray, Michael. *Classical Music Discographies. 1976–1988.* Westport, CT: Greenwood Press, 1989.

Gra/Goo   *The Gramophone Good CD Guide.* Harrow: General Gramophone Publications Limited, 1994, 1995.

Gra/Jub   *Gramophone Jubilee Book*, ed. Roger Wimbush. Harrow: Gramophone Publications Limited, 1973.

Gui/Com   *Guide to Competitions.* New York: Concert Artists Guild, 1989.

Hag/Dec   Haggin, B. H. *A Decade of Music.* New York: Horizon Press, 1973.

Hag/Mus   Haggin, B. H. *Music in the Nation.* New York: William Sloane Associates, Inc., 1949.

Hag/Thi   Haggin, B. H. *Thirty-Five Years of Music.* New York: Horizon Press, 1974.

Ham/Lis   Hamilton, David. *The Listener's Guide to Great Instrumentalists.* New York: Facts on File, Inc., 1982.

Han/Vie   Hanslick, Edouard. *Vienna's Golden Years of Music 1850–1900*, trans. Henry Pleasants III. London: Victor Gollancz, 1951.

Hei/Rhy   Heiles, William. *Rhythmic Nuance in Chopin Performances Recorded by Moriz Rosenthal, Ignaz Friedman, and Ignaz Jan Paderewski.* D.M.A. diss., University of Illinois, 1964.

Hen/Pre   Henderson, W. J. *Preludes and Studies.* New York: Longmans, Green & Co., 1891.

Her/Cla   Herring, Peter. *Classical Music on Compact Disc.* New York: Harmony Books, 1986.

Hor/Ivo   Horowitz, Joseph. *The Ivory Trade: Piano Competitions and the Business of Music.* Boston: Northeastern University Press, 1991.

Hun/Old   Huneker, James. *Old Fogy.* Philadelphia: Theodore Presser Co., 1913.

Hun/Ste   Huneker, James. *Steeplejack.* New York: Charles Scribner's Sons, 1918, 1920 (2 volumes in 1).

Hun/Uni   Huneker, James. *Unicorns.* New York: Charles Scribners's Sons, 1917.

Hun/Var   Huneker, James. *Variations.* New York: Charles Scribner's Sons, 1921.

IWWM   *International Who's Who in Music and Musician's Directory*, Eleventh edition. Cambridge, England: International Who's Who in Music, 1988.

Jac/Rev   Jacobson, Robert. *Reverberations.* New York: William Morrow and Co., 1974.

Kai/Gre   Kaiser, Joachim. *Great Pianists of our Time*, trans. D. Woodridge and George Unwin. London: George Allen and Unwin, Ltd., 1971.

Kau/Art   Kaufmann, Helen, and Eva vB. Hansl. *Artists in Music of Today.* New York: Grosset and Dunlap, 1933.

Keh/Pia   Kehler, George. *The Piano in Concert.* Metuchen, N.J.: The Scarecrow Press, Inc., 1982. 2 volumes.

Kir/Pab   Kirk, H. L. *Pablo Casals*, New York: Holt, Rinehart and Winston, 1974.

Kol/Que   Kolodin, Irving. *In Quest of Music.* New York: Doubleday and Co., Inc., 1980.

Lah/Fam   Lahee, Henry C. *Famous Pianists of Today and Yesterday*, Boston: L. C. Page and Co., 1900.

Lan/Mus   Langford, Samuel. *Musical Criticisms*, ed. Neville Cardus. London: Oxford University Press, 1929.

Lam/Mem   Lamond, Frederic. *The Memoirs of Frederic Lamond.* Foreword by Ernest Newman, Introduction and Postscript by I. T. Lamond. Glasgow: William MacLellan,1949.

Loe/Men   Loesser, Arthur. *Men, Women and Pianos.* New York: Simon & Schuster, 1954.

Lyl/Dic   Lyle, Wilson. *A Dictionary of Pianists.* New York: Schirmer Books, 1984.

Mac/Gre   Mach, Elyse. *Great Pianists Speak for Themselves*. New York:
           Dodd, Mead and Co., 1980.
Mac/Gr2   Mach, Elyse. *Great Pianists Speak for Themselves*. Volume 2.
           New York: Dodd, Mead and Co., 1988. Both Mach volumes
           are available together in a Dover (1991) paperback.
Mar/Gre   Marcus, Adele. *Great Pianists Speak*. New Jersey: Paganiniana,
           1979.
Met/Cat   Methuen-Campbell, James. *Catalogue of Recordings by Classical
           Pianists*. Volume I (Pianists born to 1871). Chipping
           Norton: Disco Epsom Limited, 1984.
Met/Cho   Methuen-Campbell, James. *Chopin Playing*. From the Composer
           to the Present Day. New York: Taplinger Publishing
           Company, 1981.
MGG   *Die Musik in Geschichte und Gegenwart*. Kassel und Basel:
           Bärenreiter Verlag, 1949-68. 14 volumes plus supplement.
Moh/My   Mohr, Franz (with Edith Schaeffer). *My Life with the Great
           Pianists*. Grand Rapids: Baker Book House, 1992.
Moo/Am   Moore, Gerald. *Am I Too Loud?: A Musical Autobiography*.
           New York: The Macmillan Company, 1962.
Neu/Art   Neuhaus, Heinrich. *The Art of Piano Playing*, trans. K. A.
           Leibovitch. London: Barrie and Jenkins, 1973.
New/GrA   *The New Grove Dictionary of American Music*, ed. H. Wiley
           Hitchcock and Stanley Sadie. London: Macmillan Press
           Limited, 1986. 4 volumes.
New/Gro   *The New Grove Dictionary of Music and Musicians*, ed. Stanley
           Sadie. London: Macmillan Publishers Limited, 1980. 20
           volumes.
Nie/Mei   Niemann, Walter. *Meister des Klaviers*. Berlin: Schuster &
           Loeffler, 1921.
Noy/Pia   Noyle, Linda. *Pianists on Playing*. Metuchen, N. J.: The
           Scarecrow Press, 1987.
O'N/Gra   O'Neil, Thomas. *The Grammys for the Record*. New York:
           Penguin Books, 1993.
Pau/Dic   Pauer, E. *A Dictionary of Pianists and Composers for the
           Pianoforte*. London: Novello, Ewer and Co., 1895.
Pay/Cel   Payne, Albert (pseud. A. Ehrlich). *Celebrated Pianists Past and
           Present*. London: Harold Reeves, n.d.
Pen/Gui   *The Penguin Guide To Compact Discs*. London: Penguin Books.
           Published variously as *The Complete Penguin Stereo Record
           and Cassette Guide, New Penguin Guide to Compact Discs and
           Cassettes, Penguin Guide to Compact Discs, Penguin Guide
           to Compact Discs, Cassettes and LPs*. 1984, 1986, 1988,
           1990.
Per/Art   *Performing Arts Index* (Review of the Arts). NewsBank, Inc.,
           1975–.
Ran/Kon   Range, Hans-Peter. *Die Konzertpianiste der Gegenwart*. Lahr/
           Schwarzwald: Moritz Schauenburg Verlag, 1966.

Rat/Cle   Rattalino, Piero. *Da Clementi a Pollini.* Duecento anni con i grandi pianisti. Milano: Ricordi/Giunti Martello, 1983.

Reu/Gre   Reuter, Florizel von. *Great People I Have Known.* Waukesha: Freeman Printing Co., 1961.

Rub/MyM   Rubinstein, Arthur. *My Many Years.* New York: Alfred A. Knopf, 1980.

Rub/MyY   Rubinstein, Arthur. *My Young Years.* New York: Alfred A. Knopf, 1973.

Sac/Vir   Sachs, Harvey. *Virtuoso.* New York: Thames and Hudson, Inc., 1982.

Sah/Not   Sahling, Herbert. *Notate zur Pianistik.* Aufsätze sowjetischer Klavierpädagogen und Interpreten. Leipzig: VEB Deutscher Verlag für Musik, 1976.

Sal/Fam   Saleski, Gdal. *Famous Musicians of Jewish Origin.* New York: Bloch Publishing Company, 1949.

Sch/Fac   Schonberg, Harold C. *Facing the Music.* New York: Summit Books, 1981.

Sch/Glo   Schonberg, Harold. C. *The Glorious Ones.* New York: Times Books, 1985.

Sch/Gre   Schonberg, Harold C. *The Great Pianists* (revised and updated). New York: Simon & Schuster, Inc., 1987.

Sch/My   Schnabel, Artur. *My Life And Music.* New York: St. Martin's Press, 1961.

Sha/Lon   Shaw, Bernard. *London Music in 1888–89 As Heard by Corno Di Bassetto.* London: Constable and Company Limited, 1937.

Sha/Mus   Shaw, Bernard. *Music In London 1890–94.* London: Constable and Company Limited, 1932. 3 volumes.

Sit/Cla   Sitsky, Larry. *The Classical Reproducing Piano Roll.* A Catalogue-Index. Westport, Connecticut: Greenwood Press, 1990. 2 volumes.

Sor/Aro   Sorabji, Kaikhosru. *Around Music.* London: The Unicorn Press, 1932.

Tho/MRL   Thomson, Virgil. *Music Right and Left.* New York: Henry Holt and Company, 1951.

Tho/Mus   Thomson, Virgil. *Music Reviewed 1940–1954.* New York: Vintage Books, 1967.

Tho/MuS   Thomson, Virgil. *The Musical Scene.* New York: Alfred A. Knopf, 1947.

Tho/Pia   Thompson, Wendy, with Fanny Waterman. *Piano Competition: The Story of the Leeds.* London: Faber and Faber, 1991.

Ung/Key   Unger-Hamilton, Clive. *Keyboard Instruments.* Minneapolis: Central Data Publishing, 1981.

Wal/The   Walter, Bruno. *Theme and Variations*, trans. James A. Galston. New York: Alfred A. Knopf, 1959.

Wod/Evi   Wodehouse, Artis S. *Evidence of 19th Century Piano Performance Practice Found in Recordings of Chopin's Nocturne, op. 15,*

	no. 2, Made by Pianists born before 1910. D.M.A. diss., Stanford, 1977.
Woo/My	Wood, Sir Henry. *My Life of Music.* London: Victor Gollancz Ltd., 1938.
WW	*Who's Who.* New York: St. Martin's Press, 1994.
WWAM	*Who's Who in American Music.* Classical Second Edition. New York: R. R. Bowker Company, 1985.
WWF	*Who's Who in France.* Paris: Editions Jacques Lafitte, 1990.
WWM	*Who's Who in Music and Musicians' Directory.* Cambridge: Melrose Press, 1992–93.
Zil/Rus	Zilberquit, Mark, Dr. *Russia's Great Modern Pianists.* Neptune, New Jersey: Paganiniana Publications, 1983.

B. ARTICLES

Bacon, Ernst. "Pianists Then and Now." *Clavier,* Nov 1981, pp. 22–25.

Brower, Harriette. "American Women Pianists: Their Views and Achievements." *Musical America,* 26 Oct 1918, pp. 18–19.

———. "Golden Age of Piano Playing." *Musical America,* 5 May 1917, p. 23.

———. "How The Master's Touch Transforms." *Musical America,* 12 July 1919, p. 10. (Bauer, Paderewski, Novaes).

———. "Principles of Piano Study: Laying the Right Foundation—Finger Action—The Best Sort of Music for Study Purposes—Questions of Memorizing." *Musical America,* 29 July 1916, p. 23.

———. "Recovering The Greater Chopin." *Musical America,* 23 Nov 1918, pp. 44–45.

———. "Vital Points in Piano Playing: Authoritative Views on Rhythm and Tone Color." *Musical America,* 26 Sept 1914, p. 11.

———. "Vital Points in Piano Playing: An Epitome of Expert Opinions on 'How to Memorize'." *Musical America,* 1 Aug 1914, p. 9.

———. "Vital Points in Piano Playing: Hints from Leading Authorities on Hand Position, Finger Action and Artistic Touch. *Musical America,* 18 July 1914, p. 9.

———. "Vital Points in Piano Playing: Noted Performers and Teachers Supply Advice on 'How to Practice'." *Musical America,* 25 July 1914, p. 9.

Chase, Gilbert. "Five Volumes of Memoirs Make Absorbing Reading." *Musical America,* 10 Nov 1938, pp. 13, 25. (Paderewski, Busoni, Clara Clemens Gabrilowitsch.)

Chasins, Abram. "The Grand Manner." *Saturday Review,* 24 Sept 1955, pp. 40, 42.

Clark, Sedgwick. "Who Wants To Be Another Horowitz?" *Village Voice,* 20 March 1978, pp. 36–37. (Argerich, Ax, Kovacevich, Lupu, Pollini, Serkin)

Crutchfield, Will. "The Lure of History and Interpretive Power." *New York Times,* 25 March 1990, sec. 2, p. 81. A suggested basic library of historic recordings on compact discs from instrumental masters of the past.

Doerschuk, Bob. "Tradition & Innovation In Bach Keyboard Performance." *Keyboard*, March 1985, pp. 13–16, 78–84. (Busoni, E. Fischer, Gould, Tureck.)

Downes, Olin. "Pianists Past and Present—Changes in Public Taste." *New York Times*, 16 May 1926, sec 8, p. 6.

Ericson, Raymond. "Many and Good." *New York Times*, 7 June 1964, sec. 10, p. 18. (Ashkenazy, Badura-Skoda, Brailowsky, Ogdon, Richter, Rosen, Rubinstein.)

"Famous Russian Pianists on the Art of Piano Study." *Etude*, March 1913, p. 171.

Goldberg, Albert. "Pianists: Victories, Vagaries." *Los Angeles Times*, 8 April 1979, pp. 72–73. (Hofmann, Rubinstein, J. Lhévinne.)

Goldsmith, Harris. "Record Reviews." *ARSC Journal*, Vol. 17, nos. 1–3, 1985, pp. 142–155. (Backhaus, Cortot, Ed. Fischer, Gieseking, Haskil.)

Hart, Philip. "The Pianist of Now and Then." *Musical Courier*, July 1961, pp. 48–51.

"Has the Art of the Piano Reached Its Zenith or Is It Capable of Further Development." *Etude*, Feb 1919, pp. 79–80; March 1919, pp. 139–140. Conference with Bauer, Grainger, Jonas, Gabrilowitsch, Hofmann, Lambert, Ganz, Hutcheson, Stojowski.

Henahan, Donal. "First the Lucky Break—and Then?" *New York Times*, 24 Jan 1988, sec. 2, p. 21. (Cliburn, Feltsman, Watts.)

Holland, Bernard, and Michael Kimmelman. "Critics Select Favorites from 87's Classical Crop." *New York Times*, 6 Dec 1987, sec. 8, pp. 29-30. (Horszowski, Kapell, Schiff.)

Husarik, Stephen. "Piano Rolls: Untapped Technical Resources." *Clavier*, April 1986, pp. 14–16.

Kammerer, Rafael. "Golden Age of Pianists Preserved on Old Records." *Musical America*, Feb 1957, pp. 28–29, 122, 172–173.

———. "Rosenthal, Cortot, and other old masters." *American Record Guide*, Nov 1957, pp. 80–81, 120.

Methuen-Campbell, James. "Leschetizky pupils on record." *Records and Recording*, Aug 1980, pp. 21–22.

———. "Polish pianists on record." Records and Recording, Jan 1979, pp. 42–45.

Michener, Charles. "Pianists—A Golden Age." *Newsweek*, 23 Jan 1978, pp. 70–72.

Morrison, Bryce. "The Russian Piano School." *Gramophone*, Feb 1993, pp. 31–32.

"Piano Concertos from Mozart to Prokofiev." *Gramophone*, 15 July 1961, p. 11. (Arrau, Cliburn, Cortot, Rubinstein.)

Schonberg, Harold C. "Great Pianists From the Past Re-Emerge." *New York Times*, 17 June 1990, pp. 23, 26. (Hess, Moiseiwitsch.)

Thompson, Oscar. "Where Are the Prodigies of Yesteryear." *Musical America*, 3 Jan 1920, pp. 5–6.

Cyprien Katsaris (ICM Artists)

Louis Kentner

Zoltan Kocsis (ICM Artists)

Stephan Kovacevich (Photo Courtesy of Sophie Baker)

Lili Kraus (Photo Courtesy of James J. Kriegsmann)

Ruth Laredo (Christian Steiner)

ERRATA

Gillespie, *Notable Twentieth-Century Pianists*
Volume 2: K-Z

In the photo essay (following page xxviii) for this volume, two photos are incorrectly captioned. The photo titled Rudolf Serkin should read Solomon, and the photo titled Solomon should read Rudolf Serkin.

Alicia de Larrocha (Christian Steiner)

Josef Lhévinne

DINU LIPATTI

his last recital

FESTIVAL INTERNATIONAL DE BESANÇON
September 16, 1950

Dinu Lipatti (Angel Records)

Radu Lupu (Photo Courtesy of Laura Lynn Miner)

Dame Moura Lympany (Credit: Christian Thompson)

Ivan Moravec (*IMG Artists*)

Guiomar Novaes

Ignace Paderewski (Courtesy Société Paderewski)

Murray Perahia (Frank Salomon Associates)

Ivo Pogorelich (ICM Artists)

András Schiff (Shirley Kirshbaum & Associates, photo courtesy of Laura Lynn Miner)

Peter Serkin (Photo Courtesy of Regina Touhey)

Rudolf Serkin

Solomon (Courtesy Bryan Crimp)

André Watts (Photo Courtesy of Arnold Newman, Courtesy *IMG Artists*)

Earl Wild (Courtesy Michael Rolland Davis)

Notable
Twentieth-Century
Pianists

KAPELL, WILLIAM: b. New York, New York, 20 September 1922; d. Half Moon Bay, California, 29 October 1953.

> Willy was a pianist first, last and always. You had to understand that. There was in him the relentless, terrible and wonderful compulsion of genius. He had to play. He had to play better than anyone else in the world. This was not vanity. It was nothing so cheap, so ephemeral, so unworthy. It was an ever deepening sense of responsibility. It was humility in the face of music.
>
> Claudia Cassidy (*Chicago Tribune*, 30 October 1953)

William Kapell died in an airplane crash more than 40 years ago. He was very young, only 31, and his concert career had been so short, barely a decade. Yet in that brief time his piano performances made such a significant impact on the world of music that obituary tributes depict Kapell as one of the greatest pianists America had produced. For instance, the discerning Virgil Thomson of the *New York Herald Tribune* wrote, "Among musicians of his generation William Kapell . . . was one of the great ones. . . . In one decade he had won a worldwide audience. At the beginning of a second he was recognized as a master to be taken seriously in the great piano repertory."

In the years following his death Kapell's recordings went out of print. Occasionally a pirated record or a tape made privately at one of his concerts would appear. And there were also some brief biographical mentions in music books/dictionaries. In 1963 Harold Schonberg included Kapell in his book *The*

Great Pianists, and *Grove's Dictionary of Music and Musicians* always retained the entry on Kapell; but for the most part, his name faded into public memory.

Despite this neglect, Kapell was never really a "lost" pianist. On the contrary, he had become a legend to those who could actually remember his brilliant piano playing and to those who knew his recordings. And undoubtedly they are responsible for all the attention paid to Kapell in the last decade. A quarter-century after Kapell's untimely death, Michael Sellers, a pianist inspired by Kapell's recordings, established (1978) the William Kapell Piano Foundation for Contemporary Music and Musicians. In 1979 the Naumburg Foundation dedicated its International Competition to Kapell's memory. On 26 October 1983 eight pianists, including four who knew Kapell personally, played a Kapell Memorial Concert at The Symphony Space in New York City, and each wrote a tribute to Kapell that was printed in the booklet distributed at the concert.

On 18 July 1985, Dr. Anna Lou Kapell Dehavenon, Kapell's widow, gave a Kapell collection (diaries, letters, photographs, programs, reviews, recordings, memorabilia, clippings) to the International Piano Archives at the University of Maryland, College Park; and the following year the IPAM published *William Kapell Remembered*, a guide to their exhibition of Kapell's life and career. In 1986 the University of Maryland International Piano Festival and Competition was renamed The University of Maryland International William Kapell Piano Competition and Festival. There are new issues of Kapell recordings, and in the 1980s music magazines published at least half a dozen articles about Kapell (see Ref.). And in 1992 the IPAM published Tim Page's *William Kapell: A Documentary Life History of the American Pianist*—immensely informative and presented in an engaging, innovative format. William Kapell will definitely be remembered.

Nothing in his immediate background explains his musical genius. His father Hyman (Harry) Kapell (a New Yorker of Spanish-Russian ancestry) and his mother (Edith Mouletski [Wolfsohn] of Polish descent) owned a bookstore in Manhattan. They were not musicians, and there is never a suggestion that Kapell was an infant prodigy. He had some piano lessons at about age eight, simply because his parents believed all children should study music, but since he had no interest in practicing, they stopped the lessons. At about age 10 something rekindled his interest. He asked for more piano lessons, and this time they took him to Dorothy Anderson LaFollette, a well-known teacher. Recognizing Kapell's innate talent, she immediately started him on three private lessons a week at her home. He progressed so rapidly that only six weeks later he was one of a group of students, chosen from various settlement schools, to play for pianist Jose Iturbi and be rewarded with a turkey dinner at the Iturbi apartment.

LaFollette worked with Kapell until he was 16 years old. Generous and painstaking, she frequently extended his lessons to three or four hours. She allowed him to practice at her home whenever he liked, and in 1935 she even took him along on a visit to her mother in La Jolla, California, where she continued his lessons and arranged his first piano recital—at a beach hotel named *Casa de Mañana*. LaFollette also arranged for Kapell to play for Rosina and Josef Lhévinne, her own teachers, and for Artur Rubinstein. (For many years Rubinstein and Kapell would get together to play for each other and exchange ideas. Details of their longtime, sometimes stormy, friendship can be found in Lowenthal, "Memories.") Most important, LaFollette laid the groundwork for Kapell's brilliant technique; and, not least, under her care the boy who once refused to practice turned into an inexhaustible, almost compulsive practicer.

In 1936 (Kapell was then attending the Columbia Grammar School) LaFollette took him to play for Olga Samaroff. One story says that Kapell himself had requested a change of teachers, but in her *Etude* article Samaroff explains that LaFollette brought Kapell to her because at that stage "his untamed qualities" were beyond LaFollette's control. "I realized just what a challenge it would be to educate such a temperamental youngster," wrote Samaroff, "but I recognized his talent at once and decided to accept him. He was awarded a scholarship with me at the Philadelphia Conservatory of Music, and so began a ten-year association with the most gifted, lovable, unpredictable, often inspiring, sometimes exasperating and altogether unique member of my large musical family." (Samaroff)

"Madame" Samaroff was the greatest musical influence of Kapell's life. Her lessons rarely touched on technical details or how to use the arms and hands. She did insist that the student pay strict attention to all indications made by the composer. "Then came interpretative suggestions, never as blueprints for performance but as aids in stimulating the student's own imagination. To get sonority in a Bach organ fugue, she would ask you to imagine yourself hearing the work in a great cathedral, full of echoes, hollows, and reverberations of tone. Then she would ask you to try to duplicate such a tone on the piano. When she wanted rich, full tone in a passage, she would write 'red-blooded' into the score." (Kapell)

Her goal with the gifted Kapell was to give him the basic musicianship that would enable him to handle *all* styles with authority, meanwhile retaining his striking individuality; in other words, allow him to mature through guided self-development. In an article for *Etude* (Feb 1954), Samaroff wrote: "Being constantly thrown on his own, but with compromising demands on my part for sound musicianship, and a vigorous development of tonal and technical means, Kapell acquired the independent interpretative insight and artistic *self-discipline* which has enabled him to curb his fiery temperament and reduce the musical exaggerations of his boyhood days to a point where all the intensity of his artistic nature can serve the re-creation of a composition without damage to the score." Later on (1948) Kapell had some coaching (on Mozart and Schubert) from Artur Schnabel.

In 1940 Kapell received a fellowship to continue his studies with Samaroff at the Juilliard Graduate School. That same year he won the Philadelphia Orchestra's Youth Contest, and on 10 February 1940 redeemed his prize—a performance of the Saint-Saëns Concerto No. 3 in G Minor with Eugene Ormandy conducting the orchestra. Kapell played so well that he was invited to perform at Robin Hood Dell that July, and on that occasion he played the Beethoven Concerto No. 3, with Charles O'Connell conducting.

At his New York debut (38 Oct 1941) at Town Hall (his prize as winner of a Walter W. Naumburg Foundation Award), Kapell's "insight as a musician" and his "flair for the piano" begat yet another award: the 1942 Town Hall

Endowment Series Award, bestowed on the artist under age 30 who, in the opinion of professional music critics and the Town Hall music committee, had given the outstanding performance at Town Hall in the preceding year. As winner of that honor, Kapell played another Town Hall recital on 20 January 1943.

Meanwhile, with Samaroff closely supervising, the 19-year-old pianist had signed (Feb 1942) a three-year contract with Arthur Judson, director of Columbia Concerts. And on 18 July 1942 Kapell's smashing performance of Aram Khachaturian's Piano Concerto, with Efrem Kurtz and the New York Philharmonic-Symphony Orchestra, thrilled the huge Lewisohn Stadium audience and, for better or worse, tagged the Khachaturian Concerto as Kapell's own. (Within six years he had played it around 30 times.)

Kapell's scintillating playing, especially his performances of romantic Russian concertos, and his prodigious technique sent his career skyrocketing, but success exacted a heavy toll—11 exhausting years of vigorous touring, recording and practicing. He toured almost every year in the United States. (Promotional flyers tell us that in a decade Kapell had made 10 tours of America, playing "four dozen times" in the city of Chicago.) He performed in Canada, made tours of Australia (1945, 1953), South America (1946, 1948, 1951), Europe (1947), Israel (1953) and in 1953 performed at the Prades Festival.

In 1948 Kapell added teaching to his hectic schedule. He taught private students right up to the time of his death, and had been appointed to begin teaching at Juilliard in the fall of 1953. His article in *Etude* (Dec 1950) shows that his teaching emphasized scales and exercises ("indispensable to technique"), finger independence, phrasing and tone production. Equally important, the article gives a précis of Olga Samaroff's approach to teaching.

Jerome Lowenthal, one of Kapell's first students, says he was a generous, dedicated teacher. To get that "steel in the fingers," Kapell had Lowenthal practice scales, arpeggios, Czerny and the right hand of the Chopin B Minor Scherzo. Sometimes Kapell would play for him (perhaps the Bach Partitas, some Schubert Dances or Chopin Mazurkas) for as much as two hours. He also made very graphic comments on Lowenthal's playing. "His unkind words were particularly memorable: my tone in Haydn was *squirrely*, my accents in Beethoven's Opus 10, No. 2, *provincial*, and as for the triplets in the *Variations sérieuses*, they should be *agitato ma non histerioso*." (Lowenthal)

William Kapell and Rebecca Anna Lou Melson married in 1948. In later interviews Mrs. Kapell (now Dr. Anna Lou Dehavenon) presents Kapell as a man who committed himself completely to whatever he undertook—performing, teaching, studying, practicing. He had, she said, a remarkable drive, an electric personality and high intelligence. Friends add that he was honest, impulsive, passionate, outspoken and generous.

Kapell knew he had a gigantic talent and on that blessing alone, he could have rested his fame. He never did. On the contrary, all his life Kapell worked hard to perfect his art. For him, being endowed with talent meant "a life of devotion and discipline and hard labor. He took his gifts not only as a privilege, but as a mandatory duty. His curiosity was insatiable." (*William Kapell Remembered*)

Kapell was never satisfied with his own artistic development. Constantly striving for higher and higher levels of perfection, he seized every opportunity to learn and grow. An anecdote of an incident in Freeport, Illinois, perfectly illustrates Kapell's insatiable artistic curiosity. At a party following Kapell's concert, someone mentioned that the local piano teacher had once studied with Isidor Philipp in Paris. Kapell sought her out, and they spent the rest of the evening talking and playing for one another. Among other things, she showed him phrasing in Chopin as she remembered learning it from Philipp. This kind of experience would be repeated whenever Kapell encountered someone from whom he thought he could learn. ("Reflections")

After each concert, the self-critical Kapell wrote in his diary his frank evaluations of his overall performance and detailed critiques of how he played each piece. Having set himself nearly impossible goals, he practiced incessantly to attain them. Early on he discovered that he must aim for "150 per cent of excellence in order to achieve on the concert platform 100 per cent of his own musical standards." Each day's schedule, at home and on tour, was arranged around practice sessions, which could, when time allowed, last seven or eight hours. At practice he always played very slowly (difficult passages not only slow but loud), even pieces he had known for years. It was the old system of practice, as his wife remembers, with the fingers lifted high. As late as 1950, Kapell himself wrote about practicing: "I was put on Hanon as a child, I still work at Hanon, and I have yet to find a finger difficulty for which Hanon does not provide a solution. . . . Scales, arpeggios and Hanon, practiced daily over the years, make one's fingers ready for any mechanical demands." (Kapell)

Kapell's unrelenting polishing and perfecting of his innate gifts surely accounts for his phenomenal technique. Writers and critics never failed to mention it. For example, in San Francisco, Alfred Frankenstein wrote, "He possesses two of the most powerful, brilliant and impeccably accurate hands in the business." And from Louis Biancolli in New York: "There was this almost unparalleled technique of his, this whirlwind virtuosity that swept through the most grueling music with astonishing facility."

With that amazingly sure technique and his enormous capacity for hard work, Kapell acquired an unusually varied repertoire at a young age—and he kept adding to it. A proud Olga Samaroff noted that even before his 24th birthday Kapell had played "seven different recital programs and ten concertos in public." His programs confirm that he had a catholic taste in music. He played works by Bach, Scarlatti, Mozart, Beethoven, Chopin, Mendelssohn, Schumann, Schubert, Liszt, Debussy, Albéniz, Villa-Lobos, Rachmaninoff, Prokofiev, Shostakovich, Khachaturian, Mussorgsky and a good showing of American music (Copland, Thomson, Ives, Sessions, Ruggles and more). Copland's Sonata and the Variations were staple items in his repertoire, and at the time of Kapell's death Copland was composing a Piano Fantasy especially for him.

Unquestionably Kapell's driving, dazzling style admirably suited the flashy Russian showpieces responsible for his initial success. Audiences went wild over them, which of course pleased his managers. But they were not enough for the ever questing Kapell. Because he had to grow, whatever the cost, Kapell avoided the trap that would later ensnare the equally dazzling, charismatic

Van Cliburn. Kapell fought, and fought hard (his own agents, concert managers), and he also worked hard "to forge a more mature mix of his innate romanticism, brilliant technique, and powerful intellect and temperament." (*William
Kapell Remembered*)

By 1947 his artistic maturity pleased even Madame Samaroff. After
playing some of Kapell's records, she wrote him a letter (26 March 1947): "It
was truly a wonderful experience . . . to realize the big step forward you have
taken in the direction you needed progress, namely, tone. Never lose that beautiful voice again. If you listen every minute and ask it of yourself and *realize that
you know how*, your playing will always have this quality which is so rare and
so necessary to great music." ("Reflections")

Reviewers obviously agreed with Samaroff. Kapell's New York debut
on 28 October 1941 at Town Hall—his reward as a Naumburg Award winner—
pleased most critics. "He has more than enough technique, but, more important,
he has imagination and sensitivity. . . . He took some tempi at a breakneck
speed, but he did not come to grief as far as the notes were concerned." (*NYT*, 29
Oct 1941) From another critic: "His enkindling imagination and sensitivity
found their fullest expression in the F major ballade of Chopin, which was not
brilliantly performed from the technical aspect but with something rarely encountered these days, a true flair for the Polish master's idiom." (*NYHT*, 29 Oct
1941)

But Kapell was to make his early mark with the Russian school, especially with his many performances of the Khatchaturian Concerto. His performance (7 Nov 1944) of Rachmaninoff's "Paganini" Rhapsody, showed once more
that young Kapell had a great talent and a brilliant technique. "If at times his
playing seemed to be lacking in the more subdued phases of pianistic artistry,
certainly he played the florid Rachmaninoff work with great conviction and
dramatic intensity." (*NYT*, 8 Nov 1944) On 25 February 1947 Kapell gave an
electric performance of the Prokofiev Concerto No. 3 in C Major in Carnegie
Hall with Eugene Ormandy and the Philadelphia Orchestra, and composer-critic
Virgil Thomson wrote one of his always pertinent comments: "William Kapell's
performance of the piano part was powerful, beautiful and in every way striking.
. . . His rendering of this difficult and exacting work was that of a master pianist
and a master musician." (*NYHT*, 26 Feb 1947)

Kapell usually played standard recital programs, with music from all periods and of all styles. Two San Francisco recitals were typical. A review of the
first recital (2 May 1950)—music by Bach (in transcription), Prokofiev, Chopin,
Mozart and Mendelssohn—included this: "Kapell possesses a keenly intelligent
sense of musical style, but he is at his best in things like the Bach 'Fantasy and
Fugue in G Minor' or Prokofieff's Seventh Sonata, which require precision, inci-
siveness, climactic power and nervous excitement. . . . Kapell was most successful in a group of three 'Songs Without Words' by Mendelssohn. . . . His Mozart
[Sonata in C Major, K. 330], however, seldom achieved much more than a
smooth, perfectly oiled purr." (©*San Francisco Chronicle*, 3 May 1950. Reprinted by permission.)

A review of the second San Francisco recital (30 Jan 1951)—music by Bach, Copland, Debussy, Liszt—was titled "Kapell Plays Some Bach–As Written." He did indeed play "original" Bach, the Partita in D Major. This and the Copland Sonata were signaled out as especially fine performances: "Kapell seems to like things whole and authentic, and the same two adjectives apply to his own interpretative talent. . . . This was amply shown in his beautifully scaled, perfectly paced Bach, and also in his performance of the Copland sonata." (*SFC*, 31 Jan 1951)

A Carnegie Hall recital (13 Jan 1953), typically eclectic, included Mozart (Sonata in B-flat Major, K. 570), Chopin (Nocturne, op. 55, no. 2 and the Polonaise-Fantasy), Mussorgsky (Pictures) and Copland (Piano Variations). From one review: "He has big equipment, he does not bluff, his musical aims are of the highest and he employs a good deal of intelligence. . . . At his best. . . William Kapell plays the piano like a master." (*NYT*, 14 Jan 1953)

Australian critics heard Kapell's very last performances in 1953, and wholeheartedly agreed that the "poet" in Kapell was now in full control. A reviewer for *Fidelio* (Perth) wrote: "Kapell has developed from a brilliant young man into an artist who is even more brilliant . . . but who now grips imagination and heart with grand performances of mature power and outstanding artistic integrity. From first to last . . . we had that deeply satisfying evidence of proportion and balance, exquisitely expressed."

No matter what he played, Kapell was a spectacular pianist. In Aaron Copland's words, "There were brilliance and drama in his playing, songfulness and excitement. On the platform he had the fire and abandon that alone can arouse audiences to fever pitch. . . . I cannot conceive of his ever having given a dull performance." (Copland)

Kapell made comparatively few recordings, and some of these are still awaiting CD format reissue. He recorded the Khachaturian Concerto with Koussevitzky and the Boston Symphony Orchestra in 1946 and the Prokofiev Concerto No. 3 with Dorati and the Dallas Symphony Orchestra in 1949. He also recorded Beethoven's Concerto No. 2 with the NBC Symphony Orchestra, Vladimir Golschmann conducting; the Rachmaninoff "Paganini" Rhapsody with Fritz Reiner and the Robin Hood Dell Orchestra; the Rachmaninoff Cello Sonata with Efrem Kurzt and the Brahms D Minor Sonata with Jascha Heifitz. Kapell also recorded the Chopin B Minor Sonata and a selection of Mazurkas; Liszt's Mephisto Waltz No. 1, Hungarian Rhapsody No. 11 and some short works. There are also recordings made from recitals, concerts and radio broadcasts.

The Khachaturian and Prokofiev Concertos initially appeared together on an RCA LP (GL85266); they are now coupled on a CD (see Discog.) together with the pianist's now legendary performance of the Liszt Mephisto Waltz No. 1. The LP album revealed Kapell as a truly dazzling pianist indeed. "There are plenty of fine, modern recordings of the Prokofieff third concerto in good, modern sound. But this performance has such power and brilliance that it is worth hearing for its own sake—and also, of course, as a memento of the art of William Kapell." (*CPD*, 26 May 1985) Recorded when Kapell was only 22 years old, the Mephisto Waltz "would have been quite enough to place him securely among our century's pianistic geniuses. . . . The nobility of his expression and the sheer perfection of his workmanship live on in his recording." (Cha/Spe, see Bibliog.)

The Brahms Concerto No. 1 in D Minor, op. 15, with Dimitri Mitropoulos and the New York Philharmonic Orchestra, comes from a live performance on 12 April 1953, a brief six months before Kapell met his tragic death. It is a reading laced with the improvisational style that often reminded his listeners of 19th-century performance practice. It is also a reading that projects the mature talents of the young pianist. "Never, for instance, have I encountered the coda of the third movement played with such energy and fire," writes one reviewer. "But perhaps the prize of the performance is the gorgeously sustained slow movement, where the rhythm is just supple enough to project the music's haunting rhapsodic character." (*Fan*, March/April 1991)

At the time of his death Kapell was recording a Bach Partita and the complete Chopin Mazurkas. Twenty-eight mazurkas have been reissued, 18 on one LP album (IPAM 1108) and 10 on a CD that also contains the Chopin Sonatas Nos. 2 and 3. Of the 18 mazurkas issued by IPAM (see Discog.), Jerome Lowenthal writes: "Kapell's Mazurkas, though totally mature in the sense that they reveal the artist to the depths of his psyche, are in every way an expression of youth—in their exuberance as in their pensiveness, in their emotionality and in their reserve, in their pride and their reticence." (Lowenthal, "William Kapell")

The collection of 10 Mazurkas on CD is equally superb, a testimony to Kapell's sensitive artistry. "The appealing simplicity of his phrasing in the mazurkas is on the level of the great Rubinstein performances." (*Fan*, Nov/Dec 1987) The "B minor Sonata [CD RCA 5998] is as impressive as any on record: there is a perfect blend of musical inspiration and virtuosity. . . . The tempos are fast throughout, though both the second subject of the first movement and the slow movement are played with great poetic feeling. This disc gives one a startling glimpse of a young artist of enormous maturity and real genius." (Met/Cho, see Bibliog.) Another writer agrees: "His scintillating playing of the Op. 58 puts the performance on a par with the great ones by Pollini, Lipatti, Rubinstein, and Gilels. . . . The Sonata No. 2 [recorded from an Australian Broadcasting Corporation broadcast on 23 Oct 1953] is indeed a rarely beautiful performance, on a par with that of the B minor. The unaffected freshness, the poetic tenderness, the deep involvement with every measure—all add up to a very touching occasion" (*Fan*, Nov/Dec 1987)

A recent CD contains two live performances (the Rachmaninoff Concerto No. 3, played on 13 April 1948, with Sir Ernest MacMillan conducting the Toronto Symphony Orchestra, and the Khachaturian Concerto, played on 20 May 1945, with the NBC Symphony Orchestra, Frank Black conducting). Overall, the Rachmaninoff performance "stands as one of the most impetuous, even hot-headed, accounts you're likely to hear. . . . Although Kapell throws off the big chordal passages with breathtaking abandon, it's the more astringent playing that challenges belief." The Khachaturian Concerto also "presses the listener along—but with such rhythmic tact that you hardly notice you're being hustled." (*Fan*, Sept/Oct 1993)

A 1994 CD by VAIA/IPA containing some Kapell broadcast performances from the years 1942–1953 features music by Bach, Debussy, Mozart, Liszt
and Mussorgsky (see Discog.). Even taking into account the generally poor
sound quality, "one is compelled musically to the edge of one's seat. The Bach
(Allemande, Courante [Partita No. 4]) is definitely a romanticization. But what
musicality, what pianism! The Mozart (Sonata, K. 570) is elegant and high-
spirited. . . . In the Debussy (Children's Corner) one can still marvel at Kapell's
shading and chiaroscuro. The Liszt Hungarian Rhapsody 6 . . . is played stupen-
dously; the 11th Rhapsody is even more thrilling. And the Mussorgsky
[Pictures] is simply unforgettable." (*ARG*, May/June 1994) A dissenting reviewer writes that Kapell "is heard in recordings that range from the inferior to
the abominable. . . . Only parts of the Eleventh Hungarian Rhapsody and the
Mussorgsky Pictures worthily illustrate Kapell's real quality; the rest of the CD
does little service to his memory." (*Gram*, Nov 1994)

SELECTED REFERENCES

"Boy Pianist Winner Of Town Hall Award." *New York Times*, 17 Feb 1942, p.
21.
Cassidy, Claudia. "In Memory of William Kapell." *Juilliard Review*, Jan 1954,
pp. 35–36. This tribute originally appeared in the *Chicago Tribune*, 30 Oct
1953.
Copland, Aaron. *Copland on Music*. Garden City, N.Y.: Doubleday & Co,
Inc., 1960, pp. 100–104.
———. "The Measure of Kapell." *Saturday Review*, 28 Nov 1953, p. 67.
Dixon, Thomas L. "William Kapell: Is Anyone Listening?" *High Fidelity/
Musical America*, June 1984, pp. MA 41–42.
Goldsmith, Harris. "Brief Candles." *High Fidelity*, Feb 1966, pp. 50–54, 112.
Kapell, William. "Technique and Musicianship." *Etude*, Dec 1950, pp. 20–21.
"The Kapell Diary—1952." *Piano Quarterly*, Winter 1983–84, pp. 12–44.
Robert Silverman, editor, Introduction by Anna Lou Kapell Dehavenon.
Lowenthal, Jerome. "Memories of William Kapell." *Clavier*, Feb 1984, pp.
36–39.
———. "William Kapell Plays Chopin Mazurkas." Liner notes, IPAM album
1108 (see Discog.).
Montparker, Carol. "In Memory of William Kapell." *Clavier*, Jan 1984, p. 29.
Obituary. *New York Times*, 30 Oct 1953, pp. 1, 48. *San Francisco Chronicle*,
30 Oct 1953, p. 3. *The Times* (London), 31 Oct 1953, p. 8.
Page, Tim. "Diary of a Gifted Pianist." *New York Times*, 21 July 1985, sec.
2, pp. 21, 28.
———. *William Kapell: A Documentary Life History of the American Pianist*.
College Park, MD: International Piano Archives, 1992. Contains a
Discography compiled by Allan Evans.
"Reflections." *Piano Quarterly*, Winter 1983–84, pp. 13–38. A special section
including an interview with Anna Lou Dehavenon (formerly Mrs. Kapell)
and various letters written to and by Kapell.

Samaroff, Olga. "William Kapell." *Etude*, Feb 1954, pp. 26, 50, 61. Reprint of an article written when Kapell was studying with Samaroff.
William Kapell Remembered. Guide to an Exhibition presented by the International Piano Archives at the University of Maryland, College Park, July 14–Oct 31, 1986. Booklet plus a small sound recording.
See also Bibliography: Cur/Bio (1948, 1954); Dow/Oli; Ewe/Li; Rat/Cle; Rub/MyM; Sal/Fam; Sch/Gre; Tho/MuS.

SELECTED REVIEWS

BH: 30 Oct 1943. *CSM*: 12 Sept 1953. *LAT*: 12 March 1946; 4 March 1949; 2 Feb 1951; 1 Aug 1952. *MA*: 10 Nov 1941; 10 Dec 1943. *MC*: 15 April 1951; 1 Feb 1953. *NYHT*: 29 Oct 1941; 21 Jan 1943; 26 Feb 1947; 29 March 1951. *NYP*: 22 Nov 1943. *NYS*: 29 Oct 1941. *NYT*: 29 Oct 1941; 19 July 1942; 21 Jan 1943; 8 Nov 1944; 1 March 1945; 26 Feb 1947; 22 March 1947; 24 June 1947; 29 July 1947; 26 June 1948; 17 Nov 1948; 21 Feb 1949; 29 March 1951; 14 Jan 1953. *SFC*: 3 May 1950; 31 Jan 1951.

SELECTED DISCOGRAPHY

Brahms: Concerto No. 1 in D Minor, op. 15; Academic Festival Overture, op. 80; Symphony No. 3 in F Major, op. 90 (Poco Allegretto). *Melodram* MEL 18009. Mitropoulos/NYPO. From a live 1953 performance.
Brahms: Intermezzo, op. 116, no. 4 (abbreviated). Chopin: Mazurka in F Minor, op. 63, no. 2. Schumann: Romance in F-sharp Major, op. 28, no. 2. Prokofiev: Sonata No. 7, op. 83 (1st and 2nd movt. excerpts). In *William Kapell Remembered*, see Ref.
Chopin: Mazurkas (10); Sonata No. 2 in B-flat Minor, op. 35; Sonata No. 3 in B Minor, op. 58. RCA (Red Seal) 5998-2.
Kapell (Legendary Performers). Khachaturian: Concerto (Koussevitzky/Boston SO). Liszt: Mephisto Waltz. Prokofiev: Concerto No. 3, op. 26 (Dorati/Dallas SO). RCA Victor 09026-60921-2.
Mozart: Concerto in A Major, K. 414 (Andante and Allegretto: Monteux/LAPO). Rachmaninoff: Concerto No. 3 in D Minor, op. 30 (MacMillan/Toronto SO). IPA 507. Live performances.
William Kapell, Vol. 1. Khachaturian: Concerto (MacMillan/Toronto SO). Rachmaninoff: Concerto No. 3 in D Minor, op. 30 (Black/NBC SO). VAI/IPA 1027 (CD). Live performances.
William Kapell, Vol. 2. Broadcast Performances, 1942–1953. Bach: Allemande and Courante (Partita No. 4 in D Major). Debussy: Children's Corner. Liszt: Hungarian Rhapsodies Nos. 6 and 11. Mozart: Sonata in B-flat Major, K. 570. Mussorgsky: Pictures at an Exhibition. VAIA/IPA 1048 (CD).
William Kapell at Carnegie Hall. Bach: Suite in A Minor, BWV 818. Brahms: Intermezzo in A-flat Major, op. 76, no. 3. Chopin: Nocturne in B-flat Minor, op. 9, no. 1. Debussy: *La Soirée dans Grenade.* Mozart: Sonata in

C Major, K. 330. Palmer: Toccata Ostinato. Shostakovich: Preludes op. 34, nos. 5, 10, 24. IPAM cassette 1101. Excerpts from two recitals played in Carnegie Hall on 28 February 1945 and 21 March 1947.
William Kapell Plays Chopin Mazurkas (18). IPAM 1108.

KATCHEN, JULIUS: b. Long Branch, New Jersey, 15 August 1926; d. Paris, France, 29 April 1969.

> The feeling of being wanted had a great bearing on the way I played.
> Julius Katchen (*New York Times*, 18 November 1962)

It is hardly surprising that Julius Katchen showed exceptional musicality and intelligence at a very early age. The Mandell Svets, his maternal grandparents, both taught at the Moscow and Warsaw conservatories, and after emigrating to America at the turn of the century they established a very successful music school in Newark, New Jersey. Lucille Svet-Katchen, Katchen's mother, was a pianist, and had studied with Isidor Philipp at the American Conservatory at Fontainebleau; his father Ira Katchen, a successful attorney, was a well-trained amateur violinist. Katchen's grandparents provided the only consistent music instruction he ever received.

At age 10 Katchen made his public debut (2 Feb 1937) at Newark's Fuld Hall under the auspices of the Young Men's and Young Women's Hebrew Association, performing the Mozart D Minor Concerto, K. 466, with Erno Rapee, music director of Radio City Music Hall, and a small orchestra comprised of players from the New York Philharmonic-Symphony Orchestra. A few months later Eugene Ormandy invited Katchen to play at a Philadelphia Orchestra rehearsal. On the appointed day Ormandy, handing his baton to assistant conductor Saul Caston, listened from the rear of the auditorium while Katchen played the entire Mozart D Minor Concerto. Impressed, Ormandy engaged Katchen to play the work with his orchestra, and that performance (21 Oct 1937, Philadelphia Academy of Music) caused such a stir that the 11-year-old Katchen was invited to repeat the concerto with the NYPSO at its annual Pension Fund benefit concert (22 Nov 1937, Carnegie Hall), with John Barbirolli conducting and Bidú Sayão sharing guest honors.

Katchen's New York recital debut (13 Nov 1938) at Town Hall showed, said the *New York Times* critic, that the 12-year-old had an extraordinary ease at the keyboard and "an extraordinary talent that tempts one to rash prophecies." The following year Katchen's performance (6 July 1939, Lewisohn Stadium) of the Schumann Concerto with the NYPSO under Efrem Kurtz, music director of the *Ballets Russes de Monte Carlo*, showed "poise, facility, feeling and a sense of style. It does not matter if he came by the emotion second-hand—and perhaps he did not. It did matter that he conveyed the romantic spirit of the music." (*NYT*, 7 July 1939)

This was the life of a musical prodigy, yet "Buddy" Katchen had a normal childhood. He was an expert swimmer and table tennis player; and if not at the piano could usually be found playing baseball and other boys' games with his friends in his backyard. Until age 14 he studied only at home, music with his grandparents and academic subjects with a teacher from one of the local public schools. At that point his father, determined that he should have a good education and normal social life, enrolled him at the local high school and stopped his public performances.

Katchen later attended Haverford College in Pennsylvania. He may have had some lessons with David Saperton during his college years, but beyond that he apparently had no further musical training. He played often at campus events, and also gave a second New York recital (3 Dec 1944), this time at Carnegie Hall. Katchen completed the four-year college course in three years, was elected to Phi Beta Kappa and graduated in 1946 first in his class, with a degree in philosophy. That year he was one of five Americans awarded fellowships by the French government in recognition of outstanding scholastic achievement.

Just two weeks after he arrived in Paris in the fall of 1946, Katchen was invited to represent the United States at the first International UNESCO Festival. At the opening concert (6 Nov 1946), broadcast to most of Europe, he played the Beethoven "Emperor" Concerto with the *Orchestre Nationale de la Radiodiffusion française*, Paul Kletsky conducting. On 9 November Katchen played the Tchaikovsky Concerto No. 1 and a week later the Schumann Concerto, both with the orchestra of the *Société des Concerts du Conservatoire*. After performing five times in eleven days, Katchen suddenly emerged as a Paris celebrity, the most talked-about performer of the season. In late December he played Gershwin's Rhapsody in Blue at the Nice Opera House; on 21 February 1947 he played his first solo recital in Paris before a large audience at the *Théâtre des Champs Elysées*; on 7 April he was soloist with the Vienna Philharmonic Orchestra; and on 24 May he was soloist with the Paris Symphony Orchestra, Otto Klemperer conducting. As Katchen wrote to his college friends, his schedule that spring included performances in Rome, Venice, Naples, Paris, London, Stockholm, Copenhagen, Zurich and Salzburg.

That autumn Katchen began an extensive American tour (Nov 1947-Feb 1948), and until his premature death at age 42 he toured regularly. Endowed with tremendous vitality, he typically gave more than 100 concerts a season. Though his adult career was brief, Katchen performed in about 45 countries on all six continents. He made an enormous impression in Europe. Paris audiences idolized him, and in Athens in 1948 he gave 12 recitals within three weeks, each time to a sold-out house. His American appearances, however, were few and scattered. After the 1947–48 tour, Katchen played again in America in 1951, stayed away for more than 11 years, and returned more often in the 1960s. He concertized about nine months of the year and spent the rest of the time at home in Paris, usually practicing in the mornings and devoting afternoons to a small group of advanced students. Although he lived all his adult life in France, Katchen never considered himself an expatriate, a word to him meaning rejection of one's country. He stayed abroad, he said, simply because Europe offered better career opportunities. He married (1956) Arlette Patoux; their son Stefan was about eight when Katchen died.

Ill with cancer, Katchen made his last American tour in the spring of 1967, and played his final concert (12 Dec 1968) just four months before his death, at London's Festival Hall—a stunning performance of Ravel's Concerto for the Left Hand with the London Symphony Orchestra, István Kertész conducting.

Katchen's substantial repertoire, based on the standard Classical and Romantic masterpieces, included more than 32 concertos or other major works for piano and orchestra. Having been taught almost exclusively by his Russian grandparents, he naturally played many works by Russian composers— Mussorgsky, Tchaikovsky, Balakirev, Rachmaninoff, Prokofiev. Living in France, he cultivated French music. He also played some contemporary works by Berg, Foss, Bergsma, Rorem and Britten. The mature Katchen, with his formidable technique and intelligent interpretative style, made his reputation playing the music of Beethoven and Brahms. He began specializing in the Brahms repertoire in the early 1960s. Between 12 April and 22 April 1964 he played all of Brahms's solo piano music in a four-recital cycle at London's Wigmore Hall. Three months later he played (21 July 1964) the two Brahms concertos at New York's Lewisohn Stadium, with Joseph Rosenstock conducting the Stadium Symphony Orchestra. Katchen later repeated the Brahms cycle in Berlin, New York, Amsterdam and Cambridge, England; he also performed Brahms's chamber music with Josef Suk and Janos Starker.

Noted for his astounding stamina and unbounded musical vitality, Katchen never showed fatigue in the massive, Bülowesque programs he loved to play. As early as age 26 he played three piano concertos (Beethoven No. 3, Rachmaninoff No. 2, the Brahms No. 2) in one evening (30 April 1953, Festival Hall) with the London Symphony Orchestra, Walter Susskind conducting. Another example: He played (23 Oct 1960, Festival Hall) Schubert's great Sonata in B-flat Major and Beethoven's Diabelli Variations. Then, in true Bülowesque fashion, he played the whole of Beethoven's "*Appassionata*" Sonata as an *encore*.

Julius Katchen, richly gifted with a phenomenal technique and musical insight, seems not always to have used both gifts equally. Katchen was a powerhouse pianist, a cast-iron virtuoso whose fingers, it was said, could play faster and more pungently than one believed possible. At one flashing, fiery performance of Balakirev's *Islamey*, "anyone could have been forgiven for assuming that he had four hands." (*TL*, 20 May 1958) Along with brilliance and power, Katchen had superior intellectual qualities. If not always inspired, his interpretations were carefully thought out. But Katchen, particularly in his early career, sometimes played like a supercharged virtuoso, sacrificing poetry and lyrical feeling for lightning speed and deluges of overwhelming sound. His tone could become harsh and brittle; his playing too fast, too strongly accented and overpedaled.

Mechanically Katchen could do almost anything. Yet often something was missing—imagination, heart, individuality, whatever that intangible something is that "distinguishes a musician with something to say from a neatly organized machine." (*TL*, 1 March 1951) But when he reined in the virtuoso, Katchen's incisive, dazzling playing often revealed a clear understanding of the emotional and spiritual depths of the music. No matter what the reviews imply, the fact remains that Julius Katchen must have been an impressive pianist. Why else would he have had so many return engagements to Europe's great music centers? His record number of appearances in Europe (one season 32 performances in the Netherlands alone) and in Great Britain (several engagements, year after year) attest to his reputation.

Reading Katchen's reviews, one can only speculate. What if after college he had not had that sudden, smashing success in Paris and instead had continued his musical studies with a renowned teacher? Remembering that Katchen had been trained almost exclusively by his grandparents and that he had not had much, if any, serious musical study after his high school years, one wonders if under the guidance of another teacher he might have been better able to employ his glittering virtuosity and musical insight. The later reviews indicate that on his own Katchen was on his way to accomplishing that goal. Had he lived longer, he might have become one of this century's truly great pianists.

Early in his career Katchen's amazing technique often got the better of him. On 14 November 1947 his recital—works by Beethoven, Bach, Mozart, Bartók, Chopin, Debussy—showed that since his last New York appearance three years earlier he had "obviously made efforts to curb his natural tendency to indulge in overspeedy tempi. . . . But his playing yesterday was still often overspeedy, and all stressed passages were banged out with a harsh, brittle tone. . . . His approach still remains too insensitive to reach the goal to which he seems to be seriously striving." (*NYT*, 15 Nov 1947) But some six years later a remarkable all-Beethoven program (7 Feb 1954), at which he played the Sonatas, ops. 110 and 111, and the Diabelli Variations, revealed Katchen as a pianist with deep musical understanding of profound music, a pianist "with the phenomenal technique of a virtuoso and the vision of a seer." (*TL*, 8 Feb 1954)

And Katchen revealed "astonishing perception and maturity" in an all-Beethoven recital (12 Feb 1956) offering four sonatas and the 32 Variations. "Technically it was a brilliant achievement. . . . He never forgets that Beethoven was a virtuoso, or that the pianoforte is an instrument of beautiful sounds." (*TL*, 13 Feb 1956) Yet within a matter of weeks the virtuoso in Katchen seemed to be overwhelming the musician. He played (19 April 1956) Beethoven's "*Appassionata*" Sonata, Schubert's "Wanderer" Fantasy, Chopin's F Minor Fantasy and Franck's Prelude, Chorale and Fugue with formidable power, "but too often seemed out to cut a dash rather than to sound the depths of each work." (*TL*, 23 April 1956)

However, in the 1960s Katchen's all-Brahms recitals and his performances of the Brahms concertos greatly enhanced his reputation as an interpreter. The 1966 reviews are glowing: "Few pianists are able to bring off the Paganini Variations with such technical wizardry, rhythmic verve and tonal brilliance. . . . It was a most impressive performance." (*TL*, 17 Jan 1966) Only a few weeks later Katchen began his stunning four-recital Brahms cycle in New York. "His deep involvement with Brahms's music . . . has not given him the airs of a pompous specialist. The Katchen approach is that of one who loves what he is doing. . . . All of Mr. Katchen's formidable technical powers were put on dazzling display in a performance that never took the easy way out." (*NYT*, 7 Feb 1966)

Katchen made his final public appearance on 12 December 1968, playing Ravel's Concerto for the Left Hand with the London Symphony Orchestra under István Kertész. Intent on testing Ravel's intention to produce the impression of a solo part for two hands, one critic closed his eyes during much of Katchen's performance: "The result was stunning. But then, Mr. Katchen is one of those extraordinary pianists who respond to this challenge with redoubled technical brilliance and rhythmic verve." (*TL*, 13 Dec 1968)

Katchen was one of the pioneers in the field of LP recordings. His recording of the Brahms Sonata in F Minor, op. 5, made for English Decca, was the first recorded piano LP. He was also the first to make a concerto recording on LP, the Rachmaninoff Concerto No. 2.

Nearly all of Katchen's recordings are excellent. Some of them, like the exciting *Islamey* and the Brahms Paganini Variations, display his exquisite technique. Others, like the Ravel Concerto and the Rachmaninoff Rhapsody, reveal his all-encompassing musicianship. And Katchen's "recording of Britten's left-hand *Diversions*, conducted by the composer, will be difficult to equal." (New/GrA, see Bibliog.)

Katchen's recordings of Brahms's complete solo piano music, recorded between 1964 and 1966, won the coveted *Grand Prix du Disque* in 1967. This splendid Brahms cycle may prove to be his most enduring memorial.

SELECTED REFERENCES

"Boy Pianist Planning Debut Here." *Newark Star-Eagle*, 18 Dec 1936, sec. 2, p. 1.
"Boy Piano Prodigy Has Athletic Aims." *New York Times*, 21 Nov 1937, sec. 2, p. 2.
"Hero from Long Branch." *Time*, 1 March 1954, p. 57.
"Julius Katchen." Alumni files, Haverford College, Haverford, PA.
Katchen, Julius. "The Wand'ring Minstrel." *The Concert Goer's Annual No. 1*, 1957, pp. 124–130.
Meadmore, W. S. "Julius Katchen." *Gramophone*, Oct 1954, pp. 191–192.
Minshull, Ray. "Julius Katchen." A Memorial Tribute by Minshull of Decca Limited (London Records).
———. "Julius Katchen." *Gramophone*, June 1969, p. 21.
"Newark Musicians, Katchen." Katchen file, Newark Public Library, Art and Music Division.
Obituary. *New York Times,* 30 April 1969, p. 47. *Philadelphia Inquirer*, 30 April 1969, p. 19. *The Times* (London), 30 April 1969, p. 12.

"Press Story on Julius Katchen." Columbia Artists Management Inc., March 1962.
Rich, Alan. "A Willing Homecomer." *New York Times*, 18 Nov 1962, sec. 2, p. 9.
See also Bibliography: Ewe/Li; New/GrA; Ran/Kon; Rat/Cle; Sal/Fam.

SELECTED REVIEWS

LAT: 20 Feb 1952. *LM*: 10–11 Nov 1946. *MA*: 10 Nov 1937. *MM*: July 1966. *MT*: March 1951. *NYT*: 23 Nov 1937; 14 Nov 1938; 7 July 1939; 4 Dec 1944; 15 Nov 1947; 1 March 1951; 23 Nov 1962; 22 July 1964; 7 Feb 1966. *S-L*: 3 Feb 1937; 22 Oct 1937. *TL*: 1 May 1953; 8 Feb 1954; 19 April 1954; 22 April 1955; 13 Feb 1956; 23 April 1956; 10 April 1958; 29 May 1958; 25 May 1959; 4 May 1960; 4 Oct 1960; 3 April 1961; 16 Oct 1963; 25 March 1964; 13 April 1964; 17 April 1964; 23 April 1964; 30 Nov 1965; 17 Jan 1966; 16 May 1966; 27 June 1966; 28 April 1967; 23 April 1968; 30 April 1968; 13 Dec 1968.

SELECTED DISCOGRAPHY

Balakirev: *Islamey*. Liszt: *Funérailles*; Hungarian Rhapsody No. 12; Mephisto Waltz No. 1. Mussorgsky: Pictures at an Exhibition. London 425961-2.
Bartók: Concerto No. 3. Ravel: Concerto in G. London CS 6487. Kertész/London SO.
Beethoven: Concerto No. 3 in C Minor, op. 37; Concerto No. 4 in G Major, op. 58. Pickwick Classics PWK 1153 (CD). Gamba/London SO.
Beethoven: Concerto No. 5 in E-flat Major, op. 73. London Cassette 417040-4LT. Gamba/London SO.
Brahms: Ballades, op. 10; Variations on a Theme by Handel, op. 24; Variations on a Theme by Paganini, op. 35. London 417644-2.
Brahms: The Complete Works for Solo Piano. London 430053-2 (6 CDs).
Brahms: Concerto No. 1 in D Minor, op. 15; Concerto No. 2 in B-flat Major, op. 83; Variations on a Theme of Paganini, op. 35; Variations and Fugue on a Theme of Handel, op. 24. London 440 612-2 (2 CDs). Monteux/London SO.
Britten: Diversions for Piano Left-Hand. London 421855-2. Britten/London SO.
Dohnányi: Variations on a Nursery Song, op. 25. Rachmaninoff: Rhapsody on a Theme of Paganini, op. 43. London Cassette 417052-4 or LP CS6153. Boult/London PO.
Franck: Prelude, Chorale and Fugue. Schumann: Symphonic Etudes, op. 13. London LL 823.
Gershwin: Concerto in F (Mantovani/Orch.); Rhapsody in Blue (Kertész/LSO). London 436570-2.
Gershwin: Rhapsody in Blue. Prokofiev: Concerto No. 3. Ravel: Concerto for the Left Hand. London 6633.

Liszt: Concerto No. 2 in A Major. Mendelssohn: Concerto No. 1 in G Minor, op. 25. Pickwick PWK 1154 (CD). Argenta/London SO.
Rachmaninoff: Concerto No. 2 in C Minor, op. 18. Balakirev: *Islamey*. London Cassette 417021-4 or LP CS6064. Solti/London SO.
Rachmaninoff: Concerto No. 2 in C Minor, op. 18; Rhapsody on a Theme of Paganini, op. 43. London 417880-2 (CD). Boult/London PO.
Rorem: Sonata No. 2. CRI ACS 6007 (CD).

KATSARIS, CYPRIEN: b. Marseilles, France, 5 May 1951.

> By way of simplification, I would describe him as a younger standard-bearer of the Jorge Bolet/Earl Wild School of Lisztian brilliance, a brilliance very much concerned with substance.
>
> Richard Freed (*Stereo Review*, November 1982)

The French-born Katsaris, son of a Greek father (businessman Erotokritos Katsaris, who could play the violin) and a Greek mother (Niki [Papadopoulos] Katsaris, who could play the guitar), spent his early childhood in Cameroon, West Africa, where his father was in the business of exporting peanut oil and soap. They were one of the few families with a classical music record collection, and, says Katsaris, "At four years old I used to listen to the *Pastoral* Symphony and developed a strong affinity for this music." (Inglis) Katsaris began piano studies in Cameroon at the age of four, and in 1964, at age 13, he enrolled at the Paris Conservatory. He studied principally with Aline van Barentzen and Monique de la Bruchollerie, received a first prize in piano in 1969 and a first prize in chamber music in 1970.

That same year (1970) Katsaris received the Albert Roussel Prize, and also earned a certificate of honor at the Tchaikovsky Competition in Moscow. In 1972 he placed ninth at the International Queen Elisabeth Competition in Brussels and received a prize from the Alex-de-Vries Foundation. In 1974 he placed first at the International Cziffra Competition in Versailles. Since then, recitals and orchestral appearances in Europe, the Americas and the Far East have gained Katsaris a reputation as one of the finest younger pianists active today.

In 1978 he took part in the first three concerts of the newly founded Philharmonic Orchestra of Mexico City and also made his American debut, playing Rachmaninoff's Concerto No. 3 with the Detroit Symphony Orchestra, Antal Dorati conducting. In 1981 he toured extensively in Czechoslovakia and East Germany. Generally speaking, Katsaris came to his New York recital debut (23 May 1986) largely unknown in America except to keyboard enthusiasts familiar with his series of recordings.

Later engagements have included performances of Mahler's *Das Lied von der Erde* in its original version for piano and soprano and tenor soloists at New York's Lincoln Center (19 Feb 1993) and in San Francisco. In April 1993 he toured Japan with the Strasbourg Philharmonic Orchestra, and returned to

Japan in June for a series of recitals and orchestral engagements. Katsaris's 1993–94 season in North America included performances in Toronto, San Francisco and Mexico (Cervantino Festival) with the Katsaris Quintet, an ensemble comprised of principal string players from Germany's foremost orchestras.

Katsaris occasionally does some teaching; for example, master classes at the Salzburg *Mozarteum*, the Royal Conservatory of The Hague and at the Music Academy in Hong Kong. Since 1977 he has been music director of the Echternach International Festival in Luxembourg.

Katsaris is also a talented composer, and he has appeared in several films: *France Panorama*, a publicity film sponsored by the French Foreign Ministry and exhibited in 70 countries; a film of the 1979 Echternach Festival, made with the assistance of Claude Chabrol and often shown on television; a film made with the Mexico City Philharmonic Orchestra on its first tour of Europe.

Katsaris handles his unusual repertoire (transcriptions of Beethoven symphonies, for example) with ease, but he is an orthodox musician whose playing is never acrobatic; his intent is purely to express musical content. His performances of Liszt's solo piano transcriptions of all the Beethoven symphonies have been widely praised. Katsaris performs the "Pastoral Symphony" with such exceptional sensitivity that the thought of its being a transcription hardly ever intrudes. It is simply a beautiful work whose medium is the keyboard. His interpretations of some of the Bach concertos are both exciting rhythmically and fascinating pianistically. His performances of Schumann's *Kinderscenen*, op. 15; *Waldscenen*, op. 82; *Albumblätter*, op. 124, show remarkable warmth and understatement. He turns them into little gems.

Critics all seem to say more or less the same things about Katsaris's Lisztian technique. *Le Figaro* reported that a Katsaris concert was, "as far as one could imagine, a concert by Liszt, himself." Another reviewer writes of "the brilliancy with which Katsaris masters the great difficulties of Liszt's score [Beethoven Symphony No. 9]. . . . It cannot be enough admired how he is able to conquer the space of the creation that makes one forget all craftsmanship." (*Fonoforum*, Nov 1984)

At his first San Francisco recital (12 Sept 1982) Katsaris played an unusual program—Liszt's *Benediction de Dieu dans la solitude*; Schumann's *Kinderscenen* and his *Etüden in Form Freier Variationen über ein Thema von Beethoven*; Liszt's piano transcription of Beethoven's Symphony No. 6. "This was by all means a distinguished musical event. . . . What is particularly impressive is his gift of contemplation, of searching out inner meanings down to the last note. . . . Here is a genuine thinker at the piano." (*SFC*, 14 Sept 1982)

Katsaris gave his New York recital debut (23 May 1986) at Alice Tully Hall. Entitled "Liszt and Beethoven: Death and Heroism," the first half consisted of eight somber Liszt works associated with death, with Venice or with Richard Wagner (Liszt's paraphrase of the *Liebestod* from *Tristan und Isolde*; and Beethoven's Sonata in A-flat Major, op. 26, with its slow movement titled "a funeral march on the death of a hero"). The last half of the program was Liszt's piano transcription of Beethoven's "Eroica" Symphony (No. 3). "Few pianists have his gift for isolation of salient voices, a particularly crucial task in a symphonic transcription. . . . The chief technical requirement is for the stamina to keep those octaves, tremolandos and filled chords coming page after page for over half an hour. Mr. Katsaris was enormously impressive in this regard; the momentum of the great work never flagged." (*NYT*, 25 May 1986)

Katsaris approached Beethoven in a uniquely roundabout fashion via Liszt's arrangements of Beethoven's symphonies, and they have helped him, he says, in understanding Beethoven: "Liszt's transcriptions are not just little arrangements to popularize the symphonic output, but real pianistic works developing the sense of colour in piano playing." (Inglis)

In a spellbinding recital (30 Jan 1988) in San Francisco—a program of works by Schubert, Beethoven and Messiaen—"Katsaris succeeded in making a powerful effect through self-restraint. . . . He has technique to burn, but never makes that the point of a performance. His performances offer little in the way of overt commentary on the material, but they are revelatory nonetheless." (*SFC*, 1 Feb 1988)

At another unconventional program, played in San Francisco on 26 January 1991, Katsaris "applied his accomplished technique to music of a patently spiritual stripe, putting its transcendent values well ahead of display of his digital facility." The only original works were Beethoven's Sonata in A-flat Major, op. 110, and the first and last items ("contemplations") from Messiaen's suite *Vingt regards sur l'enfant Jésus*. All other works were transcriptions: Bach by Wilhelm Kempff and Katsaris; Liszt arrangements of Beethoven, Schubert and Arcadelt. "The recital peaked with pellucid readings of the framing episodes of the notoriously difficult *'Vingt Regards,'* the *'Regard du père'* and the summational *'Regard de l'église d'amour'.*" (*SFE*, 28 Jan 1991)

In a 1983 interview Katsaris confessed that rather than give concerts he prefers to cut a record or to tape a television performance, "since this gives him a sense of having mastered a piece. It also frees him to explore new works." (Soulsman) In another interview Katsaris explained that for him recording is "like a concert, with the microphone the most demanding audience." (Inglis)

Record catalogues reveal a very substantial discography for a pianist as young as Katsaris. There are a number of LPs, made in the pre-CD era. He was until recently under exclusive contract to Teldec and has currently to his credit more than twenty CDs recorded for that label. He was awarded (1985) the *Grand Prix du Disque Frédéric Chopin* in Warsaw for his recording of Chopin's Ballades and Scherzos (see Discog.). His performances and his Teldec recordings of all nine Beethoven Symphonies as transcribed for piano by Franz Liszt place him in a special category of pianism. Symphony No. 9 was awarded the *Grand Prix du Disque Franz Liszt* in 1984 and the Symphonies Nos. 1 and 2 won the same award in 1989. The Symphony No. 5, the last to be recorded, completed a 10-year project. One critic wrote apropos Symphonies Nos. 1 and 2 that Katsaris "tosses these transcriptions off like there's nothing to it, with a technique that completely encompasses the notes while leaving ample room to create the illusion of orchestral textures." (*Fan*, Sept/Oct 1989)

Katsaris's album titled *Virtuoso Chamber Music* (see Discog.) contains a broad selection of seldom-heard works ranging from Bach to Gottschalk. "The playing is hair-raising in many of these selections, and there are few pianists of any age who could range as broadly through the repertory as Mr. Katsaris does here." (Libbey, "A New Pianist . . .")

Mozartiana, a disc containing works transcribed from, or inspired by, that composer is "a jackdaw's nest of trinkets; some self-serving, some of greater value . . . presented with exceptional brilliance and aplomb by Cyprien Katsaris." (*Gram*, June 1993) Lesser-known works by Beethoven and Liszt and Czerny vie with yet even lesser-known works by Gelinek, Thalberg, Bizet and Kempff. This CD offers up sheer enjoyment, its sole purpose.

Katsaris's uniformly fine readings of the 17 Chopin waltzes can hold their own with those by Lipatti and Zimerman. "The approach here is big and bold, with plenty of flair and freedom, yet it is totally free of any excess and by no means superficial or lacking in intimacy where appropriate." (Freed)

Katsaris' reading of the Brahms Concerto No. 2, op. 83, with Eliahu Inbal and the Philharmonia Orchestra (see Discog.) received mixed reviews. On the one hand: "Neither party has seized the stage. . . . Katsaris is a sensitive, thoughtful artist, whose conception of the work is orthodox and efficiently brought off, but there is no impression of commanding personality in his playing, or even keyboard strength." (*Gram*, Aug 1990) Yet another review reads: "This is one of those rarest of recordings where everything comes together. Both pianist and conductor have an expansive and compelling view of this score, and together become a countervailing and complementary unit that serves to heighten the performance of each." (*Fan*, Nov/Dec 1990)

Katsaris's first release (1992) for Sony Classical features all three Chopin Sonatas and initiates what promises to be a cycle of works by that composer. Reviewers are simultaneously pleased and bewildered with this disc. In the Sonata No. 2, "the *Marche funèbre*'s stealthy and *piano* return hammered out triple *forte* is an unpleasant bolt from the blue and Katsaris' way in the finale section of the Third Sonata's *Scherzo* of throwing the emphasis first here, then there, and then seemingly in all directions at once, is bewildering rather than lucid. Even so, such intricacy and verve can be enthralling. Katsaris' dynamics in the Second Sonata's phantom finale are hardly *sotto voce* as marked, but his whirlwind shifts of voicing and perspective, accomplished at a scarcely credible tempo, are the work of a phenomenally, if perversely gifted pianist." (*Gramophone*, June 1993. Reprinted by permission.)

Another critic finds the Chopin Sonata No. 3 in B Minor to be especially successful, "with a scherzo as fast and light as anyone's and a beautifully shaped slow movement. Opus 35 is not quite so successful. While he is able to negotiate certain difficult passages with greater ease and accuracy than even Rachmaninov and Horowitz were able to do in the studio, I find that the climax of the first movement's development section sounds glib when it should be hair-raising. . . . Many listeners will be put off . . . by Katsaris' emulation of Rachmaninoff's *fortissimo* performance of the return of the main theme in the slow movement." (*Fanfare*, March/April 1993. Reprinted by permission.)

A second Chopin album combines the Preludes, op. 28, with a goodly number of short, seldom-played works (see Discog.). One reviewer notes, "Even if you think you know the Preludes completely and have heard every conceivable interpretation, Katsaris offers surprises by the dozen. . . . Katsaris probes into every nook and cranny of Chopin's textures to unearth previously unnoticed detail." (*ARG*, Nov/Dec 1993)

SELECTED REFERENCES

Freed, Richard. "Cyprien Katsaris." *Stereo Review*, Nov 1982, p. 84.
Inglis, Anne. "Adapting To The Circumstances." (interview) *Gramophone*, Aug 1990, p. 348.
Libbey, Theodore W., Jr. "Did Franz Liszt Compose This Concerto?" *New York Times*, 13 June 1982, p. 31.
———. "A New Pianist Displays a New Piano." *New York Times*, 18 July 1982, sec. 2, p. 19.
Marum, Lisa. "Keep Your Eye On Cyprien Katsaris, Pianist." *Ovation*, July 1982, p. 38.
McLellan, Joseph. "Hands That Speak & Sing." *Washington Post*, 1 July 1983, Weekend, p. 11.
Pincus, Andrew L. "The Art of Transcription Sheds New Light on Old Work." *New York Times*, 23 Sept 1990, Arts & Leisure, pp. 28, 30.
Soulsman, Gary. "Music's power cheers pro at Liszt concerto." *Wilmington Evening Journal*, 3 Nov 1983, sec. D, p. 1.
See also Bibliography: WWF.

SELECTED REVIEWS

CT: 18 Aug 1988. *LAT*: 14 Jan 1987. *MA*: Oct 1986. *NYT*: 25 May 1986; 1 Feb 1987; 23 Feb 1993; 22 Feb 1994. *SFC*: 14 Sept 1982; 1 Feb 1988; 28 Jan 1991. *SFE*: 28 Jan 1991. *WP*: 2 July 1983.

SELECTED DISCOGRAPHY

Bach: Piano Concertos. No. 1 in D Minor, BWV 1052; No. 3 in D Major, BWV1054; No. 5 in F Minor, BWV 1056; No. 6 in F Major, BWV 1057. Teldec 9031-74779-2. Rolla/Franz Liszt CO.
Beethoven-Liszt: Symphony No. 1 in C Major, op. 21; Symphony No. 2 in D Major, op. 36. Teldec CD 8.44006 ZK.
Beethoven-Liszt: Symphony No. 3 in E-flat Major, op. 55. Teldec CD 8.43201 ZK.
Beethoven-Liszt: Symphony No. 4 in B-flat Major, op. 60; Symphony No. 8 in F Major, op. 93. Teldec CD 8.43419 ZK.
Beethoven-Liszt: Symphony No. 5 in C Minor, op. 67; Variations and Fugue in E-flat Major, op. 35. Teldec CD 2292-44921-2 ZK.

Beethoven-Liszt: Symphony No. 6 in F Major, op. 68. Teldec CD 8.42781 ZK. Also MHS 512161H (CD).

Beethoven-Liszt: Symphony No. 7 in A Major, op. 92. Teldec CD 8.43113 ZK. Also MHS 512196M (CD).

Beethoven-Liszt Symphony No. 9 in D Minor, op. 125. Teldec CD 8.42956 ZK. Also MHS 512366T (CD).

Brahms: Concerto No. 2 in B-flat Major, op. 83. Teldec CD 44936-2-ZK. Inbal/Philharmonia.

Chopin: Ballades (4) and Scherzos (4). Teldec CD 8.43053 ZK.

Chopin: Polonaises (complete). Sony Classical S2K 53967 (2 CDs).

Chopin: Sonata No. 1 in C Minor, op. 4; Sonata No. 2 in B-flat Minor, op. 35; Sonata No. 3 in B Minor, op. 58. Sony Classical SK 48483 (CD).

Chopin: Twenty-Four Preludes, op. 28; Preludes in C-sharp Minor, op. 45, in A-flat Major, op. posth.; "Wiosna" in G Minor, op. 74, no. 2; Allegretto and Mazur; Two Bourrées; Three *Ecossaises*, op. 72, no. 3; *Ecossaises*, WN 27; Bolero, op. 19; *Contredanse* in G-flat Major; *Galop Marquis* in A-flat Major; *Feuille d'album* in E Major; Allegretto in F-sharp Major; Cantabile in B-flat Major; Largo in E-flat Major; Fugue in A Minor. Sony SK 53355 (CD).

Chopin: Waltzes (19). Teldec CD 8.43056 ZK. Also MHS 512202K (CD).

Grieg: From Holberg's Time; Lyric Pieces (selections). Teldec CD 8.42925 ZK.

Liszt: Mephisto Waltzes 1-4; Bagatelle; Mephisto Polka; *Bénédiction de Dieu dans la solitude*. Teldec CD 8.42829 ZK.

Mendelssohn: Concerto No. 1 in G Minor, op. 25; Concerto No. 2 in D Minor, op. 40; Concerto in A Minor for Piano and Strings, op. posth. Teldec 9031-75860-2. Mazur/Leipzig GO.

Mozartiana. Beethoven: Eleven Variations on *Se vuol ballare* in F Major, WoO 40. Bizet: *Là ci darem la mano*. Czerny: *Fantaisie brillante*. Fischer: *Das Donnerwetter*. Gelinek: *Air des mystères d'Isis*. Katsaris: *In Memoriam Mozart*; *Mozartiana*. Kempff: *Pastorale variée*. Liszt: *Ave verum corpus*. Thalberg: Fantasia on *Don Giovanni*; *Lacrimosa*. Sony Classical SK 52551 (CD).

Schumann: *Kinderscenen*, op. 15; *Waldscenen*, op. 82; *Albumblätter*, op. 124. Teldec 9031-75863-2, formerly 8.43467.

Scriabin: Piano Music (selections from early works). EMI 1C 2LP 137 1162983.

Stravinsky: *Les Noces*. DG 423251-2. With pianists Martha Argerich, Krystian Zimerman and Homero Francesch, Leonard Bernstein conducting.

Virtuoso Chamber Music. Cziffra: *Étude de Concert* (arr. from Rimsky-Korsakov's Flight of the Bumblebee). Schumann: *Variationen über ein Theme von Clara Wieck*; *Träumerei*. Schumann-Liszt: *Widmung*. Liszt: *Csárdás obstiné*; *Soirées de Vienne*. Mozart: *Das Butterbrot*. Prokofieff: Prelude and Toccata. Chopin: Nocturne in C-sharp Minor, op. posth. Katsaris: *Improvisation d'après une sculpture d'Agam*. Gottschalk: The Banjo. J. S. Bach: Largo (Concerto BWV 1056). Teldec CD 8.42479.

⚜ ⚜ ⚜

KEMPFF, WILHELM: b. Jüterborg, Germany, 25 November 1895; d. Positano, Italy, 23 May 1991.

As a pianist he was either godlike or disastrous, sometimes within the same piece. I recall an Opus 111 that followed such a confused opening with one of the most sublime Ariettas I've ever heard. That was Kempff, great and unique but also puzzling and enigmatic.

Mitsuko Uchida (*Music and Musicians*, November 1985)

Unter dem Zimbelstern, the title of Wilhelm Kempff's autobiography, refers symbolically to his evolution as a musician born, figuratively speaking, to the sound of the organ. (*Zimbelstern* is the name of an organ stop.) Both his grandfather (Friedrich) and his father (Wilhelm) were organists and cantors, and Kempff became aware of music as a very small child hearing his father, the cantor of Jüterborg, playing organ chorales. No doubt the roots of Kempff's strong Christian faith also lay embedded in the sacred music ambience of that childhood lived under "the star of the cymbal," the *Zimbelstern.*

At age five (the family moved to Potsdam that year) Kempff began lessons in organ, piano and composition with his father, and sometimes he was allowed to sing in his father's choir at the Church of St. Nicholas. At age six Kempff began piano lessons with Ida Schmidt-Schlesicke, and at age nine he was taken to Georg Schumann, director of the Berlin *Singakademie,* to have his musical skills tested. At the examination he played and transposed some Preludes and Fugues from Bach's Well-Tempered Clavier and also improvised a fantasy and fugue on a theme by Bach. (Kempff's remarkable improvisations would prove to be a high point of his later concerts.) Schumann, mightily impressed with the young prodigy, contacted Joseph Joachim at the Berlin *Hochschule für Musik,* with the result that Joachim awarded Kempff two scholarships.

He began composition studies with Robert Kahn and piano lessons with Heinrich Barth. "My teacher Heinrich Barth," reported Kempff in his autobiography, "was a pupil of Bülow, Bülow of Liszt, Liszt of Czerny and Czerny of Beethoven." With this musical lineage Kempff could only emerge as a pianist in the so-called classical tradition. From age 15 to 18 he put aside music studies to complete his academic education at the *Viktoriagymnasium* in Potsdam, after which he returned to Berlin, where he resumed his music training at the *Hochschule* and studied music history and philosophy at the university. Upon completion of his *Hochschule* courses, he was awarded two of the coveted Mendelssohn prizes, one in piano and the other in composition.

Kempff began his professional career in 1916 when Heinrich Rudel, cantor of the Berlin cathedral, engaged him as organist and pianist to tour with the cathedral choir through Germany and Scandinavia. His piano performances so delighted Scandinavian audiences that he was invited to return for solo recitals. Performed in 1919, those enormously successful recitals prompted King Gustave of Sweden to present Kempff with the distinguished "*Artibus et Litteris*" award. In 1917 he played his first recital at the Berlin *Singakademie,* a program that included Beethoven's "*Hammerklavier*" Sonata and Brahms's

Variations on a Theme by Paganini. In 1918 he made his first appearance as soloist with the Berlin Philharmonic Orchestra, directed by Arthur Nikisch, the first of nearly 50 years of collaborations with that orchestra. For the next few years Kempff toured as a pianist, still mostly in Germany and Scandinavia. In 1924 he succeeded Max Pauer as director of the Stuttgart High School for Music, but being an administrator and also teaching master classes increasingly interfered with his concert career. He resigned in 1929.

By World War II Kempff had acquired a reputation in Europe (particularly Germany and Scandinavia), South America and Japan as one of the most convincing interpreters of the Beethoven sonatas. Since after the war he more or less followed that same concert itinerary, Kempff was 56 years old when he finally made his London debut (27 Oct 1951) at Wigmore Hall and 69 when he made his American debut (13 Oct 1964) at Carnegie Hall.

At many Kempff recitals his masterful improvisations aroused the most exciting response, perhaps because so few pianists in recent decades have had that particular talent. "His gift for improvisation, his 'unbounded delight in fashioning music instantaneously' founded Kempff's reputation, and it is still an essential criterion of his interpretative art. Abhorrence of stale routine and of the unvarying products of a merely rational reading of the printed notes dominates him to this day." (Liner notes, Beethoven Sonatas LP [1965] DG 2535 291-10)

Kempff also had a reputation for being an excellent teacher. He taught master classes at the Stuttgart High School for Music (1924–29) and summer courses (1931–41) in the *Marmorpalais* at Potsdam, along with Edwin Fischer and Walter Gieseking. In 1957 he inaugurated an annual course in Beethoven interpretation at his summer retreat in Positano, Italy, personally selecting the young pianists who would attend.

Kempff composed from childhood. His works include four symphonies, four operas, concertos for piano and for violin, ballets, string quartets, the dramatic cantata *Deutsches Schicksal* and works for piano solo (see MGG for complete list).

Kempff suffered from Parkinson's disease for the last decade of his life. He gave his final concert in 1981 in Paris. He died in Italy on 23 May 1991 at the age of 95. Seven children (in 1926 Kempff married the Baroness Helen Hiller von Gaertringen [d. 1986]) survived him.

From the outset of his long career (he was still performing in his eighties) Kempff won recognition for his fine interpretations of German Classic and Romantic works, especially the music of Beethoven (by age 16 he had mastered the 32 Beethoven Sonatas), Schubert, Schumann, Chopin and Brahms. "In the 1950s, his was the 'voice' of Beethoven for a new generation in much the same way as Schnabel's had been before the war. . . . His [Beethoven] playing was never touched by routine, and his Schubert and Schumann surveys are equally illuminating." (Layton)

When playing introspective music Kempff could sound lyrical, charming and guileless; with large-scale works he often achieved nobility of character through his clear textures, singing tone quality and restrained tempos. For the most part, he carefully avoided overt sentimentality, emphasizing instead the purely musical aspects of melody and structure. His interpretations were sound rather than brilliant, yet he had an imaginative approach to playing that never lost its freshness. And he had a "real pianissimo, one that rises gently from the keys and is even capable of color within the pianissimo dynamic." (*NYT*, 11 Dec 1965)

Kempff managed to sustain a high level of interest at his concerts. Evened out over the years, the ultimate critical assessment indicates that he achieved a nobility and breadth of line that overshadowed the deficiencies of his technique. Backed by vast experience and fine musicianship, his playing was always authoritative yet could be puzzling. "There are moments when Kempff seems temporarily possessed by a demon which makes him thump and bang, and behave generally like a flashy nineteenth-century *Klaviertiger*." (*MT*, May 1953). And, said fellow pianist Alfred Brendel: "I have had some of my greatest experiences in the concert hall on his great days. But he [Kempff] can be so variable—more so than any other great artist I know." (*RR*, June 1971)

Kempff reveled in heroic-size programs. A London recital (28 March 1953) featured two masterpieces: Bach's Goldberg Variations and Beethoven's Sonata, op. 106 ("*Hammerklavier*")! "Kempff's performance ["*Hammerklavier*"] was on a massive scale, reaching the heights and plumbing the profundities of this terrifying sonata. It was deeply thoughtful, and afforded an experience such as few other living pianists could provide." (*MT*, May 1953)

Another substantial program, performed at the Festival Hall on 18 October 1959, offered three monumental works—Beethoven's Sonata in A Major, op. 101, Schumann's Fantasy in C Major and Brahms's Sonata in F Minor. Critical reaction was undisguised disappointment. "His timing of musical sentences, of bridge passages, and rhetorical flourishes is impetuous, often naively vulgar. . . . Beautiful moments of touch and tone and pedalling are his concern, and very impressive they can be." (*TL*, 19 Oct 1959)

At a much later London recital (21 March 1965) Kempff's performance of Beethoven's Sonata in A-flat Major, op. 110, received high marks: "The limpid ease of the first movement and the controlled fire of the *Molto allegro* were alike arresting, but it was in the fugal finale that clear phrasing and fine dynamic control paid their biggest dividends. Every part sang, every entry made its full effect." (*MM*, May 1965) On 9 November 1969 Kempff played Beethoven's Concerto No. 4 with the London Philharmonic Orchestra, Lorin Maazel conducting. "Not a great, radiant performance; but all of it was intensely enjoyable. In the Allegro and Andante, particularly, Kempff's *cantabile* rang out marvellously sweet and pure, voiced as childlike as a wooden flute." (*MT*, Jan 1970)

Kempff's affiliation with *Deutsche Grammophon*, begun in 1920 when he made his first Beethoven sonata recording, lasted for more than 60 years. He recorded the 32 Beethoven sonatas three times (on electric 78s, LP discs and in stereo) and recorded the five Beethoven concertos twice. Some critics felt that Kempff's early mono recordings of the sonatas, despite some erratic and seemingly eccentric interpretations, to a great extent captured the true essence of Beethoven. The same critics usually also remarked on his consistent lack of technical control.

Kempff's last set of Beethoven sonatas, recorded for stereo LPs between January 1964 and January 1965 (see Discog.) and aided of course by far superior technical procedures, is more secure and clearly reveals his straightforward, thoughtful approach to performance. "It is a wonderful set, one of the finest things the gramophone has ever given us, not simply because it offers great music and great music-making, but because it is, over its ten-hour span, a thing of such unquenchable vitality." (*Gram*, March 1991)

On a smaller scale, a 1983 reissue of the 1962 Beethoven Concerto No. 5 with the Sonata in C Minor, op. 111, recorded in 1964 (see Discog.), offers good examples of his rich but not cloying tone, and his keen sense of rhythm, which permits the use of *rubato* without violating good taste. "Kempff's trim, at times even salon-like style is remarkable in its musicality, command of voicing and . . . apt clipped cragginess." (*Fan*, Jan/Feb 1988)

Between 1965 and 1969 Kempff recorded 11 completed Schubert sonatas plus seven which survive in two or more movements of an uncompleted whole. These performances, available as a 7-CD set, reveal Kempff's considerable talents. "Kempff is a master of pianistic intimacy and fine gradation. . . . Whatever else the character of the music may suggest to Kempff, the dynamic scale is narrow, the tonal range refined and basically monochromatic, the sense of motion always delicately calibrated. . . . Kempff is by no stretch of description always placid or imperturable, but he controls and overcontrols this music with the same finely graded sense of pace and permanently light touch that illuminate his Beethoven playing." (*Fan*, March/April 1989)

SELECTED REFERENCES

Cairns, David. "Keepers of the eternal flame." *Sunday Times* (London), 7 July 1991, sec. 5, p. 5. Arrau, Kempff, Serkin.

Gavoty, Bernard. *Wilhelm Kempff*. Lausanne: René Kister, 1954 (Series Great Concert Artists).

Goldsmith, Harris. "Beethoven and Brahms With a Master's Stamp." *High Fidelity*, Oct 1964, pp. 124–126.

Henahan, Donal. "Schubert—Transcendental Amateur." *High Fidelity*, June 1971, pp. 71–72.

Horowitz, Joseph. "The Poet and the Ponderer." *New York Times*, 23 Aug 1992, sec. 8, p. 21.

Hsu, Madeleine. "A Summer with Wilhelm Kempff." *Clavier*, Oct 1991, pp. 20–23. Reprinted from Jan 1970 *Clavier*.

Kempff, Wilhelm. *Cette Note grave*, translated from the German by Alphonse Tournier. Paris: Librairie Plon, 1955. French translation of *Unter dem Zimbelstern*.

———. *Kadenzen zu Klavierkonzerten von Ludwig van Beethoven*. Berlin: Bote & Bock, 1967.

———. *Kadenzen zu Klavierkonzerten von Wolfgang Amadeus Mozart*. Berlin: Bote & Bock, 1974.

———. *Unter dem Zimbelstern: Das Werden eines Musikers*. Stuttgart: Engelhornverlag Adolf Spemann, 1951.

Layton, Robert. "The End Of An Era." *Gramophone*, Aug 1991, pp. 50–51.

Meyer-Josten, Jürgen. "In the Right Spirit." *Records and Recording*, Nov 1975, pp. 24–25.

Obituary. *New York Times*, 25 May 1991, sec. 9, p. 29.

Schafer, Milton. "The Art of Wilhelm Kempff." *Musical America*, Oct 1964, pp. 58–59.

See also Bibliography: Bla/Gra; Dow/Oli; Ewe/Mu; Gav/Vin; Kai/Gre; MGG; New/Gro; Ran/Kon; Rat/Cle.

SELECTED REVIEWS

MM: May 1965. *MT*: Dec 1951; May 1953; Jan 1970. *NYT*: 14 Oct 1964; 11 Dec 1965; 28 Oct 1966; 11 Nov 1966; 21 Nov 1966. *SFC*: 7 Dec 1965. *TL*: 22 Dec 1952; 30 March 1953; 14 Dec 1953; 4 March 1955; 19 Oct 1959; 22 Oct 1959.

SELECTED DISCOGRAPHY

Beethoven: Concerto No. 1 in C Major, op. 15; Concerto No. 2 in B-flat Major, op. 19. DG *Galleria* 419856-2. Leitner/Berlin PO.

Beethoven: Concerto No. 3 in C Minor, op. 37; Sonata in C Minor, op. 13; Sonata in D Minor, op. 31, no. 2. DG 435 097-2. Leitner/Berlin PO.

Beethoven: Concerto No. 3 in C Minor, op. 37; Concerto No. 4 in G Major, op. 58. DG *Galleria* 419467-2. Leitner/Berlin PO.

Beethoven: Concerto No. 5 in E-flat Major, op. 73; Sonata in C Minor, op. 111. DG Galleria 419468-2. Leitner/Berlin PO.

Beethoven: Concertos (5); Rondos, op. 51. DG *Dokumente* 435 744-2GDO3 (3 CDs). Kempen/Berlin PO.

Beethoven: Sonatas. DG 429 306-2GX9 (nine discs). Rec. 1964–65.

Brahms: *Klavierstücke*, op. 118. DG 431162-2. Also Anda with Concerto No. 2.

Mozart: Concerto in A Major, K. 488; Concerto in C Minor, K. 491. DG 423885-2. Leitner/Bamberg SO.

Schubert: Sonatas (18). 7 DG 423496-2GX7.

Wilhelm Kempff in Performance. Beethoven: Concerto No. 3 in C Minor, op. 37 (Decker/ Montreal SO, 1966); Concerto No. 5 in E-flat Major, op. 73 (Ozawa/Montreal SO, 1966). Music and Arts CD-768.

Wilhelm Kempff: Radio Recordings 1945–1956. Bach: Chromatic Fantasy and Fugue, BWV 903; "*Wohl mir, dasz ich Jesum habe*" (Cantata BWV 147). Chopin: Mazurka, op. 7, no. 3; Mazurka, op. 56, no. 2. Fauré: Nocturne. Kempff: *Libellen über dem Froschteich* . Liszt: *La Gondoliera*. Mozart: *Pastorale variée*, K. Anhang (209b); Variations, K. 455. Koch/Schwann 3-1029-2.

KENTNER, LOUIS: b. Karwin, Silesia, Austria-Hungary (now Karvina, Czechoslovakia), 19 July 1905; d. London, England, 22 September 1987.

> Josef Lhévinne had a great influence on me; the sound of his playing is
> something I have carried in my ear all my life.
>
> Louis Kentner (*Kentner: A Symposium*)

Louis Kentner's Hungarian father worked as a substitute railroad stationmaster; his mother was an Austrian from Vienna; and they raised their family in Budapest. No doubt a child prodigy—Kentner felt that he could play the piano before he could talk—he was never treated as such. As a small child he was often drafted to turn pages for his father, a very bad pianist who would struggle for hours trying to read piano reductions of Puccini operas or Delibes ballets. Kentner spent these long hours matching the up-and-down lines of printed notes with his father's moving hands, and, incredibly, in this fashion he learned how to read music. His mother was his first piano teacher, but since she was, as he remembered, a timid soul suffering from migraines, she soon allowed her aggressive husband to take over. When Kentner had advanced enough to play some Czerny exercises, his father insisted that they play four-hand duets, usually reductions of Beethoven symphonies and other works far beyond his, and his father's, abilities.

At age six Kentner was accepted at the Royal Academy of Music in Budapest, where he began piano with Arnold Székely and composition with Hans Koessler. At the same time Kentner was also enrolled in elementary school, where he met a kindly singing teacher, a student of Kodály at the Academy, who helped him with rudimentary theory. In time Kentner grew dissatisfied with Székely's piano lessons and with Koessler's composition classes. His studies at the Academy "consisted of a rigidly imposed diet of scales, exercises and sonatinas by Bergmüller or Kuhlau," usually taught not by Koessler, then close to retirement, but by young ladies studying pedagogy. These early disappointments may have been exaggerated, for at that time Kentner's home life, as he later would say, was full "of tears, quarrels and door slamming."

Kentner's situation at the Academy improved greatly when he advanced to the classes of Leo Weiner and Zoltán Kodály, both of whom would become important influences in his life. He studied chamber music and composition with Weiner, whom he admired as a truly master pedagogue and universal musician, and they formed a close friendship. At Kentner's request, Weiner would evaluate his playing as he studied new repertoire, routinely visiting Kentner's home about once a week to hear him play, and give an opinion. Weiner always stayed for dinner, and if disagreements arose between father and son, Kentner could usually count on his good friend Weiner for support. Kodály, a quiet man not as easy to know as Weiner, taught Kentner theory and composition. Teacher and student shared a passion for walking and on long hikes in the hills around the city, Kodály gave Kentner sound advice on such practical matters as planning a career, concert agents and critics.

Kentner first attracted public notice at age 11 playing Chopin at an Academy concert, and at age 13 he gave his first public recital in Budapest. When he was 15 he dropped his piano studies to tour in Hungary and Austria, but he continued working on his own to refine his technique. At age 17 he went to live in Berlin, where he had an unexpectedly successful debut, and might have pursued a career had not his father's death forced him to return to Budapest to help support his mother and sister. Upon his return, he resumed his composition studies with Kodály. When the composer conceived the idea of giving all-Kodály concerts, he asked Kentner to play the piano, not just the solo piano works but all piano parts. These annual Kodály concerts became very successful.

In 1927 Kentner gave the first performance of Kodály's Marosszék Dances. It was a remarkable test of his memorizing skills. Ordered to Kodály's home on the morning of the performance, Kentner was led to a sofa in the dining room, handed a wet manuscript page, and instructed to memorize it. While the composer worked at a piano in the adjoining room—Kentner said Kodály never composed without a piano—Kentner studied each page as it was brought to him. Kodály finished by lunchtime, and Kentner took the piece home to practice it on the piano. That evening he played it on a Budapest radio program, and the next day he played the work from memory at a concert.

While living in Berlin, Kentner had twice visited London to give recitals. Although the Londoners were not visibly impressed with him, he liked everything about England and determined to settle there one day. In 1935 he finally emigrated to London with his wife (m. 1931), the Hungarian pianist Ilona Kabos. During the marriage—they divorced in 1945—they often played two-piano concerts.

New friends in London arranged three recitals to introduce Kentner's name to the British public. Having been trained at the Royal Academy in Budapest, Kentner had an affinity for, and understanding of, Liszt. In 1933 he had placed third in the Liszt Competition held in Budapest. In London he made the mistake of including works by Liszt, at that time the bête noire of Britain, on his programs, thereby provoking audiences and critics. But some of the few Liszt admirers in London made the audacious suggestion that Kentner give an all-Liszt recital, and the surprising success of that recital (27 Oct 1953) revivified his heretofore sluggish British career. To do justice to his British reputation as a Liszt specialist, Kentner learned more of the repertoire and worked on his technique. He also joined the first Committee of the Liszt Society, formed in 1951, and was president from 1965 until his death. Kentner sincerely believed that his early Liszt recitals and the work of the Liszt Society helped greatly in eradicating the British prejudice against that composer.

Since he had no intention of remaining just "the Liszt pianist" in England, Kentner spent two difficult years trying to establish himself as a generally successful pianist. His first important orchestral engagements, a series of Mozart concertos with Sir Thomas Beecham conducting the London Philharmonic Orchestra, drew fine notices for his interpretations of Mozart. During the 1940s he played the complete Well-Tempered Clavier of Bach in a series of recitals, all the Beethoven piano sonatas and all the Schubert sonatas. He also played Liszt's complete *Années de pèlerinage* for the BBC radio and, with Yehudi Menuhin, played all the Beethoven violin and piano sonatas at the Edinburgh Festival.

Menuhin and Kentner became brothers-in-law by marriage when Kentner married (29 May 1946) Griselda Gould, sister of Menuhin's wife Diana. The two musicians became close friends, and often toured and recorded together. On 30 September 1949 they introduced William Walton's Sonata for Violin and Piano, dedicated to their wives, in Zurich. With Gaspar Cassadó they formed a first-rank trio, performing mostly at the important European festivals until the great Spanish cellist's death in 1966. In 1954 Menuhin and Kentner toured India, appearing as a duo, as solo recitalists and with orchestra.

Kentner was 51 and already had a worldwide reputation when he made his very successful American debut (28 Nov 1956) at Town Hall, followed by a tour of the United States. On 21 October 1960 he inaugurated Judson Hall, formerly the Carl Fischer Hall, playing the first of seven programs presenting all 32 Beethoven sonatas. Although Kentner gave recitals right to the end of his life, these 1960 programs were his last in the United States, except for one appearance in 1979. That summer he served on the jury for the University of Maryland International Piano Competition and gave both a master class and a recital.

During the last decade of his life Kentner served on many international juries, gave a yearly recital for the Liszt Society in London and often played for the Royal Society in Dublin. He toured in Great Britain, Germany, Italy and Switzerland, and made a tour of France with Yehudi Menuhin. On his 80th birthday he played a London recital, on his 81st birthday he appeared at the Cheltenham Festival and later that same year he played at the Windsor Festival. Kentner played his final recital at the Menuhin Festival in Gstaad, Switzerland, just six weeks before his death.

A scholarly musician with catholic tastes, Kentner developed a versatile repertoire. While still in his teens, he played all the Beethoven piano concertos in Budapest, a cycle he later repeated in Paris, Venice, Zurich, London, New York and Vancouver. His repertoire also included Bach, Romantic composers like Schubert and Chopin, and many modern composers. He thoroughly enjoyed contemporary music. In Hungary he had performed not only modern works by his countrymen Kodály and Bartók but also compositions by Debussy, Ravel, Scriabin, Falla, Bloch and Casella.

In 1933 he gave the first Hungarian performance of Béla Bartók's Piano Concerto No. 2. Bartók, who had played the world premiere in Frankfurt a few days earlier at a public concert on German radio, specifically requested that Kentner introduce the concerto in Budapest. In 1942, after Kentner had settled in England, he and his first wife Ilona Kabos gave the premiere of the revised version of Bartók's Concerto for two Pianos and Percussion. And in 1945 Kentner gave the European premiere of Bartók's Concerto No. 3, with Sir Adrian Boult conducting. In 1962 Béla Bartók's son discovered his father's Scherzo, op. 2, for piano and orchestra, composed in 1905, and gave the rights of first performance to Kentner. Kentner played the world premiere (26 Feb 1963) at the Festival Hall with the London Philharmonic Orchestra under Sir Malcolm Sargent.

In England, Kentner turned his attention to British composers, performing works by Bax, Lambert, Walton, Ireland and Tippett. He gave the premiere performances of Michael Tippett's Piano Concerto No. 1, in both England and the United States; Alan Rawsthorne's revised Piano Concerto No. 1; and Sir Arthur Bliss's Triptych for piano. Even when he did not particularly like a modern work—he felt that the abolition of tonality impoverished rather than enriched music—the sympathetic Kentner tried hard to understand it.

Kentner taught for most of his life, and was an interesting and very good teacher, admired and respected by his students. He took private students and from 1974 taught quite regularly at the Yehudi Menuhin School at Stoke d'Abernon in Surrey. And he frequently gave master classes (England, Italy, Israel and Switzerland). In his eulogy, Sir Claus Moser, a pupil for six years, described his memorable lessons with Kentner. And in the Preface to *Kentner: A Symposium*, Harold Taylor described Kentner's teaching style: "While the pupil plays, he sits at the opposite end of the room . . . often listening with eyes closed. . . . The pupil is allowed to play the whole piece or movement without interruption and is always given an account of the general impression he has made, before the detailed work of teaching begins. This usually involves several journeys from the armchair to the piano stool and back again . . . for Kentner is a great believer in the virtues of demonstration and example."

Kentner's contributions to music literature include his perceptive and valuable *Piano*, really three books in one: "Understanding the Piano," "Playing the Piano" and "The Great Pianoforte Composers." He also wrote the autobiographical "Sketch of a Self-portrait" published in *Kentner: A Symposium*. A recognized Liszt performer and scholar, Kentner wrote two highly informative essays for *Franz Liszt: The Man and His Music*.

During World War II Kentner, a British citizen since 1946, played at military camps and factories, and often performed at the National Gallery lunchtime concerts organized by Myra Hess. He was also the unseen pianist who played the "Warsaw Concerto" for the film *Dangerous Moonlight* (1941), made in England during the war. Besides his long term as president of the Liszt Society, Kentner was president of the Chopin Society, founded in 1971, an honorary fellow (1970) of the Royal Academy of Music, and a Commander of the Order of the British Empire (C. B. E., June 1978).

Louis Kentner, one of the last great Romantics, never strayed from the Romantic tradition of aesthetics, sound and style. "He did not change according to fashion; he remained true to his musical upbringing and, in sharing it, he was a breath of fresh air on the concert stage. And part of that tradition were his qualities of personality and vast culture expected of artists of those days." (Laires) Kentner's playing showed a remarkable sensitivity, lucidity, and tonal beauty; he had an especially lovely way of preserving a long thematic line.

A provocative all-Liszt recital at Chelsea Town Hall on 27 October 1953 included compositions from different periods in the composer's life. "No better exponent of Liszt's piano music is to be found in this country than Mr. Kentner, who executed a physically and technically exacting task with his accustomed mastery, though injudicious use of the sustaining pedal and a tendency to explosively loud dynamics proved discomfiting in the over-resonant hall." (*TL*, 2 Nov 1953)

When Kentner made his American debut (28 Nov 1956), playing Bach-Liszt, Bartók, Kodály and Chopin, his reputation had preceded him, but even the critics were unprepared for his talent. Paul Henry Lang, the eminent musicologist and critic, wrote an all-favorable review: "Mr. Kentner is beyond doubt one of the finest pianists heard here in a long time. His technique and keyboard security are phenomenal, but this surely is the result of perfect rapport between mind and fingers." (*NYHT*, 29 Nov 1956) Another intelligent review of Kentner's American debut included: "Mr. Kentner's musicianship is solidly complemented by technical gifts of the first order. He can do just about whatever he wishes at the keyboard. . . . He has the means to be a slamming virtuoso . . . but his interests do not lie in display." (*NYT*, 29 Nov 1956)

On 20 September 1959 a Wigmore Hall recital contained equal parts of Liszt and Chopin. Kentner made Liszt's *Weinen Klagen* sound like "half a dozen cathedral organs in one with his astonishing command of sonority." Liszt's second Ballade was his most successful interpretation, "since he presented every facet of its picturesque, chivalric romantic content." (*TL*, 21 Sept 1959)

Kentner was in New York City during the months of October and November 1960, playing the entire 32 sonatas of Beethoven in a series of seven recitals. (He had performed the same series in London some 10 years earlier.) The first program (21 Oct) presented the three sonatas from Opus 2 and ended with the mighty Sonata in C Minor, op. 111. "Mr. Kentner's pianism is wonderfully vital, a quality so essential to Beethoven's music. . . . The vitality stems from the energy that seems to fill each note Mr. Kentner strikes. . . . Every note is crystal clear, in figurations, in inner voices, in the fullness of his chording." (*NYT*, 22 Oct 1960)

Even in his later years Kentner constantly strove to provide his audiences with lively, interesting, sometimes amusing programs. On 23 March 1983 the featured attraction at a Queen Elizabeth Hall recital was a performance of the *Hexameron*—"Grand bravura variations for piano on the march from Bellini's *The Puritans*"—a work written in 1837 for a charity concert given at the house of Princess Belgiojoso. Chopin, Pixis, Thalberg, Czerny, Herz and Liszt each contributed a variation, and Liszt also composed the introduction, theme statement, bridge passages and the finale. At the 1983 recital "Kentner assumed Liszt's role, while pupils from his recent South Bank master classes, taking their turns at a second piano, played one variation each by the other composers. It was a good example of highbrow entertainment music." (*MM*, July 1983)

The Kentner discography covers a wide spectrum of composers (see Taylor). Although generally known as a great Liszt interpreter, Kentner was highly regarded in Britain and on the Continent for his Chopin playing. "He recorded many of Chopin's works for Columbia on 78s, having made his first disc as early as 1928—this was recorded in Hungary and bought by Edison Bell, and is a performance of the A flat Impromptu, Op. 29, and the C-sharp Minor Fantaisie-Impromptu, Op. 66. These are beautifully shaped readings, which according to some critics the pianist has never matched." (Met/Cho, see Bibliog.) These two early Chopin recordings are available on CD, coupled with two Liszt compositions *and* Kentner's masterful 1939 reading of Beethoven's Sonata in B-flat Major, op. 106 (see Discog.). His concept of the Beethoven is intensely personal, free and romantic. "In terms of piano sound, there can be no more beautiful *Hammerklavier* on record, from the 'angelic garlands' of the first movement's first transition passage to the titanic sonorities of the fugue's trills." (Nicholls)

Kentner made LP recordings over a period of 20 years (1954–75). His Liszt recordings are excellent. In the album of operatic and dramatic fantasies (see Discog.), Kentner gives exciting, authoritative performances combining strength and poetry. And the Transcendental Etudes proved a magnificent outlet for his talents. "There is plenty of bravura in this music but it finds better effect if it is enmeshed with refinement. That's the way Louis Kentner approaches the set and that's why he is most successful." (Coh/Rec, see Bibliog.)

The reissue of many of his Liszt recordings (from the 1960s and 1970s) on a double Vox CD (see Discog.) is a welcome addition to the available Kentner discography. "Kentner's virtuosity had rusted somewhat with the passing years, but his playing remained brimful of humanity and understanding, the early *Harmonies poétiques et religieuses* and 'Faust' Waltz proving particularly musical, and the rare *Hungarian Folksongs* inspiring a real sense of poetic narrative." (*Gram*, Nov 1993)

The CD album of *Piano Favorites* (see Discog.), a disc emanating from a Qualiton LP released during the early 1970s, contains a variety of well-known pieces by various composers (Beethoven, Chopin, Liszt, Mozart, Schubert, Schumann). "The recording is beautifully warm and natural and serves Kentner's thoughtful and neatly turned playing well." (*Gram*, May 1988)

SELECTED REFERENCES

Downes, Edward. "Fast Learner." *New York Times*, 30 Dec 1956, sec. 2, p. 7.

Harrison, Vernon. "Mr. Louis Kentner, C.B.E." Memorial prepared for Kentner's publishers Kahn & Averill, London.

Kentner, Louis. "M. Béla Bartók." *London Times*, 15 Nov 1945, p. 7. An "appreciation" of the Hungarian composer.

———. "The Interpretation of Liszt's Piano Music." In *Franz Liszt: The Man and His Music*, ed. Alan Walker. New York: Taplinger, 1970, pp. 202–220.

———. *Piano.* (Yehudi Menuhin Music Guides). London: Macdonald & Co., 1976.

———. "Solo Piano Music (1827–61)." In *Franz Liszt: The Man and His Music*, pp. 79–133.

Kentner, Mrs. Louis. Letters, dated 4 Oct 1988; 11 Oct 1988.

Laires, Fernando. "Louis Kentner." *Piano Quarterly*, Winter 1987–88, p. 31.

Moser, Sir Claus. "Louis Kentner 1905–1987." Remarks made at Kentner's funeral, 28 September 1987.

Nicholls, Simon. "Louis Kentner." Liner notes for GEMM CD 9480.

Obituary. *Piano Quarterly,* Winter 1987–88, p. 31. *The Times* (London), 23 Sept 1987, p. 31.

Sabin, Robert. "Louis Kentner—Wars and Revolutions Have Never Kept Him from Working." *Musical America,* 1 Jan 1957, pp. 12–13.

Taylor, Harold, ed. *Kentner: A Symposium.* With a Foreword by Yehudi Menuhin. London: Kahn & Averill; New York: Pro-Am Music Resources Inc., 1987. (Chapter I, "Sketch of a self-portrait," is a brief Kentner autobiography.)

See also Bibliography: Bro/Mas; Ewe/Li2; IWWM; New/Gro; Ran/Kon; Rat/Cle.

SELECTED REVIEWS

GM: 9 March 1979. *MM*: July 1983. *NYHT*: 29 Nov 1956. *NYT*: 29 Nov 1956; 22 Oct 1960. *SR*: 15 Dec 1956. *Time*: 8 March 1963. *TL*: 2 Nov 1953; 1 March 1954; 21 Sept 1959; 11 Jan 1960; 27 Feb 1963; 24 April 1963. *24 Heures*: 13 Aug 1987.

SELECTED DISCOGRAPHY

Balakirev: Sonata in B-flat Minor. Liapunov: Transcendental Etudes, op. 11, nos. 10–12. Turnabout TV-S 34470, 1972.

Beethoven: Sonata in B-flat Major, op. 106 (*Hammerklavier*). Chopin: Fantaisie-Impromptu in C-sharp Minor, op. 66; Impromptu in A-flat Major, op. 29. Liszt: *Bénédiction de Dieu dans la solitude*; Hungarian Rhapsody No. 9. Pearl GEMM CD 9480.

Chopin: The Four Ballades; Barcarolle, op. 60. Saga XID 5233.

Liszt: *Années de pèlerinage* (Italie). *Odéon* PALP 1987 (1963).

Liszt: *Concerto pathétique*; Rumanian Rhapsody; Spanish Rhapsody. Turnabout TV 34444S.

Liszt: Hungarian Rhapsodies. 3 Vox CBX 5452.

Liszt: Operatic and Dramatic Fantasies. Turnabout TV 34163S.

Liszt: Piano Music. Ballade No. 2 in B Minor; Elegy No. 2; *La Lugubre gondola*; *Nuages gris*; Transcendental Etudes (12); 2 Turnabout TV 3422-25.

Louis Kentner plays Liszt. Apparitions No. 1; Ballade No. 2 in B Minor; *Bénédiction de Dieu dans la solitude*; Elegy No. 2; *La Lugubre gondola*; *Nuages gris*; *Harmonies poétiques et réligieuses*; Five Hungarian Folksongs. Four Little Piano Pieces; *Reminiscences de Don Juan*; Spinning Song from Wagner's "Flying Dutchman"; *Valse de Concert sur deux motifs de "Lucia et Parisina"*; *Valse de l'ópera "Faust" de Charles Gounod*; Wedding March and Elves' Dance from "Midsummer Night's Dream." Vox Box CDX2 5503. (2 CDs).

Piano Favorites. Beethoven: Bagatelle in A Minor ("Für Elise"). Chopin: Etudes, op. 10, nos. 3, 5, 12; Prelude, op. 28, no. 15; Waltzes, op. 64, nos. 1, 2. Liszt: *Gnomenreigen*; *Waldesrauschen*. Mozart: *Rondo a la Turca* (Sonata, K. 331). Paganini-Liszt: *La Campanella*. Schubert: *Moment musical* in F Minor, D. 780, no. 3. Schumann: *Traumerei*

(*Kinderscenen*). Wagner-Liszt: Spinning Song (*Der fliegende Holländer*). *Hungaroton* White Label CD HRC 050.

KOCSIS, ZOLTAN: b. 30 May 1952, Budapest, Hungary.

> Whatever Kocsis does, he does with a vengeance—passionately, thoroughly, conscientiously.
>
> Bálint András Varga (*High Fidelity*, January 1987)

It is an unusual concert pianist who tells an interviewer that musicians are performing too much and that there are too many mediocre performances; but Zoltán Kocsis, who made that statement, is truly an unusual pianist, particularly for his generation. "Young pianists," he says, "are not ready to go out and play so many performances. I don't want to judge them, but especially in the last 40 years, classical music has become real show business. They don't have any choice but to perform, perform, perform, keep their names in evidence or they are instantly forgotten." (Crutchfield) This is not just talk. Kocsis has built his international career slowly, preferring, unlike most of his colleagues, to give of his talent and energy at home in Hungary, where musicians have more time to prepare and more time to rehearse.

Kocsis is said to be shy, perhaps even inhibited, but he is also an articulate, outspoken critic of today's musical environment: too many performances not up to standard; too many orchestras dominated by unions; pianists conducting from the keyboard (a bad idea, says Kocsis), and so on. Airing his untempered opinions may not endear him to the musical world, but in Hungary Kocsis's strong personality and multiple musical activities have already made him, says writer Varga, "a national institution."

Even at age three Kocsis was fascinated by the piano. He started improvising, and in time was able to listen to music on the radio and play it back in the same key and the same rhythms. At age five he began music lessons with a teacher named Szmrecsany, who assigned endless technical exercises and also, when Kocsis was six, introduced him to the music of Bartók. After five years with Szmrecsany, Kocsis studied (1964–68) piano and composition at the Béla Bartók Conservatory. In 1968, at age 16, he enrolled at the Franz Liszt Academy of Music and studied principally with Pál Kadosa and Ferenc Rados.

In 1970 Kocsis's debut, a tour of Hungary and winning first prize in the Beethoven Piano Competition, sponsored by Hungarian Radio, plunged him into a career. In 1971 he played his first foreign concert, a performance in Dresden with the Dresden Philharmonic Orchestra, and that same year Kocsis toured the United States, playing Bartók's Concerto No. 1 with the Budapest Symphony Orchestra, György Lehel conducting. In 1973 he received the Liszt Prize, awarded by the Hungarian government. He was appointed assistant to Pál

Kadosa in 1973, graduated, with distinction, from the Liszt Academy in 1974, and in 1976 succeeded Kadosa as professor of piano at the Academy.

Kocsis formed a close personal and professional relationship with Sviatoslav Richter. The two played a four-hand recital of Schubert compositions at Hermann Prey's Schubertiade Festival at Hohenems, Austria, and at the 1977 Tours Festival, an event one European music critic called "the most moving concert in years."

Since that time Kocsis has concertized (about 50–60 appearances a season) mostly in Europe, and also in the Americas, Australia and the Far East. Kocsis and conductor Ivan Fischer founded (1983) the Budapest Festival Orchestra, selecting members from the Hungarian State Orchestra, Hungarian Radio Orchestra, the opera orchestra, some free-lance musicians and also students from the Liszt Academy. This new orchestra, sponsored largely by the Budapest Spring Festival and *Hungaroton* Records, played its first concert in December 1983. In 1987 Kocsis and the orchestra recorded a complete survey of Bartók's music for solo piano and orchestra—three CDs, released by Philips (see Discog.). Kocsis takes great pride in the fact that this orchestra, unlike orchestras controlled by unions, has from 15 to 20 rehearsals for each concert or recording. Kocsis also helped to establish the New Music Studio in Budapest, formed to present concerts of contemporary music by such composers as Cage, Glass, Feldman, Boulez, Stockhausen and others. In addition to all this, Kocsis has taught and composed steadily. Since 1976 he has been professor of piano at the Liszt Academy, and he has composed since early childhood.

Writer Varga says Kocsis has become a national institution in his native Hungary not only because of his piano performances and recordings but because of his "unique personality and his diverse activities." With Kocsis, "diverse" means playing concerts, composing, teaching, writing, consulting (for *Hungaroton* Records) and conducting. And with him "unique" means "unpredictable, full of contradictions, incapable of compromise." (Varga) The Hungarian government has repeatedly honored him: the Liszt Prize in 1973; in 1978 the Kossuth Prize, the government's highest award; in 1984 he was named "Merited Artist." Kocsis and his wife (m. 1986), pianist Adrienne Hauser, live in Budapest.

In two dozen British/American reviews dating from 1971 to 1992, there is not one all-out negative critique of Kocsis's playing. These particular reviews portray him as a natural talent backed by a very solid musicianship. They describe his technique as, variously, icily brilliant, heroic, dazzlingly fluent. They portray Kocsis as a pianist with (again, variously) iron fingers, steely control, superior rhythmic steadiness, rhythmic precision; and as a headstrong, strong-willed performer, with a towering sound that perfectly matches the grand vision of his interpretations. Kocsis's subtle *rubatos*, eloquence in slow movements, even his sometimes controversial hair-raising tempos, all indicate a musician who thinks for himself, and who thinks seriously, with intelligence and respect for the music he is projecting. What some critics miss is "a little caprice, a little laughter, in Kocsis' musicianship."

In the performances covered by these 20 years of reviews, Kocsis played a great deal of Bartók and Rachmaninoff; the Beethoven Concertos Nos. 4 and 5; some Liszt, Debussy, Schubert, Brahms and Bach. He chooses substantial, challenging works rather than crowd-pleasers.

Kocsis plays Bartók with great understanding and style. Only 19 years old when he made his first New York appearance (24 Nov 1971, playing Bartók's Concerto No. 1 with the Budapest Symphony Orchestra conducted by György Lehel), even at that young age Kocsis showed that he was the master of this difficult work. "He not only breezed through the considerable technical and tonal difficulties, but also did it without being percussive, and he made music as he went along." (*NYT*, 26 Nov 1971) On 19 March 1992 Kocsis played this same concerto for his debut performance with the Boston Symphony Orchestra, conducted by Marek Janowski. Although not a profound performance, it was exciting. "He played with power, command and hellbent determination. He has a prodigious technique that enables him not only to dispatch the octaves, chords and clusters that thicken the piano writing, but to bring out inner voices and details." (*BG*, 21 March 1992)

A performance (4 March 1987) of Bartók's Concerto No. 2 with the Toronto Symphony Orchestra, Andrew Davis conducting, once again confirmed Kocsis's understanding of Bartók and his own wonderful virtuosity. However, "he excelled in more than a mastery of the stringent technical demands. There were suggestions of mood changes as frequent as the shifts from soloist to orchestra in the first movement, where the percussive character of the piano was predominant. But the emotional range was much more clearly projected in the 'Night Music' of the Adagio, where lyrical piano tone also played a part. It was a quality performance." (*GloM*, 5 March 1987)

On 12 October 1983 Kocsis gave a superlative reading of Rachmaninoff's Concerto No. 3 in San Francisco, with the San Francisco Symphony Orchestra under Edo de Waart. "Kocsis took some startling liberties . . . especially in his general softening of many fortes written in the score. . . . But his finale was played at the blinding speed of a Horowitz, every note in place, every chord projected just so, but with a power you'd never conceive was stored up within that wiry frame." (*SJM*, 14 Oct 1983)

Beethoven is said to have played his Piano Concerto No. 4 fast and impetuously at its first performance. The 25-year-old Kocsis's performance of that concerto with the Dresden *Staatskapelle*, Herbert Blomstedt conducting, at the 1978 Edinburgh Festival "matched that description in the finale, which went like thunder and lightning, or in the middle of the first movement. . . . But many of us will chiefly remember his highly poetic soft playing, fires banked up with real mastery, in all three movements." (*TL*, 7 Sept 1978)

At a Carnegie Hall performance (2 Feb 1990) of the Beethoven Concerto No. 5 with the Warsaw Philharmonic Orchestra, conducted by Kazimierz Kord, Kocsis, "for his part, never let us forget for a moment his ability to fill this big hall with piano sound. . . . Mr. Kocsis' technique is totally under control; the musical instincts excellent. Raw energy, however, seems to count for a little too much in his set of values." (*NYT*, 4 Feb 1990)

A Carnegie Hall recital (26 Feb 1987) consisted of three Liszt pieces (Hungarian Rhapsody No. 5 in E Minor, *Ave Maria*, *Grosses Konzertsolo*) and Schubert's Sonata in A Major, D. 959. In the midst of Liszt's lavish virtuosity, Kocsis "showed neither the structural command . . . nor the sheer love of virtuosic display—the feeling of *joy* in playing such music—that so many pianists of the past epitomized." (*NYT*, 1 March 1987) However, when Kocsis gave this same program at Chicago's Orchestra Hall a few days later (1 March 1987), he played the Rhapsody's massive chords with weighty grandeur and "unfolded melodies with an unerring sense of when to push forth or hold back." As for the *Grosses Konzertsolo*, he "elevated its overblown technique into an inviting musical statement. . . . Kocsis sees the musical meaning within the pyrotechnics, and he always makes it vividly clear." (*CT*, 2 March 1987)

Kocsis's eclecticism and versatility were in evidence at a Los Angeles recital on 17 February 1993—a program of Beethoven, Debussy, Liszt and Schubert, the Schubert (three short pieces) being most outstanding. "From the evidence . . . he has a close rapport with, and intimate knowledge of, this composer, plus much of the temperament, astuteness and technique to hold these apparently rambling structures together. Three pieces by Debussy revealed similar expertise. . . . His playing of 'D'un cahier d'esquisses,' the Arabesque No. 1 and 'Reflets dans l'eau' became demonstrations of a consistently liquid tone and perfectly gauged dynamics." (*LAT*, 19 Feb 1993)

Zoltán Kocsis has established an impressive reputation. If as yet the final word is not in on his playing, it seems always to be exciting and certainly is never dull.

Like Glenn Gould, whose recordings he greatly admires, Kocsis prefers recording to performing live, and he records meticulously. His recordings for *Hungaroton* (i.e., Bartók Concertos Nos. 1 and 2, see Discog.), made when he was in his early twenties, show not only youthful energy and bristling technique but already signs of his elegant approach. In 1979 Philips Records signed him on, and both record companies appear prominently in his ever expanding discography.

Kocsis refutes the idea that he is a specialist in the music of Bartók; however, he certainly plays it often and has recorded much of it, including the complete works for solo piano and orchestra (Grammy, 1988). These are available on a three-CD set from Philips—the three concertos, the Rhapsody, the Scherzo and the Music for Strings, Percussion and Celesta, all recorded with the Budapest Festival Orchestra, conducted by Ivan Fischer (see Discog.). "Although the Kocsis/Fischer collaboration produces plenty of excitement, it is the sheer intelligibility of their performances that makes this release so special. At 36 Kocsis has established himself as one of the most interesting virtuosi of his generation." (Turok)

Among his numerous recordings, two beautiful Debussy albums stand out as very special (see Discog.). One of these (Philips 422404-2) won the 1990 Gramophone Award as the best instrumental recording of the year: "The terrific refinement of Kocsis's pianism is matched by a compellingly vivid piano sound from Philips and the end result provided me with some of the most exotic and colouristically evocative piano playing I have heard for a long time." (*Gram*, Oct 1990)

Kocsis's recording of two Mozart concertos was named the *Ovation* Recording of Distinction in August 1985. Playing with the Ferenc Liszt Chamber Orchestra, János Rolla conducting, Kocsis views Mozart in a robust, somewhat extroverted manner, one that is persuasively exciting. "From the very first bars, the music emerges full of life, rhythms are well sprung and melodies soar. Kocsis' technique is flawless but, more importantly, he imbues every note with energy and communication."

Kocsis is now recording all of Bartók's solo piano music. The first volume (see Discog.), a collection of Bartók's early compositions, bodes extremely well for succeeding issues. "He plays everything here with clean, technically assured sonorities, but the music never seems scrubbed up. Indeed, he plays many of these works as though he'd just written them. . . . This series could become a landmark." (*StR*, June 1993)

SELECTED REFERENCES

Crutchfield, Will. "A Pianist, Bartók Well In Hand." *New York Times*, 5 Feb 1988, sec. 3, p. 3.

Eckert, Thor, Jr. "Who will replace the honored pianists?" *Christian Science Monitor*, 21 May 1987, Arts-Leisure, pp. 25, 28.

ICM Artists, Ltd., publicity brochure 1993.

Johnson, Stephen. "Finding the Mean Tone." *Gramophone*, Feb 1990, p. 1443.

Turok, Paul. "Highly Rewarding Bartók by Kocsis." *New York Times*, 22 May 1988, p. 25.

Varga, Bálint András. "The Phenomenon Kocsis." *High Fidelity*, Jan 1987, pp. 71–72.

Waleson, Heidi. "Zoltán Kocsis: Intensity, Originality and a Passion for Bartók." *Ovation*, Aug 1988, pp. 9–10, 14.

Wiser, John D. "Fragments of a Conversation with Zoltán Kocsis." *Fanfare*, May/June 1988, pp. 338–340.

See also Bibliography: IWWM; Mac/Gr2; Sch/Gre.

SELECTED REVIEWS

BG: 21 March 1992. *CT*: 2 March 1987. *DT*: 10 Feb 1983. *FB*: 8 Oct 1984. *GloM*: 5 March 1987. *IS*: 4 April 1987. *LAT*: 31 Oct 1983; 19 Feb 1993. *MiT*: 27 March 1987; 29 Jan 1988. *MM*: July 1978; Jan 1984. *MT*: Nov 1983. *NYT*: 26 Nov 1971; 7 March 1984; 4 March 1985; 1 March 1987; 6 Feb 1988; 4 Feb 1990. *SFC*: 12 Oct 1984. *SJM*: 14 Oct 1983. *TL*: 8 Aug 1978; 7 Sept 1978.

SELECTED DISCOGRAPHY

Bach: Concerto in D Minor, BWV 1052; Concerto in E Major, BWV 1053. *Hungaroton* HCD 12916. Simon/Liszt CO.

Bartók: Allegro barbaro; 3 Hungarian Folk Songs; Hungarian Peasant Songs; 3 Rondos on Folk Tunes; Romanian Folk Dances; Sonata; Suite, op. 14. Denon CD-7813.

Bartók: Concertos for Piano Nos. 1, 2 and 3; Music for Strings, Percussion and Celesta; Rhapsody for Piano and Orchestra, op. 1; Scherzo for Piano and Orchestra. Philips 416 831-2 (3 CDs). Fischer/Budapest FO.

Bartók: For Children. *Hungaroton* HCD 12304-2.

Bartók: Works for Piano Solo, Vol. 1. 14 Bagatelles; 2 Elegies; 6 Romanian Folk Dances; Sonatine; 3 Hungarian Folk Tunes. Philips 434 104 (CD).

Beethoven: Concerto No. 4 in G Major, op. 58; Sonata in E-flat Major, op. 81a. Fidelio 1814 (CD). Lukács/Budapest SO.

Children's Corner. Bartók: *Mikrokosmos* (excerpts). Beethoven: *Sonatine* in G Major; *Sonatine* in F Major. Debussy: Children's Corner. Mozart: Sonata in C Major, K. 545. Schumann: *Kinderscenen.* Quintana 903006 (CD).

Debussy: *Arabesques*; *Berceuse héroique*; *Hommage à Haydn*; *Images* (1, 2); *L'Isle joyeuse*; *Rêverie*; *D'un cahier d'esquisses*. Philips 422404-2.

Debussy: *Estampes*; *Images* (1894); *Pour le piano*; *Suite bergamasque*. Philips 412 118-2.

Haydn: Sonata in B-flat Major, Hob. XVI:18; Sonata in C Minor, Hob. XVI:20; Sonata in E-flat Major, Hob. XVI:45; Sonata in A-flat Major, Hob. XVI:46. *Hungaroton* HCD-11618.

Liszt: Concerto No. 1 in E-flat Major; Concerto No. 2 in A Major. Dohnányi: Variations on a Nursery Song, op. 25. Philips 422380-2. Fischer/Budapest FO.

Mozart: Concerto in A Major, K. 414; Concerto in A Major, K. 488. *Hungaroton* HCD 12472. Rolla/Liszt CO.

Rachmaninoff: Concerto No. 1 in F-sharp Minor, op. 1; Concerto No. 2 in C Minor, op. 18. Philips 412881-2. De Waart/San Francisco SO.

Rachmaninoff: Concerto No. 3 in D Minor, op. 30; Concerto No. 4 in G Minor, op. 40. Philips 411475-2. De Waart/San Francisco SO.

VIDEO

Mozart on Tour Vol. 5. Concerto in A Major, K. 488. Philips 070 242-3. Belohlavek/ Virtuosi di Praga.

KOVACEVICH, STEPHEN (BISHOP): b. San Pedro, California, 17 October 1940.

> Our society . . . wants to hear a performance that's note perfect . . . which is a pity. . . . Forget about accuracy. Just go for the music.
> Stephen Bishop-Kovacevich (*The Age*, 12 May 1986)

Three decades of reviews prove conclusively that Kovacevich's credo of "going for the music" has served him well, for he ranks among the elite pianists of his generation. He began his career as Stephen Bishop, but in his mid-thirties became Stephen Bishop-Kovacevich, not as a passing whim but as a proud declaration of his Yugoslav heritage. He had been born Kovacevich (his father Nicholas Kovacevich was a Croatian immigrant, his mother Loreta [Zuban] Kovacevich a first-generation Croatian-American), but his name was changed to Bishop after his mother remarried. (Several years ago, he dropped the "Bishop" to become Stephen Kovacevich.)

He was raised in Berkeley, California, and from age 8 to 18 went across the bridge to San Francisco to study piano with Lev Shorr, a pupil of Anna Essipoff. At his first public appearance (20 Feb 1952), at age 11, Kovacevich played the Jean Françaix Concertino with the San Francisco Youth Symphony, Kurt Adler conducting. A few weeks later the 11-year-old played his first public recital (23 April 1952) at The Century Club in San Francisco, and the next day one reviewer wrote of the eleven-year-old boy's fabulous memory and well-trained hands: "He gave a long, highly varied program of classical and modern works and carried it off with a great deal of spirit and charm." (*SFC*, 24 April 1952)

The printed program for that recital claims that young Kovacevich's repertoire included concertos by Beethoven, Schumann, Mozart and Ravel. By the time he reached 14, he had already played the Schumann A Minor and the Ravel G Major concertos with the San Francisco Symphony Orchestra. The teen-age Kovacevich loved playing brilliant works by Chopin and Liszt, and Shorr let him do so; but in time Kovacevich himself felt the need to leaven his repertoire. Instinctively he turned to Beethoven's piano music, finding there exactly the right catalyst for his artistic development. Thirty years later Kovacevich told interviewer Rosslyn Beeby that at 18 he had fallen in love with Beethoven's piano music, especially the Diabelli Variations, and that he had always loved the symphonies and quartets.

In the spring of 1959 (Kovacevich was enrolled at the University of California at Berkeley from September 1958 to May 1959) he attended two Myra Hess recitals in San Francisco, and for him, "that was it." Sidney Griller of the Griller Quartet, then in residence at the Berkeley campus, arranged an audition with Dame Myra, and she agreed to take Kovacevich as a student. He went to London that summer and had two years of intensive work with Hess before her health began to fail. By that time, Kovacevich was already beginning to give his own concerts.

Like most 20-year-olds, as he remembers it, he thought he knew everything until in her quiet, regal way Myra Hess showed him how very little he actually did know. He had, for instance, no sense of sound. Shorr had given him
a solid technical foundation but his touch was heavy and unusually hard. Under
Dame Myra's guidance, Kovacevich learned to play down bravura and speed and
to think more about acquiring the right sound for each composer, even the right
sound for different periods in a composer's life. She showed him (Myra Hess
used the Matthay technique) how to achieve the "right sound" through proper application of weight and relaxation of muscles. That abstract process becomes
crystal clear with Dame Myra's wonderfully graphic explanation: Just as you
would not hold a postage stamp with a viselike grip if you were trying to figure
out how much it weighed, you should not be rigid when feeling the weight of
the keyboard.

Kovacevich launched his own professional career. He simply hired the
Wigmore Hall (five times within two years), beginning with his London debut
on 12 November 1961. "It was no lightweight program [the Berg Sonata, three
Preludes and Fugues from Bach's Well-Tempered Clavier, Book I, and
Beethoven's Diabelli Variations], and he is clearly no lightweight musician."
(*TL*, 13 Nov 1961) Renting a recital hall left him small profits, but ultimately
he began to get playing engagements. In August 1962 he substituted for an ailing Dame Myra at a Promenade Concert, playing the Beethoven Concerto No. 4,
with Sir Malcolm Sargent conducting. Within a few years, his performances
throughout Britain and in Europe earned him a reputation as one of the most talented of the young pianists. Bolstered by some excellent recordings and superb
British reviews, he returned to America and made his New York debut at Town
Hall on 9 March 1967.

Now one of the first-rank pianists on the international circuit,
Kovacevich has appeared at the major European festivals, as soloist with the
world's great orchestras, and frequently as a soloist at the BBC Henry Wood
Promenade Concerts. Besides his many engagements throughout Great Britain
(he has made his home in London since 1959), he has toured in Europe, the
United States, Japan, Israel, Australia, New Zealand, South America and the Far
East.

In 1984 Kovacevich began a second career when he conducted an all-
Beethoven program with the Houston Symphony Orchestra. On 9 May 1986 he
led the Australian Chamber Orchestra in another all-Beethoven program at the
Sydney Opera House and conducted the Piano Concerto No. 1 from the keyboard.
This performance so delighted the concert's sponsors that they offered him, and
he accepted, a three-year contract as their Principal Guest Conductor. In 1989
the ACO renewed the contract for another three years. In September 1990
Kovacevich also became Artistic Director and Principal Conductor of the Irish
Chamber Orchestra. Among others, he has conducted the Royal Liverpool
Philharmonic, New Zealand Symphony, BBC Philharmonic, Northern Sinfonia,
Scottish Chamber, Ulster, Tivoli and Gulbenkian orchestras. In January 1990
he had a huge success in his debut with the City of Birmingham Symphony, and
the orchestra re-invited him for the 1991–92 season. He made his Los Angeles

debut as pianist-conductor with the Los Angeles Philharmonic Orchestra at the Hollywood Bowl (summer 1990) performing two different all-Mozart programs.

Kovacevich claims that for him the conducting feeds the piano, that when he conducts from the keyboard he plays the piano better. Knowing how it feels to walk onstage alone and play a solo instrument, Kovacevich has a special empathy with the soloists he conducts, especially pianists. Despite hundreds of performances, as a pianist he can still inexplicably suffer from nerves. Conducting, he claims, makes him feel "a thousand times less nervous" and is "300 times more fun." However, as recently as the summer of 1989 Kovacevich told a *Los Angeles Times* interviewer that he could still say that the old thrills of playing the piano have not left him.

His critical Urtext edition of a selection of Schubert's piano music, based on autographs and first editions, was published by Oxford University Press (1972) in its *Keyboard Classics* series. Since 1987 he has held the International Chair of Piano Studies at the Royal Academy of Music. Almost half of Kovacevich's time is devoted to conducting; yet he usually plays about 50 piano concerts a year.

Whatever their criticism, reviewers almost unanimously agree that Stephen Kovacevich is an exciting pianist, known especially for his distinguished interpretations of the classical repertoire, particularly Beethoven. He also plays Bartók and Stravinsky and Berg, and he has premiered new works (Richard Rodney Bennet and John Taverner have dedicated piano concertos to him); but in general he finds "not a lot of worthwhile ideas" in contemporary music.

Kovacevich is a highly intelligent musician with deeply musical instincts; a commanding if not a "born virtuoso" technique; a very personal, bold and unaffected style; and, like his teacher Myra Hess, an often tender and beautiful sound. Conversely, negative criticisms have complained of his "wired, steely-fingered pianistic style," his "galloping tempos," or the sometimes brute force of his "cutting" musical attack. Overall, the broad spectrum of reviews attesting to his standing as one of the finest of his generation of pianists indicates that his fame rests not so much on a mighty technique or profound interpretation as on some intangible quality always present in his playing.

For example, when Kovacevich and the English Chamber Orchestra played (5 March 1978) the Mozart D Minor Concerto, K. 466, in London, "There was nothing overtly grand in his manner, yet the dexterity of his figuration in the first movement told its own tale of perfect mastery seriously applied. . . . This was piano playing to overawe." (*TL*, 7 March 1978) Again, Kovacevich's execution of the Schubert Sonata in B-flat Major at the Kennedy Center on 19 March 1987 may not have been "quite note-perfect but musically it was on an exalted plane of concentration and imagination. . . . Seldom does a player plumb as deeply beneath its lyric complexities. . . . By comparison, even the Horowitz recording seems a little too slick." (*WP*, 26 March 1987)

Kovacevich's interpretations of the last three Beethoven sonatas at the University of California at Berkeley on 30 January 1982 seemed to focus on a larger vision of the music rather than on detail. A marvel of sound, "the tone he drove from the piano was, frankly, shocking and harsh, as he emphasized the forceful energies [op. 109]. He arrived at the fugues, and they were all smoothed out into as fascinating and transparent play of counterpoint as one will hear from any master." (*SFC*, 1 Feb 1982) Another Beethoven performance (9 Jan 1985)—the "Emperor" Concerto with the Minnesota Orchestra, Neeme Järvi conducting—was "certainly not a probing reading of this majestic work, but it was a performance of dexterity, energy and, above all, muscularity. Bishop-Kovacevich has one of the brightest touches to be heard from any pianist. . . . Pianists this exciting don't come along regularly." (*SPPP*, 10 Jan 1985)

Early in his career Kovacevich earned kudos for programming Bach, Mozart and Beethoven (3 Feb 1963, Wigmore Hall), thus proving himself as being more interested in the solid substance of music than in piano playing for its own sake. "Fortunately he had a strong and incisive technique which enabled him to express himself with clarity and conviction, but it was what he actually had to reveal about the music itself that singled him out as a young artist of unusual distinction." (*TL*, 4 Feb 1963) Kovacevich has lived up to that early promise. Twenty years later, in a recital (10 Dec 1984) at St. John's Church in London, his "ease of movement and beauty of sound in Bach's Fourth Partita" moved one critic to elevate that performance into the lofty company of Dinu Lipatti's now famous, almost definitive recording of the Bach Partita No. 1. (*MT*, Feb 1985)

In a performance (8 July 1989) of Mozart's Concerto in C Major, K. 503, with Heiichiro Oyama conducting the Los Angeles Philharmonic Orchestra, Kovacevich "favored eloquence over indulgence, finesse over flash. His reading was by most standards not a particularly emotional one, but one both intelligent and personal." (*LAT*, 10 July 1989) When Kovacevich joined the London Philharmonic Orchestra, Mariss Jansons conducting, at Festival Hall on 28 November 1992 for another Mozart concerto, K. 491, in C Minor, "Janson's characteristic spontaneity was nicely offset by the more cerebral approach of the soloist. . . . [Kovacevich] allowed a dynamic sense of drama to emerge from a tight rational control. Eschewing sentimentality . . . Kovacevich nevertheless forged a powerful emotional bond with orchestra and conductor." (*TL*, 1 Dec 1992)

Most of Kovacevich's recordings are outstanding, some are magnificent. It is regrettable that so many have been cut from the catalogues. An early (1969) recording of the Diabelli Variations, his first recording for his major producer Philips, was the work with which he was said to have conquered London. These variations are of such diversity that it is all but impossible to expect one performer to realize all 33 with equal effect. "Where Bishop comes closest to that illusionary objective is not in his dexterity, velocity, or depth of insight. . . . It is rather, in his comprehension of the character and mood of every variation, his stress on the *musical* meaning they convey rather than on the 'seriousness' of the project." (*SR*, 26 July 1969) Reissued on CD (see Discog.), these variations still command admiration. Kovacevich's performance "has a clarity, poise and vitality that has commended itself to more than one generation of collectors over the past 20 years." (*Gram*, Aug 1990)

Kovacevich won an Edison Award in 1970 for his recording of the Bartók Concerto No. 2 and the Stravinsky Concerto for Piano and Wind Orchestra. "The Bartok in particular is an electrifying performance which shows Bishop's full command of the highly strung nervosity of the Hungarian's creative and emotional style. The range of touch is impressive in its completeness, and the dynamic variety ranges from a hushed, muted pianissimo to the wildest, most barbaric display of fortissimo tone which is steely without ever being offensive." (*RR*, July 1973)

Kovacevich's LPs (1970, 1976) of Bartók's three piano concertos, now on CD (see Discog.), are "readings which capture the rhythmic spring, the inner intensity, and the controlled fanaticism so crucial to the Bartók idiom." (*Gram*, May 1991) He has also made a stunning recording of the Bartók *Mikrokosmos* Book VI and the Out of Doors suite. "The characterization is brilliantly intense. *From the Diary of a Fly, Ostinato,* March, and the Bulgarian Dances themselves, as well as the savagery and combined sultry evocations of the *Out of Doors* suite, spark off a superb response. This is superlative Bartók playing." (*RR*, July 1973)

Kovacevich is fortunate in having Sir Colin Davis and either the London or the BBC Symphony Orchestras as collaborators in his distinctive, imaginative interpretations of the Beethoven concertos. In addition to the five Beethoven concertos, they have recorded the Brahms concertos, the Grieg and Schumann concertos, the Bartók No. 2 and the Stravinsky Concerto (see Discog.). Their recording of the Grieg and Schumann concertos offers refreshing versions of these two full-blown Romantic favorites. Kovacevich shines mightily in the Schumann masterpiece. "There is refinement and strength, the virtuosity sparkles, the expressive elements are perfectly integrated with the need for bravura." (Gra/Goo, see Bibliog.)

Kovacevich's readings of the poetic Schubert Sonata in B-flat Major, D. 960, and a program of Brahms piano pieces (Philips 411 137-2) are exceptional. The lyrical Schubert (see Discog.), with its leisurely first two movements, is projected with great sensitivity and warmth. The more introspective of the Brahms pieces are wonderfully personal, with a most judicious use of *rubato*. The passionate Capriccios of op. 116 are appealing emotional portraits.

Kovacevich first recorded the Brahms Concerto No. 1 in D Minor in 1980 with the London Symphony Orchestra, Sir Colin Davis conducting. In 1992 he recorded it anew, this time with the London Symphony Orchestra under Wolfgang Sawallisch, a performance nominated as *Stereo Review*'s Best Recording of the Month (May 1993). It also received the 1993 Gramophone Award in the concerto category. For one reviewer, the new Kovacevich CD on EMI "not only surpasses his own previous version but, as far as I'm concerned, pretty much *every* other recorded version." (*SR*, May 1993) More recently, Kovacevich has recorded Brahms's Concerto No. 2 in B-flat Major with the same conductor and orchestra. From one reviewer: "I don't know a generally better recent version." (*Gram*, Oct 1994)

SELECTED REFERENCES

Beeby, Rosslyn. "Pricking Pomposity." *The Age* (Melbourne, Australia), 12 May 1986, p. 14.

Bishop, Stephen. "Competing with Your own Recordings." *High Fidelity*, Feb 1975, pp. 24–25.

———. "Studying with Myra." In *Myra Hess, By Her Friends*. New York: The Vanguard Press, Inc., 1966, pp. 75–77.

Cariaga, Daniel. "Expatriate Pianist Home for a Visit." *Los Angeles Times*, 8 July 1989, sec. 5, p. 1.

———. "A Pianist Takes up Baton." *Los Angeles Times*, 11 Jan 1987, p. 62.

Clarke, Keith. "Fulfilling an Ambition." *Encore bravo*, 1987, pp. 80–81.

Goldsmith, Harris. "How Do You Like Your Chopin?" *High Fidelity*, June 1973, p. 75.

Johnson, Stephen. "A Return To The Classics." *Gramophone*, Oct 1992, p. 12.

Morrison, Bryce. "Stephen Bishop-Kovacevich." *Music and Musicians*, April 1985, p. 6.

Orga, Ates. "Stephen Bishop." *Records and Recording*, July 1973, pp. 18–23.

Program. The Century Club of San Francisco, 23 April 1952.

Wigmore, Richard. "Second Time Around." *Gramophone*, Oct 1994, pp. 14, 17.

See also Bibliography: Dub/Ref; Eld/Pia; IWWM; New/Gro.

SELECTED REVIEWS

HP: 16 July 1983. *LAT*: 10 May 1976; 17 Jan 1987; 10 July 1989; 9 July 1990. *MG*: 17 July 1985. *MM*: June 1984; Feb 1985; Nov 1985. *MT*: July 1968; Feb 1985. *NYT*: 10 March 1967; 15 Nov 1968; 14 Feb 1972; 1 March 1974; 13 March 1983. *OT*: 24 Feb 1978. *SFC*: 24 April 1952; 7 May 1976; 1 Feb 1982; 25 Feb 1986. *TL*: 13 Nov 1961; 4 Feb 1963; 4 May 1977; 15 July 1977; 6 Dec 1977; 8 Feb 1978; 7 March 1978; 4 June 1979; 7 Jan 1980; 31 March 1981; 24 Nov 1981; 7 April 1982; 11 Dec 1984; 1 Dec 1992; 11 Nov 1993. *SPPP*: 10 Jan 1985. *WP*: 26 March 1987.

SELECTED DISCOGRAPHY

Bartók: Concerto No. 2. Stravinsky: Concerto for Piano and Wind Orchestra. Philips SAL 3779. Davis/London SO.

Bartók: Mikrokosmos, Book VI; Out of Doors; Sonatina. Philips 6500013.

Bartók: Piano Concertos (complete). Philips 426 660-2. Davis/BBC SO.

Beethoven: Concerto No. 1 in C Major, op. 15; Concerto No. 4 in G Major, op. 58. EMI CD-EMX2177. Kovacevich/Australian CO.

Beethoven: Concerto No. 1 in C Major, op. 15; Concerto No. 2 in B-flat Major, op. 19. Philips 422968-2PB. Davis/BBC SO.

Beethoven: Concerto No. 3 in C Minor, op. 37; Concerto No. 4 in G Major, op. 58. Philips 426062-2PCC. Davis/London SO.

Beethoven: Concerto No. 5 in E-flat Major, op. 73 (Emperor). Philips 422482-2. Davis/London SO.

Beethoven: Sonata in C Major, op. 53; Sonata in F-sharp Major, op. 78; Sonata in A-flat Major, op. 110. EMI CDM 7 54896-2.

Beethoven: Sonata in E Minor, op. 90; Sonata in A Major, op. 101; Sonata in C Minor, op. 111. EMI 7 54599-2.

Beethoven: Sonata in A Major, op. 101; Sonata in E Major, op. 109. Philips 7800 569.

Beethoven: Variations on a Theme of Diabelli, op. 120. Philips 422 969-2PCC.

Brahms: Ballades; Scherzo op. 4; *Klavierstücke,* op. 76. Philips 411103-2.

Brahms: Concerto No. 1 in D Minor, op. 15. EMI 7 54578-2. Sawallisch/London PO, 1992. Winner of the 1993 Gramophone Award in the concerto category.

Brahms: Concerto No. 2 in B-flat Major, op. 83. EMI CDC5 55218-2. Sawallisch/London PO.

Brahms: *Klavierstücke,* op. 118; Rhapsodies; Waltzes. Philips 420750-2.

Brahms: *Klavierstücke,* op. 119; *Fantasien,* op. 116; 3 Intermezzi, op. 117. Philips 411137-2.

Grieg: Concerto in A Minor, op. 16. Schumann: Concerto in A Minor, op. 54. Philips 412923-2. Davis/BBC SO.

Mozart: Concerto in D Minor, K. 466; Concerto in A Major, K. 488. Philips 422466-2. Davis/London SO.

Schubert: Sonata in B-flat Major, D. 960. Hyperion CDA-66004.

KRAUS, LILI: b. Budapest, Hungary, 4 March 1903; d. Asheville, North Carolina, 6 November 1986.

> Goethe said we go through some periods of history which show great technical progress and some which have progress of the spirit. But the times which are remembered are the times of the spirit.
> Lili Kraus (Columbia Artists Publicity Release, 1977)

Lili Kraus was herself a passionate, resolute spirit. As a young pianist beginning her career she was, in her own words, "a wild Hungarian overflowing with effusive, undisciplined emotions." Experience and maturity restrained some of those emotions, but through good times and bad, even including three years of forced labor in a Japanese prison camp, Mme. Kraus retained her indefatigable spirit. She loved life ("I adore life, I adore beauty, I adore ugliness") and lived it to the fullest. Above all else, Lili Kraus loved music so deeply that when, after more than a year in prison away from her husband and children, she was asked what she most wanted, Kraus replied, "I would love a piano and to be reunited with my family, in that order." For Lili Kraus, music always came first.

Kraus remembered her parents as being poorly matched and living in near poverty. Her father Victor Kraus, a Czech, eked out a living sharpening knives and scissors. It was her Hungarian mother Irene (Bak) Kraus, (a singer denied a professional career because at the time it was deemed inappropriate for a lady) who insisted that her daughter learn to play the piano. At age six Kraus began piano lessons and at age eight enrolled at the Royal Academy of Music in Budapest. The first year she studied with a student teacher, the next year began piano with Arnold Székely, a pianist who had studied with Busoni. Kraus also studied theory with Zoltán Kodály and chamber music with Leo Weiner; and throughout her nine years at the Academy, she practiced regularly from two to three hours daily. She was scheduled to spend her final year in the master class of Arpád Szendy, but Szendy died before classes started.

Left without a teacher, Kraus accepted a job teaching piano to children in a small town near the Czechoslovakian border and completed her course work at the Academy by proxy. At age 17 she graduated from the Academy with highest honors and later returned to study piano with Béla Bartók. In 1923 Kraus left Budapest to attend Severin Eisenberger's master class at the Vienna Academy of Music. Completing the three-year course in one year, she stayed on in Vienna to study with Edward Steuermann, a specialist in the music of Schoenberg.

In 1924 the Vienna Academy engaged Kraus as an assistant teacher and in 1925 appointed her a full professor to teach a master class, a position she held for six years. Meanwhile, Kraus made her professional debut in 1923 in Amsterdam, performing with the *Concertgebouw* Orchestra, conducted by Willem Mengelberg. Within two years, despite her teaching duties, she had played about 45 recitals, including a performance with the Dresden Philharmonic Orchestra and one with the Berlin Philharmonic Orchestra. While in Berlin she played for Wilhelm Furtwängler, who predicted a brilliant career for Kraus and recommended that she study with Artur Schnabel. However, Eisenberger, her teacher at the time, rejected the idea, warning her that Schnabel would only turn her into a caricature of himself. Although deeply disappointed, the loyal Kraus deferred to her teacher.

In 1931 Lili Kraus married Dr. Otto Mandl, a prosperous businessman, doctor of philosophy and art patron. They had a daughter and a son and, although Dr. Mandl was about 17 years her senior, the marriage, Kraus often said, was ideal. After the Depression destroyed his business, Dr. Mandl devoted himself to his wife's career. Always at her side—not as official manager but as guide, confidant, critic, promoter and traveling companion—under his loving care, Kraus's life and career blossomed. When he learned that because of Steuermann she had given up the idea of studying with Schnabel, Dr. Mandl arranged an audition with Schnabel in Berlin. Within two months Kraus had about 20 lessons with Schnabel. In order to make life easier, the Mandls moved to Berlin, and for the next four years, until 1934, Kraus had lessons or coaching from Schnabel. Unlike her lessons with Bartók, always one-on-one private sessions, Kraus never had a private lesson with Schnabel. Sessions were always conducted with 20 to 25 auditors present. Whereas with Bartók she had studied mostly Bartók's works, occasionally a Beethoven sonata or some Liszt, Schnabel introduced her to a wider repertoire, including Mozart, Schubert, Weber and Brahms. The Mandls and the Schnabels became lifelong good friends.

Beginning in 1931 Kraus made annual concert tours, dreading the long separations from her children but driven to perform—in Europe, Great Britain, China, Japan, Australia, New Zealand and South Africa. Besides her many solo appearances, she developed an enormously successful partnership with the violinist Szymon Goldberg. Known as the Kraus-Goldberg Duo, they played throughout Europe and recorded the 10 Beethoven violin and piano sonatas. These recordings and her solo recordings added greatly to Kraus's growing international fame.

From 1932 until late 1938 the Mandl family lived on Lake Como near Tremezzo, Italy, and left only because of the fast-spreading Italian Nazi movement and the fact that Otto Mandl was Jewish. They went directly to Paris, and early in 1939 to London, where temporary papers gave them the protection of British citizenship. Kraus performed often in London up to the time England became embroiled in World War II. Disregarding the threat of war, the entire Mandl family set out with Kraus on a long concert tour due to begin in Djakarta, Indonesia (then Batavia, Java) in 1940 and finish in San Francisco in February 1943 with Kraus's American debut, a performance with the San Francisco Symphony Orchestra, conducted by Pierre Monteux. That tour never materialized. The Mandls arrived safely in Djakarta, but after the Japanese occupied Malaya, further travel became too dangerous. They took a house in Bandung, a town in the mountains above Djakarta, from which Kraus, accompanied by her husband, traveled once a month to Djarkarta to play a radio broadcast recital, a routine she continued even after the Japanese occupied Indonesia. She also gave recitals at some of the Japanese prison camps set up for women and children.

Without warning, Kraus herself was arrested (March 1942) on a false charge (conspiracy to kill the Japanese guards and release British and Australian prisoners) concocted by an imprisoned Dutch woman as a means of gaining her own freedom. As a result, Kraus spent nearly two years in a forced-labor camp located in the mountains above Djakarta. Not knowing whether her husband and children were alive (all ultimately were imprisoned) and without a piano to play or music to read, the resilient Kraus kept her spirits high by playing music in her mind, mentally going through the masterpieces in her repertoire and each time finding new values, new insights or new delights that she had hitherto not even thought of. Lili Kraus always believed that mentally performing these works over and over again, even as she scrubbed latrines and gutters, greatly improved her ability to memorize.

In December 1943 a Japanese officer, having recognized her name, allowed her to play the piano one hour a week. Three months later a Japanese symphony conductor, who had once heard Kraus play, noticed her name on a list of prisoners and interceded on her behalf. Transferred to a detention center in Djakarta, she was finally reunited with her family. For the next year and a half the four Mandls lived in what had once been a single-car garage; even so, Kraus had an old piano, courtesy of the symphony conductor. Freed in October 1945 when the Japanese surrendered Djakarta, two months later the Mandls were in Australia, Kraus having received an offer from the Australian Broadcasting Company to play a 40-concert tour. Although not ready for a tour—she weighed less than 100 pounds and her body was covered with infections—she knew that this tour meant a fresh start. The family had been stripped of everything they owned, and Dr. Mandl, a diabetic, was too ill to work after the years of imprisonment. To prepare, the indomitable Kraus practiced in the Sydney radio studios—long hours of "utter agony" in the Australian heat—and during the next 18 months played 120 concerts in Australia and New Zealand. In recognition of her "unrelenting efforts in aid of countries in need as well as for educational achievement," Kraus was granted honorary New Zealand citizenship.

With her hands grown strong and powerful from prison labor, Kraus felt fine about her playing until she made her first postwar recording in London in 1948. While her hands were indeed strong, her fingers had lost their former sensitivity, and to her horror she realized that her playing was "undisciplined, incoherent, conceited and stupid." As she told her biographer, it was "the worst Hungarian playing you have ever heard. . . . I cannot tell you the shock." It took many months for Kraus to reassess her playing, refine her technique and restore her self-image, but later that year (1948) she toured South Africa, and in 1949 she served as head of the piano department at Capetown University. Finally, after a six-year postponement, Lili Kraus made her American debut with a recital at New York's Town Hall on 6 November 1949.

Forging her way back into the front rank of pianists proved a hard task. Not yet fully restored to her old vigor and always concerned about the need to support her family, Kraus went through a phase of not playing too well. Besides, she found that some people had forgotten her earlier fame and that there were even new people in the musical world who had never heard of Lili Kraus. During 1950–54 the Mandls lived in Paris, and Kraus made many tours (Europe, North and South America, Japan, India, Australia, New Zealand) and many, many recordings. Constantly concertizing and recording, she rekindled her career. From 1954 to early 1956 the family lived in Vienna, but for the sake of her husband's frail health—he suffered a heart attack in 1952—they moved to the gentler climate of southern France, near Nice. Dr. Mandl died in 1956.

Devastated (theirs had been a very close relationship) and completely adrift (Dr. Mandl had managed everything for her), Kraus forced herself to go on, and shortly took an apartment in London. About 1963 a new manager, Alix Williamson of New York, started a whole new career for her, especially in the United States, by proposing a daring, monumental project: a concert cycle presenting all 25 Mozart piano concertos. Between May 1965 and September 1966 Kraus, Stephen Simon (a young conductor who had studied with Josef Krips) and the Mozart Festival Orchestra (drawn from members of the Vienna Symphony Orchestra) recorded all the Mozart solo piano concertos for Columbia's Epic label. Two weeks after completing the recording sessions, Kraus, Simon and the Mozart Chamber Orchestra began (4 Oct 1966) a series at New York's Town Hall, playing all the Mozart concertos in nine concerts. The following season (1967–68) Kraus played all of the Mozart piano sonatas in five recitals at Hunter

College in New York; and during the 1968–69 season she played three all-Schubert recitals at the Metropolitan Museum in New York.

With her American career burgeoning, Kraus moved to the United States in 1967 and that same year became artist-in-residence at Texas Christian University in Fort Worth, Texas, an association that began with her first master class in July 1967 and continued each summer until June 1980. Crippled with rheumatoid arthritis, she gave a final one-day class in May 1981. Although officially retired from TCU in 1983, she returned to teach a few students during the 1983–84 academic year. At her final appearance (12 June 1982 at Swarthmore College), Lili Kraus played the Mozart Concerto in D Minor, K. 466, with the Swarthmore Festival Orchestra, James Freeman conducting.

Of all the honors, awards and fulfilling performances Lili Kraus experienced during her long life, the most satisfying may have been her five-week stay in the summer of 1965 at Dr. Albert Schweitzer's compound in Lambaréné, Africa. What began as a family visit with her daughter Ruth Pope, son-in-law Dr. Fergus Pope (at that time assistant to Dr. Schweitzer) and grandchildren became an unforgettable musical experience. Each evening after Dr. Schweitzer's Bible reading, Kraus played some Mozart or Bach for him. Although he no longer played for an audience, Dr. Schweitzer often joined her at the piano, perhaps to compare the trills of the two composers or to demonstrate how accents differ. That enriching musical encounter with the great Dr. Schweitzer became one of Lili Kraus's most treasured memories, all the more poignant because Dr. Schweitzer died two months after her visit.

The story of Lili Kraus's life and career proves that she was strong, disciplined, diverse and dynamic. Whatever she undertook to do, she accomplished it with the utmost verve and an almost theatrical enjoyment. Music always came first, but Kraus was also a good amateur artist (she drew only for her family and friends); she designed her own gorgeous concert gowns; and she swam daily until illness stopped her. A devout Roman Catholic, she nevertheless practiced yoga and transcendental meditation. She described herself to her biographer as "terribly passionate, irrational, and the most undiplomatic person God ever made." (Roberson, "Lili Kraus") Others saw Lili Kraus as a charismatic, devastatingly charming Hungarian enchantress.

Kraus practiced regularly, sometimes eight hours a day, but not by playing a work over and over again. Before she ever began working with a piece at the piano she already knew it so well that the large thematic sections were clear in her mind and she had no need to work them up. On the other hand, she would spend hours perfecting a trill or trying to overcome problems. As she once explained, she had not worked on scales, octaves or double thirds *per se* for some 30 years. Instead, she practiced the difficulties she found in each work from the point of view of interpretation. "But of course for the interpretation to appear in immaculate truthfulness, technical supremacy is indispensable. Therefore, my practicing includes technical work and hard drudging drills all the time, but never divorced from the text." (Elder, "Regal Lady") Kraus had an excellent visual memory, but as she played she tried to remember the sound of the music rather than how the music looked on the printed page.

She apparently loved to teach and taught whenever her concert schedule permitted. She was only eight years old when she took her first piano pupil, a child of five, and only age 11 when she took her next student, a woman of 45. She taught at the Vienna Academy of Music (1924–31); was head of the piano department at Capetown University in 1949–50; was artist-in-residence at Texas Christian University from 1967 to 1983. In 1956 Kraus toured America in "A Day with Lili Kraus," at each stop giving a seminar in the morning, a master class in the afternoon and a recital in the evening. Some students adored her, some were disappointed, but almost all found her intensely devoted to music. Between 1962 and 1981 Kraus served on every jury at the Van Cliburn Competition.

At the very beginning of her career Kraus played a great deal of Chopin. In the 1930s she played a lot of Beethoven, especially in her performances with Szymon Goldberg, and broadened her repertoire to include Schumann, Haydn, Schubert, Brahms and Mozart. By then Kraus had a reputation for her exceptionally clear and musicianly interpretations of the Classical and early Romantic repertoire. Basically her repertoire ranged from Bach to Bartók (Kraus was an exceptional Bartók performer) and other contemporary composers. However, she did not like all modern music and absolutely refused to consider electronic attempts as musical art. Her greatest fame rests on her Mozart performances.

As with her teaching, Lili Kraus's playing is totally linked to her personality. Exuberant, dominating, radiant, she had a *grande dame* presence that took over the concert hall the moment she stepped out of the wings. Her opulent gowns, her elegant air, the way she swept onto the stage, all only added to the excitement. Her intense personality and her deep love for music sometimes carried her away, but as a performer Kraus hated anything that did not serve the music and avoided all flamboyant aspects of playing.

Critics generally agreed on the notable characteristics of Kraus's playing style: technical firmness wherein each note becomes noticeably important; a dramatic (and passionate) approach to the basic concepts of the music; careful attention to phrasing; telling dynamic contrasts; an imaginative but sensitive approach to ornamentation; and, above all, total love of, and dedication to, her art. "With her wide experience, her keyboard command and her manner of playing . . . with a combination of flair and intimacy, she is always a compelling personality. . . . One of Miss Kraus's advantages as a technician is a particularly articulate right hand. . . . Another of her gifts is for making a melody sing almost as in an aria." (*NYT*, 19 Nov 1963)

On the negative side, some critics reproached Kraus for her (to them) arbitrary interpretative ideas. In one of her performances (9 Dec 1962) of Beethoven's Prometheus Variations, "too often the rough-hewn was replaced by the simply rough, and her sometimes exaggerated dynamics led to a touch of coarseness." (*TL*, 10 Dec 1962) Reviewers also targeted Kraus's excessive rhythmic freedom. Her American debut recital (6 Nov 1949) baffled some listeners, and she disappointed a critic expecting to hear the Lili Kraus known to him through her recordings. What bothered him most was that the rhythmic liberties Kraus employed with expressiveness and charm in the first piece, a Bartók

Peasant Song, raised havoc in all the rest of the Bartók compositions and in every other work on the program. "Mozart, Haydn, Schubert and Brahms were all subjected to the same type of approach, regardless of their style, in readings that were invariably eccentric, capricious, and filled with dynamic exaggerations." (*NYT*, 7 Nov 1949)

But if the critics sometimes found fault, the public seldom did. The fact is that Lili Kraus's readings of Mozart and of Schubert can compete with those by today's finest pianists. She was a superb performer of the Mozart concertos. In 1972 her reading of the Mozart Concerto in A Major, K. 488, with the National Symphony Orchestra, Howard Mitchell conducting, prompted a rave review: "There is no one these days who plays the piano remotely like Lili Kraus. Her playing is by no means confined to the miracle that happens when she first touches the piano. Rather it begins with the orchestral introduction, at which moment she becomes one with the music. She enters totally into Mozart's conception, of which her part and that of her instrument are but one element." (*WP*, 8 March 1972)

Comparing several performances of one work reveals Kraus's highly personal interpretative style. She often played the Mozart Concerto in D Minor, K. 466, and each time it emerged in a different light. At a Kennedy Center performance (8 May 1974) with the National Symphony Orchestra under James De Preist, she played it in a "fiery, magnificent, storming fashion. Kraus was overpowering. . . . There was a divine impatience in her playing." (*WP*, 9 May 1974) When she performed (10 April 1975) that same concerto with the Atlanta Symphony Orchestra, Robert Shaw conducting, she played "in the wonderfully illuminating manner that is her own. No prim and proper Mozart this, but a performance that fleshed out the very human qualities of self-assertion, gentleness and, in the finale, sophisticated humor." (*AJ*, 11 April 1975) And when Kraus played (14 Jan 1981) that apparently favorite concerto with the Oregon Symphony Orchestra, Gunther Schuller conducting, one reviewer acknowledged that it was one of the most moving concerto performances he had heard in a long time—"rich, understated and poised, filled to overflowing with radiance and devotion." (*OS*, 15 Jan 1981)

Although the reviews of Kraus's Mozart solo recitals were mixed, often tempered with negative reactions, she remained secure in her niche as a Mozart specialist. On 1 November 1967 she played the first recital of her Mozart sonata cycle at Hunter College. "Her touch could be downright harsh, in fact, when brusqueness seemed called for in the score. Embellishments were plentiful (always where indicated, occasionally where not) and in excellent taste. Phrasing sometimes was clipped . . . but the pianist was showing us Mozart's lucidity of detail and clarity of structure, and she did so triumphantly." (*NYT*, 2 Nov 1967)

Lili Kraus is also remembered for her Schubert performances. At a London recital (8 Feb 1959) her reading of Schubert's great A Minor Sonata, op. 143, was "on a majestic scale only rarely encountered. . . . Miss Kraus managed this difficult, intensely idiosyncratic work with superb musicianship." (*TL*, 9 Feb 1959) And on 15 November 1968 when she gave the first of three Schubert recitals at New York's Metropolitan Museum, "she managed somehow to find and reveal more varieties of mood, texture, color and accent in Schubert's piano music than most other pianists ever seem to be aware of." (*NYT*, 16 Nov 1968)

Kraus's New York performance (1 Aug 1976) of Mozart (K. 310, K. 396, K. 455) and Beethoven ("*Waldstein*" Sonata, Variations, op. 35) drew glowing comments and an intelligent assessment of her playing. Kraus dropped some notes in rapid passages and sometimes her phrasing was uneven, but her playing offered something more precious—"a sense of nobility, a kind of heroic commitment that infused everything she played with an ardent, heart-pounding sense of discovery. . . . If music-making means passionate involvement, profound intelligence and immense personal conviction, then there are few artists in the world who can match pianist Lili Kraus." (*NYP*, 2 Aug 1976)

Kraus made a great many fine recordings. After World War II she began recording for various labels—*Parlophone*, *Discophiles français*, Vox, Educo— but many of her recorded performances are now out of print.

She recorded some Bach, Schumann, a substantial amount of Beethoven and Schubert. But most of her attention was given to Mozart, her beloved Mozart. She not only recorded all of Mozart's piano sonatas but the complete concertos as well. In four periods, between May 1965 and September 1966, Lili Kraus, aided by conductor Stephen Simon and members of the Vienna Symphony Orchestra, completed a landmark version of Mozart's 25 concertos. There have been more recent complete recordings of the concertos—Barenboim, Perahia, Uchida—and Kraus's version, taken as a whole, has perhaps been equaled, but certainly never surpassed. Her dedication to Mozart and her dramatically projected but classically restrained approach to this magnificent repertoire provide a textbook for anyone who would understand and appreciate the art of the Viennese master.

SELECTED REFERENCES

Ardoin, John. "A Lesson in Musical Love with Lili Kraus." *New York Times*, 1 Aug 1976, sec. 4, p. 15.

Doerschuk, Bob. "Lili Kraus: Spirited Doyenne of Mozart and Bartok." *Keyboard*, Oct 1983, pp. 52, 54, 66, 75.

Elder, Dean. "Lili Kraus . . . Regal Lady of the Keyboard." *Clavier*, Sept 1980, pp. 21–27.

———. "Making Mozart Live." *Clavier*, May-June 1971, pp. 12–18.

———. "On Mastering Mozart." *Clavier*, April 1971, pp. 11–16.

Ericson, Raymond. "A Cross and a Privilege." *New York Times*, 25 Oct 1970, sec. 2, p. 19.

Freed, Richard. "Lili Kraus, Mozartean." *Stereo Review*, Feb 1975, pp. 76–78.

Kober, Barbara. "The Indomitable Spirit of Lili Kraus." *Ovation*, Nov 1981, pp. 16–18.

Kraus, Lili. "Of Teachers and Husbands." *Piano Quarterly*, Winter 1973–74, pp. 34–35.

———. "Marriage to Mozart." *Music Journal*, Dec 1966, pp. 24, 53.

Kraus, Lili, ed. *The Complete Original Cadenzas by W. A. Mozart for his Solo Piano Concertos*. Melville, New York: Belwin-Mills Publishing Corp., 1971.

Obituary. *Asheville Citizen* (North Carolina), 7 Nov 1986, pp. 1, 10. *New York Times*, 7 Nov 1986, sec. 4, p. 18.

Reinthaler, Joan. "Lili Kraus Helps Students Find 'Elusive Musicality'." *Washington Post*, 12 Aug 1969, sec. B, pp. 1, 5.

Roberson, Steven H. "Lili Kraus: The last Interview." *Piano Quarterly*, Winter 1986–87, pp. 29–31.

————. *Lili Kraus: The Person, The Performer, and The Teacher*. Ph.D. dissertation, University of Oklahoma, 1985. Contains an extensive Kraus bibliography and discography. UMI 8521272.

Snyder, Louis. "Applause from four continents." *Christian Science Monitor*, 20 Aug 1970, p. 19.

Williamson, Alix B. "Lili Kraus Remembered." *Music and Musicians*, Jan 1987, pp. 14–15.

See also Bibliography: Cur/Bio (1975, 1987); Eld/Pia; Ewe/Mu; Mac/Gre; New/GrA; WWAM.

SELECTED REVIEWS

AJ: 11 April 1975. *CA*: 12 Oct 1975. *LAT*: 9 Dec 1949; 10 July 1956; 12 Jan 1971. *NYP*: 2 Aug 1976. *NYT*: 7 Nov 1949; 18 Oct 1958; 19 Nov 1963; 5 Oct 1966; 1 Feb 1967; 2 Nov 1967; 16 Nov 1968; 30 Oct 1970. *OS*: 15 Jan 1981. *OT*: 6 Feb 1978. *PP*: 17 Sept 1977. *PPH*: 3 Feb 1977. *SFE*: 24 July 1976. *TL*: 29 Jan 1934; 16 June 1939; 29 Oct 1951; 5 Feb 1958; 10 Feb 1958; 9 Feb 1959; 10 Dec 1962. *WP*: 12 Aug 1969; 8 March 1972; 31 July 1972; 9 May 1974. *WS*: 21 May 1979.

SELECTED DISCOGRAPHY

Bach: Chromatic Fantasy and Fugue BWV 903. Haydn: Fantasy in C Major, Hob. XVII:4. Mozart: Fantasy in D Minor, K. 397. Schubert: Wanderer Fantasy in C Major, D. 760. Vanguard VBD-25003 (CD).

Bartók: Evening in the Country; Fifteen Hungarian Peasant Songs; For Children, Vol. 1; Three Hungarian Folk Songs from Csik; Six Romanian Folk Dances; Three Rondos on Folk Tunes; Sonatina. Vanguard Classics OVC 8087 (CD).

Mozart: Concertos (complete). Columbia P12 11806/18. Simon/Vienna SO.

Mozart: Concerto in F Major, K. 413; Concerto in F Major, K. 459; Concerto in D Minor, K. 466; Rondo, K. 485; Sonata in F Major, K. 332. Vox Box CDX 5510 (2 CDs). Jorda/Pro Musica Orchestra.

Mozart: Concerto in F Major, K. 459; Concerto in D Major, K. 537. *Via Classique* 642310 (CD). Rivoli/*Orchestre de la Société Philharmonique d'Amsterdam* (1959).

Mozart: The Complete Piano Sonatas. Sony Classical 4-SM4K 47222 (CD).

Mozart: Sonata in F Major, K. 332; Variations, K. 455. Haydn: Sonata in E-
   flat Major. Schubert: Sonata in A Minor, D. 784. Vogue CD 672012.
Schubert: Impromptus, D. 899, D. 935. Vanguard Classics OVC 4068 (CD).
Schubert: Sonata in A Major, D. 664; Sonata in A Minor, D. 845. Vanguard
   Van C-10074.

VIDEO

Lili. A biographical documentary film. Fort Worth Publications, 1984.

L

LAMOND, FREDERIC: b. Glasgow, Scotland, 28 January 1868; d. Stirling, Scotland, 21 February 1948.

> At his best, he translated Beethoven's mind in the grandeur of true insight.
>
> Obituary (*Musical Times*, March 1948)

Frederic Lamond lived in Germany for more than 50 years, but he kept his British citizenship and never completely lost his Scottish accent. Without question, Lamond found an exciting, deeply satisfying life and career in Europe, especially in Germany. He studied with Liszt and von Bülow; made friends with Brahms, Richard Strauss and Anton Rubinstein; and had Rosenthal, Sauer, Siloti and Friedheim for classmates.

Lamond's father Archibald, a weaver and self-taught musician, became so involved with volunteer church music in his village of Cambuslang that he lost his business and had to move (1859) his large family to Glasgow, where he found work as a clerk in a cotton mill. Growing up in poverty, Frederic Lamond found great comfort listening to music, whether a barrel-organ or a Psalm tune. He had his first music lessons from his brother David, 19 years his senior and later a well-known piano teacher. In 1880 Lamond, at age 12, was appointed organist (his father became choirmaster) at the Newhall Parish Church in Glasgow's east end. That ended Lamond's formal education. With four organ voluntaries to prepare for each Sunday, there was no time for school, only for organ practice. About a year later father and son resigned to take better positions at the Laurieston Parish Church. Meanwhile, in 1879 he began violin lessons ("massive doses of Bach") with Henry Cooper and also sang in the chorus of the Glasgow Choral Union. In 1880 Lamond took up the oboe, three lessons a week, and studied German with his friend Carl Scheffel.

On the advice of Victor Buziau (a Belgian violinist who directed the winter performances of the GCU Concerts), Lamond was taken to Frankfurt for further study. Accompanied by his brother David and two sisters (they took in boarders to pay expenses) he arrived in Frankfurt in September 1882. In October he enrolled at the Hoch Conservatory, where he hoped to study with Clara Schumann, but since the great Clara accepted only students who had been personally recommended, Lamond was assigned to the younger faculty. He studied piano with Max Schwartz, composition with Anton Urspruch and violin with Basserman, most likely an assistant to Hugo Heerman. In 1883 the Hoch faculty quarreled. Some younger teachers, including Schwartz, opened the Raff Conservatory, with Hans von Bülow as honorary president, and Lamond and many other students followed their teachers to the new institute. That same year Lamond's performance of the Saint-Saëns Concerto No. 2 in G Minor took first place in the Raff Conservatory third examination, his prize being a ticket for a performance of *Parsifal* at Bayreuth.

In May 1884 Hans von Bülow, prominently active at the Raff Conservatory, offered a six-week course on Bach, Beethoven and Brahms, and Lamond was allowed to participate, working principally on Beethoven's Opus 106, the "*Hammerklavier*" Sonata. In the summer of 1885 Lamond took Bülow's five-week course on the same three composers. After this course and additional lessons with Bülow in Berlin, where they worked partly on the Brahms Concerto No. 2 in B-flat Major, Lamond concentrated on becoming a pianist. He venerated Bülow, a great musician he thought often misunderstood by his contemporaries. "Bülow taught me many things. . . . His example, his admonitions, his lessons. . . . I never paid him one penny for the many priceless things he taught me." (*Memoirs*) Because of Bülow, Lamond spent the autumn of 1885 at Meiningen, playing oboe in the Meiningen Ducal Orchestra, at that time directed by Bülow. Unexpectedly, and with only two days' notice, Bülow called on Lamond to play the Brahms B-flat Piano Concerto at a court concert.

During his stay in Meiningen, Lamond heard the first performance of Brahms's Symphony No. 4 in E Minor, with Bülow conducting the Ducal Orchestra. Immediately afterward Lamond, hidden behind a theater curtain, heard a repeat performance given solely for the Duke, with Brahms himself conducting.

Lamond completed his studies at the Raff Conservatory in July 1885 and set off for Weimar, fortified with a recommendation from Max Schwartz. Liszt accepted him as a pupil into a class that included Moriz Rosenthal, Alexander Siloti, Conrad Ansorge and Bernard Stavenhagen. The term "pupil of Liszt" can be greatly misleading. In his last years Liszt really had no pupils as such. In 1885, when the 17-year-old Lamond went to Weimar, Liszt was failing physically and mentally and had less than a year to live. Liszt spent only a few summer weeks at Weimar. About all his class "pupils" could do was hope for a chance to play for him. Divided into two groups, they met on alternate days at

Liszt's villa on the grounds of Weimar's grand ducal palace. Each pupil would put his music on a table, Liszt would select a piece and ask the student who had prepared it to play it for him. It may be that Liszt felt that Lamond, whom he affectionately called "*der Schotte*," was worth encouraging, for he gave Lamond opportunity to play almost all the principal pieces in his repertoire. Lamond followed Liszt to Rome in December 1885. (He adored Liszt and was forever grateful that the old master had made the effort, just a few months before his death, to attend Lamond's London recital on 15 April 1886. To be sure, Liszt's presence greatly enhanced Lamond's professional reputation.)

Lamond made a very successful Berlin debut on 17 November 1885; played three recitals (one all Beethoven, one all Brahms, one mixed program) in Vienna in February 1886; and gave his first recital in Great Britain in Glasgow on 8 March 1886. Lamond resided in Frankfurt, where he made a modest living teaching piano lessons and "music" lessons and slowly built a career as a concert pianist. When Felix Mottl invited him to play a Beethoven Concerto in Munich, Lamond seized the opportunity to arrange, on his own, three recitals, and he received excellent notices.

To further promote his career, Lamond and his younger brother Charles journeyed (Feb 1888) to St. Petersburg to introduce the pianist to Russian audiences. The British Embassy there having ignored their letters of introduction, the brothers themselves arranged a debut recital, and Lamond's playing so impressed Becker, Russia's largest piano manufacturer, that the firm sponsored a second recital. In the interval between the two recitals, Lamond met Anton Rubinstein at a court concert, conducted by Rubinstein. Appalled that the British Embassy had ignored Lamond's letters of introduction, Rubinstein made a point of informing the British Ambassador. The Embassy immediately purchased a block of tickets for Lamond's second recital, and both Rubinstein and the Ambassador attended. It was a stunning success.

Lamond's career flourished. Later that year (1888) he played the Beethoven Sonata in B-flat Major, op. 106, at one of the *Gewandhaus* chamber-music concerts in Leipzig; in March 1889 he gave five highly successful recitals in Hamburg. He played a great deal in Europe, especially in Germany, and also in Great Britain, steadily gaining fame as a great Beethoven specialist. On 23 December 1889 Lamond made his first appearance as soloist at the Glasgow Choral Union Concerts, playing the Saint-Saëns Concerto No. 4, with August Manns conducting, and also three solo works. On 5 April 1890 Lamond played the same Saint-Saëns at the Crystal Palace in London.

In 1893 he was summoned to Moscow to play Tchaikovsky's B-flat Minor Concerto. Tchaikovsky, who died that year, had himself recommended that Lamond play his Concerto in Russia. Lamond played it on 10 October 1893 with the Imperial Russian Music Society, Vassily Safonov conducting, and in his *Memoirs* admitted that on that occasion he had "dropped so many notes under the piano that one could write a symphony with them." He toured Russia in 1896 and France in 1899. Although he made his American debut in New York in 1902, Lamond did not play again in America until 1922, when he made a brief tour. He also gave lecture-recitals while on the faculty (1923–24, 1924–25) at the Eastman School of Music in Rochester, New York.

Lamond lived in Frankfurt until 1904, the year he married Irene Triesch, a German actress, and settled in Berlin. Although the demands of their separate professions often kept them apart, their marriage lasted 44 years, until Lamond's death in 1948. The Lamonds stayed in Germany during World War I. Initially imprisoned as a British citizen, Lamond was so respected by the Germans, including the Crown Prince, that he was soon released and allowed to concertize within Germany. After the war he resumed his tours in Europe and Great Britain, and in 1917 became a professor at the conservatory of The Hague. Since Irene Lamond was partly Jewish, they had to leave when the Nazi regime took power. Lamond moved to London in 1935; however, Irene Lamond first made a visit to Switzerland with her grandson, and was detained. Seven years later she finally rejoined her husband in Glasgow.

Alone in London and already in his mid-sixties, Lamond had little means of support. And he greatly missed his life in Germany. Eventually he left London for his native Glasgow, where from 1939 he taught at the Scottish National Academy of Music. Every year Lamond played four gigantic recitals at the Athenaeum Theater in Glasgow, always beginning with an all-Beethoven program. And he usually appeared at the Scottish Orchestra's opening concert each season, playing a concerto in his individual, powerfully expressive manner.

In 1941 Lamond was hit by a car. While recuperating, he practiced on an upright piano in his room at the Royal Infirmary and even left the Infirmary to play a Liszt recital on a BBC broadcast. The taxi returning him to the Infirmary had an accident, a strange coincidence, and Lamond was critically hurt. In spite of his advanced age he made a good recovery and in time was able to return to his teaching and concertizing. In 1943 he celebrated his 75th birthday performing Liszt's E-flat Concerto with the BBC Scottish Orchestra. Poor health forced him to retire at the age of 78. Lamond died 21 February 1948 at the Stirling Royal Infirmary.

Although from about age 12 he had no formal schooling, Frederic Lamond, aided by a remarkable memory, became an intelligent, highly cultivated man. He spoke German and French well and knew a little Russian and Turkish; late in life he took up the study of Gaelic and began rereading the Waverley novels. It is perhaps due to his all-around musical culture and intellectual curiosity that Lamond impressed his audiences as a musician first and a pianist second.

Most Lamond programs were gigantic. For example, a New York program (12 Nov 1902) consisted of five Beethoven sonatas, ops. 106, 110, 111 and the "*Waldstein*" and the "*Appassionata.*" At Queen's Hall on 10 May 1919, Lamond played two concertos—Beethoven's Concerto No. 5 and the Tchaikovsky Concerto No. 1. The first of his four Glasgow Athenaeum recitals in 1943 consisted of three Beethoven sonatas—op. 10, no. 2; op. 53 and the mighty "*Hammerklavier*"—and also the op. 119 Bagatelles and the *Rondo a capriccioso*. Lamond played mostly the traditional repertoire—Bach, Handel, Haydn, Mozart, Liszt, Schumann, Chopin and, most notably, Brahms and Beethoven.

From boyhood to death, Lamond's name was associated with the works of Beethoven. As he aged, he was even thought to resemble Beethoven. "I always maintain it is a pity Lamond looks so much like Beethoven," wrote Sir Henry Wood. "The average concert-goer believes he cannot play any other composer's works. This is the greatest error—for his interpretation of the Liszt, Rubinstein and Tchaikovsky concertos equals that with which his name is synonymous, *The Emperor* of Beethoven." (Woo/My, see Bibliog.)

Particularly successful with the Beethoven Sonata, op. 106 ("*Hammerklavier*"), Lamond "was the first to make this sonata as not intrinsically difficult. His strenuous surmounting of technical difficulties has brought the lineal direction of the thematics into the foreground and leads the interest from the very beginning to a clear superstructure." (Riemann) At an early New York recital (12 Nov 1902) he "played five of Beethoven's most difficult and profound sonatas, and revealed an understanding of their significance, a clear insight into some of their deepest depths, and a command of technical resources that marked him out as an artist of altogether exceptional power." (*NYT*, 13 Nov 1902)

A recital (Bach, Beethoven, Chopin, Liszt, Schumann) on 18 March 1912 in the Queen's Rooms in Glasgow drew this comment: "Lamond is one of the most virile of pianists. He is essentially a player for big music, and his reputation as an interpreter of Beethoven is one of the most significant things about him. . . . A characteristic of Lamond's Beethoven playing is its lack of sentimentality." (*ET*, 19 March 1912)

From all accounts, Lamond's 1923–25 residency in the United States was richly productive. He performed often in New York—at least five appearances in 1923 alone. On 29 March 1923 he played the Tchaikovsky Concerto No. 1 with the Philharmonic Society, conducted by Willem Mengelberg, and his performance "was a really masterly one; making no revelation in music that has become so familiar, it was distinguished not only by abundant power and sweep, but by an individually musical quality that put something more than power and sweep into it." (*NYT*, 30 March 1923)

More significant, perhaps, were the numerous programs that Lamond gave in Rochester, New York, where he taught for two seasons at the Eastman School of Music. He gave the expected recitals, but more importantly, he presented a series of lecture-recitals covering a large portion of keyboard literature. Reviews indicate that they were eminently successful. For example: "Frederic Lamond gave the second in his series of interesting and illuminating lecture recitals in Kilbourn Hall yesterday afternoon. . . . Mr. Lamond may be primarily 'a pianist for pianists'; he is an academician whose intellectuality is always a dominant characteristic of his performance, which is likewise marked by exquisite clarity, a subtle appreciation of phrasing and nuance and a consummate skill in the use of the pianistic pedal." (*RTU*, 27 Nov 1923)

In 1936 Lamond celebrated the 50th anniversary of his first appearance in London in grand style. From 31 October through 14 November he gave a series of seven historical recitals similar in scope to those seven famous Historical Concerts played by Anton Rubinstein in 1885. The first listed works by J. S. Bach, Handel, Scarlatti, Rameau, Couperin, Byrd, Bull, Haydn and Mozart; the second was devoted to music by Mendelssohn, Schubert and Weber; Schumann's music comprised the entire third concert and Chopin's the fourth; the fifth concert presented music by Brahms and Reger, the sixth was an all-Liszt program;

and the seventh, predictably, was reserved for Beethoven. Incredibly, in the midst of these taxing programs, Lamond played Beethoven's "Emperor" Concerto on 8 November, with Sir Henry Wood conducting the Queen's Hall Orchestra.

Apparently only two of the seven recitals were reviewed. Lamond was criticized a bit after his first concert for over-romanticizing music (Scarlatti, Couperin, Rameau) that was not suited to the piano. However, the Bach Chromatic Fantasy and Fugue, "which was the central and largest work in the programme . . . was played with Mr. Lamond's characteristic appreciation of its monumental qualities." (*TL*, 2 Nov 1936) The fifth recital included Brahms's Sonata No. 3 in F Minor and the "Paganini" Variations and also Reger's Variations and Fugue on a Theme by J. S. Bach: "Mr. Lamond brings a life-long experience to his task of displaying alike the invention of Brahms and the ingenuity of Reger. . . . The programme displayed his effortless technique applied to produce an experienced interpretation." (*TL*, 11 Nov 1936)

Frederic Lamond produced a small but significant collection of recordings. Despite the drawbacks of early sound-recording techniques, we can still discern the beauty of his tone, his preoccupation with the inherent musical essence in a composition. His is playing in the grand manner, impressive for its sheer command of the keyboard.

Early in his career Lamond made numerous piano rolls for Duo-Art, Ampico and Welte, including arrangements of Tchaikovsky's Symphony No. 5 and Beethoven's Symphony No. 3. A representative selection from the Duo-Art catalogue has been reissued on CD (see Discog.).

Lamond's disc recordings, made between 1919 and 1944, include seven complete Beethoven sonatas plus some isolated movements, the Emperor Concerto (No. 5) and a few Liszt compositions. From among the very few available recordings, two works emerge as representative of Lamond at his best: the Beethoven Sonata in C Minor, op. 13 (*Pathétique*) and Liszt's bravura showpiece "*Tarantella di Bravura*" on themes from *La Muette de Portici*. And a CD anthology titled *The Pupils of Liszt* (GEMM 9972, see Discog.) includes Beethoven's Rondo in G Major, op. 51, no. 2, and a rare recording of Liszt's *Liebestraum* No. 2 in E Major.

The GEMM CD 9911 (see Discog.) shows Lamond as an authentic interpreter of some of Liszt's best-known compositions. "This is exemplary and revelatory Liszt playing. The emphasis given to detail, the sculpting of sound and his luxuriating in polyphony attest to a level of musicianship no longer heard." (Evans)

The most recent disc (APR 5504) contains Lamond's complete Liszt recordings, made for HMV/Electrola between 1919 and 1936. His talents shine most brightly in the overtly technical works such as the Auber-Liszt *Tarantelle*, *Tarantella* (*Venezia e Napoli*), *Waldesrauschen* and *Feux follets*. Other performances, particularly the earlier ones, give the impression that Lamond "did not take recording too seriously at first." (Crimp)

SELECTED REFERENCES

Anderson, H. L., J. F. Perkins and Gerald Stonefield. "Frederick Lamond: the recordings." *Recorded Sound*, Jan 1977, pp. 642–651.

Bauer, Harold. *Harold Bauer: His Book*. New York: W. W. Norton, 1948, reprint by Greenwood Press, 1969, pp. 22–23.

Crimp, Bryan. "Frederic Lamond." Liner notes, APR CD 5504.

Evans, Allan. "Frederic Lamond: Liszt's Last Pupil." Liner notes, GEMM CD 9911.

"Frederic Lamond." *The Musical Age*, Feb 1904, pp. 31–32.

Henderson, A. M. "Frederic Lamond." In *Musical Memories*. London, Glasgow: The Grant Educational Co., Ltd., 1938, pp. 52–58.

Kohn, Frederick. "Frederic Lamond: a memoir." *Recorded Sound*, Jan 1977, pp. 641–642.

Lamond, Frederic. "The Indefinable Liszt." *Etude*, July 1936, pp. 419–420.

———. *Memoirs of Frederic Lamond*. With a Foreword by Ernest Newman. Introduction and Postscript by Irene Triesch Lamond. Glasgow: William McLellan, 1949.

———. "Memories of Liszt: from Glasgow to Weimar in the 1880s." *Recorded Sound*, Jan 1977, pp. 634–635.

———. "Some Vital Points Piano Students Miss." *Etude*, Sept 1923, pp. 583-584. Reprinted in Coo/Gre (see Bibliog.).

"Man Who Makes Great Music." *Glasgow Review*, No. 1, 1966, pp. 4–5.

Obituary. *London Times*, 23 Feb 1948, p. 6. *Musical Times*, March 1948, p. 93. *New York Times*, 22 Feb 1948, p. 48.

Riemann, Hugo. *Ludwig van Beethovens sämtliche Klavier-Solosonaten*. Berlin: Max Hesse's Verlag, 1920.

"Talks with Great Scots." *Scotland*, Autumn 1937, pp. 57–59.

Walker, Agnes. "Frederic Lamond (1868–1948)." *Recorded Sound*, Jan 1977, pp. 636–641.

———. "The Man Who Remembered Liszt." *Music and Musicians*, Nov 1961, p. 21.

See also Bibliography: Ald/Con; Bro/Mod; Coo/Gre; Ewe/Li; MGG; Nie/Mei; Rat/Cle; Reu/Gre; Rub/MyM; Sch/Gre; Sha/Mus; Woo/My.

SELECTED REVIEWS

ET: 27 Dec 1905; 19 March 1912; 4 Feb 1914; 15 Oct 1920; 23 April 1921; 10 Nov 1921; 12 Jan 1922; 6 April 1922; 13 Nov 1929; 16 Nov 1932. *MT*: 1 May 1890; 1 Jan 1920;1 Jan 1926; Nov 1934. *NYT*: 13 Nov 1902; 26 Nov 1902; 3 Feb 1923; 16 Feb 1923; 30 March 1923; 3 Nov 1923; 4 Dec 1924. *RTU*: 23 Oct 1923; 20 Nov 1923; 27 Nov 1923; 22 Jan 1924; 21 Oct 1924; 11 Nov 1924; 2 Dec 1924. *TL*: 19 April 1886; 7 April 1890; 22 April 1890; 5 May 1897; 5 May 1913; 28 April 1913; 14 April 1919; 12 May 1919; 20 Oct 1919; 3 Nov 1919; 13 Dec 1920; 4 April 1921; 9 March 1921; 25 March 1927; 2 Nov 1936; 11 Nov 1936.

SELECTED DISCOGRAPHY

Beethoven: *Piano Sonatas Vol. One.* Sonata in C Minor, op. 13; Sonata in C-sharp Minor, op. 27, no.2; Sonata in D Minor, op. 31, no. 2. Concert Artist Cassette CH4-TC-4004.

Frederic Lamond: The Complete Liszt Recordings 1919-1936. Cujus animam (Rossini: Stabat mater); *Erlkönig* (Schubert); *Feux follets*; *Gnomenreigen*; *Liebestraum No. 3*; Petrarch Sonnet No. 104; *Un sospiro*; *Tarantella (Venezia e Napoli)*; *Tarentelle di bravura* (Auber: *La muette de Portici*). APR 5504 (CD).

Frederic Lamond: Liszt's last pupil. Auber-Liszt: *Tarentelle di bravura.* Brahms: Capriccio in B Minor, op. 76, no. 2. Chopin: Nocturne in A-flat Major, op. 32, no. 2. Glinka-Balakirev: The Lark. Liszt: *Liebestraum* No. 3; *Feux follets*; *Waldesrauschen*; Petrarch Sonnet No. 104; *Gnomenreigen*; Concert Study in D-flat Major; Valse Impromptu; *Tarantella* from *Venezia e Napoli.* Rossini-Liszt: *Cujus animam.* Rubinstein: Barcarolle in G Minor. Schubert-Liszt: *Erlkönig.* Pearl GEMM CD 9911.

Frederic Lamond, piano. Beethoven: Sonata in C Minor, op. 111. Liszt: Concert Etudes Nos. 2 and 3. Rossini-Liszt: *Cujus animam* (from *Stabat Mater*). Strauss-Grünfeld: *Frühlingsstimmen.* Tchaikovsky-Lamond: Symphony No. 5 in E Minor, op. 64 (2nd Movt.). Weber-Lamond: Overture to *Der Freischütz.* Foné 90 F 06 CD. (Duo-Art rolls)

Frederic Lamond Plays Beethoven. Concerto No. 5 in E-flat Major, op. 73. Concert Artist Cassette CH4-TC-4021. Goossens/Royal Albert Hall Orch.

The Pupils of Liszt. Beethoven: Sonata in C Minor, op. 13. Glinka-Balakirev: The Lark. Liszt: Tarantella on Themes from Auber's *La Muette de Portici.* Pearl Opal 824/5.

The Pupils of Liszt. Beethoven: Rondo in G Major, op. 51, no. 2. Glinka-Balakirev: The Lark. Liszt: *Liebestraum* No. 2. Pearl GEMM CDS 9972 (2 CDs). A different selection from that in the LP of the same title.

Tribute to Lamond. Beethoven: Sonata in C-sharp Minor, op. 27, no. 2. Glinka-Balakirev: The Lark. Liszt: *Gnomenreigen*, plus a recorded illustrated lecture (BBC) on Liszt, narrated and performed by Lamond. Rare Recorded Editions 161.

LAREDO, RUTH: b. Detroit, Michigan, 20 November 1937.

> I wasn't a prodigy—but a talent—and never planned to be anything other than a pianist.
>
> Ruth Laredo (*High Fidelity/Musical America*, December 1974)

Without benefit of much fanfare or high-pressure promotion, Ruth Laredo has played her way into the top ranks of American pianists. The Laredo clippings—

articles, interviews, concert reviews, record reviews—delineate a refreshingly well-balanced career that has gained her fourfold fame as recitalist, concerto soloist, chamber musician and recording artist.

Within her memory, there never was a time when Ruth Laredo could not play the piano. She began picking out tunes before she was two, and by the time she reached three could play entire sonatinas by ear. She grew up surrounded by music and with music-loving parents. Her father Ben Meckler, a high school English teacher, played the banjo for a Detroit vaudeville theater during his college years. Her mother Miriam taught piano lessons at home. Laredo was taken to concerts from the time she was a toddler, but her mother wisely refrained from giving her formal instruction until she was five years old and never forced her into practicing as a duty. Laredo remembers that her love for the piano began the day she heard her first piano recital, played by Vladimir Horowitz in Detroit's vast Masonic Auditorium. Sitting just a few feet away from Horowitz (Laredo's father bought last-minute stage seats), the enthralled eight-year-old fell in love with the kind of music and the kind of playing she was hearing. She knew then that she wanted to become a pianist.

Laredo was about age 10 when her mother selected Edward Bredshall to take over her training. Obviously he was the perfect choice, for Laredo has repeatedly told interviewers that Bredshall created a wonderful atmosphere in which to study and had a wonderful way of teaching. "He made the whole world change for me and made music such fun." (*CL*, Nov 1982) Cultured and intelligent, Bredshall taught Laredo that to make music one needed to know something about life and the other arts. At some lessons they simply talked, Bredshall sharing with her his own lively interest in literature, opera, art, politics, history, "everything." During her four years with him, a lesson every Saturday afternoon at his studio in the Art Center Music School, Laredo discovered a whole new world of repertoire, including Stravinsky, Bartók, Prokofiev and Debussy.

At age 11 she played a solo recital (11 April 1949) at the Detroit Institute of Arts, and made her formal concert debut (26 July 1949) at a summer "Pops" concert, playing the last two movements of the Beethoven Concerto No. 2 with the Detroit Symphony Players, Walter Poole conducting.

Edward Bredshall died in 1952, and Laredo began lessons with Mischa Kottler, a Russian from Kiev who had studied with Alfred Cortot in Paris and Emil von Sauer in Vienna. Laredo credits Kottler, one of Detroit's most distinguished teachers, for keeping her on an even keel through what she calls the treacherous years "for any talented kid."

The Music Study Club of Detroit awarded Laredo a series of summer scholarships, making it possible for her to attend the Indian Hill summer music camp located near Tanglewood in the Massachusetts Berkshires. She loved it. There were so many other gifted young people to perform with, so many opportunities to play and such fine teachers. She studied piano with Seymour Lipkin and chamber music with violinist Berl Senofsky. Senofsky arranged an audition for her with Rudolf Serkin in Vermont, where Serkin was artistic director of the Marlboro Music Festival. Laredo played some Bach, the Beethoven Sonata, op. 101, and Chopin's A-flat Ballade. "I can see you play like a tiger," said Serkin, and accepted her as a student. In the fall of 1955 she became a Serkin pupil at the Curtis Institute in Philadelphia. For her, Serkin was not so much a piano teacher as a music teacher. "He shaped my attitude toward music—which has stayed with me throughout my adult life." (*KeCl*, May/June 1988)

Serkin made Laredo look for musical concepts she had never thought of before, and he never let her forget his cardinal rule: The greatness of the music always surpasses anybody's ability to perform it, hence the performer must serve the music no matter how much hard work that might require. "The music requires such and such," he would say, and it was up to her to study the music and discover for herself what he meant by "such and such." He never allowed her to change a score, and rather than exercises to develop technique, he assigned the Chopin Etudes. Serkin made her listen to her sound, and forced her to find a way to develop tonal control and a wide range of dynamics. Instead of explaining how she might acquire a greater sound and proper projection, Serkin assigned her grand virtuoso works—the Tchaikovsky Concerto No. 1 and the Liszt Mephisto Waltz, for example—works that absolutely demanded a big sound. Now known as a big, bold pianist, the diminutive Laredo insists that big sound has nothing to do with height or strength but how you manage to convey certain ideas.

Laredo's graduation (9 March 1960) at the Curtis Institute coincided with a celebration in honor of the 50th birthday of Samuel Barber, a Curtis alumnus. At the invitational all-Barber concert, Laredo played Barber's Sonata, op. 26, and the composer, present in the audience, made her day especially memorable by writing "*Brava, bravissima*" on her music.

On 1 June 1960 she married Jaime Laredo, a Bolivian violin prodigy she had often performed with at Curtis. A 1959 Curtis graduate, Jaime had attained immediate fame by winning first prize in the prestigious Queen Elisabeth International Music Competition in Brussels. Thus when they began concertizing together professionally, Ruth served as accompanist and the more famous Jaime as star performer. For the next few years her idea of becoming a concert pianist stayed largely on hold. In 1963 the Laredos gave more than 30 concerts in France and Italy, having been selected for the first annual exchange program of the International Federation of *Jeunesses Musicales*. In May 1964 they played together at the Casals Festival in San Juan, Puerto Rico.

Meanwhile, Ruth Laredo entered the Leventritt and Naumburg competitions, but nothing came of it; yet slowly, almost unnoticed, her solo career emerged. Sponsored by *Jeunesses Musicales*, she made her New York orchestral debut (28 March 1963) at Carnegie Hall, playing Mendelssohn's G-minor Concerto with the American Symphony Orchestra, conducted by Leopold Stokowski. On 20 March 1964 she gave a solo recital at Judson Hall in New York, playing Bach, Scriabin and Ravel's *La Valse*.

The next year Laredo toured in Europe and Israel with a group from Marlboro, performing the Bach Concerto in D Minor, BWV 1063, for three claviers and orchestra, with Rudolf and Peter Serkin. She also recorded the same concerto with Rudolf Serkin and Mieczyslaw Horszowski. On 28 January 1966 she gave a recital on the Metropolitan Museum's Young Artists' Series, and during the 1960s she also toured through the United States with the "Music from Marlboro" group. Despite these activities and her emerging prominence, her career as soloist seemed to be in limbo. When she played with her husband, critics might note her fine musicianship or talent, but more often reported that "the accompanist was Ruth Laredo." About 1969 she finally attained equal status when they formed the Jaime and Ruth Laredo Duo. Their daughter Jennifer Alexandra was born that same year.

The Laredos spent most summers at the eight-week Marlboro Music Festival in Vermont, a wholly valuable experience since there were always new people, new points of view and every week new music to learn and perform. At one memorable private affair, Laredo was invited to play some Beethoven trios with Pablo Casals and Supreme Court Justice Abe Fortas, an accomplished violinist. Her playing so pleased Fortas that he arranged for the Laredos to perform at a state dinner given at the White House (Sept 1967) in honor of the president of the Republic of Niger.

Consciously or unconsciously, Laredo was building a large and versatile piano repertoire. With Serkin she had learned mostly the standard German works, that is, a lot of Beethoven, Mozart and Bach. At the same time, Serkin encouraged her to pursue her own interests—the French and Russian composers. And during the Marlboro years, there were wonderful opportunities to expand her repertoire. When Leon Kirchner was on hand, she learned 20th-century works by Berg, Schoenberg, Webern and Bartók; when Pablo Casals was in residence, she learned more of the 19th-century repertoire. Laredo's enormous repertoire includes more than 20 concertos and ranges from Bach to Bernstein. Her fame rests on her awesome performances of the works of Rachmaninoff and Scriabin.

Laredo's first solo recording, a 1967 disc of French music for the Connoisseur Society, received unanimous critical raves for her interpretations of Ravel's *La Valse* and *Valses nobles et sentimentales*. About two years later she approached several record companies with the idea of making recordings to celebrate the upcoming centennial of the mystic Russian composer Alexander Scriabin (b. 1872). Finally, in 1970 Alan Silver of Connoisseur let her make a trial record: Scriabin's Fifth, Seventh and Ninth Sonatas and the Eight Etudes, op. 42. It proved so successful that within a year Laredo had recorded Scriabin's complete piano works for Connoisseur (10 discs, reissued by Nonesuch).

In 1971 she performed all 10 Scriabin sonatas in two recitals (9, 31 Oct) at Hunter College, and later repeated them at the 93rd Street YM-YWHA. These Scriabin recitals and Laredo's Scriabin recordings, the first in North America, sparked renewed interest in his music. Although she had been concertizing for many years and had toured extensively, it was the Scriabin performances that brought Laredo her first real public recognition. And the success of her Scriabin recordings prompted Columbia to invite her to record the complete solo piano works of Rachmaninoff in honor of his 100th birthday in 1973. Early in the 1970s Laredo gave up her accompanist role to follow her own career as concert pianist. In 1973, after receiving outstanding reviews for her solo recital on the Great Pianists Series at Lincoln Center, she signed an exclusive contract with Columbia Artists Management. That same year she played nine major works of Brahms at Alexander Schneider's New School Brahms Marathon and also appeared with the Cleveland and Guarnieri quartets.

One year later the Laredos separated. Never having been on her own professionally, she wondered if she could support herself with her concerts. She need not have worried. At her first appearance (12 Dec 1974) with the New York Philharmonic Orchestra, playing Ravel's Concerto in G under Pierre Boulez, she gave "a whipcracking performance. . . . Miss Laredo made it a true divertissement." (*NYT*, 14 Dec 1974)

The monumental Rachmaninoff project (1973–81, 7 LPs) forced Laredo to develop strength she never knew she had. Ever since she made these historic recordings—she is the first person ever to have recorded Rachmaninoff's complete solo piano works—her name has been inextricably linked with his music. In "Life with Rocky," Laredo says, "the endurance, the speed, the power required by this music is unlike any other piano writing I've ever encountered." (*Key*, Aug 1987) Soon after the release of the first album (Preludes, op. 23 and Five Pieces, op. 3), in the spring of 1974, C. F. Peters commissioned her to edit a new Urtext edition of the complete Rachmaninoff works for piano.

Laredo does not have private pupils, but she enjoys teaching and has taught all through her career—residencies, master classes or chamber-music coaching—at Banff Summer School (1985, 1987, 1989), Aspen (1975) and at the Eastern Music Festival (1988); at Kent State/Blossom (1969–71), at Yale (1977–79) and at the summer session of the School of Arts in Victoria, B.C. (1979–86). "When I teach, I say you have to hear properly, way out in the stratosphere, what the audience is receiving. You must put across what you have to say on the stage—the timing, the nuances of pedaling, the textures of various pianos in relationship to your own touch." (Rubinstein)

Laredo has played with most of the major American orchestras, toured extensively as a recitalist, is a frequent guest artist with the Cleveland and Tokyo quartets and regularly schedules time to tour with the flutist Paula Robison. Their "Paula and Ruth" recitals have won both critical acclaim and an intensely loyal following. Laredo seems only to get busier. In recent years she has been presenting "Concerts with Commentary" at the Metropolitan Museum of Art in New York, each program devoted to a single composer. The first series (1988–89) dealt with three composers with whom she has long been identified: Scriabin, Rachmaninoff and Ravel. The next series featured Chopin, Schumann and Brahms. Laredo also writes an ongoing column (Ruth Laredo's Piano Forum) for *Keyboard Classics* and has contributed to *Keynote* and other publications.

Although never straying from stylistic correctness, Ruth Laredo has always been known, recognized and admired as an individualist. A Milwaukee program (18 Jan 1977) of Rachmaninoff, Scriabin, Schumann, Liszt, Mozart and Bach "showed her as a sensitive performer with a mind of her own. Her playing never edged toward carbon-copy style of established, conventional readings. There was a freshness, a spark of individuality in all her work." (*MJ*, 20 Jan 1977)

Ruth Laredo's diminutive size and contrasting strength at the keyboard have always elicited comments from the critics, particularly concerning the difficult repertoire—Scriabin, Rachmaninoff, Ravel—that she chooses. "She is immensely strong and accurate, willing to take risks. Her technical skills are so great that she can safely attempt velocities that might be a danger to a lesser pianist." (*WE*, 3 Dec 1980) But there are other qualities in her playing. On 11 June 1985 a Detroit recital (works by Tchaikovsky, Scriabin, Bloch and Prokofiev) won high praise for beautiful tone quality, "the precise delicacy with which she phrases, the naturally modulated dynamic shifts, the combination of power and gentleness that fills her playing with such unassailable authenticity—these are the qualities that make Laredo such a special pianist." (*DFP*, 13 June 1985)

Laredo's first performance (8 Jan 1984) of Samuel Barber's Concerto, op. 38, was a triumph. Playing with the New Jersey Symphony Orchestra under Sixten Ehrling, she achieved "an interpretation that glittered, sang, thundered and thrilled." The concerto's first movement—in classically oriented sonata form— "had Miss Laredo tossing off octave runs of staggering difficulty, yet with an ease of manner and a clarity of articulation that one finds only in artists for whom technique is a strictly subordinate problem." (*S-L*, 9 Jan 1984)

Laredo's performance (3 July 1988) of Rachmaninoff's Rhapsody on a Theme of Paganini with the Detroit Symphony Orchestra, Sixten Ehrling conducting, proved to be "something special. . . . In addition to knowing this piece inside out, Laredo also enjoys playing it, and she transmitted that joy to her listeners with such enthusiasm [that] they rose to their feet at its conclusion to let her know how infectious her joy was." (*DFP*, 5 July 1988)

Although Laredo has built a substantial reputation with her distinctive readings of Scriabin, Rachmaninoff and Prokofiev, she holds her own in earlier repertoires. For example, she is a fine, sensitive Beethoven player. Laredo's performance (11 March 1982) of four Beethoven sonatas on the Kennedy Center's Beethoven Piano Sonata Series received special praise for her phrasing, which "was governed by passion and titanic strength. . . . This was great Beethoven playing and the impact was staggering." (*WP*, 13 March 1982) Her Berkeley (California) program of 8 October 1983 included music by Chopin, Rachmaninoff, Beethoven and Barber. "Laredo's view of Beethoven's C major Sonata (1796) was as impressive as it was surprising. Its showy nature and qualities prophetic of his later style were never so clear and dramatic. It was an altogether arresting performance." (*SFC*, 10 Oct 1983)

On 5 January 1991 Laredo played the Saint-Saëns Concerto No. 2 in G Minor with the Richmond Symphony Orchestra, George Manahan conducting. "The first movement was solidly comfortable in its expansive format. The runs of the fast second movement [there is no slow movement] swept along into the closing movement, a presto in which the piano buzzed like a spinning wheel." (*RNL*, 7 Jan 1991)

Ruth Laredo's large and loyal following admires just about everything she does. Indeed, there is so much to admire. Laredo's joy in music is irresistible. Words sifted from reviews spanning three decades delineate a performer who thinks big, a bold performer projecting clear, distinctive ideas of each work. Her high-voltage style—taut, tempestuous, daring—radiates energy, endurance and virtuosity. And Laredo mostly plays dashing works perfectly suited to her brilliant technique and marvelously bright tone.

The adverse complaints running through the reviews tend to be similar. Laredo's playing has too much intensity and not enough emotion; or her nervous tension sometimes leads to blurring; or her tone is too brittle; or she sometimes overpedals. Overall, the negative criticisms seem unimportant. Ruth Laredo comes through as a superb performer, a refreshing performer who makes wonderfully enjoyable music.

Laredo has a substantial discography, and at this writing a number of the LPs are available on CD. The five-CD collection of Rachmaninoff's complete works for solo piano, originally recorded on LP (Grammy, Vol. 7, 1980) during 1975–77, stands as a personal monument to one of Laredo's most admired composers. While not every item is of equal value, Laredo has in general scored a resounding interpretative triumph. For example, her reading of the Sonata No. 1 in D Minor is, wrote one reviewer, "the first I have heard that extracts the last iota of detail, in both structure and content, from the piece and does so with a true sense of the grand line." (*StR*, Jan 1981)

The 10 Scriabin Sonatas are obtainable only on cassette, but another Scriabin program (see Discog.) has been reissued on CD. Both collections are superb. "Laredo's playing is technically strong, and there is a consistent, honest passion, a rich coloring, and a fine proportioning in these deeply Romantic performances." (*Key*, Sept 1985) The complete Scriabin Sonatas are particularly fine. Laredo gives each of these compositions a distinctive, meaningful performance. "She distinguishes her interpretations with sensitive lyrical expressiveness, thoughtful modulations of tempi and dynamics, and a luxurious sense of tone and atmosphere. She thus lends an intimate dimension which is uncommon among Scriabin performances." (*ARG*, March/April 1985)

The available CDs offer ample proof of Laredo's artistry. A recital recorded in 1980 and reissued by Connoisseur Society (see Discog.) offers works by four of her favorite composers. Her playing is outstanding—"the Rachmaninoff as tasteful as the Debussy, the Debussy as richly colored as the Scriabin, each piece brought off to near-perfection in its own character." (*StR*, Dec 1986) The Prokofiev is equally fine.

Some of Laredo's finest Beethoven performances are preserved on a four-sonata CD (see Discog.). The "*Appassionata*" in particular "is beautifully formed, technically precise and emotionally powerful." (*WP*, 16 Nov 1986) And Laredo's recital of music by Albéniz and Falla offers a full hour of recorded pleasure. These are beautifully conceived and stunning performances, not always played exactly as the composer indicates, but always alive with infectious enthusiasm.

SELECTED REFERENCES

Belt, Byron. "Musician of the Month: Ruth Laredo." *High Fidelity/Musical America*, Dec 1974, pp. MA 4–5.
Clark, Robert S. "Ruth Laredo." *Stereo Review*, Oct 1974, pp. 82–84.
Gruen, John. "A Lady Tiger at the Keyboard." *New York Times*, 15 Dec 1974, sec. 2, pp. 21–22.
Kozinn, Allan. "Ruth Laredo: Powerhouse at the Piano." *Ovation*, March 1981, pp. 20–23.

Laredo, Ruth. "Life with Rocky." *Keynote* (Publication of WNCN 104 FM N.Y.), Aug 1987, pp. 7–11.
———. "New Discoveries About Rachmaninoff's Prelude Op. 3, No. 2." *Keyboard Classics*, Jan/Feb 1986, pp. 34–35.
———. *The Ruth Laredo Becoming a Musician Book.* Valley Forge, Pennsylvania: European American Music Corp., 1992.
———. "Ruth Laredo's Piano Forum: Questions." *Keyboard Classics*, May/June 1988, pp. 40, 43.
Montparker, Carol. "Rediscovering Rachmaninoff: A Visit with Ruth Laredo." *Clavier*, Sept 1986, pp. 12–16.
———. "Ruth Laredo: Dynamic Dynamo." *Clavier*, Nov 1982, pp. 10–12.
Rubinstein, Leslie. "Premier Pianist." *Stagebill*, Nov 1986.
Sperber, Gordon. "Inspired: U.S. pianist pays tribute to Russian." *Winston-Salem Journal*, 13 March 1993.
See also Bibliography: Cur/Bio (1987); Dub/Ref; IWWM; New/GrA.

SELECTED REVIEWS

BE: 18 Jan 1993. *CPD*: 14 Aug 1978. *CSM*: 28 April 1976. *DFP*: 30 Nov 1958; 10 Jan 1966; 13 June 1985; 17 April 1988; 5 July 1988. *DO*: 12 Sept 1983. *FJ*: 23 Nov 1987. *MJ*: 20 Jan 1977. *NAO*: 23 April 1990. *NYT*: 21 Jan 1966; 12 Oct 1971; 14 Dec 1974; 19 Jan 1981; 29 Sept 1987; 16 Feb 1990. *RMN*: 15 April 1990. *RNL*: 7 Jan 1991. *SFC*: 10 Oct 1983; 26 March 1990. *S-L*: 9 Jan 1984; 15 Jan 1990. *SLPD*: 14 Jan 1979. *ST*: 19 Oct 1981. *WE*: 3 Dec 1980. *WP*: 13 March 1982; 22 Nov 1986; 24 Feb 1989.

SELECTED DISCOGRAPHY

Barber: Nocturne; Sonata, op. 26; Souvenirs. Elektra/Nonesuch cassette 79032.
Beethoven: Sonatas, op. 2, no. 3; op. 49, no. 2; op. 57; op. 81a. Second Hearing GS-9007 (CD).
Chopin: Etude, op. 25, no. 4. Mazurkas, op. 6, nos. 2 and 3; op. 24, no. 2; op. 33, no. 4; op. 56, no. 2; op. 63, no. 3. Nocturne, op. 15, no.1. Scherzo, op. 20. Waltzes, op. 34, nos. 1 and 2; op. 42; op. 69, nos. 1 and 2. Electra/Nonesuch cassette 9 71450-4.
My Second Recital . Bach (arr. Hess): Jesu, Joy of Man's Desiring. Beethoven: Sonata in F-sharp Major, op. 78. Brahms: Intermezzo, op. 117, no. 1; Waltzes, op. 39 (5). Chopin: Mazurka, op. 6, no. 1; Nocturne, op. 15, no. 2; Waltz, op. 64, no. 2. Debussy: Sarabande. Khachaturian: Toccata. Mozart: *Rondo alla Turca*. Schumann: Arabesque, op. 18. Tchaikovsky: Humoresque (from *Deux Morceaux*, op. 10); June Barcarolle (The Seasons); Natha-Valse (from *Six Morceaux*, op. 51). Essay 1026 (CD).
Rachmaninoff: The Complete Solo Piano Music. Sony Classical SMK 48 468-472 (5 CDs).

Ruth Laredo plays Albéniz and De Falla. Albéniz: *Cantos de españa,* op. 232;
   Suite española. Falla: Three Dances from the Three-Cornered Hat; *El Amor
   brujo*: Suite. MCA Classics. MCAD 6265 (CD).
Ruth Laredo Recital. Debussy: *Feux d'artifice*; *Bruyères*; *La fille aux cheveux de
   lin*; *Reflets dans l'eau.* Prokofiev: Sonata No. 3 in A Minor, op. 28.
   Rachmaninoff: Prelude in C-sharp Minor, op. 3, no. 2. Scriabin: Etude in
   C-sharp Minor, op. 2, no. 1; Poem, op. 32, no. 1; Sonata No. 9 in F
   Major, op. 68 ("Black Mass"). Connoisseur Society CD 4060.
Scriabin: Etudes, op. 42; Sonatas (10). 2 Electra/Nonesuch cassettes 73035.
Scriabin: *Poeme,* op. 32, no. 1; Preludes, op. 11; Preludes, op. 74. Phoenix
   PHCD 114.

⚜ ⚜ ⚜

LARROCHA, ALICIA DE: b. Barcelona, Spain, 23 May 1923.

> I was born in Barcelona, and I have Catalan blood, but I'm a bit of a
> mixture. My father was a Catalan born in Madrid. My mother was
> from Barcelona but of Navarraise ancestry, and I also have Andalusian
> and Basque blood. I suppose you could call me a Spanish cocktail.
>
> Alicia de Larrocha (Crichton, "Lady of Spain")

Sometimes a concert pianist assumes a repertoire, whatever it may be, and lives
with it, assimilates it, to such an extent that the time comes when that repertoire
belongs to that performer. So it is with Alicia de Larrocha. This self-styled
"Spanish cocktail" long ago claimed her native piano music as her own, and her
interpretations of that music—so authentic and unique that no other readings
even come close—are the cornerstones of her fame. Larrocha has never forsaken
her Spanish roots and is still, as a very lively septuagenarian, the definitive performer of Spanish piano music. More than that, her beautifully grand yet beautifully simple readings of traditional repertoire (notably Schumann, Mozart,
Beethoven) communicate the essence of that music in an inimitable manner unmistakably her own. There is no other pianist like her and, so say some musical
experts, there may never be another pianist like her.

   She is the third of four children born to Eduardo de Larrocha and Maria
Teresa de la Calle, a pianist who had studied with Enrique Granados. Her mother's sister, also a Granados pupil, taught for many years at the *Academia Marshall*, the school Frank Marshall established as successor to the academy started
by Granados early in the century. If the story is true, before Larrocha was three
the family grand piano had become her great big black toy, something to make
noise on, something to play under. One day her banging on the keys with a
pencil forced her pianist aunt to lock the instrument, but not too much later that
same aunt started her on lessons.

   At age four Larrocha began piano studies with Frank Marshall, the only
other teacher she has ever had, and for all intents and purposes the *Academia*

Marshall became her home. "I spent all my time there," she says, "at the piano and playing games." Within a year she played a concert for a small group of Marshall's friends, including Joaquin Turina, the composer. At age 11 she made her official debut, playing the Mozart "Coronation" Concerto with Enrique Fernández Arbós and the Madrid Symphony Orchestra.

Spanish piano music fascinated her even then, but Marshall assigned her pieces from the classic repertoire—Bach and Mozart, Chopin, Schumann and Liszt—and made her wait until she was about 17 before allowing her to make a serious study of Spanish works. Disappointed at the time, she later realized Marshall was right. "Spanish music," says Larrocha, "is *very, very, very* hard. . . . If you cannot play Bach and Mozart well, you cannot play Spanish music well." (Ericson)

Since Frank Marshall lived in Spain on a British passport, he got out of the country at the outbreak of the Spanish Civil War in 1936. Larrocha studied and practiced on her own until he returned in 1939, then resumed her lessons and soon became Marshall's assistant. In 1940 she began giving concerts in Spain, Spanish Morroco and the Canary Islands. In 1947 she played in Europe, her first concert tours outside of Spanish territory.

Larrocha and Juan Torra, also a pianist and pupil at the *Academia Marshall*, married in 1950. Their son Juan Francisco was born in 1957; their daughter Alicia in 1959. And when Frank Marshall died (1959), the Torras took over the direction of the *Academia Marshall*. Together 32 years, they were unusually close, despite long separations. Larrocha depended on her husband for every detail of every aspect of her career. (Juan Torra died in 1982, and Larrocha, utterly lost in every way without him, had to cope with a whole new way of life.)

She made her London debut at Wigmore Hall on 12 January 1953; made her American debut (11 Feb 1954) in Los Angeles, playing the Mozart Concerto in A Major, K. 448, and Manuel de Falla's Nights in the Gardens of Spain with Alfred Wallenstein and the Los Angeles Philharmonic Orchestra; and played her first New York recital (16 April 1955) at Town Hall.

Between 1955 and 1965 Larrocha taught at the *Academia Marshall*, made recordings and toured regularly in Europe. However, after that initial American experience she waited 10 years before playing again in the United States. "Nobody invited me," she says. That is, until Herbert Breslin, a New York publicity agent, heard some of her wonderful recordings and persuaded her to sign with him for a series of concerts in the United States. On 29 December 1965, a full decade after her last American performance, Larrocha played the Mozart Concerto in A Major, K. 488, with the New York Philharmonic Orchestra, conducted by William Steinberg, and this time she was an unqualified success. Two weeks later just about every New York critic gave her recital (15 Jan 1966) at Hunter College rave reviews, and that year's concerts in Europe and America placed her among the best pianists of the day. Her entrancing programs of Spanish music gave American audiences something new and delightfully refreshing and gave Larrocha a faithful following that endures to this day.

One of the concert world's most durable, dependable performers, Larrocha radiates energy and relishes her life of music, even all the traveling involved. And how she has traveled! In 1977 she told an interviewer, "I tour the whole year long and I have done this for 13 or 14 years now with not one month away from it." (Duarte) For years she played upwards of 100 concerts a year, half in the United States and the rest in Europe, Central America, South America, Japan, Israel, South Africa, the Middle East, Australia and New Zealand. Recently she has slowed down, but apparently not much.

Larrocha has received many awards for her recordings: *Grand Prix du Disque* (1960, 1974); the Amsterdam Edison Award (1968, 1978); Grammy Awards (1974, 1975); *Deutscher Schallplattenpreis* (1979); *Grand Prix du Disque Franz Liszt* (1980). She received the Paderewski Memorial Medal in London in 1962; was awarded the Order *Isabel la Católica* in 1972; was named *Musical America*'s Musician of the Year in 1978; was granted the honorary degree of Doctor "*Honoris Causa*" in Music by the University of Michigan in 1979; received Spain's *Medalla de oro al merito en las bellas artes* in 1982. And in 1985 she was awarded the National Music Prize by the Spanish Ministry of Culture.

Very few writers have been able to resist mentioning Alicia de Larrocha's short stature (4' 9") and small hands. And she herself confesses that her hands have been a lifelong obsession. Indeed years of exercising (pulling, kneading, splaying and stretching her fingers to the utmost limit) have made her hands strong, muscular and capable of spanning, as she puts it, nine-plus notes. Being so tiny, Larrocha sits high at the keyboard so that when necessary she can hunch her shoulders to get more arm and body weight into the keys. Few pianists of either gender play as powerfully, fluently and accurately. "Larrocha simply plays like a great musician, as capable of achieving silky tone and cobweb delicacy as crashing power. The high position does not seem to hinder her in producing a beautiful, unforced tone, as it logically ought to do." (*NYT*, 18 July 1976)

Larrocha, the kind of pianist who listens—very carefully and very critically—to her own playing, believes that the ear is very important. "It tells you what to do . . . and you manage to do it [produce big sounds], but I cannot tell you how. Somehow you manage to produce what your ear demands. You compensate with the pedal, too, of course." (Dobratschewsky) Her own remarkable talent for self-listening gets as much attention from writers as do her small hands. For example, "Her astounding accuracy, velocity and clarity in chord registration simply seem to defy physiological explanation, and confirm . . . that the secret of musical technique lies primarily in the ear and the memory, not the fingers." (Henahan)

One of Alicia de Larrocha's most intriguing, arguably nonmusical, qualities is her stage presence. If she feels nervous, it never shows. She comes onstage very matter-of-factly, sternly confident yet somehow friendly, and always modest. After all these years of adoring audiences and admiring critics, Larrocha still seems not to know that she is one of the world's greatest pianists. A most unusual celebrity, she has never craved fame, never felt in competition with her colleagues. All Larrocha has ever wanted to do is make music and, as she says so often, she "loves everyone who makes music."

Offstage Alicia de Larrocha is, in her words, moody and unpredictable: "I am characteristically Latin, up one day, down the next, up, down, up, down."

Temperament even decides Larrocha's practicing regime. When feeling good about practicing, she might keep going through the whole day; at other times she might practice for barely a half-hour. Touring precludes regular practicing, but she studies scores in airports, on planes, etc., and practices at every opportunity (with a mute on the strings of hotel pianos), usually working on the technique involved in the pieces she has programmed.

When learning a new composition, Larrocha looks first at the work's general structure and form, next considers details (technical, sound and phrasing problems) and finally puts it all together, without using the pedal. And as Frank Marshall taught her, she learns the left hand first. "It's the most important hand in everything," says Larrocha, "in balance of sound, in *rubato*, in style. The left hand is like a column that holds the whole building, the whole monument. The melody is nothing, really—just the first thing the ear captures." (Forsht)

Larrocha describes her repertoire as not very large and representative of her "love of the moment." She prefers to be known not as a "Spanish pianist" but as a pianist who happens to be Spanish, and says her repertoire includes music of every country and every style—classic, romantic, baroque. Decades of recitals prove her right. As a child she played only traditional repertoire, mostly Bach and Mozart and works by Romantic composers, Schumann in particular. And she gained her first fame for her performances of Spanish music, especially Albéniz and Granados. "Her ability to perform Spanish music is unmatched and perhaps never will be superseded. . . . Her performances . . . capture the subtleties—as well as the distinct colors—of Spanish music. . . . Larrocha knows when to pause ever-so-slightly in a phrase, how to evoke the pastels of the Spanish landscape." (Reich)

Generally speaking, Larrocha's repertoire begins with Couperin and Bach, includes the Mozart and Beethoven sonatas and concertos, concentrates on the Romantic era and extends to post-Romantic composers such as Rachmaninoff and Granados. She plays works by fellow Spaniards, like Rodrigo and Esplá, but otherwise rarely contemporary music. Usually she keeps 12 or 13 concertos current (with a few days' notice she can ready one of many more in her repertoire); and she prepares two (formerly three or four) recital programs a season.

Alicia de Larrocha was born with marvelous musical instincts, and she has all the techniques it takes to realize them. The unanimous critical voice (put together from many, many reviews) describes her technique: ultrararified, stupendous, unerring, flawless, prodigious, tactile wizardry, near-miraculous keyboard control. It also describes her musicianship: aristocratic, suave, superb, intelligent, prodigious. Most particularly, her "magnificent sense of form and design," the "gorgeous sound of her voicing," her "exquisite phrasing" and her "artful shadings of rhythms and phrasings" have elevated Larrocha into the class of fabled pianists.

Adverse comments on Larrocha's pianism are so few (and usually tempered with compliments) as to hardly exist. Sometimes the music she plays is "less than profound," but always her playing is "nothing short of magnificent." A performance of the Beethoven Concerto No. 2 was "expert in the highest degree, and unexciting." Her Brahms Concerto No. 2 at Lincoln Center "was played carefully and intelligently . . . but monumentality of this sort is hardly her cup of tea."

At her American debut (11 Feb 1954) with Alfred Wallenstein and the Los Angeles Philharmonic Orchestra, Larrocha's performance of the Mozart Concerto in A Major, K. 488, was "restrained in scale, but not small; the passages purled and rippled, the melodies sparkled brightly and there was an incisive and well-controlled rhythmical impulse to give it all shape and form." And her reading of Falla's Nights in the Gardens of Spain "stood out with a well-calculated variety of tonal subtleties and an innate musicianly feeling for the requirements of sound ensemble." (*LAT*, 12 Feb 1954)

She played her beloved Spanish music (Albéniz, Granados, Suriñach), the Beethoven Sonata in A-flat Major, op. 110, Schumann's *Carnaval* and Herbert Murrill's *Suite française* at her New York recital debut on 16 April 1955. Reviewers hesitated over her interpretations of Beethoven and Schumann, especially her unconventional reading of *Carnaval*, yet the "deviations were always related to a firm musical esthetic, its points of stress and climax determined by an artistic awareness of a very conscious sort." Of course she played the Spanish segment of this program with "crisp rhythm, stylistic assurance, and the kind of flexibility in melodic statement that is hard for an outsider to simulate." (*SR*, 30 April 1955)

At her first New York appearance after that 10-year hiatus Larrocha gave an inspired performance (29 Dec 1965) of the Mozart Concerto in A Major, K. 488 (with William Steinberg conducting the New York Philharmonic Orchestra). "She went to the heart of the musical phrase with deftness and aplomb. . . . There was plenty of detail to her playing, the shaping of each scale with beautifully graded dynamics, the underlining of important left-hand figures." (*NYT*, 30 Dec 1965)

Larrocha has attracted a large, ardent following, especially in America. At a sold-out Hunter College recital (28 Oct 1972), "the tiny lady from Spain could do no wrong. . . . She is, after all, one of the most finished pianists before the public. . . . She played Debussy's Soirée dans Grenade with hauntingly beautiful color and utter relaxation. What with this kind of floating tone, aided by delicate pedal effects, Debussy's ideal of a piano without hammers came true." (*NYT*, 30 Oct 1972)

A London performance (2 March 1980) of the complete *Iberia* ("a recital that should go straight into the international piano archives") was an artistic triumph remarkable for its sheer sound. "No orchestra could have rivalled the range of colour Miss Larrocha drew from her piano. And whether loud or soft, sweet or dry, *joyeux* or *sanglotant* . . . her tone was always a feast for the ear." (*TL*, 3 March 1980)

Larrocha has been playing Schumann's music since she was in her teens. Her performance (29 May 1980) of the Schumann Concerto at London's Festival Hall, with Michael Tilson Thomas conducting the Philharmonia Orchestra, "gave a rare pleasure in so familiar a classic through the ravishing sensibility of her playing throughout. Nothing was forced, and nothing was false, but her endearing warmth of spirit shone through the lyrical and more vigorous passages alike." (*TL*, 30 May 1980)

Reviews of an all-Schumann recital Larrocha played during the 1987–88 season are equally laudatory. From Chicago: "De Larrocha was marvelously adept at conveying the composer's peculiar duality, as witnessed by her wide dynamic and textural contrasts, her abrupt shifts from skittish rhythmic patterns to supple lyricism." (*CT*, 16 March 1987) And from Los Angeles: "Rarely does an artist communicate as directly as Larrocha did with her adoring audience. . . . She conveyed strength and vigor without effort or exertion, and she floated melodies on edgeless moonbeams." (*LAT*, 19 Nov 1987)

Usually Larrocha's Beethoven performances receive equal compliments. On 11 May 1979 she gave a radiantly lyrical performance of the Concerto No. 4 with the Hallé Orchestra under James Loughran. "Rare is the pianist," wrote one London reviewer, "who can charm us and hold our undivided attention with every scale and bravura gesture in a classical concerto. . . . Miss de Larrocha finds the structural meaning in every slightest incident." (*DT*, 14 May 1979)

That same year (1979) she performed all five Beethoven concertos in New York with the Pittsburgh Symphony Orchestra under André Previn. And in 1989 at Ravinia, within five days the inexhaustible Larrocha performed all the Beethoven concertos as well as the complete Albéniz *Iberia*. The first program (10 Aug 1989) consisted of Beethoven's first three concertos, performed with the Chicago Symphony Orchestra, Edo de Waart conducting. Analyzing all three performances, one critic wrote, "She can thunder at the keyboard as boldly as most anyone. But De Larrocha is sparing in her use of fortissimos, saving them for critical climaxes. Instead, she prefers to make her points through the luster of her tone, the precision of her touch and the unassailable depth of her interpretations." (*CT*, 11 Aug 1989) Ten days later Larrocha concluded her Beethoven cycle, and two days after that played the complete *Iberia*—again an inimitable reading.

In Los Angeles on 2 March 1995 an ideal Larrocha program (Spanish composers in the first half, Schumann's *Carnaval* in the second half) once again reaffirmed her "kaleidoscopic musical artistry." Technically and interpretatively at her best, the 71-year-old Larrocha's playing "inspired her listeners through musical point, articulate and compelling re-creations of contrasting works and multicolored, seductive, exquisite pianism. . . . Her phrasing, musical rhetoric and command of articulation find meaning where others deliver only notes." (*LAT*, 4 March 1995)

From 1967 through 1991 Larrocha's recorded albums received 11 Grammy awards—eight of them for performances of Spanish music, the other three for Schubert (Sonata in B-flat Major, 1984), Mozart (Sonatas, 1990) and concerted music by Ravel and Fauré (1975).

Alicia de Larrocha has performed and recorded much of Mozart's music. One reviewer, surveying her discs of the complete sonatas, writes: "She has a natural affinity for the kind of crisp flexibility, pointed, graceful rhythms and bright, ringing *cantabile* that are eminently suited to this material." (*CLA*, Dec 1990) In a similar vein, a review of her recording of two Mozart concertos (K.

271 in E-flat Major and K. 467 in C Major) with Sir Colin Davis and the English Chamber Orchestra (see Discog.), states that the pianist "has proved herself to be a sympathetic and thoughtful artist in this repertory . . . the pianism is fully secure while tempos are carefully judged." Yet the critic feels a certain disappointment: "It is all rather bland and faceless, with everything done well enough but never magically or memorably." (*Gram*, Jan 1992)

There are close to 20 currently available versions of the complete concertos of Beethoven, and of course just as many different approaches, ranging from strictly objective to strictly subjective. Larrocha's performances with Riccardo Chailly conducting the Berlin Radio Symphony Orchestra appear, to some, to add little to an already overloaded catalogue. Despite her uncontested musicianship and technical expertise, "she has nothing of individual interest to tell us about any of these masterpieces." (*MA*, Nov 1987) Another view sees Larrocha as "more at home in the slow movements, which are played with a cool grace that is not unappealing." In the often strenuous first movements and the usually sparkling finales, "there is a brittleness about the interpretations, and occasionally about the touch itself." (*Gram*, Nov 1986) But a third appraisal finds these Beethoven discs "an unusually satisfying set. . . . The first three concertos combine brisk tempos, a neatly gauged dynamic scheme and rhythmic élan. The Fourth Concerto is wonderfully relaxed in its opening movement and thrillingly dark in a slow movement even more than usually restrained, while the pianist's fleet, buoyant approach to the Fifth Concerto, the 'Emperor,' downplays the swagger, concentrating instead on illuminating structural and melodic detail." (*LAT*, 1 March 1987)

EMI has reissued on CD a series of performances of Spanish music—Albéniz, Falla, Granados, Turina—originally recorded by *Hispavox* between 1958 and 1967, and issued in the United States on the Epic and Columbia labels. Larrocha has no serious competition in this repertoire except perhaps herself, for she has recorded some of the compositions several times. Although the quality of sound is not that of her later recorded performances, these earlier versions are superbly authentic and exciting realizations by one of this century's finest keyboard artists. Larrocha made four versions of *Iberia*. This CD (EMI) has the second version, originally recorded in 1962. While her third and fourth interpretations are both remarkable, in 1962 "Larrocha had exactly the right mixture of authority, imagination, and digital resourcefulness to offer a really magisterial account of the score." (*ARG*, Jan/Feb 1993) A 1988 comparison of the first three versions: "Listening to these three performances is to hear a single persistent voice. The earliest may tend more toward fleetness, with less willingness to linger, and among all three are many variations in detail—this in music which, after all, invites a measure of spontaneous interpretation." (Holland) So, in reality, the obvious difference lies primarily in the technology, the later readings being superior only in matters of sound reproduction.

The EMI Falla collection (see Discog.) comes from 1958. A later London recording contains most of the same material with of course a richer sound quality, but this early version is certainly competitive. The two Granados CDs on EMI contain 1963–67 originals and are as authentic as any interpretations could possibly be: Larrocha's teacher Frank Marshall was himself a pupil and close friend of the composer. Another version of the *Goyescas* (her fourth) appears on an RCA CD (see Discog.). However, as one listener opines, "She more or less owns this music and competes mostly with herself, and whichever de Larrocha recording of *Goyescas* you get, it's better than anyone else's." (*Fan*, May/June 1991) Turina's music is perhaps not as well known as that by the other three composers but it is eminently worthwhile, in particular the four-movement *Sanlucar de Barrameda*, one of Turina's comparatively few ventures into large-scale composition.

Larrocha's exploration of French repertoire for piano and orchestra shows convincingly that she is not restricted to the Spanish school. Fauré's seldom-heard *Fantaisie*, op. 111, is perhaps not as intrinsically interesting as his *Ballade*, op. 19, but in Larrocha's hands it becomes as definitive a performance as could be desired. The Franck Symphonic Variations, which must compete with at least a dozen fine readings, are remarkable for their fastidiousness and elegance. And the Ravel Concerto in G Major is played "sensitively and with impeccable attention to detail." (*Gram*, Sept 1987)

A recent CD combines music by Manuel de Falla with that of the Catalan composer Xavier Montsalvatge (see Discog.). For one reviewer, the high point of this program is Falla's *Fantasía bética*, Larrocha "beginning it more deliberately than in her 1974 Decca recording, displaying great tonal imagination throughout, and confirming her status as the foremost interpreter today of Spanish keyboard music." (*Gram*, Sept 1994)

SELECTED REFERENCES

Blyth, Alan. "Alicia de Larrocha." (interview) *Gramophone*, Oct 1973, p. 654.

Chase, Gilbert. "Falla: Piano Music" *Stereo Review*, Sept 1975, p. 112.

Crichton, Ronald. "Lady of Spain." (interview) *Records and Recording*, Oct 1973, pp. 30–32.

Davis, Peter G. "The Spanish Piano School and its Star Pupil." *New York Times*, 31 July 1977, sec. 2, p. 13.

Drobatschewsky, Dimitri. "A Big Sound." *Arizona Republic* (Phoenix), 14 April 1985, sec. F, p. 3.

Duarte, John. "Lady of Spain." (interview) *Records and Recording*, Dec 1977, pp. 18–19.

Ericson, Raymond. "In The Granados Tradition." *New York Times*, 2 Jan 1966, sec. 2, p. 11.

Forsht, James L. "Alicia de Larrocha: First Lady of the Piano." *Keyboard Classics*, Nov/Dec 1986, pp. 5–6.

Henahan, Donal. "They're mad about Alicia." *New York Times Magazine*, 18 July 1976, sec. 6, pp. 13–16.

Holland, Bernard. "De Larrocha Travels Once More to 'Iberia'." *New York Times*, 16 Oct 1988, pp. 31, 44.

Kuehl, Olga Llano. "Alicia de Larrocha." *Clavier*, April 1982, pp. 14–15.

Larrocha, Alicia de (with Edmund Haines). "Granados." *High Fidelity Magazine*, Dec 1967, pp. 56–58.

Livingstone, William. "Alicia de Larrocha." (interview) *Stereo Revue*, March
    1980, pp. 78–80.
Morrison, Bryce. "Alicia de Larrocha." (interview) *Music and Musicians*, Oct
    1979, pp. 21–22.
"Musical America Names Alicia de Larrocha Musician of the Year." *High
    Fidelity*, Aug 1978, pp. 88–89.
Reich, Howard. "No Easy Pieces." *Chicago Tribune*, 6 Aug 1989, sec. 13, p.
    8.
Rockwell, John. "Who Says Modern Pianists Are Un-Romantic?" *New York
    Times*, 3 June 1984, sec. 2, p. 23.
Schonberg, Harold C. "Miss De Larrocha Rules As the Queen of Pianists."
    New York Times, 22 Oct 1982, sec. 3, p. 3.
Sweeney, Louise. "Alicia de Larrocha: What I'm playing is what I love."
    Christian Science Monitor, 8 Dec 1978, sec. B, p. 16.
See also Bibliography: Cur/Bio (1968); Dub/Ref; Eld/Pia; Ewe/Mu; IWWM;
    Jac/Rev; Mac/Gre; New/Gro; WWAM.

SELECTED REVIEWS

BG: 9 April 1988. *BH*: 18 Nov 1991. *BN*: 7 April 1978; 23 Oct 1987. *CST*: 9
Nov 1987; 16 Aug 1989. *CT*: 16 March 1987; 11 Aug 1989. *DP*: 16
March 1976. *DT*: 14 May 1979. *LAT*: 12 Feb 1954; 28 Oct 1967; 18 Jan
1972; 29 July 1976; 16 March 1978; 23 Nov 1981; 9 Nov 1984; 19 Nov
1987; 28 March 1991; 24 Nov 1992; 28 Feb 1994; 4 March 1995. *MT*:
Aug 1970; April 1982. *NY*: 16 Dec 1967. *NYP*: 12 April 1976; 20 July
1989. *NYT*: 17 April 1955; 30 Dec 1965; 17 Jan 1966; 15 Dec 1966; 8
Dec 1967; 4 Oct 1969; 18 Dec 1970; 30 Oct 1972; 12 Nov 1974; 3 May
1982; 11 Oct 1982; 21 Nov 1992; 1 Dec 1993. *PP*: 27 Nov 1982. *SFC*: 4
July 1981; 17 April 1991. *SFE*: 13 Nov 1986. *SR*: 30 April 1955; 27
Dec 1969. *ST*: 11 Nov 1983. *TL*: 12 Jan 1953; 13 Oct 1978; 3 March
1980; 30 May 1980; 19 Aug 1981. *WP*: 10 Nov 1975; 7 July 1988. *WS*: 7
Aug 1978. *WT*: 14 May 1990.

SELECTED DISCOGRAPHY

Albéniz: Obras para piano. Azulejos; *Cantos de España*; *Malagueña*; *Mallorca*;
    La Vega; *Zambra granadina*; *Zaragoza*. EMI Classics CDM 7 64523-2.
Albéniz Piano Works. Iberia; *Navarra*; *Suite española* no. 1, op. 47; *Pavana-
    capricho*, op. 12; Tango (*España*, op. 165); *Puerta de tierra, Rumores de la
    caleta* (*Recuerdos de viaje*, op. 71). EMI CDMB 7 64504 (2 CDs). Second
    version of *Iberia*.
Albéniz: *Iberia* (complete); *Malagueña*; *Navarra*; *Pavana-capricho*; *Puerta de
    tierra*; *Rumores de la caleta*; Tango. Falla: *Fantasía bética*; *4 Piezas es-
    pañolas*. London 433 926-2 (2 CDs). Third version.
Albéniz: *Iberia* (complete); *Navarra*. London 417887-2 (2 CDs). Fourth ver-
    sion.

Beethoven: Concerto No. 1 in C Major, op. 15; Sonata in D Major, op. 28. RCA Victor Red Seal 09026 61676-2. Thomas/London SO. The Concerto is also available on Video (see below).

Beethoven: Concertos for Piano and Orchestra (5); "Choral" Fantasy, op. 80. London 414 391-2 (3 CDs). Chailly/Berlin RSO.

Esplá: *Sonata Española*, op. 53. Granados: *Danzas españolas* (1954). Rodrigo: *Danzas de España*. MCA Classics MCAD2-9824B.

Falla: Nights in the Gardens of Spain (Dutoit/Montreal PO); *El amor brujo*. Rodrigo: *Concierto de Aranjuéz*. London 430 703-2.

Falla: *Quatre pièces espagnoles*; *Fantasía bética*; Spanish dance No. 1 (*La vida breve*); *Serenata andaluza*; *Sinfonia* (*El Retablo de Maese Pedro*). Montsalvatge: *Divagación*; Three Divertimentos; *Si, à Mompou*; *Berceuse à la memoria de Oscar Esplá*; *Sonatine pour Yvette*. RCA Victor 61389-2.

Fauré: *Fantaisie*, op. 111. Franck: Symphonic Variations. Ravel: Concerto for the left hand; Concerto in G Major. London 417 583-2. Foster/London PO.

Granados: *Allegro de concierto*; *Danza lenta*; Twelve Spanish Dances. EMI CDM 64529-2.

Granados: *Escenas románticos*; *Goyescas*; *El pelele*; *Seis piezas sobre cantos populares españoles*; *Valses poéticos*. EMI CDBM 64524-2.

Mozart: Concerto in E-flat Major, K. 271; Concerto in C Major, K. 467. Victor Red Seal 60825 (CD). Davis/English CO.

Mozart: Concerto in E-flat Major, K. 482; Concerto in D Major, K. 537. Victor Red Seal 09026-61698-2. Davis/English CO.

Mozart: Sonatas, K. 282, 330, 332, 332. London 417 817-2.

Mozart Sonatas (complete). RCA Victor Red Seal 60407, 60453-54, 60709 (4 CDs).

Ravel: Concerto in G; Concerto for Left Hand; *Sonatine*; *Valses nobles et sentimentales*. RCA 09026-60985 (CD). Slatkin/St. Louis SO.

Schumann: Allegro in B Minor, op. 8; *Carnaval*, op. 9; *Faschingsschwank aus Wien*, op. 26. London 421 525-2.

Spanish Encores. I. Albéniz: *Malagueña*; *Pavana capricho*; *Puerta de tierra*: *Bolero*; *Rumores de la caleta*: *Malagueña*; *Sevilla*: *Sevillanas*; *Tango*. M. Albéniz: Sonata in D Major. Granados: *Andaluza*; *Valenciana o Calesera*. Mompou: *Impresiones intimas*. Soler: Sonata in D Major; Sonata in G Minor. Turina: *Sacro-monte*; *Zapateado*. London 417 639-2.

Spanish Fireworks. I. Albéniz: *Iberia* (*Triana*); *Navarra, Suite española* (*Asturias, Sevilla*). M. Albéniz: Sonata in D Major. Falla: *El amor brujo* (Dance of Terror, Ritual Fire Dance); Three-Cornered Hat (Miller's Dance). Granados: *Allegro de concierto*; *Goyescas* (*Quéjas, o la maja y el ruiseñor, El Pelele*); *Zapateado*. Mompou: *Secreto*. Turina: *Danzas gitanas* (*Sacromonte, Zapateado*). London Jubilee 417 795-2.

Turina: *Danzas fantásticas*; *Sacromonte* (*Danzas gitanas*); *Sanlucar de Barrmeda*; *Zapeado* (*Danzas andaluzas*). EMI CDM 64528-2.

VIDEO

Beethoven: Concerto No. 1 in C Major, op. 15. With Michael Tilson Thomas
and the London Symphony Orchestra. RCA Victor (Red Seal) 09026
61782-3. Volume 2 of *Dudley Moore introduces Concerto!*

LEVITZKI, MISCHA: b. Kremenchug, Russia, 25 May 1898; d. Avon-by-
the-Sea, New Jersey, 2 January 1941.

> Among the younger generation I had two successful rivals: Benno
> Moiseiwitsch and Mischa Levitzki.
>
> Artur Rubinstein (*My Many Years*)

Forty years after Mischa Levitzki's premature death, Artur Rubinstein still remembered him as one of only two "successful rivals" in the upcoming generation of pianists. Rubinstein's memorial accolade takes the measure of the young
Levitzki, and seems a fitting cap to the lavish praise heaped on him throughout
his career. It also causes all the more regret that this pianist died at the age of
42.

Mischa Levitzki, born in Russia to Russian parents, was nevertheless
an American citizen. Jacob L. and Anna (Smelanski) Levitzki, his parents, were
naturalized American citizens who at the time of his birth just happened to be
back in Russia on a long, long visit. (Levitzki was eight years old when they
returned to America.) He began violin lessons at about age three and at six
started piano lessons with a family friend, advancing so rapidly that the following year he was sent (friends raised the funds) to the Warsaw Conservatory for a
year of study with Aleksander Michalowski, a well-known pianist and teacher.

The following year the Levitzkis returned home to New York, and almost immediately the eight-year-old Mischa had a chance to play for Walter
Damrosch, conductor of the New York Symphony Society. Damrosch advised
further study at the Institute of Musical Art (now the Juilliard School), and
friends provided financial support. For the next five years Levitzki studied with
Sigismond Stojowski at the Institute, attended public schools in Brooklyn and
New York and practiced about two hours daily. It was a heavy schedule for a
boy not yet in his teens, still not overly restricted. Despite possible injury to
his hands, Levitzki was allowed to play baseball, a game he dearly loved.

Meanwhile his remarkable talent attracted more supporters, and in 1911
he was sent to Germany to study at the Berlin *Hochschule für Musik*. Only 13
years old, he met with obstacles. For one thing, the *Hochschule* only admitted
students age 16 or older. Even more upsetting, Levitzki wanted to study with
Ernst von Dohnányi, but the famed composer-teacher disapproved of *Wunder-
kinder* and specifically held to the age 16 requirement. When first approached,
Dohnányi actually refused to give Levitzki an audition but eventually relented

enough to listen to the boy play one piece. Levitzki played Raff's *La Fileuse*, and the now interested Dohnányi asked him to play another. Levitzki then played Mendelssohn's Spring Song, and played it so well that Dohnányi invited him to take the *Hochschule* examination the following day.

The next morning Levitzki explained to the 15 examiners that he would play Mendelssohn's Concerto in G Minor. Of course there was no orchestra at the ready, but Dohnányi, surprising everyone present, stepped forward to play the second-piano accompaniment. The examiners accepted Levitzki as a *Hochschule* student, and Dohnányi allowed him into his advanced class. He made exceptional progress in his four years (1911–15) with Dohnányi. In 1913 he was awarded the Mendelssohn second prize; in 1914 he received the Mendelssohn first prize.

Although well aware of Levitzki's technical skills, Dohnányi first assigned him pieces (Schumann's *Kinderscenen*, some early Beethoven sonatas) requiring less technique than Levitzki already possessed. This was Dohnányi's method for making the student, unhampered by technical difficulties, devote himself to mastering the true meaning of a work. Rather than objecting, Levitzki was only too glad to learn how to prepare a work in a careful, systematic way. At a typical lesson Dohnányi would listen carefully, without interrupting, as the student played his whole piece. He would then make corrections or suggestions, after which he sat down and played the piece from beginning to end.

Except for two hours of private tutoring, Levitzki's days in Berlin were wholly devoted to music. Unfortunately too much bicycle riding strained his right hand and arm, so that for the first year or so he had to limit his practice to two hours a day. However, as he later said, "I *thought* music constantly, lived in it, made serious theoretical studies and heard no end of concerts and opera." (Brower) During his last two years with Dohnányi he practiced about three hours daily.

Dohnányi worked with Levitzki for about a year before allowing him to perform publicly, first in Germany and Belgium. Levitzki made his official Berlin debut in March 1914 and, despite the start of World War I, he remained in Germany until 1916, making tours of Germany, Austria and Scandinavia. Once home, after five years abroad, Levitzki made his official American debut (17 Oct 1916) at Aeolian Hall in New York, and his playing caused a sensation. Rave reviews from the New York critics gave his career a spectacular start. For the next 25 years Levitzki toured extensively—in the United States (more than 20 times), Canada, Europe, Australia, New Zealand, Hawaii, Singapore, Java, Japan, China. Like pianist Shura Cherkassky, Levitzky loved traveling, even touring, and in several interviews told about the music and other interesting facts encountered in his travels in the Orient, Australia and New Zealand (Levitzki, "Music on. . .").

A composer as well as pianist, Levitzki wrote his own cadenza to the Beethoven Concerto No. 3 in C Minor, but otherwise composed mostly salon pieces—charming, well-designed works with titles typical of the time, for instance, *Arabesque valsante*, *Valse tzigane*, The Enchanted Nymph, Gavotte in

Old Style. His first published work, the Valse in A Major, came out in Australia and quickly became a popular piece with pianists everywhere.

Levitzki's last New York appearance was at the Metropolitan Opera House on 5 March 1940, playing the Saint-Saëns Concerto No. 2 in G Minor with Maurice Abravanel conducting the New York City Symphony Orchestra. Less than a year later he died (2 Jan 1941) of a heart attack at his home in New Jersey. His wife, the former Grace O'Brien of New York, survived him.

Levitzki programs dating from 1916 to the end of his life show a rather small repertoire and much repetition of the same works year after year. And in one interview he explained why. "Quality and not quantity is what really counts, always and forever in art. . . . The literature of the piano has assumed tremendous dimensions. Far better to master a worthy portion of it than to dabble in all. There is no short cut in art. Learn all well or not at all. Do not try to play twenty concertos superficially, if you have lived only years enough to master ten well. The others will come with time and study." (Levitzki, "Getting a Start. . .")

If Levitzki played Bach, it was either the well-known Chromatic Fantasy and Fugue or one of the organ works in transcription. He played a few of the Beethoven sonatas, usually the "*Appassionata*," "Moonlight" and "*Waldstein*," occasionally Opus 101 or Opus 110. He often played Schumann's Symphonic Etudes and many selections from the Chopin repertoire. Mozart's Sonata in A Major, K. 331, appeared sporadically and he often programmed the last movement separately.

He did not play contemporary music because he thought it lacked "the greatness of substance, the qualities of enduring significance" found in the works of the older masters. If he programmed a "new" composition, it would be a seldom-heard piece written by one of those same masters. He claimed that though the novelty and color of Ravel's *Jeux d'eau* had originally enchanted him, the charm ultimately wore off; however, his programs show that he played the *Jeux d'eau* to the end of his life.

Levitzki's concerto repertoire, by today's standards, was limited. He most often played the Saint-Saëns Concerto in G Minor, the Beethoven Concerto No. 3 in C Minor and Schumann's Concerto in A Minor; and less frequently played the Mozart Concerto in A Major, K. 488, and Beethoven's Concerto No. 2 in B-flat Major.

There is no question but that Levitzki had the technique to play just about anything. "There is such a thing as a natural technique," he once wrote, "and I suppose that is what I have. I think technique is a gift, just as much as the gift for musical expression. But a gift in either direction must be developed to be of real value." To improve technique, Dohnányi, like some other master pedagogues (notably Alfred Cortot and Tobias Matthay) taught the principle of relaxation, that is, supple wrists, no stiffness or tension anywhere. In addition, said Levitzki, Dohnányi was "very particular about clearness of touch, requiring the fingers to be well raised in slow and careful practice. The beginning and finishing of the phrase, its shading and balance are all thought out." (Brower)

Levitzki played without gestures, grimaces or affectations of any kind. Mature and poised at the piano, even as a youth, he appeared totally absorbed in the music. His approach to a work was equally serious, essentially intellectual and very personalized, yet he never allowed his individuality or his virtuosity to encroach on the music or lead him into excess of any kind. Some writers now classify Levitzki as a transitional pianist, on the one hand displaying an exquisitely rich, orchestral tone and the striking individuality reminiscent of Rosenthal, Paderewski, Pachmann and other titans of the old school; and on the other hand the cool, profoundly intellectual approach and complete absence of emotion advocated by some modern pianists.

Whatever camp he belongs to, Levitzki was a great pianist, and had the reviews to prove it. "Still in his early twenties," wrote one critic, "Levitzki is a ripened, magnificent pianist, one of the Olympians." (*CEA*, 10 Dec 1923) And this: "He is a musician of fine intimacies, delicacies and reserves. His style is individually his own, as is his technique, exceedingly finished, unfailing in its correctness, endless in its minute gradations. His tone is of an exquisite purity and pearly opalescence." (*NYT*, 9 Nov 1922)

Rave reviews for his American recital debut (17 Oct 1916) in New York ensured his career. "Mr. Levitzki's technical equipment is ample. . . . He has tone, too, in quantity and quality, a good feeling for color, a notable instinct for rhythm and also true repose. Best of all, he is nobly served by his ideal musical sense and fine qualities of intellect." (*MA*, 28 Oct 1916) From another source: "His [technique] is highly developed, very certain, and would be 'brilliant' if he sought brilliancy as an end in itself. But he is as little of a virtuoso as can well be imagined, and technical proficiency is to him but a means to an end." (*NYT*, 18 Oct 1916)

Glowing reviews led to more and more appearances. At his third recital (19 Jan 1917) Levitzki's "work throughout was not only of very high merit, but it seemed to give an even greater display of his pianistic gifts than before, gifts that include first of all tonal beauty, rich technical resource, and a poetic feeling combined with profound musical intelligence." (*NYS*, 20 Jan 1917) Apart from one sonata, the Mozart in A Major, K. 331, that program consisted of short compositions by Beethoven, Chopin, Scarlatti, Rubinstein and Liszt.

The highly respected critic James Huneker expressed his admiration for Levitzky in colorful prose. One of Levitzki's typically conventional Carnegie Hall programs (1 March 1919) had to compete with Galli-Curci singing at the Lexington Theater and Farrar singing at the Metropolitan! But, said Huneker, "'Kid' Levitzki was not easily daunted, either by rival attractions or by the familiar music he presented; a familiarity that bred beauty, not contempt. In sooth, his playing was beautiful. Technical surety, clarity in phrasing, a lovely touch and tone—rather say a variety of touches and an astonishing color-range, considering the limitations of the keyboard." (*NYT*, 2 March 1919)

London concertgoers and critics greatly admired Levitzki. On 20 October 1927 the major work on his recital at Queen's Hall was Beethoven's "*Appassionata*" Sonata. "In Beethoven . . . his rhythmic sense enabled him to hold the thing well together, and his reading seemed consistently thought out. . . . In his Chopin the lightness of touch of the smaller works . . . created the happiest impression." (*TL*, 21 Oct 1927)   Another Queen's Hall recital (29 Oct 1929) included works by Franck, Schumann and Chopin. And, like his recital of two years previous, "His Chopin was the most definitely successful part of his programme". (*TL*, 2 Nov 1929)

Excerpts from Levitzki's reviews sometimes sound like hero-worship. "He seems to be lacking in nothing;" "Streaming passages flowed like champagne"; "To listen to Beethoven's concerto played by Mischa Levitzki was like a wonderful dream." But critics noted his limited repertoire. For instance, a review of a Carnegie Hall recital (26 Feb 1929) praises his delightful playing, yet, "withal there is surprisingly little musical contentment to be derived from Mr. Levitzki's evenings at the keyboard. As represented in his recital of last week . . . his expositions were fashioned out of the same material as usual. He played the C minor Variations of Beethoven, the G minor Sonata of Schumann, the Prelude, Chorale and Fugue of Franck, all with the same abstract virility, the identical taken-for-granted kind of perfection." (*MA*, 10 March 1929)

Another criticism dealt with performance practice and stylistic interpretation. When Levitzki played the Mozart Concerto in A Major, K. 488, and Beethoven's Concerto No. 2 in B-flat Major at Carnegie Hall on 10 April 1937, his clean and accurate technique, carefully worked-out phrasing and suave tone were all duly noted. But, "neither of the concertos was performed in a manner to bring out the real qualities of its content to any adequate degree. There was a strange lack of variety in the treatment accorded each of these works, for the scope of the pianist's imagination seemed too limited to enable him to give either concerto its due." (*NYT*, 11 April 1937)

One of the finest testimonials to Levitzki and his art was penned by Abram Chasins, who knew him personally and bemoaned the fact that in 1957 there was not one LP to document the genius of Levitzki for those who had not heard him or known "the warmth and chivalry and magic that poured from him and his playing alike. His compelling force resided in the greatness of his talent and the greatness of his heart. He had, in counterbalance, a small repertoire and a small opinion of himself and of his truly superb art. Within his limited repertoire, however, he was a vibrant, master workman: everything was pure radiance; every note shone like a sunbeam." (Cha/Spe, see Bibliog.)

Levitzki made only a comparatively small number of recordings. He made a few acoustic discs for American Columbia between 1923 and 1925 and there was one electric recording, *La Campanella*, made in 1925. The next discs were made during 1927–33 in England for HMV, and after that he recorded very little. Levitzki's recordings appear and reappear in various collections, so that a certain amount of duplication is unavoidable. For a small, selective program of fine Levitzki performances, the Pearl CD (see Discog.) is excellent, compositions originally put to disc for HMV and Victor between 1927 and 1938. They are almost without exception expertly done. "The pianism breathes the ambience of 19th Century Europe, without the expected exaggeration and 'artistic license.' It is not surprising that Arthur Rubinstein admired Levitzki and considered him a formidable rival." (*ARG*, Jan/Feb 1993) Outstanding items in the collection are the Chopin Nocturne in F-sharp Major, op. 15, no. 2, and Valse in G-flat Major, op. 70, no. 1; Liszt's Hungarian Rhapsody No. 12 and Levitzki's own *Arabesque valsante.*

All of Levitzki's electric recordings are available in one 2-CD collection (APR 7020, see Discog.). They reveal his strengths and weaknesses. For example, one weakness lies in matters of performance practice and style. Levitzki did not have the feeling for each composer's musical style that many of his peers possessed, and he usually played Scarlatti, Beethoven or Liszt in pretty much the same way. He was also often accused of playing mechanically, with little emotional involvement. "When Levitzki is involved in a work, for example the Chopin Scherzo or Ballade, he emotes by adding vigor or fireworks to the difficult passages, or distending the phrasing somewhat." These criticisms, however, can only be applied specifically, for exceptions to the pianist's so-called shortcomings are plentiful. In fact, according to the same reviewer, "the color and charm he applies to whatever is played surpass any living pianist and suggest Friedman's influence." (*Fan*, Sept/Oct 1992)

Levitzki was not especially known as a fiery technician, but he had plenty of technique at his command. He recorded a quantity of Liszt compositions, many of which are included in the APR CD collection. "With the co-operation of Sir Landon Ronald and the LSO, he plays the E flat Concerto as a work of true musical substance and stature. . . . And even if 'Un sospiro' and the second of his two versions of 'La campanella' are slightly less distinguished, the three *Hungarian Rhapsodies* again show him at his most elegantly eloquent, as well as brilliant." (*Gram*, June 1992)

These two collections, then, contain between them most of Levitzki's studio recordings. A few others have been assembled in the Appian *Romantic Rarities* CD set (see Discog.): Gluck-Sgambati *Mélodie d'Orphée*; Tchaikovsky *Troika en traineaux.*

SELECTED REFERENCES

Brower, Harriette. "Piano Technique Merely a Gift, Says Mischa Levitzki." *Musical America*, 3 Feb 1917, p. 31.

Crimp, Bryan. "The Pianistic Genius of Mischa Levitzki." Liner notes, CDAPR 7020, 1992.

Hart, Ernest. "Seeing Mischa Levitzki At Close Range." *Musical America*, 31 May 1919, p. 35.

Levitzki, Mischa. "Getting a Start as a Virtuoso." *Etude*, Feb 1923, pp. 79–80.

———. "Music on the Other Side of the World." *Etude*, Sept 1926, pp. 635–636.

"Levitzki, Back from Tour, Tells of Music Famine in Orient." *Musical America*, 25 Feb 1922, p. 21.

"Mischa Levitzki Has Climbed High in First American Tour." *Musical America*, 24 Feb 1917.

"New Friends Honor Levitzki." *New York Times*, 13 Jan 1941, p. 11.

Obituary. *Musical America*, 10 Jan 1941, p. 32. *New York Times*, 3 Jan 1941, p. 19.

"Tour For Young Russian Pianist." *Musical America*, 4 Nov 1916, p. 43.
"Unwise to Indulge in Little-Known Music Until One Has 'Arrived,' Declares
  Levitzky." *Musical America*, 11 May 1918, p. 2.
See also Bibliography: Ald/Con; Bro/PiS; Cha/Spe; Coo/Gre; Ewe/Li; Ewe/Mu;
  New/GrA; Rat/Cle; Rub/MyM; Sal/Fam.

SELECTED REVIEWS

BET: 20 Oct 1916. *BH*: 20 Oct 1916. *CEA*: 10 Dec 1923. *CSM*: 20 Oct
  1916. *IN*: 4 April 1917. *LAT*: 30 Jan 1926. *MA*: 28 Oct 1916; 25 Nov
  1916; 27 Jan 1917; 13 April 1918; 28 Dec 1918; 29 Nov 1919. *MT*: 1
  Dec 1927. *NYA*: 18 Oct 1916; 20 Jan 1917; 23 Dec 1918. *NYS*: 18 Oct
  1916; 20 Jan 1917; 23 Dec 1918. *NYT*: 18 Oct 1916; 6 Nov 1917; 23 Dec
  1918; 2 March 1919; 9 Nov 1922; 12 Jan 1927; 27 Feb 1929; 29 Oct
  1930; 6 Dec 1930; 1 Feb 1933; 25 April 1934; 9 March 1937; 11 April
  1937; 4 Jan 1939; 6 March 1940. *NYTr*: 20 Jan 1917; 10 Nov 1918.
  SLGD: 5 Nov 1932. *SPI*: 14 Jan 1926. *ST*: 14 Jan 1926. *TL*: 21 Oct
  1927; 2 Nov 1929.

SELECTED DISCOGRAPHY

Beethoven (arr. d'Albert): *Ecossaise*. Chopin: Nocturne in F-sharp major, op.
  15, no. 2; Polonaise in A-flat major, op. 53; Scherzo No. 3 in C-sharp minor, op. 39; Waltz in G-flat major, op. 70, no. 1. Levitzki: *Arabesque valsante* in A Minor; Valse in A Major. Liszt: *Etude de Concert* No. 3 in D-
  flat Major; Hungarian Rhapsody No. 12. Mendelssohn: *Andante* and *Rondo
  capriccioso*, op. 14. Paganini (arr. Liszt): *La Campanella*. Rubinstein:
  Staccato Etude in C Major, op. 23, no. 2. Scarlatti: Sonata in A Major, K.
  113. Schumann: Sonata in G Minor, op. 22. Pearl GEMM CD 9962.
Mischa Levitzki: The complete HMV recordings 1927-33. Bach-Liszt: Prelude
  and Fugue in A Minor. Beethoven: *Ecossaise* in E-flat Major. Chopin:
  Preludes, op. 28, nos. 1, 7, 23; Waltzes, op. 64, no. 3, op. 70, no. 1;
  Ballade No. 3 in A-flat Major, op. 47; Nocturnes, op. 15, no. 2, op. 48, no.
  1; Scherzo No. 3 in C-sharp Minor, op. 39; Polonaise in A-flat Major, op.
  53. Gluck-Brahms: Gavotte. Levitzki: Waltz in A-flat Major. Liszt:
  Concerto No. 1 in E-flat Major (Ronald/LSO); *Un Sospiro*; *La Campanella*;
  Hungarian Rhapsodies nos. 6, 12, 13. Mendelssohn: *Rondo capriccioso*,
  op. 14. Moszkowski: *La Jongleuse*. Rachmaninoff: Prelude in G Minor,
  op. 23, no. 5. Rubinstein: Staccato Etude. Scarlatti: Sonata in A Major, K.
  113. Schubert-Tausig: *Marche militaire*. Schumann: Sonata No. 2 in G
  Minor, op. 22. CDAPR 7020 (2 CDs).
Mischa Levitzki plays Beethoven, Mendelssohn and Liszt. Beethoven:
  Ecossaises; Sonata in F Minor, op. 57. Debussy: Arabesque No. 1 in E
  Major. Liszt: Etude No. 3 in D- flat Major (*Un Sospiro*). Mendelssohn:
  Rondo capriccioso, op. 14. Schumann: *Fantasiestück*, op. 12, no. 2.
  Stojowski: *Valse, Danse Humoresque*. Klavier KS-116. From Duo-Art
  piano rolls.

Romantic Rarities, Volume Two. Chopin: Waltzes in A Major, op. 2, E Minor, op. posth.; Etudes, op. 10, no. 5 and op. 25, no. 1. Gluck-Sgambati: *Mélodie d'Orphée*. Levitzki: *Valse de concert*; Waltz in A Major. Liszt: *La Campanella*; Hungarian Rhapsody No. 6. Moszkowski: *La Jongleuse*, op. 52, no. 4. Tchaikovsky: *Troika en traineaux*. CDAPR 7014.

LHÉVINNE, JOSEF: b. Orel, Russia, 13 December 1874; d. Kew Gardens, New York, 2 December 1944.

> He was one of the great romantic pianists of the century, an exponent of the grand manner of Anton Rubinstein, with whom he studied. A technician inferior to none, a colorist exceeded only by Hofmann, the master of a singing line and stirring feats of virtuosity, Lhévinne stood unique.
>
> Harold C. Schonberg (*New York Times*, 21 August 1955)

The Moscow Conservatory's memorable class of 1892 produced not one, but three future musical luminaries who now "stand unique" in musical history: Sergei Rachmaninoff, Alexander Scriabin, Josef Lhévinne. That year Rachmaninoff graduated with a gold medal in composition; Lhévinne outscored Scriabin to win the gold medal in piano. Overshadowed by his colorful classmates, the reserved, unambitious Lhévinne quietly and almost in spite of himself became "one of the great romantic pianists of the century." That he did so was due in no small measure to Rosina (Bessie) Lhévinne, his wife of 46 years.

The remarkable Lhévinnes first met in 1889 when Josef, age 14 and the best piano student at the Moscow Conservatory, for a short time gave piano lessons to Rosina Bessie, age nine and a very shy, fairly new student at the Conservatory. They married in June 1898, and although Rosina only two weeks earlier had graduated from the Conservatory with a gold medal in piano, she quickly decided to forgo a career of her own in order to devote all her energies and talents to furthering her husband's career. For the rest of his life the strong, ambitious Rosina was beside him, and behind him, coaxing, guiding and supervising. Josef Lhévinne now "stands unique" in musical history, but not alone, for it is impossible to forget Rosina Lhévinne and the enormous influence she had on his career.

Josef Lhévinne was the son of Arkady Levin, a trumpeter born in Lodz (now in Poland, then under Russian domination), and Arkady must have been a superior trumpeter to support his 11 children. Josef, the ninth child, was born in Orel, halfway between Kiev and Moscow, but about two years after his birth the government allowed his father to relocate the family in Moscow. To support his huge brood in the city, Arkady had to work at two full-time positions. Away from home most of the time, he saw little of his family, but he provided a good, plain living.

Josef Lhévinne's biographer believes that living so long (until he married) in his parents' dreadfully overcrowded apartment accounts for Lhévinne's lifelong insatiable craving for unlimited space. With so many children around, he went largely unnoticed until he was three years old. That was the year his father, despite their tight quarters, offered to store a brother-in-law's old upright piano in the apartment. The next year a delighted Arkady Levin noticed that little Josef could play tunes he heard on the street and, even more, was beginning to harmonize.

Lhévinne had his first piano lessons with Nils Krysander, a Swedish-born piano teacher and choir director, and began performing in public at about age eight. At age 11 he played at one of Moscow's grand soirées—an event attended by the Grand Duke Constantine—and although dazzled by his first taste of glittering society, Lhévinne confidently played Beethoven's "Moonlight" Sonata and the Wagner-Liszt Tannhäuser March. Pleased and impressed, His Highness, who had listened most attentively, looked about for the wealthiest man present (he decided on the host) and ordered him to pay for Lhévinne's further education.

Thus in 1886 Lhévinne enrolled at the Moscow Conservatory as a pupil of Vassily Safonoff, who soon let him know that his technique was all wrong. Up to this point, playing had come easily for Lhévinne, and his teachers had allowed him to play some of the great works of Beethoven, Chopin and Liszt. However, his fingers were stiff and usually would start hurting after he had practiced a few hours. He had to go back to the basics, and Safonoff started by giving him six months of daily lessons to correct his bad habits. It was tedious. Instead of playing great works, he had to do exercises and scales. Safonoff would not allow stiffness, but neither would he allow any kind of hand motion; and to get his ideas across, he would place a small object on the back of Lhévinne's hand while he was playing scales and five-finger exercises, then watch closely to see that the object stayed put.

Safonoff also gave Lhévinne a whole new concept of playing scales—never play them mechanically, but always with attention to tone, rhythm and dynamics. Intrigued by this concept, Lhévinne developed a love for playing scales that stayed with him to the end of his life. Once he had the technique to begin learning repertoire again, he faced yet another difficulty. He had always played with music, and now discovered that for every lesson with Safonoff he had to come with the music already memorized. Fortunately, memorizing came easily. He would play a piece a few times and have it in his mind; however, like Cortot, he sometimes quite easily forgot. The demanding Safonoff was exactly right for Lhévinne, and incidentally it was Safonoff who suggested that, for professional purposes, Josef Levin become Josef Lhévinne.

Lhévinne spent the summer of 1889 working with Safonoff at Kislovodsk in the Caucasus. It was his first look at nature, and the stars, mountains, trees and streams, so different from what he knew in his crowded Moscow neighborhood, captivated him. His love for stargazing stayed with him to the end of his life.

Early in 1890 Anton Rubinstein chose Lhévinne to play at one of the most important events of the forthcoming season—the great annual benefit concert (for widows and orphans of musicians) held in the Hall of the Nobility. All that summer Lhévinne prepared, under Safonoff's direction, and on 17 November 1890 (his official Moscow debut) played the Beethoven "Emperor" Concerto with Rubinstein conducting the Moscow Symphony Society Orchestra.

Lhévinne graduated at age 17 in that distinctive 1892 class with a diploma in virtuosity and a gold medal in piano. He had spent three summers with Safonoff in the Caucasus, and now spent the summer after graduation with Rubinstein at Klein Schachwitz, near Dresden. That autumn he made a tour of some Russian rural provinces with Eugenio Giraldoni, a baritone whose father taught voice at the Moscow Conservatory, and he always felt that accompanying a singer had taught him a great deal about musical phrasing. He also made a short solo tour of eastern Europe, and about this same time joined with cellist Modest Altschuler and violinist Alexander Petschnikoff, also Conservatory graduates, to form the Moscow Historical Trio. The Trio played concerts in Russia, Poland, Austria-Hungary and Germany, but it was not too long before Lhévinne withdrew because, as Altschuler said years later, "His tone was so pure and beautiful, so vari-colored and expressive of the emotional content of the work in hand, that in spite of his artistic reticence, the piano part always stood out." (*MA*, 19 May 1906)

In August 1895 Lhévinne entered the second International Rubinstein Prize Competition, that year held in Berlin's Bechstein Hall. For the large-scale works required, Lhévinne played Beethoven's "*Hammerklavier*" Sonata, op. 106, and the Rubinstein Concerto No. 5, and won first prize: 5,000 francs and a contract with concert manager Hermann Wolff to play 40 concerts during the 1895–96 season—a wonderful start on his career. But he had only played in Moscow, Amsterdam and Paris when he was called home to fulfill his compulsory military service, and although away from the piano only a year, it took Lhévinne five years to restart his career.

After their marriage in 1898, the Lhévinnes lived a lean year in Moscow, sometimes performing at social gatherings but mostly supported by Rosina's parents. In the fall of 1899 he began teaching at the local school of the Imperial Russian Music Society in Tiflis (Tbilisi), a small but wealthy town in the Caucasus. Besides teaching, Josef gave solo recitals and sometimes performed duo recitals with Rosina. They were now self-supporting and, best of all, Tiflis was an ideal spot for Lhévinne to pursue his passion for studying the stars. The Lhévinnes might have remained there had not the ambitious Rosina realized that this comfortable environment was wrong for her husband's artistic development. He had no rivals at Tiflis, none of the competition he would face if he were on the concert circuit, and if they stayed, his career, she was sure, would stall. Josef, she decided, should be in Berlin.

They arrived in Berlin during the winter of 1901 and set up an intensive routine of practicing. Before long the great Busoni invited them to his studio. He asked Lhévinne to play certain pieces (the Schumann Toccata, the Brahms-Paganini Variations, Liszt's *Feux-follets*, Rubinstein's Octave Etude, Chopin's Octave Etude and Etude in Double Thirds) and complimented him on his playing. But Busoni said nothing else, and Lhévinne never knew what Busoni really thought of his playing. However, some fifty years later a Busoni pupil in attendance at that studio on that long ago evening finally told Rosina that at the next day's class Busoni had said, "If I put you all in one pot you would not make one Lhévinne." (Wallace, *A Century*. . .)

It was hard for Lhévinne to get back into the concert world, but ultimately his performances (Warsaw, Paris, Berlin) resulted in a contract from the Hermann Wolff management and an offer to teach at the Stern Conservatory in Berlin. He was about to accept when he was offered an appointment as full professor at the Moscow Conservatory. He decided on Moscow and began teaching there in 1902 under a contract that allowed him to make concert tours. In 1903 his performances in Warsaw, Paris, Berlin, Vienna and London recharged his career, but unfortunately not for long. While in London, Lhévinne fell off his bicycle and broke his leg. Although he was able to continue teaching, it was March 1904 before he returned to the concert platform.

In 1905 the Russian Embassy in Washington, D.C., seeking to improve Russia's image abroad, came up with the idea of sponsoring a tour of the Russian Symphony Orchestra, the ensemble that Modest Altschuler had established in New York in 1903. The tour would begin in January 1906, Lhévinne would play and his old teacher Safonoff would conduct. There were problems from the start. As Lhévinne was preparing to leave in December 1905, revolutionary uprisings trapped him in Moscow for two weeks. He finally got away on the night of 29 December 1905, but his train made it only halfway to St. Petersburg (revolutionists had torn up the tracks), and he had to bribe his way to the border on a succession of intervillage mail sleighs.

That harrowing experience was only the beginning. When he arrived in New York on 14 January 1906, Lhévinne discovered that the promised tour had been canceled because the agent in charge had gone bankrupt. It was a crushing blow. He had endured so much and come so far to play in America, and now faced the prospect of having to return to Moscow without having played even once. His good friends Altschuler and Safonoff came to the rescue. Altschuler obligingly arranged for Lhévinne to perform at the very next concert given by his Russian Symphony Orchestra. Lhévinne decided to play Rubinstein's Concerto No. 5, and Safonoff agreed to conduct. Thus Josef Lhévinne made his American debut on 27 January 1906 at Carnegie Hall.

He stunned his audience, captured the critics and next morning won a contract with Steinway and Sons—$10,000 plus expenses for an extended tour during the 1906–07 season. In the next 10 weeks Lhévinne performed 12 times (New York, Chicago, Cincinnati, New Haven), and returned home to Moscow, not a disappointed failure but the musical sensation of the season in America. He had, however, overstayed his leave from the Moscow Conservatory. They had refused to grant an extension, and he was forced to resign. The Lhévinnes spent the summer of 1906 in Paris, where he practiced from eight to ten hours a day to prepare for the long Steinway tour (by the end of the summer it included more than 60 appearances) due to start in October, and over the summer he learned many new works and relearned many old. He went to America with five possible recital programs ready. (In Paris that July, Rosina gave birth to their first child, named Constantine.)

Lhévinne played only a little during 1907–08, spending most of his time getting ready for another long Steinway tour in the 1908–09 season. And for the next five years he toured from October through June, in Europe and in the United States.

Meanwhile in 1907 the Lhévinnes had settled in Berlin. They rented a villa, set up a teaching studio and until World War I held to a demanding, over-taxing schedule. Students, many of them Americans, flocked to their studio. By 1911 Lhévinne had more than 40 students, whose lessons Rosina covered when he was away on tour, and to accommodate the steadily increasing number, in May 1914 the Lhévinnes purchased a 21-room villa in the Berlin suburb of Wannsee. Then in August, Germany and Russia declared war, the students had to leave, and for the next five years the Lhévinne entourage rattled around alone in the huge mansion, interned as resident aliens and virtually prisoners of war. Only an edict from Kaiser Wilhelm pronouncing Lhévinne "an authentic genius who is not to be disturbed" saved them from prison camp. There were condi-tions: they had to report regularly to the police, obey an 8 P.M. curfew and not give any concerts or earn money as long as Germany and Russia were at war.

Forbidden to earn money and having all his savings out of reach in Russian banks, Lhévinne had to borrow from German friends just to exist. To fill out their meagre rations, the family learned how to grow vegetables and find mushrooms in the forest. The one thing that saved his sanity was an annual visit (the first in March 1915) to Budapest to give charity concerts—trips sanc-tioned by the authorities because Lhévinne ostensibly earned no money. However, concert manager Gustav Barczy, organizer of the charity concerts, se-cretly arranged private concerts. Earning money and eating decent food on those Budapest excursions alleviated some of the stress of those wartime years.

His good friend Barczy also tricked Lhévinne into enlarging his reper-toire. Every summer Barczy wrote to Lhévinne to tell him exactly what the Beethoven Society in Budapest would want him to play on the next visit. Thus all during the war Lhévinne kept adding to his repertoire, each year works by a different composer. Only at the end of the war did he learn that those requests for specific works had come from Barczy himself, not from the music society. To keep Lhévinne working and to bolster his morale, Barczy had kept him busy adding new works to his repertoire.

Hungarian audiences and critics went wild over Lhévinne's playing. "For him nothing is impossible on the piano, and his technique, dynamics, tempo and rhythm differ from those of the best virtuosos by an inimitable natu-ralness and matter of course. . . . Lhévinne is absolutely new, something unique and unprecedented, something one can only marvel at." (*Pesti Naplo*, Budapest, 13 March 1915)

The Lhévinnes' second child, named Marianna, was born in Berlin in July 1918. The Armistice was signed on 11 November 1918, but shortly there-after civil war erupted in Russia (the Lhévinnes lost all the money they had in Russian banks), and most of Europe was in postwar chaos. America, they de-cided, was best for them, but it took nearly a year to get passports. Still, the long isolation was over; they could go freely about Berlin, and Lhévinne was free to give concerts. That year he played in Oslo, Berlin, Budapest and in Yugoslavia, and in every instance it was apparent that Lhévinne was not the same man who had played for them before the war. Audiences invariably greeted him warmly, but Lhévinne seemed diffident, aloof and deeply involved in the music.

The Lhévinnes arrived in New York on 22 October 1919. The next day Lhévinne gave a recital in Connecticut. On 26 October he played the Tchaikovsky Concerto in B-flat Minor at New York's cavernous Hippodrome, with Nikolai Sokoloff conducting the New Symphony Orchestra, and a few days later he began an extended tour (8 months, 40 cities, 50 appearances).

The Lhévinnes bought a house in Kew Gardens, Queens, and soon had a teaching studio. Lhévinne actually taught all through his career, most of the time in conjunction with his wife. She worked on students' technique and he worked with them on such refinements as the inner meaning of a phrase, how to play with freedom yet with discipline, how to fathom the depths of a composer's intentions. An excellent but demanding teacher, Lhévinne made his students memorize every work brought to a lesson, and insisted that they have complete mastery of scales, octaves, arpeggios, double thirds, double sixths.

He also taught at the Juilliard School from 1924, the year it opened, until his death, and gave master classes every summer—from 1929 to 1932 at the American Conservatory in Chicago; in 1932 at the *Mozarteum* in Salzburg. In 1933 both Lhévinnes taught summer classes in Maine (Seal Harbor and Camden) and in 1935 began classes in Colorado (Denver and Boulder). For some reason, possibly because of the growing Nazi movement he had seen while in Salzburg, Lhévinne finally became an American citizen in 1933.

Lhévinne's several articles on piano pedagogy appeared as a series in *Etude* magazine in 1906, and in 1924 they were published together as *Basic Principles in Pianoforte Playing*, a book still valuable in that it reveals the concepts behind Lhévinne's remarkable piano playing: emphasis on a singing tone, careful use of the pedal, disciplining the ear to listen, playing technical studies with attention to sound, rhythm and dynamics.

He made annual tours of the United States right up to the end of his life, starting off every season with a Carnegie Hall recital. He also made astonishingly successful tours of Latin America and three postwar tours of Europe—Nov–Dec 1926, Oct–Dec 1928, Feb–April 1937. Between February and May, 1933, Lhévinne gave 13 weekly radio broadcasts on the NBC network—half-hour programs on which he played one or two movements from a concerto and one or two solo pieces.

In the last decade of his life he actually played fewer solo recitals and many more joint recitals with Mme. Lhévinne. On 14 January 1939 they celebrated the 40th anniversary of their two-piano partnership with quite unusual performances at Carnegie Hall. They were assisted by the Juilliard Orchestra, conducted by Ernest Hutcheson and Albert Stoessel. Lhévinne played the Tchaikovsky Concerto No. 1, a work that had brought him much success through the years. Mme. Lhévinne, ending her 40-year retirement as a solo pianist, played the Chopin Concerto in E Minor. Together they played the Mozart Concerto in E-flat Major for two pianos, K. 365.

Lhévinne played his last Carnegie Hall recital on 7 November 1943 and made his final New York appearance on 31 July 1944, playing the Tchaikovsky Concerto No. 1 at Lewisohn Stadium with the New York Philharmonic-Symphony, Fabien Sevitzky conducting. In August he visited his daughter Marianna in Hollywood, California. Stricken with a heart attack, he recuperated sufficiently to return home, and died of a second heart attack on 2 December 1944. There was a memorial service at the Juilliard concert hall and tributes arrived from around the world. One of the very finest came from Artur Rubinstein: "The musical world has lost a great artist and one of the greatest pianists of our epoch. . . . Lhévinne, in my opinion, belonged to the group one could call 'aristocrats of the keyboard'. . . . His playing possessed what the French most love—'éclat,' clarity to the highest degree, the ability to project all the beauty and depth of a musical work with the ease of one who dominates all pianistic difficulties without ever 'showing them off'." (*NYHT*, 10 Dec 1944)

Like the musician, the personal Josef Lhévinne was aristocratic and reserved. Although constantly before the public, he remained an intensely private person who craved solitude and revered nature. For 26 years he spent one summer month each year all by himself at Bonnie Oaks, a Wisconsin farm where he had converted an obsolete watertower into an ideal retreat—his Steinway on the first floor, his bed and fishing gear on the second floor, his beloved telescope and astronomy books at the top. That month of silence, studying the stars at night and fishing by day when not practicing, made it possible for Josef Lhévinne to endure the outside world for the rest of the year.

Lhévinne's solo repertoire was not extensive. Like Mischa Levitzki, he programmed certain works—Schumann's Toccata, *Carnaval*, Symphonic Etudes; Brahms Sonata in F Minor, Paganini Variations; Liszt Sonata in B Minor, *Etude de Concert*, *Feux Follets*, *La Campanella*—with some consistency throughout his career. And Chopin works appeared on just about every recital program. Like Egon Petri, Lhévinne played many works in transcription—by d'Albert, Godowsky, Tausig, Busoni, Liszt, Saint-Saëns, Balakirev. But as he grew older, particularly after World War I, the transcriptions appeared less and less, noticeably replaced with music by Debussy, occasionally Ravel. As for earlier repertoire, Bach appeared only in transcription, and Handel, Mozart and Haydn were almost totally ignored. Lhévinne appears never to have played more than half a dozen Beethoven sonatas, in particular Op. 27, no. 2 ("Moonlight") and Op. 81a ("*Les Adieux*"). His repertoire with orchestra included Rubinstein's Concerto No. 4 in D Minor, op. 70, and his Concerto No. 5 in E-flat Major, op. 94; Beethoven's Concertos No. 1 in C Major, op. 15, and No. 5 in E-flat Major, op. 73; Chopin No. 2 in F Minor, op. 21; Liszt No. 1 in E-flat Major, and the Tchaikovsky Concerto No. 1 in B-flat Minor, op. 23. Lhévinne also played the Weber *Konzertstück* in F Minor, op. 79.

Lhévinne had the kind of fluid, flawless technique that drew gasps even from other great pianists. (It helped that he had huge hands.) He kept in form with about four or five hours of daily practice, seven or eight hours when preparing for a big tour. And he practiced very slowly. A pupil who often heard him practicing during the summers in Maine remembered that Lhévinne was unbelievably patient, that he could work endlessly on the shape of a phrase or the dynamics of a particular passage. "His command of dynamics of the piano from the biggest outburst to the most delicate of pianissimo was a marvel to hear." (Smith)

The most striking characteristic of Lhévinne's playing was its absolute integrity. It also made his playing controversial. He was competing in the era of Paderewski and Pachman, and critics and audiences alike were in tune with grandly brilliant, emotional playing. Although Lhévinne also played in the grand manner, his was playing of crystalline purity and refinement. His hastily put together American debut (27 Jan 1906), playing the Rubinstein Concerto No. 5 in E-flat Major, op. 94, with Safonoff and the Russian Symphony Orchestra, caused a sensation: "The real Rubinstein II is Mr. Lhévinne. He has the great Anton's technique, his dash, his bravura, his brilliancy, and a good deal of his leonine power. He can make the piano sing, too." (*NYEP*, 28 Jan 1906)

Routinely reviewers lavished praise on Lhévinne's technique, his ravishing tonal palette, his control of dynamics; and then qualified their praise because his playing often failed to reveal profound insight, poetical feeling, or emotion of any kind. Very early, in 1907, an astute critic explained Lhévinne's predicament in going against the style of the day: "Lhévinne lacks all the qualities that the uninitiated public craves but possesses everything that the musician demands. He is authoritative, sincere, unaffected. As a great artist he is the peer of any, as a poseur he is a failure. . . . Lhévinne is too great an artist for his own good." (*Musical Leader*, Chicago, 31 Jan 1907)

In spite of some criticisms, Lhévinne had an enormously successful career. *Musical America* reported that literally hundreds of people had to be turned away at Lhévinne's Aeolian Hall recital of 13 January 1913. At this point critics, too, succumbed to Lhévinne's overwhelming playing: "Yesterday he showed a warmer feeling and a firmer grasp in the purely musical qualities of what he was playing than he has before. There was a poetic touch in more than a little of it. . . . In short, Mr. Lhévinne seemed to have made an appreciable step forward toward the higher qualities of musicianship." (*NYT*, 14 Jan 1913)

But then came World War I and Lhévinne's internment in Berlin. He returned to concertizing after the war, but it was clearly evident that the years of isolation and deprivation had greatly changed him. On his first postwar American tour (1919–20), he often opened his recital with the Beethoven Sonata in E-flat Major, op. 81a ("*Les Adieux*"), playing it with "such unescapable pathos that at times it was almost unbearable to listen to." (*MA*, 10 Jan 1920) Lhévinne's colossal technique remained intact, but now he often played as though in a trance, aloof from his listeners. Even when thunderous applause roused him, he quickly retreated again into his inner world.

"With time," wrote his biographer, "the dreamy, reflective side of his personality came to predominate over the objective and direct. . . . Whether this vagueness was a result of wartime isolation or was a natural development of the artist's temperament, no one can say. Whatever the cause, the change was plain to see." (Wallace, *A Century.* . .) "Time and again he would make his somnambulistic entrance, settle down at the keyboard with an audible sigh, and play a whole recital without any signs of inspiration." (Morris) Despite all this, Lhévinne held on to his audiences. His annual Carnegie Hall recitals were sensationally successful and often the high point of the musical season.

For the rest of Lhévinne's life critics would argue over his playing. There seemed to be "little intervention of personality" in his playing, so little personality, in fact, that reviewers sometimes expressed the wish for more Lhévinne in his interpretations. It was just too reserved, too cold for some; others greatly admired its clarity, its remarkable individuality. Some found him uninspiring; others thought he was an inward poet of the piano, not so much lacking in emotion as superior to it. "Other artists," wrote an admirer, "bring out the beauty, the passion, the human, but Lhévinne's interpretations are spiritual." (*MC*, 22 April 1920)

By the late 1920s delicacy and nuance had become the outstanding characteristics of his pianism. Not incidentally, works by Anton Rubinstein disappeared from his repertoire, and works by Debussy were added. His technique now had become "marvelous not so much for its strength and brilliance . . . but more because of the control of that strength into the finest-spun delicacies and nuances." (*MiT*, 7 March 1928)

Following that phase of overrefinement, Lhévinne's playing readjusted once again. After his Carnegie Hall recital of 17 November 1940, Virgil Thomson wrote what now seems the definitive assessment of Lhévinne's pianism: "Everything he does is right and clear and complete. Everything he doesn't do is the whole list of things that mar the musical executions of lesser men. This is not to say that tenderness and poetry and personal warmth and fire are faults of musical style. . . . I am saying that Mr. Lhévinne does not need them. They would mar his style; hence he eschews them. He eschews them because his concept of piano music is an impersonal one. . . . Thus it is that Mr. Lhévinne's performance is worthy of the honorable word *academic*. And if he seems to some a little distant, let us remind ourselves that remoteness is, after all, inevitable to those who inhabit Olympus." (*NYHT*, 18 Nov 1940)

Like most early 20th-century pianists, Lhévinne made piano rolls, but unlike many of his colleagues he made many more rolls than discs. Beginning in 1906 he made a series of 29 Welte piano rolls. The 21 Ampico piano rolls date from the 1920s and they are the most valuable, for by that time the recording mechanism had been greatly improved and refined.

The Ampico rolls have been recorded on 3 LPs (see Discog.). The first volume includes an aristocratic reading of the Schumann *Papillons*, op. 2, and four Chopin pieces: two etudes, a nocturne and the Op. 53 Polonaise. Volume 2 contains mostly Liszt: some original works, a Schubert transcription (*Soirée de Vienne*), a Mendelssohn transcription (*Auf Flügeln des Gesanges*) and Liszt's arrangement of the Paganini *La Campanella*. Capping this LP of bravura playing is the formidable Tausig Fantasia on Hungarian Gypsy Songs, a work of such transcendent technical difficulty that it is seldom, if ever, programmed by today's pianists. Volume 3 of The Ampico Recordings has music by Albéniz, Schubert, Sinding, Schulz-Evler and the Beethoven "Moonlight" Sonata, op. 27, no. 2. Not pleased with the Beethoven—probably originally recorded for the Welte Company and re-edited by Ampico technicians—Lhévinne disavowed it in later years.

Lhévinne made his first disc recordings (Beethoven-Busoni, Rachmaninoff, Schumann-Tausig, Tchaikovsky) in 1920 for *Pathé-Actuelle*. He made one recording (Strauss-Schulz-Evler "Blue Danube Waltz") in 1928, otherwise his solo discs date from 1935–36, all on the Victor label. In 1955 Victor issued an LP containing most of his recordings for that label. Even then, one writer noted that, "in comparison with what Lhévinne demonstrated on that disc, all but a handful of today's pianists playing the same pieces resemble a litter of squealing kittens trying to sound like ferocious tigers." (Cha/Spe, see Discog.) Reviewing an LP reissue in 1971, Igor Kipnis wrote that Lhévinne's is "probably the most *musical* account of the Schumann Toccata [op. 7] ever recorded." He also felt strongly about the recorded Chopin compositions, particularly the Etudes and Preludes, which "would alone entitle Lhévinne to immortality." (*StR*, March 1971)

The Novello CD of Lhévinne's complete recordings (see Discog.) is a welcome reissue but a sad reminder of just how few recordings the great pianist actually did make. "That he was one of the greatest pianists of his day is proved by this disc, where his quite extraordinary technique is used totally at the service of an acutely sensitive, quite unidiosyncratic style of playing." (*Gram*, Dec 1989) The CD runs to only 71 minutes of playing time, but during that period, what a wealth of scintillating, elegant and satisfying playing! It includes Lhévinne's performances of the Beethoven-Busoni *Ecossaises* and the Schumann-Tausig *El Contrabandista*, two of the most remarkable recordings of the acoustic era. Chopin—with seven items—occupies about a third of the CD: four etudes, two preludes and the glorious A-flat Polonaise, op. 53. Lhévinne was famous for his Chopin playing. His performance of the Etude in Thirds, op. 25, no. 6, is extremely fast but maintains the utmost clarity, and the so-called "Winter Wind" Etude, op. 25, no. 11, is dazzling in its display of bravura. The Mozart Sonata for Two Pianos, K. 448, was recorded in 1939, but the Lhévinnes were dissatisfied with the results. It remained unpublished until after Josef's death.

In addition to Lhévinne's studio discs, there exist a few off-the-air recordings. Four of these, all Chopin compositions, have been included in the CD collection of *Romantic Rarities*: Volume One (see Discog.). There also exists a performance of the second and third movements of the Tchaikovsky Concerto No. 1, probably taken from one of Lhévinne's 1933 series of radio broadcasts.

Josef Lhévinne died in 1944. A quarter of a century later Glen Sherman, a Lhévinne pupil, wrote, "When I speak of Lhévinne to my students today, he sounds as remote to them as if I had studied with Chopin. It is only when they hear his recordings that they experience for themselves his enduring vitality." (Sherman)

SELECTED REFERENCES

Anderson, Harry L. "Josef Lhévinne Discography." Recorded Sound, Oct 1971, pp. 791–796.

Graham, Marianna Lhévinne, with Robert K. Wallace. "Profile of Joseph Lhévinne." *Clavier*, Dec 1981, pp. 36–37.

Hill, Edward Burlingame. "The Making of a Russian Pianist: A Talk with Josef Lhévinne." *Etude*, Oct 1906, pp. 627–628.

"Josef Lhévinne Tells How He Plays Chopin's Octave Study, Op. 25, No. 10." *Musical America*, 30 Oct 1909, p. 12.

Kipnis, Igor. "Three Great Pianists on Victrola." Stereo Review, March 1971, p. 102.

Lhévinne, Josef. "The Art of Modern Pianism." In Brower, *Modern Masters of the Keyboard* (Bro/Mod, see Bibliog.).

———. "The Art of Pianoforte Playing in Russia." *Etude*, March 1913, pp. 175–176.

———. "Basic Principles in Pianoforte Playing." Section I. *Etude*, Oct 1923, pp. 665–666.

———. "Basic Principles in Pianoforte Playing." Section II. *Etude*, Nov 1923, pp. 747–748.

———. "Basic Principles in Pianoforte Playing." Section III. *Etude*, Dec 1923, pp. 815–816.

———. "Basic Principles in Pianoforte Playing." Section IV. *Etude*, Jan 1924, pp. 17–18.

———. "Basic Principles in Pianoforte Playing." Section V. *Etude*, Feb 1924, pp. 87–88.

———. *Basic Principles in Pianoforte Playing*. Philadelphia: Theodore Presser Co., 1924. The above five articles in book form.

———. "Lhévinne Discusses Preparation of Pianists." *Musical America*, 25 Oct 1940, p. 31.

———. "My Early Life." *Ovation*, Jan 1981, pp. 23–24. Reprint from *The Gramophone Jubilee Book* (Gra/Jub, see Bibliog.).

———. "Piano Study in Russia." In Cooke, *Great Pianists on Piano Playing* (Coo/GrP, see Bibliog.).

———. "Practical Phases of Modern Pianoforte Technic." Part I. *Etude*, March 1921, pp. 151–152.

———. "Practical Phases of Modern Pianoforte Technic." Part II. *Etude*, April 1921, p. 228.

Lyle, Wilson. "Josef Lhévinne: a retrospect." *Music Review*, Aug/Nov 1989, pp. 265–269.

Morris, Edmund. "Josef Lhévinne (1874–1944): A Radio Portrait." WNCN Broadcast 27 Sept 1970.

Obituary. *Musical America*, 10 Dec 1944, p. 24. *New York Times*, 3 Dec 1944, p. 57.

Sherman, Glen. "Josef Lhévinne." *Recorded Sound*, Oct 1971, pp. 784–791.

Smith, Brooks. "The Lhévinne Legacy." *Clavier*, Dec 1981, pp. 37–38.

"A Talk with Josef Lhévinne." *New York Times*, 11 March 1906, sec. 4, p. 2.

Wallace, Robert K. *A Century of Music Making.* Bloomington: Indiana University Press, 1976.
————. "The Lhévinnes' Teaching Legacy." *Piano Quarterly*, Spring 1974, pp. 7–11.
See also Bibliography: Ald/Con; Cha/Spe; Cur/Bio (1945); Ewe/Li; Ewe/Mu; Hag/Thi; Kau/Art; Kol/Que; New/Gro; Nie/Mei; Rat/Cle; Rub/MyY; Sal/Fam; Sch/Gre; Tho/MuS.

SELECTED REVIEWS

CEA: 11 Jan 1927. *DT*: 13 Dec 1926. *FWJG*: 13 Feb 1925. *LAT*: 3 March 1909; 28 Nov 1923. *MA*: 17 Nov 1906; 1 Dec 1906; 29 Dec 1906; 19 Jan 1907; 7 Nov 1907; 15 Feb 1913; 1 May 1920; 25 Nov 1940. *MC*: 22 April 1920. *NYEP*: 28 Jan 1906; 16 Nov 1932. *NYHT*: 17 Jan 1927; 31 Oct 1927; 18 Nov 1940. *NYT*: 28 Jan 1906; 12 March 1906; 7 March 1910; 5 Jan 1912; 7 Feb 1912; 14 Jan 1913; 9 Feb 1913; 27 Oct 1919; 2 Dec 1919; 19 April 1920; 19 Jan 1922; 14 Dec 1922; 12 Feb 1924; 16 Nov 1932; 16 Jan 1938; 3 Aug 1938; 15 Jan 1939; 5 Nov 1939; 1 Aug 1944. *NYTr*: 28 Jan 1906. *NYW*: 13 Jan 1925; 31 Oct 1927. *SFC*: 15 March 1909. *SLPD*: 6 Jan 1927. *TL*: 11 Oct 1906; 26 June 1912; 27 May 1913; 31 May 1913; 7 Feb 1914.

SELECTED DISCOGRAPHY

Josef Lhévinne: The Ampico Recordings. Volume One. Chopin: Etudes, op. 10, no. 11; op. 25, no. 9; Nocturne, op. 9, no. 3; Polonaise in A-flat Major, op. 53. Rubinstein: *Kamennoi-Ostrow*, op. 10, no. 22. Schütt: *A la bien aimée.* op. 59, no. 2. Schumann: *Papillons*, op. 2. *L'Oiseau-Lyre* 414 097-1.
Josef Lhévinne: The Ampico Recordings. Volume Two. Cui: *Causerie*, op. 40, no. 6. Liszt: *Die Lorelei*; *Gondoliera*; *Liebestraum* No. 3. Mendelssohn-Liszt: On the Wings of Song. Paganini-Liszt-Busoni: *La Campanella*. Schubert-Liszt: *Soirée de Vienne*, no. 6. Tausig: Fantasia on Hungarian Gypsy Songs. *L'Oiseau-Lyre* 414 121-1.
Josef Lhévinne: The Ampico Recordings. Volume Three. Albéniz: *Córdoba* (*Chants d'Espagne*); *Sevilla* (*Suite espagnole*). Beethoven: Sonata, op. 27, no. 2. Schubert-Tausig: *March militaire*. Schulz-Evler: Blue Danube Waltz (Strauss). Sinding: The Rustle of Spring. *L'Oiseau-Lyre* 414 123-1.
Josef Lhévinne: The Complete Recordings. Beethoven-Busoni: *Ecossaises*. Chopin: Etudes, op. 10, no. 6; op. 25, nos. 6, 10-11; Polonaise, op. 53; Preludes, op. 28, nos. 16-17. Debussy-Ravel: *Fêtes* (with Rosina L.). Mozart: Sonata in D Major for two pianos, K. 448 (with Rosina L.). Rachmaninoff: Prelude in G Minor. Schumann: Toccata, op. 7. Schumann-Liszt: *Frühlingsnacht.* Schumann-Tausig: *El Contrabandista.* Strauss-Schulz-Evler: Blue Danube Waltz. Tchaikovsky: *Trepak.* Novello NVLCD 902. (produced in 1989). Also Dante HPC008 (produced in 1993).

Romantic Rarities . Vol. I. The Pathé Recordings (1920). Beethoven-Busoni: *Ecossaises.* Schumann-Tausig: *Der Contrabandiste.* Rachmaninoff: Prelude in G Minor. Tchaikovsky: *Troika en trainaux.* Off-the-air Chopin recordings: Etudes, op. 25, nos. 6, 11; Polonaise in A-flat Major, op. 53; Prelude, op. 28, no. 17. APRCD 7014.

LIPATTI, DINU (CONSTANTIN): b. Bucharest, Romania, 19 March 1917; d. Geneva, Switzerland, 2 December 1950.

> Music is a serious matter; treat it seriously!
> Dinu Lipatti (*Recorded Sound,* July 1964)

It seems sensible to assume that death cutting off the career of a famous concert pianist at the young age of 33 will almost automatically magnify that pianist's reputation. Dinu Lipatti's life exactly fits this scenario. He was a beloved celebrity, inspirer of admiration, affection and glowing critical notices wherever he performed (delicate health restricted his touring to a small area of Europe); and after his death music critics, colleagues and family published admiring, sometimes sentimental tributes. Fortunately, for a more impartial assessment of Lipatti the pianist, we have the Lipatti recordings. In the years since his death, critics unencumbered by emotion have evaluated these wonderful recordings and uniformly upheld Lipatti's lifetime reputation.

He belonged to a well-to-do, highly cultivated and intensely musical family. (His parents actually began each day by playing the Bach-Gounod *Ave Maria.*) His paternal grandfather, a melomane, played guitar and flute; his father Theodor Lipatti, an amateur violinist, had studied with Sarasate and Carl Flesch; his mother Anna (Racoviceanu) Lipatti was a good pianist; and Georges Enescu, Romania's foremost violinist and composer, was his godfather. Lipatti's mother claimed that at six months he could clap time to melodies and Czardas dances sung by the servants. At age four this precocious child played a Mozart minuet at his own christening; and at age five his performance at a local charity concert caused a sensation. "With the lack of nerves of an experienced artist this young phenomenon played by ear a Bach Prelude and several of his own compositions. . . . This was living testimony of an undoubted musical genius." (*Rampa,* 14 May 1922)

The frail Lipatti never attended school. To guard his health and not incidentally to ensure that he devoted time to music, his parents employed tutors (for such diverse subjects as literature, science, photography and wood carving); and every year through high-school age he had to sit for examinations. At age eight he began serious music study (piano, solfeggio, harmony) with Mihail Jora; when he reached age 11, Jora prepared him for the entrance examination at the Bucharest Conservatory (at that time the Royal Academy of Music and Drama), and advised him to study with Florica Musicescu. He was too young for official admittance, but Musicescu accepted the obviously talented child as her pupil, and gave him her most serious attention.

Strong forces, often conflicting, dominated Lipatti's childhood years. On the one side were his adoring parents. Immensely proud of their son's genius and anxious to have him play in public as quickly as possible, they generously supported him with teachers, books, music and whatever else he needed. On the opposite side were Lipatti's dedicated teachers, equally insistent that he should not appear in public before he had acquired a certain artistic standard. Lipatti seems to have withstood the onslaught of these powerful personalities, taking from each "only what was best for him. An extraordinary self-discipline and a striving after perfection were enhanced, in his case, by a total inner conviction of his own worth, which provided the necessary impulse to develop his natural gifts." (Tanasescu and Bargauanu) The uniquely close bond that Lipatti developed with both Jora and Musicescu lasted until his death. After he left Bucharest, he regularly (and voluminously!) reported to them on his performances, lessons, problems, life and health.

After four years (1928–32) at the Bucharest Conservatory, Lipatti received a diploma with distinction. Meanwhile, as a student he had played the Grieg Concerto, conducted by Professor Dan Simonescu, at a festival given at the Opera House. And in the summer of 1932 he played the Chopin Concerto in E Minor, conducted by Constantin Nottara, at a concert given by that year's finalists at the Conservatory. Although only age 15, his rare gifts and already highly developed talent were evident: "Besides possessing an unusual comprehension of music and a mature mastery of the instrument, his gifts are sustained by a sensitivity and temperament which make him an accomplished musician." (*Universul*, June 1932)

The following year his performance (10 Feb 1933) of the Liszt Concerto in E-flat Major also received glowing reviews: "Lipatti, who is on the threshold of maturity, appears to be endowed not only with a splendid technique but also with spiritual qualities, a fine grasp of the works performed, and a great desire to achieve the correct interpretation." (*Cuvintul*, 13 Feb 1933) The following month the 16-year-old Lipatti was called upon, with but a few days' notice, to substitute for a Polish pianist forced by illness to cancel a performance with George Georgescu and the Bucharest Philharmonic Orchestra. On that occasion Lipatti's performance of the Chopin Concerto in E Minor confirmed both his talent and his sound musical training: "He mastered the difficult solo parts, not only with assurance and technical brio, but with an artistic refinement, a sentiment of rare purity and a clarity of expression that can only serve to emphasize his precocious musical intelligence." (*Universul*, April 1933)

That same year (1933) Lipatti entered the International Piano Competition held in Vienna between 26 May and 16 June and quickly advanced to the finals. A close, contested decision by the jury (among them, Alfred Cortot, Wilhelm Backhaus, Emil von Sauer) awarded second prize to Lipatti and first prize to a Polish pianist named Boleslav Kohn, and Alfred Cortot resigned in protest. That autumn Lipatti played the Grieg Concerto with the Bucharest Philharmonic Orchestra under George Georgescu.

In August 1934 Lipatti's strong-willed mother arrived in Paris with her two sons, having on her own already obtained all passports and purchased a small apartment. She immediately took Lipatti to Cortot, at that time director of the *Ecole Normale de Musique*; and Cortot admitted Lipatti as his pupil, with the arrangement that when he himself had to be away, Lipatti would study with Yvonne Lefébure. On Cortot's advice, Lipatti began Paul Dukas's composition class in November 1934. After Dukas's death in May 1935, Lipatti studied composition and, as he put it, "music" with Nadia Boulanger. His loving friendship with Boulanger, a powerfully beneficial influence in his life (he called her his "musical guide and spiritual mother") lasted until his death.

Apart from vacations, Lipatti lived in Paris from 1934 until 1939. Duplicating his speedy progress at the Bucharest Conservatory, he quickly assumed the role of star student at the *Ecole Normale*, and his frequent performances at the *Ecole Normale* concerts did much to establish his reputation. Only a few months after he enrolled, he played (24 Dec 1934) Liszt's Concerto in E-flat Major with the school orchestra, conducted by Cortot. On 25 February 1935 he gave the first Paris performance of Georges Enescu's Piano Sonata in F-sharp Minor at an *Ecole Normale* concert. On 20 May 1935 he played his first solo recital in Paris, under the auspices of the *Ecole Normale*. At the end of his first year he received the *licence de concert*. His reputation kept growing. During his second school year he was invited to give a joint program with the Manhattan Quartet at the Geneva Conservatory on 28 October 1935 and at Montreux the following day. "Without diminishing the excellence of the American Quartet," wrote the *Tribune de Genève* (30 Oct 1935), "it must be admitted that the real surprise of the evening was the pianist Dinu Lipatti." In 1937 Lipatti attended Cortot's class in interpretation and Boulanger's class in analysis. He also took part in chamber-music evenings.

In 1936 Lipatti was introduced to Clara Haskil by Nadia Boulanger at the home of the Princesse de Polignac. Lipatti, age 19, and the middle-aged Haskil became fast friends almost immediately. Even though they were separated most of the time, due to their conflicting schedules, the two maintained a steady correspondence, Lipatti addressing Haskil in his openly affectionate way as "Dear Clarinette."

Now a celebrity in both Paris and Bucharest, Lipatti increasingly attracted attention in other countries. He gave concerts in Italy in 1938, and in 1939 gave what he called his first recital in the grand manner—a solo performance (29 March 1939) at the *Salle Pleyel* in Paris. But that July Lipatti, exhausted from concerts and concerned about the unavoidable war, canceled all concerts and returned home to Romania. Based in Bucharest until 1943, he gave many concerts in Romania and also made concert tours, often with the Bucharest Philharmonic Orchestra, in Czechoslovakia, Germany, Bulgaria, Austria and Italy. During this interval he composed, as he had always done since childhood, and also wrote music criticism and articles about the musical life in Paris, published in *Libertates*.

In 1940 Lipatti gave a two-piano concert with Madeleine Cantacuzino, who became his constant companion and, after finally obtaining her divorce, his wife. In the fall of 1943 they left Bucharest to tour in Sweden, Finland,

Germany and Switzerland. They never again lived in Bucharest. Lipatti became seriously ill in Geneva. Several months of convalescence in the Swiss mountains restored his vitality sufficiently to enable him to return to Geneva to try to pick up the threads of his career. Popular in Switzerland, on 1 April 1944 he was appointed professor at the Geneva Conservatory; however, since he had refused an offer of Swiss citizenship, he was not allowed to teach private lessons.

Lipatti's illness, ultimately diagnosed as lymphogranulomatosis, required a series of radiation treatments in 1945; and, inevitably, caused more and more concert cancellations. However, during periods of remission he played often, mostly in Switzerland, where he now had a large, loyal following, and a few concerts in Italy and Belgium. He was well enough to play the Grieg Concerto in Paris on 16 February 1947 and the Schumann Concerto in London on 11 April 1948, with the Philharmonia Orchestra, conducted by Herbert von Karajan. The release of his recordings—Lipatti had signed an exclusive contract with Columbia Records in 1946—added immensely to his fame and brought offers to play from around the world. As his condition worsened, concert programs had to be planned according to his physical strength, and planned extensive tours of the Americas and Australia had to be canceled.

Lipatti underwent another radiation series and blood transfusions in the summer of 1948. All 40 concerts projected for the first four months of 1949 were canceled; but in February 1950 he was able to play the Schumann Concerto with Ernest Ansermet in Geneva. That summer Walter Legge arrived in Geneva with a team of Columbia technicians and a fully equipped recording van. Bolstered by injections of the then new drug cortisone, Lipatti recorded steadily between July 3 and 12. After those sessions, he gave only two more performances. He played the Mozart Concerto in C Major, K. 467, on 23 August 1950 at Lucerne with Herbert von Karajan conducting, and played a recital—his final appearance—at Besançon on 16 September 1950. Only his indomitable spirit and massive injections got him through that last performance; even then, he lacked the strength to finish the final group, the complete Chopin Waltzes. Instead of playing the last Waltz, he concluded that recital with one of his favorite works, Myra Hess's arrangement of Bach's Jesu, Joy of Man's Desiring.

During his brief life, Dinu Lipatti accomplished a great deal as pianist, teacher and composer. His compositions were well received in his lifetime. Lipatti himself often played his Concertino in Classical Style for Piano and Chamber Orchestra. His *Symphonie Concertante* for Two Pianos and String Orchestra, op. 5, had its premier in Paris in 1939, with Clara Haskil and Lipatti at the keyboards. His fine solo work, the Sonatina for Left Hand, was written in 1941.

He was equally respected for his teaching (1944-49) at the Geneva Conservatory. Essentially, he advised students to find the spirit of the work, then have the courage to express it aloud with confidence. The word "truth" played an important part in Lipatti's vocabulary and teaching. That did not mean the text, or an accent or crescendo in the right place; it meant "the real spirit of the work, the totality of the composer's intentions."

Dinu Lipatti's pianism and musicianship were mostly innate, not acquired. Even as a small child, his emerging talent astounded Florica Musicescu. "What was so impressive, apart from his power to assimilate ideas and his stamina, was his amazing pianistic dexterity. He could instantly reproduce any musical idea with uncanny precision, without the slightest hesitation, in its entire harmonic structure—a feat which would normally require hours of work." (Tanasescu and Bargauanu) These wonderful natural abilities were reinforced by unusually large hands that could reach a twelfth and a remarkable dedication to work. A perfectionist who prepared every minute detail of every work he played, Lipatti sometimes worked on a composition for years before being satisfied with his performance. He refused to play in public any work not on his schedule (planned years in advance) of works to be studied. For example, he allowed four years for preparing the Beethoven "Emperor" Concerto and three years for the Tchaikovsky Concerto No. 1.

Walter Legge, who knew Lipatti well from their years of making recordings, described him as "a good man in the highest sense, and a particularly sensitive one. He was in all things an aristocrat of the finest fibre, temperamentally incapable of vulgarity in thought or deed. He was fastidious and distinguished in all he did." (Legge) With those words Legge describes both Lipatti the man and Lipatti the performer. A sensitive, aristocratic and fastidious pianist, Lipatti always sought the finest means of artistic expression. His approach has been described as embodying the detachment of a scientist and the intuition of an artist; nevertheless, in performance Lipatti tried for the greatest freedom possible—a balance between reason and feeling, between careful analysis and spontaneity.

Lipatti never played in the Americas or Australia and only rarely in England, and his frail health restricted touring to a fairly small area of Europe (Romania, France, Switzerland, Italy, Czechoslovakia, Germany, Austria, Bulgaria, Finland, Sweden). Thus, the available reviews of his live performances are largely limited to those published in the biography by Tanasescu and Bargauanu. On the whole, these reviews, like those of his recordings, reveal Lipatti as a pianist with an impeccable technique and as a sensitive, understanding interpreter who penetrated deeply into the meaning of the music. The recurring descriptive adjectives—orderly, controlled, formal, intelligent, precise, refined, impeccable, artistic—define a playing style of unusual brilliance, eloquence and elegance. In the lovely phrasing of Francis Poulenc, Dinu Lipatti was "an artist of divine spirituality."

As frequently happens, qualities admired by one critic disturbed others. While uniformly acknowledging Lipatti as a great musician and great talent, some reviewers found his playing too formal, too perfect—and lacking the feeling, lyricism and spontaneity Lipatti himself sought. Poor reviews are in the minority. In every country he played, Lipatti typically received extraordinarily complimentary notices.

Paris audiences apparently loved Lipatti from the start. He had been there only a few months and was completely unknown when he played Georges Enescu's Sonata in F-sharp Minor at an *Ecole Normale de Musique* concert (25 Feb 1935) and was brought out for six enthusiastic curtain calls. At his first

Paris recital (20 May 1935) critics raved over his transcendental virtuosity: "It is rare to come across a marriage between first-rate technical achievement and the finest qualities of musicianship, but this is so in the case of Dinu Lipatti. . . . His pianism is endowed with extraordinary sonorities which are never superficial even when playing a most subtle *pianissimo*, nor ever harsh in *forte*, retaining a constant and carefully controlled richness of tone." (*La Revue Musicale,* June 1935)

As in Paris, Lipatti quickly enchanted audiences in Switzerland. The solo pieces he played at a joint concert (28 Oct 1935) with the Manhattan Quartet received more coverage than the compositions played by the chamber ensemble. "He played a most interesting Bach-Busoni transcription [Toccata in C] which proves that in the hands of a master a transcription can become a new creation. . . . Cortot is right: Dinu Lipatti is 'one of the great pianists of tomorrow, if not already one of today'." (*Tribune de Genève*, 30 Oct 1935)

A recital in Rome drew similar notices: "This excellent pianist, by making use of an impeccable technique, has proved that he is endowed with outstanding artistic qualities. I admired his lightness of touch and the mastery of his craft which reached such a high degree of perfection in all the pieces that—if we may say so—it was the interpretation of a genius." (*Poppolo di Roma*, 29 Jan 1938)

Up to the time he performed that first recital "in the grand manner," in Paris on 26 March 1939, Lipatti had been judged as an uncommonly talented student; but after that Paris recital critics considered him as a competing concert artist. "We do not know what to praise most, his technical mastery or his profound musical understanding. In Dinu Lipatti the two are intimately linked, one sustaining the other." (*L'Art Musical*, 21 April 1939)

When Lipatti played in Stockholm, Swedish critics pointed out his power, the clarity of his readings and the elegance and nobility of his musical conception: "What is so rare in an artist who possesses such intensity and such an extraordinary technique is the degree to which he avoids falling into the trap of empty virtuosity by placing it at the service of artistic values." (*Allehanda*, 14 Sept 1943)

Lipatti, Herbert von Karajan and the Philharmonia Orchestra recorded the Schumann Concerto in A Minor in London on April 9 and 10 of 1948, and the following day played the same concerto at a public concert. "Mr. Lipatti's is a masculine approach . . . but out of the strong came forth not only sweetness of tone but rhythm that could be tender as well as vigorous. Nothing showed the sheer musical quality of these two artists [more clearly] than the transition from slow movement to finale, which was not a mechanical link but a transformation." (*TL*, 13 April 1948)

Lipatti, a perfectionist, loved recording because he could repeat a work—or a passage—as many times as it took to satisfy his ideal conception. In 1937 he and Nadia Boulanger, his piano-duet partner, recorded a selection of seven Brahms Waltzes (HMV DB5061) and, with a vocal quartet, the *Liebeslieder* Waltzes (HMV DB5057-9). Other than these early recordings, Lipatti recorded only with Walter Legge, music director for Columbia Records.

Under an exclusive contract with Columbia, signed in January 1946, Lipatti made the records that now stand as his musical testament.

The first Columbia recordings were made in Zurich in July 1946. However, the matrixes were damaged and eventually had to be destroyed. Most of Lipatti's official recording sessions were done in England at four different periods. At the first (Oct–Nov 1946) he recorded Liszt's *La Leggierezza* and a Chopin Waltz. The second session (Feb–March 1947) produced two Scarlatti sonatas, a Chopin nocturne and the B Minor Sonata. In September of that same year (1947) Lipatti recorded the Grieg Concerto in A Minor with the Philharmonia Orchestra, conducted by Alceo Galliera; the Chopin Waltz in A-flat Major, op. 34, no. 1; the Liszt *Sonetta del Petrarca* No. 104; and the Scarlatti Sonata in E Major, K. 380. During his last visit to London, in April 1948, he recorded the Schumann Concerto in A Minor, with Herbert von Karajan conducting the Philharmonia Orchestra; Ravel's *Alborada del gracioso*; and the Chopin Barcarolle.

Cortisone injections brought about a temporary reversal in Lipatti's illness in May 1950, and his doctor urged Walter Legge to come to Geneva and record while the pianist was in comparatively good health. Legge arrived with technicians and a fully equipped recording van; and in June and July Lipatti recorded some Bach (Partita No. 1 in B-flat Major, two organ chorale-preludes, a ravishing performance of the Siciliano from the Sonata No. 2 for Flute and Harpsichord in the Wilhelm Kempff arrangement); Chopin (the Waltzes and the Mazurka in C-sharp Minor, op. 50, no. 3); Mozart (Sonata in A Minor, K. 310) and Bach's Jesu, Joy of Man's Desiring in the Myra Hess transcription.

The Bach Concerto in D Minor, BWV 1052, comes from a private recording of Lipatti's performance (2 Oct 1947) with the Amsterdam *Concertgebouw* Orchestra, conducted by Eduard van Beinum. This recording—Busoni version—may offend self-proclaimed purists, but certainly not admirers of superb playing. This performance "carries a sense of occasion, a sense that something new is happening and unfolding. Lipatti's playing is beautiful in tone, carefully sculpted, and always alive to the musical line." (*Fan*, March/April 1990)

The Chopin Concerto No. 1 in E Minor, op. 11, comes from a private recording of Lipatti's performance (7 Feb 1950) with the Zurich *Tonhalle* Orchestra, conducted by Otto Ackermann. (Another recording of the Chopin No. 1, with an unknown orchestra and conductor, was eventually discovered to be spurious.) The Mozart Concerto in C Major, K. 467, was taken from a radio broadcast of a concert (23 Aug 1950) at the Lucerne *Kunsthaus*, with Herbert von Karajan conducting the Lucerne Festival Orchestra.

There are two recordings of the Schumann Concerto in A Minor, op. 54. The first, a studio version, was made on 9–10 April 1948, with Herbert von Karajan and the Philharmonia Orchestra. The second is from a radio broadcast of a concert (22 Feb 1950) at Geneva's Victoria Hall, with the *Orchestre de la Suisse Romande*, Ernest Ansermet conducting. Both of these recordings are eminently worthwhile. Evaluating the one made with von Karajan, one critic wrote that he "loved the performance for its youthful freshness and élan no less than for its absolute truthfulness to both letter and spirit of the score." (*Gram*, July 1989)

The collections in the *EMI Références* series (see Discog.) are no less distinguished: "His playing is at all times free of exaggeration or mannerism, of old-fashioned cliches of interpretation. It is playing of classic purity and elegance." (*Fan*, July/Aug 1989)

Irving Kolodin's sympathetic and articulate critique (1957) of *Dinu Lipatti: His Last Recital* (see Discog.) emphasizes the pianist's great performances of the Mozart Sonata in A Minor, K. 310, and the Bach Partita No. 1 in B-flat Major: "Expressively he reaches beyond the horizon of our previous knowledge of him in the slow movement of the Mozart, insinuating into those seemingly placid patterns a kind of affection and understanding few 'interpreters' of this composer ever convey. The sarabande of the Partita is similarly lit by a clarity of mind and a warmth of spirit not given to many." (Kolodin, "Lipatti's Last. . .") The welcome reissue of this album in CD format prompted another critic to further praises: "For Mozart he [Lipatti] finds a wonderfully translucent sound-world, rich in subtleties of colouring." And as for the two Schubert Impromptus, "the musical message is all the more affecting for its totally selfless simplicity and purity of expression." (*Gram*, Dec 1994)

How do we as listeners evaluate Lipatti's playing? His devoted followers will maintain that all his recordings are wonderful, which, it must be admitted, is pretty close to the truth. All the available recordings show the meticulous care which Lipatti gave to literally every note, the elegant cantabile of his melodic lines, the careful phrasing and tasteful virtuosity. But above all what shows most clearly is Lipatti's serious dedication to his art, a dedication he maintained to the very end. "It must be said, once again, that not a single note left to us by this noble young artist shows anything other than the highest integrity." (Goldsmith)

SELECTED REFERENCES

Boulanger, Nadia. "In Remembrance of Lipatti." *Saturday Review*, 30 May 1953, pp. 45, 47.
Dinu Lipatti: His Last Recital. Booklet to accompany Album Angel LP 3556B.
"Dinu Lipatti—1917–1950." *Newsweek*, 25 May 1953, p. 90.
Goldsmith, Harris. "Brief Candles." *High Fidelity*, Feb 1966, pp. 50–54, 112.
"In Memoriam." *New Yorker*, 23 May 1953, p. 111.
In Memoriam Dinu Lipatti 1917–1950. Geneva: Editions Labor et Fides, 1970. Contains 28 tributes written by friends and colleagues.
Kolodin, Irving. "The Late Lipatti Memorialized." *Saturday Review*, 23 May 1953, p. 51.
———. "Lipatti's Last Recital." *Saturday Review*, 27 April 1957, pp. 41, 52.
Legge, Walter. "Dinu Lipatti." *Gramophone*, Feb 1951, p. 193. This article was reprinted in *The Gramophone Jubilee Book* (Gra/Jub, see Bibliog.).
Lewis, Leonne. "Memories of Dinu Lipatti." *Clavier*, July/Aug 1992, pp. 20–23.

Lipatti, Anna. *La Vie du pianiste Dinu Lipatti*. Paris: *Editions du vieux Columbier*, 1954.

Lipatti, Madeleine. "Dinu Lipatti: Son dernier recital." *Le Guide du Concert*, 27 Dec 1957, p. 464.

" Lipatti's Last." *Time*, 10 June 1957, pp. 71–72.

Monsaingeon, Bruno. *Mademoiselle* (Conversations with Nadia Boulanger), trans. Robyn Marsack. Manchester: Carcanet Press Ltd., 1985, pp. 76–78.

Obituary. *The Times* (London), 5 Dec 1950, p. 6.

Schonberg, Harold C. "Records: Lipatti." *New York Times*, 11 Oct 1953, sec. 10, p. 9.

Siki, Béla. "Dinu Lipatti." *Recorded Sound*, July 1964, pp. 232–237.

————. "Reflections on Dinu Lipatti." *Clavier*, Feb 1995, pp. 15–17.

Spycket, Jerome. *Clara Haskil*. Lausanne: Edition Payot, 1975.

Tanasescu, Dragos. *Dinu Lipatti Remembered*. New York: Musical Scope Publishers, 1971.

Tanasescu, Dragos, and Grigore Bargauanu. *Lipatti*. (translated by Carola Grindea and Anne Goosens) London: Kahn & Averill, 1988. Foreword by Yehudi Menuhin.

Tubeuf, André. "The Legacy." Liner essay for EMI Références album C 051-01696.

See also Bibliography: Gra/Jub; Hag/Dec; Hag/Thi; New/Gro; Rat/Cle; Rub/MyM.

SELECTED REVIEWS

Adeverul, 12 June 1932. *Allehanda*, 14 Sept 1943. *Curentul*, 5 Oct 1939. *Cuvintul*, 13 Feb 1933. *TL*: 13 April 1948.

SELECTED DISCOGRAPHY

Bach (arr. Busoni): Concerto in D Minor, BWV 1052 (Beinum/*Concertgebouw*). Chopin: Concerto No. 1 in E Minor, op. 11 (Ackermann/*Tonhalle* Orch.); Nocturne in D-flat Major, op. 27, no. 2; Etudes in E Minor, op. 25, no. 5; in G-flat Major, op. 10, no. 5. Jecklin-Disco JD 541-2.

Bach: Partita No. 1 in B-flat Major, BWV 825. Bach-Busoni: *Nun komm, der heiden Heiland*, BWV 599; *Ich ruf zu dir*, BWV 639. Bach-Hess: *Jesus bleibet meine Freude*, BWV 147. Bach-Kempff: Siciliana from Flute Sonata, BWV 1031. Mozart: Sonata in A Minor, K. 310. Scarlatti: Sonatas in D Minor, K. 9, in E Major, K. 380. Schubert: Impromptus in E-flat Major, D. 899, no. 2; in G-flat Major, D. 899, no. 3. EMI *Références* CDH-69800 (Great Recordings of the Century).

Brahms: Waltzes op. 39, nos. 1, 2, 5–6, 10, 14–15 (w/Nadia Boulanger). Chopin: Sonata No. 3 in B Minor, op. 58. Enesco: Sonata No. 3 in D Major, op. 25. Liszt: *Sonetto 104 del Petrarca*. Ravel: *Alborada del gracioso*. EMI *Références* CDH 7 63038-2.

Chopin: Concerto No. 1 in E Minor, op. 11 (Ackermann/*Tonhalle* Orch.).
   Grieg: Concerto in A Minor, op. 16 (Galliera/Philharmonia). EMI
   Références CDH 63497-2.
Chopin: Waltzes; Barcarolle in F-sharp Major, op. 60; Nocturne in D-flat Major,
   op. 27, no. 2; Mazurka in C-sharp Minor, op. 50, no. 3. EMI Classics
   CDH-69802.
Dinu Lipatti. A 7 LP collection including all of the above minus the Bach
   Concerto and Chopin Etudes but with the addition of the Schumann
   Concerto, op. 54 (with von Karajan). EMI 15 3780 3.
Dinu Lipatti: His Last Recital (Besançon Festival, 16 Sept 1950). Bach: Partita
   No. 1 in B-flat Major, BWV 825. Mozart: Sonata in A Minor, K. 310.
   Schubert: Impromptus in G-flat Major, D. 899, no. 3, in E-flat Major, D.
   899, no. 2. Chopin: Waltzes (13). Angel LP 3556B. Includes an essay by
   Walter Legge. Reissued on CD, EMI Références H5 65166-2.

⚜ ⚜ ⚜

LORTIE, LOUIS: b. Montreal, Canada, 27 April 1959.

> Lortie is a pianist who projects the idea of perfection after only the first
> notes and he makes certain that the evening will be musically interest-
> ing.
>
> *Trouw* (24 October 1989)

Louis Lortie was already seven years old—and had not studied music—when his
family moved to a new house and discovered a piano and a few music books left
behind in the basement. Attracted to the keyboard, Lortie begged his parents
(both played the piano, but very little) to teach him to read music. He began
lessons and, as he remembers it, one of his first attempts was Schumann's "The
Happy Farmer." Lortie also remembers that although his parents were not especially musical, his grandmother, living with the family at the time, gave him
the encouragement he needed. He was still age seven when he began proper
lessons at the *Ecole de Musique Wilfrid-Pelletier* in Montreal, studying succes-
sively with Nicole Pontbriand-Beaudoin and Sister Simone Martin. He had more
advanced instruction from Yvonne Hubert at Montreal's *Ecole Normale de
Musique*.

   Although a comparatively late starter in music, Lortie at age nine began
entering the Canadian Music Competitions, and for five successive years (1968–
72) he was awarded a prize. As recipient of the Montreal Symphony Orchestra
Prize, the 13-year-old Lortie made his debut with that orchestra in 1972. In
1973 (and again in 1975) he received a prize at the Czechoslovakian radio's
Concertino Praga. In 1975, at age 16, Lortie received a prize in both the CBC
National Talent Competition and the Canadian Music Competitions' International Stepping Stones contest. Meanwhile, he was giving recitals and appearing on
the CBC.

Accepted to study technique with Dieter Weber in Vienna during 1975–76, Lortie discovered on arrival that Weber was too ill to teach. Lortie later enrolled at Indiana University. He had classes with Josef Gingold and Janos Starker and studied piano with Menahem Pressler, but, dissatisfied with his piano instruction, he left the University after just three months. He also had occasional "most stimulating" lessons with Leon Fleisher in Baltimore.

In 1978 Lortie was chosen by Andrew Davis, conductor of the Toronto Symphony Orchestra, to play the Liszt Concerto No. 1 on the TSO's tour of Japan and China. Before leaving, they played the Liszt at Toronto's Massey Hall (Lortie's debut performance), and on the tour had great success in Tokyo, Beijing, Shanghai and Canton. The Peoples' Republic of China invited Lortie to return in 1983 to give recitals in Shanghai and Beijing and to make a tour with the Shanghai Philharmonic Orchestra. In September 1984 Lortie placed first at the Busoni International Piano Competition in Bolzano, Italy, and two weeks later won fourth prize at the Leeds International Competition in Great Britain.

Lortie's career developed quickly during 1985. He made his American debut in Washington, D.C., on 13 April; made his London orchestral debut (14 Nov) playing the Beethoven Concerto No. 4 with the London Symphony Orchestra, conducted by Andrew Davis; and made his London recital debut on 21 November 1985. In 1987 he made his New York recital debut (18 March) and, to mark the 50th anniversary of composer Maurice Ravel's death, played all the Ravel solo piano works in two recitals for both the CBC and the BBC.

Lortie plays more than half of his concerts in Great Britain and Europe (Germany, France, Italy, Belgium, the Netherlands, Scandinavia), the rest mostly in North America. In 1984 he was awarded the Virginia P. Moore Prize, given by the Canada Council, and in 1986 he received the *Grand Prix* of the *Conseil des arts de la Communauté urbaine de Montréal.* In 1987 the Canada Council named him "Performer of the Year." In 1990 Lortie received the Juno Award for the best classical album (20th Century Original Piano Transcriptions, see Discog.). In 1991 his recording of Beethoven Variations, op. 34 and op. 35 (see Discog.) received the Dutch Edison Award.

Louis Lortie often tells interviewers that he does not have favorite composers, that he wants "to play things that are best for a certain stage in my life." Music written before Bach is not for him, and he does not play Bach either because, he says, "the experience of playing Bach on the harpsichord has made it difficult for him to interpret it at the piano, but after Mozart his repertoire is, as he admits, fairly conventional. 'I'm not afraid of the great works, and I'm not really interested in exploring backwaters'." (Johnson)

Programs from the years 1985–95 indicate that Lortie's recent repertoire consists chiefly of works by Liszt, Ravel and Chopin; that he often plays Beethoven, Brahms and Schumann; and less frequently plays works by Mozart and Stravinsky. His orchestral performances over this period included the Liszt Concerto No. 1 in E-flat Major; Ravel's Concerto in G; the Chopin Concerto No. 2 in F Minor; the Schumann Concerto; Mozart's Concerto in A Major, K. 488; the Beethoven Concerto No. 4 in G Major.

Lortie frequently programs complete sets of pieces. He likes "to see what a composer is doing with a genre. For example, each of the four Chopin Scherzos I am playing on the debut Atlantic tour represents a period. They cover a 20-year span. The first, written when Chopin was 20 or 21, is very jubilant, like the studies. The fourth, written a year or two before he died, is almost impressionistic." (*CH*, 28 Jan 1987)

Lortie is exceptionally well equipped to play the demanding works he programs. "He is a wonderfully gifted pianist, instantly engaging in his musical manner; the technique is solid as a rock. He also has that rare gift of *listening* intently to what he plays, forever colouring, shading, emphasizing, minutely adjusting." (*FT*, 5 Nov 1986) Five years later another reviewer said it this way: "He has personality, strong feelings about the music he plays, the technical resources to express those feelings, and . . . a palpable regard for his listeners." (*LAT*, 27 April 1991)

Those excellent descriptions of Lortie's playing reappear, in one mode or another, in most of the Lortie reviews. One critic sees his "engaging" musical manner as "a warm, communicative personality which establishes a rapid rapport with the audience." (*MT*, Feb 1986) And another describes it as a "strong pianistic personality made up of equal parts virtuoso and poet. The combination, it hardly needs be said, is rare." (*LAT*, 1 Aug 1993)

Reviewers dwell on that theme—that Lortie is equal parts poet and virtuoso, a bravura pianist yet at the same time one whose performances shimmer with poetic beauty. It is true that he is not given to showy technical displays, even with the dazzling virtuosic repertoire he frequently plays. "He appears indifferent to external colour, preferring to revel in the iridescence of reverberation. For Lortie the pedal is a paint brush." (Pedersen, "Fiery Lortie. . .")

Lortie's elegant playing rests on a subtle range of colors, not a multi-layered orchestral sound but "minute varieties of the normal piano sound." Achieving what he calls the "pearly" sound is never his goal. What fascinates him is the concept of changing the quality of sound from one composer to another, that is, finding the right sound for each composer and his particular style. "A special relationship to a composer that involves sound production is my greatest interest," he says. "If you play Mozart with a sound more appropriate for Ravel, that is not good." (*Fan*, Jan/Feb 1991)

If critics sometimes question or disparage his sensitive, carefully considered readings, all seem to agree that they are logical, lucid and faithful in both spirit and style to the music he is playing. There is also little doubt about Lortie's "solid as a rock" technique. "Unlike so many of today's young pianists, who are keyboard athletes with plenty of technique but little sense of communication, the Canadian Louis Lortie is something of an aristocrat. . . . He revealed a powerful technique that was never flaunted as an end in itself but was always used to express a highly poetic purpose." (*GM*, 29 April 1986)

Typically, the very qualities pleasing some critics disturb others. Some find that Lortie's style and temperament make for heavy going, that essentially his understated, nonflamboyant playing is "saying that much of the 19th century piano literature assumed to be entertaining and diverting has a very serious side to its character." (*SFC*, 23 Feb 1993) Others find that despite Lortie's intensity there is a coolness and reserve in his playing. He is, to be sure, a performer with "sufficient personality and intellect to hold the sophisticated listener's interest for an entire evening. Still, it must be said that this program [half Chopin, half Ravel] never reached an emotional temperature of memorable heat." (*LAT*, 12 Dec 1987)

Lortie performed all 27 Chopin Etudes at his Washington, D.C., debut (13 April 1985), and it was a phenomenal recital. "Everything was direct and clear. His legatos were silken . . . his staccatos, arpeggios and runs had absolute rhythmic integrity. . . . Lortie handled with aplomb not only the technical hurdles, but the musical and emotional ones." (*WP*, 15 April 1985)

A review of his London debut recital (21 Nov 1985) at Wigmore Hall reads: "He has a warm, communicative personality which establishes a rapid rapport with the audience. He also has the ability to invest a phrase with a flash of new tone-colour, or to give it a palpable rhythmic lift. . . . In Chopin's Op. 10 Etudes, Lortie grasped every opportunity to communicate something worthwhile. . . . It was a display of bravura tempered by delicacy, passion by sensibility, of the kind for which Chopin the pianist was himself renowned." (*MT*, Feb 1986)

On 12 October 1989 Lortie opened the *Meesterpianisten* series at Amsterdam's *Concertgebouw*, playing a most strenuous program: Stravinsky's *Trois mouvements de Petrouchka*, the *Jeux d'eau* and *Sonatine* of Ravel plus the entire *Années de pèlerinage: Italie* of Liszt. Again, rave notices: "Never in the history of this venue have we seen playing with such pleasure and impeccable style." (*Trouw*, 24 Oct 1989); "An unbelievable debut Sunday night in the Grand Hall." (*Het Parool*, 23 Oct 1989); "Brilliance, spontaneity and high-caliber style are united in Lortie. In one word, Lortie is a master." (*Algemeen Dagblad*, 24 Oct 1989)

The first half of an unusual San Francisco recital (21 Feb 1993) had two extended works: Schumann's *Bunte Blätter*, op. 99, and the Brahms Variations on a Theme by Robert Schumann, op. 9 (the theme comes from the fourth Schumann [Op. 99] piece). Lortie gave an unusual performance of Schumann's seldom-performed collection. His "forceful and intense approach to the Schumann was startling and even unsettling. He treated the work as if it were a song cycle with a unifying mood. . . . The Brahms Variations was quite another and greatly satisfying story, played with sensitive regard for the connected moods of a set conceived as a unified work." (*SFC*, 23 Feb 1993)

Lortie's career appears to be flourishing, and his performances continue to fulfill the promise of his earlier days. His performance (29 July 1993) of Liszt's Concerto No. 1 with the Los Angeles Philharmonic Orchestra, Hermann Michael conducting, "restored one listener's faith in the future of keyboard playing and in the continuing tradition of Romantic pianism. Here was a handsomely colored, full-out technical display that also reinstated the nobility and lyricism of the overexposed concerto." (*LAT*, 31 July 1993) And for a Pasadena, California, recital (25 Jan 1995): "He has the fingers of a keyboard wizard, the poetic bent of one born to play music of the Romantics and a strong personality. His Chopin program . . . offered solid musical values and treasurable individual performances." (*LAT*, 27 Jan 1995)

Lortie's recording of the Chopin Etudes (see Discog.) has received contradictory reviews. One unusually harsh account states that in Lortie "we have the modern style in excelsis. He plays all 27 Chopin Etudes with simply amazing technique and a complete lack of poetry. . . . It is a pity that Mr. Lortie lacks the color and rhythmic flexibility to go along with his remarkable fingers." (*NYT*, 1 March 1987) On the other hand, another reviewer rates this as "the finest set of Chopin Etudes on disc. Even Pollini's superlative set now takes second place. . . . It's the eloquence Lortie finds in even the fast Etudes that is so compelling and exceptional." (*SFC*, 8 Feb 1987)

Lortie also recorded the Chopin Concerto in F Minor, op. 21, and it appears coupled with the Schumann Concerto in A Minor, op. 54. A reviewer who finds that Lortie brings strength and authority as well as some tenderness to the Schumann also writes: "I confess to feeling at times that this fine artist could be a little more yielding and melting with the music. . . . Yet his playing is always shapely and his fingerwork impeccable. . . . The performance of the Chopin is rather a weighty affair. . . . But the piano part is characteristically imaginative and Lortie plays it with great authority." (*Gram*, Nov 1992)

In his recording of the "Italian" volume of Liszt's *Années de pèlerinage*, "Lortie proves himself an artist of exceptional finesse whose response to the music's romance is as sympathetic as his tone is round and warm." However, this reviewer ends his appraisal with one caveat: "I still have the feeling that this distinguished French-Canadian artist is perhaps more temperamentally attuned to the half-Gallic Chopin than to Liszt." (*Gram*, Sept 1991) But, writes another critic, "This is the volume of the Years of Pilgrimage most suited to Lortie's aristocratic, soft-spoken artistry. . . . I found great allure in his unwillingness to indulge in rhetoric, and his rhythmic clarity and slightly cool tone prevent introversion from turning into limpness." (*ARG*, March/April 1992)

Lortie has recorded Ravel's compositions for solo piano on two CDs and the two concertos on a third (see Discog.). The first CD of solo music includes among other things the *Pavane, Tombeau de Couperin, Jeux d'eau, Valses nobles et sentimentales* and closes with a scintillating account of *La Valse*. As observed by one critic, "Everything on the disc is played with total keyboard mastery as well as the keenest ear for texture and timbre. . . . The recital comes over with exceptional vividness and immediacy." (*Gram*, May 1989)

The second volume of Ravel's solo keyboard music contains *Gaspard de la nuit, Miroirs* and the *Sonatine*. Reactions vary. One critic admits that Lortie possesses the necessary style and technique and that "his playing throughout has admirable fingerwork, clean pedalling, tasteful phrasing and often a limpid beauty that in itself is attractive. . . . [But] "I confess a feeling of disappointment with a *Gaspard* that is short of atmosphere." (*Gram*, Oct 1989) But another reviewer feels that Lortie's "account of 'Gaspard de la nuit,' a work that has fared extremely well on records, is among the most moving and satisfying I have heard." (*WT*, 31 Jan 1990)

The two Ravel concertos, which appear on a single CD along with the Fauré Ballade, op. 19, were recorded with the London Symphony Orchestra, Rafael Frühbeck de Burgos conducting. One pleased reviewer describes Lortie's performance of Ravel's Concerto for the Left Hand as filling "the air with the sounds of spectacle—grand displays of musical light and color from piano and orchestra that dazzle the ear and the mind. . . . His brilliant tone and exuberant agility follow Ravel to the limits of excitement." The Concerto in G "sparkles and shines with the richly variegated spectrum of the modern orchestra." (*CDR*, June 1990)

Another Lortie CD combines Schumann's sometimes enigmatic *Bunte Blätter*, op. 99, and Brahms's Variations on the fourth piece in the Schumann collection. Lortie's "interpretation is as conceptually sound, beautifully expressed, and musically satisfying as you could wish. His playing is natural, subtly nuanced, full of grace and sensitivity." (*ARG*, Nov/Dec 1994)

SELECTED REFERENCES

Epstein, David. "The Canadian Music Competition." *Musical America*, Feb 1976, pp. 14–15.

Gerber, Leslie. "Conversation with Louis Lortie." *Fanfare*, Jan/Feb 1991, pp. 439–441.

Johnson, Stephen. "Adding To Our Knowledge." *Gramophone*, Jan 1987, p. 985.

Morrison, Bryce. "Louis Lortie." (interview) *Music and Musicians*, June 1989, pp. 5–6.

Pedersen, Stephen. "All the world's a stage for Montreal pianist Louis Lortie." *The Chronicle-Herald* (Halifax), 28 Jan 1987.

———. "Fiery Lortie—Canada's proudest boast." *The Mail-Star* (Halifax), 30 Jan 1987.

Potvin, Gilles. "Louis Lortie." *Encyclopedia of Music in Canada*, 1992, pp. 773–774.

Regan, Tom. "Lortie downplays romantic ideals." *The Daily News* (Halifax), 29 Jan 1987, p. 16.

Smith, Craig. "Lortie brings technical flair to renditions of Chopin music." *New Mexican* (Santa Fe, NM), 17 Sept 1993.

Smith, Harriet. "Themes and Variations." *Gramophone*, August 1994, pp. 22–23.

See also Bibliography: New/Gro.

SELECTED REVIEWS

CPD: 23 July 1990. *CT*: 10 Aug 1988. *DT*: 6 Nov 1986. *FT*: 5 Nov 1986. *GloM*: 29 Nov 1990. *GM*: 29 April 1986. *LAT*: 9 Dec 1986; 12 Dec 1987; 27 April 1991; 31 July 1993. 1 Aug 1993; 27 Jan 1995. *MT*: Jan 1986; Feb 1986. *NYT*: 22 March 1987; 7 March 1990; 30 Aug 1990. *PI*: 13 Feb 1993. *SFC*: 22 March 1986; 21 Feb 1989; 11 March 1991; 23 Feb 1993. *SFE*: 25 Jan 1995. *SLPD*: 24 Jan 1991. *SPPP*: 17 Feb 1989. *TL*: 15 Nov 1985. *WP*: 15 April 1985; 24 June 1988; 26 Sept 1989; 3 Feb 1990; 6 Feb 1990; 30 June 1993. *WT*: 31 Jan 1990; 5 Feb 1990; 17 Feb 1993.

SELECTED DISCOGRAPHY

Beethoven: Bagatelle in A Minor (*Für Elise*); Rondo in C Major, op. 51, no. 1; Rondo in G Major, op. 51, no. 2; Variations in F Major, op. 34; Variations in E-flat Major, op. 35 ("Eroica" Variations). Chandos CHAN-8616 (CD).

Beethoven: Sonata in C Minor, op. 10, no. 1; Sonata in F Major, op. 10, no. 2; Sonata in D Major, op. 10, no. 3. Chandos CHAN-9101 (CD).

Beethoven: Sonata in C Minor, op. 13; Sonata in C Major, op. 53; Sonata in E-flat Major, op. 81a. Chandos CHAN-9024 (CD).

Brahms: Variations on a Theme by R. Schumann, op. 9. Schumann: *Blumenstück* in D flat, op. 19; *Bunte Blätter*, op. 99. Chandos CHAN-9289 (CD).

Chopin: Concerto No. 2 in F Minor, op. 21. Schumann: Concerto in A Minor, op. 54. Chandos CHAN-9061 (CD). Järvi/Philharmonia.

Chopin: Etudes (complete). Chandos CHAN-8482 (CD), also Musical Heritage Society MHS 512141X (CD).

Liszt: Three Concert Studies (*Il Lamento, La Leggierezza, Un Sospiro*); Sonata in B Minor. Chandos CHAN-8548 (CD).

Mozart: Concerto in A Major, K. 414; Concerto in E-flat Major, K. 449. MHS 512034Y (CD). Turovsky/*I Musici de Montreal*.

Ravel: Concerto in D Major for Left Hand; Concerto in G Major. Fauré: Ballade, op. 19. Chandos CHAN-8773 (CD). Frühbeck de Burgos/London SO.

Ravel: Piano Works, Vol. 1. Jeux d'eau; Pavane pour une infante défunte; Sérénade grotesque; Le Tombeau de Couperin; La Valse; Valses nobles et sentimentales. Chandos CHAN-8620 (CD).

Ravel: Piano Works, Vol. 2. *Gaspard de la nuit; A la manière de Borodine; A la manière de Chabrier; Menuet antique; Menuet sur le nom de Haydn; Miroirs; Prélude; Sonatine.* Chandos CHAN-8647 (CD).

20th Century Original Piano Transcriptions. Gershwin: Rhapsody in Blue. Prokofiev: 3 Pieces from Romeo and Juliet (op. 75). Stravinsky: 3 Movements from Petrushka. Chandos CHAN-8733 (CD).

LUPU, RADU: b. Galati, Romania, 30 November 1945.

> The Romanian pianist is an authentic melancholy romantic. He glowers . . . and with no apparent regard for his audience, he plunges into each composition as if it existed only in a solitary inner world.
> Robert Commanday (*San Francisco Chronicle*, 21 March 1981)

From need or by nature most performing artists seek publicity and crave attention—but not Radu Lupu. To public and press alike he appears indifferent, difficult, even antisocial. However, interviewers discover that underneath his public facade the real Lupu is amenable, warm and responsive. The fact is that Radu Lupu is not antisocial but shy. He abhors the competitive, commercial aspect of concertizing and, to the extent possible, avoids unnecessary publicity. Unfortunately, his onstage behavior only fuels the rumors about his difficult personality, since Lupu ignores rather than woos an audience. He comes onstage intense and unsmiling, immediately begins playing and seldom even turns his head toward the audience.

Critics fare no better, for Lupu is a rare performer in that he usually ignores reviews of his performances. He stopped reading criticisms when he realized that he could get good reviews when he personally felt he had not played well and, vice versa, get poor reviews for what he considered a good performance. The nonconforming Lupu has become a famous pianist in a generation that has produced a fairly large number of famous pianists—Argerich, Ax, Barenboim, Kovacevich, Dichter, Gutiérrez, Ohlsson, Pollini. Where Lupu ranks in this illustrious company is, of course, as subjective and capricious as the opinions concerning his personality and performances.

No one else in his immediate family was musical. His father was an attorney, his mother a linguist. Lupu began piano lessons with Lia Busuioceanu when he was six years old, and he made his first public appearance at age 12 at Brasov, Romania, playing a program of his own compositions. At age 14 he studied for some months at the Bucharest Conservatory with Cella Delavrancea and Florica Musicescu, the professor who had taught Dinu Lipatti. From 1961 to 1969 Lupu studied in Moscow on a scholarship. He was a pupil of Galia Eqiazarova at the Moscow pre-conservatory (1961–63); and at the Moscow Conservatory (1963–69) he studied with Heinrich Neuhaus, his son Stanislav Neuhaus and Helene Kaspina. Looking back, Lupu is grateful for what he learned from his teachers in Moscow and also grateful that his first teacher took him to orchestral concerts. At the same time he thinks of himself as being autodidactic, having taken "some from Furtwängler, Toscanini, everywhere . . . more and more since I left Moscow." (*CL*, May-June 1981)

In 1966 Lupu gave recitals in Moscow and Leningrad, and in September of that year he took first prize at the second Van Cliburn Piano Competition held at Fort Worth, Texas. He was also awarded two other prizes—a prize for best performance of a work (Willard Straight's Structure) especially composed for the competition and another prize for best performance of Aaron Copeland's Sonata (second movement). Despite these remarkable achievements, the 20-year-old Lupu wisely elected to return to his studies at the Moscow Conservatory rather than begin a concert career. In 1967 he won the International Competition Georges Enescu in Bucharest and in 1969, his final year at the Moscow Conservatory, he took first prize at the Leeds International Piano Competition. That same year Lupu made his London recital debut (27 Nov 1969), and finally began his concert career.

In 1972 two important engagements established his reputation in America: a performance (in New York) with the Cleveland Orchestra, Daniel Barenboim conducting, and a performance with the Chicago Symphony Orchestra, Carlo Maria Giulini conducting. Engagements with the New York

Philharmonic Orchestra followed, and for two years Lupu toured the United States, making appearances in almost every major city. For nearly 20 years now he has been a major presence on the international music scene, performing regularly as soloist and recitalist in Europe, Great Britain and the United States. He has also performed in Israel and toured China with the European Community Youth Orchestra.

Lupu does not accept pupils. He may agree to listen to someone play and give his opinion, but he does not teach on a regular basis. He is married to Elisabeth Wilson, a fellow student at the Moscow Conservatory, and they make their home in London.

Radu Lupu's intensely personal playing style—intelligent, quiet, deeply serious—is easily recognizable. It reveals how thoroughly Lupu prepares his performances—"each phrase, each note, each pause placed precisely within his own commanding scheme of the music's development." (*DT*, 1 Dec 1985) His careful preparation (his "manic delight in analysis," as one interviewer perceived it) begins with his first reading the work in question away from the piano. If there are musical problems, he solves them mentally before going to the piano to figure out how to produce the effects he wants. Lupu loves the preparation process, and he also loves practicing as long as he can concentrate on the music without getting tired. According to Murray Perahia, Lupu's good friend with whom he often plays and records piano duets (see Discog.), Lupu is a genius who hardly needs to practice. He hears a piece once and can just about play it through.

Subtlety, finesse, eloquence, insight, integrity; poetic, gentle, sensitive, refined, elegant—one or more of these identifying words appear in almost every Lupu review. Some critics may complain that Lupu's lyrical playing lacks fire; or that it is too aloof; or that it is so inwardly concentrated that the listener is shut out. But if flair is missing in his music, Lupu more than "makes up in poetic seriousness rendered by what might be called self-effacing technique. He doesn't dazzle with pointillistic runs and cosmic banging." (*NYT*, 29 Jan 1991) His playing is warm, sincere and always in good taste. Lupu has an acute sense of rhythm and a wonderful gift for fitting phrases together. Not afraid of *rubato*, he uses it skillfully for musical enhancement. Ritardandos may occur where not indicated in the score, but with Lupu they make musical sense. Dynamic shading in every degree possible, from very soft to very loud, often appears in his personal reading of a score, but again is kept within the bounds of good taste. Lupu is a splendid musician, never a showman. Integrity governs every measure of his playing.

His interpretative powers seem to find their finest expression with Beethoven, Brahms, Mozart and, above all, he has become one of the great Schubert pianists of our day. At his London debut recital (27 Nov 1969) Lupu played (Schubert Impromptus D. 899 and D. 935 and Beethoven 32 Variations in C Minor) with great sensitivity. "He can produce a *pianissimo* of unearthly Richter quietness, a clarion Gilels *fortissimo*, a sharp and marvellously evocative Cherkassky ghost-chord, struck fierce and loud with the soft pedal down, all with the greatest of ease." (*MT*, Jan 1970) A Hunter College program (16 Feb 1974) included Schubert's great posthumous Sonata in B-flat Major, an arduous interpretative test for any pianist. Favoring "a generally quiet range of dynamics that was almost hypnotic in its delicacy of nuance and expression . . . he drew the listener into the very heart of the music and made its every change of detail and direction a momentous event." (*NYT*, 18 Feb 1974)

If Lupu is at his greatest with Schubert, he is almost equally recognized for his Brahms interpretations. His impressive performance (10 Feb 1980) of the notoriously difficult Brahms Sonata No. 3 in F Major at Avery Fisher Hall "had rhythmic flexibility, plasticity of phrase and a nice balance of freedom and license. The slow movements, taken at excruciatingly deliberate speeds, caught the essentially Brahmsian tone of sweet regret." (*NYT*, 11 Feb 1980) In his performance (27 Feb 1987) of Brahms's Concerto No. 1 with the Los Angeles Philharmonic Orchestra, André Previn conducting, Lupu found the essence of Brahms, playing the big first movement "with a compelling force and authority. He articulated the slow movement with a kind of mystically ethereal lyricism that he alone, among his contemporaries, can achieve." (*LAHE*, 2 March 1987)

Lupu often performs Mozart concertos. His playing (20 Aug 1982) of the Mozart A Major Concerto, K. 488, with England's National Youth Orchestra, Christopher Seaman conducting, "was a wonder of delicate under-statement. For some, Mr. Lupu's periodic retreat into near-inaudibility may have seemed precious or self-conscious, yet such contained beauty of expression, backed by pianism of the greatest subtlety and finesse, is rare indeed." (*DT*, 23 Aug 1982) A performance of "rare and eloquent proportion" describes Lupu's reading at a 1986 Queen Elizabeth Hall concert of the Mozart Concerto K. 491 with the English Chamber Orchestra, Sir Colin Davis conducting: "Few pianists would dare such complete simplicity in their handling [in the slow movement] of all those gentle insistent repeated notes. Few indeed, could." (*TL*, 27 Sept 1986)

In September 1979 Lupu and the Los Angeles Philharmonic Orchestra under Lawrence Foster performed all five Beethoven concertos in four concerts at the Hollywood Bowl. Lupu's reading of the Concerto No. 2 was distinguished more for cool intellect than warmth of response. Concerto No. 3 was remark-able for its brilliance, reflection, arrogance and profundity, but, any "stretches of harshness in Lupu's playing were offset by evaporative pianissimos, glowingly adhesive legatos, and an absolutely lucid, frequently inspired account of the indi-vidual phrase." (*LAHE*, 6 Sept 1979)

At a Fort Worth, Texas, recital (12 Feb 1985) that began with two Beethoven sonatas (op. 109 and op. 110) and concluded with the Schumann Fantasia in C Major, Lupu found a wealth of inner voices and accents that lesser pianists either do not recognize or cannot illuminate. At all times "the sonori-ties of his playing had rare depth and beauty . . . whether a thundering *forte* or a whispered *pianissimo*. . . . But above all, there was a richness of poetic thought that turns a recital into a feast." (*DMN*, 15 Feb 1985)

On 27 March 1994 Lupu played the Mozart Concerto in A Major, K. 488, in London with Sir Colin Davis and the London Symphony Orchestra. "As ever, Lupu's control of the quietest playing that has possibly ever been heard in a live performance of this concerto was total in the slow movement. Notes

seemed to drop out of the air and into place . . . imperceptibly phrased into life."
(*TL*, 28 March 1994)

"Magical" and "mystical" also crop up frequently in the Lupu reviews.
It may be that his greatest gift is his ability to entrance an audience, an undefin-
able quality that transcends technique and general musicianship.

Radu Lupu has made comparatively few recordings—mostly works of
Beethoven, Schubert and Brahms, and some excellent Mozart recordings. He
made his recording debut with London (Decca) Records, a recording of
Beethoven's Concerto No. 3 that was awarded the *Grand Prix du Disque* for 1972
(see Discog.). The middle movement, with its slow, deliberate tempo and lovely
interplay between piano and orchestra, and the superbly articulated finale make
this one of the finest recordings of the Beethoven Concerto No. 3.

Four Schubert discs (see Discog.) stand out for sheer beauty and musical qualities. The collection of Schubert Impromptus (D. 899 and D. 935), in
particular, is an absolute delight. The implied (but deceptive) simplicity of most
of these pieces is maintained through Lupu's sustained, controlled lyricism.
Tempos are never hurried, and the fine balance between melodic line and accompaniment is preserved with innate sensitivity.

Lupu has made two fine Brahms recordings. The incredibly difficult
Sonata No. 3 in F Minor, op. 5 (see Discog.) is almost a symphony for piano,
and Lupu creates a monumental keyboard landmark from its five highly contrasted movements. But the Brahms recital album (Piano Music, see Discog.) is
perhaps the most attractive for the discophile. "What is most treasurable about it
is the quiet rapture of some of the most quintessentially Brahmsian moments. .
. . This remains as fine a selection of Brahms's piano works as you are likely to
find on one record." (*Gram*, Aug 1987)

SELECTED REFERENCES

Beigel, Greta. "Romanian Pianist Lupu: An Insecure Winner." *Los Angeles
    Times*, 7 Sept 1979, sec. 4, pp. 1, 22–23.
Freed, Richard. "Mozart for Two Pianos." *Stereo Review*, Jan 1992, p. 73.
Hume, Paul. "Keeping Up with the Cliburns (and the Joneses)." *Saturday
    Review of Literature*, 29 Oct 1966, pp. 56–57, 72.
Lupu, Radu. Biographical notes, *New York Public Library* clippings file.
Montparker, Carol. "Murray Perahia and Radu Lupu: Friendship and Music at
    the Highest Level." *Clavier,* July-Aug 1985, pp. 32–34.
———. "Radu Lupu: Acclaim in Spite of Himself." *Clavier*, May-June 1981,
    pp. 10–14.
———. "Radu Lupu in Conversation." *Clavier*, July-Aug 1992, pp. 12–16.
Rockwell, John. "Who Says Modern Pianists Are Un-Romantic?" *New York
    Times*, 3 June 1984, sec. 2, p. 23.
"Success by Short Cut." *Time*, 21 Oct 1966, p. 96.
Woodward, Ian. "Wonderboy." *Christian Science Monitor*, 10 Sept 1970, p.
    19.
See also Bibliography: IWWM; Kol/Que; New/Gro; Rat/Cle.

SELECTED REVIEWS

BaS: 8 Nov 1976; 8 Feb 1980. *BG*: 14 Feb 1987. *CST*: 10 Aug 1977; 12 Feb
1988; 24 Jan 1989. *CT*: 9 March 1984; 23 Jan 1990; 1 Feb 1991. *DMN*:
15 Feb 1985. *DT*: 23 Aug 1982; 1 Dec 1985. *GM*: 1 Dec 1985. *G-M*: 17
March 1982; 20 Feb 1985. *Gram*: Aug 1987. *LAHE*: 6 Sept 1979; 2
March 1987. *LAT*: 11 Feb 1974; 16 Feb 1976; 6 Sept 1979; 19 March
1981; 6 Feb 1990; 7 Feb 1995. *MH*: 7 April 1975. *MM*: Aug 1983; Aug
1985. *MT*: Jan 1970; June 1983; Feb 1987. *NY*: 23 Feb 1976; 25 Feb
1980. *NYP*: 13 April 1967. *NYT*: 13 April 1967; 18 Feb 1974; 6 Feb
1976; 11 Feb 1980; 12 March 1982; 14 March 1988; 29 Jan 1991; 16 Feb
1991. *PI*: 10 Feb 1984; 29 Jan 1991; 14 Feb 1992; 17 Jan 1995. *SFC*: 27
Jan 1978; 21 March 1981. *STL*: 29 Oct 1978. *TL*: 28 Nov 1969; 21 Sept
1979; 27 Sept 1986; 9 Nov 1986; 31 May 1990; 22 Oct 1992; 28 March
1994. *WP*: 17 Jan 1990.

SELECTED DISCOGRAPHY

Beethoven: Concerto No. 1 in C Major, op. 15; Concerto No. 2 in B-flat Major,
op. 19. Decca 6.42602 AZ. Mehta/Israel PO.
Beethoven: Concerto No. 3 in C Minor, op. 37; Thirty-Two Variations on an
Original Theme. London CS 6715. Foster/London SO.
Beethoven: Concerto No. 5 in E-flat Major, op. 73. London 400050-2.
Mehta/Israel PO.
Beethoven: Sonata in C Minor, op. 13; Sonata in C-sharp Minor, op. 27, no. 2;
Sonata in C Major, op. 53. London 421031-2.
Brahms: Piano Music. Ops. 79, 117, 118, 119. London 417599-2.
Brahms: Sonata No. 3 in F Minor, op. 5; Sextet, op. 18 (Theme and Variations,
arr.) London 417122-2.
Grieg: Concerto in A Minor, op. 16. Schumann: Concerto in A Minor, op. 54.
London 414432-2. Previn/London SO.
Mozart: Concerto No. 12 in A Major, K. 414; Concerto No. 21 in C Major, K.
467. London 417773-2. Segal/English CO.
Mozart: Sonata in D Major, K. 448. Schubert: Fantasia in F Minor, D. 940.
Sony Classical MK-39511 (CD). With Murray Perahia.
Schubert: Impromptus D. 899 and D. 935. London 411711-2.
Schubert: Sonata in Λ Major, D. 664; Sonata in B-flat Major, D. 960. London
440295-2.
Schubert: Sonata in A Minor, D. 845; Sonata in G Major, D. 894. London
416640-2.
Schubert: Sonata in C Minor, D. 958; *Moments musicaux*. London 417785-2.
Schumann: *Humoreske*, op. 20; *Kinderscenen*, op. 15; *Kreisleriana*, op. 16.
Decca 440 496-2.

VIDEO

Mozart on Tour Vol. 6.   Concerto in F Major, K. 459.   Philips 440 070 243-3.
Zinman/*Deutsche Kammerphilharmonie.*

LYMPANY, MOURA: b. Saltash (Cornwall), England, 18 August 1916.

> If anything I am more resilient and excited about concerts than ever.
> I'm a Leo, you see—outgoing, strong, disciplined and hard working; in-
> dispensable qualities for a pianist.
>
> Moura Lympany (*Gramophone*, September 1989)

Moura Lympany has every right to be proud of being a Leo. In 1989, when she
made the statement quoted above to interviewer Bryce Morrison, Lympany was
73 years old and happily celebrating 60 years of giving concerts. She is now
recognized as one of England's finest pianists. She is also a survivor. Holding
on to her career has never been easy, and along the way she has endured enough
for two lifetimes: two divorces, the loss of four infant sons (one stillborn, twins
miscarried at 5 months, one who died after 35 hours), two operations for breast
cancer. By any criteria, Dame Moura has proved herself an exceptionally resilient Leo.

   She began life as Mary Gertrude Johnstone, daughter of Beatrice
Limpenny and Captain John Johnstone. Her intelligent, ambitious mother had
for several years tutored the children of a wealthy banking family in St.
Petersburg, Russia. Treated more as a member of the family than a servant,
Beatrice Limpenny returned to England in 1915 (at the height of World War I)
with a deep love for everything Russian. She was then 35 years old, an ener-
getic, cultivated woman conversant in several languages and with a good head for
business. The handsome Captain Johnstone, on the other hand, had little ambition and no visible means of support. She knew, and he actually warned her,
that he would not make a good husband. She nevertheless married him and most
of the time supported him.

   The Johnstones named their first child Mary, but always called her
Moura, the Russian diminutive for Mary, and they raised her and her two
younger brothers in Teignmouth, on the south Devon coast, in a house her
clever mother had purchased with her savings. Mrs. Johnstone wanted her children to have the best education possible, but although she taught piano, cello,
Russian, German and French lessons, it was hard to save money for tuition. An
advertisement in a Catholic magazine settled the problem for Moura. The ad offered a place at the *Couvent des Soeurs de Marie* in Tongeren (Tongres),
Belgium, for only £5 a term. Thus during the Easter holiday of 1923 Moura,
not quite seven years old, sailed alone on the Ostend ferry, with a name tag at-
tached to her coat. What might have been a miserable, lonely childhood became

instead some of the happiest years of her life. She already knew French, and both the nuns and the Belgian family who took her in on holidays treated her so kindly that she would love Belgium and the Belgians for the rest of her life.

The piano fascinated her even as a toddler. Once her mother had taught her the right-hand notes, she spent hours trying to invent tunes or copy the ones she heard her mother play. As soon as she started piano lessons at school, the nuns, realizing her innate talent, arranged piano lessons twice a month with Professor Jules Debefve at the Liege Conservatory. By the time she was nine, she was practicing five hours a day, and could play all 48 Bach Preludes and Fugues. After four years in Belgium, the little English girl not only spoke French all the time, but had become thoroughly European in her manners. When she finally returned home for a visit, an uncle, outraged to find her so "foreign," insisted that she remain in England to be "re-Anglicized."

Mrs. Johnstone, now on the lookout for an inexpensive London school, negotiated a low board-and-tuition fee at the Convent School of Our Lady of Sion in London, where she had once taught, and that ended Moura's four immensely happy years at Tongeren. She began private piano lessons with Ambrose Coviello, a professor at London's Royal Academy of Music, and at his suggestion applied (1929) for the Ada Lewis Scholarship at the RAM. On holiday that summer at the seaside town of Bexhill, she heard her first professional concert—an orchestral program, conducted by Basil Cameron, at the White Rock Pavilion in Hastings. Hearing the concert was so exciting that the 12-year-old Lympany agitated for permission to ask Basil Cameron if she could play for him. She easily passed the audition, and Cameron engaged her to play the Mendelssohn Concerto No. 1 in G Minor at Harrogate, Yorkshire, on 8 August 1929.

When the matter of publicity arose, Cameron asked Mrs. Johnstone for Moura's full name. He thought "Moura" was a good concert name, but rejected the "Johnstone." As Lympany tells the story in her autobiography, Cameron then asked her mother for her maiden name. "'Limpenny,' she answered, stressing the first syllable. 'A bit better,' remarked the conductor. . . . 'What about the old spelling,' my mother suggested helpfully. 'It is Lympany.' 'Perfect!' exclaimed Basil Cameron." (Lympany, *Moura Lympany*) In those few moments Moura Johnstone became Moura Lympany.

The concert was a splendid success, and shortly afterward the 13-year-old pianist learned that she had won the Ada Lewis Scholarship and would enter the Royal Academy of Music that September. (Meanwhile she would still be a boarder at Our Lady of Sion.) She continued her studies with Ambrose Coviello at the RAM and graduated (1932) with highest honors. In June of that year, still only 15 years old, she played the Grieg Concerto at the annual RAM Queen's Hall concert, with Sir Henry Wood conducting the RAM orchestra.

Lympany then had nine months of study with Paul Weingarten in Vienna, where, courtesy of her shrewd mother, she received room and board at the *Dritte Bezirk* convent in exchange for speaking English with the other girls. With Weingarten, Lympany worked mostly on romantic works, notably the Rachmaninoff Concerto No. 2 in C Minor. That summer (1933) she entered the Liszt Piano Competition in Budapest, but made no showing. (Annie Fischer placed first, Louis Kentner third.) She returned to England and went to work as an accompanist for a singing teacher.

Winning the Elizabeth Stokes Scholarship enabled her to have advanced study with Coviello, but after two terms, Lympany's mother arranged for private lessons with Mathilde Verne, a strict pedagogue and famous as the teacher who had trained Solomon. "She disciplined me," says Lympany. "Up to then I had a natural instinct and technique." (Elder, "The Legendary...") Verne put her on a regular practice routine (four hours a day, broken into one-hour sessions) and made her do exercises (stretching, thirds, sixths, octaves). Since then Lympany has practiced four hours a day and religiously done those exercises. And she has never forgotten Verne's secrets of good practice: *regularity*, no matter how you feel, no matter what you think you have to do; and *mental control*, that is, always being aware of how you play every note and why you played it that particular way. Verne arranged Lympany's first professional recital, at the Wigmore Hall, and about this same time Lympany played the Schumann Concerto with Sir Thomas Beecham at Croydon.

Mathilde Verne died unexpectedly in 1936. Lympany had had only a brief year with Verne, but has always been grateful for those productive lessons. She might not have known where to turn next, but her ever-on-the-alert mother managed to get her an audition with the British Women's Symphony, and that organization engaged Lympany to play the Delius Concerto and Vincent d'Indy's Symphony on a French Mountain Air. Since she knew neither work, a friend suggested she seek help from Tobias Matthay, one of England's greatest pedagogues. He not only helped her; he turned out to be the "guiding musical light" of her life.

Matthay taught her, she says, "how to take interpretation out of the realm of vague feeling and to project it, consciously, as a planned pattern of musical thought." (*Etude*, May 1949) He made her realize that she had to stop phrasing by instinct, as she had always done. "You must learn to phrase. . . . Always go towards the next note. A phrase is leading to the next phrase; know where a phrase is leading and where the climax is that you're going toward." (Elder, "The Legendary...") Matthay also taught her how to study away from the piano, and ever since she usually takes a score to bed in the evening and phrases it in the way Matthay had showed her. For instance, she remembers working on the Mendelssohn *Variations sérieuses* in bed, singing them to herself to see where the phrases were going.

All told, Lympany studied with Matthay for 10 years. In June 1938, two years after she began working with him, he suggested that she enter the Ysaÿe Piano Competition (now called the Queen Elisabeth of Belgium International Music Competition). Emil Gilels captured first prize and Moura Lympany, then age 21, placed second. Judge Artur Rubinstein was so taken with her playing that he induced his concert manager in Paris to arrange a tour for Lympany in the 1938–39 season: Belgium, France, Holland, Italy, Scandinavia, Spain, Portugal.

Meanwhile, in 1939 Lympany married Colin Defries, a businessman and amateur pianist. Although he was 32 years her senior, it was a happy relationship; her husband took care of all her concert affairs, and when she practiced concertos, he always played the orchestral accompaniments on a second piano.

Unfortunately Lympany's well-launched career came to a halt during World War II. She gave a few concerts during the war years, but most of the time traveled about Britain playing for hospitalized soldiers, factory workers and dock hands. Early in 1940 the Society for Cultural Relations with the USSR organized a concert of new Russian works never performed in England. The Society asked Clifford Curzon to play the Khachaturian Concerto. Unable to accept, Curzon suggested Lympany in his stead. Gifted with a wonderful memory, she learned the work in just one month and in the spring of 1940 played the Khachaturian Concerto at Queen's Hall under the baton of composer Alan Bush.

Khachaturian's concerto created a sensation. England had never heard anything like it. And Lympany adored it. "It was new, it was modern, it had fantastic pace, it was a thrilling work, and somehow it suited the warlike mood of the nation and the time." As for young Moura Lympany's playing, it took the critics by surprise. Her "virtuosity was as unexpected, as dazzling, and as agreeable to concertgoers in wartime London as a friendly firework in the blackout." (Lympany, *Moura Lympany*) The Khachaturian Concerto made her famous. She played it just about everywhere and recorded it for Decca Records; and incidentally it gave her a reputation as a Russian "specialist."

In the spring of 1945 the British Council sent Moura Lympany, by then one of Britain's foremost pianists, and Sir Adrian Boult to play in the newly liberated Paris. She played the Rawsthorne Piano Concerto No. 1, a work she had learned for the occasion, and also, once again, the Khachaturian Concerto, with Boult conducting the *Orchestre du Conservatoire*. The following year (May 1946) the British Council chose the same two musicians to represent Britain at the first Prague International Festival ("Prague Spring") organized after the war. Lympany played the John Ireland Piano Concerto, with Sir Adrian Boult conducting, and also gave a solo recital. The Paris and Prague assignments were the first of many cultural missions for Lympany. She was one of the first British pianists to tour the USSR after the war and, as she puts it, "It was my destiny to give the fantastic Khachaturian Concerto its first performance in London, Paris, Milan, Brussels and Australia."

Lympany was made a Fellow of the Royal Academy of Musicians in 1948, the year in which she also made her American debut. (She had vacationed in America in 1946, during which time she broadcast four times, twice from New York City and twice from Montreal.) At the request of an admirer (her recordings had made her well known in America), she gave her first American performance in Seattle, then on 24 November 1948 made an enormously successful formal debut at New York's Town Hall.

On this fateful trip to America, Lympany met Bennet Korn, vice-president of Dumont Television. He was her own age, and they fell instantly in love. In 1950 Lympany divorced her husband of ten years, and in 1951 married Korn. They lived in New York and Long Island, and for three years Lympany pretty much stayed away from the concert stage. But she kept up her practicing. During this marriage she gave some concerts in the United States, made brief tours of England, and in 1956 made a short tour of Czechoslovakia and Russia as soloist with the London Philharmonic Orchestra. Deeply in love, Lympany gave most of her time to her home and husband.

In 1960 she returned from a five-week tour of Australia and discovered that her husband had fallen in love with another woman. After the divorce (1961) she had a miserable year alone in New York, often taking comfort in sleeping pills, before making up her mind to go home to London and get busy recharging her career. That proved by no means easy. Away from the concert stage for a decade, Lympany had been virtually forgotten by the music world. In her autobiography she recalls that a "whole new generation of young whiz-kids at the piano had come up, and I was eclipsed." But she kept going.

In 1969 Lympany required surgery for cancer of the left breast, but three months after the operation she played (30 Oct 1969) both Cyril Scott's Concerto and Prokofiev's Piano Concerto No. 4, op. 53, for the left hand, at the Royal Festival Hall. Disturbed by her reviews and not satisfied with her playing in general, she went to Ilona Kabos, a pedagogue famous for helping concert pianists, to find out what had gone wrong with her playing. Kabos was just what Lympany needed. Confidante as well as teacher, Kabos helped Lympany to regain her shattered self-confidence. "She was pitiless and disapproving," Lympany says in her autobiography, "but continued to teach me where and how I was going wrong. She could tell if I was faking a passage I did not know too well technically, or any emotion I did not really feel. But she never destroyed me or my individuality. That was her great strength."

Lympany tested herself playing charity concerts and, pushed on by Kabos, gave a recital (20 Jan 1972) at Queen Elizabeth Hall: the Haydn E Minor Sonata, Schumann F-sharp Minor Sonata in the first half and the 24 Chopin Preludes in the second half. A reviewer not wholly satisfied with the way Lympany played the Chopin Preludes, nevertheless applauded her "heroic playing" in the Schumann and her "clear, quiet, almost private, performance" of the Haydn. (*TL*, 21 Jan 1972) Undaunted, Lympany gave more concerts in England and, on short notice, substituted for Gina Bachauer, playing three concerts in Yugoslavia.

In 1973 Lympany saw a throat specialist about a chronic irritated throat and cough. He ordered her to leave London for a warm, dry climate and not to talk for a month. She rented a small house in Rasiguères, a tiny village (population 150) near Perpignan in southern France, close to the Spanish border; spent nearly two years there and fell in love with the town, the people and the vineyards. (The feeling has been returned. The villagers have named a wine in her honor—*Cuvée Moura Lympany*.) Rasiguères, she says, has been her salvation. She eventually purchased a house and vineyard there and usually spends part of every year in the village and, since 1983, the rest of the time at her apartment in Monte Carlo.

The year 1979 (the 50th anniversary of her debut at age 12) began most auspiciously. On 6 January she was appointed a Commander of the British Empire (C.B.E.), and later that anniversary year Belgium awarded her the *Decoration de Commandeur de l'Ordre de la Couronne du Royaume de Belgique*, in recognition of her services to that country. On 13 June 1992 Lympany was made a Dame Commander of the British Empire.

In 1980 Lympany began planning a festival at Rasiguères. The first one, named the *Festival de la Musique et du Vin Rasiguères*, took place in June 1981 and was enormously successful, thanks to the help of friends like Victoria de los Angeles, Elizabeth Harewood, Larry Adler and Edward Heath. In 1986 Lympany inaugurated another festival, the Festival of the Seven Chapels, in Guidel, Brittany, under the patronage of Prince Louis de Polignac.

Meanwhile, in September 1983 she underwent a second breast operation and —always resilient—bounded back. In 1989 she celebrated the 60th anniversary of her debut with an all-Chopin recital (10 Sept 1989) at the Royal Festival Hall, and was overwhelmed by astonishing reviews proclaiming her the "Amazing Lympany," "Queen of the Ivories," a "Poet of the Piano."

In her 1991 autobiography the strong-minded Dame Moura wrote that she is in excellent health, has learned to cope, has no intention of failing and is far too busy to think about old age. She looks to a future of more concerts, directing and developing the two festivals (Rasiguères, Guidel) and enjoying her havens in Monte Carlo and Rasiguères.

In choosing her repertoire Lympany followed "treasured advice" from her teacher Tobias Matthay, who insisted that pianists should play works for which they are physically and temperamentally suited. Virtuoso works like the Rachmaninoff concertos and preludes came easily to Lympany; and Matthay taught her not to resist the inclination to be a virtuoso player. As a result, the Rachmaninoff and Khachaturian concertos early on established her career.

Over the course of that career she has played almost 60 concertos or other works with orchestra, which is not too surprising, given her quick memory. In addition to the standard concertos (Beethoven, Brahms, Chopin, Grieg, Rachmaninoff, Tchaikovsky, etc.) she has also played concerted works by Berkeley, Delius, Ireland, Rawsthorne, Scott, Williamson, among others. Her solo repertoire, equally eclectic, ranges from Bach and Scarlatti through Mozart, Beethoven, the Romantics and Impressionists to Bartók, Schoenberg and Samuel Barber.

Because of her great success with the Rachmaninoff and Khachaturian concertos and her reputation as a romantic virtuoso player, Lympany hesitated about playing Beethoven. When she finally set her mind to playing Beethoven's Variations in C Minor, she went "in fear and trepidation" to Artur Schnabel to ask how to play the work. Having convinced herself that she was not a Beethoven player, her Beethoven playing was timid, stiff and hesitant, but Schnabel changed her concept of the Variations. She had been treating them as an exercise. He showed her how to approach them as the true work of beauty they really are. In another attempt to get away from her romantic, virtuoso reputation, she had had some lessons with Edward Steuermann while living in America during her second marriage. Steuermann, who had studied with Schoenberg, had a completely different approach from Matthay. "He was a tremendous brain, a great stickler for what is written, Germanic and classical." (Lympany, *Moura Lympany*)

Lympany invariably approaches a work the way Matthay taught her, that is, she plays the piece through and through until she feels she has an understanding of it. Next she works on the technical difficulties, then phrases the piece the way Matthay had taught her to do. All her life she has practiced as Verne taught her to do, four hours regularly, always paying attention to what she is doing, and always including the exercises Verne taught her. To keep in form, Lympany also does a few variants on Hanon and some Chopin studies, most of the time the same ones.

She has never done any teaching but, unlike many of her colleagues, she approves of piano competitions. Despite any drawbacks, Lympany believes that competitions give young pianists something to work toward and help them to build endurance and self-confidence.

In her own words, Lympany is a practitioner of what she calls the English school of pianism—not the flashy kind of playing but the kind where everything is done without exaggeration; and her keyboard manner, quiet and without extraneous motions or gestures, bears this out. Her appeal, wrote one critic, "lies in her dignified approach to music, in her reliability. She radiates assurance to her listeners that while she may not deal in extreme excitations, she will never go far wrong either." (*NYT*, 10 Nov 1981)

Critics admire her clear, lucid and obviously carefully thought-out playing. They admire her ability to let the musical phrase have time to breathe, to phrase a line or a fragment thereof with a feeling for subtle nuance that brings the music to life. She can be heroic without resorting to bombast, tender without melting into sentimentality, virtuosic without recourse to vulgar display. But even admiring critics sometimes find that Lympany's playing lacks warmth and abandon, that sometimes its very refinement makes it sound too serious. One recurring criticism has been that Lympany's tendency to use identical pedaling and *rubato* throughout a program gives the music an impersonal, at times monotonous, sound.

What matters is that this remarkably strong pianist has sustained her concert career for more than six decades (she has an enormous following in Great Britain); and since her 60th anniversary celebrations in 1989, Dame Moura "has again become a celebrity, and the rapidly thinning ranks of artists in her generation make her performances all the more prized." (Elder, "The Legendary. . .")

Lympany played a long and daring program for her American recital debut (24 Nov 1948) at Town Hall, and one critic responded with the kind of long, analytical review usually accorded only the seasoned, well-established performer. In part: "Miss Lympany's performances . . . had a refreshing and irresistible wholesomeness, a freedom from exaggerations, an impeccable taste, a sanity, and at the same time a definite individuality, which, combined with first-rate virtuosity, made her performances noteworthy. Her pianism was unusually clean-cut and at the same time unusually poised and controlled." (*NYT*, 25 Nov 1948)

Lympany's Carnegie Hall recital on 20 November 1957 earned a resounding bravo. She had, in the view of one critic, finally found herself: "She has arrived at a point where they [her interpretations] must be taken on her own terms. For the playing was completely authoritative and of a piece, and it automatically placed her among the ranks of the world's important pianists." (*NYT*, 21 Nov 1957)

As one of the judges for the 1983 University of Maryland's Piano Festival and Competition (in 1986 renamed for William Kapell), Lympany gave a solo recital (21 July 1983) of three well-known works—the Beethoven "Moonlight" Sonata; Schumann's Fantasia, op. 17; and the Brahms "Handel" Variations, op. 24. "Lympany commanded a performance marked by a dramatic understatement of themes. Her playing was extremely clean and lucid. . . . She was just as impressive for her swift keyboard technique as she was for her refined sense of style." (*WP*, 22 July 1983)

Lympany's performance (4 June 1983) of the Mozart Concerto in B-flat Major, K. 456, with the St. Louis Symphony Orchestra, Raymond Leppard conducting, "was careful without being overly cautious; you got the feeling that every detail of every note was pondered before it was presented. The voice of the piano was perfectly integrated into the sound of the orchestra, the gentle tone she drew from the concert grand would have made an early music specialist weep for joy." (*SLPD*, 7 June 1983)

At her all-Chopin London recital (10 Sept 1989) celebrating her 60 years on the concert platform, Lympany played "with all the agility and enthusiasm of youth and with all the maturity and subtlety of experience. . . . [Hers] is a practical, no-nonsense approach, in which the music itself guides the way she thinks about it." (*DT*, 12 Sept 1989)

In 1992 Dame Moura returned as judge and soloist to the University of Maryland's William Kapell Piano Competition and Festival. Her all-Chopin recital (17 July 1992) —the 24 Preludes and the Sonata in B Minor—prompted this: "Chopin's music epitomizes the piano, and Lympany's playing sums up an old-school style; the combination can be most compelling. Lympany opened with the Preludes, Op. 28. Her characteristic legato and singing melodic line were at once evident. Some might object to pedaling that was overly generous in passages. . . . But no one could argue with the limpid tone, gentle phrasing and overall elegance she brought to these 24 masterpieces. . . . The remainder of the program was devoted to the B Minor Sonata, where Lympany produced handsome weight in the keys, economical and relaxed at the same time." (Kate Rivers, *WP*, 20 July 1992. Reprinted by permission.)

On 9 October 1994 a Boston audience "heard a living legend," Dame Moura at age 78, playing a herculean program (Beethoven's 32 Variations in C Minor, Mozart's C Major Sonata, K. 330, Brahms's Paganini Variations (Book II), Debussy's *Reflets dans l'eau*, Rachmaninoff's Preludes, op. 32, nos. 5 and 10, Liszt's *Les jeux d'eaux à la Villa d'Este* and Polonaise in E Major) and playing it "with stunning artistry." An insightful review of that recital reads: "Most striking is her ability to change sound and musical personality for each composer. Though this approach is not always prized by pianists, such radical change of voices added a thrilling depth and variety to a recital that made complete sense." (Peter Catalano, *American Record Guide*, March/April 1995. Reprinted by permission.)

Lympany made many recordings from the 1940s to the 1960s. Initially Decca asked her to record Rachmaninoff's 24 Preludes. As she relates, "I knew two of them, but Matthay taught me the others; I learned them and recorded them as I went along. They received very good notices, and in the early 1950s I redid them for long-playing records." (Elder, "The Legendary. . .") Decca also arranged for her to do the Rachmaninoff Concerto No. 3, the Khachaturian and the Saint-Saëns No. 2, followed by the Schumann, the Liszt E Flat and the Grieg concertos. She later made some recordings for EMI. To date, several of these early recordings (Decca and HMV [EMI]) have been reissued on CD.

One LP (2 discs) and seven CD collections provide an overview of the pianist's repertoire. The LP, titled *The Lympany Legend* (see Discog.), contains an elegant collection of EMI recordings dating from 1947 through 1952 (large-scale, substantial works like the Schumann Symphonic Etudes and the Brahms-Paganini Variations [Book I]) that reaffirm Lympany's reputation for both tremendous technique and musicianship. Two toccatas—by Ravel and Prokofiev—and Liszt's Mephisto Waltz No. 1 are scintillating and exciting. Shorter compositions by Brahms, Albéniz, Chopin, Debussy, Granados and Shostakovich round out this notable collection.

There are also two CD collections, each titled *Best-Loved Piano Classics* (see Discog.). Recorded in 1988 and 1991, these albums contain mostly short, very well-known and time-tested favorites played by a seasoned artist in her seventies. They offer generous samplings of music from all periods: Baroque (Bach, Handel, Daquin); Classic (Mozart, Haydn); a wide spectrum of Romantic music from Beethoven through Chopin, Liszt, Schumann; works by Debussy and Ravel. Here "Moura Lympany displays her limpid sound, plastic phrasing, and brilliant technique. The distinguished British pianist plans the smallest details, yet her playing possesses remarkable spontaneity." (*CL*, Jan 1991) These two collections are among the finest recitals of their kind to be found anywhere.

In England mere mention of the Khachaturian Concerto in D-flat Major brings to mind the name of Moura Lympany. Her recording of this concerto with Anatole Fistoulari and the London Philharmonic Orchestra was made in 1953. The Saint-Saëns Concerto No. 2 in G Minor was recorded with Jean Martinon conducting the same orchestra in 1951. These two concertos were later issued together on a single Olympia CD (see Discog.) to celebrate the pianist's 60 years on the concert stage. One reviewer particularly relished the "brilliantly played first-movement cadenza and the nocturne-like *Andante* of the Khachaturian, and the Saint-Saëns performance . . . where the playing glistens with virtuosity, panache and charm." (*Gram*, Sept 1989)

Lympany has programmed and recorded Russian music and Russian concertos so frequently that she (contrary to her inclinations) became known as a Russian "specialist." Her recordings of Prokofiev's Concertos No. 1 in D-flat Major and No. 3 in C Major were made for EMI in 1958, with Walter Susskind conducting the Philharmonia Orchestra, and are now available in CD reissue (see Discog.). The one-movement D flat Concerto "is played simply and straightforwardly but it emerges as a strong and youthfully ebullient piece." And in the

C major Concerto "there is plenty of virtuosity and excitement." (*Gram*, Dec 1986)

In her "Russian" period, Lympany also recorded the first three Rachmaninoff concertos: No. 1 in F-sharp Minor, op. 1, in 1954; No. 2 in C Minor, op. 18, in 1953; and No. 3 in D Minor, op. 30, in 1952. She played the first two concertos with the Philharmonia Orchestra, conducted by Nicolai Malko. Anthony Collins led the New Symphony Orchestra in Concerto No. 3, and Lympany's reading of this difficult concerto ranks among the finest ever. "What a marvelously deft and imaginative performance it is, full of personality and poetry, yet crystal clear and totally free of spurious interpretative points." (*Gram*, March 1988) The two Prokofiev and three Rachmaninoff concertos have been combined by Olympia and issued in two separate CDs (see Discog.).

The Rachmaninoff Preludes are again available, for Lympany recorded them for CD in 1993. "This is Dame Moura Lympany's third recording of the Rachmaninoff Preludes and it is in many ways her finest. For here is glowing evidence that recreative energy, richly coloured and modified by time, can live on more heartwarmingly than ever." (*Gram*, Feb 1994)

A program of Debussy's music (see Discog.) adds another distinctive collection to the Lympany discography. "Subtle and distinctive, this is among the most memorable of recent Debussy recitals. Dame Moura may have lost some of her delicious lightness, her nonchalant pianistic prowess, yet as she nears her eightieth birthday her playing is more sensitive and exploratory than ever." (*Gram*, Oct 1994) In 1995 Lympany recorded the Chopin Preludes, op. 28, for Erato.

Still awaiting reissue are Lympany's 1960 recordings of the Chopin Nocturnes (available on cassette, see Discog.), the Chopin Sonata in B Minor, the Schumann Fantasy, the Beethoven Concerto No. 5 and the *Sonata Pathétique*, op. 13. The Beethoven, on LP, was issued in 1957 by the Book-of-the-Month Club as one of their Music Appreciation Records. The "Emperor" performance was conducted by Thomas Scherman with the Stadium Concerts Symphony Orchestra.

SELECTED REFERENCES

Elder, Dean. "The Legendary Lympany." *Clavier*, Feb 1992, pp. 10–17.
———. "Moura Lympany's Technical Regimen." *Clavier*, Feb 1992, pp. 18–19.
Foss, Hubert. "Moura Lympany: A Great British Pianist." *The Canon*, July 1951, pp. 593–596.
Hamilton, Allan. "I just loved the piano." *London Times*, 17 Aug 1991, p. 46.
Kammerer, Rafael. "Moura Lympany: Artist of Wide Interests." *Musical America*, March 1958, pp. 9–10.
Lympany, Moura. "On Becoming a Better Pianist." *Etude*, May 1949, pp. 281, 324.
———. "Report on Antipodes: Australia's musical life is full, colorful and varied." *Musical Courier*, June 1960, p. 11.

Lympany, Moura, and Margot Strickland. *Moura Lympany: Her Autobi-
ography*. London: Peter Owen, 1991.
Morrison, Bryce. "Cornish at Heart." *Gramophone*, Sept 1989, p. 409.
"Moura Lympany at 70." *Music and Musicians*, Sept 1986, pp. 6–7.
Myers, Leslie. "Symphony has Lympany tonight." *Clarion-Ledger* (Jackson,
Mississippi), 6 Jan 1989, sec. C, p. 1.
Shulgold, Marc. "Lympany '84: Toast of Rasiguères." *Los Angeles Times*, 10
March 1984, sec. 5, p. 9.
Stringer, Robin. "The Days of Wine and Music." *Telegraph Sunday Magazine*,
10 June 1979, pp. 43–45.
See also Bibliography: Ewe/Li; IWWM; New/Gro; Ran/Kon; Rat/Cle.

SELECTED REVIEWS

ARG: March/April 1995. *DT*: 12 Sept 1989. *GM*: 22 Aug 1991. *LAT*: 26
Nov 1956; 15 Aug 1958; 26 Aug 1961; 15 Feb 1965; 12 March 1984; 19
Nov 1988. *MM*: Feb 1974; Dec 1984; Feb 1985. *MO*: May 1980. *MT*:
Feb 1985. *NYT*: 25 Nov 1948; 7 Jan 1950; 13 Dec 1954; 21 Nov 1957;
18 June 1965; 10 Nov 1981. *SLPD*: 7 June 1983. *STL*: 20 July 1975; 29
Oct 1978. *TL*: 21 June 1943; 25 May 1946; 22 April 1955; 14 May 1956;
6 March 1958; 29 April 1959; 1 Nov 1969; 21 Jan 1972; 27 Feb 1973; 30
Nov 1974; 20 Oct 1978; 13 Sept 1989. *WP*: 22 July 1983; 20 July 1992.

SELECTED DISCOGRAPHY

Beethoven: Concerto No. 5 in E-flat Major, op. 73; Sonata in C Minor, op. 13.
Music Appreciation Records MAR 5713.
Best-Loved Piano Classics. Albéniz-Godowsky: Tango. Beethoven: *Für Elise*;
Minuet in G. Brahms: Waltz No. 15. Chaminade: *Automne*. Chopin:
Etudes, op. 10, nos. 4 and 5; Fantaisie-Impromptu. Debussy: *Clair de lune*;
Golliwog's Cakewalk. Dvořák: Humoresque. Falla: Ritual Fire Dance.
Granados: The Maiden and the Nightingale. Liszt: *Un Sospiro*.
MacDowell: To a Wild Rose. Mozart: *Rondo alla turca*. Rachmaninoff:
Prelude in C-sharp Minor. Rubinstein: Melody in F. Schumann:
Träumerei. EMI CDZ 7 62523 2.
Best-Loved Piano Classics 2. Albéniz: *Malagueña (España)*. Bach-Hess: Jesu,
Joy of Man's Desiring. Beethoven: Sonata, op. 27, no. 2 (1. Adagio
sostenuto); *Rondo a capriccioso*, op. 129. Chopin: Mazurka, op. 17, no. 4;
Waltzes, op. 64, no. 2, op. 70, no. 1. Daquin: *Le Coucou*. Debussy: *La
Cathédrale engloutie*; *La Fille aux cheveux de lin*; *Reflets dans l'eau*.
Handel: Air and Variations (Suite No. 5). Paderewski: *Menuet célèbre*, op.
14, no. 1. Ravel: *Jeux d'eau*. Satie: *Gymnopédie* No. 1. Schumann: *Der
Vogel als Prophet*. Scriabin: Etude, op. 8, no. 12. EMI CDZ 7 67204 2.
Chopin: Nocturnes Nos. 1–19. Maestro cassette MCS2 5001.

Debussy: *Deux Arabesques*; Children's Corner; *La plus que lente*; *Poissons d'or (Images)*; *Prélude, Le petit nègre (Suite bergamesque)*; *Des pas sur la neige, La terrasse des audiences du clair de lune, Ondine, Feux d'artifice* (Preludes); *Pour les cinq doigts, Pour les arpèges composés* (Etudes); *L'Isle joyeuse*. EMI Classics for Pleasure 5 68237 2.

The Lympany Legend. Albéniz-Godowsky: Tango in D. Brahms: Intermezzo, op. 117, no. 2; Variations on a theme of Paganini, op. 35 (Book II). Chopin: *Fantasie-Impromptu*, op. 66. Debussy: *Clair de lune (Suite Bergamasque)*. Granados: *Quéjas, o la Maja y el ruiseñor (Goyescas)*. Liszt: *Feux follets*; *Les jeux d'eaux à a Villa d'Este*; Mephisto Waltz No. 1; Polonaise No. 2. Prokofiev: Toccata, op. 11. Schumann: Symphonic Etudes, op. 13; *Vogel als Prophet (Waldscenen)*. Shostakovich: Three Fantastic Dances, op. 1. Turina: *Rapsodia sinfonica*. Imprimatur DIMP 2 MONO. Susskind/PO.

The Lympany Legend Vol. 1. Prokofiev: Concerto No. 1 in D-flat Major, op. 10. Rachmaninoff: Concerto No. 1 in F-sharp Minor, op. 1; Concerto No. 2 in C Minor, op. 18. Olympia OCD 190. Susskind/Philharmonia.

The Lympany Legend Vol. 2. Prokofiev: Concerto No. 3 in C Major, op. 26 (Susskind/ Philharmonia). Rachmaninoff: Concerto No. 3 in D Minor, op. 30 (Collins/New SO). Olympia OCD 191.

Moura Lympany: 60 Years On The Concert Stage. Khachaturian: Concerto in D-flat Major (Fistoulari, London PO). Saint-Saëns: Concerto No. 2 in G Minor, op. 22 (Martinon/London PO). Olympia OCD 236.

Rachmaninoff: 24 Preludes. Erato 4509-91714 (CD).

$\mathcal{M}$

MICHELANGELI, ARTURO BENEDETTI: b. Brescia, Italy, 5 January 1920; d. Lugano, Switzerland, 12 June 1995.

> I do not play for others—only for myself and in the service of the composer. It makes no difference to me whether there's an audience or not.
>
> Michelangeli (*New York Times,* 21 August 1977)

The reclusive, controversial Michelangeli meant what he said. He detested playing in public, disliked recording and fanatically guarded his privacy—all major ingredients in creating the myth and gossip enveloping, often beclouding, the true facts of his life. He rarely granted interviews, tried to omit biographical data from his program notes and shunned both the media and his adoring following. Four interviews (1960, 1966, 1973, 1977) published in English reveal a long-standing and remarkably consistent unapproachableness. Whether by nature or by deliberate planning, by the time Michelangeli reached age 40 he had become an enigma and a legend, "as much of a mystery to his students as he was to his ardent admirers." (Holcman)

He was still mysterious at age 70. There have always been pianists who have tried to create a personal mystique based almost as much on capricious behavior and reclusiveness as on technical skill, but "few have managed to achieve this status as effortlessly as Arturo Benedetti Michelangeli." (*TL,* 27 April 1990) This unenviable reputation resulted largely from artistic infractions: canceling appearances, interrupting tours, stalking out of recording sessions and, even less endearing, an obvious disdain for both audiences and critics. It may be that his unorthodox behavior was due to the fact that he was an extreme

perfectionist. A pianist whose obsession with playing only a perfect piano
outdid even that of Glenn Gould, Michelangeli worked on his piano and its
pedals, always with his personal tuner, for hours before every concert, every
recording session, every time he played. Tuning, toning, coloring and
equalizing, he strove for a degree of precision almost impossible to obtain.
There were times, noted more than one critic, when Michelangeli's piano seemed
more important than the music.

Biographical information on Michelangeli is not only scant but inconsistent. He began learning the violin at the early age of three, and at age four
began violin and organ studies at the Venturi Musical Institute in Brescia. He
himself reported that having pneumonia and later contracting tuberculosis made
it physically impossible for him to handle the violin, so that at about age 10 he
began piano studies with Giovanni Maria Anfossi at the Milan Conservatory.
Michelangeli received his diploma in piano from that Conservatory in 1933, and
thereafter, though he was only age 13, he was largely self-taught. There is no
mention of teachers beyond this age; and in 1973 Michelangeli, then age 53,
claimed that he had "lived and studied a bit almost everywhere—I traveled all
round Europe with my grandmother, and studied mainly by myself." (Gill)

To please his father, who strongly objected to his having a career in
music, Michelangeli studied medicine for a few years, but irrevocably returned to
music. On his own without family aid, he earned money as a church organist
and also spent about a year—dates are vague—at the Franciscan monastery at
Laverna, reportedly recuperating from a relapse of the tuberculosis. All through
these years he must have continued with his piano practice and study, for at age
19 he competed in the first International Piano Competition in Geneva. At the
final concert the nine-member jury, led by Cortot and including Paderewski,
unanimously awarded him the first prize; and critics hailed him as "the new
Liszt." That same year Michelangeli was appointed professor of piano at the
Martini Conservatory in Bologna, where he spent two productive years teaching
and concertizing.

In 1940 at his Rome debut at the *Teatro Ardiano*, Michelangeli's superbly elegant playing created "the biggest musical sensation in Italy for quite
some time." (*NYT*, 11 Feb 1940) The lavish reviews clearly indicate that
somehow, and mostly on his own without guidance from a celebrated pedagogue,
Michelangeli had managed to acquire "not only a piano technique like steel and
mercury, but a musical insight that was at once idiosyncratic but effective, dark
with pessimism yet capable of warming the heart." (Morrison)

But Michelangeli's promising start evaporated under the pressures of
war. He served in the Italian air force, later became active in the Italian under-
ground resistance movement. Immediately after the war he returned to his concert
career. In the Gill interview Michelangeli claimed that agent Harold Holt, having heard a Michelangeli recording, invited him to perform in England. As
Michelangeli recalled it, he lived in England for two years after the war and, because he had refused to play with what he considered the "poor" English orchestras of that time, Holt brought over the best European orchestras and conductors
for him to play with. If such performances took place, reviews are not listed in
The Times (London) index; however, there is a review dated 16 December 1946

of Michelangeli and the London Symphony Orchestra, directed by Warwick Braithwaite, performing the Liszt Concerto in E-flat Major and Franck's Symphonic Variations.

On his first tour of the United States during 1948–49, Michelangeli made his orchestral debut at Carnegie Hall on 28 November 1948, playing the Schumann Concerto with the New York Philharmonic-Symphony Orchestra, conducted by Dimitri Mitropoulos; and traveled to the Pacific Coast to play Haydn's Concerto in D Major and the Franck Symphonic Variations with the Los Angeles Philharmonic Orchestra, conducted by Alfred Wallenstein. He gave his first New York recital at Carnegie Hall on 30 January 1949. American critics were not wholly enthusiastic, and Michelangeli for his part did not care for America. Yet abroad he quickly gained a reputation as one of his generation's finest pianists: the phenomenal Michelangeli who, "although appearing but rarely on the world's concert platform . . . is idolized even by some distinguished rivals." (*SR*, 30 July 1960)

Rumors of poor health were always a part of the Michelangeli mystique, although he appeared as a powerful-looking man with large hands (able to span a twelfth). In his youth he loved to fly planes and race fast cars. For whatever reason, he began to divide his time between performing and teaching. And whether because of ill health or because he detested performing in public, for many years he gave concerts only when exactly in the mood or when he needed money to support his generous student programs.

With typically eccentric dedication, Michelangeli for many years devoted most of his time and energies to teaching at the International Academy, a school he founded and wholly supported. He and his wife, also a pianist, would rent a villa, sometimes a palace, at different locations (Brescia, Arezzo, Bolzano, Bologna, etc.), install a fleet of pianos and personally train anywhere from 15 to 30 hand-picked gifted students from around the world. They were able to refuse government aid and to board and teach students free of charge because Michelangeli's occasional concerts in Italy at exorbitant fees enabled him to support the entire project.

Opinions vary as to Michelangeli's success as a pedagogue. (Martha Argerich believed that she learned very little with Michelangeli. Maurizio Pollini claimed that he "learned some very fine things.") Erratic and temperamental, Michelangeli would dismiss a student at a moment's notice if he or she failed to show the expected talent and enthusiasm. Lessons, always private, took place day or night according to the maestro's inclination and could last from 20 minutes to three hours. He developed each student according to his or her personality, never using a set method or technique for teaching. Most important, Michelangeli tried to make his students think. "When I sit at the keyboard, I am lost. And I think of what I play, and of the sound that comes forth, which is the product of the mind. Today's young musicians are afraid to think. They do everything in order *not* to think." (Gruen) As for the physical aspects of playing, he stressed the importance of tonal qualities and tried to eliminate the (to him) percussiveness and ugliness of piano sound.

Teaching became Michelangeli's whole way of life, but ultimately it tired him out, and in the early 1960s he returned to the concert circuit. He made tours of South America and the Soviet Union, made his first Paris appearance (24 Jan 1965) in many years, and also toured Japan in 1965. In 1966, after a 15-year absence, Michelangeli returned to America for a coast-to-coast tour. For unknown reasons, he left Italy in 1965 to make his permanent home in Lugano, Switzerland. In the 1977 interview he said that he was living in Lugano and had not played in Italy for the last ten years. His only explanation: "It bores me to play in Italy."

After returning to the concert stage, this outlandish pianist survived through a combination of remarkable talent, perseverance and showmanship, the latter projected through his colorful, though withdrawn stage presence and his idiosyncratic temperament. Always considering only his own moods and feelings, Michelangeli ignored audiences and agents, balked at applause, stalked away from encores and as much as possible shunned personal contacts. Public and press alike undoubtedly put up with this undependable, often surly pianist solely because of his talent. Particularly annoying was his lifelong habit of frequent concert cancellations, sometimes on short notice, because of illness or an imperfect piano. For example, in 1973 his personal piano, shipped from Hamburg to London, had been allowed to sit in a damp warehouse. Michelangeli not only refused to play his piano in that condition, but insisted that he could not find a suitable substitute piano in all of London. Again, of five concerts scheduled in Japan in 1980, he played only one, canceling all others because he was not pleased with the condition of his own piano and claimed that none he tried in Japan was satisfactory.

Two hours' reading (more than enough to ingest the few articles in English) about such cantankerous behavior can arouse indignation, even contempt. On the other hand, two hours' listening to Michelangeli's music can be enthralling.

Over the years Michelangeli deliberately pared down his repertoire. He began with an eclectic group of composers: Chopin, early Beethoven, Bach and Bach-Busoni, Mozart, Schumann, Brahms, Granados, Mompou, Albéniz, Grieg, Galuppi, Scarlatti. In the 1960s he was performing all of the Beethoven Sonatas and Mozart Concertos; all the piano works of Chopin and Debussy; some Bach, Schumann and Brahms; some works by old Italian composers and some by modern composers. At the time he claimed to have no prejudices against contemporary music, that in fact at age 16 he had been the first pianist to introduce Schoenberg's works in Italy. Yet 13 years later, in the Gill interview, Michelangeli disparaged all music written during the previous 20 years, describing modern composers as "noisemakers" and piano pieces by such 20th-century composers as Schoenberg, Messiaen and Stockhausen as "experiments" and "abortions."

By the late 1970s Michelangeli's repertoire had dwindled to a comparatively few composers. He had already eliminated Bach: "I only play Bach on the organ, though never in public." And from that time Michelangeli stubbornly stripped his repertoire to the point that, judging from available programs, he was playing almost exclusively works by Chopin, Beethoven, Debussy, Ravel and Schumann.

In like manner Michelangeli steadily and deliberately refined his playing style to the degree that it is difficult now to believe that at the outset of his career critics called him "the Italian Liszt" because of his lively impetuosity, luminous tone and his smoldering performances of Spanish music—all descriptions totally foreign to the unique style for which Michelangeli is famous. A more severe Michelangeli developing in the 1950s showed less warmth, less drama and a more restricted tonal palette, and thereafter he seemed to have become obsessed with the idea of stripping tonal color to its utmost austere limits. His mature playing style was remarkable for immaculate technique, elegant precision, interpretative insight and stark, almost monochromatic tone color.

For admirers, his "pianism is unique—uncompromising, original and breathtaking in the overall scale of interpretation: long phrases, meticulously judged tempi and exquisite, delicately varied sounds drawn from the piano." (Mottley) Devotees marvel at the way Michelangeli's polished, perfectionist playing presents music so sparingly, yet with such insight and clarity, and they point out his beautiful tonal quality. That tone quality, Michelangeli believed, resulted from his early organ and violin studies. Concerning his tone, he said that one must not think of piano sound, "but of a combination of the violin and the organ."

For some critics this same much-admired purity and perfection makes Michelangeli's playing too tight, too cold, too remote. For such critics, his powerful, original playing lacks spontaneity, imagination and deep understanding.

Flamboyant virtuosity, not polish and perfection, attracted attention at young Michelangeli's Rome debut in 1940. "His dazzling technique, transcending all difficulties, permits his entire concentration in the higher spheres of his art. . . . His command of tone color and dynamic range is no less extraordinary." (*NYT*, 11 Feb 1940) Six years later he played Liszt's Concerto in E-flat Major and Franck's Symphonic Variations at his London orchestral debut (15 Dec 1946), and even then the virtuoso style of Liszt "suited the pianist better than the intimate poetry of César Franck." (*TL*, 16 Dec 1946)

By the time he made his American orchestral debut (18 Nov 1948)—he was then age 28—Michelangeli's style had changed noticeably. "He was completely sure of himself, which his beautiful piano tone entitled him to be. . . . He played Schumann's music intimately and not in the exterior virtuoso manner. [He] . . . assured us, by his performance, that the Schumann Concerto is neither a display piece nor a classic inspiration. . . . There was only one defect. . . . The performance was just too authoritative, too intelligent, too skillful and certain of itself to stir the listener or move him deeply." (*NYT*, 19 Nov 1948)

Michelangeli received only lukewarm notices at his Los Angeles debut on 13 January 1949: "He is a fluent pianist and his work is distinguished by a facile sort of surface polish and an impersonal and remote approach that almost never penetrates beyond exterior qualities. Frankly, we have heard numerous students give equally satisfactory performances of Haydn's Concerto in D Major and the César Franck Symphonic Variations." (*LAT*, 14 Jan 1949)

Through the years Michelangeli's playing usually delighted audiences and, to be sure, some critics, but most reviewers seemed admiring yet perplexed. A Carnegie Hall program (21 Jan 1966) including the Bach-Busoni Chaconne, Beethoven's Sonata in C Minor, op. 111, the Debussy *Images* and Chopin's *Berceuse* and his Scherzo in B-flat Minor produced a typical critical mixture of praise and caution. After noting that the Beethoven Op. 111 asks for something beyond physical command, one critic wrote: "Michelangeli has all of that and a good deal more, including the control of tonal values to make the opening of the Arietta suitably sublime. What he lacks is patience with structure, interest in architecture, to sustain a long line of thought and carry through a saturating mood. . . . Scholarship behind him, Michelangeli applied himself to the two sets of Debussy *Images*, with quite miraculous results. *Reflets dans l'eau* was not merely liquid in its rippling sonorities, but also reflective in its utilization of them; and the *Cloches à travers les feuilles* rang all the bell changes Debussy imparted to his imagery." (*SR*, 5 Feb 1966)

A critic disturbed by that same recital wrote both a review (*NYT*, 22 Jan 1966) and an article (*NYT*, 6 Feb 1966) devoted to Michelangeli's fine yet puzzling performance. Granting that Michelangeli could do anything at the piano, and that he was a superb technician, a master of tone color and obviously an intellectual, this critic still contended that Michelangeli's "musical ideas are, by most current standards, weird. He illustrates a kind of romanticism that went out of vogue as far back as the turn of this century. At least, many of his devices are romantic: the lingering on notes, the slowdown to introduce new musical material. . . . He really is a modern pianist who tries to be romantic, but he simply does not feel romanticism. All of his romantic devices sound arbitrarily superimposed, and, as such, forced and artificial." (Schonberg) This critic also reported that while most professional musicians hated that recital—many pianists actually walked out—Michelangeli's eccentric playing absolutely mesmerized the nonprofessionals in the audience.

It must be remembered that part of the Michelangeli mystique was the unpredictability of his performances. A Los Angeles recital (20 Nov 1966) completely free of Michelangeli's well-advertised eccentricities received high marks from a critic who in 1949 had thought his playing prosaic. But this time Michelangeli "enthralled a capacity audience with piano playing of a type rare, and in some respects not surpassed, even in a world overpopulated with fine pianists. . . . He excites by revealing what is in the music and what is within himself, never by any superficial display, though the smoothness and agility of his technique are phenomenal. Even more phenomenal is his unerring control of every imaginable shade of tone color and nuance." (*LAT*, 22 Nov 1966)

A Washington, D.C., recital (15 March 1970) devoted to Beethoven and Chopin was, according to one reviewer, "a true revelation, and certainly one of the most remarkable recitals I have heard in a full lifetime of concert-going." Michelangeli's reading of the Beethoven Sonata in C Minor, op. 111, emanated such "transcendental loveliness" that this critic could recall only one other live performance, one by Artur Schnabel, that had moved him so deeply. With his Chopin, Michelangeli clearly demonstrated the difference in stature between Beethoven and Chopin. "To Michelangeli, Chopin was an inspired composer of salon pieces. . . . The glitter of those lovely ornaments, the impetuous, self-generating rhythms, the graceful, effeminate melodies were swept clean of the dulling patina of familiarity. They came from Michelangeli's fingers so bright and shiny and exciting that they might have been written yesterday." (*WS*, 16 March 1970)

Michelangeli offered a "cool and clipped" reading (3 May 1990) of Beethoven's Concerto No. 3 with Michael Tilson Thomas and the London Symphony Orchestra. From start to finish, Michelangeli "was holding phrases neatly apart, resisting any dynamic continuity. . . . The tone was uniformly dry, but not in the clattering upper treble, the counterpoint banally clear." (*TL*, 4 May 1990)

Michelangeli's London recital (10 May 1990) fared little better. Beethoven's Sonata in B-flat Major, op. 22, was "dispatched with seeming indifference, and Op. 111 with cool, dispassionate mastery. Then came Chopin: the great Mazurka op. 33, no. 4, with wondrous inflections and no trace of dance; the first Scherzo, its fleet outer sections broken by little hesitations and flurries, the exquisite line at its centre teased beyond song or endurance." (*MT*, Aug 1990) *The Times* critic was a bit more charitable although in Op. 22 she felt "the tension was focused on the man, and, as if uncomfortably aware of the fact himself, Michelangeli gave the piece a rough ride. . . . That total freedom from the awareness of the performing self was achieved in the Arietta of the Sonata, Op. 111. . . . After the interval came Chopin and some of the richest playing Michelangeli has offered London for some time." (*TL*, 12 May 1990)

Obviously the enigmatic Michelangeli never changed. But his recordings should be preserved. Even if in his frigidity he does not gratify you, he will utterly astonish you as you listen to him performing flawlessly, as if alone and exclusively for himself.

Michelangeli had a reputation for being difficult in recording sessions. In 1960 *Time* reported: "During rare recording sessions, he will sit pondering for hours before placing hands to keys, or walk out to take the speeding air in his car. Or he may smash an offending disk over his knees, as he did at Naples a few years ago, destroying two weeks' work." (*Time*, 19 Sept 1960) And fifteen years later another writer noted that, above all, Michelangelo "demands absolute perfection from himself and refuses to commit a single note to tape until he is fully satisfied with his own performance." (Mottley) The fact is that in recording, as in concerts, everything depended on the will (or whim) of the maestro (his preferred mode of address). The crew recorded what he wanted, when he wanted, where he wanted and for as long as he wanted.

The completed recordings are often just as capricious, and choosing the right ones takes a bit of listening and comparing. Debussy's Children's Corner, recorded live at a Lugano concert in 1968, and Ravel's *Gaspard de la nuit*, recorded live in Turin in 1962, appear on a *Nuova Era* CD, along with some Italian cembalo pieces. "These performances exhibit all of Michelangeli's faults and virtues—a highly idiosyncratic interpretive approach, a very great sense of tempo and rubato, though always tempered with a sense of classical balance and proportion, a seamless legato coupled with a varied and often very subtle coloristic palette, and an awesome virtuoso technique." (*Fanfare*, Sept/Oct 1989. Reprinted by permission)

One of Michelangeli's finest concerto discs couples the Rachmaninoff Concerto No. 4 with the Ravel Concerto in G Major (rec. 1957). The Ravel is certainly a very good performance; the Rachmaninoff is a superb performance. Michelangeli's pianism allows "musical conceptions to materialize which might not dawn on others. It is not a question of structure, in the narrow sense of the awareness of overall proportions . . . but the way structure is projected and the way it is transmuted into emotional drama." (*Gram*, Sept 1988)

In general, in playing the music of Debussy and Ravel, Michelangeli had few peers. He recorded both books of Debussy Preludes (see Discog.). According to one listener, the recording of Book I (1978) "is undoubtedly Michelangeli's finest since the 1957 Ravel and Rachmaninov Concertos. The playing contains all the legendary Michelangeli hallmarks, allied to which is a welcome degree of warmth. . . . The staggering articulation, tonal range . . . and dynamic control . . . [are] little short of miraculous." (*RR*, Nov 1978) And, even if one cannot agree with everything in Book II, as one reviewer remarked, "if you go along with him, however, I think you will be intrigued and delighted by some heightened perceptions. . . . Michelangeli shows what magic can be achieved through an exceptional control of sonority and the ability to produce effects of perspective." (*Gram*, March 1989) The Ravel CD (Concerto in G, *Gaspard de la nuit, Valses nobles et sentimentales*) is exceptionally fine. "Few others have captured the frigid grandeur of 'Ondine' with such aloof precision; and no one else . . . has darted through 'Scarbo' with such sinistrally playful agility. But his highly accentuated, disruptively modernistic reading of *Valses nobles et sentimentales* is very nearly as good." (*Fan*, March/April 1991)

Michelangeli was definitely not a great Beethovenist. The reissue of Op. 111, originally recorded in 1965, can in no way compare with the great readings by Schnabel, Serkin, or Backhaus. The performance is somewhat disquieting, basically a disregard of many indications by the composer himself. And Michelangeli's Mozart frequently suffers a similar fate. His recordings of the Mozart Concertos K. 466 and K. 503 offer no challenge to the older ones by Anda or the newer ones by Uchida. One harsh critic writes that Michelangeli's pair of performances "gives little indication that the pianist has any feeling for or understanding of two of Mozart's greatest contributions to the concerto literature. Phrasing is often mannered and fussy, and dynamic variances are virtually ignored. . . . This is undoubtedly the worst Mozart record I have heard in years." (*ARG*, May/June 1991) Another critic attempts to give the pianist his just due: "His exquisitely jeweled keyboard filigree is beyond reproach for tone, touch, and technical assurance. . . . Yet fascinating as Michelangeli's playing almost always is, it can be equally frustrating when his sheer charisma draws our attention from the composer's art to the performer's artifice." (*MA*, July 1991)

Not all of Michelangeli's recorded Mozart readings have received such negative reactions. For example, a critic reviewing a CD containing a 1955 performance of the Mozart Concerto in B-flat Major, K. 450, and also some Chopin compositions (see Discog.) finds that Michelangeli's Mozart playing "exhibits to a large degree the qualities which have distinguished Michelangeli's art: lucid articulation, unruffled tonal beauty, and a perfection of execution akin to a lapidarian's." And this reviewer waxes ecstatic about Michelangeli's Chopin: "Overpowering playing by one of the greatest masters of the century." (*Fan*, Nov/Dec 1988) A complete Chopin recital (*Foné* 90 F 32, see Discog.) recorded in 1967 and remastered in 1991 "comes close to the status of a historical recording. Here is truly sensational playing and artistry of a rarified quality, sometimes even a little intimidating in its brilliance." (*ARG*, Nov/Dec 1992)

A recent 6-CD collection (*Fonit Cetra*) groups live performances from Italian Radio sources made over a number of years. "Most of this collection, with rare exception, is music-making on the most exalted level." (*ARG*, Nov/Dec 1994) Also, in evaluating the discography of this eccentric, tremendous pianist, one should not forget the numerous 78 rpm discs that he made years ago. Some of these have been put to CD (Melodram 28019). They exhibit the exhilarating virtuosity of the youthful Michelangeli and a warmth and subjectivity that is often missing from his later recordings.

SELECTED REFERENCES

Chissell, Joan. "Top price, top value for Michelangeli." *The Times* (London), 29 Jan 1972, p. 7. A fine review of a Debussy CD.

Crimp, Bryan. "Pursuit of Perfection." *Records and Recording*, Nov 1978, pp. 20–22.

"The Diamond Touch." *Newsweek*, 24 Jan 1966, p. 81.

Driver, Paul. "A Touch of Temperament." *Sunday Times* (London), 2 June 1985, p. 43. A comparison between Michelangeli and Murray Perahia.

Gill, Dominic. "Michelangeli." *Music and Musicians*, June 1973, pp. 28–31.

Gruen, John. "Michelangeli Will Play Here Again Next Year—Maybe." *New York Times*, 21 Aug 1977, sec. 2, pp. 13–14.

Hall, Raymond. "Italian Piano Discovery." *New York Times*, 11 Feb 1940, sec. 9, p. 7.

Holcman, Jan. "Pianist Without Portfolio." *Saturday Review*, 30 July 1960, pp. 33–35.

Klein, Howard. "An Enigma and a Legend at 46." *New York Times*, 16 Jan 1966, sec. 2, p. 17.

Manildi, Donald. "Arturo Benedetti Michelangeli: In Performance." Liner notes, *Arturo Benedetti Michelangeli Live!* (see Discog.)

McMullen, Roy. "Michelangeli and the Machine." *High Fidelity*, Jan 1966, pp. 46–49.

Morrison, Richard. "Driving force hits the keys: Arturo Benedetti Michelangeli." *The Times* (London), 27 April 1990, p. 20.

Mottley, David. "A Living Legend." *Records and Recording*, Sept 1975, p. 12.

Schonberg, Harold C. "Romanticism and The Modern Mind." *New York Times*, 6 Feb 1966, sec. 2, p. 13.

See also Bibliography: Ewe/Mu; Gav/Vin; Kai/Gre; Met/Cho; New/Gro; Ran/Kon; Rat/Cle; Rub/MyM; Sch/Gre.

SELECTED REVIEWS

BG: 18 Nov 1968. *BH*: 18 Nov 1968. *LAT*: 14 Jan 1949; 22 Nov 1966. *MA*: Feb 1969. *MM*: Aug 1985; July 1987. *MT*: April 1957; May 1957; June 1982; Aug 1985; May 1987; Aug 1990. *NW*: 29 Nov 1948. *NY*: 6 Feb 1965. *NYT*: 11 Feb 1940; 19 Nov 1948; 31 Jan 1949; 21 Jan 1950; 7 Jan 1966; 22 Jan 1966; 3 Nov 1966; 27 Nov 1968. *SFC*: 15 Nov 1966. *SR*: 5 Feb 1966. *STL*: 25 March 1973; 2 June 1985. *TL*: 16 Dec 1946; 27 Feb 1957; 5 March 1957; 29 June 1959; 12 May 1961; 15 May 1961; 9 June 1965; 19 March 1973; 14 April 1982; 28 May 1985; 20 March 1987; 30 March 1987; 4 May 1990; 12 May 1990. *WS*: 16 March 1970.

SELECTED DISCOGRAPHY

Albéniz: *Malagueña*, op. 71, no. 8. Bach-Busoni: Chaconne. Beethoven: Sonata in C Major, op. 2, no. 3. Brahms: Variations on a theme by Paganini, op. 35. Granados: *Andaluza*, op. 37, no. 5. Grieg: Melancholy, op. 47, no. 5; At the cradle, op. 68, no. 5. Mompou: Canción y danza No. 1. Scarlatti: Sonata in D Minor, K. 9; Sonata in C Minor, K. 11. EMI Classics CDH 64490-2. Recorded from 1939 to 1942.

Arturo Benedetti Michelangeli Live! Beethoven: Concerto in E-flat Major, op. 73 (Celibidache/Paris SO). Haydn: Concerto in D Major, Hob. VIII:2 (Orizio/Brescia FO). Music and Arts CD-296.

Arturo Benedetti Michelangeli 1942-1943. Bach: Italian Concerto. Chopin: *Berceuse*, op. 57; Mazurka, op. 33, no. 4. Grieg: *Erotik*. Scarlatti: Sonata in B Minor, K. 27; Sonata in D Major, K. 96. Pellegrino: Allegro. Teldec 4509-93671-2

Bach-Busoni: Chaconne. Beethoven: Sonata in C Major, op. 2, no. 3. Brahms: Variations on a Theme by Paganini. Debussy: *Images*, Book I. Scarlatti: Four Sonatas. Schumann: Concerto in A Minor, op. 54; *Faschingsschwank aus Wien*. Melodram CD 28019 (2 CDs). Rowicki/Warsaw PO.

Beethoven: Concerto No. 1 in C Major, op. 15; Sonata in E-flat Major, op. 7. DG 419 249-2. Recorded from live performances. Giulini/Vienna SO.

Beethoven: Concerto No. 5 in E-flat Major, op. 73 (Steinberg/NYPO); Sonata in C Minor, op. 111. Debussy: Children's Corner. Grieg: Concerto in A Minor, op. 16 (Rossi/RAI-Roma). Ravel: *Gaspard de la nuit*. Memories HR 4368/69 (2 CDs). Public Performances 1961–68.

Chopin: *Andante spianato and Grande Polonaise*, op. 22; Ballade in G Minor, op. 23; Scherzo in B Minor, op. 31. Mozart Concerto in B-flat Major, K. 450. Fonit-Cetra CDE 1021. Rossi/RAI di Torino.

Chopin: *Andante spianato and Grande Polonaise*, op. 22; Ballade in G Minor, op. 23; Six Mazurkas; Sonata No. 2 in B-flat Minor, op. 35. Foné 90 F 32 (CD).

Debussy: Children's Corner. Galuppi: Sonata in C. Ravel: *Gaspard de la nuit*. Scarlatti: *Quattro Esercizi per Clavicembalo*. *Nuova Era* 2216 (CD).

Debussy: *Images* I and II; Children's Corner. DG 415 372-2.

Debussy: Preludes, Book I. DG 413 450-2.

Debussy: Preludes, Book II. DG 427 391-2.

Grieg: Concerto in A Minor, op. 16. Schumann: Concerto in A Minor, op. 54. Teldec Historic 9031-76439-2. Recorded in 1942. Gallieri, Pedrotti/La Scala Theater Orchestra.

Michelangeli. Beethoven: Concerto No. 5. Haydn: Concerto in D Major. Mozart: Concertos Nos. 13, 15, 20, 23. Schumann: Concerto in A Minor. Liszt: Concerto No. 1. Chopin: Scherzo No. 2; Ballade No. 1; Fantasy in F Minor; 3 Waltzes; 3 Mazurkas. Debussy: *Images*; 2 Preludes; Children's Corner. *Fonit Cetra* 2002 (6 CDs). Live performances from Italian radio.

Mozart: Concerto in B-flat Major, K. 450 (Rossi/RAI Torino); Concerto in A Major, K. 488 (Giulini/RAI Rome). *Fonit Cetra* CDAR 2004.

Mozart: Concerto in D Minor, K. 466; Concerto in C Major, K. 503. DG 429 353 (CD). Garben/North German RO.

Rachmaninoff: Concerto No. 4 in G Minor, op. 40; Ravel: Concerto in G. EMI CDC7 49326-2. Gracis/Philharmonia.

Ravel: Concerto in G; *Gaspard de la nuit*; *Valses nobles et sentimentales*. Galuppi: Sonata in C. Hunt (Arkadia) CD 904. Sanzogno/RAI-Turin.

Schumann: *Carnaval*, op. 9; *Faschungsschwank aus Wien*, op. 26. DG 423321-2. Recorded in 1957 for the BBC Transcription service.

Schumann: *Carnaval*, op. 9. Album for the Young, op. 68 (Nos. 37–39). EMI Angel CDC 7 49325-2. Recorded in 1975.

MOISEIWITSCH, BENNO: b. Odessa, Russia, 22 February 1890; d. London, England, 9 April 1963.

> In his great days Moiseiwitsch was the most disciplined of pianists. Of all the Leschetitzky pupils, he well may have been the most naturally gifted. He had a technique that put him on a par with Hofmann, Rachmaninoff and Lhévinne, and he had tone to match.
> Harold C. Schonberg (*New York Times*, 21 April 1963)

Odessa, a Ukranian seaport on the Black Sea, has spawned a remarkable number of truly great pianists—Barere, Cherkassky, Gilels, Pachmann and Benno Moiseiwitsch. Moiseiwitsch lived in Odessa until he was 15 years old, one of seven children raised by David Leon Moiseiwitsch, a horse breeder and farmer, and Esther (Miropolsky) Moiseiwitsch, a cultivated, musically gifted woman. The moment his mother realized that he could pick out tunes on the family piano, she started his lessons; and as soon as he could read music, she arranged weekly lessons with a professional piano teacher. At about age seven Moiseiwitsch began lessons with Dmitri Klimov at the Odessa Imperial School of Music.

At age nine he won the Rubinstein Stipendiary Prize, awarded to the student with exceptional talent and high grades. Since the winner retained the prize until he left the Imperial School, the competition was held only in those years when the prize was available. Moiseiwitsch held the prize until he left the school at age 15. By that time he was already a pianist of unusual promise, but Odessa offered few opportunities for advancement and, besides, these were the uneasy times preceding the revolution of 1905. Under the circumstances, the extended Moiseiwitsch family agreed that it would be wise to send Benno and his older brother John to London to join relatives living there.

Moiseiwitsch's application for admission to London's Royal Academy of Music was rejected because, as the family story goes, his audition proved he was too far advanced. Another family parley—letters back and forth to Odessa and meetings in London—decided that Moiseiwitsch should study with the great Leschetizky in Vienna. Sasha Konievsky, a brother-in-law and prominent businessman, accompanied him to Vienna and arranged a hearing with Leschetizky. Moiseiwitsch played some Bach and Chopin's "Revolutionary" Etude, and for his pains received a typical Leschetizky response: "I can play this better with my left foot. . . . I don't want *bravura* or exhibitionism. Go and practice for a couple of months until you've mastered real control. Then you can come back and we'll see what progress you've made." (Moiseiwitsch, M.)

That stinging rejection shocked the 15-year-old into working more intensely than he had ever done in his life. He practiced diligently (scales, thirds, sixths, repeated notes), sometimes 10 hours a day, and at his second tryout Leschetizky accepted him. That signaled a momentous turning point in his career. In later years Moiseiwitsch often said that when he went to Leschetizky he had a good technique and nothing else, that he owed a great deal to this master who had a special gift for knowing how to develop each pupil's individuality. Leschetizky, he said, turned what talent he had into a deep love for the piano. Moiseiwitsch became one of Leschetizky's most famous pupils and to the end of his life remained an ardent disciple.

Leschetizky dismissed him when he was age 18. He returned to London and gave a pre-debut recital (1 Oct 1908) at the Town Hall in Reading, but had to wait more than a year to make his professional London debut (8 Feb 1910) at Bechstein Hall. After that successful debut Moiseiwitsch's career moved ahead without pause, and by 1914, said Sir Henry Wood, he had established a fine reputation in England. (Moiseiwitsch never returned to Russia and in 1937 became a British subject.)

He made his New York debut at Carnegie Hall on 29 November 1919, and within a few years had become as popular with American audiences as with audiences on the Continent and in Britain. Over the course of his half-century career Moiseiwitsch made more than 20 American tours, three tours of the Far East, four tours of South America and six tours of Australia and New Zealand.

He was at his prime during World War II, and he pushed himself hard. He played all over Britain (more than 800 concerts) in bombed-out halls, unheated buildings, even during air raids, and at some of the concerts performed as many as three major concertos. For just one cause alone, Lady Churchill's "Aid to Russia" fund, he gave more than 100 concerts; and in 1946 Moiseiwitsch was awarded the C. B. E. (Order of Commander of the British Empire) for his unstinting wartime services.

His Carnegie Hall recital of 8 February 1947, his first American appearance in 14 years, was a glorious success. Moiseiwitsch remained active to the end of his life, but critical comments indicate that after the war his playing showed a decline, which is not surprising. That endless round of performances during the war had drained his energies, just as so much repetition of the same works (by popular demand) had robbed his playing of some of its spontaneity. After the war there was at times a noticeable difference. Sometimes he played beautifully, at other times he seemed worn out. His playing lacked form, and he sometimes emphasized subsidiary detail in a way which distracted, rather than enhanced, the effect.

On 23 March 1958 Moiseiwitsch celebrated the 50th anniversary of his concert career, playing three Rachmaninoff works (Concerto No. 1, Concerto No. 2, Rhapsody on a Theme of Paganini) with the Symphony of the Air, conducted by Leon Barzin, at Carnegie Hall. In 1959 the Royal Philharmonic Society named him a life member. In 1960 he played at the 100th Promenade Concert, at Albert Hall. On 19 July 1961 he played the "Emperor" Concerto at Lewisohn Stadium, one of his last American appearances with orchestra; and his last American tour ended on 28 February 1963. Only a month later Moiseiwitsch had a stroke and died in a London hospital on 9 April 1963.

He had lived life to the fullest. He was genial, generous and a witty raconteur. He enjoyed tobacco, spirits and gourmet food. An avid gambler, he played a lot of poker. He loved books and the theater. In 1914 he had married Daisy Kennedy, an Australian violinist. They had two daughters, and divorced about 1924. In 1929 Moiseiwitsch married Anita Gensburger. They had one son, and this marriage lasted until her death in 1956.

Moiseiwitsch had no interest in teaching, although he frequently wrote about pianism and problems of technique and style; and certainly he never tired of extolling the virtues of Leschetizky's teaching. Leschetizky had made Moiseiwitsch a great pianist, and Moiseiwitsch idolized him. Leschetizky had taught him not to play to an audience, but always to play to himself and, most important, to *listen* to himself very seriously. "All of his teaching," said Moiseiwitsch, "was grounded in fundamental beauty of tone and emphasis on expressive color. Individuality, not method, made him the wonderful teacher he was." (Goodwin)

Thus Moiseiwitsch's playing was in every respect the Leschetizky way of playing. In one term or another, critics and writers on music invariably define him as a "pianist in the grand tradition" and his style as "playing in the grand manner." Moiseiwitsch himself, trying to define what he thought critics meant, wrote: "In the broadest sense, they mean a style of playing which penetrates deeper than the physical conquering of the piano. It concerns itself with the release of music. The 'grand style' moved listeners through interpretation. . . . Interpretation does not mean borrowing 'effects' to round out the rendition of a given work. It means learning how to think musically in approaching all works." (Moiseiwitsch, "Playing. . .")

Labels, grand or otherwise, made little impression on Moiseiwitsch. As he put it, he simply tried to play as Leschetizky had taught him, "with a singing tone, attention to all the voices in the music, and the slight changes in time values that are known as rubato. If that is the 'grand tradition,' then it applies to me." (Ericson)

He was, by any definition, a romantic pianist. "You're a natural born romantic," Leschetizky had told him. "That's all right. Don't worry. You're in good company. So was Beethoven." This "born" Romantic naturally approached the piano with a romantic view. Believing that the performer took precedence over the composer, he thus felt free to take liberties with tempo and rhythm, highlight inner voices, emphasize tonal shading, make expressive ritards. Moiseiwitsch's attitude toward the printed score must scandalize today's mechanically precise pianists, yet in his prime the old Romantic was a very disciplined pianist.

Moiseiwitsch felt that interpretations must always be different, arguing that just as no person feels the same on different days, so a pianist's playing is never exactly the same at different performances. Each time the playing must reflect the artist's mood and his ideas. Moiseiwitsch fortunately had the "ability to see into a composer's mind and to transmit the essence of his imagination through musical color. It is this that has helped to place him among the outstanding pianists of the century." (Goodwin)

His brother recorded that Moiseiwitsch tried to practice a few hours every day, even when traveling. On long train rides and in hotels he played on a dummy keyboard with the usual padded hammers but no strings. He actually liked practicing away from the piano, which is to say that he would go through an entire piece mentally, usually hearing in his mind things which escaped him when he was physically practicing. At the piano he would try to incorporate into his playing what he had learned mentally.

Up to World War II Moiseiwitsch played a large, varied repertoire. He kept as many as 20 concertos ready to play on notice and played solo works by just about every major composer from the Baroque (Couperin, Daquin, Rameau, Scarlatti) to the 20th century (Poulenc, Prokofiev, Rachmaninoff, Khatchaturian), excluding, however, Mozart and Haydn. He frequently programmed seldom-heard music, for example, works by Medtner, Palmgren, Hummel, Rubbra, Rawsthorne, Tcherepnin. In fact, Sir Henry Wood said that Moiseiwitsch had introduced more new piano works before the public than any other pianist he knew.

Moiseiwitsch mostly played works by Romantic composers, especially Chopin and Schumann, his favorite. "In the depths of my heart," he said during a radio talk broadcast over the BBC in the late 1950s, "Schumann is and always was my favourite composer." (Gibb)

Moiseiwitsch made a good impression at his London recital debut (8 Feb 1910) at Bechstein Hall: "In the slow movement of Beethoven's Sonata ["*Appassionata*"] he was a little apt to over-emphasize the sforzandos, but . . . elsewhere he showed a most refreshing absence of any tendency to exaggeration, and infused a freshness into his playing that was as striking as it was pleasing." (*TL*, 9 Feb 1910)

Just about every New York newspaper reported on Moiseiwitsch's New York recital debut in Carnegie Hall on 29 November 1919. One critic complained of the program's "preposterous length" and the pianist's "appalling liberality," and summed up Moiseiwitsch as "not a big or a commanding figure despite some exquisite traits, or the propounder of momentously eloquent and soul-searching messages. . . . He is a miniaturist of unfailing taste." (*MA*, 6 Dec 1919) Yet most reviews were highly complimentary. For example, "He has a beautiful touch. He is more than a mere technician, for he has brains, a soul, as well as the fleetest of fingers. He never bangs. A staccato, clarity itself; a singing touch." (*NYW*, 30 Nov 1919)

Moiseiwitsch's first Boston recital (23 Feb 1920) augmented his reputation. His long programs still bothered some reviewers, but even these were captivated by his playing. As always, critics noted Moiseiwitsch's quiet stage manner: "He attends strictly to the business in hand without playing to the gallery. . . . One forgets the player and thinks, as he obviously does, only of the music. . . . He never blurs a note, never pounds, never loses the lustrous tone which is his rarest merit." (*BG*, 24 Feb 1920)

A performance (19 Nov 1920) with the Chicago Symphony Orchestra, Frederick Stock conducting, illustrates Moiseiwitsch's eclectic concerto repertoire. He not only played the Schumann Concerto in A Minor but also Ernest Schelling's "Fantastic Suite" for piano and orchestra. All the reviews were wonderful. For example, "There is a splendor about his art that is like the unearthly beauty of distant and unconquered heights of cloud veiled mountains." (*CT*, 20 Nov 1920) "His interpretations glowed with fire and he played with the buoyant exuberance of youth, neither mellowed nor spoiled by the disillusions of riper experience." (*CHE*, 20 Nov 1920)

"In his great days, up to World War II, Moiseiwitsch was one of the supreme pianists. He had everything—technique, a glorious sound, poetry, strength when needed, an easygoing and unmannered musical mind." (Schonberg, "A Lyrical Pianist. . .") A taxing Town Hall program (17 Nov 1934)—Bach-Busoni, Brahms-Paganini, Schumann, Chopin-Liszt and Liszt-Busoni—highlighted the Beethoven "*Waldstein*" Sonata. The Beethoven performance particularly impressed one reviewer with its "sustained, singing themes and crisp, light passage work, its unforced eloquence heightening a sombre mood." (*NYT*, 18 Nov 1934) And at his first Carnegie Hall recital (8 Dec 1947) in 14 years, the audience "heard a formidable pianist, one of the best in the world. It heard playing of power and passion, in which brilliant virtuosity was always under the control of a disciplined and imaginative mind." (*NYT*, 9 Dec 1947)

However, some sharply critical reviews confirm that Moiseiwitsch's playing declined after the war. He made a poor showing at London's Festival Hall on 7 November 1954, especially in a group of 12 studies by Chopin. "He treated them merely as technical show pieces, devoid of all poetry, and gabbled them off far too hurriedly for clear articulation of detail or, in fact, any finesse of phrasing." (*TL*, 8 Nov 1954)

Compliments counterbalanced most of the disapproving statements. Take, for instance, a critique of a recital in Los Angeles on 5 February 1960: "He played his repertoire with a sweep and a commanding sense for big lines and cumulative effects. Even if he was no longer able technically to carry out all his intentions and could no more dazzle with brilliance, there was still the feeling of elegant showmanship, of a musical nobility and of interpretations eminently true to style." (*LAT*, 7 Feb 1960)

A review of Moiseiwitsch's last appearance with orchestra in New York (19 July 1961), titled "Glorious Evening at Stadium," reads: "Mr. Moiseiwitsch's part in the proceedings consisted of a transcendent performance of Beethoven's 'Emperor' Concerto. His conception was, perhaps, less heroic than some, but definitely more poetic and wise than most." (*NYT*, 20 July 1961)

Olin Downes had this to say: "Distinguished artists are less often consistent and irreproachable in what they do than lesser men who are more concerned with the facts. Mr. Moiseiwitsch always impressed and challenged the listener, and at his best fascinated him by the individuality, the sensitiveness and grandeur of his style." (Goodwin)

Moiseiwitsch recorded over a long period of time. His finest playing is found in the pre-World War II recordings. These early discs include the Liszt Hungarian Fantasy (1939) and *La Leggierezza* (1941), the Mendelssohn-Rachmaninoff "Midsummer Night's Dream" Scherzo (1939) and the Weber-Tausig Invitation to the Dance (1939).

He was with HMV from 1916 to 1930, and returned to that company in 1937. The first period is represented on a 1987 double LP album *The Early Recordings* (see Discog.), which contains a fascinating and eclectic collection of mostly short compositions. Most of these are engaging examples of the pianist in top form. Even in the scarcely believable virtuosity heard in the Strauss-Godowsky *Fledermaus* Paraphrase, the beauty and elegance of his phrasing are as much in evidence as the pyrotechnics. And "Moiseiwitsch's technical sureness and clarity are at once evident in Daquin's *Le Coucou*, which has an impressive purity for its day, while Debussy's 'Jardins sous la pluie' from the *Estampes* . . . also impresses through its neat agility and immaculate style. Ravel's *Jeux d'eau* has a fine balance of elegance and poetry. . . . What emerges from the four sides, even in such a sequence of brief pieces, is Moiseiwitsch's sense of style, his sureness of technique, and the beauty and range of sound at his command." (*Gram*, Feb 1988)

The second HMV album contains Rachmaninoff works recorded between 1937 and 1948. The larger works—Concertos Nos. 1 and 2, Paganini Rhapsody—are certainly fine and impeccably played. But the competition in this repertoire today has produced some overwhelmingly exciting and beautiful playing which seriously competes with Moiseiwitsch's readings. Overall the two LP albums get high marks. "What's most striking in all of these performances is the grace and elegance of the playing: the shading of dynamics, the variety of tone, the subtlety of his voicing, the languorousness that never goes slack, and the utter transparency of music that sounds thick in almost any other hands." (*Fan*, May/June 1988)

A CD reissue of Beethoven's Concerto No. 3 in C Minor, op. 37, places Moiseiwitsch as a front contender in that composer's music and also gives us yet another different concept of Beethoven's style. It was recorded in 1950 for

HMV, Malcolm Sargent conducting the Philharmonia Orchestra. Here Moiseiwitsch "projects vivacity, pastel color, and melting tone that add up to an engrossing, communicative experience. . . . Some of today's firebrands have more accurate techniques; Moiseiwitsch instead provides poetry." (*CL*, April 1990)

A 2-CD collection (APR 7005, see Discog.) presents a fine sampling of Moiseiwitsch recordings made between 1938 and 1950. Some works from *The Early Recordings* are also included, but the CD format makes these discs most desirable. According to one critic, this collection shows that Moiseiwitsch's playing "appealed to both music-lover and connoisseur alike. His natural gifts of poeticism and spontaneity never left him throughout his very long career and fortunately there are enough good records that bear witness to his artistry." (*Gram*, Sept 1990)

A Centenary Celebration, a 1990 reissue of early Moiseiwitsch recordings, includes two performances with the London Philharmonic Orchestra: Beethoven's Concerto No. 5, recorded in 1938 with George Szell conducting; and the Liszt Hungarian Fantasy, recorded in 1939, with Constant Lambert. There is a later (1963) recorded broadcast version of the Beethoven with Sir Malcolm Sargent, but the 1938 performance shows Moiseiwitsch at his best, "a performance that is transparently first-rate. . . . The combination of authority and sensitivity can be witnessed in the special way that he takes his time over phrasing." (*Gram*, Oct 1991)

An even later historic reissue (Testament SBT1023) contains three works originally recorded in 1952–53—the Brahms Variations and Fugue on a Theme by Handel, op. 24, Schumann's Fantasia in C Major, op. 17, and *Fantasiestücke*, op. 12. "We have here performances of the *Fantasie* and *Fantasiestücke* which are the most compelling, intelligent, tonally luscious, and exciting ever recorded. . . . There is plenty of substance provided by Moiseiwitsch [in the Brahms], especially in the way he adapts his virtuosity to rip through the digital difficulties, taking risky tempos and rendering the musical content before the pyrotechnics." (*Fan*, Jan/Feb 1994)

Moiseiwitsch still ranks as one of the great romantic pianists of the century. "It would be unjust to allow his memory to be characterised by the occasional imperfections of his last years as some critics have tried to do. There are imperishable qualities in the recordings he made, and through these we are reminded why the great Rachmaninoff himself avowed Moiseiwitsch to be the favourite interpreter of his works." (Gibb)

SELECTED REFERENCES

Ardoin, John. "Moiseiwitsch at 72." *Musical America*, March 1962, pp. 10–11.

Crimp, Bryan. *Benno Moiseiwitsch: An HMV Discography*. Hexham: Appian Publications, 1990.

Ericson, Raymond. "Leschetizky Memoir." *New York Times*, 22 Jan 1961, sec. 2, p. 9.

Gibb, James. "Benno Moiseiwitsch remembered." *Musical Times*, Feb 1990, pp. 86–87.

Goodwin, Noel. "Moiseiwitsch." *Musical America*, May 1957, pp. 9–10.
Kipnis, Igor. "A Moiseiwitsch Postscript." *Clavier*, Feb 1990, pp. 23–24.
Mathews, George. "Benno and Me." *Clavier*, Feb 1990, pp. 19–22.
Moiseiwitsch, Benno. "Leschetizky." *Piano Teacher*, Jan/Feb 1963, pp. 3–4.
———. "Light and Shade in an Artist's Life." (interview with Harriette Brower). *Etude*, Nov 1927, pp. 821–822.
———. "New Tendencies in Pianistic Art." *Etude*, May 1920, pp. 295–296.
———. "Playing in the Grand Style." *Etude*, Feb 1950, pp. 18–19, 56.
———. "Sergei Rachmaninov, 1873–1943." *The Gramophone Jubilee Book*, ed. Roger Wimbush. Harrow: Gramophone Publications Limited, 1973, pp. 178–181.
———. "Trends in Piano Playing." (interview with Myles Fellowes). *Etude*, Nov 1955, pp. 26, 39, 44.
Moiseiwitsch, Maurice. *Moiseiwitsch*. London: Frederick Muller Limited, 1965.
Obituary. *Musical America*, May 1963, p. 51. *Musical Times*, May 1963, p. 358; June 1963, p. 430. *New York Herald Tribune*, 10 April 1963, p. 28. *New York Times*, 10 April 1963, p. 39.
Schonberg, Harold C. "Great Pianists From the Past Re-emerge." *New York Times*, 17 June 1990, sec. 2, pp. 23, 26. CD Reviews of Hess and Moiseiwitsch.
———. "A Link Is Gone." *New York Times*, 21 April 1963, sec. 2, p. 11.
———. "A Lyrical Pianist Who Had Everything." *New York Times*, 31 Jan 1988, p. 24.
See also Bibliography: Ald/Con; Bro/Mas; Bro/Mod; Cha/Spe; Dow/Oli; Ewe/Li; Lan/Mus; New/Gro; Sal/Fam; Woo/My.

SELECTED REVIEWS

BG: 24 Feb 1920. *BH*: 24 Feb 1920. *CEP*: 20 Nov 1920. *CHE*: 20 Nov 1920. *CT*: 20 Nov 1920. *LAT*: 6 April 1949; 7 Feb 1960; 5 Aug 1961. *MA*: 6 Dec 1919; 14 Jan 1929. *MT*: 1 Nov 1921; 1 Nov 1926. *NYEP*: 1 Dec 1919. *NYS*: 30 Nov 1919; 29 Dec 1919. *NYT*: 30 Nov 1919; 29 Dec 1919; 5 Nov 1922; 17 Oct 1926; 27 March 1927; 14 Nov 1934; 18 Nov 1934; 9 Dec 1947; 14 Nov 1949; 27 Feb 1950; 22 March 1952; 11 Nov 1953; 24 Feb 1955; 24 March 1958; 20 July 1961. *NYTr*: 30 Nov 1919. *NYW*: 30 Nov 1919. *TL*: 9 Feb 1910; 22 Nov 1911; 9 March 1914; 8 June 1914; 2 April 1917; 28 Jan 1918; 30 June 1919; 29 May 1922; 25 Sept 1922; 29 Sept 1924; 11 Feb 1930; 8 Nov 1954; 5 Nov 1956; 9 Dec 1958; 5 Oct 1959; 19 Nov 1960.

SELECTED DISCOGRAPHY

Beethoven: Concerto No. 3 in C Minor, op. 37. Schumann: Fantasia, op. 17. IPAM 1109 (CD). Sargent/Philharmonia.
Beethoven: Concerto No. 5 in E-flat Major, op. 73. Delius: Concerto in C Minor. Bruno Walter Society BWS 725. Sargent/SO.

Benno Moiseiwitsch: A Centenary Celebration. Beethoven: Concerto No. 5 in E-flat Major, op. 73 (Szell/London PO). Liszt: Hungarian Fantasy (Lambert/London PO). Medtner: Fairy Tale, op. 34, no. 2. Prokofiev: *Suggestion diabolique*, op. 4, no. 4. Strauss-Godowsky: Paraphrase on *Die Fledermaus.* Koch International Classics 3-7035-2.

Benno Moiseiwitsch: The Complete Rachmaninov Recordings 1937–48. Concerto No. 1 in F-sharp Minor, op. 1 (Sargent/Philharmonia); Concerto No. 2 in C Minor, op. 18 (Goehr/London PO); Lilacs, op. 21, no. 5; *Moment musical* in E Minor, op. 16, no. 4; Preludes, op. 3, no. 2, op. 23, no. 5, op. 32, nos. 5, 10, 12; Rhapsody on a theme of Paganini, op. 43 (Cameron/London PO); Scherzo from "A Midsummer Night's Dream" (Mendelssohn). Archive Piano Recordings APR 7004 (2 LPs).

Benno Moiseiwitsch: The Complete Rachmaninov Recordings 1937–43. APR 5505 (CD). Same contents as the above LPs, with the omission of Concerto No. 1. and Lilacs, op. 21, no. 5.

Benno Moiseiwitsch: The Early Recordings 1916–30. Beethoven: Andante in F Major. Brahms: Capriccio in B Minor, op. 76, no. 2; Intermezzo in C Major, op. 119, no. 3; Rhapsody in E-flat Major, op. 119, no. 4. Chopin: Ballade in A-flat Major, op. 47; Etudes, op. 10, nos. 4, 10, 11, op. 25, no. 3; Impromptu in A-flat Major, op. 29; Scherzo in B-flat Minor, op. 31; Waltz in E Minor, op. posth. Daquin: *Le Coucou.* Debussy: *Clair de lune*; *Jardins sous la pluie*; Minstrels. Delibes: *Passepied.* Granados: *Andaluza*, *Rondalla* (*Danzas Españolas*). Henselt: *Si oiseau j'étais.* Hummel: Rondo in E-flat Major, op. 11. Mendelssohn: Songs Without Words, op. 19, no. 3, op. 53, no. 4. Moszkowski: *La Jongleuse*, op. 52, no. 4. Rameau: *Gavotte et Variations.* Ravel: *Jeux d'eau.* Scarlatti-Tausig: Pastorale and Capriccio. Scriabin: Nocturne for the left hand, op. 9, no. 2. Strauss-Godowsky: Concert paraphrase on *Die Fledermaus.* Weber: Presto (Sonata No. 1). Archive Piano Recordings APR 7003 (2 LPs).

Benno Moiseiwitsch: Solo Piano Recordings 1938–50. Beethoven: Andante in F Major; Rondo in C Major, op. 51, no. 1. Chopin: Barcarolle in F-sharp minor, op. 60; Nocturne No. 2 in E-flat Major, op. 9, no. 2; Polonaise No. 9 in B-flat Major, op. 71, no. 2. Debussy: *Clair de lune* (*Suite bergamasque*); *Jardins sous la pluie* (*Estampes*); Toccata (*Pour le piano*). Liszt: *Etude de Concert* No. 2 in F minor; Hungarian Rhapsody No. 2 in C-sharp minor; *Liebestraum* No. 3 in A-flat Major. Mendelssohn: Scherzo in E minor, op. 16, no. 2. Mussorgsky: Pictures at an Exhibition. Ravel: *Toccata* (*Le Tombeau de Couperin*). Schumann: Romance in F-sharp Major, op. 28, no. 2. Weber: Presto (Sonata No. 1 in C Major); *Rondo brillant* in D-flat Major (arr. Tausig). Wagner-Liszt: Tannhaüser Overture, S. 442. CDAPR 7005 (2 CDs).

Brahms: Variations and Fugue on a Theme by Handel, op. 24. Schumann: Fantasia in C Major, op. 17; *Fantasiestücke*, op. 12. Testament SBT1023 (CD).

Pupils of Leschetizky. Leschetizky: Arabesque in A-flat Major. Weber: *Perpetuum Mobile.* OPAL CD 9839.

Rachmaninoff: Concerto No. 2 in C Minor, op. 18 (1955); Rhapsody on a
Theme of Paganini, op. 43 (1955); Prelude, op. 32, no. 5 (1956); Prelude,
op. 32, no. 10 (1941); *Moment musical*, op. 16, no. 4; Lilacs, op. 21, no.
5 (1948); Scherzo from "A Midsummer Night's Dream," op. 61
(Mendelssohn arr. Rachmaninoff). EMI CDH7 63788-2. Rignold/Phil-
harmonia.

MORAVEC, IVAN: b. Prague, Czechoslovakia, 9 November 1930.

> It is so easy to kill an artist. If he dares to play really personally he
> gets beaten down by the critics and loses his courage. You have to be
> able to say, "Excuse me, this is the way I'm convinced the music
> should sound."
>
> Ivan Moravec (*Providence Journal-Bulletin*, 7 November 1986)

Ivan Moravec, now in his mid-sixties, still has, as he has always had, the
courage to uphold his personal ideas as to how music should sound. Like other
pianists who play with a clearly recognizable personality, Moravec is sometimes
criticized for his highly individual approach to music; but the substantial following he has built up over the years ranks him among the foremost pianists of his
day.

Although not a child prodigy, even as a small boy Moravec took delight in musical sound—not piano music, interestingly enough, but the beautiful (and romantic) voices of opera singers. His father, an attorney and good amateur pianist, adored opera and had a large record collection, including many
Caruso records. Moravec remembers turning pages as his father played piano reductions of Puccini and Verdi scores and remembers feeling tearful because he
thought Caruso's voice was so beautiful. These early musical experiences made
a lasting impression. In 1988 Moravec told an interviewer: "An intense singing
tone is, for me, the utmost performance. Perhaps in the piano playing, I was
looking for a similar quality. The tone on the piano dies quickly; it really needs
double effort to produce the illusion of a long tone." (Brown)

The singing voice may have been Moravec's first love, but piano
recordings (some by Walter Gieseking, available in Prague during World War II,
and some by Ignaz Friedman) also made a tremendous impression on him. At
about age seven he began piano lessons at the Prague Conservatory with Erna
Grünfeld, a niece of the celebrated pianist Alfred Grünfeld. At age 16 Moravec
played on Prague Radio; at age 18 he received a first prize in piano from the
Conservatory. But then injuries from an earlier skating accident derailed his budding career, and for six years, from age 18 to 24, severe pain in his arms, hands
and neck kept Moravec from playing public concerts. During this frustrating period he had some coaching (1952–53) from Ilona Kurz at the Prague Academy of
Musical Arts; he did some teaching; and, as one might guess, spent hours listen-

ing to vocal music. He takes a sanguine view of the enforced hiatus. "Painful experiences," says Moravec, "mean that you mature in other ways. When I was able to play again, I built things with more efficiency, and when an older player learns a new piece, he knows the style better and it means more to him. Perhaps if I had been completely healthy, with muscles like a bull, my style would have been absolutely different." (Wigler)

Those years away from performing at such a critical age partly explain Moravec's slow-moving career, but there are also political reasons to consider. Although he has lived all his life in Czechoslovakia, for decades a Communist country wherein the State controlled all the arts, Moravec never joined the Communist Party. It seems safe to assume that the State concert agency had little interest in promoting the career of a pianist who was not a member of the Party. But illness and politics are not alone responsible for Moravec's slowly developing career; there is also the pianist himself. Ivan Moravec is a sensitive rather than a sensational virtuoso. Neither his quiet, introspective nature nor his sincere, straightforward playing makes good material for a publicity build-up— and that suits him perfectly. Moravec wants plenty of time, sometimes years, to prepare a work before playing it in concert; and he wants ample time ahead at concerts in order to make a thorough check of the piano he will be playing. There are pianists who almost yearly make several tours involving 100-plus per-formances. Moravec insists on going at his own, slower pace.

When he returned to performing in 1954 after that six-year break, he played mostly in Czechoslovakia, Poland, Hungary and Italy. Attending Arturo Michelangeli's master classes in Arezzo, Italy, in 1957 and 1958 confirmed his own ideas on interpretation, and also boosted his self-confidence. At age 28, Moravec made his London debut (2 May 1959), and good reviews from London prompted the owners of the newly formed Connoisseur Society to ask the Czech concert agency to send them tapes of Moravec's playing. Astounded by those tapes, Connoisseur sent Moravec a Prague–New York round-trip ticket, and the end result was a dozen or so records, produced between 1962 and 1969, that gave Moravec high standing among a small corps of serious music lovers.

Meanwhile, at the 1961 Prague Spring Festival, George Szell, the Czech-born conductor of the Cleveland Orchestra, heard some Moravec tapes and made plans for Moravec to play a week of performances (in Cleveland and New York) with his orchestra. Those concerts, played in 1964, might have led to a prosperous career in North America, but Moravec refused to compromise his convictions, and he and Szell argued from the start. Already upset because Moravec chose a Baldwin piano instead of a Steinway, Szell became enraged at Moravec's romantic reading of the Beethoven Concerto No. 4. Instead of a tri-umph, Moravec's New York debut performance (17 Feb 1964) turned into a near disaster. Years later, Stephen Sell, assistant to Szell when Moravec made his debut, told an interviewer that he thought Moravec's playing was the most beau-tiful he had ever heard in his young life. The problem, he said, was that "Szell wanted to teach his interpretation to all the soloists who worked with him, and Moravec refused to yield to that." Moravec's version of the incident, reported in the same interview, is even more revealing: "Szell was bitter because he was used to having his own way and he felt humiliated by me in front of musicians whom he regarded as his employees." (Wigler)

The Szell contretemps is an important reminder of Moravec's unshakable belief in his own concept of how music should sound, but it may also have marked him as being difficult to work with. Certainly, it was some years before he was invited to perform with another important American orchestra, and 25 years passed before he made his first appearance (13 Jan 1989) with the New York Philharmonic Orchestra. Statistics from the *New York Times* Index (1964–1980) indicate that Moravec played the Beethoven Concerto No. 4 with Szell and the Cleveland Orchestra in New York on 17 February 1964, played his New York debut recital at Philharmonic Hall on 20 October 1968, and then did not appear again in New York for 10 years—on 7 February 1978, at the Metropolitan Museum of Art. Despite his 10-year absence, tickets to that recital were sold out long in advance, very likely to longtime devotees who knew Moravec's Connoisseur recordings. He has always had a faithful core following, and it has steadily increased, especially since his playing on the soundtrack of the 1984 film *Amadeus* introduced his name to a much wider audience.

Since 1980 Moravec, still traveling at his own pace, has performed regularly in the United States and Canada, giving solo recitals, performing with major orchestras and at prestigious festivals. In London, *The Times* Index covering a 30-year period (1959–89) shows less than 10 Moravec performances (1959, 1962, 1964, 1968, 1975, 1985, 1988); but he has performed extensively elsewhere: Amsterdam, Paris, Berlin, Dresden, Munich, Vienna, Rome, Florence, Milan, Moscow, St. Petersburg, Sophia, Bucharest, Istanbul, Ankara.

Moravec and his wife Suzanna, who always travels with him, still live in Prague. Their family is grown, and they have grandchildren. He has been a regular soloist with the Czech Philharmonic Orchestra since 1975, and in 1979 received the title of Merited Artist.

Moravec has taught at the Prague Academy of Musical Arts since 1969 and has also held hugely successful master classes in Prague, Czechoslovakia, and in Italy. Basically his teaching derives from the concept that the teacher must guide the student in developing his or her personal style and must take particular pains to keep students from becoming carbon copies of the teacher. He requires students to record their practicing, listen to it very carefully and make a detailed self-analysis. Unlike many pedagogues, he advises his students to also listen to other pianists' recordings of the work they are preparing—not to imitate, but to learn.

Moravec uses this same comparison-listening method in his master classes. He will play three or four tapes (without identifying the pianists) of one movement from a large-scale work (for example, the first movement of Beethoven's "Moonlight" Sonata) and invite the students to discuss each interpretation. Moravec believes that comparing three or four interpretations (tone, *rubato*, dynamics, sensitivity, etc.) is very helpful for students. He of course has been listening to, and learning from, recordings since he was a teenager, and he still believes that hearing a great performance over and over again makes it possible for a musician to attain a higher level of that performance.

Moravec's following has grown in the last dozen or so years, but he still seems not to be up there in the "greatest pianists" category. Granted, he has few of the attributes often admired today; that is, he is not glamorous or eccentric, not a dazzling technician and does not perform a large repertoire. Yet the mild-mannered, patrician Moravec seems to have something that many of today's pianists lack and, in truth, most likely would not want. This subtle, hard-to-define quality has been attributed to Moravec's "intense calm coupled with his sense of dramatic pause. No other major pianist equals him in this precious quality, except possibly Solomon." (*HF*, July 1984)

Of course, being a perfectionist who takes time for everything, including time to become familiar with the pianos he is to play, also sets Moravec apart in today's musical world. Having the piano just right is almost an obsession with him. Whenever possible, he gets to a concert location in time to choose the right piano ("get to know it like an old friend"); if he cannot choose a piano, then he works with the local technician to get the action on the hall concert grand exactly the way he wants it. And if the technician is unable to achieve the desired action, Moravec gets out his own tools and works on the piano. He has been known to cancel a performance because of a hopeless piano.

Such careful attention to the piano no doubt helps in achieving the full, rich singing tone he draws from the instrument. Then, too, Moravec, all his life fascinated with the singing voice, constantly strives to re-create that kind of sound ("a long-lasting, shining, intense tone") on the piano. For him, imagination is the key. If you hear the music inwardly, he says, and "if your image is clear and intense, you will force your hand to produce the sound you want. Generally, I produce the tone by using the weight of my arm. The tone doesn't come out as I want if I use only the fingers." (Elder)

Rather than work on purely technical exercises at practice sessions, Moravec usually works on the pieces he is readying for performance. He imagines how he wants a piece to sound, tries to achieve that particular sound, then imagines an even better sound and, as his imagination expands, his playing, he feels, gets better and better. "When I start to practice a piece," he says, "my first consideration is to find the most intelligent possible reading, but I am usually frustrated because there is a gap between the image of the music in my mind and what actually comes out of the piano. However, if a pianist has a rich imagination and willpower, I believe he can do anything. Also, I am patient." (Plaskin) In the course of his studies he will change his fingering many times, sometimes to make it technically easier, at other times to get a better sound. "Fingering," he says, "is just not a question of speed or of accommodation, but chords sound very differently if you just have a sophisticated fingering which really helps your hand press more profoundly and more intensively into the keys." (*PQ*, Summer 1981)

Moravec's careful, deliberate approach to a work requires lots of time (sometimes as long as two years to prepare a large-scale work) to overcome the technical problems and also what he calls "sound-touch" problems of a piece. Details are explored in depth, then integrated into the whole structure. As he tells interviewers, he believes he has a good feeling for the tension of music.

"The *detail* of interpretation comes through learning a piece, but the most important thing one can catch is the feeling of the piece as a *whole*." Understanding
the music as a whole (that is, striving for "the big line") and not as a series of
separate segments is highly important to Moravec. The danger, he says, is that
the pianist can fix on one trivial detail to such an extent that he loses the big
line.

His constant probing and polishing of a work and the fact that he studies and restudies everything he performs precludes a fast-growing repertoire.
Moravec mostly plays works by Mozart, Beethoven, Chopin, Schumann,
Brahms, Franck, Ravel, Debussy, Dvořak, Smetana, Suk, Janáček; and his in-
depth studies produce sensitive, intelligent and very personal interpretations. For
some listeners they are too free, too highly individual. As he explains, "I make
constant changes in how I play. It is not that I intend to change, but more subtle or intelligent ideas occur in my mind, and I try to follow them." (Doerschuk)
Having discovered—or rediscovered—what he personally feels is the inner
essence of a work, Moravec plays it with absolute conviction.

His playing style, if we judge by critical appraisals, is not easy to define. Performing his favorite repertoire (Mozart, Beethoven, Chopin, Debussy),
Moravec reveals a patrician poetic sense that has been termed by one critic as being Romantic, but not heroic. Moravec's playing may be too patrician for some
critics, even though he can at times unleash dramatic fireworks. In the sum, he
is at his "remarkable best at something much harder to achieve: the ability to
play a sustained legato line pianissimo, maintaining clarity of texture and playing with absolute adherence to rhythmic detail." (Wigler)

At a University of Maryland recital (13 July 1987) Moravec's performance of Bach's Chromatic Fantasy and Fugue emerged as an intensely felt masterpiece delineating in proper perspective the contrast between the Fantasy's variegated interplay of improvisatory-like sections and the disciplined, elegant,
neatly articulated Fugue. Although he played the first movement of Beethoven's
"Moonlight" Sonata more slowly than usual, Moravec endowed the work with
an uncommonly fresh and engaging approach. In Debussy's Children's Corner,
he blended the harmonic colors to perfection and shaded each interpretation with
the appropriate dynamics. His Chopin—two Scherzos, op. 31 and op. 39—was
memorable, exciting, a true projection of that composer's sometimes elusive
style. This was effortless playing; nothing seemed too difficult.

A critique of Moravec's London debut (2 May 1959) at Wigmore Hall
elaborated on Moravec's sense of style and clarity of expression: "His touch is
eloquently expressive: balm to the ear in Mozart, a searing tongue of fire in the
dramatic variations of Beethoven's 32 in C minor, strong and heady wine in
Chopin's F minor ballade." (*TL*, 4 May 1959) A week later Moravec gave a
performance (9 May 1959) of the Prokofiev Concerto No. 1 in D-flat Major, op.
10, with the London Royal Philharmonic Orchestra, conducted by Gunnar
Staern, remarkable for "its clear, gleaming, yet unmetallic brilliance, its rhythmic alacrity and its deep musical sympathy and warm *cantabile* in the slow
movement." (*TL*, 11 May 1959)

No such applause greeted Moravec's New York debut at Carnegie Hall on 17 February 1964—that notorious performance of the Beethoven Concerto No. 4 with George Szell and the Cleveland Orchestra. But even though Moravec had to wait some years before another engagement with a major American orchestra, his reputation continued to grow, thanks to his excellent recordings. His recordings have almost always garnered the highest of ratings. His recitals fare differently, largely because of widely contrasting critical opinions on Moravec's interpretative approach. Three reviews of a Chicago recital (1 Feb 1978) provide a perfect example. One critic describes Moravec as "a pianist with a fine sense of structure and proportion and a limited sense of color and nuance." (*CST*, 2 Feb 1978) For another reviewer, "It seemed as if four or five different pianists were playing, one for each style and composer represented on the program." (*CDN*, 2 Feb 1978) And a third critic raved: "Pianism of this quality comes along far too infrequently, but when it does, connoisseurs rejoice." (*CT*, 2 Feb 1978)

In recent years, such conflicting views have given way to generally excellent reviews. A San Francisco recital (20 Nov 1982) included pieces by Debussy and Chopin and *ended* with Beethoven's "*Appassionata*" Sonata. "The pianist as painter was the intellectual base of Moravec's Debussy, and seldom have the impressionistic studies been so clear and so suggestive of nuance at the same time. . . . Moravec's Chopin included four Nocturnes and the Scherzo in B Minor, beautifully sung, tastefully accented, a treat even for the many pianists who were in the audience. In intensity, it was all leading up to Beethoven's 'Appassionata' Sonata. One was simply unprepared for the power that was unleashed in Moravec's Beethoven, with its wave after wave of beautiful sound, its perfectly weighted chords and ornamental effects. . . . With Moravec's keen insights, it was like hearing the Appassionata for the first time." (*SFC*, 22 Nov 1982)

Incredibly, Moravec's ("shamefully belated") debut with the New York Philharmonic Orchestra took place on 13 January 1989, when he played the Schumann Concerto in A Minor, Felix Kruglikov conducting. It was piano playing, said one reviewer, "that was warm, idiomatic and always attuned to the shifting emotional landscape of Schumann's world. Mr. Moravec has plenty of technique, but he didn't advertise it any more than he advertised himself. He simply played the music, beautifully." (*NYT*, 14 Jan 1989)

A recital played on 7 January 1993, in Princeton, New Jersey, with works by Haydn, Schubert, Debussy and Chopin, prompted an overview of Moravec's playing: "He is a lyric muse. No matter what the work, Moravec found the singing lines in it. . . . When playing Schubert's final large work, the B-flat Sonata, the melodies soared without ceasing, nearly oblivious to the accompaniments and harmonies supporting them. It was Schubert played with the ultimate in classical restraint and proportion. . . . The Debussy [*Pour le piano*] sparkled. The swatches of color glistened. Never have the scales been so clear. All the dramatic contrasts and dynamic excitement jumped off the page. . . . The Chopin Barcarolle and Ballade were, indeed, impeccable in technique and nuance but reserved. There were times one prayed for an earth-shattering crash or for some spiritual vision rising beyond temporal concerns." (*Star-Ledger* [Newark], 9 Jan 1993. Reprinted by permission)

Moravec made over a dozen recordings with the Connoisseur Society label between 1962 and 1969. Many of them won awards and were listed among "Best Recordings of the Year" by magazines such as *High Fidelity*, *Saturday Review*, and *Stereo Review*. When the Connoisseur Society ceased to exist, Moravec's recordings became collector's items. (They are now gradually being reissued on CD, see Discog.) In the early 1980s Moravec became affiliated with the Moss Music Group (*Vox Cum Laude*) and Nonesuch Records. His recordings and CD reissues on these labels and the *Supraphon* label attest to his talent.

Reviews of Moravec's recitals and recordings indicate that he is indisputedly one of the finest Chopin players of this century. His Chopin somehow gives the impression that this is the unique realization, that Chopin should sound no other way. His 1966 Connoisseur Society recording of the complete Nocturnes—now in CD reissue—stands as one of the great Chopin recordings of all time (Grammy, 1966), partly because of "the quite incomparable richness and realism of the recording, but mainly because of the beauty, depth, hypnotic concentration, and intensity of personal expression that Moravec brought to his interpretations of these pieces." (*ARG*, March/April 1992) A reissue of Moravec's 1965 Chopin Preludes for VAIA (see Discog.) was praised for the "dreamy tone and utterly perfect interpretations. . . . This is one of the two or three great Chopin pianists to record in modern sound." (*ARG*, Jan/Feb 1994)

Schumann presents a different style of romanticism than that of Chopin, and Moravec delineates this convincingly in his recording of the *Kinderscenen*, op. 15. Recorded in Prague, it is part of a CD taken from three recitals in that city in 1987 and 1988 (see Discog.). Each of the tiny miniatures becomes in essence a tiny tone poem, but Moravec's mastery ties them together in harmonious unity. On a much larger scale, Moravec's recording (*Supraphon* 11 0650-2) of the Schumann Concerto in A Minor, op. 54, with Vaclav Neumann conducting the Czech Philharmonic Orchestra, is truly masterful. There are literally dozens of Schumann Concerto recordings, but one cannot refrain from agreeing that Moravec's version is "surely one of the two or three finest performances of that elusive work ever committed to disc." (*HF*, July 1984)

It is difficult to read anything but praise in reviews of Moravec's recordings. For example, a most interesting Beethoven CD containing the Concerto No. 4 (with Martin Turnovsky and the Orchestra of the Vienna *Musikverein*), the seldom-played Sonata in E Minor, op. 90, and the popular 32 Variations on an Original Theme in C Minor (see Discog.) elicited this critique: "Moravec, the most refined of pianists, never indulges in mannered exaggeration. But neither does he homogenize the work's [Concerto No. 4] contrasts, its whispering *pianissimo* passages followed by forte outbursts. With his vast tonal palette and subtle sense of tempo variation, Moravec can give those contrasts full due." (*Fan*, May/June 1993)

His Brahms recordings earn similar raves. Moravec's 1989 recording of both Brahms Concertos with the Czech Philharmonic Orchestra, Jiri Belohlavek conducting, are magnificent: "All the right ingredients are here: the burnished refinement of the Czech Philharmonic captured in all its splendor, extraordinary rapport between Moravec and Belohlavek, and the playing of a soloist who combines meticulous attention to detail with an iron grasp of the Brahms idiom." (*ARG*, July/Aug 1992)

The Dorian CD 90172 couples the Brahms Concerto No. 1 and the Schumann Concerto, both made from live performances (Schumann in 1992, Brahms in 1993) with the Dallas Symphony Orchestra, Eduardo Mata conducting. While in no wise belittling the older versions, one critic writes, "What sets the Moravec/Mata [Brahms] apart is that extra edge generated by an occasion where all the right conditions coalesce. . . . Much the same can be said about the Schumann. The previous Moravec recording, with Vaclav Neumann, ranked as one of the best, but this is even better." (*ARG*, Jan/Feb 1994)

A recent Vox Box album (5103) contains recordings of Debussy (*Estampes, Images,*) and Chopin (mazurkas, waltzes, polonaises) made in 1982–83. Moravec's "performances here are impeccable in every respect. . . . Others offer more spontaneity, wit, and excitement but nobody creates a more evocative atmosphere or more beautiful sounds than Moravec." (*ARG*, Sept/Oct 1994)

SELECTED REFERENCES

Brown, Peggy. "Mozart Helped Boost a Pianist's Career." *Long Island Newsday*, 22 Jan 1988, sec. D, p. 5.

Commanday, Robert. "Ivan Moravec Brings Czech Music to Life." *San Francisco Chronicle*, 15 Oct 1984, p. 43.

Dawson, Eric. "Czech pianist has the spirit of a master." *Calgary Herald,* 10 Feb 1989.

Doerschuk, Bob. "Ivan Moravec: Reflections of a Czech Virtuoso." *Keyboard*, Jan 1983, pp. 18–24.

Elder, Dean. "Ivan Moravec: Conquering Chopin's Scherzo in C-sharp Minor." *Clavier*, Feb 1985, pp. 6–11.

Fisk, Josiah. "Czech pianist Moravec's playing has personality." *Boston Herald*, 11 Nov 1989.

Goodfriend, James. "Ivan Moravec: a pianist who prepares every note." *Stereo Review*, Jan 1981, pp. 90–91.

Gray, Channing. "Moravec, the master craftsman." *Providence Journal*, 7 Nov 1986.

Gray, Patricia. "Ivan Moravec: Portrait of the Artist and the Man." *Piano Quarterly*, Summer 1977, pp. 5–10.

———. "A Sort of Inner Radar." (interview) *Piano Quarterly*, Summer 1981, pp. 21–25.

Koehler, Ray. "Pianist displays quiet sensitivity." *Reading Eagle*, 9 Nov 1986.

Plaskin, Glenn. "A Pianist Reaches for a Wider Audience." *New York Times*, 24 Oct 1982, sec. 2, p. 17.

Rockwell, John. "Who Says Modern Pianists Are Un-Romantic?" *New York Times*, 3 June 1984, sec. 2, pp. 23, 26.

Shulgold, Marc. "Jet-age Concert World can't put Stopwatch on Talents of
   Czech Pianist Ivan Moravec." *Rocky Mountain News* (Denver, Colorado),
   22 Feb 1989.
Wigler, Stephen. "In Age of Hype, Fame Eludes Unhyped Pianist." *Baltimore
   Sun*, 8 Nov 1987, sec. M, pp. 1, 9.
See also Bibliography: New/Gro; Ran/Kon; WWAM.

SELECTED REVIEWS

BE: 10 Aug 1991. *CDN*: 2 Feb 1978. *CE*: 5 Nov 1984; 22 April 1989. *CPD*:
   14 Feb 1986; 16 Feb 1991. *CST*: 3 Feb 1978; 15 Dec 1986. *CT*: 2 Feb
   1978; 15 Dec 1986; 13 Nov 1989. *LAT*: 5 Feb 1982; 1 July 1994. *MH*: 4
   March 1982. *MJ*: 10 Feb 1978. *MM*: May 1983; June 1985. *MiT*: 5
   April 1985. *MT*: June 1959. *NYT*: 18 Feb 1964; 21 Oct 1968; 9 Feb
   1978; 2 March 1980; 26 Oct 1982; 28 March 1984; 14 Jan 1989. *PI*: 7
   Nov 1987. *PJ*: 24 Nov 1987. *RE*: 10 Nov 1986. *SFC*: 8 Feb 1982; 22
   Nov 1982; 12 March 1984; 15 Oct 1984; 20 Jan 1986; 8 Feb 1988; 13 Feb
   1989; 12 July 1991. *SFE*: 17 Feb 1978. *S-L*: 9 Jan 1993. *SM*: 16 Aug
   1986. *TL*: 4 May 1959; 11 May 1959; 28 April 1962; 7 March 1968; 11
   Dec 1975; 30 April 1985. *WP*: 14 July 1987; 10 May 1989.

SELECTED DISCOGRAPHY

Bach: Chromatic Fantasy and Fugue. Mozart: Sonata in B-flat Major, K. 333-
   315c. Schumann: *Kinderscenen*, op. 15. *Supraphon* 11 0359-2.
Beethoven: Concerto No. 3 in C Minor; Symphony No. 5. *Supraphon* 11
   0719-2. Neumann/Czech PO.
Brahms: Concerto No. 1 in D Minor, op. 15. Schumann: Concerto in A Minor,
   op. 54. Dorian DOR 90172 (CD). Mata/Dallas SO. Recorded from live
   performances.
Brahms: Concerto No. 1 in D Minor, op. 15: Intermezzi, op. 118, nos. 1 and 2.
   Supraphon 11 1274-2. Belohlavek/Czech PO.
Brahms: Concerto No. 2 in B-flat Major, op. 83. *Supraphon* 11 0953-2.
   Belohlavek/Czech PO.
Chopin: Barcarolle; Etude, op. 25, no. 7; Preludes; Scherzo No. 1. VAIA 1039
   (CD). Originally issued in 1965 by Connoisseur Society.
Chopin: Etudes, op. 25, nos. 1 and 7; Mazurkas, op. 7, no. 5, op. 41, no. 1,
   op. 56, no. 2, op. 68, no. 4; Scherzos (4). Dorian DOR-90140 (CD).
Chopin: Nocturnes (complete). Nonesuch 79233 (2 CDs). Originally issued in
   1966 by Connoisseur Society.
Franck: Symphonic Variations. Schumann: Concerto in A Minor, op. 54.
   Supraphon 11 0650-2. Neumann/Czech PO.
Ivan Moravec: French Keyboard Masterpieces. Debussy: Children's Corner;
   Claire de Lune: Pour le piano; Jardins sous la pluie (Estampes); Preludes,
   Book I: *La Cathédrale engloutie, Les Collines d'Anacapri*; Preludes, Book II:
   *Feuilles mortes, Feux d'artifice, Ondine, La puerta del vino, La Terrasse des
   audiences du clair de lune*. Franck: Prelude, Chorale and Fugue. Ravel:

Sonatine. VAIA 1043-2 (2 CDs). Originally issued in 1964 and 1969 by Connoisseur Society.

Ivan Moravec: Live in Prague. Smetana: 4 Czech Dances; Poetic Polka, op. 8, no. 2; Souvenir of Pilsen. Korte: Piano Sonata. Suk: Love Song, op. 7, no. 1; *Humoreska*, op. 7, no. 2. Elektra/Nonesuch 79146-2.

Ivan Moravec plays Beethoven. Concerto No. 4 in G Major, op. 58; Sonata in E Minor, op. 90; Variations in C Minor. VAIA 1021 (CD). Turnovsky/Vienna *Musikverein.* Originally issued by Connoisseur Society.

Ivan Moravec plays Beethoven, Vol. 2. Sonata in C Minor, op. 13; Sonata in C-sharp Minor, op. 27, no. 2; Sonata in F Minor, op. 57; Sonata in E-flat Major, op. 81a. VAIA 1092 (CD). Originally issued by Connoisseur Society.

Ivan Moravec plays Chopin. Ballades (4); Mazurkas, op. 7, no. 2, op. 17, no. 4, op. 24, no. 2, op. 50, no. 3, op. 63, no. 3. VAIA 1092 (CD). Originally issued by Connoisseur Society.

Ivan Moravec plays Chopin. Mazurkas in B-flat Major, op. 7, no. 1; C-sharp Minor, op. 30, no. 4; B Minor, op. 33, no. 4; F Minor, op. 63, no. 2; A Minor, op. 68, no. 2; Polonaise in C-sharp Minor, op. 26, no. 1; Polonaise Fantasie in A-flat Major, op. 61; Waltzes in A Minor, op. 34, no. 2; C-sharp Minor, op. 64, no. 2; E Minor, op. posth. MMG/*Vox Cum Laude* MCD 10016.

Ivan Moravec plays Debussy and Chopin. Debussy: *Estampes*; *Images.* Chopin: Mazurkas, op. 7, no. 1, op. 30, no. 4, op. 33, no. 4, op. 63, no. 2, op. 68, no. 2; Polonaises, op. 26, no. 1, op. 61; Waltzes, op. 34, no. 2, op. 64, no. 2, op. posth. Vox Box CDX 5103 (2 CD).

Mozart: Concerto in A Major, K. 488; Concerto In C Major, K. 503. *Supraphon* 11 0271-2. Vlach/Czech SO.

NOVAES, GUIOMAR: b. São João da Boa Vista (São Paulo district), Brazil, 28 February 1895; d. São Paulo, Brazil, 7 March, 1979.

> Her approach to music was said to be invariably elegant, poetic and intensely individual in her interpretations.
>
> Obituary (*New York Times*, 9 March 1979)

The pronounced and abiding individuality of her playing established Guiomar Novaes as one of the most personal pianists of this century. Even in her teens she had an unwavering confidence in her own approach to music and throughout more than 60 years of playing before the public, Novaes never changed her style. She played, always, in her own fashion, according to her own instincts, and she had the talent and authority to carry it off not only convincingly, but with elegance and charm.

Not even that eminent pedagogue Isidor Philipp could induce Novaes to change her way of playing. She always listened attentively to his suggestions and corrections concerning a piece, but then, as Philipp later told the story, when Novaes played the piece a second time for him, she played it exactly as she had done before. "The little Novaes," said Philipp, "was a force of nature." In time she won him over, and he let her be.

Where, one wonders, did Novaes's marvelous musical talent and that enormous self-confidence come from? She detested giving interviews, consequently there are few, and these contain scant, sometimes conflicting information. For example, one writer reports that Novaes was the 17th of 19 children, another that she was the third youngest of 17 children, and yet another speaks of

Novaes's mother raising 11 children. Suffice to say that her parents Anna (de Menezes) Novaes and Manoel da Cruz Novaes produced a huge family in São Pãulo. (Novaes happened to be born in the village of São João da Boa Vista only because her mother was there on an extended vacation.)

It was by no means a musical family. Novaes's father was in business and her mother was fully occupied raising children, although she had sung in a church choir before her marriage. But Novaes, as she herself said, "was always considered a musical child." Although she had not had piano lessons before entering kindergarten at age four, she was able to play on the piano the songs sung by the class. "No one had taught me the notes," she said, "but I knew where to find them; and I played because it seemed the only natural thing to do." (Novaes, "Simplicity. . .")

At about age six Novaes began lessons with Luigi Chiafarelli, a contemporary of Busoni in Italy who had been trained in Germany and made a point of returning to Europe every year to keep abreast of musical developments. Novaes had a weekly lesson with Chiafarelli, additional lessons with his assistant and every week participated in the class held at Chiafarelli's home. A prodigy, she progressed rapidly. She made her first public appearance at age seven and soon after undertook a tour of the São Pãolo district. By age 11, the year her father died, Novaes was playing the organ at the children's Mass at a local church. Meanwhile she also attended school, studying languages, history, literature and mathematics.

At age 14 Novaes, with a grant from the Brazilian government, a chaperone and a letter of recommendation from Chiafarelli to Isidor Philipp, arrived (13 Nov 1909) in Paris to apply for admittance to the Paris Conservatory. It was, she discovered, the last day to apply for enrollment and just two days before the first entrance examination. Reports on those examinations differ, but it seems certain that nearly 390 applicants were applying for 11 vacancies, only two of which were available to foreign students. All reports confirm that the petite 14-year-old Novaes's playing caused a sensation. At the first examination she played the Bach Prelude and Fugue in C-sharp Major from Book I of the Well-Tempered Clavier, the Liszt-Paganini Etude No. 4 in E Major, the Chopin A Flat Ballade and part of Schumann's *Carnaval*. Stunned by her Chopin playing, the jurors (among them Fauré, Debussy and Moszkowski) asked her to play the Ballade again at her second examination and ultimately they awarded her first place among all those applicants.

Novaes studied at the Paris Conservatory for two years, having three lessons a week with Isidor Philipp, practicing on the other days and also attending school to study French, German, Italian, history, geography, mathematics, literature and art. She made her Paris orchestral debut in January 1911 with the Châtelet Orchestra under Gabriel Pierné. After receiving her *premier prix* in piano in July 1911, the 16-year-old gave some performances in France, England, Switzerland, Germany and Italy, then had about two years at home in Brazil practicing and studying on her own.

In 1915 Brazil's ambassador to the United States took Novaes and her mother to New York, and her enormously successful American debut (11 Nov 1915) led to an American tour and a second one in 1916–17. Over the course of the following three years, much of it spent in the United States (she gave concerts and also had advanced coaching from Sigismond Stojowski in New York), Novaes laid the foundation of her long career. For more than 60 years she toured regularly in North America and South America and, less frequently, in Europe.

After her marriage (1922) to Octavio Pinto, a Brazilian civil engineer and also composer and pianist, Novaes continued with her career, sometimes playing her husband's piano pieces in her recitals and, while traveling from concert to concert, writing voluminous letters to her son and daughter. Often tempted to retire to have more time with her family, especially after her husband's death in 1950, Novaes always returned to her beloved piano. A recital at Hunter College on 2 December 1972 proved to be her final New York appearance. Guiomar Novaes suffered a stroke on 31 January 1979 and died in São Paulo on 7 March.

The epitome of the Romantic pianist, Novaes played more with heart, ears and instincts than with intellect, and it is no surprise that she was at her absolute best playing Chopin (she ranks as one of the greatest Chopinists of her time) and Schumann (audiences clamored to hear her play *Carnaval*). And just as she instinctively knew *how* she should play, Novaes always knew *what* to play. By today's standards hers was a modest repertoire with few, if any, thundering showpieces.

Many of her recital programs (as drafted from reviews taken from each decade of her 60-year career) began with Bach (either original or in transcription), or with a Scarlatti sonata or a French *clavecin* piece. Almost every program included a Beethoven work, usually a sonata, and also one or more pieces by Chopin. Schumann, especially *Carnaval*, appeared often. Over the years Novaes filled out her programs with works by diverse composers, such as Mendelssohn, Franck, Debussy, Moszkowski, Daquin, Gluck, Gottschalk, Villa-Lobos, Albéniz, Pinto and Halffter. The reviews indicate that Novaes's basic concerto repertoire, also small by today's standards, included the Grieg, Schumann and Chopin concertos, the Mozart Concerto in D Minor, K. 466, the Saint-Saëns Concerto No. 4 and the Beethoven Concertos Nos. 4 and 5.

During her student years she practiced about four or five hours a day, usually playing the standard exercises (Cramer, Czerny, Philipp) for technique and building up her repertoire. Once on the concert circuit, Novaes devoted her practice sessions to the pieces she was performing that current season. Surprisingly, we have an in-depth view of one of these sessions because the usually reticent Novaes once allowed a critic to listen while she practiced at Town Hall.

He reported that for two hours Novaes worked painstakingly on Beethoven's "*Waldstein*" Sonata. Beginning at the slowest possible tempo and playing each hand separately, she gradually worked up to half tempo, repeating "certain figures again and again, uncovering little melodies hidden in the passagework, testing the spaces between chords for the precise measure of silence." Finally, apparently satisfied, Novaes played the sonata up to tempo, "pouring out the great music in a liquid cascade that . . . glowed with an inner radiance." (*Time*, 13 Dec 1954) Why had Novaes, who by 1954 had been concertizing for

40 years, practiced so hard and so long on a piece she knew so well? Because, she explained to the critic, each time she played a work she played it differently, always discovering something new that made her wonder why she had not uncovered it before.

Her heavy concert schedule left little time for teaching, but Novaes willingly gave advice to young pianists, particularly to Nelson Freire, another Brazilian pianist. "Guiomar has inspired me a lot," Freire told interviewer Dean Elder. "It wasn't what she said—she said almost nothing—but it was the way she said it. It's hard to explain." (*CL*, Jan 1977) Novaes also outlined general advice for students in an *Etude* article (Aug 1927): Mastering piano technique in the early stages of development is vital; the best practice is slow practice, and the slower the better; developing a beautiful and varied tone quality is of prime importance. "Preparation for the depression of each key must be just as perfect as that of any instrumentalist or singer," wrote Novaes, "and the actual sounding of the tone must be finely regulated or the resultant tone will be of inferior quality with no further chance of improving upon it."

Clearly Novaes's piano playing was instinctive more than scholarly. She had an unerring sense of rhythm and seemed always to play spontaneously and effortlessly (making her fluid technique appear easy), and with a warmth and charm that captivated audiences. It follows that music always came easily to Novaes, that playing the piano was never a duty or drudgery. "I have always worked only when I felt like it," she said. "I don't believe in long hours, unless one is preoccupied with technique. And one shouldn't be because technique is such a minor matter." (Rich) "Naturally I have to prepare everything," she told another interviewer, "but when I am in public I never think of technique. I just play as I feel, as I think I should play. . . . I let myself go and give my mood of the moment." (Elder)

Whatever her mood, Novaes's playing had the utmost clarity. An honest performer, she used her fleet and flowing technique only to enhance the music, never for showy effect. The numerous critiques of her playing confirm her reputation as one of the most intensely personal pianists of her time. Not that she changed the notes—Novaes was always faithful to the composer—but she had a special gift for bringing out inner voices that most pianists completely ignored. She was also known for the utterly beautiful tone she drew from the piano, a tone ("iridescent," "melting," "ringing"), said more than one reviewer, that had a depth that seemed bottomless. Other critics insisted that her tone was equally as lustrous, lyrical and hypnotic as the wondrous tone of Paderewski.

Even critics disturbed by Novaes's intensely personal readings of well-known works greatly enjoyed her playing, largely because Novaes "was always saying something musically, and saying it with a complete mastery of the idiom. . . . Her taste is fastidious without becoming precious." (*MA*, 10 March 1941) Another reviewer conceded that even though there were times when he had "to stand on his head in reorientation of convictions" in order to understand Novaes's approach, it was worth it, "just for the pleasure of observing how imagination and authority—no matter how capricious—can produce a fascinating and provocative example of re-creation." (Cha/Spe, see Bibliog.)

Yet another writer, although puzzled by Novaes's reading of the Schumann *Carnaval,* still found it deeply absorbing and a "sign of Novaes's magnificent artistry that she could so persuasively reconstruct the scale of interest in one of the most personal masterpieces in piano literature." (*CT*, 22 March 1926) And some 15 years later another critic had this to say: "Though her interpretative ideas often travel the lesser known paths, one can be sure that there is a continuity and a long-range viewpoint that makes everything right." (*NYWT*, 9 March 1942)

A study of more than 80 reviews (written by diverse reviewers over the course of her long career) proves incontestably that critics greatly admired Novaes's playing. There are a few unfavorable comments ("emotional immaturity," "overdone pedaling," "extreme contrasts in dynamics and tempos," "too literal playing," "too brilliant playing") in the very earliest reviews; the rest are mostly accolades.

In retrospect, Richard Aldrich's perceptive review of Novaes's American debut recital (11 Nov 1915) served as a prototype for many later reviews. Aldrich admired Novaes's swift, fluent and generally accurate technique; her remarkably full, round and richly colored tone ("which even in the loudest passages never lost its beauty"); and the abundance of musical feeling evident in her brilliant playing. Not brilliancy for its own, said Aldrich, for Novaes's playing was graceful, charming and poetic, radiating glowing vitality, with no attempt to dazzle or make a personal display. On the negative side, Aldrich pointed out Novaes's sometimes extreme contrasts in dynamics or tempos, but, for him, they were not frequent enough "to seriously disturb her listeners; and there is very much in her playing to give them great artistic pleasure." (Ald/Con, see Bibliog.)

W. J. Henderson's early description of Novaes's performance (27 Oct 1918) of the Chopin Ballade No. 1 in G Minor may be flowery, but it, too, provided fitting phrases for later generations of reviewers: "Whether she strikes out massive phrases in grandiose utterance or betrays Chopin's most tender confidences in the half-heard breathing of a whispered caress, she never gives the impression of sheer force or violent contact. Her velvet fingers plunge down into the cool depths of the keys as swimmers into the heart of a sunlit sea, and around them all is moist, lucent, radiant." (*NYS*, 28 Oct 1918)

The witty James Huneker's review of Novaes's performance (13 March 1919) of the Grieg Concerto with the New York Philharmonic-Society, Josef Stransky conducting, also supplied pertinent phrases for later Novaes critiques: "Her rhythm was positively electrifying and her tone massive . . . her touch, i.e., her voice, was as velvety as the mellowest Chianti." (*NYT*, 14 March 1919)

An early (unidentified) British critic also provided pertinent descriptive phrases for later reviews of Novaes's playing: "Her Chopin [Sonata in B-flat Minor] was never sentimental, nor yet febrile. Rather we were conscious of an extraordinary fierceness in her interpretation of the music, even the softer passages revealing, as it were, the claw under the silk glove. . . . Here was an example of Chopin-playing perfect in its own way." (*MT*, 1 Dec 1925)

An all-Chopin program played during the 1924-25 season drew uniform praise. For example, "Mme. Novaes is as impressive in the power with which she renders compositions as in her delicacy and sureness of touch." (*NYEP*, 13 April 1925) Again, Novaes's performance (27 Oct 1938) of the Beethoven Concerto No. 4 in G Major, op. 58, inspired accolades. Her reading was "one of exquisite tone and technical brilliance. Particularly to be admired are her accomplishments in the scale and passage interludes where each fleeting note is cleanly articulated and crisp without the loss of legato. . . . Deep musical feeling is [demanded] and Miss Novaes met the requirements in musicality and imagination." (*MA*, 10 Nov 1938)

Reviews from successive decades follow the same pattern. A Novaes recital (22 Feb 1941) at Town Hall proved to be "delectable" all the way around: a truly poetic, aristocratic and elegant performance of the Chopin Sonata in B Minor, op. 58; a fastidious, exquisite performance of two Scarlatti sonatas; an unsurpassable performance of Debussy's *Poissons d'or*; and a most interesting reading of the Beethoven Sonata in D Minor, op. 31, no. 2. "One might well have asked for a stronger, more incisive playing . . . but it was a pleasure to hear an 'un-Beethovenish' performance of the work, for a change. . . . If Miss Novaes erred in making the music too transparent and graceful, it was in the right direction." (*MA*, 10 March 1941) When Novaes played the Beethoven Sonata in C Major, op. 53 ("*Waldstein*"), at a Hunter College recital (16 Oct 1960), hers was not, as one critic expressed it, "a metaphysical, star-groping Beethoven." She "played the music naturally and her approach was primarily lyric. Even when she built up the last movement with immense power, it was still essentially a lyric reading." (*NYT*, 17 Oct 1960)

At her Town Hall recital of 8 March 1942, "It was inescapably evident that Mme. Novaes is now one of the representative interpreters of our day—capable of the ultimate eloquence, the seizing imagery, the wash of sound to realize completely works as diverse as the D major toccata of Bach and the twenty-four preludes of Chopin." (*NYS*, 9 March 1942)

A Los Angeles recital (11 Jan 1952), an "exhibition of superlative music making," inspired an exceptionally complimentary review. Novaes opened the recital with Bach's Organ Prelude in G Minor and from the very first notes she created an improvisatory atmosphere that held throughout the program. Everything she played seemed to emanate from "a spontaneous outpouring of inspiration that had just struck that very moment. Of course nothing so polished or perfected is ever improvised; it is only great art that can make it appear so. And the sort of art Miss Novaes displayed is still one of the rarest things in the world of music." (*LAT*, 12 Jan 1952)

Fifty years after her first New York appearance, Novaes, age 71 and still in top form, played (3 March 1966) the Mozart Concerto in D Minor, K. 466, with the New York Philharmonic Orchestra, Thomas Schippers conducting. "Musically, of course, she is ageless," wrote one critic, "for the values in her art are untouched either by time or by fashion. . . . [Her Mozart] had its overtones of drama, but also its undertones of sentiment, all within a classic conception of balance and proportion." (*SR*, 19 March 1966) Novaes, wrote another critic, "filled the music with the beautiful ringing tone that is hers; the intuitive outlining of phrases, so clear yet so sensitively molded; the way she suddenly throws into relief certain subsidiary figurations that seem both original and right." (*NYT*, 4 March 1966)

Later that year a San Francisco recital (13 Nov 1966) convinced one bedazzled reviewer that Novaes was like a good wine: "After 50 years on the American concert stage, she's better than ever. . . . Miss Novaes is a phenomenon of the times. . . . Her technical mastery, poetics, and keyboard accuracy are at a peak." (*SFC*, 15 Nov 1966)

That would have been the perfect moment for retirement, but Novaes apparently could not give up concertizing. Six years later, at age 77, her untidy, detached playing all through the first half of her Hunter College recital (2 Dec 1972) wrung the hearts of those who remembered "the Novaes of the velvet paws, the Novaes of indescribable elegance and fluent technique." But then, somehow, the great Novaes of old was there for the second half: "The playing was strong and confident, with clear articulation, correct pedaling and a refined feeling for dynamics." (*NYT*, 4 Dec 1972)

Novaes made a large number of recordings, including most of Chopin's major works. (A complete discography can be found in James Methuen-Campbell's article in *Records and Recording*, May 1979.) She made a few records in the 1920s, but most of her discs were produced between 1950 and 1970. Many have been reissued on cassette and CD (see Discog.).

Several knowledgeable writers of music (Chasins, Elder, etc.) who heard Novaes in concert insist that her recordings rarely equal her high concert standards, largely because she was stimulated by an audience and obviously missed that interaction when playing alone in the recording studio. "Her genius," said Chasins, "lay in doing naturally what comes naturally. Her entire nature is evidently stimulated and enhanced by audiences as they are by her presence, for it is primarily on the platform that the full force of her personality is freely expressed and significantly revealed." (*SR*, 31 March 1956) And from Nelson Freire, who knew Novaes well: "It was a struggle for her to make records. She's spontaneous; she does many things just once." (*CL*, Jan 1977) Those comments help to explain why the quality of Novaes's recordings varies considerably.

Her Chopin discs are particularly outstanding. The cassette entitled *Chopin Favorites* (see Discog.) provides an excellent introduction to the art of Novaes. Crystalline clarity, articulation and glistening cascades of sound in the Scherzo in C-sharp Minor, op. 39, place it among the great performances of all times, and the same high musical quality is present in her playing of the "Minute" Waltz, the Impromptu, op. 36, the Etude, op. 10, no. 3, and the great Fantasy in F Minor, op. 49. The *Berceuse* is noticeably uneven, with wrong notes marring the limpid flow of Chopin's arabesques.

The delicate rhythmic patterns and Novaes's obvious empathy with the music place her collection of Chopin mazurkas (11 on cassette) right alongside the illustrious mazurka recordings of Rubinstein and Horowitz. Her recordings of the F Minor Concerto, op. 21, and the complete 24 Preludes are also excellent. Famous in her day for her interpretations of the Chopin sonatas, Novaes's recorded version of the Sonata in B-flat Minor, particularly the Finale, is a delight to hear.

But her recordings of the Chopin nocturnes and etudes do not measure up to the all-around high performance standards of her recordings of the sonatas and preludes. To be sure, some are fine, for example, the difficult Nocturne in C Minor, op. 48, no. 1, and the Etude in E Major, op. 10, no. 3; but there are numerous instances where one is puzzled by exaggerated *rubato* and unexpected tempo changes that seemingly contradict the composer's intent. Then, too, Novaes simply was not technically equipped to play some of the etudes, all too evident when one compares her recording of Op. 10, no. 1, with that of Moriz Rosenthal!

As with Chopin, Novaes had an affinity for playing Schumann, and it shines through in the Schumann works she recorded. Two of the best are the *Papillons,* op. 2, and the *Kinderscenen*, op. 15, where the romanticism of the composer meets and blends with the sensitive, emotional nature of the performing artist. Schumann's great Concerto in A Minor, op. 54, as performed by Novaes, is vibrant rhythmically and unfolds with an outstanding feeling for and understanding of Schumann's style. The *Carnaval*, op. 9, which Novaes loved to play in concert (and audiences loved to hear), is also given a loving, dedicated performance.

Novaes's other recordings are mostly interesting, if sometimes overpersonalized examples of her talent. Her Beethoven recordings include a fine Op. 111 ("among the best on record" [Wigler]), a performance of the lyrical Concerto No. 4, op. 58, that unequivocally places her among the great 20th-century pianists and a magisterial reading of the Concerto No. 5, op. 73 ("Emperor"), that fully substantiates Novaes's reputation as an outstanding keyboard artist.

SELECTED REFERENCES

Chasins, Abram. "The Realm of Queen Guiomar." *Saturday Review*, 31 March 1956, pp. 40–41.

Cooper, Frank. "The Grandest Piano Concert of Modern Times." *Clavier*, Jan 1971, pp. 12–14, 21.

Elder, Dean. "Guiomar Novaes—an Interview." *Clavier*, Oct 1971, pp. 10–20.

Finck, Henry. "Guiomar Novaes of Brazil." In *My Adventures in the Golden Age of Music* (Fin/My, see Bibliog.), pp. 315–318.

Kinscella, Hazel G. "'Mechanical Memory' comes from too much fast practice, says Guiomar Novaes." *Musical America*, 9 Feb 1918, p. 31.

Methuen-Campbell, James. "Guiomar Novaes: An Appreciation." *Records and Recording*, May 1979, pp. 27–28. Includes a discography.

Novaes, Guiomar. "Simplicity as a Background for Art." (interview with Rose Heylbut). *Etude*, March 1939, pp. 153–154.

———. "Technic and Beauty in Piano Playing." *Etude*, Aug 1927, pp. 565–566.

Obituary. *New York Times*, 9 March 1979, sec. 2, p. 6.

Oliveira, José da Veiga. "*Guiomar Novaes—Uma Plenitude Artistica.*" *Revista Do Arquivo Municipal*, 1981, pp. 7–30.

Peeler, Clare. "Guiomar Wants Americans to Understand her Brazil Better."
    Musical America, 22 June 1918, p. 31.
Rich, Alan. "Guava Paste, Chopin and Brazil." *New York Times*, 15 July
    1962, sec. 2, p. 7.
Rockwell, John. "Guiomar Novaes Declines To Call It a Piano Finale." *New
    York Times*, 2 Dec 1972, p. 42.
Rust, Roberta. "Remembering Guiomar Novaes." *Clavier*, April 1991, pp. 20–
    22.
Schonberg, Harold C. "Her Right-to-the-Heart-of-It Style Brought Sheer
    Pleasure and Delight to Audiences." *New York Times*, 9 March 1979, sec.
    2, p. 6.
Wigler, Stephen. "The Girl From Brazil." *Classical Pulse*, Dec 1994, p. 24.
See also Bibliography: Bro/Pia; Cha/Spe; Coo/Gre; Cur/Bio (1953); Woo/My.

SELECTED REVIEWS

LAT: 4 Jan 1952; 12 Jan 1952; 30 April 1958; 16 July 1958; 4 Dec 1962; 18
Nov 1968. *MA*: 20 Nov 1915; 29 April 1916; 2 Dec 1916; 10 Nov 1917; 9
Nov 1918; 25 Dec 1937; 10 Nov 1938; 10 March 1941; Jan 1961. *MT*: 1
Dec 1925; 1 Jan 1926. *NYEP*: 13 April 1925; 5 Dec 1932. *NYS*: 28 Oct
1918; 13 April 1925; 9 March 1942. *NYT*: 12 Nov 1915; 23 Nov 1916;
19 March 1917; 28 Oct 1918; 14 March 1919; 15 Feb 1920; 17 April
1921; 24 Jan 1923; 4 Dec 1932; 13 Dec 1936; 3 March 1940; 27 Oct 1946;
23 Nov 1947; 9 Nov 1952; 10 Nov 1957; 28 June 1958; 19 Oct 1959; 4
March 1966; 21 March 1966; 24 Oct 1966; 4 Dec 1972. *NYW*: 28 March
1920. *SFC*: 15 Nov 1966. *SR*: 19 March 1966. *TL*: 7 Oct 1912; 23 Oct
1912; 7 May 1913; 27 May 1913; 1 May 1967.

SELECTED DISCOGRAPHY

The Art of Guiomar Novaes. Vol. 1. Chopin: Ballade in A-flat Major, op. 47;
    Ballade in F Minor, op. 52; *Berceuse*, op. 57; 3 *Ecosaisses*, op. 72; Etude
    in G-flat Major, op. 10, no. 5; Etude in G-flat Major, op. 25, no. 9;
    Polonaise in F-sharp Minor, op. 44; Polonaise in A-flat Major, op. 53.
    Vanguard Classics OVC 8071 (CD).
Beethoven: Concerto No. 4 in G Major, op. 58; Sonata in C-sharp Minor, op.
    27, no. 2. Allegro cassette ACS-8050. Swarowsky/Vienna Pro Musica
    SO.
Beethoven: Sonata in C-sharp Minor, op. 27, no. 2; Sonata in E-flat Major, op.
    81a; Sonata in C Minor, op. 111. Vanguard Classics OVC 8072 (CD).
Chopin Favorites. *Berceuse*, op. 57; Etude in E Major, op. 10, no. 3; Fantasy
    in F Minor, op. 49; Nocturne in F-sharp Major, op. 15, no. 5; Impromptu
    in F-sharp Major, op. 36; Scherzo in C-sharp Minor, op. 39; Waltz in D-
    flat Major, op. 64, no. 1. Allegro cassette ACS-8094.
Chopin: Mazurkas (11). Allegro cassette ACS-8132.
Chopin: Preludes, op. 28; Sonata in B-flat Minor, op. 35. Vox STPL 510.940.

Chopin: Sonata No. 2 in B-flat Minor, op. 35; Sonata No. 3 in B Minor, op.
    58. Allegro cassette ACS 8078.
Chopin: Waltzes. Vox PL 8170.
The Classical Novaes. Beethoven: Concerto No. 5 in E-flat Major, op. 73
    (Perlea/ Bamberg SO). Mozart: Concerto in E-flat Major, K. 271; Concerto
    in D Minor, K. 466 (Swarowsky/Vienna SO); Sonata in G Major, K. 283;
    Sonata in A Major, K. 331; Sonata in C Major, K. 545. Vox Legends
    CDX2 5512 (2 CDs). Rec. early 1950s.
The Complete Victor 78 rpm Recordings, 1919-1927. Albéniz (arr. Godowsky):
    Tango in D Major. Beethoven (arr. Rubinstein): Turkish March. Chopin:
    Mazurka in D Major, op. 33, no. 2. Gluck (arr. Friedman): Dance of the
    Blessed Spirits. Gluck (arr. Brahms): Gavotte. Gottschalk: *Hymne
    National Brésilien.* Ibert: The Little White Donkey. Levy: Brazilian
    Tango. Liszt: *Gnomenreigen*; *Waldesrauschen.* MacDowell: Witches'
    Dance, op. 17, no. 2. Mendelssohn: Spring Song, op. 62, no. 6.
    Moszkowski: *Guitarre*, op. 45, no. 2; *La Jongleuse*, op. 52, no. 4.
    Paderewski: Nocturne in B-flat Major, op. 16, no. 4. Philipp: *Feux follets*,
    op. 24, no. 3. Rubinstein: Nocturne in G Major, op. 75, no. 8. Villa-
    Lobos: *O Polichinelo.* Music and Arts CD-702.
Debussy: Preludes (Book I). Allegro cassette ACS 8136.
Guiomar Novaes/Otto Klemperer. Bach: Prelude in G Minor. Beethoven:
    Concerto No. 4 in G Major, op. 58; Turkish March (arr. A. Rubinstein).
    Brahms: Capriccio in D Minor, op. 76; Intermezzo in B-flat Minor, op.
    117, no. 2; Waltz in A-flat Major, Op. 39, no. 15. Chopin: Concerto No.
    2 in F Minor, op. 21. Gluck: Dance of the Blessed Spirits (arr. Sgambati).
    Saint-Saëns: *Caprice sur les airs de Ballet d'Alceste.* Schumann: Concerto
    in A Minor, op. 54. Vox Legends CDX2 5501 (2 CDs).
    Klemperer/Vienna SO. Rec. late 1950s and early 1960s.
Guiomar Novaes plays Chopin. Etudes, op. 10; Etudes, op. 25; Nocturnes;
    Sonata in B-flat Minor, op. 35. Vox Legends CDX3 3501 (3 CDs). Rec.
    mid-1950s.
The Romantic Novaes. Chopin: *Berceuse*, op. 57; Concerto No. 1 in E Minor,
    op. 11 (Perlea/Bamberg SO); Impromptu in F-sharp Major, op. 36; *Trois
    Nouvelles Etudes*; Scherzo No. 1 in B Minor, op. 20; Scherzo No. 3 in C
    Minor, op. 39; Sonata in B Minor, op. 58. Falla: Nights in the Gardens of
    Spain. Grieg: Concerto in A Minor, op. 16. Vox Legends CDX2 5513 (2
    CDs). Swarowsky/Vienna SO.
Schumann: *Carnaval*, op. 9. *Kinderscenen*, op. 15; *Papillons*, op. 2. Turnabout
    TV 34164S.

O

OGDON, JOHN ANDREW HOWARD: b. 27 January 1937, Mansfield Woodhouse, Nottinghamshire, England; d. London, England, 1 August 1989.

> Even in an age when glittering technique is almost taken for granted, Ogdon's facility for both the fine-spun and the fantastic is prodigious.
>
> *Time* (22 February 1971)

Through most of the 1960s John Ogdon, a gentle giant with a prodigious high-powered talent, reigned as Britain's most acclaimed, most sought-after young pianist. By the early 1970s recurring bouts of mental illness began to interrupt his steamrolling career, and ultimately forced it to a halt. After years of intermittent hospitalizations, recovery periods and relapses, Ogdon resumed his career in 1981, playing very well if not with his former electrifying style. However, reviews from later in the 1980s show that there were times when the old Ogdon—awesome and often astonishing—reappeared. Fighting mental illness, Ogdon failed to fulfill the great promise of his early career, but "he was an artist who in his last, much-applauded performances, as in his first, established a unique niche for himself in British music-making." (Greenfield)

John Ogdon's personal and musical development ties directly to his background. His father Howard Ogdon, an English teacher and amateur musician, was a highly intelligent eccentric who suffered a breakdown, spent three years in a mental hospital and later wrote a book about his illness (Ogdon, Howard). John Ogdon's mother, Dorothy, nurtured and protected both her husband and her talented youngest child, John. She waited on, picked up after, and so thoroughly spoiled John that he grew up disorganized, dependent and unable to take care of himself in the ordinary routine of daily living. As an adult, this ambling hulk of a man still expected—and needed—someone to look after him.

He was a slow learner when it came to walking and talking, but Ogdon played the piano at age five and began composing when he was nine. A Miss Houseley gave him his first formal piano lessons when he was six. About a year later his family moved to Manchester, where he was enrolled at the Royal Northern College of Music to study piano with Iso Elinson and composition with Richard Hall. Ogdon was 10 years old when his parents stopped his music studies and sent him to the Manchester Grammar School for his general education. However, on his own he kept up his music, practicing a lot of Czerny and, from about age 12, stacks of music he got from the library, especially piano arrangements of symphonies.

At age 16 Ogdon returned to the RNCM. Not knowing whether he wanted to be a pianist or a composer, he studied piano with Claude Biggs, a Bach specialist, and composition with Thomas Pitfield. Ogdon practiced intensively at college, and he also became aware of modern music through contact with "New Music, Manchester," a group of young composers, among them Peter Maxwell Davies, Harrison Birtwistle, Alexander Goehr and Elgar Howarth. Endowed with a phenomenal memory (Biggs claimed that Ogdon could learn in one week what other students took months to learn) and an incredible sight-reading ability, Ogdon was the one always called upon to play the new works. This group made him so conscious of modern music, especially that of the second Viennese school, that his first public concerts included Webern's Variations, Davies's Trumpet Sonata and Goehr's Three Clarinet Pieces. Ogdon took all honors in his class, and on 11 July 1956 played the Brahms Concerto No. 1 with the student orchestra, conducted by Sir John Barbirolli, considered a hero in Manchester for turning the Hallé into one of England's finest orchestras.

After graduation, Ogdon returned as a part-time student for advanced studies. With a grant from the RNCM, he studied (winter 1957–58) with Egon Petri in Basel, Switzerland, three months of training that proved to be a key factor in his musical development. In 10 three-hour sessions Petri, a student of Ogdon's idol Ferruccio Busoni, led Ogdon to a broader understanding of Busoni, stimulated his interest in Alkan, another neglected composer, and coached him on works by Beethoven, Chopin and Brahms. Petri was very clear in explaining his interpretations and his technique, and his in-depth analysis of each work had an impressive, lasting influence on Ogdon.

Ogdon returned to England early in 1958 and stayed with his mother in Manchester, composing and practicing. Later that year he began making regular trips to London to study with Denis Matthews, who, Ogdon always felt, gave him a real feeling for Classical style. Ogdon played the Beethoven Concerto No. 3 with the BBC Northern Orchestra on a radio program; played Liszt's *Totentanz* with the Royal Liverpool Philharmonic Orchestra; and in November 1958 returned to Liverpool to play the Busoni Concerto for Piano, Orchestra and Men's Chorus with the RLPO, conducted by John Pritchard. Ogdon's powerful, confident and brilliant playing and the fact that he played the mammoth, unfamiliar work without a score absolutely astounded his listeners. Early in 1959 he began making regular trips to Liverpool to study with Gordon Green. In May he took second prize in the first Liverpool International Piano Concerto Competition. He made his Proms debut (8 Aug 1959) with the London Symphony Orchestra, Basil Cameron conducting, and made his London recital debut (29 Sept 1959) at Wigmore Hall. The prestigious music agency of Ibbs and Tillett signed Ogdon as a client and by the end of that busy year had him playing all over Great Britain. John Ogdon and Brenda Lucas, a pianist he had met at the RNCM, married in July 1960 and settled in Manchester.

In January 1961 Ogdon took first prize in a Franz Liszt Competition, held in London, with an "inspired" performance of Liszt's B Minor Sonata. Not a traditional event but a promotion for a film about Liszt (*Song Without End*), this was nonetheless a competition with high standards. Louis Kentner headed the jury, the event had broad media coverage and the finals were televised. The publicity generated by winning the competition, plus the success of his first recording (1960) galvanized Ogdon's already fast-moving British career. He had so many bookings and, at his agents' request, substituted for so many indisposed pianists that he acquired the nickname "Slogger Ogger."

To prepare for the 1962 Tchaikovsky Competition, he took lessons in London with the Hungarian teacher Ilona Kabos. At the competition Ogdon's performance of the Liszt E-flat Concerto received a four-minute ovation from the Moscow audience and advanced him to the finals. First, however, the over-booked pianist had to return to London to play the Tchaikovsky Concerto No. 1 at Festival Hall, after which he flew back to Moscow and played the same concerto in the competition finals. The jury, headed by Emil Gilels, awarded a joint first prize to John Ogdon and Vladimir Ashkenazy. Ogdon's career skyrocketed. Requests for him to play came from around the world—it is said that he once traveled 30,000 miles in one month—and the impresario Sol Hurok became his American agent. For nearly a dozen years Ogdon's life was a constant round of appearances: solo recitals, performances with orchestra, radio and television events, interviews, not to mention recording sessions, parties and receptions.

To be nearer to London, the musical hub of Great Britain, the Ogdon family (a daughter was born in 1961) moved from Manchester to Isleworth, Middlesex. Besides his countless engagements in Great Britain, during the 1960s and early 1970s Ogdon toured in the United States, the Far East, Israel, Australia, New Zealand, South Africa, Kenya and in Europe on both sides of the Iron Curtain. Jet lag apparently never bothered him. He accepted every engagement he could cram into his schedule and, although now internationally famous, would still substitute for indisposed colleagues, even those of lesser fame. Besides concertizing, he recorded (eventually more than 40 records), added to his repertoire and continued to promote modern music. Somehow, he also found time to compose (over 200 works in his lifetime). By the time he was 25, Ogdon had become "the most talked about and admired of the young English musicians, considered by many to be the successor of the legendary Busoni." (*NYT*, 15 July 1962)

John Ogdon began to show behavioral changes as early as the late 1960s, and the word "demonic" sometimes appeared in his reviews. It had nothing to do with playing loud or brilliantly or fast. What critics and audiences began to sense was some kind of inner intensity that, while it never seemed to show offstage, would sometimes completely overtake him during performances, leaving him euphoric and dripping with perspiration. For some reason, in September 1965 Ogdon signed with a new agent, Basil Horsefield, and soon after, Hurok dropped Ogdon from his roster. Within two years Ogdon's concerto bookings had dropped so much that in 1967 he asked Ibbs and Tillett to take him back. By 1968 he was again playing too often and pushing himself too hard, but his growing fame and fortune enabled him to move his family (now four, Richard having been born in 1965) into the prestigious neighborhood of Chester Terrace, London. However, the signs were already present (friends and colleagues worried because he was drinking and smoking heavily) that Ogdon's inner conflicts and the pressures of his high-powered celebrity and expensive social life were taking a severe toll.

Ogdon began the 1970s with his usual nonstop schedule. Although by 1972 he was obviously more erratic, dogmatic, impatient and ill-tempered, he still went on tour, gave master classes, taught and composed, unable or unwilling to stop. Finally aware of his increasingly aggressive, irrational behavior and fearing that he had his father's illness, he sought help from a psychiatrist. Ahead of him lay sad years—suicide attempts, costly hospitalizations and treatments, cycles of relapses and recoveries, canceled performances. Treated with drugs, he was well enough in 1975 to accept a position as professor of piano at the University of Indiana Music School in Bloomington. In August 1976 the Ogdon family, now overloaded with debt because of extravagance and his illness, made a new start in Bloomington. The University allowed him to concertize—amazingly, the drugs had not affected his wonderful memory—but in time he had so many engagements that the university administration began to complain of his absences. In the midst of this new success, Ogdon suffered a relapse and again began to cancel concerts, but between bouts of illness, he played in Iran and Japan. At the end of 1978 he was admitted to a Bloomington hospital and treated with Lithium. It proved to be a lifesaver. He had to resign his teaching position, but he stayed in Bloomington until late in 1980.

After a three-year absence, on 5 February 1981 Ogdon (substituting for the late Hans Richter-Haaser) gave a London performance that, said one critic, was sketchy by the standards of Ogdon's glorious youthful period, "but powerfully felt and projected, and with moments of exquisite delicacy." (*TL*, 6 Feb 1981) Although in and out of hospitals, often admitting himself as a patient, Ogdon was able to perform—in England, France, Italy, Sweden, Germany and the Soviet Union.

Unexpectedly, after just one day in the hospital, John Ogdon died of bronchopneumonia on 1 August 1989, at the age of 52. He may never have regained his former fame, but he never lost his formidable technique, his musical imagination or his unique ability to surprise an audience with the power and intelligence of his playing. Only a year before his death Ogdon gave a stupendous performance (14 July 1988, Queen Elizabeth Hall) of Kaikhosru Sorabji's gargantuan piano work *Opus clavicembalisticum*, a 252-page score of awesome technical challenges. One after another, Ogdon conquered every technical improbability—"the epic chordal cascades, the frenetic chromatic lines racing five ways simultaneously, the complex chains of emphasis needed to make even partial sense of the fugues." (*TL*, 15 July 1988) John Ogdon, always a pianistic original, never an orthodox pianist, remained a magnificent pianist to the end.

Ogdon was no ordinary pianist. He was an unusual man and unorthodox musician, one whose propensities for unusual programming and lengthy recitals prevented him from becoming a "popular" pianist. Not a specialist in the commonly understood meaning of the word, he was indeed a specialist in the unusual, the neglected, the new. He seldom gave what could be called a "standard" recital, and when he did, it was usually a heroic one featuring works bristling with formidable problems. For example, a 1973 London recital included *two* Beethoven sonatas—op. 57 and op. 109—*two* Chopin Ballades and *three* virtuoso pieces by Liszt. Being a composer as well as performer, Ogdon relished programming 20th-century keyboard music on his recitals, giving particular emphasis to British composers.

Ogdon was always famous for his technical prowess. When, as a student, he played the Brahms Concerto No. 1 in Manchester (11 July 1956), a critic commented: "Where the concerto was technically most demanding, the pianist was most impressive: his heavy chords and double trills were forceful and exact, and he stroked the keyboard elegantly in the soft legato arpeggios." (*GM*, 12 July 1956) And when Ogdon played Liszt's Concerto No. 1 for his London Proms debut (8 Aug 1959), his technical skills were in full sail: "In so far as prestidigitation and sheer exuberance were concerned . . . Mr. Ogdon passed his test with flying colours." (*TL*, 10 Aug 1959)

Ogdon's New York debut (16 Jan 1964) was a qualified success. "He seemed like a very thoughtful pianist, with decided lyric gifts [Beethoven Sonata in E major, op. 109]. Then came the Brahms Variations on a Theme of Paganini, and Mr. Ogdon began playing too fast. . . . Busoni's Sonatina Secondo, however, won back the interest, for it was full of mystery and odd colors." (*NYT*, 17 Jan 1964)

Ogdon continued to receive plaudits for his great physical command of the keyboard and, at the same time, frequent questionings as to his supposed lack of emotional involvement and choice of repertoire. Yet his career flourished. Fellow musicians displayed a healthy respect for the wondrous things that he could accomplish at the piano. A review ("Recital by Most Musical Pianist") of a London recital (11 April 1965) defines Ogdon at the height of his career: "Mr. John Ogdon is about five times as musical as any other pianist in this country, and though that does not mean that he plays consistently with such finish (or even with such persuasiveness) as some of his colleagues, the virtue illumines his recitals. His musicality is proclaimed in his repertory, which changes all the time . . . and it can be heard in his ability to play a simple piece with complete, spontaneous directness so that it sounds more marvellous than the most heaven-storming flight of rhetorical eloquence." (*TL*, 12 April 1965)

When Ogdon played four Scriabin sonatas on a Los Angeles recital (19 Jan 1973), he revealed, at least for one critic, a special affinity for Scriabin's music. "The technical challenges are colossal and he met them head on with effortless virtuosity. The interpretative insights were on a comparable level; it would be hard to imagine a clearer exposition of all the variegated tonal effects, the emotional frenzies, the sudden relapses into what Scriabin called 'soul states'." (*LAT*, 22 Jan 1973) Ogdon's sympathetic bond with Scriabin showed again at an all-Scriabin recital (sonatas and etudes) at a 1977 festival in Charleston, South Carolina: "Scriabin's piano music is very thick textured, busy as Times Square at high noon, but Ogdon untangled it, held up the important strands for us all to hear, and never once made it sound unwieldy." (*CNC*, 5 June 1977)

Ogdon's performance of Busoni's complex *Fantasia contrappuntistica,* the high point of a "characteristically hefty programme" in London on 23 April 1986, produced an intricately favorable review. "He charted a lucid course through Busoni's vast tracts of labyrinthine counterpoint and homed in unerringly on the penultimate 'Corale' section, a masterstroke of keyboard sonority, with the work's opening chord-sequence returning in mystical, stratospheric regions while an ostinato quaver figure growls in the lightless depths below." (*MT*, July 1986)

On 14 July 1988, John Ogdon gave the first complete performance in England of Kaikhosru Sorabji's gargantuan *Opus clavicembalisticum.* By any criteria, Ogdon's 240-minute musical marathon was amazing. The work abounds in incredible technical hurdles and "Ogdon conquered them, one after another, with magnificent resource and sheer guts. . . . Four hours after starting, he seemed to be playing more brilliantly than ever. Finally, a somewhat stunned audience rose in euphoric acclaim." (*TL*, 15 July 1988)

Ogdon made a number of recordings during his short and intermittently brilliant career. Many of the LPs are no longer available. These include an album of Nielsen compositions (RCA Red Seal LSC-3002), the great Beethoven Sonata, op. 106 (RCA Red Seal LSC-3213) and the Alkan Concerto for Solo Piano (RCA Red Seal LSC-3192). However, a number of his discs are now in CD reissue, the finest being those made when Ogdon was in his prime. One of these, the Busoni Concerto (Grammy, 1968), shows Ogdon as the keyboard giant that he was. As one critic wrote, "This 1967 recording of Busoni's piano concerto catches him at the zenith of his career and in the blush of one of his most resplendent triumphs." (*Fan*, July/Aug 1990) Here the pianist's strengths shine forth in great style. The seemingly effortless technique, enchanting variety of tone and touch, artful phrasing—all are present in abundance.

The case for the other large Busoni work which Ogdon recorded, the formidable *Fantasia contrappuntistica* (see Discog.) is not as compelling or persuasive. He put it to disc after his emergence from bouts with mental illness. Originally appearing in LP format with Busoni's Fantasia after J. S. Bach (Altarus 2-9074), it was later reissued on CD, considerably enhanced and with the addition of the Toccata, among the composer's last completed works for the piano. Knowledgeable opinions on the disc differ. One review of the LP called this "a performance so powerfully culminatory that one can almost imagine it being recorded in a single 'take.'. . . Ogdon's comprehension of this idealistic synthesis and coexistence of styles, his ability to emphasize both the *Fantasia's* disparity and its unity is perhaps the most praiseworthy (and the most deeply

Busonian) aspect of this remarkable performance." (*Gram*, Oct 1988) The same critic, writing of the later CD collection, felt that Ogdon's brilliance in all three completed "a Busonian triple self-portrait: grandly magisterial in the *Fantasia contrappuntistica*, profoundly and movingly meditative in the *Fantasia nach J. S. Bach*, bitterly contemplating defeat in the *Toccata*." (*Gram*, July 1989)

Another reviewer reacted to Ogdon's performances on LP somewhat differently: "In the works at hand his tempos are massively deliberate with little or no gain in clarity, but with a great softening of edge. . . . The *Fantasia contrappuntistica* [was] slugged out amid alternately limp and pedantic feints which carry it to a side break at the end of the third fugue." (*Fan*, Sept/Oct 1987) Again the same critic found the CD format "alternately rough-hewn and sculpted but always granitic, anguishing, and monumental. The preference for massive sonorities often pushes both the instrument and the recording to their limits." (*Fan*, Sept/Oct 1989)

Another "monumental" performance of a monumental composition, the *Opus clavicembalisticum* of Kaikhosru Sorabji, as recorded by Ogdon, requires four CDs (see Discog.). The complex fugues, theme with 40 variations, passacaglia with 81 variations—all demand a transcendental technique. It is a formidable task even for the listener, but, wrote one reviewer, "From the hammered-out single notes of the raga-like opening to the closing pages . . . is an epic journey in which one experiences spectacular feats of virtuosity, discovers immensely still, quiet pools of lyricism, risks being buried under avalanches of notes and pummelled by all manner of eruptive violence; and afterwards is never quite the same again." (Driver)

The recordings of Franck, Fauré and Grieg (see Discog.) reveal another side of Ogdon. These lovely examples of late 19th-century piano repertoire require a sensitive, yet controlled command of the keyboard, a delicate balance between classic restraint and romantic abandon. Ogdon achieves all this in these readings.

SELECTED REFERENCES

Alexander, John. "John Ogdon—A Discography." *Music and Musicians*, Feb 1987, p. 13.

Blyth, Alan. "Ogdon: composer and pianist." *Music and Musicians*, April 1968, pp. 22, 49.

Driver, Paul. "Lap of honour for a marathon man." *Sunday Times* (London), 13 Oct 1991, Records, p. 15.

Greenfield, Edward. "Power and patience." *The Times*, 2 Aug 1989, p. 2.

Longworth, R. C. "When Titans Crumble." *Chicago Tribune*, 30 Aug 1989, sec. 13, pp. 32, 34.

Matthew-Walker, Robert. "John Ogdon at 50." *Music and Musicians*, Feb 1987, p. 12.

Obituary. *Gramophone*, Sept 1989, p. 426; *New York Times*, 2 Aug 1989, sec. 4, p. 22; *The Times* (London), 2 Aug 1989, p. 16.

Ogdon, Brenda Lucas. "Madly Gifted: A Musician's Struggle with Insanity." *The Sunday Times* (London), 21 June 1981, pp. 33–34.

Ogdon, Brenda Lucas, and Michael Kerr. *Virtuoso: The Story of John Ogdon.* London: Hamish Hamilton, 1981.
Ogdon, J. A. Howard. *The Kingdom Of The Lost.* London: The Bodley Head, 1947.
Ogdon, John. "The Romantic Tradition," in *Keyboard Music,* ed. Denis Matthews. Middlesex: Penguin Books, 1972, pp. 209–258.
———. "Solo Piano Music (1861–86)," in *Liszt: The Man and His Music,* ed. Alan Walker. New York: Taplinger, 1970, pp. 134–167.
Owen, Michael. "Playing for real—Ogdon is back." *The Times* (London), 1 Feb 1981, p. 32.
"Unromantic Romantic." *Time,* 22 Feb 1971, p. 78.
"Why John Ogdon is smiling." *The Sunday Times* (London), 1 Feb 1981, p. 32.
See also Bibliography: IWWM; Kai/Gre; Kol/Que; Mac/Gr2; Rat/Cle.

SELECTED REVIEWS

CNC: 5 June 1977. *GM*: 12 July 1956. *LAT*: 22 Jan 1973; 9 Aug 1973. *MM*: June 1965. *MT*: June 1969; March 1972; July 1973; July 1986. *NYT*: 17 Jan 1964; 15 Feb 1964; 8 May 1965; 3 March 1966; 17 Jan 1974. *TL*: 10 Aug 1959; 1 Oct 1959; 12 March 1960; 6 Feb 1961; 25 April 1964; 12 April 1965; 10 May 1967; 8 June 1967; 15 July 1967; 2 Feb 1968; 25 April 1969; 9 Feb 1972; 22 May 1973; 24 May 1978; 6 Feb 1981; 19 March 1981; 15 July 1988.

SELECTED DISCOGRAPHY

Alwyn: Fantasy-Waltzes; 12 Preludes. Chandos CHAN 8399 (CD). Rec. 1984.
Beethoven: Sonata in C Minor, op. 13; Sonata in C-sharp Minor, op. 27, no. 2; Sonata in F Minor, op. 57. IMP PCD 828.
Busoni: Concerto in C Major, op. 39. Angel CDM 7 69850 2. Revenaugh/Royal PO.
Busoni: *Fantasia Contrappuntistica*; Fantasia after J. S. Bach; Toccata. Continuum CCD 1006.
Franck: Symphonic Variations (Barbirolli/PO). Grieg: Concerto in A Minor, op. 16. Schumann: Concerto in A Minor, op. 54 (Berglund/New PO). Encore CDE 7 67772-2.
The John Ogdon Collection. IMP Classics (3 CDs). Contains "Beethoven Piano Sonatas," PCD 828 (see above); "John Ogdon Plays Chopin," PCD 834 (see below); and "Virtuoso," PCD 920 (see below).
John Ogdon Plays Chopin. Barcarolle in F-sharp Major, op. 60; *Berceuse* in D-flat Major, op. 57; Fantasy in F Minor, op. 49; Nocturne in F Major, op. 15, no. 1; Polonaise in C Minor, op. 40, no. 1; Sonata No. 3 in B Minor, op. 58. IMP PCD 834.
Mendelssohn: Concerto No. 1 in G Minor, op. 25; Concerto No. 2 in D Minor, op. 40. Klavier KCD-11029. Ceccato/London SO.

Rachmaninoff: Concerto No. 1 in F-sharp Minor, op. 1; Concerto No. 2 in C Minor, op. 18. Collins Classics 10882 (CD). Rozhdestvensky/London SO.

Rachmaninoff: Suite No. 1, op. 5; Suite No. 2, op. 17; Russian Rhapsody; Prelude in C-sharp Minor, op. 3, no. 2. MHS 513327A (CD). With Brenda Lucas.

Sorabji: *Opus Clavicembalisticum.* Altarus 9075 (4 CDs).

Stravinsky: Capriccio. Decca (The Classic Sound) 443 577. Also Pulcinella and *Apollon musagète.* Marriner/ASMF.

Virtuoso. Beethoven: Bagatelle in A Minor (*Für Elise*). Brahms: Rhapsody in G Minor, op. 79, no. 2. Chopin: Polonaise in A-flat Major, op. 53. Debussy: *La Fille aux cheveux de lin.* Mendelssohn: Songs Without Words, op. 38, no. 2; op. 53, no. 5; op. 62, no. 6. Mozart: Rondo alla turca (Sonata, K. 331). Mussorgsky: The Old Castle. Ravel: *Laideronnette, imperatice des pagodes*; *Pavane pour une Infante défunte.* Satie: *Gymnopédie* no. 1. Schubert: *Moment Musical* no. 3 in F Minor. Tchaikovsky: Barcarolle, op. 39, no. 6. IMP Classics PCD 920.

VIDEO

Virtuoso. A BBC Television drama based on the book by Brenda Lucas Ogdon and Michael Kerr.

OHLSSON, GARRICK: b. White Plains, New York, 3 April 1948.

> The way he breathes within a phrase makes the music rise above its own beautiful self to something very close to ecstasy. In matters of tonal shading, there is additional magic, as he spins out the merest thread of a melody or cascades down the keyboard with a glorious wash of sound.
>
> John Schneider (*Atlanta Journal*, 21 April 1978)

The Ohlsson family was not especially musical, and he was not a child prodigy; in fact, Ohlsson began piano lessons at the somewhat late age of eight. Alvar Ohlsson, his Swedish father, had gone into business in the United States after World War II; Paulyne (Rosta) Ohlsson, his Italian mother, worked as a travel agent. Both parents had had childhood piano lessons, and they gave their only child his first lessons with Thomas Lishman at the Westchester Conservatory. At age 12 Ohlsson performed Paul Creston's "Fantasy" with a youth orchestra, conducted by the composer. He studied (1961–66) with Sascha Gorodnitzki in the preparatory department at Juilliard, and at age 15 he won first prize in a Westchester competition. Meanwhile he excelled at mathematics and languages at White Plains High School, and after graduating in 1966 he began piano studies privately with Olga Barabini of Rye, New York, his most important, most influential teacher. In 1966 he also transferred to the college division at Juilliard, where he worked with Gorodnitzki (1966–68) and Rosina Lhévinne (1968–71). Ohlsson graduated from Juilliard with a Bachelor of Music in 1971.

He had meanwhile in 1966 won the Busoni Piano Competition at Bolzano, Italy; in 1968 won first prize at the Montreal International Piano Competition; and on 5 January 1970 had made his New York recital debut at the Grace Rainey Rogers Auditorium of the Metropolitan Museum of Art. A reviewer who singled out Ohlsson's courage in undertaking Ravel's very difficult *Gaspard de la nuit* granted that although his performance may have been lacking in some elements of fantasy and imagination, "it was all there technically, and he flashed through the fearsome difficulties of 'Scarbo,' such as the intricate handcrossings, with a fluency that never faltered." (*NYT*, 6 Jan 1970)

Certainly Ohlsson was ready to begin a concert career, yet in 1970 he had just nine bookings for the coming year. Two major piano competitions were held that year (1970)—the Tchaikovsky in Moscow and the Chopin in Warsaw—and Ohlsson elected to enter the Chopin because, as he later said, "I wanted to spend a year studying his music intensively. Since the music of Chopin is an essential part of the repertory of any serious pianist, it would all be music I could use later in my career, no matter what happened at Warsaw." (O'Reilly) His efforts paid off handsomely.

Ohlsson dominated that 1970 Chopin Competition. Clearly the favorite of audiences, he placed first (Mitsuko Uchida placed second) and also won prizes for best performances of a mazurka and best concerto performance. His career took flight the moment he won that gold medal in Warsaw. Being the first American to win the Chopin Competition, Ohlsson, like Van Cliburn a dozen years earlier, became an overnight sensation on both sides of the Atlantic. Officials of the Warsaw Philharmonic Orchestra immediately asked him if the next week he could play (as substitute for an ailing Leon Fleisher) the Ravel Concerto for Left Hand Alone. He fortunately had the work in his repertoire and gave two performances, with Witold Rowicki conducting. An intensive 12-day tour of Poland followed, in the course of which Ohlsson became so popular with the concert-going, Chopin-loving Polish audiences that he has since made about a dozen tours of that country.

He was still touring Poland when Eugene Ormandy invited him to play the Chopin Concerto No. 1 in E Minor, his contest concerto, with the Philadelphia Orchestra in Philadelphia and also in New York (10 Nov 1970). Next came an all-Chopin recital (29 Nov 1970) in Washington, D.C., a New York concert (13 Dec 1970), and a performance (17 Dec 1970) for President and Mrs. Richard Nixon at the White House. And when Ohlsson made his debut (4 Feb 1971) with the New York Philharmonic Orchestra, playing Beethoven's Concerto No. 1 in C Major, with Seiji Ozawa conducting, one critic predicted that, "he'll be around, and we shall be hearing much more from him." (*NYT*, 6 Feb 1971)

Ohlsson has more than fulfilled that prophesy. Between 1971 and 1973 he gave almost 200 performances: dozens in the United States; tours (1971–72) of Germany, Yugoslavia, Italy and Austria; a three-week tour of Japan (June

1972); and his London orchestral debut (1 July 1972), playing the Rachmaninoff Concerto No. 3 with the New Philharmonia Orchestra, conducted by Edo de Waart. Ohlsson has performed with the finest orchestras in Europe and America and had the rare distinction of playing with all five of London's orchestras during a single season (1977–78). In 1980 he celebrated the tenth anniversary of his Warsaw competition victory with an extensive world tour.

He started off his career with a killing schedule and in 1973 decided to pare it down—from about 90 to, say, 65 appearances a season. But 20 years later Ohlsson was still extremely active. In the 1990–91 season he played 13 different concertos in 25 orchestral engagements, about 15 recitals and five chamber concerts. His 1991–92 season included a tour of Great Britain with the Czech Philharmonic Orchestra, a tour of the United States with the Royal Liverpool Philharmonic Orchestra, about 15 other concerto performances with European and American orchestras and recitals in Berlin, London, New York, Milan and Prague. He has cut back a little, but Garrick Ohlsson truly enjoys performing, and his tours take him around the world—North America, Europe, the Far East, New Zealand.

He also likes to play chamber music and to accompany vocalists and has performed with sopranos Jessye Norman and Magda Oliveiro, clarinettist Richard Stoltzman, cellist Heinrich Schiff, violinist Gil Shaham and with the Cleveland, Emerson, Guarnieri, Takács and Tokyo string quartets.

Ohlsson has many interests and abilities outside of music. He is fluent in German, Spanish, French and Italian and can get by in Swedish and Polish. His promotional material says that he is interested in wines, Oriental art and history, science fiction and psychology and that he is a "veteran" bicyclist.

On 13 May 1994 Ohlsson was awarded the Avery Fisher Prize in recognition of his outstanding achievement and excellence.

Ohlsson's passion for learning new works accounts for his exceptionally large, eclectic repertoire. Winning the Chopin Competition marked him for a time as mostly a Chopin specialist, but since the early 1970s he has added more than 200 works to his repertoire. His programs show that he plays Haydn, Mozart, Beethoven, Chopin, Liszt, Brahms, Ravel, Grieg, Bartók, Rachmaninoff, Scriabin, Prokofiev; also unusual items like the Busoni Concerto and several seldom-heard works by Weber (see Discog.); and contemporary works, such as Charles Wuorinen's extremely difficult Concerto No. 3, which Ohlsson premiered (4 May 1984) with the Albany Symphony Orchestra, Julius Hegyi conducting.

Ohlsson has an amazingly large, diverse concerto repertoire. As recently as the 1990–91 season he performed concertos by Barber, Bartók, Beethoven, Brahms, Dvořák, Grieg, Mozart, Prokofiev, Ravel and Tchaikovsky; and the next season added concerted works by Franck, Ravel and Shostakovich.

The bottom line of course is that Ohlsson has the memory and more than enough technique to play such a repertoire. His technique, say reviewers, is superlative, masterful, magnificent. As a youth he maintained "his fleet fingers and galloping dexterity" by practicing a great deal, but most of his life he has practiced about four hours a day. He considers technique as a means to an end, not as a distinct entity. In other words, Ohlsson's technique is not dedicated to dazzling his hearers. The music and musicianship come first; being a stage performer is always secondary.

He approaches a work by first working with it in small units. "I try to build the piece phrase by phrase. If the notation doesn't make sense, I try to talk to the composer to see what it means. If necessary, I go note by note, which takes patience and a lot of time." (Novik)

As a very young pianist he had an imitation-Horowitz, highly virtuosic way of playing. For instance, at the Montreal competition the 20-year-old Ohlsson "played as though his life depended on it, and he thrived on the audience reaction, moving on to even greater heights as the concert progressed. . . . With time and experience to temper some of the exuberance and provide even more attention to detail, he may well become one of the greats of the century." (*G-M*, 19 June 1968)

And Ohlsson has done exactly that. Rather than coasting along for years repeatedly playing his "winning" competition pieces, he has steadily and deliberately developed his musicianship and enriched his repertoire. The Horowitz-type playing has long since been retired in favor of clarity, lucid textures and tone color. "One of the most striking aspects of his talent is that so big a man [6 feet 4 inches, around 200 pounds] can play with such delicacy and finesse. From the first he has been a fastidious artist who plays fortissimos without pounding, has a technique equal to the demands of any music yet written, and is possessed of a sense of rhythm that is unfailing." (O'Reilly)

As soon as he returned home from winning the Warsaw competition, Ohlsson gave two performances (Philadelphia, New York) of the Chopin Concerto No. 1 (his competition concerto) with Eugene Ormandy and the Philadelphia Orchestra. The New York audience "heard a performance of impressive technical command and an interpretation . . . that had the imprimatur of Chopin's native land. . . . [Ohlsson] curved Chopin's lyrical phrases gracefully and sensitively, sixtyfourth-note runs cascaded brilliantly and always Chopin's most note-clotted measures made utter, limpid sense." (*NYT*, 12 Nov 1970)

On 5 August 1971 Ohlsson again played "his" Chopin concerto at the Hollywood Bowl with Kazuyoshi Akirjama conducting the Los Angeles Philharmonic Orchestra. He is "what James Huneker used to call a pianissimist, a light-fingered pianist who can articulate the trickiest passages effortlessly with the shimmering tone so essential to Chopin. He can make the piano sing limpidly, and he employs the treacherous Chopin rubato with admirable discretion." (*LAT*, 7 Aug 1971)

Four years later a review of a New York recital (6 Jan 1975) clearly showed that Ohlsson had overcome any temptation to rest on his competition laurels. He played a very demanding program—one of the less familiar Haydn sonatas; two massive Liszt works (*Bénédiction de Dieu dans la solitude*, *Funérailles*), Chopin's 24 Preludes, op. 28—and proved that he had become a thinker as well as a phenomenal technician. "This was not merely a good piano recital; it was also an important one, and it put Mr. Ohlsson right up in the rank of major pianists. . . . Bigness permeated everything in the program. . . .

Romantic pianism, as practiced by its greatest exponents, was an aristocratic art, and Mr. Ohlsson's performances had that kind of aristocratic approach." (*NYT*, 7 Jan 1975)

In a collection of about 100 reviews, it is difficult to find an all-out poor response to Ohlsson's playing. On 31 July 1978 he played the Brahms Concerto No. 2 with the BBC Symphony Orchestra, conducted by James Loughran. Ohlsson placed his talents "at the service of every bar and achieved his effects, most impressively, through the kind of agility and mobile phrasing that one associates more with Chopin than with Brahms. . . . Mr. Ohlsson showed that a fortissimo can be rendered as much by trenchant articulation as by weight." (*TL*, 1 Aug 1978)

Ohlsson's Carnegie Hall program of 21 September 1980 produced one of his very few bad reviews. "Even though the playing was polished, the music itself was rough and clouded. In the first movement of the impulsively nervy Beethoven sonata [Op. 2, no. 2], it was unclear in espressivo moments just what was being expressed. . . . The Chopin Ballade [No. 4] seemed composed of virtuosic episodes with a few fleeting beautiful moments—and without narrative drive." (*NYT*, 22 Sept 1980)

On the other hand, Ohlsson's recital of 20th-century music played in Chicago on 6 Jan 1985 (it included both the Prokofiev Sonata No. 8 and the Samuel Barber Sonata, op. 26) proved a rousing success. "Ohlsson grappled with the dissonances and experimental harmonies in these works and unfailingly managed to illuminate them through effortless technique and masterful musical phrasing enhanced by the creamy tone of the Bösendorfer piano he played." (*CST*, 7 Jan 1985) Another critic noted that Ohlsson "tends to be a serious and expressively restrained interpreter rather than a flashy one, but at those moments when energy and stamina are required, he delivers in spades." This critic was particularly captivated by the Barber Sonata. "The bluesy Adagio rarely has sounded so idiomatic, and the horrendously difficult fugue could boast more than enough blazing virtuosity to send Horowitz into green-eyed fits." (*CT*, 7 Jan 1985)

When Ohlsson played (8 Feb 1991) the Grieg Concerto in A Minor with the Boston Symphony Orchestra, Robert Spano conducting, he made it sound as fresh and exciting as when it was first heard. "Ohlsson's performance was leisurely, detailed, observant, and superbly played; it sang and it danced, and pianist and conductor seemed to be having the time of their lives working together. Ohlsson is now surely the pianist of choice among those out on the circuit playing the big bowwow repertory. He has a real sound, his own . . . and he is *interesting*." (*BG*, 9 Feb 1991)

An all-Chopin recital (14 Feb 1993) at Town Hall drew this comment: "He has always been sensitive enough to find and highlight the music's most graceful nuances, yet he is more inclined toward the dramatic side of Romanticism than toward the perfumed, dreamy image of Chopin that was once the norm." (*NYT*, 15 Feb 1993)

Ohlsson has made recordings for several labels, including EMI, Delos and Telarc. The Chopin discs he made in the 1970s for EMI—the Scherzos, the 16 Polonaises, the F Minor Fantasy and the concertos—have been well received.

Ohlsson "displays excellent schooling in everything that he does and is a basically serious player, whose Chopin has an aristocratic grandeur of conception. .
. . Little in his artistry is left to chance, but he never sounds calculated; he has
the ability to allow the music to inspire him." (Met/Cho, see Bibliog.) The
two Chopin Concertos made in 1976 with the Polish Radio National Symphony
Orchestra have been reissued on a single CD (see Discog.). A critic noting that
the orchestra is badly placed, nevertheless admired "the way Ohlsson states the
main theme of the first movement of the First Concerto, the way he enters in
the Second Concerto, and his ability to maintain a sense of continuity in the extended passage work." (Fan, March/April 1989)

　　　　Ohlsson has completed 5 CD albums (see Discog.) under his contract
with Arabesque to record the complete works of Chopin, and one must agree that
they "place him in the forefront of modern-day Chopin interpreters. . . . This is a
pianist of brilliance and formidable technique, yet an artist of keen sensitivity to
mood, color, and expression." (ARG, July/Aug 1992)

　　　　During the period April 1987 to February 1988, Ohlsson gave no concerts. Instead he worked on repertoire and also recorded the four sonatas of Carl
Maria von Weber. The response has been overwhelmingly enthusiastic. Written
by a master of Romantic opera who was also a master pianist, these sonatas are
tinged with myriad operatic reminiscences. They require a secure technique and
above all great discretion to keep them from becoming maudlin. Ohlsson plays
all four as though he had been there at the time of their inception. This album
was named the 1989 "Solo Instrumental Record of the Year" by Ovation magazine. "These sonatas deserve and repay repeated hearings, and Garrick Ohlsson
has provided benchmark recordings of all four of them." (OV, Aug 1989)

　　　　Ohlsson worked on Busoni's mammoth (70 minutes) Concerto for
Piano, Orchestra and Men's Chorus for a year, took it on tour with the Cleveland
Orchestra, under the baton of Christoph von Dohnányi, and also recorded it (see
Discog.). His recorded performance is a magnificent combination of artistry and
musicianship rarely encountered: "A landmark recording, awesome and indispensable. . . . It is Ohlsson's distinction that he knows, bar by bar, what is required
and can give it due measure with seamless, seeming ease." (Fan, March/April
1990) And this: "One doubts . . . whether the concerto has ever been played
with such virtuosity, from the conductor and his players as well as the soloist. .
. . Ohlsson and Dohnányi have the gravity and the largeness of view to convey
the work's vision as well as its pianistic triumphalism." (Gram, April 1990)

　　　　From the heroic framework and complex workings of the Busoni
Concerto to Debussy's short, atmospheric, impressionistic studies involves quite
a stylistic and artistic changeover, but Ohlsson is the quintessential pianist, at
home with most composers and periods. His recording of the Debussy Etudes
and the Suite bergamasque may not have won the kind of lavish praise bestowed
on his Busoni recording, but a reviewer who claimed not even to like the
Debussy Etudes, recommends this "imaginatively played recording." Ohlsson
"makes the intellectual content of the music so interesting. . . . I find his playing deeply satisfying and illuminating." (Fan, Jan/Feb 1990) Another reviewer
writes that Ohlsson's "sonorities are often more reminiscent of Rachmaninoff

and Bartók than of French piano music. His tone is full and rounded and he very much stresses the melodic side of the music." (*Gram*, Feb 1990)

In 1986 Ohlsson recorded Charles Wuorinen's Concerto No. 3 with the San Francisco Symphony, Herbert Blomstedt conducting. The work is laced with incredible technical and rhythmic problems. "Wuorinen has himself fittingly described his finale as 'a hip-swinging wing-ding.' The virtuoso repertory holds no terrors for a pianist of Ohlsson's formidable technical endowment, but even he forthrightly calls that movement 'hard as hell . . . a bit like an aerobics class'." (*HF*, July 1989) From another commentator: "With its manic energy levels and shrapnel-like bursts of notes, the Stravinsky-tinged music has all the repose of a prison riot. Mr. Ohlsson, however, tosses off the irregular rhythms and note patterns with such panache that the momentum becomes irresistible. A cynic might even argue that this is a case of a spectacular performance making a work sound better than it is." (*NYT*, 18 June 1989) Another contemporary work, Henri Lazarof's *Tableaux* ("After Kandinsky") for piano and orchestra, was recorded by Ohlsson with Gerard Schwarz and the Seattle Symphony Orchestra. Their 1987 performance received a 1990 Grammy award.

SELECTED REFERENCES

Bender, William. "Chopin with Pow." *Time*, 30 Nov 1970, p. 57.

DeVinney, Richard. "Ohlsson Takes His Music Around the World." *Grand Rapids Press*, 14 Dec 1986.

DuVal, Linda. "Garrick Ohlsson." *Gazette Telegraph*, 24 Oct 1986, sec. D, pp. 1, 7.

Faron, James. "U. S. Pianist, 22, Wins in Warsaw." *New York Times*, 25 Oct 1970, p. 80.

Fleming, Shirley. "Garrick Ohlsson: musician of the month." *High Fidelity/ Musical America*, March 1971, pp. MA 8–9.

Fruchter, Rena. "Pianist Finds Own Mold." *New York Times* (New Jersey edition), 14 Jan 1990, sec. 12, p. 11.

Horowitz, Joseph. "How a Horowitz Emulator Turned Into Garrick Ohlsson." *New York Times*, 17 April 1977, sec. 2, p. 15.

Jones, Robert. "The Promoter." *Sunday News*, 23 May, 1976, (Leisure), p. 16.

Novik, Ylda. "Garrick Ohlsson: Music is the Driving Force." *Piano Quarterly*, Fall 1977, pp. 40–43.

O'Reilly, F. Warren. "Garrick Ohlsson: the making of a piano giant." *Washington Times*, 6 July 1983, sec. B, pp. 1–2.

Salzman, Eric. "Reviving Busoni." *Stereo Review*, Feb 1990, p. 153.

Shear, Nancy. "Garrick Ohlsson on Building a Career." *Music Magazine*, Nov/Dec 1982, pp. 22–25.

See also Bibliography: Cur/Bio (1975); Eld/Pia; Ewe/Mu; IWWM; Mar/Gre; New/Gro; WWAM.

SELECTED REVIEWS

AJ: 3 May 1976; 21 April 1978. *BaS*: 15 Jan 1983. *BG*: 30 Jan 1989; 9 Feb 1991. *BH*: 30 Jan 1989. *C-J*: 29 Feb 1976. *CPD*: 14 Jan 1989; 21 July 1990. *CST*: 8 Jan 1977; 17 Dec 1979; 7 Jan 1985. *CT*: 7 Jan 1985; 20 Sept 1988. *GloM*: 18 March 1986; 1 Feb 1989. *HA*: 10 March 1980. *LAHE*: 28 Aug 1986. *LAT*: 7 Aug 1971; 26 Jan 1991. *MG*: 19 June 1968. *MiT*: 12 Oct 1979. *NYT*: 6 Jan 1970; 12 Nov 1970; 7 Jan 1975; 22 Sept 1980; 11 Oct 1984; 12 Aug 1990; 11 April 1992; 15 Feb 1993. *ORE:* 4 Feb 1986. *PI*: 20 Jan 1990; 29 Oct 1991. *PP*: 9 Jan 1987. *SFC*: 18 July 1986; 15 June 1991; 15 Jan 1993. *SPI*: 19 Nov 1986. *SPPP*: 1 Aug 1990. *ST*: 19 Nov 1986; 23 May 1991; 15 Oct 1991; 26 Jan 1995. *TL*: 3 July 1972; 1 Aug 1978; 20 May 1980; 27 May 1986. *WP*: 1 July 1985; 2 June 1992; 18 July 1994.

SELECTED DISCOGRAPHY

Beethoven: Sonata in F Minor, op. 2, no. 1; Sonata in F Minor, op. 57; Sonata in E Major, op. 109. Arabesque Z6638 (CD).

Busoni: Concerto in C Major, op. 39. Telarc CD-80207. Dohnányi/Cleveland SO.

Chopin: Concerto No. 1 in E Minor, op. 11; Concerto No. 2 in F Minor, op. 21. EMI Eminence CD-EMX 2133. Maksymiuk/Polish Radio NSO.

Chopin: Complete Works, Vol. I: Sonata No. 1 in C Minor, op. 4; Sonata No. 2 in B-flat Minor, op. 35; Sonata No. 3 in B Minor, op. 58. Arabesque 6628 (CD).

Chopin: Complete Works, Vol. II: Preludes, op. 28; Prelude No. 14; Prelude in A Flat; Rondo (à la Mazur) in F, op. 5; Rondo in C Minor, op. 1. Arabesque 6629 (CD).

Chopin: Complete Works, Vol. III: Ballades (4); Rondo in E-flat Major, op. 16; Rondo in C Major, op. 73. Arabesque 6630 (CD).

Chopin: Complete Works, Vol. IV: Scherzi and Variations. Arabesque Z6633 (CD).

Chopin: Complete Works, Vol. V: Polonaises and Impromptus. Arabesque Z6642-2 (CD).

Debussy: *Suite bergamasque*; Etudes (12). Arabesque CD Z-6601.

Haydn: Sonata in C Major, Hob. XVI:50; Sonata in D Major, Hob. XVI:51; Sonata in E-flat Major, Hob. XVI:52; Variations in F Minor, Hob. XVII:6; Adagio in F Major, Hob. XVII:9. Arabesque Z6625 (CD).

Lazarof: Tableaux for Piano and Orchestra. Delos DE 3069 (CD). Schwarz/ Seattle SO.

Liszt: Concerto No. 1 in E-flat Major; Concerto No. 2 in A Major. Seraphim cassette 4ZG-60431. Atzmon/New PO.

Rachmaninoff: Concerto No. 3 in D Minor, op. 30. *Nuova Era* 6721-DM (CD). Caracciolo/RAI di Milano. Recorded from the 1966 Busoni Competition.

Scriabin: Concerto in F-sharp Minor, op. 20. *Supraphon* 10 4149-2. Pesek/ Czech PO.

Weber: Sonatas (4); Invitation to the Dance; *Momento capriccioso*, op. 12; *Rondo brillante*, J. 252. Arabesque Z-6584-2 (2 CDs).

Wuorinen: Concerto No. 3. Elektra/Nonesuch 79185-2. Blomstedt/San Francisco SO.

$\mathcal{P}$

PACHMANN, VLADIMIR DE: b. Odessa, USSR, 27 July 1848; d. Rome, Italy, 6 January 1933.

> With Pachmann it was all a question of style, and to try to think of the value of the music apart from its expression would be, to him, a radical mistake. A beautiful and appropriate touch, and not ideas, was the foundation of artistic playing.
>
> Erik Brewerton (*Musical Times*, February 1933)

Never mind that Vladimir de Pachmann comes out of the pages of music history sounding more like a P. T. Barnum buffoon than a concert pianist, or that his piano recitals sound like vaudeville high jinx. History also records that Pachmann's ravishingly beautiful Chopin playing has secured him a unique place in the annals of keyboard history.

Vladimir de Pachmann, the first of that remarkable group of Odessa-born pianists (Barere, Cherkassky, Gilels and Moiseiwitsch), was the youngest of 13 children born to Vincent de Pachmann, a professor at Odessa University and also an amateur violinist. At about age six Pachmann began violin lessons with his father and a few years later started piano lessons. At age 18 he enrolled at the Vienna Conservatory, where he studied piano with Joseph Dachs and harmony with Anton Bruckner and graduated with a gold medal in 1869. Those years at the Conservatory were all the formal training Pachmann ever had; for the rest of his life he was a self-taught pianist.

He returned to Odessa and gave a few well-received recitals. But then in 1870 he heard a performance by Carl Tausig (the great Liszt pupil was on his final tour of Russia), and Tausig's overwhelming artistry left Pachmann besieged with self-doubts. Although he was only 22 years old and had just begun his career, he withdrew from concertizing to work on his own. Eight years of study and self-discipline produced "a unique technical equipment which included a tone of extreme refinement and glowing color, and an execution of unfailing clarity." (*MA*, 10 Jan 1933)

After that eight-year break, Pachmann returned to the concert stage with performances in Berlin, Leipzig and other German cities, but his playing was still not exactly as he wanted it to be, and once again he withdrew to study, this time for two years. Although an onstage clown, Pachmann was a serious, dedicated musician, and all his life, not only during those 10 years of arduous study on his own, he searched for the perfect way in piano playing. As he later told interviewers, he knew that the piano could yield a tone which, though he had never heard it, he knew was possible; and he had determined to keep working until he knew how to produce that special tone.

In 1880 Pachmann scheduled concerts in Vienna, but he was so terrified at the thought of facing an audience after 10 years away that he twice postponed the first recital. On the third attempt he made it out onto the stage and played his recital—and received a thunderous ovation. Three immensely successful concerts in Vienna and three equally sensational concerts in Paris bolstered his confidence and ensured his career. Pachmann made his London debut on 20 May 1882, playing the Chopin F Minor Concerto at one of Mr. Ganz's concerts, and made his American debut (7 April 1890) with an all-Chopin recital at New York's Chickering Hall. A performer almost to the end of his life, he toured often in Britain, Europe and the United States.

In 1884 Pachmann married Margaret Oakey, an Australian pianist and former student. They had two sons, and divorced in 1892. Reportedly there were other marriages. In 1885 Denmark made Pachmann a Knight of the Order of Dannebrog; in 1916 the Royal Philharmonic Society awarded him its Gold Medal.

Throughout his career Pachmann consistently played a few large-scale works: four Beethoven sonatas—Op. 13 ("*Pathétique*"), Op. 26 in A-flat Major, Op. 27, no. 2 ("Moonlight") and Op. 53 ("*Waldstein*"); Schumann's *Davidsbundlertänze* and the Sonata No. 1 in G Minor, op. 11; and the Mozart Sonata in A Major, K. 331. Some programs show the Weber Sonata in A-flat Major, op. 39, and small-scale works by Liszt and Mendelssohn. Very early programs reveal that even then Pachmann played many all-Chopin recitals, and increasingly Chopin dominated his repertoire. Most pianists of his time usually programmed only the large-scale Chopin works because they thought the smaller pieces too intimate for the concert hall. Pachmann, however, played Chopin's smaller pieces "and discovered a way of producing a tone that sounded throughout the largest hall yet preserved its intimate character." (Blickstein)

A pianist who never stopped working and studying, Pachmann practiced every day. As he explained to interviewers, "First I play scales for sixteen minutes every morning. No one can play scales as I do. Then I practice Godowsky for technique. Every morning I give to Godowsky, and a few octave studies of Joseffy for legato."

Although always well-prepared, Pachmann dreaded going out to play before an audience, and nerves partly account for his peculiar behavior. François Pallottelli, Pachmann's longtime secretary, reported that early in his career the pianist had discovered that he felt less nervous if he busied himself smiling and gesticulating as he came onstage. The facial contortions and monkeyshines grew worse with each passing year. While playing, Pachmann talked incessantly, to himself and to the audience; he made faces, fiddled excessively with the piano stool, sometimes even crawled under the piano to find, as he put it, "the wrong notes he had accidentally hit."

His wild behavior irritated some critics to the extreme. George Bernard Shaw described Pachmann's London concert of 17 August 1889 as a "Pachmann performance with accompaniments by Chopin." James Huneker, one of America's foremost critics, nicknamed Pachmann "the Chopinzee," an insult that stayed with the pianist to the end of his life. And, wrote a reviewer in 1907, "Mr. de Pachmann now goes so far as to interpret his music sometimes to fit his pantomime, and so actually distorts it that he may make what he considers a witty point himself. It is, of course, all hideously inartistic and annoying to those who wish to enjoy the truly remarkable and beautiful qualities of Mr. de Pachmann's art. They injure the art as well as disturb the listener." (*NYT*, 27 Nov 1907)

All the same, reviews and articles of Pachmann's own time make it clear that he drew large audiences and, of greater interest, that some of the most important music critics of the time were able to overlook his performing shenanigans. Even in his later years, when Pachmann's eccentricities often overshadowed his playing, "the careful listener and watcher would, however, be rewarded by a few moments, perhaps a single etude or prelude of Chopin, which could only be described by the word perfect. Ten minutes of such playing of Chopin, in which everything needful to be said was said through a touch on the keys of pearl-like smoothness, a control which was without a hint of strain, a naturalness in expression which made all the intellectualists seem mere fumblers—this was . . . the revelation of the supreme artist in Pachmann." (*TL*, 8 Jan 1933)

He was at his finest in works demanding extreme delicacy of touch, and in this respect he probably had few superiors. His playing showed many of the legendary characteristics of Chopin's own playing, and he was by general consent a near ideal interpreter. Pachmann developed an astounding *pianissimo* technique that restored to Chopin's music the sonorities of the early pianos, and he mastered the delicate intonation of the instrument so thoroughly that in his last years his sound rarely rose above a *piano*. "His importance in interpreting Chopin's works lay in his closeness to the composer's era and his ability to capture the 'right' atmosphere for a work; for this last attribute, he was feted throughout Europe as an authoritative interpreter." (Met/Cho, see Bibliog.)

Pachmann's peculiar, inimitable interpretations sorely tried the patience of some critics. To begin with, as the "king of pianists" (his own words) he felt free to do anything he liked with the music. The character of a work meant nothing to him. He had no desire to be intellectual or dramatic; what mattered to Pachmann, particularly with Chopin, was beautiful playing. He often mutilated compositions by inserting arpeggios between phrases and extra chords at the end of certain works, but despite his alterations and additions, Pachmann at his best gave his listeners "not only the rarest and most triumphant interpretations of Chopin, but the choicest and most legitimate examples of pure playing that we have had in our day. . . . Pachmann at his highest is truly supreme." (Hill)

A more objective analysis, written by the composer Sorabji in 1932, begins, "Before his extravagances and eccentricities had almost entirely swamped his artistry, that is to say up to within fifteen or even ten years ago, his playing of the smaller [Chopin] nocturnes, waltzes, etudes and mazurkas was exquisite— the almost unlimited range of his gradations of tone within a *mezzo forte* and an unbelievable *quasi niente*, the amazing fluidity and limpid liquidity of his finger work, his delicious dainty staccato, the marvellous cantilena, the exquisite phrasing and the wonderfully delicate fantasy of the whole, all made his playing of these things an enchantment and a delight." However, continues Sorabji, Pachmann "was a lamentable failure in works on a large scale or cast in a heroic mould; his lack of intellectual staying power, grasp, personal force, or ability to think in big sweeps, the essential smallness of his style and his musical outlook has been pitifully revealed." (Sorabji)

Pachmann remains an enigma. He lived in a world of his own, and his playing was unlike that of any other pianist. He played a limited repertoire and behaved outlandishly. Why did he become one of the great pianists of his day? The answer, said those who heard him, lies in the uniquely alluring sound that Pachmann drew from the piano.

Right from the start—playing the Chopin Concerto in F Minor for his London debut (20 May 1882) on one of the orchestral concerts of Wilhelm Ganz at St. James Hall—Pachmann showed himself to be "a born Chopin player. . . . His touch is of the utmost delicacy; the subtlest gradations of time and strength are to him as natural as they were to the composer when he wrote; there is, indeed, about his playing that charm of dreamy poetry of which those speak with enthusiasm who heard Chopin himself." (*TL*, 23 May 1882)

His first American engagement, a series (7–10 April 1890) of three all-Chopin recitals at New York's Chickering Hall, proved so successful that he gave a total of five performances, one with the assistance of his wife. On 11 April 1890 Pachmann performed the Chopin Concerto in F Minor with Frank Van der Stücken conducting; and on 25 April Pachmann gave a program of selected compositions from his first three recitals. At his debut recital (7 April 1890) Pachmann played with "a very clean and smooth legato. . . . His tone color is very soft and agreeable. . . . His playing is full of delightful nuances. . . . His cantabile is sweet and well sustained, and his octave playing is neat. On the other hand, his range of dynamic effects is not large. His limits appear to lie between an extremely delicate pianissimo and a fairly sonorous forte." (*NYT*, 8 April 1890).

Pachmann's performance (9 April 1892) of the Chopin F Minor Concerto at New York's Metropolitan Opera House, with Anton Seidl conducting the orchestra of the New York Philharmonic Society, received unequivocally mixed reviews. For example, "Mr. de Pachmann has strong musical instinct, he has a rare gift of touch, and he has exceptional technical accomplishments; but he has little variety of tone, less power, and no mental grasp at all." (*NYT*, 11 April 1892) The same theme runs through a review of an all-Chopin recital (1 Nov 1892) in London: "Of the many works by Chopin, among which was the beautiful sonata in B minor, a few were played to absolute perfection, and some creditably, while some were completely spoilt by exaggeration." (*TL*, 2 Nov 1892) And at a London performance (15 Nov 1892) of the Schumann *Carnaval*, Pachmann "drowned [the finale] in showers of wrong notes." (*TL*, 16 Nov 1892)

Almost any Pachmann program could contain both beautiful and cata-strophic playing. An appraisal from a review of his 9 January 1894 recital at New York's Chickering Hall is typical: "The eminent Russian virtuoso was heard by a large audience and was heartily applauded in spite of his indulgence in a good deal of eccentricity. . . . There was only one fault about this programme, and that was that M. de Pachmann did not play it. In two of the Schumann numbers his memory failed him and he left the pieces incomplete. He began the Mendelssohn variations, tangled himself all up in them and emerged into a Chopin fantasia, which must have puzzled lovers of Mendelssohn tremendously. M. de Pachmann did play the Weber sonata [A-flat Major] neatly, and he gave a dazzling exhibition of his technical skill in the second of the Chopin etudes, a study in chromatic thirds." (Courtesy of *The New York Times*, 10 Jan 1894)

With so many of Pachmann's peers giving serious performances, one might well wonder at Pachmann's success, for he *was* eminently successful. His entire adulthood was spent as a touring concert pianist and he never seemed to want for performance dates. Why, then, the adulation on the part of the audi-ence? Pachmann was a showman, he depended on his antics and unconventional stage deportment to create an aura that would sustain recitals of inconsistent artistry. But always there were moments of utterly beautiful playing.

For example this, after a New York recital of 14 November 1904: "His tone, his gradation of dynamics below certain well-defined limits of sonority, the exquisite clarity and perfect articulation of even his ultimate pianissimos, are such as no other man can surpass." (*NYT*, 15 Nov 1904) And these remarks concerning a program given in Kansas City, Missouri, on 20 February 1912: "He was in his happiest mood, and gave bountifully of his wonderful art. The greater part of his program was made up of Chopin, and such beauty of tone as he produced, and such perfect understanding of the composer's purpose, one sel-dom has the opportunity of enjoying." (*MA*, 2 March 1912)

Pachmann never lost his ability to create controversy. At age 75 and about to embark on an American tour after an absence of 10 years, Pachmann, when asked by reporters who was the greatest pianist in the world, modestly replied that he, Pachmann, was "'the grandest player. . . . 'What about the musi-cal critics?' 'The only critics in the world are in Berlin, Rome and Boston.' 'What about the New York musical critics?' 'They are capricious'." (*NYT*, 23 Aug 1923)

At his final farewell recital (there were many) in New York on 13 April 1925 Pachmann managed to exit as a true artist of exceptional ability and talent.

It was an unusual program—the Mozart Fantasia in C Minor, K. 475, the rest all Chopin. On the one hand, his performance of the Chopin Scherzo in B-flat Minor was "balderdash," something to be ignored along with Pachmann's other "foolings." However, his "masterly interpretation of the Mozart C minor Fantasia . . . would in itself have done much to justify the occasion. For when Mr. de Pachmann is greatest . . . it is realized that this extraordinary man, a virtuoso, at 76, of astonishing qualities, and on occasion a great poet of his instrument, has achieved and forgotten more than many a pianist ever knew." (*NYT*, 14 April 1925)

Pachmann made a substantial number of piano rolls for English Duo-Art and for Welte, and he recorded much of the same repertoire on disc, two notable exceptions being the Mozart Sonata in A Major, K. 331 (Welte) and Bach's Italian Concerto (Welte).

He made comparatively few recordings. As record producer F. W. Gaisberg laconically noted, "when Vladimir de Pachmann came to us to record, all seriousness was laid aside and we settled down to an hour's variety show." (Gai/Mus, see Bibliog.) Pachmann recorded some of the earliest classical piano discs ever made. The earliest ones, made for the Gramophone and Typewriter Co., date from 1906. The later ones appeared on Victor, HMV and English Columbia labels. Pachmann was age 58 when he began recording on disc and he continued to make records until 1927, when he was nearing eighty. His recorded repertoire includes a few compositions by Liszt, Mendelssohn, Schumann, Weber and Brahms, the rest are mostly short compositions by Chopin.

The discs he made before World War I and a few later ones from 1925 and 1927 show a pianist of high order. The Chopin recordings include the Barcarolle and *Berceuse*, a number of nocturnes, preludes, waltzes, etudes, mazurkas, two impromptus, one ballade, one polonaise and two sonata movements. Some of the most impressive performances are found in the Nocturnes, particularly op. 9, no. 2, in E-flat Major and op. 15, no. 1, in F Major. Later discs of the Nocturne in E Minor, op. posth., and the Mazurka in A-flat Major, op. 50, no. 2, show Pachmann at his very best.

Some of Pachmann's finest performances are on the 1911–1912 recordings he made for the Victor Company. These have been reissued on a Pearl LP (see Discog.). A more recent collection, an Opal CD (see Discog.), reveals the "real" Pachmann. "With the exception of the Mazurka, op. 24, no. 4, all the Chopin here comes from before the First World War and gives us a fascinating glimpse of what must have been a highly distinctive and artistic pianist." (*Fan*, July/Aug 1989)

SELECTED REFERENCES

"Antics." *Time*, 27 Oct 1924, p. 12.

Benko, Gregor. "Vladimir de Pachmann Discography." *International Piano Library*.

Blickstein, Edward. "More Than a Clown." *High Fidelity*, July 1969, pp. 59–62.

Brewerton, Erik. "Pachmann—An Impression." *Musical Times*, Feb 1933, pp. 125–126.

"Degrees in Musical Virtuosity." *New York Times*, 30 Aug 1923, p. 12.

"De Pachmann Says 'I'm Greatest Pianist'." *New York Times*, 29 Aug 1923, p. 3.

Hill, Edward Burlingame. "A True Interpreter of Chopin." *Etude*, Jan 1905, p. 19.

"How De Pachmann Plays Chopin." *Saturday Evening Post*, 17 Oct 1903, p. 5.

Nettheim, Nigel. "De Pachmann's Piano Fingerings." *Clavier*, March 1992, pp. 14–16.

Obituary. *The Times* (London), 8 Jan 1933, p. 14. *Musical America*, 10 Jan 1933, p. 33.

Pachmann, Vladimir de. "How to Play Chopin." *Etude*, Oct 1908, p. 629.

———. "Originality in Pianoforte Playing." *Etude*, Oct 1911, p. 657.

———. "Should Piano Playing Undergo a Radical Reform?" *Etude*, Dec 1923, pp. 819–820.

———. "Work, the Secret of Pianistic Success." *Etude*, Nov 1911, p. 734.

Peyser, H. F. "Critics? They Are A 'Canaille'—A Set Of Villainous Rascals!" *Musical America*, 8 July 1911, p. 3.

"The Puzzling de Pachmann, as His Manager Sees Him." *Musical America*, 23 June 1917, p. 35.

Sorabji, Kaikhosru. "Pachmann and Chopin." In *Around Music*. London: The Unicorn Press, 1932, pp. 176–177.

Symons, Arthur. "Pachmann and the Piano." In *Plays, Acting, and Music*. London: Duckworth & Co., 1903, pp. 68–71.

See also Bibliography: Ald/Con; Bro/Mod; Car/Tal; Coo/Gre; Coo/GrP; Dow/Oli; Ful/Doo; Gol/Jou; Hun/Old; Hun/Ste; Hun/Uni; Hun/Var; Kol/Que; Lah/Fam; Lan/Mus; Nie/Mei; Pay/Cel; Rat/Cle; Rub/MyM; Rub/MyY; Sha/Lon; Sha/Mus; Woo/My.

SELECTED REVIEWS

MA: 2 Nov 1907; 23 Nov 1907; 6 May 1911; 28 Oct 1911; 11 Nov 1911; 25 Nov 1911; 23 Dec 1911; 10 Feb 1912; 2 March 1912; 16 March 1912; 20 April 1912. *MT*: 1 April 1921. *NYT*: 8 April 1890; 9 April 1990; 10 April 1890; 12 April 1990; 26 April 1990; 7 Feb 1992; 11 April 1892; 25 Oct 1893; 10 Jan 1894; 15 Nov 1904; 20 Nov 1907; 27 Nov 1907; 21 Oct 1911; 14 April 1912; 23 Oct 1923; 17 Nov 1923; 18 March 1924; 18 Oct 1924. *TL*: 23 May 1882; 3 June 1887; 2 Nov 1892; 16 Nov 1892; 7 June 1901; 25 June 1901; 26 May 1902; 10 April 1911.

SELECTED DISCOGRAPHY

The Compositions of Franz Liszt. Etude de Concert No. 2 in F Minor; *Rigoletto* Paraphrase. Recorded from Welte piano rolls.

Keyboard Giants of the Past. Chopin: Impromptu in F-sharp Major, op. 36. RCA Victor SP-33-143 (LP).

Vladimir de Pachmann. Chopin: Barcarolle, op. 60; Etudes, op. 10, no. 5, op. 25, no. 3; Impromptu in A-flat Major, op. 29; Mazurkas, op. 25, no. 4, op. 33, no. 3, op. 50, no. 2, op. 67, no. 4; Nocturnes, op. 9, no. 2, op. 27, no. 2, op. 37, no. 2; Preludes, op. 28, nos. 15, 23–24; Sonata in B Minor, op. 58 (Scherzo). Raff: *La Fileuse*, op. 15, no. 2. Schumann: Novelette in F Major, op. 21, no. 1. Verdi-Liszt: *"Rigoletto" Paraphrase de Concert.* Opal CD 9840.

Vladimir de Pachmann Plays Chopin, Mendelssohn and Schumann. Chopin: Ballade No. 3 in A-flat Major, op. 47; Etude in G-flat Major, op. 10, no. 5; Etude in E Minor, op. 25, no. 5; Etude in B Minor, op. 25, no. 10; Funeral March from Sonata, op. 35; Nocturne in F Major, op. 15, no. 1; Nocturne in G Major, op. 37, no. 2; Prelude in D Minor, op. 28, no. 24; Waltzes, op. 64, nos. 1–2. Mendelssohn: *Rondo capriccioso*, op. 14; Spinning Song, op. 67, no. 4; Spring Song, op. 62, no. 6; Venetian Gondola Song, op. 30, no. 6. Schumann: The Prophet Bird, op. 82, no. 7. Pearl GEMM 103 (LP).

⚜ ⚜ ⚜

PADEREWSKI, IGNACE JAN: b. Kurylówka, Poland, 18 November 1860; d. New York, New York, 29 June 1941.

> Being no pyrotechnician with fireworks at his fingertips, he had to maximise different attributes, qualities which more superficially brilliant pianists often neglect: eloquence that could become oratorical; a *cantabile* that could reach the back of the gallery, even in *pianissimo*; phrasing as much determined by breathing as a singer's; and pedalling like a 'wash' in a water-colour painting.
>
> Ronald Stevenson (*The Paderewski Paradox*)

By no means a child prodigy, Ignace Paderewski owed his runaway fame on the concert stage to his indomitable will and persistent practicing—year after year, often eight hours at a stretch. Almost every piano teacher he studied with discouraged the idea of a concert career—even Leschetizky said it was too late—yet Paderewski persevered. His enthralling piano technique was made, not born, and it took an ironclad will to create, sustain and control it.

His parents belonged to the fiercely patriotic but largely impoverished Polish gentry living in the western Ukraine, once part of the Polish Republic. His mother Polixena (Nowicka) Paderewska, daughter of an exiled professor from the University of Vilnius, died shortly after Paderewski's birth, leaving her husband Jan, employed as an estate manager, to raise Paderewski and his sister Antonina, two years older.

When at about age three Paderewski began picking out melodies on the family's old Graff piano, his father hired an elderly violinist named Runowski to give both children music lessons. Runowski knew nothing about the piano; he merely beat time as the children played simple duets. The children advanced to weekly (then monthly) music lessons with Peter Sowinski, who taught them how to play simple salon pieces and four-hand arrangements of themes from Rossini and Donizetti operas, but unfortunately they learned very little about piano technique, not even basic fingering. All his life Paderewski would regret that as a child he had not learned how to play correctly and how to practice. With his innate musical ability and talent for improvisation, young Paderewski was able to compose little compositions, and by the time he was 12 he had played a few local concerts, mostly charity affairs. In 1868 Michael Babianski came into the family as tutor and began teaching Paderewski French grammar, geography and history. Paderewski's academic education was under way, but he realized that he was not making any progress with the piano.

Even after he had been admitted to the Warsaw Conservatory in 1872, his piano teacher Julian Janotha allowed him to continue playing in his own unorthodox fashion. To add to his frustration, his quick progress in harmony and counterpoint with Gustaw Roguski fostered the idea that Paderewski was at the Conservatory to become a composer, not a pianist. As a composition student, he was required to learn the orchestral instruments, and he ended up a reluctant first trombone in the school orchestra. He also composed a few minor works, but never neglected the piano, working mostly by himself because his teachers (he also studied technique and repertoire with Rudolf Strobl, Jan Sliwinski and Pawel Schlözer) insisted that he could never become a concert pianist. During these sometimes stormy years, Paderewski (twice expelled for refusing to attend orchestra rehearsals) lived in the home of Edward Kerntopf, eldest son of the Warsaw piano manufacturer, who became a generous supporter and lasting friend.

After graduation (1878), the Conservatory immediately hired Paderewski as a piano instructor, yet no one encouraged him as a pianist. For the next three years he taught, composed some piano works, began work on his Violin Sonata and frequently visited the salon of Helena Gorska, wife of the violinist Wladyslaw Gorski. That social environment made him keenly aware of his own superficial education, and he initiated a self-improvement program (he taught himself Latin, mathematics, history and Polish literature) that would continue for the rest of his life. Paderewski's lifelong habit of learning was so successful that the historian William Milligan Sloane once described him as the best-educated man he had ever met.

At the start of 1880 Paderewski married Antonina Korsak, a student at the Conservatory, only to be widowed that same year when Antonina died shortly after the birth of their son Alfred on 1 October. (Although not apparent at birth, Alfred had a congenital illness, spent most of his life confined to a wheelchair, and died at age 21.) After his wife's death, Paderewski left his infant son with his mother-in-law, worked extra hard teaching and composing and saved his money for study abroad.

Prodded by Helena Gorska, his devoted friend and counselor, in 1882 he studied composition with Friedrich Kiel in Berlin for about seven months, working 10 to 12 hours daily, and was always grateful to Kiel for being the very first teacher to encourage his ambition to become a concert pianist. Out of funds, Paderewski returned to Warsaw. The Conservatory rehired him to teach piano, and he earned extra income from writing newspaper articles and teaching private lessons. Even so, he practiced obsessively to improve his technique, and with his extra money hired four tutors to give him evening lessons (Latin, mathematics, literature, history) between eight P.M. and midnight.

Early in 1884 Paderewski returned to Berlin to study orchestration with Heinrich Urban. That summer, while vacationing in the Tatra Mountains, he met the famous Polish actress Modjeska (Helena Modrzejewska). When Paderewski played for her, Modjeska felt his intensity to be almost hypnotic, and her theatrical instincts instantly sensed his mesmerizing stage quality. Modjeska urged him to become a concert pianist. She backed her advice by appearing with Paderewski in a concert in Kraków and then giving him all the profits so that he could go to Vienna to study with Leschetizky.

Paderewski was about to be 24, very old for a student, when he arrived in Vienna in October 1884. Worse than that, his unconventional fingering and shabby work habits appalled Leschetizky, who accepted him reluctantly, most likely because he admired Paderewski's natural technique, his tone and his effective pedaling. Leschetizky (he never charged Paderewski for a single lesson) made him begin with humiliating finger exercises and Czerny studies. Paderewski also studied with Leschetizky's wife, the pianist Anna Essipoff, who made a point of introducing him to the culture and charm of Vienna. Under Leschetizky's guidance Paderewski learned a Saint-Saëns Concerto, a few Bach pieces, one of the easier Beethoven sonatas, a Schumann sonata and a few short compositions. Out of money, Paderewski returned to Warsaw in February 1885, and on 9 April gave a concert there of his own compositions—many solo works and, with Gorski, the Violin Sonata.

From July 1885 he taught for nearly a year at the Strasbourg Conservatory. He also played concerts in Strasbourg and elsewhere in Alsace, gaining recognition as a pianist and meeting influential Parisians who urged him to do recitals in Paris. Early in 1887 the always supportive Edward Kerntopf gave Paderewski funds for a year in Vienna, where he had about 16 more lessons with Leschetizky; studied the rest of the time with Essipoff; and worked endless hours on Czerny and Clementi studies.

His first Paris recital, held at the *Salle Erard* on 3 March 1888, drew a full house, thanks to the Gorskis (living in Paris, they rounded up the expatriate Poles) and Anna Essipoff (on tour in France, she spread word of the recital in musical circles). Five days later Paderewski gave a recital of his own works, with Gorski again playing the Violin Sonata; they repeated this concert 10 days later, and Paderewski also played the Saint-Saëns Piano Concerto No. 4 at a Lamoureux concert at the *Cirque d'été*. Within a month and without realizing it, he had become the sensation of Paris. It was not simply his playing that thrilled the Parisians. Paderewski's onstage presence radiated with that indefinable quality Modjeska had recognized back in 1884. He was inundated with invitations to play, but knew only the limited repertoire he had prepared in Vienna with Leschetizky. Working feverishly, he produced a second program within three weeks, then played wherever he was asked, including the French provinces and Brussels.

Paderewski's meagre repertoire could not possibly sustain a concert career. In late October 1888 he left for Vienna, hoping to work again with

Leschetizky, but ultimately produced two programs largely on his own because Leschetizky was away and, when he returned, he had little free time. Early in 1889 Paderewski gave an immensely successful recital at Vienna's Bösendorfer Hall. That spring he returned to Paris with three more programs prepared.

Further, he had gained confidence in himself as a pianist and was gaining some recognition as a composer. (His famous Minuet, op. 14, no. 1, would eventually sell in the millions.) An avid composer, especially in his youth, Paderewski's Opus 1 appeared in 1876, and over a period of 40 years he composed many works distributed among 24 opus numbers. He apparently stopped composing around 1917. Most of his compositions are for piano (see Zamoyski for complete list). Many were regularly performed during his lifetime, but are no longer heard. His opera *Manru* had several performances early in the century, then disappeared. Neither the Polish Fantasy (piano and orchestra) nor the Sonata is heard today, and his genuinely fine Concerto in A Minor receives only an occasional performance.

Paderewski made highly successful tours through Belgium, the Netherlands, the French provinces, Germany, Hungary, Bohemia and Poland, then at the end of 1889 returned to Paris. He loved Paris. He could be with Alfred, now nine and living in Paris with Helena Gorska, and he could also mingle with famous musicians like Gounod, Massenet, d'Indy, Widor, Fauré and especially Saint-Saëns, with whom he formed a lifelong friendship.

Paderewski's first London recital (8 May 1890, St. James's Hall) drew a small audience and a cool reception, possibly because his agent had crassly billed him as "the lion of Paris." But by the time he had completed some 40 appearances, public and private, he had become the darling of London society. His first American tour (Nov 1891–March 1892), arranged by the House of Steinway to promote its pianos, proved to be brutal and exhausting. The horrified Paderewski discovered that in the first week alone he was expected to play six concertos as well as solos. To fulfill this incredible contract (in Europe a pianist might play just six concertos in an entire season), after each concert he practiced nights at the Steinway warehouse, exhausting his whole being and inflaming his nerves.

Although his first American concert (17 Nov 1891), held at Carnegie Hall with Walter Damrosch conducting, was a sensational success, Paderewski was too spent physically and emotionally to realize it. Success followed success. By 1904 Paderewski's annual American tour was earning him well over a million dollars, and a contemporary journalist estimated that for each piece he played, including encores, Paderewski was averaging about $1,000.

Paderewski toured all the time—repeated tours of America and Europe, tours in South America, Australia, New Zealand and South Africa. His repertoire held to the classics—Beethoven, Brahms, Schumann, Mendelssohn, Liszt, Chopin; some popular pieces by Anton Rubinstein or other contemporary composers; and his own compositions.

He yearned for free time for composing, reading, studying or simply enjoying his estates, but always needing more money, he had to keep touring. It took every penny Paderewski made to support his growing responsibilities and his legendary generosity. He had a kind (and costly) nature, loved to give presents, send flowers and make people happy. He gave whenever asked or wherever he saw a need.

Paderewski's lasting relationship with Helena Gorska, his devoted companion and foster mother of Alfred, blossomed into a love affair. Her marriage to Gorski was finally annulled, and she and Paderewski married in Warsaw in May 1898. They lived at the Villa Riond-Bosson, his Swiss estate at Morges on Lake Geneva. Paderewski now had to support Helena and her son; Alfred, with his medical needs and personal attendants; his widowed sister Antonina, who managed the large and very expensive household. And he spent exorbitantly large sums on lands in Poland and elsewhere.

An ardently patriotic Pole, Paderewski also donated vast sums to the cause of Polish independence. In 1910 his stirring speech at Kraków made him a hero with politicians and peasants alike. It may have been the first step in his career as a statesman. When World War I struck Europe in 1914, Paderewski set up Polish relief committees in Vevey, Paris and London, and spent the rest of the war in America raising millions for Polish famine relief, working for Polish independence and giving concerts to aid America's war efforts. Fluent in several languages, Paderewski turned out to be a remarkable speaker in English. As at the piano, on the rostrum he kept his audience spellbound, delivering his words with a sense of timing and musicality. He made about 340 speeches and played nearly as many concerts.

When he returned to Europe after the war, Paderewski stood as a symbolic figure of Poland itself, without question the person most Poles felt they could trust. In 1919 he served as the first Premier of Poland, and he represented Poland at the Paris Peace Conference. Incredibly, this pianist from the concert stage emerged from the Peace Conference with a reputation as an incomparable orator, linguist and one who knew the history of Europe better than most professional statesmen. Disillusioned in his dream of Polish independence, Paderewski resigned from the Conference in 1920, but continued his fight for Polish independence as the Polish delegate to the League of Nations.

By 1922 he needed money desperately. Vast amounts of his fortune had been spent on Poland and his countrymen, his estates were heavily mortgaged and he had not had any concert income for about five years. To recoup, he began an American tour on 22 November 1922, and his return to the concert stage "created nearly as great a sensation as his debut had done more than thirty years previously. He was now honoured not only as a great pianist, but also as a distinguished statesman whose efforts had been largely responsible for the rebirth of his country." (*Paderewski plays Chopin*, Liner notes, GEMM CD 9397, see Discog.)

In America Paderewski lived like a grand potentate, traveling in a private railway car with a piano, a full entourage (usually including a secretary, valet, piano tuner, tour manager, masseuse, chef, two porters) and often friends with whom to play bridge or billiards. His every move and everything about him—health, wealth, habits, clothing and flowing hair—fascinated the American press and public. People queued early in the morning for his concerts and rose to their feet when he came onstage. Audiences stood on their chairs to cheer, and some left only when movers rolled the piano from the stage. He even sparked a

Paderewski industry: dolls, wigs, shampoos, soaps, candles, iron pills, toys and more.

Such hysterical acclaim, more familiar to a 20th-century rock star than a Victorian concert pianist, obscures Paderewski's performance. People either worshipped him or dismissed him as a charlatan; seemingly there was no middle ground. Paderewski himself was keenly attuned to his audience, how it responded, and in fact often played intently to just one person. Pablo Casals, for example, felt that when he heard Paderewski play at the *Salle Erard* the pianist stared at him throughout the concert. At introductions later, Paderewski declared, "I already know this young man; tonight I played for him. This youth is *prédestiné.*" (Kir/Pab, see Bibliog.)

Though he made fewer tours in the 1930s and at times played very badly, Paderewski's loyal audiences still thronged to hear him. He was 78 when he began his 20th and final American tour in February 1939. After suffering a heart attack on 25 May, he canceled the rest of the tour and returned to Switzerland.

When World War II overtook Europe, Paderewski left for America, hoping once again to serve the Polish cause. Although 80 and very frail, he wrote letters, made radio talks and met with important people to warn them that Hitler had to be stopped. On 22 June 1941 he made a long speech at a rally of World War I Polish-American veterans, nearly collapsing in the heat as people crowded around to touch him, kiss his hands, even his clothes. Within a few days Paderewski had pneumonia. He died on 29 June at the Buckingham Hotel in New York City.

As in his life, thousands came to see Paderewski. Day and night, crowds filed by his glass-covered coffin, first at the hotel, later at St. Patrick's Cathedral. An estimated 35,000 people stood in the rain to watch the horse-drawn caisson bearing his coffin process to Pennsylvania Station. By order of President Roosevelt, Paderewski was honored with a 19-gun salute and (in accordance with Paderewski's request) buried at Arlington National Cemetery to await the day when his body could be returned to a free Poland. Thanks to a new generation of Polish patriots, Poland is once again a free nation. On 5 July 1992 Paderewski's remains were reinterred in Warsaw's St. John Cathedral.

Just as he always needed money, Paderewski needed constant reassurance from an audience to bolster his self-confidence. A latecomer to fame, he apparently never trusted his talent, and all his life depended on long, hard practice sessions. Obviously, Paderewski's mesmerizing onstage presence masked an insecure, nerve-wracked man. "Toward the end of his career, Paderewski always started his concerts late; it was a great irritation, and the audience would start clapping—a quarter of an hour, twenty minutes. And he was offstage with his hands in hot water because of an arthritic condition! Then he'd come on and play like an angel." (Gil/Boo, see Bibliog.)

From the very start of his concert career to its zenith, Paderewski seemingly could do no wrong. Probably the high point of that incredible career came during the final decade of the 19th century. Later, critics began to notice blurred textures, erratic rhythms, poor technique and the asynchronous treatment of chords. For example, a 1905 review included this: "Some of the pounding that he did yesterday was scandalous and knew no measure; and this was never an element in Paderewski's spell in those earlier days. . . . It seems as if in some way he has lost something of that instinctive sense of proportion that used to characterize everything he did." (*NYT*, 26 March 1905)

To be completely fair, Paderewski's playing should be evaluated at its peak, when indeed it must have been splendid. Some of the finest appreciations of Paderewski the man and the artist were written after his death. For example, we have a long and eminently fair appraisal of the pianist from the highly respected Olin Downes: "The generations who knew the art of Ignace Paderewski at the height of his powers were fortunate indeed. There was not and there will not be a pianist like him. He absorbed great 'traditions,' but they were the frame of his unique individuality and communicative power. His playing was that of a poet and romanticist. Its impassioned eloquence was companioned by the seduction of his singing tone and the glamorous beauty which he evoked . . . from the instrument of wires and keys. In the later period he became more enamored of line than of color, and was often careless of detail and of tone-quality per se. . . . But always, when the mood seized him, he could sing with an ineffable simplicity and a wistfulness that haunted the memory, the song of a little Impromptu of Schubert, [just] as he could summon the bardic utterance of a Chopin polonaise or the communings of a late sonata by Beethoven.

"Paderewski, in any place or period, would have stood forth from his contemporaries, and probably in much the same light in which he stands today. He was never a man for precise measurements and he never could have escaped the consequences of greatness. . . . It was because of the essence of his being that Paderewski was able to evoke the sounds that he did from the instrument." (Downes, "Passing . . .")

About the same time, critic and editor Leonard Liebling, who had studied piano with Leopold Godowsky, devoted one of his columns titled "Variations" to Paderewski: "Paderewski was just Paderewski, that was all. A marvelous artist of unique individuality and flaming personality, with irresistible charm. . . . Specifically he had a full, rich, pulsing tone that bore no relation to the hard stabbing he did in his later years. He was a genius with the pedal, and as a colorist. He made his tone do anything he listed—sing, exult, thunder, sentimentalize, even sob. . . . He left one actually limp with his inescapable rhythmic drive and emotional heat in Chopin's A-flat Polonaise or that in F-sharp minor; even the hackneyed A major took on a martial nobility which I have never heard from any other pianist." (*MA*, 15 April 1941)

A more contemporary commentary on Paderewski's control of sound comes from the late eminent pianist Sir Clifford Curzon: "A pianist without a beautiful and appropriate sound is like a human being in cardboard clothes. You have to clothe your music in the right sound. Paderewski used to have this to perfection. I shall never forget his performance of Schumann's F sharp minor Sonata. The start of the slow movement was extraordinary for the reason I've mentioned." (*MM*, Feb 1979)

These descriptions depict Paderewski in his prime, and he was indeed a glorious performer. However, by the 1930s his performances had begun to deteriorate, possibly because of his turbulent personal life. Near the end of his life his playing could in no way be compared with that of the earlier, great Paderewski, and it is a pity that he felt compelled to continue playing in public.

Paderewski made almost 100 recordings during a period of more than 25 years—from June 1911 to November 1938. Since by 1930 his playing tended to be unpredictable and erratic, the earlier recordings are the best, even though they are acoustic recordings with considerable surface noise. In the first decade of this century Paderewski made about 20 rolls for the Welte-Mignon Reproducing Piano. In the 1930s about 30 rolls were issued by Duo-Art. (*Paderewski Plays*, see Discog; Sit/Cla, see Bibliog.)

A fine collection (6 LPs) of Paderewski's recordings, assembled for the Pearl historical series in Britain, contains at least one version of almost every significant composition recorded by Paderewski (and issued) between 1911 and 1937. The later CDs contain compositions chosen mostly from the original six-volume set (see Discog.).

Despite the dynamic and tonal restrictions of the early discs, they reveal a great deal of Paderewski's magnetic pianism. "The recordings demonstrate that Paderewski's greatest technical accomplishments were his quick and delicate right-hand passage-work—scales, glissandi and so on. Where his technique often let him down was in heavier, complicated chord passages, octave passages and the like. Distinguishing marks of Paderewski's playing were his frequent separation of left and right hands—something which modern listeners are unaccustomed to, but which was common enough in Paderewski's youth and earlier— and a freedom of movement within the basic tempo he chose for a given piece or section of a piece." (Sac/Vir, see Bibliog.)

Paderewski made his first acoustic recordings at his estate at Morges in July 1911. The Chopin Polonaise, op. 40, no. 1, reveals the strength and intensity of his playing but overall is unimpressive. On the other hand, the Schubert-Liszt "Hark, Hark the Lark" contains some fine, stylish playing.

The intriguing 1912 recordings contain three excerpts from Schumann's *Fantasiestücke*, op. 12, that border on the sublime, especially the fine tonal control and dreamy expression of *Des Abends* and the intimate tonal picture projected, despite some interpretative exaggerations, in *Warum*. There is also Anton Rubinstein's *Valse Caprice*. Brilliantly played, this offers a rare opportunity to hear the music of this composer who was so popular during Paderewski's time. Mendelssohn's Hunting Song, op. 19, no. 3, is a delight, and some of the Chopin Etudes (op. 25, nos. 1, 2, 7) are especially well performed, even by contemporary standards, but others contain much inaccurate, rhythmically distorted playing. The Liszt *Etude de concert* No. 2 almost approaches perfection.

In the 1917 recordings, made before Paderewski gave up playing to fight for the Polish cause, he gives an impression of being relaxed. In the Chopin Nocturne, op. 15, no. 2, one of the most beautiful of these recordings, the chromatic ornamentation is indescribably lovely.

In 1922 Paderewski returned to concertizing and to recording. Liszt's Hungarian Rhapsody No. 10, with its noble opening and thrilling octave glissandi, is one of the very best of Paderewski's 1922 efforts. An unsentimental performance of Chopin's *Berceuse* and Liszt's arrangement of Chopin's song "My Joys" are both notable complements to the 1917 recordings. The highlight of the 1924 discs is the sparkling performance of the Spinning Chorus from The Flying Dutchman (Wagner-Liszt). Paderewski also plays his own Nocturne, op. 16, no. 4, a good example of one of his very best works.

The 1937 recordings contain three works—one each by Haydn, Mozart and Beethoven (see Discog.)—showing that at age 77 Paderewski was still capable of extremely beautiful playing. (Most of the music had been heard a year earlier in the film "Moonlight Sonata," which starred the pianist.) The Haydn Variations alone, said the reviewer for *Gramophone* (March 1938) made this record a necessity to the admirer of Paderewski's incomparable genius. And his playing of the Beethoven Sonata (op. 27, no. 2), particularly the first movement, shows the famous tonal beauty still in place. In August 1937 another *Gramophone* reviewer wrote ecstatically of Paderewski's reading of the Mozart Rondo, K. 511: "Every note is a joy: touch, tone, expression are those of a master. I was completely enchanted."

Paderewski recorded many Chopin pieces. While some of his interpretations may vary stylistically from what we expect today, there is no denying the delicacy of touch, the excitement and the freedom of phrasing that characterize the finest Paderewski playing. "What's most striking here is how vividly Paderewski gives each piece a distinctive character: from the quiet intensity of op. 25/7 to the impish irony of the elegant op. 64/2 to the volcanic seriousness of the 'Revolutionary Étude,' from the sweetness of the Berceuse to the crispness of op. 33/2 to the almost brutal charge through op. 18, Paderewski's Chopin has a dizzying variety of color and mood." (*Fanfare*, March/April 1989. Reprinted by permission.)

SELECTED REFERENCES

Altman, Elenore. "The Paderewski Legend." *Piano Teacher*, Nov/Dec 1964, pp. 2–6.

Baughan, Edward A. *Ignaz Jan Paderewski*. London: John Lane, The Bodley Head, 1908.

Chasins, Abram. "The Art of Paderewski." *Saturday Review of Literature*, 24 Nov 1956, pp. 48–49.

Downes, Olin. "Paderewski, Conqueror of His Destiny." *New York Times Magazine*, 2 Nov 1930, pp. 4–5, 23.

———. "Passing of a Hero." *New York Times*, 6 July 1941, sec. 9, p. 5.

Duleba, Wladyslaw, and Zofia Sokolowska. *Paderewski*. Translated by Wiktor Litwinski. New York: The Kosciuszko Foundation, 1979.

Gerstenzang, James. "Bush and Poles Honor Patriot, New Freedoms." *Los Angeles Times*, 6 July 1992, sec. A, pp. 1, 6.

Haughton, John Alan. "Paderewski, Lion of Music and Hero of Poland, Dies at 80." *Musical America*, July 1941, pp. 7, 33.

Hodgson, Leslie. "The Incomparable Pianist." *Musical America*, Aug 1941, p. 7.

Hoskins, Janina W. *Ignacy Jan Paderewski (1860–1941): A Biographical Sketch and a Selective List of Reading Materials.* Washington: Library of Congress, 1984.

House, Edward M. "Paderewski: The Paradox of Europe." *Harper's Magazine,* Dec 1925, pp. 30–36.

Landau, Rom. *Ignace Paderewski: Musician and Statesman.* New York: Crown Publishers, 1934.

Liebling, Leonard. "Variations." *Musical America,* 15 April 1941, p. 33.

Mason, William. "Paderewski: A Critical Study." *Century Library of Music,* vol. 18, ed. Ignace Jan Paderewski. New York: The Century Co., 1900, pp. 577–584.

Paderewski, Ignace Jan. "Breadth in Musical Art Work." *Etude,* Feb 1915, pp. 89–90.

———. "Chopin." *Etude,* Feb 1926, pp. 95–96.

———. "Reflections from a Musical Life." *Etude,* Nov 1936, pp. 683–684.

Paderewski, Ignace Jan, and Mary Lawton. *The Paderewski Memoirs.* New York: Charles Scribner's Sons, 1938.

Ringle, Ken. "Paderewski's last journey home." *Washington Post,* 27 June 1992, sec. C, p. 1.

Société Paderewski. The Society publishes a volume of *Annales* and operates a small museum. Address: Centre Culturel, Place du Casino 1, CH-1110 Morges, Switzerland.

Stevenson, Ronald. *The Paderewski Paradox.* Lincoln: The Klavar Music Foundation, 1992.

Strakacz, Aniela. *Paderewski As I Knew Him.* Translated by Halina Chybowska. New Brunswick: Rutgers University Press, 1949.

Zamoyski, Adam. *Paderewski.* New York: Atheneum, 1982.

See also Bibliography: Bro/Mas; Bro/Pia; Car/Ful; Dan/Con; Dow/Oli; Fin/My; Fin/Suc; Ful/Doo; Gol/Jou; Hun/Old; Hun/Ste; Kol/Que; Lan/Mus; Met/Cho; Rub/MyM; Rub/MyY; Sac/Vir; Sch/Glo; Sch/Gre.

SELECTED REVIEWS

MA: 2 Nov 1907; 9 Nov 1907; 6 Feb 1909; 5 Feb 1910; 22 Nov 1913; 6 Dec 1913; 27 Nov 1915; 25 Dec 1915; 10 Nov 1930. *MT*: 1 June 1890; 1 July 1890; 1 Aug 1923; 1 Nov 1931. *NYT*: 24 Jan 1892; 27 Jan 1892; 30 Jan 1892; 3 Feb 1909; 2 Nov 1913; 16 Nov 1913; 30 Nov 1913; 8 March 1914; 6 Nov 1916; 10 Jan 1917; 1 April 1917; 23 Nov 1922; 17 Dec 1922; 27 Feb 1939. *TL*: 17 June 1897; 4 July 1901.

SELECTED DISCOGRAPHY

The Art of Paderewski. Vol. 1. Beethoven: Sonata in C-sharp Minor, op. 27, no. 2. Haydn: Andante and Variations in F Minor. Mozart: Rondo in A Minor, K. 511. Paderewski: *Cracovienne fantastique,* op. 14, no. 6; *Mélodie,* op. 8, no. 3 (*Chants du Voyageur*); Minuet in G Major, op. 14, no. 1; Nocturne in B-flat Major, op. 14, no. 6. Schubert: Impromptu in A-

flat Major, D. 935, no. 2; Impromptu in B-flat Major, D. 935, no. 3;
Moment Musical in A-flat Major, D. 780, no. 2. Pearl GEMM 9499 (CD).
The Art of Paderewski. Vol. 3. Brahms: Hungarian Dances 6–7. Debussy:
Preludes Book I (1, 2, 3, 12); *Reflets dans l'eau.* Mendelssohn: Songs
without Words, op. 19, no. 3, op. 53, no. 4, op. 67, no. 4. Rubinstein:
Valse Caprice, op. 118. Schumann: *Fantasiestücke*, op. 12, nos. 1–3;
Nachtstücke, op. 23, no. 4; Prophet Bird. Strauss-Tausig: One Lives but
Once. Pearl 9109 (CD).
Paderewski. Beethoven: Sonata in C-sharp Minor, op. 27, no. 2. Chopin:
Etudes, op. 10, no. 3, op. 25, nos. 8–9; Nocturne, op. 15, no. 2;
Polonaise, op. 53; Sonata No. 2, op. 35 (3rd and 4th movts.). Liszt: *La
Campanella*; Hungarian Rhapsody No. 10. Paderewski: Minuet, op. 14, no.
1. Rachmaninoff: Prelude, op. 32, no. 12. Schumann: *Nachtstücke*, op.
23, no. 4. Strauss-Tausig: *Man lebt nur einmal.* Wagner-Schelling:
Prelude to *Tristan und Isolde.* RCA Victor 09026-60923-2.
Paderewski. Pearl LP GEMM 126, 140, 150, 179, 196, 279. Six LPs contain-
ing at least one version of every significant Paderewski recording.
Paderewski Plays Chopin. Vol. I. *Berceuse*, op. 57; Etudes in C Minor, op.
10, no. 12, A-flat Major, op. 25, no. 1, F Minor, op. 25, no. 2, C-sharp
Minor, op. 25, no. 7, A Minor, op. 25, no. 11; Mazurkas in D Major, op.
33, no. 2, A-flat Major, op. 59, no. 2, F-sharp Minor, op. 59, no. 3;
Nocturnes in F Major, op. 15, no. 1, F-sharp Major, op. 15, no. 2;
Polonaises in E-flat Minor, op. 26, no. 2, A-flat Major, op. 53; Preludes in
D-flat Major, op. 28, no. 15, A-flat Major, op. 28, no. 17; Waltzes in C-
sharp Minor, op. 64, no. 2, A-flat Major, op. 42, E-flat Major, op. 18.
Pearl GEMM CD 9323. Chosen from the above six-volume LP set.
Paderewski Plays Chopin. Vol. II. Ballade in F Minor, op. 52; Etudes in E
Major, op. 10, no. 3, G-flat Major, op. 10, no. 5, C Major, op. 10, no. 7,
G-sharp Minor, op. 25, no. 6, G-flat Major, op. 25, no. 9; Maiden's Wish
(arr. Liszt); Mazurkas in A Minor, op. 17, no. 4, C-sharp Minor, op. 63,
no. 3; My Joys (arr. Liszt); Nocturnes in E-flat Major, op. 9, no. 2, B
Major, op. 62, no. 1, E Major, op. 62, no. 2; Polonaise in A Major, op.
40, no. 1; Sonata in B-flat Minor, op. 35 (3rd movt.); Valse in A-flat
Major, op. 34, no. 1; Pearl GEMM CD 9397. Chosen from the above six-
volume LP set.
Paderewski Plays Concert No. 1. Chopin: Ballades, op. 23, op. 47; Mazurka,
op. 24, no. 4; Nocturne, op. 37, no. 2; Polonaise, op. 40, no. 1; *Valse
brillante*, op. 34, no. 1. Debussy: Reflections in the Water. Mendelssohn:
Spinning Song. Schubert: Impromptu, D. 935, no. 2. Schubert-Liszt:
Hark, Hark the Lark. Klavier KS 127. Recorded from piano rolls.
Paderewski Plays Concert No. 2. Beethoven: Sonata, op. 27, no. 2. Chopin:
Scherzo in C-sharp Minor, op. 39. Liszt: Hungarian Rhapsodies Nos. 2 and
10. Schubert-Liszt: *Soirée de Vienne.* Wagner-Liszt: Isoldes Love Death.
Klavier KS 129. Recorded from piano rolls.

PERAHIA, MURRAY: b. New York City, New York, 19 April 1947.

> Poet of the piano may be a trite phrase but it completely describes
> Perahia. He makes music effortlessly and with a beguiling spontaneity
> that always reflects the composer more than the performer. At least
> 99% of the time he makes you feel that you are finally hearing the per-
> fect performance of whatever he may be playing.
> Albert Goldberg (*Los Angeles Times*, 7 November 1979)

Count Murray Perahia (and also Emanuel Ax, Horacio Gutiérrez, Radu Lupu,
Garrick Ohlsson, Peter Serkin) among that new generation of pianists born in
the latter half of the 1940s—a new generation, says Perahia, immensely influenced by Artur Schnabel and Edwin Fischer, great pianists who repudiated the
idea of virtuosity for the sake of virtuosity and refused to play the crowd-pleasing
pieces audiences wanted to hear.

Murray Perahia, the epitome of the Schnabel-Fischer concept, was born
with a great gift for music, and his father encouraged his musical interests; but
Perahia was never a performing piano prodigy. Quite the opposite, for it took
him about 20 years to decide that he really wanted to be a concert pianist. Born
and trained in New York City, he is the son of David and Flora Perahia (both
born in Greece but descendants of Spanish Sephardic Jews evicted from Spain in
1492), who emigrated to America in the 1930s.

David Perahia loved music, especially opera, and he saw to it that his
son discovered music at a very early age. Murray Perahia heard his first concert,
at Lewisohn Stadium, before he was four years old (and reportedly sat amazingly
still), and before long his father began taking him to the opera every Saturday
during the season. Although only four, Perahia could sing some of the tunes he
heard at the opera and sometimes pick them out on a toy piano.

From age four to six Perahia studied music with Lilly Aseal, a neighborhood teacher, and apparently had a wonderful time spending hours at the piano
just playing and improvising. He never thought of it as practice; it was great
fun. At age six he started lessons with Jeannette Haien, assistant to Abram
Chasins on his WQXR radio program. She was only 22 years old, and Perahia
happened to be her first pupil, thus he became, as he later expressed it, her "project." Their twice weekly sessions sometimes lasted more than two hours, and
Haien gave him a solid musical foundation—not merely piano lessons but also
theory, harmony, composition and ear training through four-part dictation.
Perahia learned a great deal musically, but Haien's increasing control of his life
bothered him. When he left her at age 17, he was uncertain about continuing
with the piano, confused because he felt he was playing only for Haien, playing
her way without knowing *why* he was doing this or that.

Perahia knew that he wanted to do something in music, but he just was
not sure which direction to take. He was 17 years old, had completed his studies
with Haien and also had graduated (1964) from the New York High School of the
Performing Arts. The question was, what to do next? He wanted to play as
much chamber music as he could, he wanted to study conducting and he had by

no means abandoned the piano; in fact, his piano playing at the high school had made him something of a star. Having decided to study technique on his own, in 1964 Perahia enrolled at the Mannes School of Music as a conducting major with Carl Bamberger.

In 1965 he won the Kosciusko Chopin Prize and also auditioned successfully for Young Concert Artists, his "prize" being management services and a debut recital at Carnegie Recital Hall. After hearing that debut performance (10 Jan 1966), one encouraging reviewer wrote: "For scope, temperament and sheer vitality of thought, Perahia must be regarded as a comer of the first magnitude." (*MA*, April 1966)

The Mannes years were most productive. Along with his conducting classes—geared more to score-reading than actually conducting an orchestra—Perahia studied counterpoint, theory and Schenker analysis. He also studied chamber music with Arthur Balsam and studied piano on his own. Trying to find his personal way of making music, not Haien's way, Perahia came to the conclusion that the only way to start, to make sense out of music, was to understand structure. In later years he would often say that he felt that these years of studying the piano alone had been most beneficial to his playing and his career.

Perahia was still a Mannes student when he launched his career with a chamber-music concert at the Library of Congress in Washington, D.C. As he remembers it, "My very first professional engagement was with Boris Kroyt, violist of the Budapest Quartet, and [clarinettist] Harold Wright. . . . I think I was 18 or 19 at the time. Vox put out a recording of that concert. It was my first recording and my first paid engagement." (Delacoma)

Several summers at the Marlboro Music School and Festival in Vermont essentially completed Perahia's training. Marlboro gave him the opportunity to perform and study with great musicians like Rudolf Serkin (Perahia sometimes played four-hand music with Serkin); Pablo Casals (for whom Perahia sometimes played in private); Alexander Schneider (Perahia often played with Schneider's chamber orchestra); and especially Mieczyslaw Horszowski, one of the truly great pianists of the century. "Horszowski was always my idol," says Perahia. "I loved his playing for its incredible understanding. I suppose I'm a bit academic, maybe pedantic, in my upbringing, and the kind of pianist who appeals to me is one who tries to get at what the music is about." (Blyth)

Perahia played an enormous amount of chamber music at Marlboro and, possibly because of Horszowski's influence, began practicing the piano more seriously. In 1968 he signed with Frank Salomon, an agent who was also manager of the Marlboro Music Festival. Although Perahia graduated (1969) from Mannes with a B.S. in conducting, he was performing more as chamber pianist, accompanist or soloist than as conductor. The previous year his performance (27 Dec 1968) of the Bach Concertos Nos. 4 and 6 with Alexander Schneider and his chamber orchestra at Carnegie Hall had earned both applause and bravos.

After graduation Perahia taught at Mannes for a time; he was for a year Rudolf Serkin's teaching assistant at the Curtis Institute of Music; and he was also performing, but mostly chamber music, especially on the "Music from Marlboro" tours. Although most definitely interested in the piano, he hesitated to commit himself to becoming a solo pianist and having to learn all that repertoire. In retrospect, it would seem that the events of 1972 made the decision for him.

In the spring of that year (1972) Perahia within one week appeared as soloist with two New York orchestras. He first played (4 March 1972) with the *Music Aeterna* Orchestra, Frederic Waldman conducting, at Carnegie Hall, giving a "graceful, fluent, crystal clear" performance of the Mozart Concerto in C Major, K. 467, and a "sensitive, feeling" reading of the Chopin Concerto No. 1. "Clearly this was Mr. Perahia's evening, and he made the most of it." (*NYT*, 6 March 1972) Only a few days later Perahia made an "auspicious" debut (10 March 1972), playing the Mozart Concerto in G Major, K. 453, with the New York Philharmonic Orchestra, István Kertész conducting. In that same busy year Perahia signed a contract with Columbia records, the beginning of his two-decade affiliation with CBS Masterworks, now Sony Classical records.

The crowning achievement of 1972 came in September when Perahia won (the first American ever to do so) the Leeds International Piano Competition in England. His prize included more than 50 engagements—with major orchestras in London, other orchestras throughout the British Isles, the Israel Philharmonic Orchestra and the *Concertgebouw* Orchestra; and also a solo recital debut at London's Queen Elizabeth Hall and appearances on BBC television and radio.

Perahia's playing at those many performances resulting from winning at Leeds propelled him into a career as a concert pianist, and from the start it has gone immensely well. His playing at the 1973 Aldeburgh Festival led to a beneficial, indeed inspiring, association with Benjamin Britten and Peter Pears, founders of the festival. When Britten became too ill to perform, Perahia took over as accompanist for Pears's lieder recitals in both England and the United States. It was an invaluable experience, especially in that he often went to Britten for ideas on various song cycles, and that led to talks on other musical matters. Britten—a remarkable pianist, says Perahia—gave him advice on performing the Schumann Piano Concerto and the Chopin Preludes. For years Perahia played regularly at Aldeburgh and from 1981 through 1989 was artistic co-director. He was later appointed honorary director of the Britten-Pears School for Advanced Musical Studies.

On 9 January 1975 Perahia was one of the first recipients of the Avery Fisher Award, and the $5,000 stipend made it possible for him to stop giving concerts in order to learn new repertoire. Overnight success had plunged him headlong into a busy concert career, but he was well aware that he was becoming known as a Chopin and Schumann specialist. He needed to broaden his repertoire then, and ever since, whenever possible Perahia has taken some time away from the concert platform to study new works, even some he may never play in public. Ever the musician first and a pianist second, it matters not that he may not play them in public because, as he says, "I am more interested in the ideas behind the music than in one instrument."

It is typical of Perahia's whole attitude toward music that he disapproves of piano competitions, even despite what he gained from winning the Leeds competition. Generally speaking, says Perahia, competitions have contributed to "what I find a too intense, almost exclusive, concentration on technical brilliance and technical perfection among today's younger pianists. They tend to lose sight of, or neglect, problems that are more musical, more musically substantive, than purely technical." (Pleasants)

Perahia has lived in London since 1973, mainly because it has been so much easier to get from there to his many repeat performances in Great Britain and on the Continent. But he has made almost annual tours of the United States and has toured in Canada, Japan and Israel. He has put down deep roots in his adopted city. His wife Ninette (m. 1981) is British and their two sons were born in London. In 1987 Perahia was made a Fellow of the Royal College of Music.

Perahia began playing and conducting the Mozart concertos with student ensembles at the Mannes School of Music, and throughout his career he has made a speciality of those concertos, "which he plays with a magnificent combination of majestic elegance and an almost Romantic passion." (Kozinn) Perahia's programs encompassing the years 1966 to the present indicate that he also plays the Schumann Concerto, the Grieg Concerto, the Brahms Concerto No. 2, the Mendelssohn Concertos Nos. 1 and 2 and the Chopin and Beethoven concertos.

Those same programs show that Perahia's earliest solo repertoire consisted almost exclusively of works by Schumann, Chopin and Schubert, and that gradually he added works by Scarlatti, Haydn, Bartók, Mendelssohn, Brahms and Beethoven. The fact is that Perahia has continually, if slowly, enriched his repertoire. The 1986 programs include both the Tippett Sonata No. 1 and the Berg Sonata. The 1989 programs reveal a new Perahia, playing overtly virtuosic works by Liszt (Hungarian Rhapsody No. 12, Spanish Rhapsody, Mephisto Waltz, *Waldesrauschen, Au bord d'une source*), Rachmaninoff (four *Etudes tableaux*), Schumann (*Faschingsschwank aus Wien*, op. 26).

To maintain that repertoire, Perahia practices about five or six hours a day, using a metronome because, he says, "it's important to keep a rhythmic pulse." But when asked his views on playing with feeling and *rubato* or strict time, Perahia quotes Artur Schnabel: "I play with feeling and in time." Basically, Perahia believes in "playing everything with a certain amount of *rubato*, though it has to be very subtle and with what I would term 'harmonic' *rubato*, rather than great heaves and sighs, which I tend not to favor." (Long)

Perahia studies every work with meticulous attention to detail. He starts on a new composition by playing it through to get a sense of direction, phrase design, points of tension. Next he works out the technique needed to articulate what he has discovered in the first reading. The final stage is polishing, reevaluating certain ideas and reworking some passages. Study away from the piano is also vastly important. Perahia believes that learning as much as possible about the composer of the piece—his other music, life, letters, temperament, how and where he lived—will add insight to the music making.

He developed his personal interpretative approach working on the piano on his own while at Mannes, his goal being to try to get away from a set interpretation, to find a way of making music which was completely his own. In the end, he came to the conclusion that the only way to make sense out of music was to understand its structure. His interpretations—lyrical, direct and deceptively effortless—result from hard, disciplined work (he never takes a single bar for granted) and reflect his deep concern for form and structure. His steadfast desire to express the poetry and inner meaning of the music, not obvious virtuosity, has caused more than one critic to mark Perahia as the most poetically expressive pianist since Dinu Lipatti.

At his New York recital debut (10 Jan 1966, Carnegie Recital Hall), Perahia's "massive, clearly articulated style" reminded one critic of Cortot, "and Perahia's resemblance to that artist was further reinforced by an inclination to add octaves or 'woolly' his sonority at certain climactic interludes. What Perahia needs most now is the experience to channel and soften his daring, unconventional impetuosity." (*MA*, April 1966) Six years later his experience showed in a performance (4 March 1972) of the Mozart Concerto in C Major, K. 467, and the Chopin Concerto in E Minor with the *Musica Aeterna* Orchestra, conducted by Frederic Waldman. In the Mozart, "his playing—graceful, fluent, crystal clear—dovetailed perfectly with the gracious orchestral sound." And his reading of the Chopin was "a conception that made its impact through flexibility rather than virtuosity. . . . It was all warmth and lyricism, with carefully shaded dynamics, and an elegant feel." (*NYT*, 6 March 1972)

Perahia gave a cool, thoroughly intelligent performance of the Mozart Concerto in C Minor, K. 491, at his London concerto debut (18 Jan 1973) with the Royal Philharmonic Orchestra, Sir Charles Groves conducting. "Runs and rapid arpeggios flowed with a consistency that immediately recalled Mozart's favourite description, 'like oil and butter.' For dramatic as well as contemplative music he allowed himself plenty of time; his articulation of phrases was a joy to be savoured." (*TL*, 19 Jan 1973) At his London recital debut (13 Feb 1973), the introductory group of Scarlatti sonatas displayed the most essential characteristics of Perahia's style—"his exceptionally incisive articulation, his liking for a translucent sound-world, his unerring sense of shape and proportion, his way of seeking expression, in its purest and simplest form." (*TL*, 14 Feb 1973)

Perahia's performance (5 Jan 1984) of the Schumann Concerto in A Minor with the Cleveland Orchestra, conducted by Erich Leinsdorf, was for one reviewer an absorbing "blend of fire and delicacy that suited the piece wonderfully. Schumann's lyrical statements were given especially affectionate handling by the pianist, who also could send sonorities roaring when required." (*ABJ*, 6 Jan 1984) When Perahia played Schumann's *Faschingsschwank* in San Francisco on 3 April 1989, his "fearless technical control propelled the rambling opening. The freshness and alert rhythms of the three short inner sections seemed spun from unearthly fabric and the bravura give-and-take of the finale matched velocity to masterful articulation." (*SFE*, 4 April 1989)

Perahia's performance (7 April 1989) of Chopin's Concerto No. 2 in F Minor with the Fort Worth Chamber Orchestra, José-Luis Garcia conducting, "was neither the neurotic nor the hothouse performance one sometimes encounters, but rather Chopin that was relaxed yet frequently impetuous. Perahia's playing might be described best as 'passionately elegant'." (*DMN*, 9 April 1987)

Perahia's recitals most often draw glowing reviews. In Boston (12 March 1989), "he treated Liszt's gypsy dance tunes as heartfelt folksong, without a trace of sentimentality. And his playing abounded in the qualities for which he is so esteemed: scrupulous clarity, careful articulation of the musical design, vivid imagination and—yes—a poetic lyricism." (*BG*, 14 March 1989) And a review of a performance (19 March 1989) in Chicago: "One had to hear Perahia's account of Beethoven's Sonata No. 26 in E-flat Major [*Les Adieux*], however, to realize the emotional range of his Beethoven. Perahia elegantly brought across the 'story line' of the sonata, in which Beethoven expresses sadness at the departure of a friend and joy at the return." (*CT*, 20 March 1989)

A small critical minority finds that at times Perahia's playing turns cold and inexpressive; and a few critics think that his playing is small-scaled. To which Perahia responds: "I don't deliberately feel any preciousness about playing. I feel, yes, that the voices should be clear. . . . I love the idea that everything is contrapuntal. I don't like massive chordal structures without any voice-leading. In other words, for me music is basically lyrical, and banging or tonal crashes for their own sake disturb me aesthetically." (Elder) And most critics seem to agree that, "for all the moonlit effects in Perahia's pianism, he is no miniaturist—he can attack the instrument with real fury, though he never sacrifices beauty of sound." (*BG*, 7 Nov 1978)

In the early 1990s a mysterious problem with his right thumb kept Perahia away from public performance for nearly two years. He returned to the concert platform (13 Feb 1994) with a London performance of the Beethoven Concerto No. 4 in G Major, with James Levine conducting the Philharmonic Orchestra. "From its opening notes, that sense of blithe grace, co-existing with strength and breadth and so characteristic of Perahia's Beethoven, began to shape the work. . . . The perfection of phrasing, to say nothing of the mighty strength of its last, long trill [slow movement], transported it to another element, at least one world apart." (*TL*, 15 Feb 1994)

Just about every recording that Perahia has made during the past 20 years is still readily available—a worthy tribute to the beauty and enduring qualities of Perahia's artistry. Even his debut recording—Schumann *Davidsbündlertänze*, op. 6, and *Fantaisiestücke*, op. 12—still competes favorably with more recent readings by others. And Sony Classical's issue of an 11–CD retrospective collection is evidence enough of Perahia's staying power in the recording studio.

A number of his recordings have received Grammy awards—for the Mendelssohn Concertos (1975); Mozart Concertos (1978); a Bartók recital (1981); both Beethoven's "Emperor" Concerto *and* a group of sonatas (1987); a duo recital with Sir George Solti (1988); and the *Aldeburgh Recital* (1991).

Over a period of nine years Perahia and the English Chamber Orchestra, Perahia conducting, recorded all of the Mozart solo piano concertos. In these performances he "achieves power through serenity." In the D minor [K. 466] and C minor [K. 491] concertos, "Mr. Perahia's performances are remarkably subdued. . . . Mr. Perahia . . . floats above conflict, with utter faith in the music to express itself. Mozart's melodic and harmonic patterns are not used as means to self-expression; one senses rather a love for the form itself—a radiant affection for the rise and fall of phrases, and for the precise calculations of tempo which will allow them to breathe naturally." (*NYT*, 1 June 1986)

Perahia has also recorded three Mozart sonatas: K. 310 in A Minor, K. 331 in A Major, K. 533/494 in F Major. "Perahia seems here to have found the key—or separate keys—to the very essence of these works. He gives the impression that he is not so much *making* them turn out this way or that, as simply *enabling* each work to manifest its own remarkable character. . . . Subtlety and imaginativeness go hand in hand in the judicious ornamentation." (*StR*, March 1993)

A good way to approach Perahia's very comprehensive discography is to consider one or more of the three "sampler" albums available, that is, collections of representative compositions by various composers of various periods. The earliest of these, *A Portrait of Murray Perahia*, contains performances recorded in 1982–83. Most of the compositions—i.e., Chopin's Fantaisie-Impromptu and "Raindrop" Prelude, the Beethoven "*Appassionata*" Sonata, Mendelssohn's *Rondo capriccioso* and the Schubert Impromptu in G-flat Major—are familiar to the average audience. Perahia shows his complete mastery of styles here, and he also offers an excerpt from his Mozart concerto cycle, the Rondo in D Major, K. 382.

The second collection, titled *The Aldeburgh Recital*, includes the 32 Variations of Beethoven; Liszt's virtuosic Hungarian Rhapsody No.12 and Consolation No. 3; Schumann's *Faschingsschwank aus Wien*; and three Rachmaninoff *Etudes-Tableaux*. Perahia's affectionate reading of the Schumann "reminds us that Schumann really has no more eloquent champion." And all the performances on this disc "are enlivening in the very best sense, taking the music absolutely on its own terms, touching all the emotional bases and glorying in the virtually orchestral range of colors." (*StR*, June 1991) This recital, with the addition of Beethoven's Sonata in C Major, op. 2, no. 3, is available in video format (*Murray Perahia in Performance*, see Video).

The third "sampler," a more extensive one, is titled *Tout l'art du piano*. Included in this 2-CD collection are compositions by Beethoven (Concerto No. 5, op. 73, Sonata, op. 31, no. 3), Chopin (11 Preludes from Op. 28), Liszt (Hungarian Rhapsody No. 12), Mendelssohn (*Variations sérieuses*, op. 54), Mozart (Concerto in C Major, K. 467) and Schubert (2 Impromptus). Perahia's artistry is grandly displayed here.

Perahia has recorded (3 CDs) the five Beethoven concertos with Bernard Haitink conducting Amsterdam's famed *Concertgebouw* Orchestra. He has also recorded all five concertos in a three-video format with Sir Neville Marriner conducting the Academy of St. Martin in the Fields. The readings with Haitink are arguably superior, and for one reviewer this cycle is "far and away the most consistently accomplished of those currently available." In particular, "Perahia's account of the C minor Concerto is a joy from start to finish, wonderfully conceived, executed, conducted and recorded." (*Gram*, Jan 1989)

One could go on and on. A coupling of Franck's Prelude, Chorale and Fugue with a group of Liszt compositions (see Discog.) is outstanding. One reviewer places Perahia's "patrician" account of the Franck in the company of other distinguished readings by Rubinstein, Cherkassky and Bolet. (*ARG*, March/April 1992) As to the Liszt, Perahia's "range of keyboard colour in the concluding *Rhapsodie espagnole* is as ear-catching as are his rhythmic spring, his teasing

caprice and his exuberant climaxes." (*Gram*, Oct 1991) Other superb performances: Chopin Sonatas Nos. 2 and 3; Schumann and Grieg Concertos in A
Minor; Schumann *Papillons* and Symphonic Etudes.

Perahia's first recording after his nearly two-year absence from the concert platform and recording studio was a Chopin album, highlighted by the four
Ballades. "This is surely the greatest, certainly the richest, of all his many and
exemplary recordings. . . . Now, to supreme clarity, tonal elegance and musical
perspective, he adds an even stronger poetic profile, a surer sense of the inflam-
matory rhetoric underpinning Chopin's surface equilibrium." (*Gram*, Dec 1994)

SELECTED REFERENCES

Apone, Carl. "Bronx Pianist Won British Hearts." *Pittsburgh Press*, 20 Feb
    1983, sec. J, p. 3.
Blyth, Alan. "Murray Perahia." (interview) *Gramophone*, Feb 1975, p. 1463.
Cameron, Dan F. "A Conversation with Murray Perahia." *Ovation*, Feb 1988,
    pp. 12–16.
Delacoma, Wynne. "Pianist Perahia weaves magic with Mozart." *Chicago Sun
    Times*, 20 Oct 1991, (Show) p. 5.
Driver, Paul. "A Touch of Temperament." *Sunday Times* (London), 2 June
    1985, p. 43. A comparison of Perahia with Arturo Michelangeli.
Duarte, John. "Murray Perahia." (interview) *Records and Recording*, May 1982,
    pp. 5–7.
Dyer, Richard. "Perahia Wants To Play It All." *Boston Globe*, 29 March 1981,
    sec. A, p. 21.
Elder, Dean. "Beyond Virtuosity with Murray Perahia." *Clavier*, Sept 1981,
    pp. 20–25.
Goldsmith, Harris. "The Aristocratic Art of Murray Perahia." *Musical America*,
    July 1989, pp. 71–73.
Greenfield, Edward. "Welcome Back." *Gramophone*, Dec 1994, p. 32.
Holland, Bernard. "Murray Perahia—An Artist Evolves." *New York Times*, 21
    April 1985, pp. 21–22.
Kerner, Leighton. "The Singing Piano." *Village Voice*, 14 Feb 1984, p. 86.
Kimmelman, Michael. "With Plenty of Time to Think, A Pianist Redirects His
    Career." *New York Times*, 3 April 1994, sec. 2, p. 25.
Kozinn, Allan. "Murray Perahia: Classical Piano's Reluctant Superstar."
    Keyboard, April 1982, pp. 22–28.
Long, Raymond K. "The Probing Pianism of Murray Perahia." *Ovation*, Dec
    1981, pp. 8–10, 12.
Pleasants, Henry. "Murray Perahia." *Stereo Review*, Nov 1991, p. 108.
Rich, Alan. "Marlboro Man at the Piano." *Newsweek*, 13 May 1985, pp. 81–
    82.
Rockwell, John. "Seeking Greener Grass Beyond Familiar Fences." *New York
    Times*, 27 May 1990, sec. 2, p. 19.
Schonberg, Harold C. "Pianists at the Podium—Old Tradition, New Interest."
    New York Times, 26 April 1987, pp. 21, 34.

Shawe-Taylor, Desmond. "The art of Murray Perahia." *Sunday Times* (London), 18 Feb 1973, p. 37.
See also Bibliography: Cur/Bio (1982); Dub/Ref; Hag/Dec; IWWM; Mac/Gr2; New/Gro; Rat/Cle; Sch/Gre; WWAM.

SELECTED REVIEWS

ABJ: 6 Jan 1984. *ARG*: July/Aug 1994. *BaS*: 8 March 1976. *BG*: 23 April 1977; 14 March 1989; 3 Nov 1990. *CPD*: 9 Nov 1981; 21 March 1988. *CSM*: 1 May 1985. *CT*: 20 March 1989. *DMN*: 21 Feb 1986; 9 April 1987; 19 Nov 1990. *DT*: 26 May 1986. *FT*: 27 May 1986. *GloM*: 14 April 1989. *GM*: 14 Feb 1973; 26 May 1986; 15 Nov 1991. *LAT*: 6 Nov 1978; 7 Nov 1979; 10 Nov 1979; 23 Nov 1981; 18 March 1986; 24 March 1987; 7 April 1989; 29 Oct 1990; 18 March 1994. *MA*: April 1966. *MT*: April 1973; Dec 1974; Aug 1982; March 1988. *NY*: 24 Dec 1979; 27 April 1981. *NYT*: 11 Jan 1966; 28 Dec 1968; 6 March 1972; 11 March 1972; 9 March 1974; 18 Dec 1979; 29 April 1985; 17 Sept 1987; 12 April 1989; 30 Sept 1989; 12 Nov 1990; 11 April 1994. *PI*: 13 April 1990. *SFC*: 15 March 1994. *SFE*: 4 April 1989. *TL*: 19 Jan 1973; 14 Feb 1973; 14 June 1976; 8 Nov 1991; 15 Feb 1994. *WP*: 6 March 1989; 21 April 1990.

SELECTED DISCOGRAPHY

The Aldeburgh Recital. Beethoven: 32 Variations in C Minor. Liszt: Consolation No. 3 in D-flat Major; Hungarian Rhapsody No. 12. Rachmaninoff: *Etudes-Tableaux*, op. 33, no. 2, op. 39, nos. 5, 6, 9. Schumann: *Faschingsschwank aus Wien*, op. 26. Sony Classical SK 46437 (CD).
The Art of Murray Perahia. Sony Classical SX11 48153 (11 CDs). A compilation of Perahia's most popular recordings selected from his 20-year recording career with CBS/Sony.
Beethoven: Concertos (5). CBS M3K-44575 (3 CDs). Haitink/*Concertgebouw*.
Beethoven: Sonata in D Minor, op. 31, no. 2 ("Tempest"); Sonata in E-flat Major, op. 31, no. 3; Sonata in E-flat Major, op. 81a ("*Les Adieux*"). CBS MK-42319 (CD).
Brahms: Capriccio in B Minor, op. 76, no. 2; Intermezzo in E-flat Minor, op. 118, no. 6; Rhapsody in B Minor, op. 79, no. 1; Rhapsody in E-flat Major, op. 119, no. 4; Sonata No. 3 in F Minor, op. 5. Sony Classical SK-47181 (CD).
Chopin: Ballades (4); Etudes, op. 10, nos. 3-4; Mazurkas, op. 7, no. 3, op. 17, no. 4, op. 33, no. 2; Nocturne, op. 15, no. 1; Waltzes, ops. 18, 42. Sony Classical SK 64 399 (CD).
Chopin: Concerto No. 1 in E Minor, op. 11; Concerto No. 2 in F Minor, op. 21. Sony Classical SK 44922 (CD). Mehta/Israel PO.

Chopin: Sonata No. 2 in B-flat Minor, op. 35; Sonata No. 3 in B Minor. CBS MK-32780 (CD).

Grieg: Concerto in A Minor, op. 16. Schumann: Concerto in A Minor, op. 54. CBS MK-44899 (CD). Davis/Bavarian RSO.

Mendelssohn: Concerto No. 1 in G Minor, op. 25; Concerto No. 2 in D Minor, op. 40; Prelude and Fugue in E Minor, op. 35, no. 1; *Rondo capriccioso*, op. 14; *Variations sérieuses*, op. 54. CBS MK 42401 (CD). Marriner/ASMF.

Mozart: Complete solo concerti. Sony Classical SX12K 46441 (12 CDs). Perahia/English CO.

Mozart: Sonata in A Minor, K. 310; Sonata in A Major, K. 331; Sonata in F Major, K. 533/494. Sony Classical 48233 (CD).

Mozart: Sonata in D Major, K. 448. Schubert: Fantasy in F Minor, D. 940. CBS MK 39511 (CD). With Radu Lupu.

Murray Perahia Plays Franck and Liszt. Franck: *Prélude, Choral et Fugue*. Liszt: *Au bord d'une source*; *Gnomenreigen*; Mephisto Waltz No. 1; Petrarch Sonnet 104; Spanish Rhapsody; *Waldesrauschen*. Sony Classical 47180 (CD).

A Portrait of Murray Perahia. Beethoven: Sonata in F Minor, op. 57 (*"Appassionata"*). Chopin: Fantaisie-Impromptu, op. 66; Preludes, op. 28, nos. 6–7, 13. Mendelssohn: *Rondo capriccioso*, op. 14. Mozart: Rondo in D Major, K. 382. Schubert: Impromptu in G-flat Major, D. 899, no. 3. CBS MK-42448 (CD). A splendid "sampler."

Schubert: Sonata in A Major, D. 959. Schumann: Sonata in G Minor, op. 22. CBS MK-44569 (CD).

Schumann: *Davidsbündlertänze*, op. 6; *Fantasiestücke*, op. 12. CBS MK-32299 (CD).

Schumann: *Papillons*, op. 2; Symphonic Etudes, op. 13. CBS MK-34539 (CD).

Tout l'art du piano. Beethoven: Concerto No. 5 in E-flat, op. 73 (Haitink/*Concertgebouw*); Sonata in D Minor, op. 31, no. 2. Chopin: Preludes (11), op. 28. Liszt: Hungarian Rhapsody No. 12. Mendelssohn: *Variations sérieuses*, op. 54. Mozart: Concerto in C Major, K. 467 (Perahia/English CO). Schubert Impromptu in A-flat Major, D. 899, no. 4; Impromptu in F Minor, D. 935, no. 4. Sony Classical S2K 48127 (2 CDs).

VIDEO

Murray Perahia in Performance. Beethoven: Sonata in C Major, op. 2, no. 3; 32 Variations in C Minor. Liszt: Consolation No. 3 in D-flat Major; Hungarian Rhapsody No. 12. Rachmaninoff: 4 *Études Tableaux* (op. 33, no. 2; op. 39, nos. 5, 6 and 9). Schumann: *Faschingsschwank aus Wien*, op. 26. Sony Classical SHV 45987.

Murray Perahia's Mozart. Concerto in C Major, K. 467; Concerto in B-flat Major, K. 595. Sony Classical SHV 46393. Perahia/CO of Europe.

Perahia Plays Beethoven. Concerto No. 1 in C Major, op. 15. Concerto No. 3 in C Minor, op. 37. Home Vision BEE 01. Marriner/ASMF.
Perahia Plays Beethoven. Concerto No. 2 in B-flat Major, op. 19. Concerto No. 4 in G Major, op. 58. Home Vision BEE 02. Marriner/ASMF.
Perahia Plays Beethoven. Concerto No. 5 in E-flat Major, op. 73. Home Vision BEE 03. Marriner/ASMF.

PERLEMUTER, VLADO: b. 26 May 1904, Kowno (now Kaunas), Lithuania.

> He is a pianist who has no successor yet—the last in a long line of cultivated, superb musicians, whose dedication to their art is limitless and reverential.
>
> James Methuen-Campbell (*Records and Recording*, April 1979)

The venerable Vlado Perlemuter, now in his nineties, symbolizes the great tradition of French pianism flourishing from the era of Francis Planté (1839–1934) through that of Robert Casadesus (1899–1977). Although long recognized as one of France's most important pianists, Perlemuter is actually not French, not by birth or by blood—his parents were Polish Jews, born in Lithuania. However, considering the fact that they took him to live in France when he was barely four years old and that ever since (excluding a few years during and just after World War II) France has been his home, Vlado Perlemuter is of course "a French pianist."

His father was a singer (throat problems ended his career) and may have been responsible for Perlemuter's having piano lessons at an early age. At age 11 Perlemuter began two years of training with Moritz Moszkowski, a teacher who demanded absolute clarity and, for technique, loose wrists and relaxed arms. Working with Moszkowski's *Fifteen Studies in Virtuosity* (drills for acquiring virtuosity and for developing "the independence of the fingers to an equal extent in both hands") gave Perlemuter a strong technical foundation and most likely accounts for his lifelong concern with "finding the most expressive or dramatic choice of fingering."

At age 13 he was admitted to Alfred Cortot's piano class at the Paris Conservatory, a wholly new experience in lessons. Moszkowski had rarely played for students. Cortot, on the other hand, listened to the student play (just one movement of a sonata, say, or one of the Chopin Ballades), made a few general comments and then played for the student. Moszkowski inspired his students to clarity and discipline in their playing. Cortot concentrated on interpretation, on accent and phrasing and tempo, and on the actual quality of sound.

At age 15 Perlemuter received a *premier prix* in piano for his playing of Fauré's Theme and Variations—especially interesting because Fauré, at the time director of the Paris Conservatory, was chairman of the jury at that examination.

In 1920, at age 16, Perlemuter received the *prix d'honneur*, for his performance of Paul Dukas's Variations, Interlude and Finale on a Theme by Rameau. And in 1921 Perlemuter crowned his academic achievements by winning the *Prix Diémer*, the prize in a triennial competition established at the Conservatory by Professor Louis Diémer for those students who had obtained a *premier prix* during the previous 10 years. Still only age 17, in 1921 Perlemuter began classes in harmony and counterpoint and "neglected the piano for the next three years."

Perlemuter's first hearing of Ravel's *Jeux d'eau* so delighted him that he devoted two years (1925–27) to learning all of that composer's solo piano music. Not only that, through the offices of a friend of a friend, Perlemuter had the rare opportunity of having Ravel himself explain just how the works should be played. For about six months (1927) Perlemuter had coaching sessions several times a week at Ravel's home at Montfort L'Amaury, and two years later he performed (1929) all of Ravel's solo piano works in two Paris recitals.

Perlemuter was appointed assistant professor of piano at the Paris Conservatory in 1938, but World War II and the ensuing chaos in Europe interrupted both his teaching and his concert career for several years. He and his wife (Jacqueline Delevaux, m. 1937) stayed in Paris too long to be able to escape to the United States, as so many Jewish musicians had done, and in 1942 just barely made their way, with the Gestapo in pursuit, to Free France and eventually to Switzerland. These were not happy years. As an immigrant, Perlemuter was forbidden to perform publicly in Switzerland, a setback that, coming so soon after his precarious flight to freedom, caused a breakdown. He spent about three years in a sanatorium, by 1950 was again performing in Paris and in 1951 resumed teaching at the Paris Conservatory, a post he held until 1977.

Perlemuter has made his concert career mostly in Europe (France, Switzerland, Belgium, Germany, Spain, Scandinavia, Bulgaria, Turkey), North Africa and Japan, and has performed often in Great Britain.

He was Resident Pianist at Indiana University, Bloomington, for the 1962–63 academic year, but according to the University's archives, he gave no recitals there. While in the United States he played Franck's Symphonic Variations with the Boston Symphony Orchestra, Charles Munch conducting. He apparently left America before his university contract had expired and has returned only occasionally, usually to judge piano competitions and, very rarely, to give concerts.

Perlemuter has had a long and distinguished teaching career. Apart from his more than 40 years at the Paris Conservatory, he has held master classes in Canada, Japan and Great Britain; and he has served on competition juries in Austria, Hungary, Italy, Poland, Canada and the United States. Like his teacher Moszkowski, Perlemuter urges his students to work on Moszkowski's *Fifteen Studies in Virtuosity*; unlike Moszkowski, Perlemuter often plays for his students. Just a month before his 80th birthday he gave a Chopin recital (15 April 1984) at London's Elizabeth Hall, and he had "stamina in reserve for all the Etudes of Op. 25, though it is expressive nuance and his intimacy of keyboard manner that make Perlemuter so rightly venerated a teacher and, essentially, a musician's pianist." (*STL*, 22 April 1984)

France has honored her adopted son. Perlemuter is both an *Officier de la Légion d'honneur* and *Commandeur des Arts et des Lettres.* In 1972 he was made an Honorary Fellow of the Royal Academy of Music in London. His recording of the Chopin Etudes was awarded a *Grand Prix du Disque* in 1988.

Vlado Perlemuter is a refined, articulate, insightful and sincere pianist—a self-effacing virtuoso whose playing is meant to reveal, not to bedazzle. In other words, it is a shining example of the great French tradition of piano playing embodied in the art of his teacher Alfred Cortot. That tradition sees music "as essentially civilized discourse, a language in which sensibility is always balanced by sense." (*DT*, 2 Feb 1979)

His playing is remarkable for his uncommon range of tonal color (exceptionally subtle rather than strikingly rich); his masterful but unshowy technique; and the "orchestral sound" he has developed. The idea of creating an "orchestral sound" in piano playing may have taken root when Perlemuter, only in his early twenties, worked so closely with Ravel. In his book on Ravel, Perlemuter recalls how Ravel insisted that certain of his works (*Gaspard de la nuit*, for example) demanded a new range of sonorities, evocations of orchestral instruments, and in fact a polyphony of different strands of color that had to be perfectly balanced and controlled.

By way of confirmation, we have two critiques, written 65 years ago, showing that even then Perlemuter applied color delicately and abstained from showoff virtuosity. "M. Vlado Perlemuter," wrote a *Le Ménestral* critic in 1923, "knows how to give the right value either to a low note of great expressive power or to one perched perilously high—he shades them like a touch of pink on a grey background." And that same year a critic for *Le Courrier* noted "the absence of irrelevant *rubato*, of exaggerated phrasing and of wayward nuances" in Perlemuter's playing.

Only scant information is available as to how Perlemuter works. In 1974 he gave a 14-week series of recitals for the BBC, and at the time Sir William Glock, who had been head of music at the BBC for 13 years and knew Perlemuter well, published an article in which he tells about Perlemuter's unrelenting self-criticism and his hours and hours of slow practice. Despite half a century of performing, Perlemuter still practices very slowly, with the left hand, even pieces that he has known all his life. Perhaps most interesting is Sir William's view that Perlemuter's "poetic intentions imply, impose rather, a complete independence of the two hands and a mastery of the greatest possible range of tone-colour. . . . In general, though, the left hand territory seems particularly close to him. This may be partly a matter of temperament, because he inclines more to depth than to brilliance, but partly also because he has always discovered each piece of music through the left hand—read it, as it were, from the bass upwards." (Glock)

Perlemuter is always very nervous before a performance. There can be many wrong notes, sometimes memory lapses. He employs a limited dynamic range and frequently uses the pedal overgenerously, increasingly so with the passing years.

Although he has a fairly large repertoire, Perlemuter is best known for his highly personalized interpretations of the works of Chopin and Ravel. His Chopin is simple and architectural, understated, never lush or flamboyant. His readings may not please everyone, but they have strong critical support. For example, "It is in his playing of Chopin that Perlemuter excels the most. Especially in the Etudes, the Ballades and the Mazurkas he achieves, at his best, a wonderful range of tone-colour, a rhythmic subtlety, and a balance between line and detail that would be difficult to surpass." (New/Gro, see Bibliog.) And this more recent appraisal: "Nowadays, indeed, we probably prefer our Chopin to offer greater tonal allure, a sharper sense of surprise, both pianistic and interpretative. Or at least some of us do: those at the Elizabeth Hall appeared to disagree, and it must be said that, notwithstanding wrong notes and many frailties of voicing, the message of Perlemuter's Chopin emerged plainly and unscathed." (*MT*, June 1984)

Perlemuter's Ravel interpretations are equally fine. An orchestral style permeates his playing of Ravel's lush sonorities, dance rhythms, intricate keyboard figurations. His personal approach to Ravel is explained in *Ravel According to Ravel (Ravel d'après Ravel)*, the book resulting from programs Perlemuter played (1950) on French radio—programs on which he not only played all of Ravel's complete solo piano music, but also discussed Ravel's objectives with Hélène Jourdan-Morhange. Their conversations, with an added section on Ravel's two piano concertos, were published in Lausanne in 1953 and in English translation in 1989.

Regarding Perlemuter's distinctive Ravel readings, we have this from a review of his London program of 24 April 1980: "The Prelude of Ravel's Tombeau de Couperin has very many notes, yet Vlado Perlemuter's performance made it seem as if every note had been pondered: the exact yet apparently spontaneous shaping of every phrase was the result of long thought." Perlemuter's Ondine was "a magical experience, a kaleidoscope of shining, translucent phrases, with every thread in the texture logically followed through." (*TL*, 25 April 1980)

And this: "What gives Vlado Perlemuter's Ravel playing its stamp of authority . . . is the utter clarity and directness of [his] readings. . . . There is a markedly undemonstrative nature about Perlemuter's playing—he is particularly sparing with rubato quirks—and many of his speeds . . . are on the brisk side. But he remains a master both of textural delineation . . . and of tonal variety." (*TL*, 11 May 1987)

Perlemuter played both Ravel and Chopin at a recital at Newport, Rhode Island, on 19 July 1989, "a very great event," said one critic, remarkable for "Perlemuter's undimmed imagination, majestic musical understanding and apparently undimmed stamina at the keyboard. . . . The most striking feature of Perlemuter's playing [may be] its absolutely unflagging rhythmic energy. . . . Above all and in everything Perlemuter's playing is considered, imaginative and decisive." (*BG*, 21 July 1989)

A year later, at age 86, he gave a Wigmore Hall recital (30 May 1990) of music by Debussy, Chopin, Fauré and Ravel. Noting that the venerable pianist scrambled many a passage, that "wrong notes are legion," and that "one spent much of the time worrying whether or not Perlemuter would get through a piece, and sometimes naughtily hankered for the accuracy of fingerwork to which these days we are accustomed," the critic evaluated Perlemuter's more positive qualities: "a frankness of interpretative approach, a French clarity of outline and brightness of sound, a sense of drama, and, I suppose, the traditional authority of one who was taught to play Fauré by Fauré and Ravel by Ravel." (*STL*, 3 June 1990)

It is possible that the accumulation of wrong notes is due in part to the advanced age of the pianist, for earlier commentaries make little mention of this. At a Queen Elizabeth Hall recital (1 Feb 1979) Perlemuter's performance of the Schumann *Kreisleriana* was "a performance noted for its great variety of texture and mood. Every note that he plays has a beautiful tone and is magnificently proportioned." (Methuen-Campbell)

Perlemuter's five Chopin albums on CD for Nimbus include one containing, among other works, the four Ballades and the *Polonaise-fantaisie*, op. 61 (see Discog.). Here Perlemuter shows "an overall consistency of style in his approach that places the interpretations in a somewhat distant era from our own. Things are unhurried. Phrases are allowed to make their effect through subtle suggestion, rather than by direct and defined statement." (*Gram*, April 1990)

Perlemuter's recording of the Chopin Etudes places these works in their proper perspective as both viable technical studies and beautiful examples of tonal art. Perlemuter may not have the stunning technique of some of his colleagues, but he "has musical perceptions and a warm spirit that shine through every measure and that make his Chopin playing highly satisfying. . . . All 27 have refreshing insights and subtle turns of phrase that could only have come from a lifetime of thinking about the music." (*Fan*, Jan/Feb 1988)

In Perlemuter's Ravel recordings for Nimbus, age has affected his technique (he was in his seventies), yet these are "delightful, deeply sympathetic readings; the sense of spontaneity is a joy. There may be Ravel recordings which bring more dazzling virtuoso displays, but none more persuasive." (Pen/Gui [1986], see Bibliog.)

The CD of works by Bach, Chopin and Debussy (see Discog.) includes the suite *Pour le piano*, Book I of the *Images* and the scintillating *L'Isle joyeuse*. "He plays Debussy in the same tradition of great interpreters of French music, with a shimmering sound and complete control of tone colors." (*Fan*, Nov/Dec 1987) And Perlemuter's elegantly played Fauré, now on CD, should convert even the most unconvinced to that composer's music (see Discog.).

Given the many, many fine Beethoven recordings by pianists reared in the German-Austrian tradition, one might overlook a Perlemuter recording of a Beethoven recital—two sonatas (op. 81a and op. 57) and the "Eroica" Variations, op. 35. One critic, admittedly a long-standing admirer, puts this recording in a positive perspective. "He plays on the grand scale, with a big, commanding sound and sometimes highly extroverted style. His Chopin and Ravel recordings are outstanding, but I find nothing he does to be without interest. . . . This is one of the best performances of the Variations I have ever heard, beautifully characterized in every respect." (*Fan*, Nov/Dec 1989)

SELECTED REFERENCES

Dyer, Richard. "Perlemuter still makes you listen." *Boston Globe*, 21 July 1989, p. 28.

Elder, Dean. "Perlemuter on Ravel." *Clavier*, March 1982, pp. 18–20.

Glock, Sir William. "Master of the Subtle Left." *Sunday Times* (London), 3 March 1974, Magazine Section, pp. 85–86, 88.

Methuen-Campbell, James. "A master of nuance." *Records and Recording*, April 1979, pp. 16–18.

The Newport Music Festival. Program and information guide for the 1989 season.

Perlemuter, Vlado, and Hélène Jourdan-Morhange. *Ravel d'après Ravel*. Lausanne: Editions du Cervin, 1970. English edition, *Ravel according to Ravel*. London: Kahn & Averill, 1989.

Salter, Lionel. "Word of Mouth." *Gramophone*, May 1989, pp. 1702–1703.

"Vlado Perlemuter." *Guide du Concert et du disque*, 10 Feb 1956, title page.

See also Bibliography: Met/Cho; New/Gro; WWF.

SELECTED REVIEWS

BG: 21 July 1989. *DT*: 2 Feb 1979. *MT*: June 1984; July 1987. *STL*: 22 April 1984; 17 May 1987; 3 June 1990. *TL*: 16 Dec 1960; 26 Jan 1962; 21 Feb 1962; 27 Jan 1964; 15 Nov 1965; 27 Feb 1967; 22 Feb 1974; 25 April 1980; 25 April 1983; 25 May 1985; 11 May 1987; 17 May 1987.

SELECTED DISCOGRAPHY

Bach: Italian Concerto. Chopin: Mazurkas, op. 17, no. 4; op. 30, no. 4; op. 50, no. 3; *Tarantelle,* op. 43. Debussy: *Images* (I); *L'Isle joyeuse*; *Pour le piano*. Nimbus NI 5080 (CD).

Beethoven: Sonata in C Major, op. 53. Chopin: Scherzo No. 3 in C-sharp Minor, op. 39. Mendelssohn: *Variations sérieuses*. Ravel: *Ma Mère l'Oye* (with A. Farmer). Nimbus NI 5340 (CD).

Beethoven: Sonata in F Minor, op. 57 ("*Appassionata*"); Sonata in E-flat Major, op. 81a ("*Les Adieux*"); Variations and Fugue in E-flat Major, op. 35 ("*Eroica*"). Nimbus NI 5133 (CD).

Chopin: Ballades (4); Polonaise No. 5 in F-sharp Minor, op. 44; Polonaise-fantaisie, op. 61. Nimbus NI 5209 (CD).

Chopin: Barcarolle, op. 60; Sonata No. 2 in B-flat Minor, op. 35; Sonata No. 3 in B Minor, op. 58. Nimbus NI 5038 (CD).

Chopin: *Berceuse*, op. 57; Preludes, op. 28, op. 45; Fantaisie in F Minor, op. 49. Nimbus NI 5064 (CD).

Chopin: Etudes, op. 10; Etudes, op. 25. *Trois nouvelles études*. Nimbus NI 5095 (CD).

Chopin: Nocturnes. op. 9, no. 3; op. 15, nos. 1, 2 and 3; op. 27, nos. 1 and 2; op. 48, nos. 1 and 2; op. 55, no. 2; op. 62, no. 1. Nimbus NI 5012 (CD).

Fauré: Barcarolle, op. 66; Impromptu no. 2; Nocturnes, nos. 1, 6, 7, 12, 13; Theme and Variations, op. 73. Nimbus NI 5165 (CD).

Liszt: Sonata in B Minor. Schumann: Fantasia in C Major, op. 17. Nimbus NI 5299.

Ravel: Piano Works Vol. 1. *Gaspard de la nuit*; *Jeux d'eau*; *Miroirs*; *Pavane pour une Infante défunte*. Nimbus NI 5005 (CD). Rec. 1973, 1983.

Ravel: Piano Works Vol. 2. *A la manière de Borodine*; *A la manière de Chabrier*; *Menuet antique*; *Menuet sur le nom d'Haydn*; *Prélude*; *Sonatine*; *Le Tombeau de Couperin*; *Valses nobles et sentimentales*. Nimbus NI 5011 (CD) Rec. 1984.

Schumann: Symphonic Etudes, op. 13; *Kreisleriana*, op. 16. Nimbus NI 5108 (CD).

Vlado Perlemuter plays Ravel. Concerto in G Major; Concerto for Left Hand; *Gaspard de la nuit*; *Jeux d'eau*; *Menuet sur le nom de Haydn*; *Menuet antique*; *Miroirs*; *Pavane*; *Prélude*; *Sonatine*; *Le Tombeau de Couperin*; *Valses nobles et sentimentales*. Vox Legends CDX2 5507 (2 CD). Horenstein/ Concerts Colorme. Rec. 1955.

PETRI, EGON: b. Hanover, Germany, 23 March 1881; d. Berkeley, California, 27 May 1962.

> The pianists of today have marvellous digital clarity and generally do all the right things—but they lack that spark of musical greatness that Petri and pianists of his generation used to have. This, it seems, can never be handed down.
>
> *Musical Times*, July 1962

Surely, Egon Petri's extraordinary musical talent—his "spark of musical greatness," as the obituary describes it—was "handed down." His mother Katharina (Tornauer) Petri was a musician (she taught violin and voice) and his paternal forebears, of Dutch lineage, had produced a line of musicians. Petri's great-grandfather was an organist, his grandfather played the oboe and his father was Henri Willem Petri, a teacher and distinguished violinist. He was concertmaster of the orchestra of Hanover's Royal Theater at the time of Petri's birth, two years later was appointed concertmaster of the famous *Gewandhaus* Orchestra in Leipzig and six years after that, in 1889, became first violinist in the orchestra of the Dresden Royal Opera. Thus Petri lived his first eight years in three different and always lively musical surroundings.

Petri's own first instrument was the violin. From age five to ten he studied with his mother, and thereafter with his father, who insisted that his son must also learn other instruments—piano, organ and French horn. In addition, Petri studied composition with Hermann Kretzschmar and Felix Draeseke. He developed rapidly and as a teenager played second violin in his father's string quartet. Meanwhile he received a sound academic education at the *Kreuzschule* in Leipzig.

His family settled in Berlin in 1889 and shortly thereafter Petri began a more serious study of the piano in Berlin with the famous Teresa Carreño. Although only 11 years old, he never forgot how she insisted on his developing strong fingers and a "quiet" arm. As Carreño explained, "You must be able to carry a glass of water on the back of your hand as you play." Not that he abandoned the violin. He still practiced assiduously, played violin in his father's string quartet and also, from 1889 to 1901, played violin in the orchestra of the Dresden Royal Opera.

At that point his father decided that Petri had to choose his instrument—piano or violin—for further study. It was not an easy decision. Early in 1900 Paderewski had heard Petri play in Dresden and advised him to continue with the piano. On the other hand, when the great violinist Joseph Joachim heard Petri play the violin, he urged him to study with him at the Berlin *Hochschule für Musik*. Petri chose the piano, and later in 1901 enrolled in Ferruccio Busoni's master class in piano at Weimar. Although Petri had only about a dozen "official" lessons with Busoni, their friendship lasted until Busoni's death in 1924. Without doubt, Busoni was the greatest musical influence in his life. Busoni also recommended Petri to concert managers and conductors and, by turning over to Petri students he himself was unable to accept, started Petri on his lifelong teaching career.

Petri made his debut in Holland in 1902 and began making tours of Europe. In 1905 he married Maria Schoen (they had two sons and a daughter), and that same year was appointed, with Busoni's help, as professor of piano at the Royal College of Music in Manchester, England. His yearly tours while at Manchester (1905–11) greatly enhanced his reputation in Europe, and in 1911, realizing that living in Manchester (then a "provincial" city) was bad for his career, he resigned. Between 1911 and 1917 he lived in Berlin—teaching and performing in Germany, Austria and Poland. For several years he also served as Busoni's assistant, and later often said that during that stay in Berlin he became Busoni's friend, disciple and daily companion. He attended all of Busoni's concerts, observed him as he practiced and sat in on his master classes. Petri also assisted Busoni with his 25-volume *Busoni-Ausgabe* of the keyboard works of J. S. Bach, an edition begun in 1894, completed in 1923.

For the rest of his life Petri maintained two careers—concertizing and teaching. He taught at the resort town of Zakopane in Poland from 1917 through 1919, at the Basel Conservatory in Switzerland in 1920 and from 1921 to 1925 he was professor of piano at the Berlin *Hochschule für Musik*. During all these years, Petri also played a great many piano recitals in Europe, supposedly more than 300 over a five-year period. In 1923 he made a grand sweep of Russia—31 performances in 40 days in large cities, small towns, even villages. His phenomenal success with Russian audiences—Petri was the first west European artist allowed to perform in Russia after the 1917 revolution—resulted in several more tours of Russia.

In 1927 the Petris settled in Zakopane. He made concert tours every year and every summer pianists from around the world came to study with him.

After his highly successful American debut on 11 January 1932, he made four consecutive tours of the United States and also taught a series of classes (1934–35) at the Malkin Conservatory in Boston. Then in August of 1939, just six days before the Nazis invaded Poland, the Dutch consul at Kraków warned the Petris of their imminent danger. They managed to escape to Holland on the last train out of Poland before the invasion, but Petri's treasures—books, manuscripts and a great collection of letters from Busoni—all had to be abandoned. When the Nazis threatened Holland, the Petris left for the United States, Petri's home for the rest of his life.

At his Town Hall recital (25 Feb 1940)—his first New York appearance in four years—Petri, said one critic, was "at the height of his powers." From September 1940 until 1946 he was Visiting Professor of Music at Cornell University in Ithaca, New York. Meanwhile he played a great many piano recitals, including a series of Sunday recitals on NBC radio, and gave lectures. Although illness compelled him to reduce his concert schedule (his last concert in New York was in 1945), Petri continued to teach and to record. From 1947 to 1957 he taught piano at Mills College in Oakland, California.

Petri obviously enjoyed teaching and for more than 60 years taught consistently. Grant Johannesen, John Ogdon and Earl Wild all at one time studied with him. As a teacher he was, so some students thought, more interested in textual accuracy than artistic expression. According to one pupil, in Petri's approach to keyboard pedagogy there was no routine of exercises and scales. On the contrary, Petri encouraged each student to recognize his or her own problems and create exercises to solve them. Petri did not approve of hours of monotonous repetition, and often recommended transposition and rhythmic variation.

Petri himself was fond of quoting a Liszt dictum: "It is not so much the practicing of technique which is important, but the technique of practicing." And in that regard he told his students that "slow practice was not necessarily good practice, just as 'driving slowly does not mean carefully'. . . . The most liberal of teachers, he told his students, 'Don't believe anything I tell you but try out'." (Holcman) For himself and for his students, Petri always believed that nothing can equal independent experimentation.

After a 17-year absence, Petri returned to Europe in 1957 to give master classes at the Basel Academy of Music, but, owing to bad planning, only three students enrolled (John Ogdon was one), and Petri stayed less than a year. During his final three years, actually to within a month of his death, Petri held a weekly class at the San Francisco Conservatory. He kept performing, though not often, almost to the end of his life. In 1959 he played his final Beethoven cycle at the San Francisco Museum of Art—all 32 sonatas in a series of six recitals. And in 1960, nearly 80 years old, he gave his final public concert. Egon Petri died of a stroke on 27 May 1962 at Herrick Memorial Hospital in Berkeley, California.

Petri was well-read, bright, witty, and fluent in Dutch, German, Polish and English. Although some writers portray him as haughty and distant, his friends and students say differently. "Devoid of affectation, he was kindly and easily approachable. He loved life and company, had a quick sense of humour, enjoyed a joke, and was often uninhibitedly gay. Even correction was often mixed with teasing." (Wills)

Egon Petri's vast repertoire included music from all periods. He played several Mozart sonatas, all the Beethoven sonatas, much Chopin (especially the preludes and etudes), Liszt (even all-Liszt recitals), and also Schumann and Brahms. He played both of César Franck's large-scale solo works. When playing with orchestra, Petri seemed to prefer flamboyant compositions like Tchaikovsky's Concerto No. 1, the Liszt concertos and also Liszt's *Totentanz* and *Rhapsodie espagnole*.

However, Egon Petri was at his absolute finest playing a type of keyboard work considered anathema by many pianists of his day and ours—the piano transcription. "I think," he once said, "that all transcriptions should be considered as the transcriber's additions or interpretation, rather than the faithful reproduction of the original into another medium. . . . It can all be reduced to the problem of whether the end justifies the means, whether the psychological disruption of an entity is counterbalanced with a new vital expression." (*Liszt: The Famous Piano Transcriptions*, Liner notes)

Petri programmed all types of transcriptions. For example, in 1932, the year of his American debut, his three Town Hall recitals (between January and April) included these transcriptions: "Bach-Busoni (Four Chorale-Preludes); Bach-Busoni ("Ste. Anne" Organ Prelude and Fugue); Schubert-Liszt (Six Song Transcriptions); Liszt ("Don Juan" Fantasy) and Liszt (*Etudes d'exécution transcendante d'après Paganini*). The way Petri played this last work inspired one commentator to write, "I cannot think of them without applying the word transcendent to the monumental playing of those works by Busoni's pupil Egon Petri." (Cha/Spe, see Bibliog.)

Petri not only played many transcriptions on his programs, he designed recitals that would be unthinkable today—for their length if for no other reason. His extraordinary physical and mental stamina confounded his colleagues. One astounding all-Liszt recital included the Don Juan Fantasy and two sonatas (the B Minor and the Dante). That kind of monumental program was the rule rather than the exception with Petri. At one New York Town Hall recital (15 Feb 1936) he played the Mozart Sonata in B-flat Major, K. 333; the Bach Goldberg Variations as arranged by Busoni; Liszt's Sonata in B Minor; Medtner's *Deux Contes*, op. 20; Busoni's *Fantasia sopra "Carmen"* and Prokofiev's Toccata. Only a pianist endowed with a superlative memory could play such a program.

The experience of the Baldwin Piano Company agent who met Petri at the pier when he arrived in New York for his American debut (11 Jan 1932) convincingly attests to Petri's memory. When the agent asked Petri what he would be playing at his debut, Petri handed him a book—it looked like a whole catalogue of piano music—and asked him to select the works he felt would be "timely and appropriate." Petri was not boasting. As the agent later discovered, the "catalogue" was actually Petri's repertoire.

Critics portray Petri as a very sedate, very serious virtuoso deeply committed to his art. Their reviews are peppered with words like "self-effacing," "unostentatious," "sincerity," "honesty." They praise his flawless musicianship and exceptional technique, yet what they most admired was Petri's lifelong vitality and drive.

But, while acknowledging Petri's powerful style and discerning musicianship, some critics felt compelled to also mention that his playing was too logical or too cerebral or that it lacked sentiment, poetry, elegance and grace. There were also complaints about Petri's out-of-the-ordinary, overlong programs and his frequently slipshod execution of difficult passages. Petri had the technique, but had no interest in showing it off. It may be that he never bothered to give extra time to practicing those difficult technical passages.

His many faithful supporters insisted that he was a pianist who had attained an impeccable balance between the intellectual and emotional approach to music. For them, his comprehensive musicianship and powerful style more than compensated for any lack of sentiment or poetry. For example, this from the *Musical Times* (July 1962): "Petri's approach to piano playing was characterized by a complete avoidance of sentimentality, which tended to make people think him cold and detached. This was not true, however; his playing always had great charm."

An especially perceptive summation of Petri's pianism comes from writer Samuel Lipman, himself a pianist, who heard Petri play many recitals and who as a teenager had played for Petri: "He had a beautiful piano sound, and an imposing, always straightforward way of demonstrating, rather than interpreting, the works he programmed. His chief virtue as an artist—in addition, of course, to the bright and pellucid sound he drew from the instrument—was his manifest honesty; there was no artifice in his playing." (Lipman)

The concert by Manchester's famed Hallé Orchestra on 23 March 1911 was a "farewell" to both Hans Richter, the conductor, and Egon Petri, the pianist. "Mr. Petri has not only proved himself a player of the highest rank, but he has taught us new ways of dealing with the difficult economic problem of placing good music before the public." At this "farewell," Petri's performance of the Franck Symphonic Variations was "masterly in the control of tone and intensity of quiet expression." And his performance of Liszt's *Totentanz* "won its way into favour not by brilliance only but by fantastic pianissimos austerely controlled, pertinence of style, and beauty of quiet melodic tone. There was plenty of power and brilliance also when the occasion came." (*GM*, 24 March 1911)

Petri played Beethoven's mighty "*Hammerklavier*" Sonata, op. 106, at an early London recital (26 Feb 1922): "Such judicious grading of tone was to be achieved only by the coolest head and a finger control which one is tempted to call unsurpassable." (*MT*, 1 April 1922) Another reviewer agreed: "Mr. Petri's willingness to give the outline absolute clearness and leave it, showed him to be a Beethoven player of the highest type even more decisively than the driving force which he lent to the first movement or the electric swiftness applied to the fugal exposition." (*TL*, 27 Feb 1922)

A performance (11 Oct 1929) of the six Liszt Paganini Studies revealed "a virtuosity which easily beat the mere *bravura* pianists at their own game, and then added . . . a sense of fun in the exhilaration of performing with apparent ease these almost impossible feats of prestidigitation." (*MT*, 1 Nov 1929)

Petri's New York Town Hall debut (11 Jan 1932) drew mixed reactions. "He is a virtuoso by reason of his abilities and attainments; but he makes that tarnished word seem curiously unsuited to a musicianship so genuine and sincere and fine." (*NYHT*, 12 Jan 1932) Another critic added his compliments: "His voicing in the Bach Chorale Preludes was of astonishing clearness and variety of sonority and color." Concerning the Beethoven Sonata, op. 111, "From the standpoint of a 'reading,' authoritative, aware of every line, detail, development of Beethoven's fantasy, this was past mastery." But, continued this reviewer, "the principal defect was the merciless logic and visibility of analysis. . . . There were two things the listener wanted and did not always find. One was tonal beauty and sensuous coloring. Another was a freer style, which would leave more to the imagination." (*NYT*, 12 Jan 1932)

A 1934 London recital drew a caustic review: "Though his tone is always deep, it has no especial beauty; he seems to have power without brilliance, agility without elegance. His is not a typical virtuosity; very often his playing seems to be built upon a series of technical tricks and an enormous stamina. He is infinitely more successful in Bach and Mozart than in Beethoven and Brahms." This review also mentions Petri's performance (21 Feb 1934) of the Busoni Concerto for the BBC. "Petri played it fittingly, in the 'grand manner', with enormous waves and washes of colour, but little differentiation. . . . One's admiration was for Petri's power and endurance in playing a pianoforte part so lavish in its means, so meagre in its result." (*MT*, April 1934)

Petri's London performance (19 Oct 1935) of the Beethoven Sonata in B-flat Major, op. 106, *and* the Liszt Sonata in B Minor also fared badly. "He is not a stylist; his playing is not elegant or colourful or miraculously subtle in a pianistic sense; he is not on terms of intimacy with the keyboard but holds it, rather, under arrest. Neither do his interpretations betray a deep or vivid personality. They are not notable for grandeur, optimism, or striking imagination. . . . What is most to be admired in his playing is its devotion to certain thunderous conceptions which make his performances magnificent to those in sympathy with them and, when applied to the right music, extremely exhilarating to those who are not." (*MT*, Dec 1935)

Despite the critics, Petri maintained a solid reputation, but he never enjoyed anything like the popularity of a Horowitz, a Rubinstein, a Rosenthal or a Lhévinne. The fault was certainly not in his playing, but rather in his repertoire. He designed long and weighty programs. He would play music by unknown composers like Alkan, often to the annoyance of his audience. He played many works by Busoni, a composer whose compositions were practically ignored. And finally, he played more transcriptions than any other pianist at a time when such compositions were considered unsuitable, even "trashy."

Petri's many recordings are divided among 78s, LPs and radio broadcast tapes; most of the studio recordings were made for Columbia. Even though some major items are still out of print, a number have been reissued and are presently available. Some recordings were made late in Petri's life. The dell'-

Arte records, for instance, were produced from broadcast tapes which he made in his mid-seventies. Even here, while the technical dexterity is somewhat diminished, the tonal control, phrasing and general artistic concepts are intact.

There are three substantial CD collections of Petri recorded performances. The most comprehensive studio recordings are found in a three-set collection (2 CDs each) issued by Appian Publications (see Discog.), recordings originally made between 1929 and 1942. A slightly less comprehensive but nonetheless excellent collection of Petri recordings is that issued by Pearl (GEMM, see Discog.) in three CD albums. (The unusual item in this collection is the four-movement Alkan Symphony, op. 39.) Finally, a four-CD album by Music and Arts (see Discog.) contains performances from Petri's concerts and radio broadcasts during the period 1954–1962. There are many items here that are not found in the other collections.

In Petri's fine recording of the Brahms-Paganini Variations, his treatment of these variations is symphonic. Among the later recordings, Petri's 1951 performance of the Bach Chromatic Fantasy and Fugue (Busoni Edition), made in Petri's living room, is one of the best. "At Petri's hands, the famous rolled chords in the *Fantasy* seem like a force of nature. He makes the *Fugue* crystal-clear and, as Bach fugues should be but so rarely are, inexorable. Here is Bach presented not as an ineffable contrapuntalist but as a god-like titan; here is Bach conceived as the all-powerful father of our entire music." (Lipman)

Among the performances with orchestra one could cite the superb Liszt Concerto No. 2 that Petri recorded in 1938 with Leslie Heward and the London Philharmonic Orchestra (CDAPR 7023, see Discog.). And "the 1940 Minneapolis recording of the *Spanish Rhapsody*, led by Mitropoulos, still packs a mighty wallop even today." (*ARG*, Sept/Oct 1993) The Liszt solo compositions in the same collection are equally noteworthy. "The *Rigoletto* Paraphrase has enormous panache, and there is still more in the *Faust* Waltz, but in neither does Petri let things get out of hand. His account of 'La ricordanza' conversely, is notable for its refinement and eloquence." (*Gram*, Nov 1993)

SELECTED REFERENCES

Dent, Edward J. *Ferruccio Busoni*. Oxford: Oxford University Press, 1933.

Holcman, Jan. "Petri in Retrospect." *Saturday Review*, 25 May 1963, pp. 55–56.

"Individual Teaching Is the Best in the Judgment of Egon Petri." *Musical America*, 10 March 1934.

Lipman, Samuel. "Egon Petri: the musician as virtuoso." *New Criterion*, April 1992, pp. 45–51.

Obituary. *Musical Times*, July 1962, p. 489. *New York Times*, 28 May 1962, p. 29. *The Times* (London), 29 May 1962, p. 17.

Petri, Egon. "Problems of Piano Playing and Teaching." In Simon, Robert Edward, *Be Your Own Music Critic*. New York: Doubleday & Company, Inc., 1941, pp. 137–164.

"The Recordings of Egon Petri." *78 RPM*, No. 7, Sept 1969, pp. 21–28.

Rockwell, John. "Who Says Modern Pianists Are Un-Romantic?" *New York Times*, 3 June 1984, sec. 2, p. 23.
Syer, Jamie K. "Egon Petri and the Piano Transcription." Typed essay dated 11 May 1978. Yale Sound Archive.
Wills, John. "Egon Petri." *Recorded Sound*, July 1970, pp. 639–642.
See also Bibliography: Cur/Bio (1942, 1962); Ewe/Li; Ewe/Mu; NieMei; Rat/Cle; Sch/Gre.

SELECTED REVIEWS

GM: 24 March 1911. *MA*: 10 March 1941; May 1944; 10 Sept 1945; July 1959. *MT*: 1 April 1922; 1 Nov 1929; April 1934; Dec 1935. *NYHT*: 12 Jan 1932. *NYT*: 12 Jan 1932; 18 April 1932; 19 Dec 1932; 16 Feb 1936; 25 Feb 1940; 10 March 1940; 25 April 1940; 30 Dec 1940; 27 Feb 1941; 31 Oct 1942; 9 May 1944; 6 Dec 1944; 10 Oct 1945; 10 March 1947. *TL*: 12 Feb 1912; 24 Feb 1913; 26 May 1913; 28 Feb 1914; 12 March 1914; 27 Feb 1922; 27 Oct 1931; 26 Feb 1934; 19 Oct 1935; 30 Oct 1936.

SELECTED DISCOGRAPHY

The Art of Egon Petri (Concert Performances and Broadcasts, 1954–1962). Bach-Busoni: Prelude, Fugue and Allegro. Bach-Petri: I Stand Before Thy Throne; Minuet; Sheep may safely graze. Beethoven: Sonata in E Minor, op. 90; Sonata in E Major, op. 109; Sonata in A-flat Major, op. 110; Sonata in C Minor, op. 111. Busoni: *All'Italia*; Indian Diary; *Perpetuum Mobile* and *Fantasia Contrappuntistica*. Chopin: Nocturne in F-sharp Major, op. 15, no. 2; Nocturne in D-flat Major, op. 27, no. 2; Polonaise in A-flat Major, op. 53; Preludes, op. 28. Gluck-Brahms: Gavotte. Gluck-Sgambati: Dance of the Blessed Spirits. Haydn: Variations, Hob. XVII:6. Liszt: *Venezia e Napoli*. Medtner: Fairy Tales, op. 20, nos. 1 and 2; *Danza festiva*. Mozart-Busoni: Andante from Concerto, K. 271. Schubert-Liszt: *Die Forelle*. Schubert-Tausig: *Andante Varié*, op. 84, no. 1. Schumann: Fantasy Pieces, op. 12. Music and Arts CD-772 (4 CDs).
Busoni/Petri play Busoni. Busoni: "*All'Italia*" (Elegy No. 2); Fantasia after music by Bach; Indian Diary, Book I; *Sonatina No. 3 ad usum infantis*; *Sonatina No. 6 super Carmen*. Liszt-Busoni: Spanish Rhapsody. Mozart-Busoni: *Don Giovanni* Serenade. Pearl GEMM CD 9347.
Egon Petri: His recordings 1929–42, Vol. 1. The 1929 Electrola Recordings: Chopin: Waltz No. 5. Liszt: *Gnomenreigen*. Paganini-Liszt: Etude No. 5. Schubert-Liszt: *Auf dem Wasser zu singen*; *Die Forelle*; *Liebesbotschaft*. Wagner-Liszt: Spinning Chorus. The Later Liszt transcription recordings: Gounod: *Valse de l'opéra Faust*. Schubert: *Gretchen am Spinnrade*; *Der Lindenbaum*; *Soirée de Vienne* No. 6. Verdi: *Rigoletto* Paraphrase. The solo Liszt recordings: Mazeppa; *La ricordanza*; *Un sospiro*. The concerto recordings: Liszt-Busoni: *Rhapsodie espagnole* (Mitropoulos/Minneapolis SO). Liszt: Concerto No. 2 in A Major (Heward/London PO); Fantasia on Beethoven's "Ruins of Athens" (Heward/London PO). Tchaikovsky:

Concerto No. 1 in B-flat Minor (Goehr/London PO). CDAPR 7023 (2 CDs).

Egon Petri: His recordings 1929–42, Vol. 2. Beethoven: Sonata in C-sharp Minor, op. 27, no. 2; Sonata in F-sharp Major, op. 78; Sonata in E Minor, op. 90; Sonata in C Minor, op. 111. Brahms: Rhapsodies, op. 79; Rhapsody, op. 119, no. 4; Variations and Fugue on a theme by Handel, op. 24; Variations on a theme by Paganini, op. 35. CDAPR 7024 (2 CDs).

Egon Petri: His recordings 1929–42, Vol. 3. Bach-Busoni: *Ich ruf' zu dir, Herr Jesu Christ*; *In dir ist Freude*; *Nun freut euch, lieben Christen gmein*; *Wachet auf, ruft uns die Stimme*. Bach-Petri: Menuet. Busoni: *Albumblatt* No. 3; *An die Jugend* No. 3; Elegie No. 2; Fantasia after J. S. Bach; *Indianisches Tagebuch*; Serenade (Mozart: *Don Giovanni*); Sonatinas Nos. 3 and 6. Chopin: Preludes, Op. 28. Franck: *Prélude, choral et fugue*. Gluck-Sgambati: *Mélodie*. Schubert-Tausig: Andante and Variations. CDAPR 7027 (2 CDs).

Egon Petri: Volume I. Bach-Busoni: Chromatic Fantasy and Fugue. Bach-Petri: Menuet. Beethoven: Sonata in F-sharp Major, op. 78. Brahms: Variations on a theme of Paganini (Books I and II). Gluck-Sgambati: *Orphée: Mélodie*. Gounod-Liszt: Faust Waltz Fantasie. Liszt: Concert Study in D-flat Major (*Un Sospiro*); *Gnomenreigen*; Mazeppa (Trancendental Etude). Schubert-Liszt: *Die Forelle*; *Liebesbotschaft*; *Soirée de Vienne* No. 6. Pearl GEMM CD 9916.

Egon Petri: Volume II. Alkan: Symphony, op. 39. Bach-Busoni: *Nun komm' der Heiden Heiland*; Prelude, Fugue and Allegro in E-flat Major, BWV 998; *Wachet auf, ruft uns die Stimme*. Chopin: Etude in A-flat Major, op. 25, no. 1; Valse in A-flat Major, op. 42. Liszt: *Gnomenreigen*; Paganini Etude No. 5 ("*La Chasse*"); Transcendental Etude No. 9 ("*Ricordanza*"). Schubert-Liszt: *Auf dem Wasser zu singen*; *Die Forelle*; *Liebesbotschaft*. Verdi-Liszt: *Rigoletto* Paraphrase. Wagner-Liszt: Spinning Chorus from Flying Dutchman. Pearl GEMM CD 9966.

Egon Petri: Volume III. Bach: Capriccio on the Departure of his Beloved Brother, BWV 992. Brahms: Variations and Fugue on a Theme by Handel, op. 24. Busoni: *Albumblatt No. 3, All'Italia*. Chopin: Ballade, op. 47; Nocturne, op. 27, no. 2. Liszt: *Sonnetti del Patrarca* Nos. 47, 104 and 123. Schubert-Liszt: *Gretchen am Spinnrade*. Schubert/Tausig: Andante and Variations. Pearl GEMM CD 9078.

Liszt: Famous Piano Transcriptions from Mozart to Mendelssohn . Beethoven: Adelaide. Gounod: Waltz from Gounod's *Faust*. Liszt (arr. Busoni): Mephisto Waltz. Mendelssohn: Paraphrase on Wedding March and Elfin Chorus from Mendelssohn's "Midsummer Night's Dream." Mozart: Fantasie on two motives from Mozart's *Marriage of Figaro*. Westminster XWN 18968 (LP).

PLANTÉ, FRANCIS: b. Orthez, Lower Pyrenees, France, 2 March 1839; d. St. Avit near Mont-de-Marsan, France, 19 December 1934.

> Planté's was the longest, and incontestably, one of the unique careers of musical history. He carried French and all pianism to one of its highest summits, his long life testifying to an unbroken record of loyalty to his instrument and of service to Music and mankind.
>
> Irving Schwerké (*Recorded Sound*, July 1969)

Spanning 84 years—from a prodigy performance played at age seven up to his final recital (19 July 1930) played when he was 91 years old—Planté's career is indeed singular and one of the longest in musical history. Although officially retired in 1895, he generously played charity concerts and even came out of retirement during World War I. And whether on or off the concert platform, throughout his long life, "Planté never let a day pass without passing several hours at the piano." (*NYHT*, 20 Dec 1934)

Pierre Planté, his father, settled in Orthez in the French Pyrenees, married (1831) Suzanne-Eleanore Lafitte Labère de Lembeye and had four sons: Gaston, a renowned physicist who produced the first electric storage battery; Leopold, an attorney; Francis the pianist; and Henri, who died at age four. About a year after Francis Planté's birth, the family left Orthez to take advantage of the greater educational and cultural opportunities available in Paris, where they fortuitously chose a residence near that of one Madame de Saint-Aubert, a pupil of Franz Liszt. Planté was not quite four years old when Saint-Aubert began his musical instruction, and he always credited her with forming and disciplining his natural musical temperament. He made his first public appearance at age seven, playing the Beethoven Sonata, op. 2, no. 3, at a charity concert.

Although not yet 10, he was accepted at the Paris Conservatory on 5 January 1849, and admitted to Antoine Marmontel's piano class. He received a first prize in piano (1 July 1850), then spent about three years (1850–53) performing, especially at the chamber-music evenings organized by violinist Jean-Delphin Alard and cellist Auguste-Joseph Franchomme. In 1853 Planté returned to the Conservatory to study harmony with Emmanuel Bazin, and in 1855 he won a prize in harmony.

Planté's solo recitals in Paris made him an instant celebrity, catapulted to youthful fame because of what later would be called his "legendary floating tone." That tone, apparently totally free of any percussive hammer quality, caused a mild sensation. Charles-Marie Widor once ruefully admitted that he could produce the Planté tone, but only on one key at a time while Planté did it on the entire keyboard all the time. Upon hearing Planté play, his good friend Saint-Saëns once asked, "*Donne-moi donc, mon cher Francis, l'adresse de ton marchand de velours.*" According to Planté's pupils, at lessons he would instruct them to "mentalize the tone first, then try to realize it. Listen *for* tone, not listen *to* tone."

During those heady days in Paris, young Planté often visited the salon of Mme. Pierre Erard, a music patron who sponsored concerts at the Chateau de la Muette. Through her, Planté met Anton Rubinstein, Liszt, Gounod and Wagner; became especially close friends with Saint-Saëns (they loved to play pranks on each other, all the more fun if done in public); and found affectionate foster parents in Gioacchino Rossini and his wife. The Rossinis would introduce Planté as their adopted son, and he in turn referred to Rossini as "il papa secondo." At one of the Rossini soirees, Planté played two-piano works with Liszt. In time, all the applause and attention spoiled him, and he grew careless about his playing. Realizing what was happening, Planté sensibly gave up concertizing and withdrew to study and practice.

In the late 1860s he returned to performing, and for a quarter of a century toured frequently. He made his first London appearance on 1 May 1878, playing the Mendelssohn D Minor Concerto with the Royal Philharmonic Society Orchestra, but performed mostly in Europe, garnering fame as a virtuoso pianist and as the greatest living exponent of the French keyboard tradition. By 1895 Planté was tired of performing and of being away from France so much of the time. He gave up concertizing, but until the end of his life he continued to play countless charity concerts.

In retirement Planté, an avid hunter, lived the life of a country gentleman at his estate at Mont-de-Marsan on the Basque coast, leaving the region only for exceptional occasions like the piano festival held at the Sarah Bernhardt Theater in Paris (18–20 June 1907), which featured Alfred Cortot, Louis Diémer, Raoul Pugno, Eduard Risler and Planté. He never neglected his music. Blessed with enormous energy and good health, all his life he had been a tireless worker, practicing about eight hours a day when concertizing. Although "retired," Planté still practiced five or six hours daily. As he would tell his students, the intense practice was meant to perfect technique to the point of never having to think about it but be able to maintain it at a high level, thus be free to work on creating music.

After his wife (m. 1869) died in 1908, Planté became a recluse, playing publicly only for the most worthy causes until World War I brought him out of seclusion. He gave about 50 wartime charity concerts, unusual events because the eccentric Planté had decided not to play in view of the audience. Determined to perform these wartime concerts in a reposeful, meditative atmosphere, whenever possible he played in churches, crypts or chapels. A screen shielded him from the audience (there were some concerts, however, at which this self-effacement was not feasible), and applause was not permitted. Planté designed his programs to suit the places in which they were given: religious music and introspective works such as nocturnes, ariosos and the like. More than 5,000 people attended Planté's wartime concert held in June 1916 in the crypt of Saint-Honoré d'Eylau in Paris. His awesome performance—the program included the second movement of his own transcription of Beethoven's Seventh Symphony—was greeted by a "reverential, prayerful silence; not a hand lifted in applause; a single pianist giving the impression of an entire orchestra." (Schwerké)

When one of his sons (he had 3 sons, 2 daughters) was killed in 1917, Planté again withdrew from public life, dividing his time between his piano, his friends and hunting. He still practiced five or six hours a day, and even in his nineties the Planté magic was still very much in evidence. He gave a farewell concert (3 April 1930) at Mont-de-Marsan to benefit victims of a flood in southwest France, and played again (19 July 1930) in the church at Solignac (Haute Vienne). He was then 91, and his program consisted of 21 of his favorite works. Planté's rich, productive life ended on 19 December 1934.

France honored Planté with the cross of *Chevalier de la Légion d'honneur* (1876) and with the rosette of *Officier de la Légion d'honneur* (1920). In 1931 he was elected *Commandeur de la Légion d'honneur*.

Although he never embraced teaching as a profession, Planté was considered an excellent teacher, and he helped many students, always free of charge. Known for his own prodigious facility, he never tried to teach technique. He advised his students not to "play" the piano, but simply to try to make music. He played for his students and shared his wisdom and experience with them. They learned, said one pupil, almost without realizing it. Musicianship always came first, and he rejected any work meant only for exhibiting the pianist's technique. A firm traditionalist, Planté nevertheless had very strong personal ideas on interpretation. For example, he abhorred the idea of playing Bach in a dry and detached manner. "On paper you may intellectualize Bach all you want to," he said, "but when you play Bach to people remember that Bach wrote for people."

Planté never undertook the study of a new piece without first having read it away from the piano, possibly two or three times, believing that this saved much time in learning the piece. It was a method, he said, that he had learned from Liszt. Planté was also a great advocate of five-finger exercises, which he did all the time, whether dining, riding, walking, visiting, no matter where. He would make technical exercises of any difficult passages he encountered in a work, would play them first with each hand singly, then with the hands together, always working very slowly and pianissimo in order to keep relaxed.

Planté, who played mostly a traditional classical repertoire, was also highly regarded for his interest in new music. He was one of the first to play Liszt's music in public, and he continued to program contemporary music right down to his final recitals, playing works by Poulenc, Stravinsky and Prokofiev. He could also look back on playing such "moderns" as Mendelssohn, Thalberg, Debussy, MacDowell and Saint-Saëns. Planté became especially famous for his brilliant interpretations of Liszt, Mozart and Saint-Saëns.

In the course of his long devotion to the piano, an unusual career spanning eight decades, Frances Planté acquired a reputation for upholding his own lofty musical standards and the high principles of the French keyboard tradition. His audiences adored him. As with Fritz Kreisler, it was said that a kind of special, loving feeling flowed between him and them. He often performed without a set program (these unstructured recitals could last for hours), and he would talk to his audience as he played, explaining the meaning of the music or perhaps describing the technical difficulties.

Marmontel recalled that even at age 10 Planté had an astonishing facility and remarkable maturity: "Where Planté excels and remains an incomparable model is in the conduct of sound, in the art of modulating it, of nuancing it to an infinite degree. . . . The articulation is so alive, the legato so well observed, the melodic succession so well managed that the sound becomes fused, aerial, vocal, in a word, like the spun-out notes of a singer would be." (*Amis de Marquèze* album, Liner Notes, see Discog.) Rossini expressed his admiration in a letter (18 June 1857) to Planté: "I love and appreciate your extraordinary talent. . . . You possess that which one cannot acquire: the elegance of sentiment and the execution of the consummate artist." (Lenoir and Nahuque)

Hector Berlioz, then music critic for the *Journal des Debats*, reviewed (13 Feb 1860) a Planté performance of the Beethoven "Emperor" Concerto. "M. Planté is one of the young pianists of our era who does the greatest honor to the teaching of the Paris Conservatory. He performed the beautiful Concerto of Beethoven with fire, often with much grace and a complete understanding of the Beethoven style. Here is a pianist-musician who looks for his success only in the faithful and intelligent interpretation of masterpieces and does not give in to those antiharmonic and antirhythmic excesses of which pianists are often guilty." (Fabre, *La Vie. . .*)

Newspaper and periodical reviews, as we know them, were rare in Planté's era. What usually appeared was a general overview of the concert with due attention given to the attendant society, the environs and the like. For example, *L'Art Musical*, a contemporary Parisian periodical, described a Planté concert in the 7 May 1874 issue, but gave far more space to the distinguished Parisian audience, the resplendent lights and the elegant dresses before noting that "With his extraordinary talent, M. Francis Planté performed the concerto in G minor of Mendelssohn, a *Morceau de Concert* of Schumann and the finale of Weber's *Concert-Stück*, accompanied by artists chosen from the conservatory orchestra, and directed by M. Sauzay. He was also heard alone, moreover, in his own transcriptions of works by different composers—Mendelssohn, Gluck, Boccherini, Liszt, Chopin—and he was enthusiastically applauded."

Later that same month Planté played at a soiree, an event "captured" by the same periodical. "The salon and adjoining rooms overflowed with . . . the elite of all aristocracies, that of talent, that of intelligence and that of fortune. The eminent pianist enraptured this select, discriminating audience, by playing some new music on one of the excellent Franco-American pianos, a Steinway, which had quite individual effects. M. Planté began with the *andante* and *allegro* from Weber's first sonata, then he played the *Gavotte* of Gluck in his own admirable transcription, then a *Caprice* by Mendelssohn; the *Danse des Almées*, also well transcribed by the pianist; a virtuoso etude by M. F. Mathias; another etude, passionate, by M. Marmontel; second *allegro* of Weber; the *Air hongrois* of Liszt and the eighth *Polonaise* of Chopin. . . . I have not forgotten the magnificent ballade of Chopin also, which is actually a musical poem. I have kept it for the last, I might say almost as the clasp of this precious necklace of musical pearls." (*L'Art Musical*, 21 May 1874)

Robert Casadesus, another great pianist, has left us a later, more intimate glimpse of Francis Planté. In a 1970 interview Casadesus recalls a long afternoon (5 hours!) making music with Planté, already in his nineties. Planté played some Chopin Etudes and the Barcarolle for Robert and his wife Gaby, playing, said Casadesus, "as I imagine Chopin played them." The amazing nonagenarian played the Mozart Concerto in D Minor with Mme. Casadesus and the Liszt Concerto in A Major with Robert. "He played," said Casadesus, "with wonderful legato, never brilliant." (Eld/Pia, see Bibliog.)

Planté's recording career lasted a brief two days. Just thinking about a recording studio made him nervous and, besides, he was convinced that he needed a live audience to do his best. When he arranged a piano festival to celebrate the 83rd anniversary of his career and also his upcoming 90th birthday, Columbia Records urged Planté to come to Paris and record the programs, but he refused. The festival, held 10 May 1928 at the Modern Cinema at Mont-de-Marsan, consisted of the 89-year-old Planté playing one program in the afternoon and a different program in the evening. Irving Schwerké, determined to preserve the event, arranged to have Columbia Records send recording technicians and equipment to Planté's home at Mont-de-Marsan. Planté recorded for two days (July 3 and 4) and refused to do more.

Planté's complete known recordings are presently available on one LP, which is issued under two separate record labels. These LP albums have the same music, but the French disc *Hommage au pianiste Francis Planté* contains, in addition, a Chopin etude transferred from an earlier piano roll Planté had made in 1910. The French album is also a deluxe presentation with copious notes and pictures. (An Opal CD reissue contains 10 items from the LP collections.) Like so many of his contemporaries, Planté enjoyed transcribing. Three of his transcriptions can be heard on all three discs: Mephisto's Serenade by Berlioz (an arrangement applauded by the composer); Menuet by Boccherini; and Gluck's Gavotte.

The 19th-century Erard grand piano used for the recording partly accounts for Planté's tonal palette and singing touch. The strings are strung straight in parallel, not overlapping like those in later pianos. The bass register is shallower and its resonance serves as a foundation of a greatly enriched tonal body. One reviewer considers the Chopin Etudes to be the most rewarding: "In general, Planté's tempos are much slower than we are used to hearing today. [But] along comes Op. 25, No. 1, played very quickly and with superb control, Chopin with the most lovely floating poetry. . . . It becomes apparent that Planté could still do pretty much what he wanted to, and that tempos are slow because that was how he wanted to play." (*ARSC*, 1985)

On the whole, Planté's performances make us realize how close most of the music in this album is to the dance. "That, for instance, is what makes his recording of the Chopin, op. 10, no. 5, with its strutting bass, sound so vibrant and unhackneyed; and it's what gives the special character to his pungent account of the Berlioz. Yet fresh, even startling, as his interpretations may be, they're always fresh because of their illumination, not their eccentricity: Planté was no de Pachmann, and his playing, while not quite decorous, is never tasteless." (*Fan*, Jan/Feb 1988) An interesting footnote: Planté and Pachmann were the only two pianists born during Chopin's lifetime to live long enough to make gramophone records by the electrical process.

Listening to Planté's recordings, one has no difficulty recognizing him as one of this (and the last!) century's master pianists. He takes us back to the era of Schumann, Chopin and Mendelssohn. Planté managed *bel canto* on the keyboard as surely as a singer does with the voice. The romantic piano tradition is beautifully preserved here.

SELECTED REFERENCES

Barranx, Serge. "Francis Planté." *Revue régionaliste des Pyrenées*, Feb–April 1935, pp. 580–600.

Dandelot, Arthur. *Francis Planté: une belle vie d'artiste*. Paris: Editions et publications Edouard Dupont, 1928.

Fabre, Michel. *Le Souvenir de Francis Planté*. Pau: Imp. Marrimpouey, 1973.

———. *La Vie de Francis Planté où la sonate d'un virtuose*. Pau: Imprimerie de Navarre, 1982.

Gerber, Leslie. "Francis Planté Reissued Again." *Association for Recorded Sound Collection Journal*, Vol. 17, nos. 1–3, 1985, pp. 163–164.

Lenoir, Auguste, and Jean de Nahuque. *Francis Planté, doyen des pianistes*. Hossegor: Librairie Chabas, 1931.

Obituary. *New York Herald-Tribune*, 20 Dec 1934, p. 26. *New York Times*, 20 Dec 1934, p. 26.

Schwerké, Irving. "Francis Planté: Patriarch of the Piano." *Recorded Sound*, July 1969, pp. 474–494.

See also Bibliography: New/Gro; Nie/Mei; Pau/Dic; Pay/Cel; Rat/Cle; Reu/Gre; Sch/Gre.

SELECTED REVIEWS

L'Art Musical: 7 May 1874; 21 May 1874; 18 May 1876. *Journal des Debats*, 13 Feb 1860.

SELECTED DISCOGRAPHY

Francis Planté: His Complete Published Recordings. Berlioz: "Serenade" from *La Damnation de Faust*. Boccherini: Minuet. Chopin: Etudes, op. 10, nos. 4, 5, 7; op. 25, nos. 1, 2, 9, 11. Gluck: Gavotte from *Iphigénie en Aulide*. Mendelssohn: Scherzo, op. 16, no. 2; Songs without Words, op. 19, no. 3; op. 62, no. 6; op. 67, nos. 4 and 6. Schumann: Romance, op. 28, no. 2; Romance, op. 32, no. 3; At the Fountain (arr. Debussy). Opal 832.

Hommage au Pianiste Francis Planté. Same pieces as above, with the addition of a 1910 Hupfeld piano roll of the Chopin Etude, op. 25, no. 2. Sabres: *Edition des Amis de Marquèze*.

Ricardo Viñes and Francis Planté. Opal CD 9857. A selection of 10 items from the above Opal LP collection.

POGORELICH, IVO: b. Belgrade, Yugoslavia, 20 October 1958.

> Whether one likes Mr. Pogorelich or his playing, he is difficult to ignore.
>
> Bernard Holland (*New York Times*, 16 February 1986)

Relatively unknown when he entered the 1980 Frédéric Chopin Piano Competition in Warsaw, Ivo Pogorelich came out of it an overnight celebrity— ironically, not because he won. Pogorelich was actually eliminated in the third round, presumably because of his controversial interpretations, flamboyant attire and eccentric behavior; but his loss sparked a public scandal, elaborately covered by the media, and the publicity propelled him into a first-rate concert career. Pogorelich long ago proved that he is a compelling pianist and a riveting personality, but how he plays is still controversial.

Interviewers have learned comparatively little about his family or childhood, but obviously he was not a child prodigy. His father Ivan Pogorelich played the double bass in a Belgrade orchestra, so as a child Pogorelich must have heard a lot of music. Furthermore, his parents began taking him to the opera as early as age six and started him on piano lessons at age seven. (They also gave him English lessons, which accounts for his adult fluency.) If the piano captured his interest, he failed to show it; on the contrary, he hated practicing. But he was learning, and he had talent.

Sent to Moscow at age 13, Pogorelich studied five years with Yevgeny Timakhin at the Central Music School and in 1975 moved on to the Moscow Conservatory, where he worked principally with Vera Gornostaeva and Yevgeny Malinin. Both of those teachers had studied with the great pedagogue Heinrich Neuhaus, yet in several interviews Pogorelich has passed off their classes as merely a matter of attendance. "I would go to their classes and play," he says. "That was it. Nothing really happened."

He was, he claims, so bored at the Conservatory that he was on the verge of leaving before graduation. (Apparently the Conservatory was not thrilled with Pogorelich either. Reports are that he was nearly expelled, more than once, because of lack of interest.) But in 1976 everything changed. As the story goes, Pogorelich played a Chopin piece at a Moscow reception held at the home of a prominent Russian scientist, and Alice Kezeradze, the scientist's pianist wife, remarked that he was not doing justice to his talent. Piqued by her comments on his playing, at age 17 Pogorelich began private lessons with Kezeradze, simultaneously completing his courses at the Conservatory ("making only token appearances," he says) and graduating in 1980. Controversial even at that age, he says that the school authorities "took issue with my interpretations; the usual story, they wanted to hear what they wanted to hear. I have been dogged with this sort of orthodoxy and preconception all my life." (Morrison)

Pogorelich's marriage, at age 22, to Kezeradze, 14 years his senior, caused a break with his parents. He and his new family—Kezeradze had a six-year-old son—lived in Yugoslavia for about a year and a half, since then have acquired homes in London and Scotland. Kezeradze—wife, teacher, mentor, confidante, protector—seemingly dominates Pogorelich's life and career. Dismissing his years of training at the Moscow Conservatory, he claims that everything he knows he learned from her, that she absolutely transformed him, as he repeatedly says, "from being an ordinary pianist into something exceptional." Kezeradze made him work for a perfect technique ("a necessity"). She also gave him "an insight into the progressive treatment of sound as it developed in the 18th and 19th centuries . . . and taught him how to take advantage of large, modern, powerful pianos." (Stephen)

Pogorelich toured America in 1978 (more than 40 cities and towns) as soloist with the Dubrovnik Festival Orchestra, but reviews are elusive, so it would seem that at the time Pogorelich's playing made little impact. That same year (1978) he took first prize at the Allesandro Casagrande Competition in Terni, Italy, and in 1980 first prize at the Montreal International Music Competition. Nevertheless, he was still comparatively unknown when he entered the 1980 Frédéric Chopin Competition in Warsaw. He was eliminated in the third round, but the Association of Music Critics in Poland awarded Pogorelich a special prize (for displaying new insight and "opening up a completely modern and novel approach to Chopin's music"), and even the jurors eventually recognized his "extraordinarily original talent as an artist."

Pogorelich hardly needed such compliments, for he had passionate support from judge Martha Argerich, herself winner of the Chopin Competition in 1965. Even more exciting, the ensuing publicity and becoming a cult hero immediately propelled him into the spotlight. Implausibly, the winners of that 1980 competition dispersed without fanfare, while loser Pogorelich, says his press agency biography, shot overnight to stardom—"an undisputed youth idol, the 'Rock Star of Classical Music'."

His supporters quickly arranged a Warsaw recital for 30 October 1980, tickets sold out in short order and Pogorelich performed it before 3,000 riotous fans chanting "Ivo, Ivo." With that kind of publicity, it is no wonder that offers to play came from London, Amsterdam, Munich and Tokyo, or that *Deutsche Grammophon* (still his label) signed him to an exclusive three-year recording contract, or that his first recording, an all-Chopin program made in 1981, reportedly sold 100,000 copies in just three days.

Pogorelich's Carnegie Hall debut (19 May 1981) and his London orchestral debut (16 June 1981), playing the Prokofiev Concerto No. 3 with the Philharmonia Orchestra, conducted by Seiji Ozawa, greatly enhanced his reputation; others (in Paris, Madrid, Brussels, Amsterdam, Rome, Milan) firmly launched his career; and ever since Pogorelich has performed internationally. Over the years he has modified his attire and behavior, but his interpretations still provoke controversy.

Pogorelich is an enormously generous celebrity. He plays about 80 concerts a season and makes recordings, yet finds time to give charity concerts for a diverse array of organizations and gives his time, talent and money in support of young people, especially young musicians.

In articles and interviews, he comes across as an overly dramatic personality who thrives on making outrageous statements, many of them unintentionally hilarious. For instance—and for the record—the following:

"I am the world's greatest pianist, and the cleverest and most experienced young man in the world." (*DFP*, 1 Nov 1984)

"Think of the possibilities I have as the idol of so many people, which I certainly am." (*MA*, May 1984)

"I make even the smallest pieces into monuments." (*NW*, 1 June 1981)

"With a few exceptions, [America] is still a musically uneducated country, by and large." (*KeM*, May 1986)

"New York concerts are boring. They need excitement. They need me." (*OV*, Feb 1987)

"[Artur] Rubinstein was a bad pianist. . . . He possessed some of the worse taste. And his technique was limited, definitely." (*OV*, Feb 1987)

"Kapell was a dilettante and Lipatti lacked technical control." (Dub/Eve, see Bibliog.)

Obviously someone or something has led Ivo Pogorelich to believe that he is the greatest pianist in the world. Overall, critical consensus is not so sure. Many critics still query Pogorelich's extremely individual interpretations; others detect a lack of the musical understanding which Pogorelich himself feels he has in such abundance. Certainly there has never been any doubt about Pogorelich's talent and tremendous technique. But a survey of some 50 reviews from the years 1981 through 1995 makes one wonder if an overload of individuality is detracting from the listener's pleasure. And it seems inevitable that nonmusical characteristics—those arrogant comments and Pogorelich's public persona (self-absorbed, self-confident, often contemptuous)—sometimes will come to the listener's mind and spoil the performances. Some reviewers have been so affected; and the exasperated mutterings one sometimes hears at a Pogorelich recital indicate that audiences, too, can be bothered by nonmusical factors.

He has enormous talent, he is absolutely dedicated to his art and he works hard. Describing to interviewers how he works, Pogorelich explains that he approaches music like a method actor, immersing himself in the era in which the music was written in an effort to know it intimately. Pogorelich explains: "This begins, of course, with a careful reading of the scores; everything else is left to the artist and to his musical intuition. But that intuition is good *only* if it is based on a very professional knowledge and approach." (Rhein)

Pogorelich's programs show a very small repertoire, at least according to reviews covering the 15 years since he won the Chopin Competition. He claims, however, that what he performs in public represents a very small portion of an enormous repertoire he plays in private. In 1982 his repertoire allowed, in his words, "two recital programs and two different concertos for one season." Four years later he stated that he never prepares and plays more than one recital program per season.

Year-by-year reviews (1981–1995) of Pogorelich performances provide a general outline of his performing repertoire—Bach (2 English Suites), Beethoven (4 sonatas), Brahms (around 6 short works), Chopin (2 sonatas, 24 Preludes, several scherzos, polonaises and nocturnes), Haydn (2 sonatas), Liszt (Sonata, 3 Etudes), Prokofiev (2 sonatas, Romeo and Juliet), Rachmaninoff (Sonata No. 2), Scarlatti (around 15 sonatas), Ravel (*Gaspard, Valses nobles*), Schumann

(Symphonic Etudes, Toccata), Scriabin (2 sonatas and several shorter works), plus a few individual works by other composers.

This same set of reviews indicates that Pogorelich played the following works with orchestra: Chopin: Concerto No. 2, Franck: Symphonic Variations, Prokofiev: Concerto No. 3, Tchaikovsky: Concerto No. 1. By any standards, past or present, that is a very small orchestral repertoire for an international concert artist. "If Ivo Pogorelich is playing a concerto," chided one critic, "it stands more than a good chance of being Tchaikovsky's First. . . . And he does play the piece stunningly well, if controversially. But has he nothing to say about any of the other riches of the piano's concerto repertoire? Some of us are beginning to wonder." (*TL*, 8 Nov 1986)

Pogorelich prefers playing solo recitals because, he says, most orchestras and conductors are not willing to spend as much time and care over detail as he does. This scrupulous attention to detail can cause problems, like the 1984 incident with conductor Herbert von Karajan. Pogorelich's painfully slow tempos at a rehearsal of the Tchaikovsky Concerto No. 1 so disturbed Karajan that he canceled not only their planned recording but also Pogorelich's next day's live performance.

Pogorelich has accumulated an intriguing mix of reviews. Some are outright raves, some downright negative, and some uncertain. And they seem to be fairly evenly divided. The bad reviews range from honest criticism to overt sarcasm, perhaps unavoidable, perhaps not. On 23 November 1982 Pogorelich performed ("or rather toyed with") the Franck Symphonic Variations with Neville Marriner and the London Symphony Orchestra. "He made such a self-indulgent meal of the introduction that one feared the theme would never get off the ground; when it finally arrived, it was stroked rather than played. . . . It came close to self-admiration: St. Cecilia would surely not have been amused." (*TL*, 24 Nov 1982)

A lengthy review covering Pogorelich's New York recital (12 April 1984) and his performance (25 April 1984) of Tchaikovsky's Concerto No. 1 with the Boston Symphony Orchestra, Seiji Ozawa conducting, includes: "Pogorelich ravished his fans and irritated his critics. . . . He is quite simply a cult figure whose followers cheer his best and his worst with equal decibels of ecstasy. . . . In order to maintain his image as virtuoso, Pogorelich abruptly tries to make up for habitual swoonings by speedily punching out loud and fast sections of music for all they're worth. . . . He has trouble with octaves, at unexpected times. . . . His tone is often pinched to the point of tinniness. . . . Most of all he needs to surrender some of his wilfulness." (*MA*, Oct 1984)

Every year, even into the 1990s, this type of derogatory review has continued to plague Pogorelich. To illustrate: "Ivo Pogorelich's piano recital [7 May 1987] at Barbican Hall was everything our musical life can do without. . . . Pogorelich doesn't so much make music as a kind of negative theatre. He rides through the musical capitals of the world on a bubble of hype, but the defiant brilliance and untouchable manner which originally won him note seem remarkably unappetising now." (*STL*, 17 May 1987) The next year a Carnegie Hall recital (16 Feb 1988) "was alternately agreeable and exasperating. . . .

Pogorelich is a gifted young man, but somebody, somewhere, seems to have convinced him that he is an interpretive genius, which he most emphatically is not. . . . Pogorelich's way with the Romantics . . . has been mannered and eccentric. More to the point, it has been *uninteresting*, mannered and eccentric. . . . Though there have been a few artists possessing the genius to elevate egoism to an art form, Pogorelich is not in their number." (*LIN*, 18 Feb 1988)

"There isn't much Ivo Pogorelich cannot do at the piano, except perhaps play the music properly." Thus began a review of two identical Los Angeles recitals (17–18 Jan 1989). Pogorelich's spellbinding technique may have been in top form, but also present was the "almost constant defacement of the music. . . . Both Brahms Rhapsodies . . . were brutally distended, most of all by capricious tempos. . . . The Liszt [B Minor Sonata] seemed . . . fragmented into unrelated, jagged objects lined up merely to demonstrate how Pogorelich can play slow and fast, soft and loud. An evening of nothing but C-major scales could have achieved that purpose equally well and saved poor Franz Liszt the havoc wrought upon his music. . . . Even the wondrous set of Chopin Preludes didn't escape the indignity of being forced to serve as the pianist's hobbyhorses. . . . No go, Pogo." (*LAHE*, 21 Jan 1989)

And in San Francisco on 3 March 1992, "it took no more than the first few measures of pianist Ivo Pogorelich's Tuesday night recital for the old familiar feelings of bewilderment and exasperation to come flooding back. . . . He pushed and pulled at tempos, slowing down the slow and speeding up the fast. He dissected melodic lines, subjecting each note to the minutest scrutiny; sometimes he reassembled them afterwards, and sometimes not. . . . For every breathtaking textural or technical coup, there were two or three passages of sheer decadent mannerism." (*SFC*, 5 March 1992)

These predominantly negative reviews can be matched with about an equal number of highly enthusiastic critiques. For example, this glowing review of a Los Angeles recital on 24 August 1983: "He somehow manages to reach for the impossible and make the effort seem not only rational and worthwhile but simple. . . . The secret of the pianist's uncommon success lay, no doubt, in his unerring command of proportion, his keen expressive focus, his interpretive originality and, perhaps most important, his unflagging conviction that dramatic climaxes exert maximum force only when set off by passages of contrasting moderation." (*LAT*, 26 Aug 1983)

Pogorelich, said a Chicago critic after hearing "a magnificent performance" (28 Oct 1984), represents "a kind of throwback to the great succession of romantic interpreters, dazzling performers who also dared to play with great freedom, spontaneity and individuality. Pogorelich clearly seeks to carry the composer's ideas to the outer limits of expressive possibility. Paying lip service to 'traditional' interpretation doesn't interest him; communication does." (*CT*, 29 Oct 1984)

Pogorelich's Los Angeles recital of 18 February 1986 earned him an A+ all the way: "He is a virtuoso of staggering accomplishments, but others command comparable techniques. Few of his contemporaries, however, exhibit such an exhaustive range of color, from Horowitzian thunder to sustained sounds that are perfectly clear but barely audible." (*LAT*, 20 Feb 1986)

Pogorelich continues to bewilder some audiences and critics. One review of his Carnegie Hall recital on 13 March 1992 was titled "The Provocateur Who Lurks within the Pianist." The critic enjoyed the Chopin Nocturnes ("refined and considered") and the Ravel *Valses nobles et sentimentales* ("skillful and sweet"). But the Chopin Sonata was arguably eccentric. "He took the Largo of Chopin's B-minor Piano Sonata at a tempo so slow that the music disintegrated into ponderous caresses. . . . Pogorelich is still uncertain about his allegiances to audiences, to music, to himself, to his career or even to his recordings. The provocateur is always just beneath the surface." (*NYT*, 16 March 1992)

The provocateur was alive and well at a Denville, New Jersey, recital (3 April 1993), a program of 12 Scarlatti sonatas, two short Brahms pieces and the Liszt Sonata in B Minor. The *pièce de résistance* was, of course, the Sonata and reportedly "this performance went from magnificence to magnificence." After the Liszt, which concluded the program, Pogorelich, as an encore, played Balakirev's *Islamey*, a substantial virtuoso piece in its own right. "Only two things can follow the Liszt B minor and still preserve the sonata's integrity: Nothing at all (no encore), or else music of a drastically different yet serious character, such as works by Bach. What you do not play is another slamfest." (S-L, 5 April 1993)

So from these reviews we have Ivo Pogorelich—an anesthetizing, joyless, willful pianist. But we also have Ivo Pogorelich—a passionate, brilliant, matchless pianist. Clearly, the final determination is yet to be made, and it may take time. British and American newspaper indexes since 1993 record far fewer Pogorelich performances than previously. For instance, his London performance of 10 November 1992 was his first appearance there in five years (*TL*, 12 Nov 1992)

Pogorelich remains the unpredictable pianist. For example, two Pasadena, California, recitals played within ten months were so completely different they might have been performed by two different pianists. The first recital (31 May 1994), a demanding program of Mussorgsky and Chopin, was "remarkable for its musical distortion, for its pounding, for its vanity. It was, in a word, awful." The same critic reviewed the second recital (22 March 1995), works by Mozart and Schumann, and heard a totally different kind of pianist who "didn't sound at all like the man from 10 months ago. . . . This time [he] played like an angel. . . . The music sang and danced and sighed and roared and shimmered and declaimed and made beautiful sense." (*LAT*, 24 March 1995)

To date, Pogorelich has a smallish but representative discography extending from Bach and Scarlatti to Prokofiev. Like his live recitals and concerts, his recordings evoke mixed reactions. For example, his CD of the Ravel *Gaspard de la nuit* can compare favorably with the finest recorded performances of this composition. At the other extreme, his album of Brahms's music seems sadly perverse and uninformed.

Pogorelich's CD of the Chopin Preludes, op. 28 (see Discog.) drew mixed reviews. A reviewer "gripped from first note to last by the vividness and boldness of the imaginative conception, no less than by some very remarkable piano playing," was at the same time "subconsciously aware of listening to someone determined to shed 'new light' on the music at any price, and sometimes that price is too high." (*Gram*, May 1990)

Pogorelich's recording coupling the Liszt Sonata in B Minor and the Scriabin Sonata No. 2 (see Discog.) makes for a comparatively stingy (48 minutes) CD. The pianist's reading is rhythmically free and notably declamatory, albeit highly expressive and expansive, but "the extremely aggressive banging of chords, while certainly idiomatic to Liszt, does pale after 20–25 minutes. Pogorelich is most pleasing in the quiet passages, which he plays with a dreamy, ecstatic expression. . . . Pogorelich plays Scriabin's Second Sonata incandescently, in a white heat of fervor." (*ARG*, Sept/Oct 1992) However, in comparing Pogorelich's Liszt with that of Brendel and Zimerman, another critic finds that while it challenges convention at every point, the "entire performance is magnificently unsettling and is in no sense the Liszt Sonata of received wisdom. [Nevertheless] one has only to turn to earlier and outstanding performances by Brendel and Zimerman to hear how true greatness is possible without resort to so much self-conscious sifting and analysis." (*Gram*, June 1992)

Pogorelich's reading of Tchaikovsky's Concerto No. 1 with the London Symphony Orchestra, Claudio Abbado conducting, won a Recording of Distinction Award from *Ovation* in February 1987. "The piece may be treated with condescension by many sophisticated listeners, but from his richly heroic opening to the rush of adrenaline that caps the coda, Pogorelich reminds us just how much musical substance there is in it."

Pogorelich's recording of Bach's English Suites, Nos. 2 and 3 (see Discog.), is the result of a long involvement with Bach's music. He played the Suite No. 2 about 40 times in concert, worked up the Suite No. 3 in G Minor to his satisfaction and then recorded both on a single CD. For one critic, these readings present the pianist's talents in the proper light. "There one finds a big technique and bracing energy united to create straight-forward and exciting performances." (*LIN*, 18 Feb 1988) One may disagree with Pogorelich's stylistic ideas, but these Bach performances command both respect and admiration. He takes repeats for just about every dance in the suite, including Sarabandes, which means that a single CD can accommodate only two suites instead of the customary three. "These are deeply considered readings as well as marvellous displays of pianistic control, bubbling joyous in the Preludes, raptly contemplative in the Sarabandes." (*Gram*, Dec 1986)

Pogorelich's recording of 15 sonatas by Domenico Scarlatti, another pre-Romantic composer, is also excellent (see Discog.). "Overall, this is an attractively played collection, with stunning articulation for the ornaments and plenty of sparkling fingerwork to bring Scarlatti's vivid personality to life." (*Gram*, Jan 1993) Admittedly these are personal interpretations, but they are convincing, intelligently conceived and played with consummate musicianship.

In the Classic category, the only available recorded Mozart work—the Sonata, K. 331— appears on one of Pogorelich's videos (see Discog.). He has, however, recorded two Haydn sonatas, and the one in A-flat Major also appears on video. Using less restraint than he did for his Baroque interpretations, Pogorelich applies some romantic performance practices, to the delight of some and the chagrin of others. As one reviewer expressed it, "Pogorelich's Haydn is pianism of a high order, liquid enough for Chopin and expressive enough for Rachmaninov. If you can imagine such odd bedfellows, or even if you can't, this disc should provide much pleasure." (*Fan*, May/June 1993) A more severe reviewer asks some disquieting questions: "Why must the staccatos always be so pointed and clipped, even in the slow movements? And why must the passage-work be so light and fleet that it often sounds tossed off and insignificant?" (*ARG*, May/June 1993)

Pogorelich's two *Deutsche Grammophon* videos (see Discog.) have also drawn mixed reactions. The first video, recorded at the *Castello Reale di Racconigi* in Piedmont, Italy, is a recital featuring the Haydn Sonata in A-flat Major, Hob. XVI:46, Mozart's Sonata in A Major, K. 331, and a substantial Chopin group, highlighted by the Sonata No. 3 in B Minor, op. 58. Pogorelich's playing is controlled, often intense and strongly felt. The more moderate tempos are taken more slowly than usual, especially in the central portion of the Chopin scherzo movement.

The second video (Chopin and Scriabin) was recorded at the Villa Contarini in Piazzola, Italy. One very disappointed critic noted that Pogorelich has become known for his "great technical facility, and an inclination to play loudly where the music says soft, and softly where the music says loud. Judging from this video, he still refuses to follow the directions in the music." This critic also disapproved of Pogorelich's gyrations at the keyboard. "The sound approach that results from all this tense posturing is, understandably, pounding, pounding and more pounding." (*MA*, Jan/Feb 1992) Comparing that critique with another, one might almost assume that the two reviewers were writing about two different performances. We have this: "The playing is as great as I have ever heard. . . . Pogorelich unites tempos, taste, temperament, and tone in intense, inspired performances. His technique is mammoth, his phrasing and singing tone breathtaking." (*CL*, March 1992)

SELECTED REFERENCES

Beigel, Greta. "Pogorelich: Poseur, or the Prince of Pianists?" *Los Angeles Times*, 15 July 1981, sec. 6, p. 6.

Darnton, Nina. "Yugoslav Pianist Stirring Music World." *New York Times*, 1 Nov 1980, p. 16.

Doerschuk, Bob. "Shock Waves From A Daring Young Virtuoso." *Keyboard*, May 1986, pp. 70–76, 81–90.

Elder, Dean. "Ivo Pogorelich: Sensational New Star." *Clavier*, Jan 1982, pp. 16–19.

Holland, Bernard. "Flamboyance and Virtuosity Are Pogorelich's Trademarks." *New York Times*, 16 Feb 1986, pp. 25–26.

Jolly, James. "Bach, Pogorelich and the Piano." *Gramophone*, Dec 1986, p. 806.

Keener, Andrew. "Ivo Pogorelich." (interview) *Hi-Fi News & Record Review*, Dec 1981, pp. 85–86.

Malitz, Nancy. "Ivo Pogorelich." *Ovation*, Feb 1987, pp. 12–18.

Morrison, Bryce. "From Competition to Competition." (interview) *Gramophone*, Jan 1993, pp. 8–9.

Perlmutter, Donna. "Pogorelich: Pianist Does It His Way." *Los Angeles Times*, 17 Feb 1986, pp. 1, 5.

Rhein, John von. "Punk crescendo subsides: 'Poet' Ivo settles down to the real score." *Chicago Tribune*, 28 Oct 1984, sec. 13, p. 16.

Stearns, David Patrick. "Ivo Pogorelich: The brash pianist with the punk image still has surprises up his sleeve." *Musical America*, May 1984, pp. 4–5, 10–11.

Stephen, Andrew. "I, Pogorelich." *Sunday Times* (London), 10 Feb 1985, Magazine, pp. 38–40.

Welles, Merida. "Ivo Pogorelich: Piano Fortissimo." *International Herald Tribune*, 19 June 1981, p. 16.

Zukerman, Eugenia. "Pogorelich: the fire breather." *Vogue*, April 1984, p. 111.

See also Bibliography: Cur/Bio (1988); Dub/Ref; Mac/Gr2.

SELECTED REVIEWS

BG: 29 Aug 1983. *CPD*: 11 Nov 1984; 9 Jan 1989. *CSM*: 2 May 1984; 5 March 1986. *CT*: 18 Feb 1983; 29 Oct 1984; 7 Feb 1986. *DFP*: 1 Nov 1984. *LAHE*: 26 Aug 1983; 21 Jan 1989. *LAT*: 18 July 1981; 26 Aug 1983; 20 Nov 1984; 20 Feb 1986; 9 Feb 1988; 19 Jan 1989; 1 May 1990; 2 June 1994; 24 March 1995. *LIN*: 18 Feb 1988. *MA*: Oct 1984. *MT*: Nov 1982; April 1985; Jan 1987. *NW*: 1 June 1981. *NY*: 7 May 1984. *NYT*: 20 May 1981; 13 April 1984; 23 Feb 1986; 13 Jan 1989; 16 March 1992; 18 May 1994. *SFC*: 12 Feb 1986; 5 March 1992; 14 April 1993. *SFE*: 11 Feb 1986; 4 May 1990. *S-L*: 5 April 1993. *SMU*: 29 Aug 1983. *STL*: 17 May 1987. *TL*: 23 April 1981; 17 June 1981; 23 Sept 1981; 2 Oct 1981; 16 Sept 1982; 24 Nov 1982; 11 June 1984; 19 Feb 1985; 18 June 1986; 8 Nov 1986; 17 May 1987; 14 May 1992; 12 Nov 1992. *WP*: 25 March 1993. *WSJ*: 2 July 1981.

SELECTED DISCOGRAPHY

Bach: English Suite No. 2 in A Minor, BWV 807; English Suite No. 3 in G Minor, BWV 808. DG 415 480-2.

Beethoven: Sonata in C Minor, op. 111. Schumann: Symphonic Etudes, op. 13; Toccata, op. 7. DG 410520-2.

Chopin: Concerto No. 2 in F Minor, op. 21; Polonaise in F-sharp Minor, op. 44. DG 410 507-2. Abbado/Chicago SO.

Chopin: Etudes, op. 10, nos. 8 and 10, op. 25, no. 6; Nocturne in E-flat Major, op. 55, no. 2; Prelude in C-sharp Minor, op. 45; Scherzo in C-sharp Minor, op. 39; Sonata No. 2 in B-flat Minor, op. 35. DG 415 123-2.

Chopin: Preludes, op. 28. DG 429 227-2.

Liszt: Sonata in B minor. Scriabin: Sonata No. 2, op. 19. DG 429 391-2.

Pogorelich in Concert. Chopin: Ballade in F Major, op. 38; Etudes in F Major, op. 10, no. 8, A-flat Major, op. 10, no. 10, G-sharp Minor, op. 25, no. 6; Mazurkas, op. 59; Nocturne in E-flat Major, op. 55, no. 2; Polonaise in F-sharp Minor, op. 44; Preludes, op. 28, nos. 21-24; Prelude in C-sharp Minor, op. 45; Scherzo in C-sharp Minor, op. 39. Master 23 004 (CD). Recorded live in Warsaw, 30 Oct 1980.

Ravel: *Gaspard de la nuit.* Prokofiev: Sonata No. 6 in A Major, op. 82. DG 413363-2.

Scarlatti: Sonatas: D Minor, K. 1; G Minor, K. 8; D Minor, K. 9; C Minor, K. 11; G Major, K. 13; E Major, K. 20; B Minor, K. 87; E Minor, K. 98; D Major, K. 119; E Major, K. 135; C Major, K. 159; E Major, K. 380; G Minor, K. 450; C Major, K. 487; B-flat Major, K. 529. DG 435 855-2.

Tchaikovsky: Concerto No. 1 in B-flat Minor, op. 23. DG 415 122-2. Abbado/London SO.

VIDEO

Ivo Pogorelich. Chopin: Nocturne in E-flat Major, op. 55, no. 2; Polonaise in C Minor, op. 40, no. 2; Prelude in C-sharp Minor, op. 45; Sonata No. 3 in B Minor, op. 58. Haydn: Sonata in A-flat Major, Hob. XVI:46. Mozart: Sonata in A Major, K. 331. *Deutsche Grammophon* 072 217-3.

Ivo Pogorelich in Villa Contarini. Chopin: Polonaise in F-sharp Minor, op. 44; Prelude, op. 28, no. 21; Sonata No. 2 in B-flat Minor, op. 35. Scriabin: Two Poems, op. 32; Etude in F-sharp Minor, op. 8, no. 2. *Deutsche Grammophon* 072 245-3.

✤ ✤ ✤

POLLINI, MAURIZIO: b. Milan, Italy, 5 January 1942.

> Pollini stands as an example of a wholly modern kind of artistry, a kind which less adventurous spirits do not try to emulate, and which even those with similar ambitions can scarcely hope to match.
>
> David Fanning (*Gramophone*, May 1989)

Maurizio Pollini was known as a child prodigy, and small wonder! As a youngster he could memorize a 10-page piano composition in 15 minutes; at age 11 he gave a public recital; at 14 he played the complete Chopin Etudes in concert; at age 15 he placed second at the 1957 Geneva International Competition (no first prize was given); and at 17 he was awarded first place in the *Concorso Pianistico Internazionale 'Ettore Pozzoli.'*

His father Gino Pollini, a pioneer in contemporary architectural design, played the violin; and his mother Renata (Melotti) Pollini was a singer. Pollini remembers, "My parents were deeply musical, I loved music from the earliest age. My musical interests weren't specifically pianistic; if anything, I was fascinated by the orchestra." (Botsford) At age five, Pollini began piano lessons with Carlo Lonati. Many years later Pollini spoke of his teachers. "Lonati was a very good teacher. I studied with him until I was 13, and then with Carlo Vidusso [at the Milan Conservatory] five years. They gave me a good instrumental basis, and with them I was very soon free to play a great part of the repertoire. . . . In 1961, I had a few lessons from Michelangeli, who gave me some helpful advice for the sound and the technique." (Horowitz)

After Pollini graduated (1959) from the Milan Conservatory, Vidusso urged him to enter the prestigious International Chopin Piano Competition in Warsaw. That year (1960) Pollini was the youngest foreign entrant in a field of about 80 contestants, but the jury (which included Nadia Boulanger, Dmitri Kabalevsky, Witold Malcuzynski, and Artur Rubinstein) unanimously awarded him first place. This terse statement by Rubinstein echoed the feelings of the others: "Technically he already plays better than any of us on the jury."

Even before the announcement of his victory, EMI of England offered Pollini a recording contract. It was finally signed in Milan two weeks after the competition, and within a month Pollini was in London recording his competition concerto (the Chopin E Minor) with Paul Kletzki and the London Philharmonia Orchestra. The recording has since become a classic of its kind (see Discog.).

Despite his exciting success Pollini, aware that he was not mature enough as a musician, refused to commit himself to the routine of regular concert tours. As he explained, "After I won the Chopin competition, I was naturally enough asked to play Chopin the whole time, and it was partly to get away from that kind of concentration on one composer, that I went away to study and make my repertory as wide as possible." (Blyth) He canceled a projected tour of the United States arranged by impresario Sol Hurok, remained "on sabbatical" for almost seven years and emerged in 1968 ready to compete against the foremost pianists of the time. Since then, Pollini has established a major international career—in Europe, Great Britain, the United States and Japan.

A shy man, Pollini grants few interviews, and even these are sketchy. In between the 35 to 50 or so concerts he plays a year, he lives in Milan with his wife Marilisa. He finds relaxation in playing cards, swimming and chess. A Marxist in his youth, Pollini was once (at a "Concert for Peace in Vietnam" given near the end of the Vietnam War) hissed off the stage as he attempted to read an anti-American manifesto. In today's political atmosphere, while perhaps still adhering to the tenets of pure communism, Pollini prefers to remain silent.

An ardent advocate of contemporary culture, Pollini, through lectures and specially designed concerts, has done much to promote contemporary music. He feels as strongly committed to composers like Schoenberg, Webern, Stockhausen, Boulez and Nono as he does to composers of the Romantic or Classic schools. In 1974, commemorating the centenary year of Arnold Schoenberg's birth, Pollini performed Schoenberg's complete solo piano music in several important music centers, earning high praise for his clarity of expression, the refinement and freshness of his pianism, and his great desire to bring this music to public attention.

Pollini's stupendous repertoire includes most of the 19th-century standard repertoire—Beethoven, Chopin, Schumann, Schubert—and also a great number of 20th-century works—by Stravinsky, Bartók, Schoenberg, Prokofiev, Boulez and others. He is one of today's most convincing interpreters of contemporary keyboard repertoire. Critics, even those who are not totally comfortable with contemporary music, have been won over by Pollini's artistry and great understanding of 20th-century music idioms. Pollini is equally successful with the music of Chopin and other 19th-century composers. In fact, James Methuen-Campbell states unequivocally that "Maurizio Pollini is the greatest pianist, and the greatest Chopin player, to have emerged from Italy since the Second World War." (Met/Cho, see Bibliog.)

Maurizio Pollini's playing has countless admirers and comparatively few detractors. An admirer writes: "He is closest to the modern, linear, no-nonsense school of young virtuosos, yet even here his sensitivity, maturity and breadth of interests make him very much his own man." (*NYT*, 13 March 1977) Detractors dislike his objective, analytical approach. For example, "Pollini's reputation as an 'intellectual' player probably comes from this: that he seems to want to know every chord, every note, every colour, every rhythm he produces. The mind refuses to let the fingers get away with what comes naturally to them." (Griffiths) Nevertheless, Pollini is a consummate musician. His technical powers are unsurpassed, his lyrical gifts commanding, his choice of programming (Beethoven and Boulez sonatas on one recital!) energizing.

A keen observer sums up Pollini's playing thusly: "Even in an age when a juggernaut technique tends to be taken for granted, Pollini's is outstanding. Triphammer octaves, high-velocity passage work, densely woven inner voices, all are managed with breathtaking ease and control. . . . Stylistically, he favors clean, sharp-edged, objective interpretations, free of flourishes and exaggerations even in the most romantic repertory. . . . Everything he does arises from such a deep, individualized conception, and is brought off with such musicality and unforced virtuosity, that it carries its own commanding authority." (*Time*, 21 April 1980)

Another writer sees Pollini as "a great keyboard artist of the rarest sort—one who plays with note-perfect accuracy and meticulous respect for the composer's intentions while asserting his own highly personal ideas and feelings about the music." (Michener)

A long, fine essay in the *New York Times Magazine* (1 March 1987) is one of the best commentaries yet to be written about Maurizio Pollini, and is *must* reading for anyone seeking an in-depth discussion. The author finds three special characteristics that distinguish Pollini from other living pianists. "The first is performance: you go to hear Horowitz or Ashkenazy as pianists; when Pollini plays, you go to hear Chopin or Beethoven. It is the music that counts, not the performer. The second is a matter of repertory. Pollini's is vast in range, giving equal importance to the literature of the past and present. . . . The third is style. Pollini's is elegant, clear, lucid and specifically modern."

In 1968 Pollini played an all-Chopin program (26 Sept 1968) at London's Elizabeth Hall. One critic remembers this as "one of the greatest concert performances of his life so far. It seemed as though Pollini had steeled himself to the realities of the performing world by rigid discipline, and practice. His technique had become his armour, and the actual tone of the piano not a mirror but a sword." (Widdicombe)

Pollini made his New York concerto debut (1 Nov 1968) at Carnegie Hall, playing the Chopin Concerto No. 2 with the Detroit Symphony Orchestra, conducted by Sixten Ehrling. "It was not a particularly auspicious debut, in fact not a very imaginative performance. It not only was too literal, but it also lacked the rise and fall of phrase. Passagework tended to sound like scales. . . . With all his skill, Mr. Pollini failed to suggest that he was deeply involved in the music." (*NYT*, 2 Nov 1968)

His New York recital debut at Hunter College (16 Nov 1968)—a program of works by Chopin, Bartók, Schoenberg and Stravinsky—received cautious praise: "The 26-year-old Italian has about as swift and steely a set of fingers as any pianist today. . . . Mr. Pollini played the G minor Ballade beautifully, if somewhat coolly . . . [and] produced exquisite sonorities in the penultimate movement of 'Out of Doors' (Bartók). Then he played the work's toccata-like final movement, and the fireworks began. . . . Then the blockbuster came— Stravinsky's 'Petrouchka' pieces. The performances were dazzling. Mr. Pollini's drive and endurance seemed inexhaustible, and the audience was overwhelmed. Can he play Beethoven? Does he play Bach? Who cares when he plays Chopin, Bartók and Stravinsky so splendidly." (© *The New York Times Company*, 18 Nov 1968. Reprinted by permission.)

At a London recital (20 Oct 1974) Pollini played (in addition to a Beethoven sonata and the Schubert "Wanderer" Fantasy) the complete piano works of Schoenberg, "a recital in themselves, with absolute accuracy, clarity and sense. He left no doubt where the metre 'shifts', i.e. from 3/4 to 6/8, and he differentiated clearly between principal lines and subsidiary parts, and between legato and staccato parts. It was probably one of the most eloquent tributes to Schoenberg heard during the centenary celebration." (*MT*, Dec 1974)

Schoenberg's music seems almost conventional when compared with Luigi Nono's *Sofferte onde serene*, a work written for Pollini and often performed by him. It appeared on a Festival Hall program (8 Oct 1979) along with music by Chopin and Liszt. "The Nono piece," wrote one reviewer, "has the pianist in dialogue with a pre-recorded tape, a morass of echoes, thuds and splashes which I cannot profess to have assimilated or understood, yet found exhilarating in comparison with more conventional seascapes, and breathtaking in Pollini's execution." (*MT*, Dec 1979) When Pollini played (5 March 1982) this same composition for a recital at New York's Avery Fisher Hall, "A number of people marched out, loudly, during the Nono. But it is still admirable to try to confront piano buffs with the music of our time, and perhaps some who stayed had their ears opened." (*NYT*, 7 March 1982)

Even playing a more standard repertoire, Pollini can still provide unconventional programs. The first half of a Boston recital (22 March 1987) featured Chopin works composed between 1843 and 1845—two nocturnes, three mazurkas, the *Polonaise-fantaisie* and the Barcarolle. In the view of one critic, "Pollini's superbly regulated technique has a built-in disadvantage—it can smooth too many things out, make too many rough places plain. This happened a bit too often in the opening Chopin group, which eliminated elements of contrast that are composed into the music." The last part of the program consisted of all 12 of the Debussy Etudes: "When the etudes are played as Pollini did, they sound even more full of the colorful play of imagination than Debussy's most famous pieces." (*BG*, 23 March 1987. Reprinted courtesy of *The Boston Globe*)

Paradoxically, the exact same program played (26 Oct 1987) at London's Festival Hall was a disappointment to a critic who felt that Pollini had not fulfilled his original potential, that his was not great Chopin playing and "even in the rarified sound-world of Debussy's Etudes he was not entirely at ease. . . . Pollini managed to make *Pour les octaves* actually sound like the study it is not, rather than the brilliant concert waltz it is." (*FT*, 27 Oct 1987)

Then there is this critique of an all-Chopin recital (18 March 1990) in Chicago's Orchestra Hall: "He is a mature pianist at the peak of his form. Few artists have as splendid a technique under such firm control. . . . And few are better prepared to argue a case for Chopin as a serious composer—not a mere purveyor of salon-miniatures." (*CT*, 19 March 1990)

Pollini's 1992–93 recital programs included the incredible Boulez Sonata No. 2, but his San Francisco recital on 4 April 1993 was entirely conventional—two Beethoven sonatas (F-sharp Minor, op. 78, F Minor, op. 57) and one Schubert sonata (G Major, D. 894). A reviewer regretfully noting the absence of the Boulez Sonata nevertheless continued, "The authority of Pollini's playing remains a wonder, even if his readings do not attain any great individuality. . . . Every bar Pollini attacks possesses a rounded quality and an even, translucent sonority. There is no blur or fuzziness in even the most heavily pedaled passage, yet the sound envelops the listener. There is no loss of musical line or inaudibility when the score dips down to a pianissimo." (*SFE*, 5 April 1993)

Pollini's recordings have won many prestigious international awards: a 1979 Grammy Award for his recording of the Bartók Concertos with the Chicago Symphony Orchestra and Claudio Abbado; the 1979 *Grand Prix International du Disque* for his recording of the Webern Piano Variations and Boulez's Second Piano Sonata; the *Prix Caecilia Bruxelles*; the *Deutscher Schallplattenpreis*; and *Gramophone's* Award for Best Instrumental Record of 1977 (late Beethoven Sonatas).

Pollini, an exclusive recording artist for *Deutsche Grammophon* since 1971, has recorded works by Bartók, Beethoven, Boulez, Chopin, Liszt, Prokofiev, Schoenberg, Schubert, Schumann, Stravinsky and Webern. His recording of the complete solo piano music of Arnold Schoenberg (see Discog.) is a masterwork of virtuosity and musicianship. The clarity and the incredible observance of each expressive indication in the score stand as a tribute to the composer and his concepts. "No pianist has set out on this journey with the elegance of these readings of Op. 11, nor completed the traversal with such security and firm sense of direction, and even the occasional flash of humor." (*Fan*, Nov/Dec 1988)

Equally impressive is Pollini's recording of music by Boulez, Prokofiev, Stravinsky and Webern, a reissue on CD of music originally recorded in 1972 and 1978. A typical appraisal appeared in *Gramophone* (Nov 1986): "His recording of *Petrushka*, already legendary, goes so far into the realms of the uncanny as to beggar description. . . . Hearing the performance [Prokofiev Sonata No. 7] as a whole, it is remarkable how Pollini brings out the desolation behind its propulsiveness, the chill behind its warmth, and all with coruscating pianistic flair. . . . On to the Webern *Variations* and another performance of the most phenomenal precision and acute expressive poise, every note precisely weighted, coloured, above all felt. . . . Fifteen years ago I would have doubted the sanity of anyone professing admiration for the Boulez Second Sonata. . . . But abandoning oneself to the sweep of Pollini's virtuosity, I cannot believe that the fierce purity of this titanic anti-sonata will leave many listeners indifferent." (Reprinted by permission.)

Pollini's understanding of the Chopin "style" gives his readings of the Sonatas (see Discog.) a compelling authority. "Though aware that Chopin would not be Chopin without rubato, he never allows it to undermine the music's structure." (*Gram*, Aug 1986) The Pollini CD of Chopin Sonatas Nos. 2 and 3 was named a Recording of Distinction by *Ovation* (May 1987), the reviewer commenting that, "as on all of his recordings, his breath-taking technical control serves not for display but rather for the elucidation of the music's structure. . . . Still, for all their formal rigor, these are emotionally compelling performances." Pollini's magnificent 1960 LP recording of the Chopin Concerto No. 1 in E Minor is back on the shelves in a beautiful CD also containing several solo works (see Discog.). A review of the LP version of the concerto points out Pollini's amazing articulation, rhythm, pedaling and phraseology: "Time and time again one is charmed by the evenness of Pollini's scales, the flow of his legato, the way he maintains continuity of line." (*ARG*, May 1961).

Pollini's recording of the Liszt Sonata in B Minor (see Discog.) is technically flawless and beautifully structured. What is unexpected—given Pollini's sometime reputation for cool, intellectual readings—is the pure passion projected. "It seems not so much that Pollini has got inside the soul of the music but that the music has got inside him and used him, without mercy, for its own ends. . . . While the pianism can soberly be described as sensational, it is never sensationalist. Its expressive and virtuosic extremes are always subordinate to wholeness of vision." (*Gram*, July 1990)

Pollini's various Schubert recordings compare favorably with those by Alfred Brendel, even those by Schnabel. Pollini's "romanticism" may not always equal that of others in variety of color and command of *rubato*, but it is nonetheless beautiful to hear. In his recording pairing the famed "Wanderer" Fantasy with the Sonata in A Minor, D. 845 (see Discog.), the Sonata "is a reading of controlled passion with an extraordinary tension between dynamic freedom and remorseless rhythmic grip—a wholly modern, wholly compelling conception. His *Wanderer* conveys a liquid quality in the slow movement and an effortless virtuosity overall which are unrivalled, the finale arpeggios and first movement octaves not so much breath-taking as jaw-dropping." (*Gram*, Aug 1987)

Recordings of the five Beethoven concertos are no longer a rarity. However, among those available, the interpretations of Pollini and the Vienna Philharmonic Orchestra (see Discog.) stand, if not at the very top, very close indeed. We still have the glorious performances by Leon Fleisher, Artur Schnabel and Wilhelm Kempff, but Pollini is a leading contender in his generation. Technically and musically this is superb playing—exceptional concerto playing and exceptional Beethoven. And a new complete set, taken from 1992–93 live performances with Claudio Abbado and the Berlin Philharmonic Orchestra, is equally attractive.

Pollini's CD of late Beethoven sonatas (Grammy, 1978) contains wonderful performances recorded in 1976 and 1978. The "*Hammerklavier*," op. 106, in particular is notable for the pianist's dazzling technical command and musicianship. "Not only can he stand up to the accumulated momentum, but he can also build on it so as to leave the impression of one huge exhalation of creative breath. . . . In the last three sonatas there are others who stop to peer deeper into some of the psychic chasms, but Pollini's mastery of integration and continuous growth, and his ability to hold potentially conflicting musical demands in balance, are again sources of wonder." (*Gram*, July 1990)

SELECTED REFERENCES

Blyth, Alan. "Maurizio Pollini." (interview) *Gramophone*, May 1975, p. 1045.

Botsford, Keith. "The Pollini Sound." *New York Times Magazine*, 1 March 1987, pp. 30, 46–47, 53, 81.

Fanning, David. "Maurizio Pollini." (interview) *Gramophone*, May 1989, pp. 1711–1712.

―――. "Pollini." *Gramophone*, Feb 1990, p. 1440.

Griffiths, Paul. "Key to a Mastermind's Skill." *London Times*, 2 June 1990, p. 40.

Horowitz, Joseph. "Pollini's 'Modern' Pianism." *New York Times*, 1 April 1979, sec. 4, pp. 23–24.

Mellor, David. "All in good time." *Gramophone*, Aug 1994, pp. 20–21.

Michener, Charles. "Piano Conversations." *Newsweek*, 16 April 1979, p. 70.

Oestreich, James R. "If Apollo Had Played the Piano Instead of a Lyre. . ." *New York Times,* 21 March 1993, sec. 2, pp. 27–28.

Page, Tim. "Pollini: Shy, Intense, 'the Best'." *Long Island Newsday*, 29 March 1988, sec. 2, p. 3.

"Reluctant Cinderella." *Time*, 21 April 1980, p. 96.

Rockwell, John. "Pollini—The Prodigy Has Reached Maturity." *New York Times*, 13 March 1977, sec. 2, p. 22.

―――. "Who Says Modern Pianists Are Un-Romantic?" *New York Times*, 3 June 1984, sec. 2, p. 23.

Swed, Mark. "No-Nonsense Pianist Maurizio Pollini." *Wall Street Journal*, 31 March 1988, p. 20.

Widdicombe, Gillian. "Maurizio Pollini." (interview) *Records and Recording*, Dec 1974, pp. 14–15.

See also Bibliography: Cur/Bio (1980); IWWM; New/Gro; Nie/Mei; Ran/Kon; Rat/Cle; Rub/MyM; Sch/Gre.

SELECTED REVIEWS

ARG: July/Aug 1993. *BG*: 23 March 1987; 26 Feb 1990. *BH*: 26 Feb 1990. *CSM*: 1 May 1985. *CST*: 1 March 1982; 19 March 1990. *CT*: 1 March 1982; 28 March 1988; 19 March 1990; 23 March 1993. *GM*: 28 Oct 1991. *LADN*: 14 March 1991. *LAHE*: 29 March 1980; 18 March 1982. *LAT*: 16 March 1978; 2 April 1993. *MA*: Feb 1969. *MM*: Feb 1974; Jan 1978. *MT*: Dec 1974; March 1977; July 1980; Jan 1985; Dec 1985. *NY*: 27 April 1981; 22 March 1982 11 April 1983. *NYP*: 19 Feb 1976; 17 March 1980; 28 March 1987. *NYT*: 2 Nov 1968; 18 Nov 1968; 7 March 1982; 27 March 1987; 16 March 1989; 26 March 1992; 9 March 1993. *PI*: 22 March 1991; 14 March 1993. *SFC*: 19 March 1991; 31 March 1992; 6 April 1993. *SFE*: 19 March 1991; 5 April 1993. *TL*: 27 Oct 1987; 26 Oct 1990; 28 Oct 1991; 20 Dec 1991; 6 Nov 1992; 5 Nov 1993. *WP*: 13 March 1989.

SELECTED DISCOGRAPHY

Bartók: Concerto No. 1; Concerto No. 2. DG 415 371-2. Abbado/Chicago SO.
Beethoven: Concertos (complete). DG 419 793-2 (3 CDs). Jochum (1, 2), Böhm (3-5)/ Vienna PO.
Beethoven: Concertos (complete). DG 439 770-2 (3 CDs). Abbado/Berlin PO.
Beethoven: Late Piano Sonatas. Sonata in A Major, op. 101; Sonata in B-flat Major, op. 106; Sonata in E Major, op. 109; Sonata in A-flat Major, op. 110; Sonata in C Minor, op. 111. DG 419 199-2 (2 CDs).
Boulez: Sonata No. 2. Prokofiev: Sonata No. 7, op. 83. Stravinsky: Three Movements from *"Petrouchka."* Webern: Variations for Piano, op. 27. DG 419 202-2.
Brahms: Concerto No. 1 in D Minor, op. 15. DG (Galleria) 419 470-2. Böhm/Vienna PO.
Chopin: Concerto No. 1 in E Minor, op. 11; Ballade No. 1 in G Minor; Nocturnes, op. 15, nos. 1–2, op. 27, nos. 1–2; Polonaise, op. 53. EMI Classics CDM-64354. Recorded in 1960 and 1968. Kletzki/Philharmonia.
Chopin: Etudes (op. 10, op. 25). DG 413 794-2.
Chopin: Sonata No. 2 in B-flat Minor, op. 35; Sonata No. 3 in B Minor, op. 58. DG 415 346-2.
Liszt: Sonata in B Minor; *Nuages gris*; *Unstern-Sinistre*; *R.W. Venezia*; *La lugubre gondola.* DG 427322-2.
Mozart: Concerto in F Major, K. 459; Concerto in A Major, K. 488. DG 429-812-2. See also Video. Böhm/Vienna PO.
Nono: *Como una ola de fuerza y luz* (soprano, piano, orchestra and tape); *Contrepunto dialettico alla mente* (voices and tape); *Sofferte onde serene* (piano and tape). DG 423248-2. Abbado/Bavarian RSO.

Schoenberg: The Piano Music. Three Piano Pieces, op. 11; Six Little Piano Pieces, op. 19; Five Piano Pieces, op. 23; Suite for Piano, op. 25; Piano Piece op. 33a; Piano Piece op. 33b. DG 423 249-2.

Schubert: Allegretto in C Minor, D. 915; *Drei Klavierstücke*, D. 946; Sonata in C Minor, D. 598; Sonata in A Major, D. 959; Sonata in B-flat Major, D. 960. DG 419 229-2 (2 CDs).

Schubert: Fantasy in C Major, D. 760 ("Wanderer"); Sonata in A Minor, D. 845. DG 419 672-2.

Schumann: *Davidsbündlertänze, op. 6*; *Kreisleriana*, op. 16. Exclusive EX92T31 (CD).

Schumann: Fantasia in C Major, op. 17; Sonata No. 1 in F-sharp Minor, op. 11. DG 423 134-2.

VIDEO

Brahms: Concerto No. 2 in B-flat Major, op. 83. DG 440 072 293-3. Abbado/Vienna PO.

Mozart: Concerto in F Major, K. 459; Concerto in A Major, K. 488. DG 440 072 202 -3. Böhm/Vienna PO.

RACHMANINOFF, SERGEI VASSILIEVITCH: b. Novgorod, Russia, 1 April 1873; d. Beverly Hills, California, 28 March 1943.

> He was not only a great composer and a great artist, but also a great gentleman. The words of Shakespeare come to mind as being fitting to Rachmaninoff. 'He was a man; take him for all in all, we shall not look upon his like again.'
>
> A. M. Henderson (*Etude*, April 1954)

He had already, within his lifetime, been designated "the great Rachmaninoff." Since his death he has become, more than any other pianist, the idol of later generations of concert pianists. And even now, a half-century after his death, Sergei Rachmaninoff still reigns as the ultimate pianist.

Born on an estate in Oneg, in the Novgorod district, until he was nine years old Rachmaninoff lived in the easy, cultivated environment of Russia's landowning gentry. Everyone in his family seemed to be musical to some degree. Arkady Rachmaninoff, his grandfather, had studied piano with John Field and played "brilliantly," but of course not for money, only at social soirees and charity events. Vassily Rachmaninoff, his father, also played the piano; and his mother Lubov (Boutakova) Rachmaninoff reputedly had lessons with Anton Rubinstein.

Rachmaninoff had some piano instruction from his mother, starting at about age four, and later began regular lessons with Anna Ornatskaya, a student from the St. Petersburg Conservatory. He was about eight the year his father, unfortunately a gambler and inept manager, lost Oneg, the last of six estates constituting Lubov Boutakova's rich dowry, thus abruptly ending Rach-maninoff's happy, comfortable life in the country. One upsetting event followed another. Of necessity, the family moved into a flat in St. Petersburg; not long after, the parents separated, the children staying with their mother; and thereafter Rachmaninoff rarely saw his father.

There was money only for essentials, but Ornatskaya found a scholar-ship for Sergei in the junior division of the St. Petersburg Conservatory, where Vladimir Demiansky was to prepare him for advanced study with Gustav Cross, Ornatskaya's own teacher. One can only speculate as to why that did not hap-pen. Considering Rachmaninoff's innate musical instincts and splendid talents, it is puzzling that he was not a recognized child prodigy. Even more puzzling is his absolutely dismal record at the St. Petersburg Conservatory. He was inatten-tive and often truant, yet the pre-teen Rachmaninoff was always chosen to per-form at student concerts, so he must have been playing exceptionally well. Nevertheless, he was due to be expelled at the end of his third year. One theory says that his parents' separation caused his bad behavior. Another theory ex-plains that the precocious Rachmaninoff was so far advanced that he simply grew bored.

His anxious mother sought advice from her nephew, pianist Alexander Siloti, and, after hearing Rachmaninoff play, Siloti used his influence to get Rachmaninoff accepted in the lower division of the Moscow Conservatory as a student of Nikolai Sverev, Siloti's own teacher. Rachmaninoff, age 12, had reached a major turning point in his life. Studying with Nikolai Zverev, he quickly discovered, meant iron discipline, constant supervision and a regular rou-tine of practice. Besides all the hard work, he had to live in Zverev's apartment (along with two other pupils, customary in that era), which meant that his teacher controlled every aspect of his life.

Zverev was far more concerned with the music than with simply per-fecting a student's piano playing. To that end, he took his charges to concerts and operas and, to make them familiar with the great orchestral and chamber works of the classical tradition, he made them play, from memory, four-hand pi-ano arrangements of these great works, either with each other or with a hired pi-anist. Thanks to Zverev, that first academic year Rachmaninoff heard Anton Rubinstein's seven "historical" recitals, played in Moscow in January and Feb-ruary 1886, and for the rest of his life promoted Rubinstein as the greatest of all pianists.

Never in his life had Rachmaninoff worked so hard, never been so stim-ulated. And he blossomed, advancing so rapidly in one year that he was awarded a Rubinstein Scholarship and began appearing in student concerts. In 1886 he entered Anton Arensky's harmony class and in 1888 moved into the senior de-partment of the Conservatory, where he studied piano with Siloti, a new member of the faculty. Hard-working and serious, Rachmaninoff had become one of the school's best pianists and certainly was its most exciting pianist. But all along he had also been composing, and it was understood (in 1889 he received the highest possible grade in music theory) that he would become a composer, not a pianist. Seeking quiet and privacy for composing, in the fall of 1889 (he would be studying counterpoint with Sergei Taneyev and harmony and orchestration with Anton Arensky) Rachmaninoff asked Zverev if he might have a private room in the apartment with a piano for his use alone. That seemingly reasonable request so enraged Zverev that he ordered Rachmaninoff to leave the apartment.

At age 16 Rachmaninoff had reached yet another turning point in his life. Taken in by the Satins (his maternal aunt and her husband), he not only had his own room and privacy to compose, but for the first time since leaving Oneg, Rachmaninoff had a real—and very happy—family life. In the summer of 1890 the Satins took him to Ivanovka, their large family estate near Tambov, some 200 miles southeast of Moscow, and for Rachmaninoff, having been confined for four years to the close quarters of Zverev's apartment, it was like a homecoming. Ivanovka filled a large void in his life, and for the next quarter of a century it was "his beloved summer retreat and an irreplaceable source of spiritual refreshment." (Martyn)

Siloti resigned at the end of the 1890–91 academic year, and Rachmaninoff, not wanting to sign on with a new piano teacher, boldly requested permission to take the examination for his piano diploma a year early, even though in just three weeks he would have to learn two large works: Beethoven's *"Waldstein"* Sonata and the first movement of Chopin's Sonata in B-flat Minor. His request approved, Rachmaninoff passed the 1891 piano examination with highest honors. In 1892, for his final examination in composition, he had to compose an opera, in piano score, based on a story by Alexander Pushkin. Within a month the remarkable 19-year-old turned in his opera, titled *Aleko*, not simply in piano score, but fully orchestrated; and he passed with highest honors.

After leaving the Conservatory all his efforts went into composing, but he earned money with the piano, sometimes teaching piano lessons and occasionally playing in concerts. For example, on 26 September 1892 Rachmaninoff performed at the Moscow Electrical Exhibition, playing the first movement of Rubinstein's Concerto No. 4 in D Minor, some works by Chopin, some by Liszt and some of his own works, including the newly composed Prelude in C-sharp Minor. In later life Rachmaninoff would say that his career as a pianist began with that concert. However, for a good many years his maturing talents for composing and for conducting overshadowed his piano performances.

Other early piano performances included the premiere (30 Nov 1893) of his Fantasy-Pictures (First Suite) for two pianos, performed by Rachmaninoff and Paul Pabst; and in 1895 a tour (he left before it ended) in Russia and Poland as accompanist for Teresina Tua, an Italian violinist. All of this was to earn money. His composing career was not going so well. The abject failure of his Symphony No. 1, first performed in March 1897 with Glazunov conducting, brought on such a deep depression that for three years he was unable to compose.

That same year (1897) he was hired as an assistant conductor of the Mamontov Private Opera, a company owned by a wealthy businessman, but that source of income dried up when Mamontov went into debtor's prison in 1899. In the meantime Alexander Siloti's performance of Rachmaninoff's Prelude in C-sharp Minor at a London concert in 1898 caused such a furor that the London Philharmonic Society invited Rachmaninoff to appear in London the following season in a triple role as pianist-composer-conductor. At that concert (19 April 1899) he played his famous Prelude and the *Élégie* from the same set of pieces, op. 3; he also conducted his orchestral fantasy The Rock.

His long-lasting depression had kept him from composing a new concerto for that London performance, but in 1900 treatments by Dr. Nicolai Dahl, a specialist in hypnosis and autosuggestion, finally enabled Rachmaninoff to start composing again. That summer in Italy he sketched out the outline of his Concerto No. 2 in C Minor. He finished it back home in Russia, and the instant success of this celebrated concerto lifted his spirits and restored his confidence as a composer. Greater happiness and stability came into his life with his marriage in 1902 to his cousin Natalia Satina, a daughter of the Satins who had taken him in. Irina, the Rachmaninoff's first child, was born in 1903; Tatiana was born in 1907. The family spent winters in Moscow, summers at Ivanovka.

In these years Rachmaninoff was not only composing prolifically, but for two seasons, from 1904 through 1906, he also conducted the Imperial Opera Company at the Bolshoi Theater. Although he had not abandoned the piano, he rarely, if ever, gave solo recitals; and whenever he appeared with an orchestra or with other artists, he played almost exclusively his own compositions. But Rachmaninoff was a sensational pianist and, besides, possessed an intangible mystique that overwhelmed audiences. Inevitably, he appeared more and more as a pianist.

Besieged with offers (an American tour, a return contract at the Imperial Opera, a contract to conduct 10 symphonic concerts in Moscow), Rachmaninoff refused them all because he wanted more time for composing. In November 1906 he retreated with his family to Dresden, Germany, always of course returning to Ivanovka each summer. That phase of his life ended in 1909. Having finally agreed to tour America, he once again made Moscow his base of operations.

His first American tour (about 20 performances in the Northeast) began with a rush: a solo recital (4 Nov 1909) at Smith College in Northhampton, Massachusetts; a performance (13 Nov) of his Concerto No. 2 in New York, with Max Fiedler conducting the Boston Symphony Orchestra; a recital (20 Nov) of his own piano works at Carnegie Hall; and a performance (28 Nov) of his newly written Concerto No. 3 in D Minor, with Walter Damrosch conducting the New York Symphony Orchestra. At the end of that tour, he refused all offers to stay, returned to Russia and, with profits from the tour, in 1910 took over the management of his beloved Ivanovka.

Rachmaninoff's multiple talents as pianist-composer-conductor created diverse demands on his time, all the more of a problem since he took his responsibilities most seriously. From 1909 he was for three years vice-president of the Imperial Russian Music Society, which entailed inspections of the many rural music schools. He also, between 1911 and 1913, often conducted the Moscow Philharmonic Orchestra. And, with his growing fame as a pianist, he toured all over Russia, and in Europe and England. Unable to juggle all the demands on his time, in the autumn of 1912 he went off to Italy to compose. During the First World War he played concerts for soldiers and war victims in Russia.

The 1917 Bolshevik Revolution created yet another, most drastic, turning point in Rachmaninoff's life. Fortunately, an invitation to give a series of concerts in Stockholm, Sweden, in early 1918 provided the means of getting him and his family out from under the authoritarian Bolshevik government. Unfortunately, they forfeited everything—wealth and possessions—and many of Rachmaninoff's friends believed that being uprooted forever from his homeland, especially from Ivanovka, his place of rest and renewal, accounted for his chronic sadness. Although he found great fame and wealth in the West and finally, in 1943, became an American citizen, to the day of his death Rachmaninoff remained homesick for Russia—a yearning so deep that, wherever the family set up housekeeping, he re-created to the fullest extent possible the old-world Russian atmosphere of Ivanovka—its look, furnishings, mood, food—and he spoke Russian as much as possible.

Rachmaninoff practiced from eight to ten hours daily to prepare for those 1918 concerts in Stockholm, and his enormous success made him realize that being a concert pianist was his best means of earning income and that America was the place where he could make the most money. He was already 45 years old and had played in public only a very limited piano repertoire, chiefly his own works, thus his first concern was to enlarge his performing repertoire. Thanks to the discipline developed in those years with Zverev, he prepared the necessary recital programs and arrived (with his family) in America, on 10 November 1918, to begin a new, very productive phase of his life. His reputation had preceded him. Within weeks he had acquired a manager, had a contract with Steinway to use their pianos, a contract with Edison to make gramophone recordings and a contract with Ampico to make reproducing rolls.

Almost immediately Rachmaninoff plunged into what he later would describe as his *perpetuum mobile*, an endless round of concert tours that gave him financial security and artistic satisfaction. Although he frequently complained of exhaustion, of the tension and strain of playing so often for the public, the truth is that Rachmaninoff loved to play concerts. "If you deprive me of them, I shall wither away," he told his friend A. J. Swann. Besides, although one would never guess from his grim concert-platform countenance, he loved his idolizing audiences and drew inspiration from their enthusiasm.

Rachmaninoff's new concert life began with a recital in Providence, Rhode Island, on 8 December 1918; a week later he played in Boston; then in New York played his first Carnegie Hall recital (21 Dec 1918) since the 1909–10 tour. Although he still had a fairly limited repertoire to offer other than his own works (Rachmaninoff would add to this repertoire almost every year for the rest of his concert life), his astounding technique and sincere musicianship "attracted the admiration and envy of many musicians." And he diligently built up programs. "His superb training and astonishing memory again came to his aid, and with a secretary, a manager, a piano and much appreciated help from all quarters, Rachmaninoff quickly adapted to his new life." (Walker)

His arduous schedule called for six months each year touring the United States in his private railway car, one month of each year performing (playing and conducting) in Great Britain and/or Europe, and five months resting, composing and practicing. For the next-quarter century Rachmaninoff spent winters in New

York and summers in Europe, sometimes in Dresden, more often in France, and, from 1930 to 1939, at the Villa Senar (named for the first two initials of his name, the first two of his wife's name and the family initial), an estate he purchased at Hertenstein on Lake Lucerne in Switzerland. Peaceful and beautiful, it eased some of the pain of losing Ivanovka.

Rachmaninoff's performance at the Lucerne Festival on 11 August 1939 was, as it turned out, his final appearance in Europe. Two days later, with the Hitler threat spreading over Europe, he left for New York. That autumn he marked the 30th anniversary of his American debut with a series of all-Rachmaninoff concerts performed with the Philadelphia Orchestra, conducted by Eugene Ormandy. At the first concert (26 Nov 1939) he played his revised Piano Concerto No. 1 and also the Paganini Rhapsody; the orchestra performed his Symphony No. 1 in E Minor. At the second concert (10 Dec 1939) Ormandy conducted Rachmaninoff's tone poem The Isle of the Dead, and Rachmaninoff played his Concertos Nos. 2 and 3. At the third concert (13 Dec 1939) Rachmaninoff conducted two of his own works: the Symphony No. 3 and the Choral Symphony titled The Bells.

Although gravely ill in 1940, he kept on playing. In May 1942 he gave up his home on Long Island, New York, and purchased a house in Beverly Hills, California, planning, he said, to make a farewell tour during the 1942–43 season, then retire to compose. He began a long tour in the fall of 1942, had to cancel appearances, and began again in February 1943. A concert in Knoxville, Tennessee, on 7 February 1943, proved to be Rachmaninoff's final public appearance. The rest of the tour was canceled, he returned to his home in Beverly Hills, and died of cancer on 28 March 1943, three days before his 70th birthday. Requiem Masses were celebrated at the Los Angeles Russian Orthodox Church, and he was buried in Valhalla, New York.

Composing, concertizing and conducting left Rachmaninoff little time for teaching. However, in 1933 he consented to work with Gina Bachauer. For three years she studied with him as his schedule allowed, following him to Paris, Rome, London, wherever necessary. "It was the greatest thing in my musical life," said Bachauer. "He was a wonderful teacher—not in the sense of teaching technique—but in a broader sense. For him, everything that was technique was so easy—it came naturally to him—that he had no idea how to deal with the technical problems of lesser human beings. . . . In discussing the musical content of a work, its design and architecture, he was superb. These lessons, or as I prefer to call them, discussions, were of tremendous value to me. Apart from all his illuminating words on musical interpretation, he took the time to mark my scores of his concertos with fingerings, phrasings, and pedalings." The great Rachmaninoff also gave her some very practical advice: "When performing at a concert, a musician must always have the feeling that the particular work he is playing at that moment is the greatest music ever written. Also, the performer must give the best that is in him, even if he is playing in the smallest town in the most terrible theater, even if the audience is only one person." (Bachauer)

All through school, on his later tours through Russia, on his first tour of America in 1909–10 and, apart from some Scriabin concerts in 1914–15, up until 1917 Rachmaninoff played almost exclusively his own works in public. At age 45, the year he decided to become a serious concert pianist, he began conscientiously enlarging his repertoire, each year adding a certain number of works to his programs. Barrie Martyn's comprehensive, well-documented book *Rachmaninoff: Composer, Pianist, Conductor,* the definitive source for information on Rachmaninoff's performing repertoire, lists the complete repertoire by composer (pp. 417–38) and also, under "Concert Statistics" (pp. 387–95), new works added each year. These lists show that Rachmaninoff played a great deal of Chopin and Liszt, some Beethoven, Scarlatti, Bach, Debussy, Grieg, Schubert, Schumann, very little Mozart, his own works, of course, and some by his Russian contemporaries.

Rachmaninoff was a towering musician. "He had one of the more remarkable minds in musical history," wrote Harold Schonberg in a column commemorating the 100th anniversary of Rachmaninoff's birth, "and he was one of the greatest pianists who ever lived." (*NYT,* 1 April 1973)

Indeed few pianists have ever had the natural gifts bestowed on Sergei Rachmaninoff. He could sight-read anything and transpose at will; he had an unbelievable memory and an uncanny ability for absorbing (and retaining) a score, even long, complex ones, with just one hearing. For example, Rachmaninoff heard (from an adjoining room) Alexander Glazunov play his recently completed Symphony No. 5 on the piano. Although that was the first time Rachmaninoff had ever heard the work, as soon as Glazunov had finished, he went to the piano and played the work through. Another incident comes from the pianist and teacher Alexander Goldenweiser: "I remember how Siloti . . . told Rachmaninoff to learn the well-known Brahms *Variations and Fugue on a Theme of Handel.* This was on a Wednesday, and it was but three days later that Rachmaninoff played them like a master. It was his practice to memorize everything he heard, no matter how complicated it was." (Walker)

Rachmaninoff had another special gift. Like Paderewski, he possessed an intangible mystique that captured (some said "hypnotized") an audience the moment he appeared on the concert platform. This phenomenon had nothing to do with showmanship (on the contrary, onstage Rachmaninoff always appeared unsmiling, even grim), but there was a peculiar aura of seriousness and simplicity radiating from his presence that inevitably aroused the greatest admiration and utmost respect. Oftentimes an audience rose to its feet as one when Rachmaninoff first came out to begin a concert.

Obviously endowed with a natural technique, before he reached his teens he was playing the piano well enough to be chosen to perform at student concerts at the St. Petersburg Conservatory, and this despite the fact that he was a terrible student who ignored practicing. And stories abound about his spectacular piano playing at the Moscow Conservatory. Besides, the mature Rachmaninoff also had enormous hands, capable of spanning a twelfth, to fortify that technique. But he never depended on his natural gifts. Having decided, at age 45, to concentrate on being a professional virtuoso, he worked relentlessly to develop those innate talents into the nearly infallible technique ("the accuracy and precision of his technique were an unceasing marvel") that stunned his colleagues.

He actually enjoyed practicing, and was, he often said, a great believer in scales and arpeggios. He liked to warm up with Hanon exercises, playing them in all keys and different rhythmic patterns, and with half an hour of Czerny's Opus 740. His way of practicing, he told friends, was "to peer into every corner and take out every screw so that later it can more easily be put together into one complete whole." Rachmaninoff would take individual phrases, one after another, from the works he was preparing, change each one into an exercise and play it up and down the entire keyboard over and over again. Using a pocket metronome, he would start off at a very slow setting, never increasing the speed until he felt wholly satisfied with his performance at each stage.

Although he had a peerless technique, his was not a thunder-and-lightning virtuosity overpowering the music. To be sure, Rachmaninoff played in the grand manner, yet his playing was never exaggerated, never theatrical. Reviewers, in fact, seemed compelled to point out his remarkable intellect and his unique talent for simplicity, for being self-effacing and sensational all at the same time. For example, "No one projects a musical ideal, a dramatic emotion, with less of self-advertisement in the communication." (*NYT*, 20 Feb 1927) And this: "The gigantic simplicity of the presentation is one of the greatest attributes of this composer-pianist." (*NYT*, 28 Nov 1937)

Most particularly, Rachmaninoff's playing was distinguished for its profound integrity, its commanding, evocative power and a splendid breadth of style—a style of crystalline clarity, even in complex textures, yet always virile and rhythmically forceful. A master of the long line and the significance of details in relation to the whole, Rachmaninoff's playing, said Richard Aldrich, was "a synthesis, rather than analysis, of the vital elements that go to make up a great composition." (*NYT*, 20 Oct 1919)

Every one of his "powerfully sculptured interpretations" carried the imprint of his own personality; and they were always the same. Totally independent and trusting his own taste, Rachmaninoff never yielded to temporary influences or musical fads. Even though he often made tactful alterations of notes, and even harmonies, Rachmaninoff's playing never seemed spontaneous. In truth, once he had worked out his own elegant reading of a work, he played it that way forever. Normally, such repetition would bore audiences. With Rachmaninoff, however, the sheer force of his personality held audiences spellbound. "He was the most fascinating pianist of them all since Busoni," said Artur Rubinstein. "He had the secret of the golden, living tone which comes from the heart and which is inimitable." (Rub/MyM, see Bibliog.)

The few unfavorable criticisms—playing that was too cerebral, too severe, too harsh in tone—pertain to very early performances or some that Rachmaninoff gave while ill, often in pain. Even so, most critics agreed that he possessed vast resources of artistic and pianistic power, that until the very end he retained his impressive command over the keyboard. There are countless descriptions (in books, columns, articles) of Rachmaninoff's unique and fabulous playing. The following are especially to the point.

This was written in 1929: "It is doubtful if any pianist since Busoni possesses a mind as vigorous as Rachmaninoff's, or an equipment as all-embracing as his. He begins, apparently, where most pianists leave off; he can afford

to discard possessions to which they still must cling, and his imagination penetrates to regions which they have not yet discovered or into which they dare not
venture. He can also take little liberties with scores which might sound imper-
tinent if indulged in by players of lesser wisdom, but which, in his case, have
almost the effect of being authorized by the composers." (*MA*, 25 Feb 1929)

This was written in 1958: "Rachmaninoff's pianism represents far more
than 'an art of playing'—it should actually be called the art of 'speaking' the piano. The shortest phrase was long enough for him to convey a dramatic message. A master of intonation, punctuation, and culmination, Rachmaninoff was
able to impose his individual concepts with a despotic authority which was irresistible, whether his ideas did or did not correspond with usual preferences." (*SR*,
30 Aug 1958)

Finally, this from Harold Schonberg, written on the anniversary of
Rachmaninoff's 100th birthday: "When Rachmaninoff played, it was a unity.
Everything was perfectly planned, perfectly proportioned. Melodies were outlined with radiant authority; counterbalancing inner voices were brought out in
chamber-music style. And those marvelous fingers were incapable of striking a
wrong note. In an age of spectacular technicians, Rachmaninoff was peerless.
Complicated figurations . . . suddenly unraveled themselves in crystalline purity.
The playing was at all times elegant. But it had inevitability rather than spontaneity. Rachmaninoff never gave the impression that he was doing something
on the spur of the moment. . . . With Rachmaninoff, you felt that it would be
the same next year, and the years after that." (© *The New York Times
Company*, 1 April 1973. Reprinted by permission.)

Rachmaninoff made a number of piano rolls, recording exclusively for
Ampico. Many are available in both LP and CD format (see Discog.) and, unlike some early rolls, Rachmaninoff's are actually quite special. And the CD
transfers, said one critic, were the best transfers of piano rolls that he had heard
to date. "The bass of the instrument has a sonority that is usually lacking and
one can feel the individual style of the pianist throughout." (*Gram*, June 1990)
Another reviewer writes: "These Ampico piano recordings represent the best efforts with piano rolls thus far. In truth, Rachmaninoff does sound as though he
is in one's very presence in a way that is impossible with disc transfers going
back several decades." (*ARG*, July/Aug 1991)

Rachmaninoff's acoustic recordings, made from 1919 to 1924, number
67 sides, of which 32 were issued. Victor came out with the first electrical
recordings in March 1925, and Rachmaninoff was soon recording with the new
improved technique. He recorded his own Concerto No. 2 twice, in 1923–24
acoustically and in 1929 with the electric process, both with Leopold Stokowski
and the Philadelphia Orchestra. To accommodate the acoustic recording horns for
the early disc, the orchestra was drastically reduced, but the entire Philadelphia
Orchestra was present in all its glory for the 1929 version.

A substantial amount of Rachmaninoff's solo repertoire is now avail-
able on two CDs, with only a little duplication. One CD collection (RCA
Victor 7766-2, see Discog.) includes almost all of the electric 78s that
Rachmaninoff made of his own piano music from April 1925 to February 1942,

plus nine of his imaginative, skillful transcriptions. These performances "stand as one of the truly important legacies of the early years of the gramophone industry." (*Gram*, May 1990) Rachmaninoff's readings are models of perfection. His incredibly balanced control between melody and accompaniment is always in evidence and some of his performances, for example the *Polka de W. R.* and the *Liebesfreud*, have an almost unrestrained gaiety and effervescence. The collection stands as a memorial to both the composer and the pianist.

The other CD (GEMM 9457) is a more general collection (no Rachmaninoff original compositions) extending from the acoustic recording era (1921–24) through the early years of electric recordings (1925–36). Rachmaninoff began his long association with RCA Victor in 1920, and this CD presents a broad sampling of music from Daquin to Bizet. Naturally some of the acoustic discs (Bizet's Minuet, Tchaikovsky's Waltz, Debussy's Golliwog's Cakewalk and three Chopin Waltzes) have an inferior sound quality, but they radiate the Rachmaninoff charm and genius. In the electric recordings, his legendary technique shines through in the Scherzo from Mendelssohn's "Midsummer Night's Dream," Liszt's *Gnomenreigen* and the transcendental transcription that Tausig made of the Strauss waltz *Man lebt nur einmal.* And two Chopin Waltzes receive rhythmically exciting, musically stimulating performances that make Rachmaninoff's readings appear close to definitive. The Baroque era is vividly represented by a Bach Sarabande and Handel's "Harmonious Blacksmith" variations from the Suite No. 5. Also intriguing are Beethoven's 32 Variations in C Minor, even though because of 78 rpm space limitations the original 32 had to be reduced to 24.

To this day, Rachmaninoff's performance of the Schumann *Carnaval*, op. 9, remains a landmark in recording history. "Here is, as W. J. Henderson put it, 'genius understanding genius.' It is extraordinary, too, that the recording technicians of 1929 could have achieved such excellence of sound." (Liner notes, Fidelio 8822, see Discog.)

Rachmaninoff's magnificent performances of his four concertos and the Paganini Rhapsody are available in CD format (see Discog.): Concerto No. 2 (1929) and the Paganini Rhapsody (1934) with Leopold Stokowski and the Philadelphia Orchestra; Concerto No. 1 (1939-40), Concerto No. 3 (1939) and Concerto No. 4 (1941) with Eugene Ormandy and the same orchestra. And for Rachmaninoff devotees, his complete recordings have been reissued by RCA on a series of 10 CDs (see Discog.).

SELECTED REFERENCES

Bachauer, Gina. "My Study with Rachmaninoff." *Clavier*, Oct 1973, pp. 12–14, 16.

Belaiev, Victor. "Sergei Rakhmaninov." *Musical Quarterly*, July 1927, pp. 359–376.

Bertensson, Serge. "Rachmaninoff as I Knew Him." *Etude*, March 1948, pp. 138, 193.

Bertensson, Serge, and Jay Leyda. *Sergei Rachmaninoff, A Lifetime in Music.* New York: New York University Press, 1956.

Buketoff, Igor. "My Lessons with Rachmaninoff." (interview with Allan Kozinn). *Keyboard Classics*, Sept/Oct 1984, pp. 7–9.

――――. "The man behind the dour mask." *New York Times*, 4 April 1993, sec. 2, pp. 31, 38. Reprinted in *The AMICA Bulletin*, May/June 1993, pp. 120–122.

Chasins, Abram. "The Rachmaninoff Legacy—I." *Saturday Review*, 29 Oct 1955, pp. 37–39, 64.

――――. "The Rachmaninoff Legacy—II." *Saturday Review*, 26 Nov 1955, pp. 46, 70–72.

Culshaw, John. *Sergei Rachmaninoff.* London: Dennis Dobson, 1949.

Hill, Edward Burlingame. "Sergei Rachmaninoff." *Etude*, May 1905, p. 185.

Hodgson, Leslie. "Rachmaninoff, the Pianist." *Musical America*, 10 April 1943, pp. 6, 26, 33.

Holcman, Jan. "Hidden Treasures of Rachmaninoff." *Saturday Review*, 30 Aug 1958, pp. 31–33.

Kipnis, Igor. "Three Great Pianists on Victrola." *Stereo Review*, March 1971, p. 102.

Martyn, Barrie. *Rachmaninoff: Composer, Pianist, Conductor.* Aldershot: Scolar Press, 1990.

Moiseiwitsch, Benno. "Rachmaninoff Remembered." *The Music Magazine*, May 1962, pp. 14–15, 41.

Norris, Geoffrey. *Rakhmaninov.* London: J. M. Dent & Sons, Ltd., 1976.

Obituary. *Los Angeles Times*, 29 March 1943, p. 1. *Musical America*, 10 April 1943, pp. 7, 27. *Musical Times*, April 1943, pp. 127–128. *New York Times*, 29 March 1943, pp. 1, 11; 30 March 1943, p. 20. *San Francisco Chronicle*, 29 March 1943, p. 14.

"The Passing of a Giant." *Etude*, May 1943, pp. 291, 294.

Piggott, Patrick. *Rachmaninov.* London: Faber and Faber, 1978.

Rachmaninoff, Sergei. "The Artist and the Gramophone." *Gramophone Jubilee Book*, (Gra/Jub, see Bibliog.), pp. 99–102. Reprinted from a 1931 interview.

――――. "Interpretation Depends on Talent and Personality." *Etude*, April 1932, pp. 239–240.

――――. "Music Should Speak from the Heart." (interview with David Ewen). *Etude*, Dec 1941, pp. 804, 848.

――――. "New Lights on the Art of the Piano." *Etude*, April 1923, pp. 223–224.

――――. "Ten Important Attributes of Beautiful Pianoforte Playing." *Etude*, March 1910, pp. 153–154.

"Rachmaninoff's Trilemma." *The Times* (London), 2 April 1943, p. 6.

Riesemann, Oskar von. *Rachmaninoff's Recollections.* Freeport, New York: Books for Libraries Press, 1970.

Schonberg, Harold E. "Did Rachmaninoff Collaborate With God?" *New York Times*, 1 April 1973, sec. 2, p. 17.

Seroff, Victor. *Rachmaninoff.* London: Cassell & Co., Ltd., 1951.

Swan, A. J., and Katherine Swan. "Rachmaninoff: Personal Reminiscences, Part I." *Musical Quarterly*, Jan 1944, pp. 1–19.

————. "Rachmaninoff: Personal Reminiscences, Part II." *Musical Quarterly*,
    April 1944, pp. 174–191.
Threfall, Robert. *Sergei Rachmaninoff*. London: Boosey & Hawkes, 1973.
Tibbetts, John C. "Remembering Rachmaninoff." *American Record Guide*,
    Jan/Feb 1993, pp. 6–8, 10, 14.
Walker, Robert. *Rachmaninoff*. London: Omnibus Press, 1980.
Walsh, Stephen. "Sergei Rachmaninoff: 1873–1943." *Tempo*, June 1973, pp.
    12–21.
See also Bibliography: Ald/Con; Bro/Mas; Bro/Mod; Car/Del; Cha/Spe;
    Coo/GrP; Cur/Bio (1943); Dan/Con; Dow/Oli; Ewe/Li; Ewe/Mu; Ham/Lis;
    Kau/Art; Kol/Que; Met/Cho; MGG; New/GrA; New/Gro; Nie/Gre;
    Rub/MyM; Rub/MyY; Sch/Fac; Sch/Glo; Sch/Gre; Tho/Mus; Woo/My.

SELECTED REVIEWS

KJ: 22 Jan 1925. *MA*: 13 Nov 1909; 20 Nov 1909; 27 Nov 1909; 4 Dec 1909;
    11 Dec 1909; 1 Jan 1910; 22 Jan 1910; 17 Dec 1910; 1 Feb 1919; 26
    March 1927; 25 Feb 1928; 14 April 1928; 25 Feb 1929; 10 Jan 1935; 10
    Dec 1937. *MT*: 1 June 1922; 1 Dec 1929; 25 Feb 1931. *NYT*: 29 Nov
    1909; 17 Jan 1910; 22 Dec 1918; 24 Jan 1919; 30 Jan 1919; 20 Oct 1919;
    8 Dec 1919; 20 Dec 1920; 20 Feb 1927; 25 June 1933; 14 Jan 1936; 6 Dec
    1936; 6 Jan 1937; 28 Nov 1937; 9 Nov 1938; 13 Nov 1938; 30 Dec 1938;
    12 Nov 1939; 26 Nov 1939; 27 Nov 1939; 4 Dec 1939; 11 Dec 1939; 10
    Nov 1940; 28 Feb 1941; 2 Nov 1941; 19 Dec 1941; 8 Nov 1942; 18 Dec
    1942. *PS*: 15 March. *TL*: 8 May 1922; 22 May 1922.

SELECTED DISCOGRAPHY

The Art of Rachmaninoff. Schubert: Duo, D. 574 (with Fritz Kreisler).
    Rachmaninoff: Rhapsody on a theme of Paganini, op. 43. Schumann:
    Carnaval, op. 9. Fidelio 8822 (CD). Stokowski/PO.
Bach: Sarabande (Partita No. 4). Beethoven: 32 Variations in C Minor. Bizet:
    Minuet (*L'Arlésienne*). Chopin: Waltzes in E-flat Major, op. 18, D-flat
    Major, op. 64, no. 1, C-sharp Minor, op. 64, no. 2, A-flat Major, op. 64,
    no. 3, B Minor, op. 69, no. 2. Debussy: Golliwog's Cakewalk (Children's
    Corner). Handel: Air and Variations (Suite No. 5). Liszt: *Gnomenreigen*
    (*Etude de Concert*). Mendelssohn: Spinning Song, op. 67, no. 4; Scherzo
    op. 21, no. 2. Mussorgsky: Hopak. Schubert: Impromptu in A-flat Major,
    D. 899, no. 4. Schubert-Liszt: *Das Wandern*. Strauss-Tausig: One Lives
    but Once, op. 167. Tchaikovsky: *Troika en traineaux* (The Months); Waltz
    in A Flat, op. 40, no. 8. Pearl GEMM CD 9457.
Rachmaninoff: Complete Recordings. RCA Victor Gold Seal. 09026-61265
    (10 CDs). Winner of the 1993 Gramophone Award for a Historical record-
    ing.
Rachmaninoff: Concerto No. 2 in C Minor, op. 18 (Stokowski/Phil. Orch.);
    Concerto No. 3 in D Minor, op. 30 (Ormandy/Phil. Orch.). RCA Red Seal
    5997-2, also MHS 512525F (CD).

Rachmaninoff plays Rachmaninoff. Concerto No. 1 in F-sharp Minor, op. 1. Concerto No. 4 in G Minor, op. 40 (Ormandy/Phil. Orch.). Rhapsody on a Theme of Paganini, op. 43 (Stokowski/Phil. Orch.). RCA 6659-2, also Musical Heritage Society MHS 512705Z.

Rachmaninoff: Solo Works and Transcriptions. Rachmaninoff: Preludes, op. 3, no. 2, op. 23, no. 10, op. 32, nos. 3, 6 and 7; *Etudes-tableaux*, op. 33, nos. 2 and 7, op. 39, no. 6; *Morceaux de fantaisie*, op. 3 (*Mélodie*, Serenade); *Morceaux de salon*, op. 10 (Humoresque). *Moment musical*, op. 16, no. 2; *Polka de W. R.*; Oriental Sketch; Daisies, op. 38, no. 3; Lilacs, op. 21, no. 5. Bach: Preludio, Gavotte, Gigue (Violin Partita No. 3). Kreisler: *Liebesfreud.* Mendelssohn: Scherzo ("Midsummer Night's Dream"). Rimsky-Korsakov: The Flight of the Bumblebee. Schubert: *Wohin?* Tchaikovsky: Cradle Song, op. 16, no. 1. RCA Victor Gold Seal 7766-2.

Sergei Rachmaninoff: The Ampico Piano Recordings, 1919–29. Kreisler-Rachmaninoff: *Liebesleid*; *Liebesfreud.* Mussorgsky-Rachmaninoff: Gopak. Rachmaninoff: *Cinq morceaux de fantaisie*, op. 3; *Morceaux de salon*, op. 10 (Barcarolle, Humoresque). Prelude in G Minor, op. 23, no. 5; *Etudes-tableaux*, op. 39, nos. 4 and 6; Lilacs, op. 21, no. 5; *Polka de W. R.* Rimsky-Korsakov-Rachmaninoff: The Flight of the Bumblebee. Schubert-Rachmaninoff: *Wohin?* Smith-Rachmaninoff: The Star-Spangled Banner. London 425 964-2.

Sergei Rachmaninoff Plays Concert II. Beethoven-Rubinstein: Turkish March (The Ruins of Athens). Henselt: Were I a Bird, op. 2, no. 6. Mendelssohn: Spinning Song. Rachmaninoff: *Etude-tableau*, op. 39, no. 4; Lilacs; *Mélodie*, op. 3, no. 3. Rimsky-Korsakoff-Rachmaninoff: Flight of the Bumblebee. Rubinstein: Barcarolle No. 2. Schubert: Impromptu in A-flat Major. Schubert-Liszt: Wandering. Klavier KS 107. Recorded from Ampico piano rolls.

Sergei Rachmaninoff Plays Concert III. Bach: Sarabande (Partita No. 4). Bizet: Minuet. Chopin: Nocturne in F Major, op. 15, no. 4. Gluck-Sgambati: *Mélodie.* Paderewski: Minuet in G Major. Rachmaninoff: Barcarolle; Humoresque; Polichinelle, op. 3, no. 4; *Polka de W. R.* Tchaikovsky: *Troika en traineau*, op. 37, no. 11; Valse. Klavier KS 123. Recorded from Ampico piano rolls.

RICHTER, SVIATOSLAV TEOFILOVICH: b. Zhitomir, near Kiev, USSR, 20 March 1915.

> In the complicated and untidy sea in which we live today he swims totally alone and he is not concerned with any influences from the ugly side of life. He is like a white swan and he only goes where he wants to go.
>
> Midori Kawashimi (*Friends of Sviatoslav Richter*, Bulletin No. 10, December 1989)

"Going only where he wants to go and doing only what he wants to do" early on marked Sviatoslav Richter as a notoriously unpredictable performer. True, he has erratically canceled concerts in just about every year of his career, blaming the sometimes last-minute withdrawals on illness, depression, overscheduling, or simply his feeling that everything was not just right. True as well is the fact that he often makes program changes. And most likely it is also true (and how many times expressed in print!) that Richter is eccentric and moody. But none of this is for effect, nor is he, in any sense of the word, a flamboyant showman. A very private, very sincere and immensely honest pianist, everything Richter does musically reflects his deep conviction that what he is doing is right. Perhaps for that reason the incredible number of disappointing concert cancellations and Richter's habit of refusing to accommodate an audience have not damaged his reputation as one of this century's master pianists. In fact, Richter has a most active and faithful following: *The Friends of Sviatoslav Richter*, a society founded in his honor, publishes periodic bulletins reporting on Richter's activities (see *Preface*), and has published a "Discography 1948–1994," edited by Falk Schwarz.

Nothing in Richter's childhood or youth even hints of his great future. Anna and Teofil Richter, his parents, were musicians (his father taught piano and organ at the Odessa Conservatory) and on both sides most of his forebears were either musicians or artists. Yet Richter had a haphazard introduction to music— some early lessons with his father and, at about age six, some lessons with a Czech harpist. Strangest of all, Richter had no early conservatory training. But he had a natural and insatiable curiosity about music. By the time he was 14 years old he had worked his way through all of Wagner's operas; at age 15 he became an accompanist with the Odessa Philharmonic Society; and at age 18 he was hired as a *répétiteur* at the Odessa Opera—work from which he gained a knowledge of opera not common in a concert pianist and, more important, an intense desire to make the piano, like the vocalists, "sing." As *répétiteur*, he always tried to play as if in a concert, like an orchestra.

Not until the relatively advanced age of 18 did Richter begin seriously studying piano literature and practicing in his own untaught way. A year later, in May 1934, he felt confident enough to give his first public piano recital—an all-Chopin program presented at the House of Engineers in Odessa. Along with his other wide-ranging musical interests, he continued to practice the piano and often played at house parties.

In 1937, at the late age of 22 and still a self-taught pianist, Richter joined Heinrich Neuhaus's piano class at the Moscow Conservatory, and in less than a year, said the grateful Richter later, "Neuhaus freed my hands, really liberated them." Amazed at Richter's memory and his instinctive ability to play many different styles of music, Neuhaus wisely refrained from making drastic changes in his playing. Under Neuhaus's sensitive nurturing, Richter matured as a pianist, with his originality intact. He performed often as a student in Moscow. On 26 November 1940 he played the premier performance of Prokofiev's Piano Sonata No. 6 at the Moscow Conservatory. In July 1942 he played his first full Moscow recital, and on 18 January 1943 he gave the premier performance of Prokofiev's Sonata No. 7 at the Trade Unions Hall.

These were the years of World War II, and in 1941 German troops had invaded the Soviet Union. As a student, Richter's life apparently was not too disrupted by the war; however, his father (considered suspect because he had a German name and had given music lessons at the German consulate in Odessa) was arrested by the Soviet police and died while in custody. Richter's mother later married her late husband's younger brother, and the two of them left Odessa along with the retreating Axis troops. They eventually settled in Germany, but for nearly 18 years Richter believed that his mother, like his father, had died during the war. Mother and son were reunited in 1960.

Richter graduated from the Moscow Conservatory in 1944, and in 1945 he shared first prize in the All-Union Piano Competition in Moscow. In 1946 he married Nina Dorliak, a concert soprano and teacher, and for some years he accompanied her in recitals. He was now in his thirties, late for starting a concert career, but Richter quickly established a reputation in the Soviet Union. He made his first appearance outside of the USSR at the Prague Spring Festival in 1956, but another decade passed before he was allowed to perform in the West. Meanwhile he toured extensively behind the Iron Curtain (the Soviet Union, Czechoslovakia, Poland, Hungary, Bulgaria) and in China, in 1957.

On 29 May 1958 Richter made his first contact with musicians from the West when he joined the touring Philadelphia Orchestra and conductor Eugene Ormandy for a performance of the Prokofiev Concerto No. 5 at the Moscow Conservatory. The composition was new to the orchestra and Richter had only an hour to rehearse, nevertheless "orchestra and soloist sailed through the piece with astonishing rapport, immediately sensed by the audience. 'All the time,' said conductor Eugene Ormandy, 'electricity was flowing back and forth.' Richter gave Prokofiev's tongue-in-cheek score a kaleidoscopic range." (*Time*, 16 June 1958)

For more than a decade the USSR had recognized Richter as one of its greatest living pianists and as early as 1949 had awarded him the Stalin Prize for his contribution to Russian cultural life. Yet it was 1960 before he was allowed to perform beyond Soviet bloc countries; and then for the first few years he was forcibly accompanied by an official government "secretary." On 10 May 1960 Richter finally made his first appearance out from under the Iron Curtain—a recital of Beethoven sonatas in Helsinki, Finland. That October he toured the United States for the first time, making his American debut (15 Oct 1960) in

Chicago with a performance of the Brahms Concerto No. 2 with the Chicago Symphony Orchestra, Erich Leinsdorf conducting.

Richter's first New York recitals—five at Carnegie Hall within 12 days (19–30 Oct 1960)—drew roars from stunned audiences and rapturous reviews from four different *New York Times* critics. He made his London debut with a Festival Hall recital on 8 July 1961. With the help of fellow artists, he inaugurated (23 June 1964) the Touraine Festival, and he has often performed there at the concerts held in the magnificent *Grange de Meslay*, a 13th-century barn outside Tours. In retrospect, the 1960s may have been Richter's finest decade. He was at the height of his powers. "To the best of our knowledge no concerts were cancelled in 1965, 1966 and 1967, and in 1966 he probably played more concerts than in any of the following years apart from 1986. It was all bright and clear and the repertoire was so amazingly rich and varied that Richter really lived up to all praise and glory." (Schwartz, "The Unplayed Concerts")

In the fall of 1970 Richter took Japan by storm, playing 19 concerts with 5 different programs in 5 weeks and arousing such adulation that he has returned again and again. Utterly exhausted, he reduced his concert schedule drastically, and all through that decade crises of one sort or another (illness, depression, fatigue, the political climate) led to more and more concert cancellations and program alterations. ("The Unplayed Concerts," an article by Falk Schwarz in Bulletin No. 13 [Sept 1990] chronicles the cancellations—truly an amazing number—from 1961 through 1989.)

Richter started off the 1980s with a year marred by frequent illness and bouts of depression. And although 1981 began auspiciously with a superb tour of Japan, he had a grave letdown at that year's festival at Tours. Although he had not played Liszt's Transcendental Etudes in concert for 23 years, for some reason he included several in that Tours recital. "But what Richter only seemed to realize during the concert was that he as well had become 23 years older—and the playing just didn't work." (Bulletin No. 10, Dec 1989) The shock of not being able to get through the Liszt Etudes brought on a deep depression ("My hands want to play but my head is totally empty," Richter told friends). In just two years he canceled 40 concerts—15 in France, 13 in Italy, 12 in England. As it turned out, the performance at the 1981 Touraine Festival was the last time Richter played without music.

For the next few years there were more concerts with other musicians than solo recitals, either because Richter was too nervous, too tired or too deeply depressed to perform alone. There is also the possibility that he may have been simply indulging his delight in playing chamber music. But these were erratic years. After canceling 40 performances within just two years, Richter, who had never played more than 120 concerts in a year, in 1986 performed a staggering total of 150 concerts. He began with a tour of western Europe; toured the Soviet Union (more than 50 towns, from Novgorod in the west to Chabarovsky in the east); interrupted the Soviet tour to perform in Japan; then concluded his Soviet tour, east to west. (Bulletins No. 5, Sept 1988, and No. 6, Dec 1988, detail this remarkable tour "along the main railways in the Soviet Union.")

That concert marathon in 1986 exacted a heavy toll. Ill for most of 1987, Richter made a small comeback in 1988; in April 1989 underwent heart surgery in Zurich; and, after a long period of recuperation, played his first concert in 10 months on 29 January 1990, at Aix-en-Provence in France. That March he was taken ill again and had more surgery, this time in Munich. But Richter has refused to retire. In the early months of 1994 he toured in Japan, South Korea and Okinawa, and, although he turned 80 in March and in July had to have a pacemaker inserted, he reappeared in Milan, Italy, in early September, playing the Beethoven Concerto No. 1, with Ashkenazy conducting. The last word from *The Friends of Sviatoslav Richter* reports that Richter, as always going his own inimitable way, was performing (a program of five Beethoven sonatas) in Germany in November 1994.

The very complex Sviatoslav Richter is highly intelligent, cultivated and, depending on the writer, elusive, self-contained, inaccessible, remote or withdrawn. Without question, he is a genuine eccentric, one of his eccentricities being that he cannot enjoy hearing another pianist play a concert. Unable to stop himself from analyzing the other pianist's playing and comparing it to what he would do, he gets no enjoyment from the performance.

He has never done any teaching. His wife reports that while he feels he is not cut out to be a teacher, at the same time he wants to be in contact with young musicians, that he has a need to pass on what he knows.

In 1960 Richter received the Lenin Prize and was named People's Artist of the USSR. In Tours in 1985 France's Minister of Culture bestowed on Richter the honorary title of *Chevalier des Arts et Lettres*. In 1992 he received an honorary doctorate from Oxford University and also the Gold Medal from the Royal Philharmonic Society in London. His recording of the Brahms Concerto No. 2 with Erich Leinsdorf and the Chicago Symphony Orchestra won a Grammy award in 1960; an album of Schubert compositions received the *Grand Prix du Disque* in 1964.

Sviatoslav Richter surely fits the idea of the "born" pianist. How else could one explain his progress on the piano without benefit of traditional training until he went to Heinrich Neuhaus at the age of 22? Besides, writers and reviewers have thoroughly documented Richter's great gifts: prodigious memory, extraordinary (and fascinating!) musical mind, phenomenal sight-reading ability. Neuhaus went so far as to say that Richter could sight-read a piece for the first time—not only a piano composition but anything, whether an opera, symphony, chamber music—and immediately give an almost perfect reading. "The rhythm in Richter's performances makes one feel that the whole work, even if it is of gigantic proportions, lies before him like an immense landscape, revealed to the eye at a single glance and in all its details. . . . Such unity, such structure, such a wide musical and artistic horizon as his I have never encountered in any of the pianists I have known." (Neuhaus)

Richter has also been endowed with enormous hands capable of playing tenths and simultaneously playing thirds between thumb and forefinger. Yet for all his natural gifts, this pianist is a hard worker, so conscientious that on occasion he has remained in the concert hall after playing a recital and practiced his program for the next day's concert. He practices religiously. Even on tour he will practice three or four hours on the day of a performance, otherwise five hours a day. When not on tour, he will practice five, seven, even ten hours a day. In recent years he has tried to set a minimum daily practice time, and if he misses a day he does his utmost to make up the hours.

Inordinately self-critical, Richter practices very slowly, and with unlimited patience will repeat and repeat a problem passage until he feels he has it right. Andrei Gavrilov, who some years ago co-performed all of Handel's Suites with Richter, says that "Richter is capable of learning one bar for an hour, or two, or three hours; more than once I witnessed him while practicing playing one page at least seventy times." (Zil/Rus, see Bibliog.)

For many years Richter maintained a wide-ranging, catholic repertoire, at one point including around 40 concertos and as many different recital programs. Bulletin No. 10 (Dec 1989) of *The Friends of Sviatoslav Richter* gives a survey of the repertoire, based on some 1,400 concerts played from 1960 through 1989, and lists the specific works Richter performed in each of those years. Overall, he has mostly played Bach, Haydn, Beethoven, Schumann, Schubert, Debussy, Chopin, Brahms and of course Russian composers (Prokofiev, Rachmaninoff, Scriabin, Mussorgsky, Shostakovich). In 1986 Richter performed what he called his "testament," seven recitals, five of them devoted to a single composer (Beethoven, Brahms, Chopin, Haydn, Schumann), the rest including works by Brahms, Britten, Chopin, Debussy, Grieg, Hindemith, Ravel, Shostakovich and Tchaikovsky.

Richter is a scrupulously honest, confident interpreter. His highly personal approach to a work derives from his peculiar ability to know, the moment he begins working on a piece, just what he is going to do with it. Critics may frequently disagree with his unorthodox ideas and extremely subjective interpretations, but none question his integrity and sincerity. He does not listen to other pianists' recordings of a work he is preparing for a concert, for, as he says, "When I open a score, I immediately know for certain how I should play it." (Anther)

More than 30 years ago a critic made this astute (and still applicable) appraisal of Richter as interpreter: "In general, Richter is not an artist to be fully 'understood' at once, although he may be at once appreciated. It takes less time to like his playing than to grow accustomed to some of his conceptions, and the fact that we can accept these interpretations before fully comprehending their logic shows how convincing they are or, at least, how magnetic his stage personality is." (Holcman, "Sviatoslav Richter")

Richter's "magnetic" stage personality is different, to say the least. He appears completely aloof and shows no feelings whatsoever for an audience. "I don't consider the public," he tells interviewers. "My whole interest is my approaching encounter with the composer and his music."

Richter's choice of the Yamaha piano has elicited almost as much comment as his aloofness. He tried out a Yamaha CF at the Menton Music Festival in 1969, used a Yamaha on his first tour of Japan in 1970 and ever since has played his own special CF model. The Yamaha company has built two pianos for him and transports them wherever he desires. Richter loves the "neutral" sound of the Yamaha, which, he says, allows him to develop his personal style and feeling. But often audiences and some critics have complained of the Yamaha's harsh, overbright sound.

Richter began having the score on the piano in 1981, the year he had difficulty playing some of the Liszt Etudes at the Touraine Festival. Ever since he has performed with the music in front of him, a small reading-lamp to see by and a discreet page-turner at his side. He also insists that hall lights be dimmed to nearly nothing when he plays, claiming that it is better for the audience not to be able to see the pianist's hands or his facial expressions or his physical gestures, that removing such distractions will induce the audience to think more about the music. Richter "exhorts young pianists to adopt his 'healthy and natural method' as early as possible and to put in the 'hard work' to try to play as freely with the score as they would without." (Driver)

With so many concert cancellations and utter detachment from the audience, how has Richter held his reputation? The reviews of his performances—good, bad and indifferent—tell why.

Before he ever played in the West, Richter's reputation was such that American critics went to Helsinki, Finland, to hear his first performance (10 May 1960) outside the Soviet Union. "His bravura passages had a grandeur with no hint of pounding, his pianissimos a feather lightness, and his crescendos or decrescendos were so tightly controlled that they seemed to swell and diminish like the modulations of a well-trained voice." (*Time*, 23 May 1960) "People could hardly believe their ears," wrote another reviewer. "After the first sonata, there was enormous applause; after the next one they started tapping their feet, which, in Helsinki, is their expression of the utmost admiration, and after the *Appassionata* one feared that the floor might give way." (Maslowski)

The same kind of rave notices greeted Richter's first American performances. When he played (15 Oct 1960) the Brahms Concerto No. 2 in B-flat Major with Erich Leinsdorf conducting the Chicago Symphony Orchestra, "it was evident that Mr. Richter ranks among the foremost performers of our time. Conviction, strength, and intelligence informed every bar of his performance. It was one of the most deeply impressive I have ever heard." (*MA*, Nov 1960) And at his New York debut recital (19 Oct 1960) in Carnegie Hall (he played five Beethoven sonatas), Richter "displayed all the technical virtuosity expected of him; a sinewy and remarkably sensitive rhythm, ringing bravura power coupled with a feathery pianissimo touch, the ability to swell or diminish from one to the other with remarkable control." (*Time*, 31 Oct 1960)

One of the best explanations of the Richter "magic" says that "it probably stems from superb tonal artistry. As a meticulous executant he achieves extraordinary clarity both of note and phrase. Whether he feathers a non legato or makes taut a brilliant fortissimo, he is still capable of most seductive lyric playing. He pedals with exceptional awareness of what values pedaling contributes. Beyond all these attributes he communicates positive ideas of interpretation." (*CSM*, 29 Oct 1960)

Richter's solo recitals on his first American tour were almost unequivocal triumphs, yet his orchestral debut (18 Dec 1960) with the New York Philharmonic Orchestra, Leonard Bernstein conducting, disappointed one critic.

Richter's performance of the Tchaikovsky Concerto No. 1 had some "exciting moments," despite some technical problems at the start. "Nor did the stop-and-start interpretation, with phrases drawn out and then rushed, and with long ritards that were supposed to be expressive, do much honor to the pianist or to the music." Richter also played the Liszt Concerto No. 2, and even it was "highly mannered. Because of the pianist's and the conductor's constant experimentation with tempos, the work sounded disconnected." (*NYT*, 19 Dec 1960)

One of Richter's first appearances in London—a program (12 July 1961) of three large, difficult works [the Schubert Sonata in B-flat Major, the Schumann Sonata in G Minor and also Schumann's Fantasia]—elicited a telling critique. This particular critic was annoyed at Richter's unusually slow tempos throughout the Schubert Sonata, "the impression of hurry and some confusion" in the Schumann Sonata and the "muddle and mis-hits" in the Schumann Fantasia. But the review concludes with this: "To me there seems no doubt that Richter is a great pianist. I have heard enough to thrill me: a pianist who can use the piano in every legitimate and musical way—who had song in his heart and rare agility in his fingers and hands, who never attempts to improve music by discovering new effects of counter-melodies—an artist who has a belief in his choice of music, and whose great art is placed in affectionate service to the composer as a first and last aim." (*MT*, Sept 1961)

Richter played Schumann's *Bunte Blätter*, op. 99, and the Mussorgsky Pictures at an Exhibition at New York's Metropolitan Museum of Art on 24 January 1970. "Determined not to overplay [the Schumann] and in an effort to catch the singing, lyric quality, he did a great deal of pianissimo playing. He is a pianist with incredible control of dynamics, and his soft playing has any number of delicate shadings." And he played the Mussorgsky Pictures "with such drive, such subtlety, such color and imagination as to make it a new experience." (*NYT*, 26 Jan 1970)

A London recital (25 Sept 1977) at Festival Hall was "a miracle of understatement. . . . Such was the delicacy and subtlety of his art that the merest swell from a *pianissimo* to a *piano* signified more than many a rival's *fortissimo fuoco*." Richter's crystalline sensitivity shone its brightest in the Debussy: Each movement of the *Suite bergamasque* "had the fragile grace of a Watteau or Fragonard. . . . In *Estampes* he was never more magical than in his evocation of the delicate little gamelan-inspired tinkles supporting artfully detached strands of tunes in '*Pagodes*'." (*TL*, 26 Sept 1977)

In 1989, following a decade's absence from London, the 74-year-old Richter gave four London recitals, and evidently showed little evidence of his age. When it was all over, one writer looked back retrospectively. "He really is the most amazing pianist I have ever heard, and I make that assertion from the experience of 40 years of music-going, during which I must have heard *every* keyboard virtuoso from Schnabel, Gieseking and Backhaus to Brendel, Ashkenazy and Schiff, with Rubinstein spanning the lot, and not forgetting Arrau. . . . Richter's technique is the most consummate the piano has ever encountered." (Levin)

Three years later another London recital (27 May 1992) included the Haydn Variations in F Minor, Beethoven's Sonata in A-flat Major, op. 110, and works by Chopin, Debussy and Scriabin. Disappointed, one critic reported, "From my excellent vantage point on the fifth row, where I could only see the man and not the myth, I gained the impression of a fair to indifferent concert; of playing that was mettled and serious, but delivered less than it intended, and didn't always intend very convincingly. . . . One left the concert assured that Richter's technique is fairly undecayed by age, but wondering whether it is artistically healthy for a pianist to be a legend." (Driver)

The next year a London recital (21 Nov 1993) received mixed reviews. The Bach Prelude, Fugue and Allegro, BWV 998, was "overpedalled, under-characterized, muddy and often ponderous." And even with the complicated Fantasia, Adagio and Fugue in C Minor, BWV 906/968, he still seemed like "a sleeping giant." But with Schubert's 'Wanderer' Fantasy, "the greatness in Richter did finally shine through. From the first bars—crashed out like a challenge—this was an interpretation of massive scale and audacity. . . . The heroic spirit of this monumental piece was utterly captured. It was a glorious climax to a sombre recital." (*TL*, 23 Nov 1993)

Richter may have more recordings to his credit than any living pianist, despite his assertion that he despises making records. Like Murray Perahia, Richter has enjoyed the experience of having most of his recordings remain in print, even the early ones. The latest Schwann Artist Issue lists more than 50 available Richter recordings.

From 1948 to 1956 he completed more than 40 sides of 78 rpm discs for *Melodiya*, the USSR record company. In 1952 he began making LP recordings of concertos (Glazunov, Prokofiev, Rachmaninoff, Schumann and Tchaikovsky) and of solo piano works (Beethoven, Mussorgsky, Rachmaninoff, Schubert, Schumann and Tchaikovsky). His association with *Melodiya* lasted until 1959. Since Richter was still not allowed to come to the West, the West went to Richter. In Warsaw, during 1959, *Deutsche Grammophon* made three Richter recordings of concertos and solo pieces by Mozart, Prokofiev, Rachmaninoff and Schumann. Since 1960 Richter has made many recordings for different Western labels. Perhaps over half of the records in his enormous discography were taken from live performances, many of them on small pirate labels (Italian), many of them currently issued on CD by Music and Arts. He all but abandoned studio recording after the 1960s, but if he had not, Richter would not have been Richter.

Numerous collections of Richter recordings (Olympia, London, Philips) are presently available. EMI's 4-CD collection *Sviatoslav Richter: Un Portrait* (see Discog.) contains some of Richter's very best performances and provides a tantalizing overview of the work of this masterful, musicianly pianist. The most ambitious collection, *Sviatoslav Richter: The Authorised Recordings*, contains 21 CDs in a nine-box set. Consisting of both live and studio performances encompassing three decades, this vast compilation received the 1994 Gramophone Award for Special Achievement. (For an in-depth discussion of this last collection by Alexander Morin, see *ARG*, Nov/Dec 1994, pp. 233–236.)

A Schumann CD (DG *Dokumente*, see Discog.) contains recordings mostly from 1956-62—*Waldscenen*, op. 82; *Fantasiestücke*, op. 12; March, op.

76, no. 2; *Novelette*, op. 21, no. 1; Toccata, op. 7; ABEGG Variations, op. 1 (1962). The original recordings won high praise: "Richter reveals himself as an illuminative, contemplative, and evocative master of the Schumann palette. Despite questionable pedal-prolongations, his 'Des Abends' is the most meaningful I know. In 'Einsame Blumen' he offers unusual legatissimo effects, while his finger-precision in 'Traumeswirren' surpasses even that of Horowitz. Particularly beautiful are those sections in which Richter applies his neat technique of two dynamic levels between voices or separate notes in chords ('Waldscenen')." (*SR*, 25 July 1959) The CD reissue won the same enthusiasm. "You need only hear the opening bars of 'Des Abends,' the first of the Op. 12 *Fantasiestücke*, to realize anew how very close to his heart Schumann has always been. Like 'Warum?' from the same set, he plays it with an intimately tender, poetic fantasy all his own, never allowing sentiment to degenerate into sentimentality in his loving lingerings." (*Gram*, Nov 1992)

A collection of live performances (1958, 1964, 1969) groups two Schubert sonatas (C Minor, D. 958; E Minor, D. 566) and the seldom-heard Anselm Huttenbrenner Variations, D. 576. Actually they appear on two labels (see Discog.), one having been pirated from the other. One reviewer finds these performances utterly magnificent. "I don't think anybody has played D. 958 better on records, not even Richter in the studio, and hardly anyone else has even bothered with the other two pieces." (*Fan*, May/June 1993) Richter recorded a number of Schubert sonatas. Two CDs made from the 1964 and 1966 Aldeburgh Festival recitals offer three incomparable sonata readings. There are also two sonatas from 1979 reissued on Olympia (288). Here, for one reviewer, Richter's "legendary power of concentration results in some of the most mesmerizing Schubert playing I've heard." (*ARG*, Jan/Feb 1993)

Richter's performance of Book 2 of the Debussy Preludes and two Chopin works at the 1968 Prague Spring Festival were recorded and eventually united on a Pyramid CD (see Discog.). The quality of the sound is a bit muffled, but if one wishes to hear Richter playing Debussy, this is the collection. The added bonus of the Chopin—Ballade in G Minor, op. 23, and *Rondo à la Mazur*, op. 5—is a considerable plus. "The Ballade is as dramatic and exciting as I could want to hear. But perhaps even more of a discovery is the Rondo." (*Fan*, March/April 1993)

A new reissue (see Discog.) has three Prokofiev sonatas taken from 1956 and 1965 performances in Prague. For Richter's fans and those who admire Prokofiev's music, this is a major release. Another reissue, the Concerto No. 1 in D-flat Major, op. 10 (rec. 1954) with Karel Ancerl and the Prague Symphony Orchestra, again confirms Richter as a definitive Prokofiev interpreter. He plays "with all the éclat, fleetness, and fire the music demands. He captures the sardonic grotesquery of I, the rich eloquence of II, and the wit and fury of III." This reissue also contains Tchaikovsky's Concerto No. 1, performed with the Czech Philharmonic Orchestra (see Discog.). While bemoaning the existence of so many recorded versions of the Tchaikovsky, the same critic wrote, "Still, when I played some of the alternatives I realized that Richter is as good as the best of them." (*ARG*, March/April 1993)

An all-Scriabin recital, performed in Warsaw on 27 October 1972, was recorded. The CD—3 sonatas, 24 preludes, 5 etudes and the Poem, op. 52 (see Discog.)—"finds the pianist in top form. . . . All-Scriabin recitals are rare enough to begin with; even rarer is this transcendental level of artistry." (*ARG*, Nov/Dec 1992)

Although he has played a substantial amount of Chopin, Richter seems to have recorded very little. A CD reissue taken from his 1979 recitals in Japan has 12 Preludes from Op. 28 and a group of Schumann pieces. The Chopin pieces "compare favorably with the best versions. . . . Three stand out as memorable. No. 4 is a haunting lament; 7 captures the mazurka rhythm as well as the simplicity; and 21, played at the end, takes on the quality of a benediction." (*ARG*, Jan/Feb 1993)

Richter recorded the Brahms Concerto No. 2 twice in a studio, and the version with Leinsdorf and the Chicago Symphony Orchestra (Grammy, 1960) is the better of the two. Leinsdorf, a last-minute replacement for an ailing Fritz Reiner, draws the very finest from the orchestra, matching the peerless playing of the pianist. On CD the Brahms Concerto is coupled with the Beethoven Sonata in F Minor, op. 57. The Brahms, says one critic, "has something that no other performance has, and many of us will think it the best ever as long as we live. . . . Don't miss it." (*ARG*, March/April 1993)

One of Richter's recordings comes from live performances (July 1988) at Germany's Schleswig-Holstein Festival (see Discog.). Presenting the Brahms Sonata No. 1 in C Major, op. 1, with four Liszt pieces seems a bit incongruous, but the pianist's mastery in both somehow makes everything fit perfectly. In the Brahms "there is much to enjoy, not least the delicacy and fine texture of the playing—and make no mistake, there's no shortage of power. . . . This is, none the less, a thoughtful reading rather than a virtuoso one and to be appreciated as such. . . . The four Liszt pieces are also unfailingly interesting." (*Gram*, April 1992)

Richter has also recorded magisterial performances of Bach's first and third English Suites (see Discog.). This is piano Bach, not harpsichord Bach, and Richter uses the piano resources here as artfully as he does elsewhere. "Making no effort to imitate harpsichord sounds and accents, he uses all the tonal and dynamic resources of the piano to convey the musical content of these apparently formal exercises. His articulation and voicing are crystalline, and the constant movement and inner dynamism of his tempos and phrasing clarify and vivify the melodic and harmonic structure of the music. . . . There is never a dull moment in this performance, never a note out of place or wrongly accented." (*American Record Guide*, March/April 1993. Reprinted by permission.)

Richter's all-embracing repertoire includes surprisingly little Mozart, but what there is compensates with quality for quantity. An album issued by Memories (HR 4366-67) includes the Concerto, K. 482, two sonatas (K. 283 and K. 309) and *La belle Françoise* Variations, K. 353, plus the gracious support of the English Chamber Orchestra and, finally, Benjamin Britten, both conducting and joining with Richter in the Sonata, K. 521, for Piano Four-Hands. The Variations K. 353 and Sonata K. 309 date from a 1968 Prague recital, the rest stem from Aldeburgh (1966–67). Richter's approach to Mozart is not scholarly.

He "does not romanticize the music, but he does use the full resources of the modern piano. . . . These performances are real musts, especially the collaborations between the two great artists." (*Fan*, Nov/Dec 1991) Three delightful Music and Arts discs (see Discog.) also feature Richter and Britten in piano duets by Debussy, Mozart, Schubert and Schumann.

SELECTED REFERENCES

Anther, Eric. "Richter: son bloc-notes." (trans. David Brown) *The Friends of Sviatoslav Richter*, Bulletin No. 11, March 1990, pp. 10–16.

Bowers, Faubion. "Richter on Scriabin." *Saturday Review*, 12 June 1965, pp. 58–59.

Craxton, Harold. "Sviatoslav Richter." *Musical Times*, Sept 1961, pp. 558–559.

"Debut to Remember." *Time*, 31 Oct 1960, p. 34.

Delson, V., and Ralph Parker. "Two Views of Sviatoslav Richter." *Saturday Review*, 15 Oct 1960, pp. 64–66, 71.

Driver, Paul. "Keys lock up the Legend." *Sunday Times* (London), 31 May 1992, sec. 7, p. 14.

The Friends of Sviatoslav Richter. Bulletin issued quarterly at Low Warden Barns, Hexham NE46 4SN, England. Each bulletin contains a variety of information, including reviews and articles from various books and periodicals.

"Genius Unbound." *Time*, 4 Jan 1963, p. 33.

"Hearing is Believing." *Time*, 7 Nov 1960, p. 63.

Henahan, Donal. "How to Keep a Public Endlessly Fascinated." *New York Times*, 15 May 1983, sec. 2, p. 19.

Holcman, Jan. "Keyboard Left To Right." *Saturday Review*, 25 July 1959, pp. 33–35.

———. "Sviatoslav Richter." *Saturday Review*, 26 Nov 1960, pp. 43, 45, 59, 61–63.

Kawashima, Midori. "The Richter I Know." *The Friends of Sviatoslav Richter*, Bulletin No. 10, Dec 1989, pp. 25–30.

"Legend from Moscow." *Time*, 23 May 1960, p. 63.

"Legendary Virtuoso." *Time*, 16 June 1958, p. 38.

Levin, Bernard. "Mastery at Full Stretch." *The Times* (London), 3 April 1989, p. 14.

Maslowski, Igor B. "Meeting Richter in Helsinki." *The Gramophone Jubilee Book*, pp. 275–278.

Meyer-Josten, Jürgen. *Sviatoslav Richter*. Frankfurt: Henry Litolff's Verlag, 1981.

———. "Sviatoslav Richter in Conversation." *Recorded Sound*, July 1983, pp. 9–16.

"Mr. Sviatoslav Richter Discusses his Repertoire." *The Times* (London), 25 July 1961, p. 15.

"Moody Master's Smash U.S. Debut." *Life*, 31 Oct 1960, pp. 69–75.

Moor, Paul. "Sviatoslav Becomes Svyetchik." *High Fidelity*, Oct 1962, pp. 46–52, 146–147.

Morrison, Bryce. "The New Testament." *Gramophone*, March 1993, pp. 18–19.

Neuhaus, Heinrich. *The Art Of Piano Playing*. (trans. K. A. Leibovitch) London: Barrie & Jenkins, 1973.

Richter, Sviatoslav. "A Pianist Views America." *Music Journal*, March 1961, pp. 10, 64.

———. "Sergei Prokofiev." In *The Friends of Sviatoslav Richter*, Bulletin No. 11, March 1990, pp. 18–32.

———. "Some Thoughts about Soviet Music." In *The Friends of Sviatoslav Richter*, Bulletin No. 11, March 1990, pp. 33–36.

Schneerson, Grigori. "For the First Time in London." *Music and Musicians*, March 1961, pp. 6–7, 31.

Schnittke, Alfred. "Svyatoslav Richter." *Music in the USSR*, July/Sept 1985, pp. 11–12.

Schonberg, Harold C. "An Evaluation of Richter." *New York Times*, 8 Jan 1961, sec. 2, p. 9.

Schwartz, Falk. "Sviatoslav Richter—Discography (1948–1994)." *The Friends of Sviatoslav Richter*, Bulletin No. 28/29, June 1994.

———. "The Unplayed Concerts." *The Friends of Sviatoslav Richter*, Bulletin No. 13, Sept 1990, pp. 22–30.

Stewart, Gordon. "Six Characters in Search of a Pianist." *The Friends of Sviatoslav Richter*, Bulletin No. 13, Sept 1990, pp. 14–17. Transcribed from a BBC intermission discussion on 20 March 1989.

"Sviatoslav Richter." *Music and Musicians*, July 1961, p. 5.

"They Call Him a Giant." *Newsweek*, 17 Oct 1960, p. 106.

Wigler, Stephen. "At 79, Richter has some surprises for us." *Baltimore Sun*, 11 April 1993, sec. K, p. 1.

See also Bibliography: Cur/Bio (1961); Ewe/Li; Gav/Vin; Hag/Thi; Kai/Gre; New/Gro; Ran/Kon; Rat/Cle; Rub/MyM; Sch/Fac; Zil/Rus.

SELECTED REVIEWS

CSM: 29 Oct 1960. *LAT*: 11 Nov 1960; 18 Nov 1960; 1 June 1965. *LM*: 28 June 1988. *MA*: Nov 1960. *MM*: Nov 1964. *MT*: March 1963; Dec 1968. *NYT*: 30 May 1958; 20 Oct 1960; 24 Oct 1960; 31 Oct 1960; 19 Dec 1960; 16 April 1965;20 April 1965; 26 Jan 1970; 17 March 1970. *STL*: 22 June 1975; 11 July 1976; 2 Oct 1977; 2 April 1989; 31 May 1992. *TL*: 10 July 1961; 11 July 1961; 13 July 1961; 17 July 1961; 19 July 1961; 28 Jan 1963; 4 Feb 1963; 21 Oct 1968; 20 Oct 1969; 13 June 1975; 19 June 1975; 26 Sept 1977; 4 April 1979; 12 April 1979; 21 March 1989; 30 March 1989; 3 April 1989; 30 May 1992; 23 Nov 1993.

SELECTED DISCOGRAPHY

Bach: English Suite No. 1 in A Major, BWV 809; English Suite No. 3 in G Minor, BWV 811. Stradivarius STR 33334 (CD).

Bach: The Well-Tempered Clavier, Book II. *Le Chant du Monde* LDC 278 528/29 (2 CDs).

Bartók: Concerto No. 2 (Svetlanov/Soviet State SO). Britten: Concerto in D Major, op. 13 (Britten/New Philharmonia). AS 324 (CD).

Beethoven: Concerto No. 3 in C Minor, op. 37. Mozart: Concerto in E-flat Major, K. 482. EMI Classics CDM 64750. Muti/PO.

Beethoven: Sonata in D Minor, op. 31, no. 2; Sonata in E-flat Major, op. 31, no. 3; Sonata in F Minor, op. 57. Praga PR 254021 (CD).

Beethoven: Sonata in E Minor, op. 90; Sonata in A Major, op. 101; Sonata in B-flat Major, op. 106. Praga PR 254022 (CD).

Beethoven: Sonata in A-flat Major, op. 110; "Diabelli" Variations, op. 120. Praga PR 254023 (CD).

Brahms: Concerto No. 2 in B-flat Major, op. 83. Beethoven: Sonata in F Minor, op. 57. RCA Gold Seal 07863-56518-2. Leinsdorf/Chicago SO. Recorded during Richter's first U.S.A. tour in 1960.

Brahms: Sonata No. 1 in C Major, op. 1; Sonata No. 2 in F-sharp Minor, op. 2. London 436457-2. Live from *Teatro del Bibbiena*, Mantua, 1987.

Brahms: Sonata No. 1 in C Major, op. 1. Liszt: Consolation No. 6; *Harmonies du Soir*; Hungarian Rhapsody No. 17; Scherzo and March. RCA 60859-2. Taken from live performances at the 1988 Schleswig-Holstein Festival.

Chopin: Preludes, op. 28, nos. 2, 4–11, 13, 21, 23. Schumann: Fantasy Pieces, op. 12, nos. 5, 7; Novelettes, op. 21, nos. 2, 4, 8. Olympia OCD 287. Recorded from Richter's 1979 Japan recitals.

Debussy: Preludes, Book 2. Chopin: Ballade in G Minor, op. 23; *Rondo à la Mazur*. Pyramid 13507 (CD). Recorded live at the 1968 Prague Spring Festival.

Dvořak: Concerto in G Minor, op. 33 (Kondrashin/London SO). Grieg: Concerto in A Minor, op. 16 (Oistrakh/Bergen SO). Intaglio ING 751 (CD).

Liszt: Concerto No. 1 in E-flat Major; Concerto No. 2 in A Major. Philips 434163-2. Kondrashin/London SO.

Liszt: Fantasia on Hungarian Folk-tunes; *Funérailles*; Sonata in B Minor. Philips 422 137-2. Ferencsik/Budapest Philharmonia SO Recorded live, 1960.

Mussorgsky: Pictures at an Exhibition. Chopin: Etude, op. 10, no. 3. Liszt: Transcendental Etudes Nos. 5 and 11; *Valses oubliées* nos. 1 and 2. Schubert: *Moments musicaux* No. 1; Impromptus, op. 90, nos. 2 and 4. Philips 420774-2.

Mussorgsky: Pictures at an Exhibition. Prokofiev: Sonata No. 4 in C Minor, op. 29; *Visions fugitives*, op. 22. AS 334 (CD).

Prokofiev: Concerto No. 1 in D-flat Major, op. 10 (Ancerl/Prague SO). Tchaikovsky: Concerto No. 1 in B-flat Minor, op. 23 (Ancerl/Czech PO). *Supraphon* 11 0268-2 (CD). From 1953.

Prokofiev: Concerto No. 5 in G Minor, op. 55 (Rowicki/Warsaw PO). Rachmaninoff: Concerto No. 2 in C Minor, op. 18 (Wislocki/Warsaw PO). DG 415119-2.

Prokofiev: Sonata No. 2 in D Minor, op. 14; Sonata No. 6 in A Major, op. 82; Sonata No. 9 in C Major, op. 103. *Le Chant du Monde*/Praga PR 250 015 (CD). Recorded live from 1956 and 1965 Prague performances.

Richter in Recital. Debussy: *La Cathédrale engloutie*; *La Danse de Puck*; *Des pas sur la neige*; *La Sérénade interrompue* (Preludes, Book I). Haydn: Sonata in E-flat Major, Hob. XVI/49. Prokofiev: *Suggestion diabolique*, op. 4, no. 4. Vanguard Classics OVC 8076 (CD).

Richter in Vienna. Bartók: Three Burlesques. Hindemith: Suite, op. 26. Prokofiev: Sonata No. 2 in D Minor, op. 14. Shostakovich: Preludes and Fugues, op. 87, nos. 19 and 20. Stravinsky: Piano-Rag Music. Szymanowski: Calypso, *l'Ile des Sirènes* (*Metopes*, op. 29). Webern: Variations, op. 27. London 436 451-2 (2 CDs). Recorded at Vienna's Yamaha Center, 1989.

Richter plays Liszt. Concerto No. 2 in A Major (Ferencsik/Hungarian SO, 1961); *Funérailles* (1958); Hungarian Fantasia (Ferencsik/Hungarian SO, 1961); Sonata in B Minor (1971). Music and Arts CD-760. Taken from live performances.

Richter plays Mozart. Concerto in E-flat, K. 482; Sonata in G Major, K. 283; Sonata in C Major, K. 309; Sonata in C Major, K. 521 (with Britten); 12 Variations on *La belle Françoise*, K. 353. Memories HR 4366/67 (CD). Britten/English CO.

Schubert: Impromptus, D. 899, nos. 2, 4; Sonata in A Major, D. 664; Sonata in A Minor, D. 784. Olympia OLY 286 (CD).

Schubert: Sonata in E Minor, D. 566; Sonata in B-flat Major, D. 960. Music and Arts CD-642. Recorded live at the 1964 Aldeburgh Festival.

Schubert: Sonata in C Minor, D. 958; Sonata in E Minor, D. 566 (unfinished); Variations on a Theme of Anselm Huttenbrenner, D. 576. Notes PGP 11011 (CD). A duplicate of the 1989 AS disc AS 325. Recorded from 1958, 1964, 1969.

Schumann: Fantasia in C Major, op. 17; *Faschingsschwank aus Wien*, op. 26; *Papillons*, op. 2. EMI Classics CDM 7 64625-2.

Schumann: *Fantasiestücke*, op. 12 (*Des Abends*; *Aufschwung*; *Warum?*; *In der Nacht*; *Traumes Wirren*; *Ende von Lied*); March in G Minor, op. 76, no. 2; *Novelette* in F Major, op. 21, no. 1; Theme and Variations on the name "Abegg," op. 1; Toccata in C, op. 7; *Waldscenen*, op. 82. DG (*Dokumente*) 435 751-2.

Schumann: *Fantasiestücke*, op. 21; Symphonic Etudes, op. 13; Toccata, op. 7. AS-326. Live recording.

Scriabin: Etudes, op. 42, nos. 2-6; Poem, op. 52, no. 1; 24 Preludes from ops. 11, 13, 37, 39, 59, 74; Sonatas nos. 2, 5, 9. *Arkadia* GL 910 (CD).

Sviatoslav Richter. Olympia OCD 286–288, 334–337, 338, 339, 536, 537 (13 CDs). An extensive anthology in 11 volumes.

Sviatoslav Richter: The Authorised Recordings. Philips 442 464-2. A collection of 21 CDs in 9 boxed sets, with illustrated book.

Sviatoslav Richter: Concert Performances and Broadcasts, 1958–1976.
Beethoven: Sonata in F Minor, op. 2, no. 1 (1975); Sonata in C Major, op.
2, no. 3 (1975); Sonata in E-flat Major, op. 7 (1975); Sonata in G Major,
op. 14, no. 2; Sonata in E Minor, op. 90; Sonata in C Minor, op. 111
(1975); Rondo in B-flat Major for Piano and Orchestra (Kondrashin/Moscow
Youth SO). Variations and Fugue in E-flat, op. 35. Mussorgsky: Pictures
at an Exhibition (1958). Prokofiev: Sonata No. 4 in C Minor, op. 29
(1966). Rachmaninoff: *Etudes tableaux*, op. 39, nos. 3 and 4. Schumann:
Faschingsschwank aus Wien, op. 26 (1976). Scriabin: Sonata No. 9, op.
68 (1966). Tchaikovsky: The Seasons: May, June, November and January
(1966). Music and Arts CD-775 (4 CDs).
Sviatoslav Richter: Un Portrait. Beethoven: *Andante favori* in F Major; Sonata
in F Minor, op. 2, no. 1; Sonata in D Major, op. 10, no. 3; Sonata in D
Minor, op. 31, no. 2. Berg: Chamber Concerto for Violin, Piano and 13
Wind Instruments (with violinist Oleg Kagan). Prokofiev: Concerto No. 5
in G Minor, op. 55. Schubert: Fantasy in C Major ("Wanderer"), D. 760;
Sonata in A Major, D. 664. Schumann: Fantasia in C Major, op. 17;
Papillons, op. 2; Sonata in G Minor, op. 22. EMI CMS7 64429-2 (4
CDs).
Sviatoslav Richter Plays Liszt. Concerto No. 2 in A Major; *Funérailles*;
Hungarian Fantasy; Sonata in B Minor. Music and Arts CD-760.
Ferencsik/Hungarian SO. Live Performances.
Sviatoslav Richter Plays Scriabin, Debussy, Prokofiev. Debussy: *Estampes*;
Les Collines d'Anacapri, Le Vent dans la Plaine, Voiles (Preludes, Book I).
Prokofiev: Sonata No. 8 in B-flat Major, op. 84; *Visions Fugitives*, op. 22,
nos. 3, 6, 9. Scriabin: Sonata No. 5 in F-sharp Major, op. 53. DG
(*Dokumente*) 423 573-2.
Sviatoslav Richter with Benjamin Britten. Debussy: *En blanc et noir.* Mozart:
Sonata in D Major, K. 448. Schumann: *Bilder aus Osten*, op. 66. Music
and Arts CD-709. Recorded from Aldeburgh Festival recitals in 1966
(Schumann) and 1967 (Debussy, Mozart).
Sviatoslav Richter with Benjamin Britten. Mozart: Sonata in C Major, K. 521.
Schubert: Grand Duo Sonata in C Major, D. 812. Music and Arts CD-721.
Recorded from Aldeburgh Festival recitals in 1965 (Schubert) and 1966
(Mozart).
Sviatoslav Richter with Benjamin Britten. Schubert: Andante varié, D. 823
(1965); Fantasie in F Minor, D. 940 (1965); Variations on an original
theme in A-flat Major, D. 813 (1964). Solos by Richter: Three *Moments
musicaux* from D. 780. Recorded from Aldeburgh Festival recitals. Music
and Arts CD-722.
Tchaikovsky: Concerto No. 1 in B-flat Minor, op. 23. Rachmaninoff: Preludes,
op. 23, nos. 2, 5, 7, op. 32, nos. 1, 2. DG (Galleria) 419 068-2. Karajan/
Vienna SO.

ROSEN, CHARLES: b. New York City, New York, 5 May 1927.

> I'll always be called an intellectual pianist—I'm resigned to it.
> Charles Rosen (*New York Times*, 16 Oct 1977)

Charles Rosen, distinguished pianist, is all too often submerged by Charles Rosen, distinguished intellectual. Granted, the two are inextricably one, and each influences the other. The exceptionally intelligent, scholarly Rosen is indeed, as the promotional material puts it, "a writer and lecturer of extraordinary perception in the fields of music, literature and intellectual history." That said, we concentrate on Charles Rosen, famous pianist.

He was already interested in the piano by age three, and within a year could pick out tunes that he heard his mother playing. By the time he was five it was clear that he had a photographic memory and near total recall. "'Charles was the center of our household,' states his younger brother Don, director of ichthyology at New York's Museum of Natural History. 'People came as much to view this phenomenon as to visit our parents.' He remembers his brother perfecting technical passages at the piano while simultaneously reading a novel and, from a very early age, instantly reducing orchestral scores to the keyboard." (Higgins)

In 1934 his playing amazed famed pianist Leopold Godowsky. Rosen was only seven years old, but that same year his parents—Irwin Rosen, an architect, and Anita Rosen, a former actress—enrolled him in the Juilliard School. He had four years at Juilliard and at age 11 became a pupil of Moriz Rosenthal and his wife Hedwig Kanner-Rosenthal. Since they had accepted him on the condition that he must study music theory, simultaneously Rosen had lessons in theory and composition with Karl Weigl. Moriz Rosenthal died in 1946, but Rosen studied with Mme. Rosenthal another eight years.

Rosen received a B.A. (1947, *summa cum laude*), M.A. (1949) and Ph.D. (1951) in Romance languages, all from Princeton University, meanwhile also pursuing other interests—mathematics, philosophy, art and literature. In 1951 he recorded the complete Debussy Etudes; the money from that album financed his New York debut (20 March 1951); and that successful recital earned him a Fulbright grant to study in Paris. In 1953, Rosen spent a short time teaching French literature and the history of civilization at the Massachusetts Institute of Technology. But then two more highly successful New York recitals and a contract with Columbia Artists turned his attention rather exclusively to concerts and recording. Rosen has performed widely in America and Europe. In 1971 he joined the music faculty of the State University of New York at Stony Brook. Currently (1995) he is Professor of Music and Social Thought at the University of Chicago.

In 1972 Rosen's book *The Classical Style* won both the National Book Award for Arts and Letters and the A.S.C.A.P. Deems Taylor Award. His other publications include *Sonata Forms* (1980), a smaller monograph on Schoenberg (1975), *The Musical Languages of Elliott Carter* (1984), *The Frontiers of Meaning* (1994), and, with art historian Henri Zerner, *Romanticism and Realism*

(1984). He has written many articles for periodicals and provided Introductions for the Garland Early Romantic Opera Facsimiles.

Rosen received a Guggenheim Award and twice served as a Phi Beta Kappa visiting scholar. He has received honorary doctorates from the Universities of Leeds and Cambridge in England and Trinity College in Dublin. He occupied the Charles Elliott Norton Chair of Poetry at Harvard University in 1980–81 and in 1987–88 he was George Eastman Professor at Oxford University. In 1992 he was awarded the George Peabody Medal for outstanding contributions to music in America. Rosen's series of six Charles Elliott Norton Lectures, "The Romantic Generation: Music 1827–1850," delivered at Harvard, were expanded and published, with accompanying CD, by Harvard University Press in 1995.

A strong personality with strong ideas, "Charles Rosen is always right, to the delight of his friends and the dismay of his enemies, two groups that thrive in about equal abundance." There is no argument concerning Rosen's prodigious musical gifts. It is his approach to music that stirs up controversy. Elliott Carter, an admirer, describes Rosen's approach this way: "What Charles has done over the years is to examine closely the cultural and musical background of each of the important periods that produced the familiar musical classics, including those of the very recent past. . . . Consequently, his interpretations of music of any period are informed with a very deep perception of what characterizes that period in our eyes and, as well, what is meaningful in it for us. He is not concerned primarily with nostalgia for the past, but with the ways its works deserve our admiration and can convince us of their artistic value. He just wants to get back to fundamentals, to the basic facts of musical life." (Higgins)

On the subject of interpretation, Rosen himself says, "There is no such thing as an authentic performance of a work, at least an interesting and original work, and what is more, there never was one. We are either too early or too late. And yet—it must be emphasized—the work of music remains unchanged behind this relativity, fixed, unswerving, and above all, in principle, accessible." (Rosen, "Should Music. . .")

Rosen can sight-read just about any score that is placed in front of him, and he commands an enormous repertoire—Bach through the Classic and Romantic eras to the present. Twentieth-century composers—Bartók, Martinů, Stravinsky, Dallapiccola, Schoenberg, Boulez, Carter—are conspicuously represented on his solo recitals. In 1961 Rosen and Ralph Kirkpatrick premiered Elliott Carter's Double Concerto for Piano and Harpsichord. A 1978 recital (9 Aug) at the University of Maryland consisted of just two works—the Sonata No. 3 of Pierre Boulez and Elliott Carter's Piano Sonata. Rosen often programs works by Beethoven (in particular the later sonatas [Ops. 106–111] and the "Diabelli" Variations) and many works of Chopin, Schumann and Debussy, but less Ravel (*Gaspard de la nuit*) and Liszt (*Réminiscences de Don Juan*). He plays more solo recitals than concertos—the Liszt No. 1, Beethoven Nos. 1 and 5 and the Mozart Concertos in E-flat Major, K. 449, D Minor, K. 466, and C Major, K. 503.

Rosen's pianism is outstanding in many ways. He has a special ability for analyzing musical architecture and his pointed and expressive phrasing is sometimes spectacular. Every note that he plays in performance has been well thought out, analyzed and given its special emphasis in the scheme of things. And he has a prodigious technique. However, sometimes Rosen's great keyboard talents fail to produce a fully satisfying performance. There are moments when one feels that "everything is clear, but without that indefinable magic." (*HF*, April 1972) As another writer explains, "There is a deliberate dryness and bluntness in his style which restricts the range of pianistic color and forbids any self-indulgence." (*NY*, 24 Nov 1980)

Despite the sometimes severely critical reviews, Rosen has achieved almost cult status. His often small but notably elite audience is invariably loyal; and Rosen, an undeniably brilliant musician, rewards them with performances that, in their eyes, approach perfection.

Rosen's Town Hall debut recital (20 March 1951) was moderately successful. He proved himself to be at ease in a variety of styles, showing "the makings of a subtle miniaturist" in a Debussy Etude; a "flair for bravura playing" in Bartók's Romanian Dance; and a poignant approach to the Haydn Sonata in A-flat Major. But "the total impression Mr. Rosen left was that his talents, both as a musician and as a technician, are not yet very well integrated. The playing from selection to selection was uneven. Often in the same composition there were some parts that were lovely and some that just seemed to be deftly fingered. . . . Beethoven's Sonata in E, Op. 109, was the pianist's major undertaking. Parts of it were thoughtful and impressive, but his reading was episodic and he often seemed beyond his depth." (© *The New York Times Company*, 21 March 1951. Reprinted by permission.)

A review of a New York recital (15 Nov 1960) is typical: "He is still a pianist with a very special talent but also with a very specialized appeal. Nothing less than Beethoven's 'Hammerklavier' Sonata opened the program. . . . Mr. Rosen's technique is almost entirely percussive. This does mean that the tone is ever ugly. On the contrary, it always has ringing sound, at soft or loud levels. . . . But there was never a satisfactory legato in the playing, and the differentiation of voices was achieved through opposing them at varying levels of loudness. The Hammerklavier became a dry point rather than a richly dramatic canvas." (© *The New York Times Company*, 16 Nov 1960. Reprinted by permission.)

Fifteen years later at a University of California (Berkeley) recital (7 Nov 1975) Rosen treated the same sonata to "some oddly questionable" playing. "He dashed off its proclamatory first movement not nobly but at a hasty, tight clip. His playing of the enormous last-movement fugue was too lean and terse. But the sonata's slow movement bloomed beautifully." Rosen did better with the other monumental Beethoven work on this program—the "Diabelli" Variations. "Throughout it all, Rosen played with marvelous technical facility, revealing in all the variations pianistic devices and moods that were individualized and never monotonous in their range from exquisite sensitivity to entertainment, sadness,

majesty, surprise, abruptness and in the end a most kindly, delicate minuet."
(*San Francisco Examiner*, 8 Nov 1975. Reprinted by permission.)

Rosen's interpretation of another Beethoven work (Sonata in C-sharp
Minor, op. 27, no. 2, the "Moonlight") at a San Jose, California, performance
(16 Jan 1984) drew this caustic comment: "Lucky the moon was out; as for his
piano, it produced precious few moonbeams. The approach was formal, straight-
laced—a professor's reading, not a romantic's. . . . Rosen does not illuminate the
music so much as render it. He is at heart a strict classicist and strong technician who abhors sentimentality. In the process he often overlooks the sentiment
as well in his tightly reined playing." (*SJM*, 18 Jan 1984)

Rosen has fared better with Chopin. At an all-Chopin recital (4 Oct
1987) in Chicago he received kudos for his "ability to analyze musical architecture" and his "gift for finding the most convincing tempo, the most striking dynamics and the most sensitive tonal shadings. . . . He is able to reach out and
touch you with his music in a manner few can rival." (*CST*, 5 Oct 1987) A different reviewer of that same recital felt that Rosen's Chopin playing was both
probing and eloquent: "Despite Rosen's nostalgic way with a phrase, his readings
are also filled with new, intriguing ideas. His tempos defy predictability, his
textures bring out hidden voices. Rosen's Chopin, in short, combines the old
and the new, the scholarly and the spontaneous, as no one else's does." (*CT*, 5
Oct 1987)

Rosen seldom if ever gets a poor review for his performances of con-
temporary music. On 9 August 1978 he played the Elliott Carter Sonata and the
Sonata No. 3 of Boulez at the University of Maryland. "Characteristically, the
Carter 'Sonata' is a prickly, complex work, requiring intense concentration from
both performer and listener. . . . Rosen's performance was powerful, combining,
like the work itself, the highest technical, intellectual and emotional resources.
It was a case of one passionate intellect meeting another." (*WP*, 11 Aug 1978)
Years later Rosen played (22 Oct 1991) Carter's Night Fantasies at Columbia
University. "Mr. Rosen, in his atmospheric account, presented a vivid, three-di-
mensional picture of its many streams of activity." (*NYT*, 26 Oct 1991)

At his New York recital of 7 October 1993, Rosen's playing of Chopin
(Nocturne, op. 62, no. 1, Barcarolle, four mazurkas) and Liszt (three song transcriptions) received mixed criticism: "Mr. Rosen's thoughtfulness worked for and
against this music. His fastidious sense of proportion in the Mazurkas balanced
the constraints of dance movement with melodic freedom. Yet most of the
Barcarolle was stifled by its own rectitude, that is until the up-tempo coda shook
loose some unsuspected abandon in Mr. Rosen's personality. . . . Great Liszt pianists play as if beside themselves, as if gripped by a heaven-sent loss of control. This is an idea to which Mr. Rosen's clear head does not respond. His
technique, moreover, controls but does not command. The grim determination
with which he attacked bravura passages hardly served to liberate their spirit."
On this same program, "Schumann's *Davidsbündlertänze* seemed more empa-
thetic to Mr. Rosen's upright and attentive musicality. The dance rhythms and
lyric surges thrived under his discerning gaze; the final moments went past dis-
cernment and produced something very beautiful indeed." (© *The New York
Times Company*, 11 Oct 1993. Reprinted by permission.)

Rosen has recorded a substantial number of works, but some of the finest are still awaiting reissue on CD. His Bach album (see Discog.) elicited mostly rave reviews. "It [Art of Fugue] is the music of eternity, and Rosen's transcendent art brings its timelessness home to us. This is the greatest single act of pianism that I have ever encountered. No Bach devotee and no lover of the piano should miss it. . . . On top of all this Rosen gives us a golden-toned reading of the Goldberg Variations [now available in CD reissue] . . . a convincing account of a work which can be viewed from many angles, provided the vision be informed by self-denying integrity. This is the hallmark of Rosen's art throughout this notable set." (*RR*, March 1969)

Rosen's finest recordings are those in which his phenomenal technical talents combine with his never-ending search for historical truth and his active analytical predilection to create or rather re-create distinct works of art. His Ravel (*Gaspard de la nuit, Le Tombeau de Couperin*), meticulous and imaginative, is a joy to hear. His Carter (Night Fantasies, Sonata) and Boulez (Sonatas Nos. 1 and 3) recordings reflect his delight in this music. He treats many Beethoven works as Classic rather than early Romantic; seen in this light, his recordings of many of the sonatas are convincing performances of Rosen the pianist and Rosen the scholar, both inextricably entwined.

His album (3 LPs) of Schumann compositions titled "The Revolutionary Masterpieces" was issued by Nonesuch in 1984. "Claiming that Schumann's revisions for publication tended to dilute and conventionalize his first thoughts, Rosen has reverted whenever possible to the earliest known state of the music. . . . An overview leaves one with the feeling that this is a body of music leaner in texture, clearer in harmonic direction, even more immediate in expressive power, and in some ways better integrated in structure than many pianists are equipped to reveal." (*Fan*, Nov/Dec 1984) Conversely, we have this from another reviewer: "The fact that most of these performances are of first editions rather than the more commonly heard versions [e.g., Poems for the Piano stands as the first version of the Fantasy in C Major, op. 17] simply did not carry for me the emotional or scholarly punch that it might for some." (*MA*, July 1986) Although not recommending these performances as a first choice, this reviewer concludes that Rosen comes just about as close as is possible to being the modern successor to the great Egon Petri.

"The Revolutionary Masterpiece" collection has been reissued in a series of three CDs on the Globe label (see Discog.). Volume One of the CD collection contains the Op. 6 *Davidsbündlertänze* and the Impromptus on a Theme of Clara Wieck, op. 5. Those interested in original versions will find these volumes instructive. Always technically and intellectually in control, Rosen's interpretations are "tonally on the dry side, texturally of stark and brilliant clarity, and by no means lacking in expressivity." (*Fan*, Jan/Feb 1989) Volume Two contains two large-scale Schumann works—the *Carnaval*, op. 9, and the Sonata in F-sharp Minor, op. 11. A disappointed critic wrote, "*Carnaval* is a curious mixture of perceptive detail and sometimes careless execution. . . . There are wonderful moments here, but there are also far too many lapses for comfort. Even this is preferable to the sonata, played with so little animation that I find it very dull." (*Fan*, May/June 1989)

Rosen's 2-CD collection of seven Beethoven sonatas, subtitled "The Great Middle Period Sonatas," originally appeared as a set of three Nonesuch LPs. "The performances are notable for their sober clarity, particularly in Rosen's control of movement and transparency in passagework. . . . Recommended without warmth, which is just how Rosen plays." (*Fan*, Nov/Dec 1989) However, Rosen's 1968–70 collection of late-period Beethoven sonatas (Grammy, 1972), recently reissued by Sony Classical, fares considerably better. "Certainly, this is playing of high intelligence, sensitivity and great physical vigour. It is also intensely craftsmanlike—the work of a master pianist fascinated by a craft far greater than his own but which he none the less understands intimately." (*Gram*, Nov 1994)

Rosen's collection of Chopin works for solo piano (Music and Arts, see Discog.) fails to match the superb readings of other pianists. "Too many passages are belabored strenuously. Now and then there is the groundless interpretative eccentricity . . . but it does not add up to a coherent style." (*ARG*, Jan/Feb 1991) A second opinion points out the "clotted" texture from the pedaling in the Sonata No. 2 and the deliberation in the "demonic" Scherzo movement. Yet, "in the Polonaise-fantaisie and the Barcarolle, both so often allowed to meander, there is much to admire in Rosen's strong sense of direction, though in the latter, in particular, I wished he had given just a little more thought to matters of tonal refinement and sheer sensuous beauty." Detecting a lack of "a slightly more malleable lyrical flow" in Rosen's reading of the Ballades, the critic concludes: "Could it be that searching intellectual analysis of this music has ever so slightly blunted his sense of wonder?" (*Gram*, April 1991)

Rosen has recorded two of Elliott Carter's most substantial works for piano solo—the Night Fantasies and the Piano Sonata (see Discog.). The first, written in 1980, was jointly commissioned by Rosen, Paul Jacobs, Gilbert Kalish and Ursula Oppens. According to the liner notes, with this work Carter wished "to capture the fanciful, changeable quality of our inner life at a time when it is not dominated by strong, directive intentions or desires—to capture the poetic moodiness that, in an earlier romantic context, I enjoy in works of Robert Schumann like *Kreisleriana*, *Carnaval* and *Davidsbündlertänze*." But, writes one critic, "despite the neoromantic rhetoric, *Night Fantasies* is a hard-edged piece that demands more intellect than intuition [and] Rosen—with his extraordinary clarification of the music's juxtapositions (in particular, its simultaneous layering of different rhythms and dynamics)" makes as strong a case for it as possible. In the Piano Sonata, written in the years 1945–46, while Rosen "may not catch the drift of the lyrical opening of the second movement, he's completely at home in the Prokofievan toccata-like music that follows—and he breezes through the Coplandesque passages in the first movement with an uncharacteristic playfulness." (*Fanfare*, March/April 1989. Reprinted by permission.)

A number of Rosen's earlier recordings are well worth reissue. These include his Epic LP of two Ravel masterpieces—*Gaspard de la nuit* and *Le Tombeau de Couperin*. There are also three Haydn Sonatas (perhaps still available on Vanguard Cardinal cassette C 10131); several LP collections of

Beethoven sonatas; and also Rosen's performances of Bach's Art of Fugue and the Boulez Sonatas Nos. 1 and 3.

SELECTED REFERENCES

Blyth, Alan. "Not just a pianist." *Music and Musicians*, Dec 1969, pp. 26, 74.

Crankshaw, Geoffrey. "20th-Century Bach." *Records and Recording*, March 1969, pp. 24, 25.

Higgins, Joan. "Charles Rosen—Artist, Scholar, or Polymath?" *High Fidelity*, Nov 1975, pp. 83–88.

Horowitz, Joseph. "Charles Rosen—The Ph.D. at the Keyboard." *New York Times*, 16 Oct 1977, pp. 21, 28.

Margles, Pamela. "The Dual Career of Charles Rosen." *Music Magazine*, Sept/Oct 1981, pp. 12–16.

Norris, Christopher. "Charles Rosen." (interview) *Music and Musicians*, March 1977, pp. 30–34.

Rosen, Charles. *Arnold Schoenberg*. New York: The Viking Press, 1975.

————. *The Classical Style: Haydn, Mozart, Beethoven*. New York: The Viking Press, 1971.

————. "Do We Need a New Way to Play the Classics?" *New York Times*, 19 March 1972, p. 26.

————. *The Frontiers of Meaning*. Three Informal Lectures on Music. New York: Hill and Wang, 1994.

————. *The Musical Language of Elliott Carter*. Washington: Library of Congress, 1984.

————. "The Necessity of Being a Musician." *American Record Guide*, Nov/Dec 1992, p. 6.

————. "The Proper Study of Music." *Perspectives of New Music*, Fall 1962, pp. 80–88.

————. "The Quandary of the Writing Pianist." *Clavier*, March 1984, p. 34.

————. *The Romantic Generation*. Cambridge: Harvard University Press, 1995. An illustrative CD accompanies the book.

————. "The Romantic Pedal." In Gil/Boo, see Bibliog., pp. 106–113.

————. "Should Music Be Played 'Wrong'?" *High Fidelity*, May 1971, pp. 54–58.

————. *Sonata Forms*. New York: W. W. Norton and Co., 1980.

————. "Where Ravel ends and Debussy begins." *Clavier*, Dec 1967, pp. 14–17.

Rosen, Charles, and Henri Zerner. *Romanticism and Realism—The Mythology of Nineteenth Century Art*. New York: The Viking Press, 1984.

Silverman, Robert J. "An Interview with Charles Rosen." *Piano Quarterly*, Winter 1990–91, pp. 19–28.

Swed, Mark. "Revealing Secrets is Pianist's Forte." *Los Angeles Herald Examiner*, 17 July 1987.

Wagner, Jeffrey. "The Classical Style of Charles Rosen." *Clavier*, March 1984, pp. 12–16.

See also Bibliography: Dub/Ref; Hag/Dec; New/Gro; Ran/Kon; WWAM.

SELECTED REVIEWS

AJ: 11 June 1979; 11 April 1985 *BaS*: 17 Oct 1980. *BH*: 23 June 1990. *CST*:
17 Nov 1975; 5 Oct 1987. *CT*: 18 Nov 1975; 5 Oct 1987. *HF*: July
1973. *KCS*: 10 March 1982. *LAHE*: 26 Jan 1977. *LAT*: 8 Jan 1968; 24
Jan 1977; 18 April 1980; 18 April 1983. *LIN*: 18 June 1986. *MT*: June
1978. *NY*: 24 Nov 1980. *NYT*: 21 March 1951; 18 Dec 1952; 4 Nov
1953; 16 Oct 1954; 16 Nov 1960; 28 Oct 1980; 11 April 1983; 26 Oct
1991; 11 Oct 1993. *PEB*: 17 Aug 1980. *PI*: 17 Aug 1980. *SFC*: 26 June
1981; 21 June 1984. *SFE*: 8 Nov 1975; 15 Oct 1979. *SJM*: 13 Oct 1979;
18 Jan 1984. *SLPD*: 24 Sept 1979. *SMU*: 8 April 1986. *TL*: 1 April
1977. *WP*: 11 Aug 1978; 1 July 1992.

SELECTED DISCOGRAPHY

Bach: Art of Fugue; Musical Offering (2 Ricercari); Goldberg Variations. CBS
77309 (3 LPs).
Bach: Goldberg Variations. Sony Classical SBK 48173 (CD).
Beethoven: Sonata in G Major, op. 31, no. 1; Sonata in D Minor, op. 31, no.
2; Sonata in E-flat Major, op. 31, no. 3; Sonata in C Major, op. 53
(*"Waldstein"*); Sonata in F Minor, op. 57 (*"Appassionata"*); Sonata in F-
sharp Major, op. 78; Sonata in E-flat Major, op. 81a (*"Les Adieux"*).
Globe GLO 2-5018 (2 CDs).
Beethoven: Sonata in E Minor, op. 90; Sonata in A Major, op. 101; Sonata in
B-flat Major, op. 106; Sonata in E Major, op. 109; Sonata in A-flat Major,
op. 110; Sonata in C Minor, op. 111. Sony Classical SB2K53531 (2
CDs).
Boulez: Sonata No. 1; Sonata No. 3 (Trope and Constellation-Miroir). Colum-
bia M 32161 (LP).
Carter, Elliott: Night Fantasies; Piano Sonata. *Etcetera* KTC 1008 (CD).
Chopin: Ballade No. 1 in G Minor, op. 23; Ballade No. 3 in A-flat Major, op.
47; Barcarolle in F-sharp Major, op. 60; Polonaise-fantaisie in A-flat Major,
op. 61; Sonata No. 2 in B-flat Minor, op. 35. Music and Arts CD-609.
Chopin: Mazurkas (24). Globe GLO 5028 (CD).
Liszt: Concerto No. 1 in E-flat Major. Chopin: Concerto No. 1 in E Minor,
op. 11. CBS MYK-37804 (CD). Pritchard/New Philharmonia.
Ravel: *Gaspard de la nuit*; *Le Tombeau de Couperin*. Epic LC 3589 (LP).
Schumann: The Revolutionary Masterpieces, Vol. 1. *Davidsbündlertänze*, op. 6;
Impromptus on a Theme of Clara Wieck, op. 5. Globe GLO-5001 (CD).
Schumann: The Revolutionary Masterpieces, Vol. 2. *Carnaval*, op. 9: Sonata in
F-sharp Minor, op. 11 Globe GLO-5009 (CD).
Schumann: The Revolutionary Masterpieces, Vol. 3. *Kreisleriana*, op. 16;
Poems for the Piano (Fantasia in C, first version), op. 17. Globe GLO-
5012 (CD).

ROSENTHAL, MORIZ: b. Lemberg, Poland (now L'vov, Russian Ukraine), 18 December 1862; d. New York City, New York, 3 September 1946.

> When Moriz Rosenthal died . . . a tradition of heroic playing and heroic living died with him. This powerful little man with abnormally long arms and the muscles of a wrestler could swim the Hellespont one day and hold an audience spellbound with his playing the next.
>
> Louis Biancolli (*HiFi/Stereo Review*, February 1965)

So far as he ever knew, Moriz Rosenthal, one of the titans in the history of pianism, was the first musician born into his family; but even as a small child he made everyone around him aware of his obvious enthusiasm for music. At the sound of music, any music—a street organ, band concert, someone playing the piano—he stopped in his tracks, stubbornly refusing to move until he had heard the music through. Rosenthal was about age seven when his father Leo Rosenthal, a professor at the Lemberg Academy, bought him an old Conrad Graff piano. He learned to play so well on his own that when he was eight his father hired a local musician named Galloth to give him piano lessons. Galloth was not a pianist—he played viola in the Lemberg Civic Theater—but, as Rosenthal recalled, "He was familiar with the piano, and he taught me the elements of what I needed to know—how to hold my hands, how to read notes, how to discover and understand the relationship between keys and scales and chords. . . . He had a nice sense of music and an especial veneration for Schubert, and he started me on the way I have traveled." (*Etude*, Nov 1938)

From age 10 to 12 Rosenthal studied piano with Karol Mikuli, at that time director of the Lemberg Conservatory and once a favorite pupil of Chopin. Mikuli made Rosenthal aware of technique, but not technique merely for show or speed. "He opened my eyes to the beautiful balance of notes in a scale; to the perfection of clean, clear, orderly playing." (*Etude*, Nov 1938) Mikuli adhered to the Chopin traditions of touch and legato playing, of phrasing and interpretation. "Mikuli was very careful, very thorough in giving me a good foundation and in requiring me to cultivate the pure legato touch. This he accomplished through many technical forms and exercises, which I had to play in all keys, both major and minor, and with much Czerny and continuous study of the Bach Fugues." (*Etude*, March 1928) Rosenthal made his first public appearance when he was 11, playing Chopin's Rondo in C Major, op. 73, for two pianos, with Mikuli at the second keyboard.

In 1875 Rosenthal's parents moved to Vienna, where the 13-year-old Moriz began piano studies with Rafael Joseffy, a pupil of Liszt. Whereas Mikuli had always insisted on the closest legato, the most exact connection of tones, Joseffy taught a half-staccato touch, which was quite the opposite. Mikuli's style, in the Chopin manner, was smooth and flowing; Joseffy's, in the Liszt manner, was more scintillating and brilliant. Without entirely forsaking Mikuli's legato manner of playing, Rosenthal tried to cultivate the detached, brilliant, delicate style epitomized in Joseffy's playing. He made such remarkable progress with Joseffy that within a year he made a sensational recital debut (1876) in Vienna's Bösendorfer Hall, playing the Chopin Concerto in F Minor, op. 21 (with Joseffy at the second piano), Beethoven's 32 Variations in C Minor, a Chopin group and Liszt's *La Campanella*. Hearing this recital prompted Bösendorfer, the piano manufacturer, to take Rosenthal to play for Liszt. At the audition, held in October 1876 during one of Liszt's frequent visits to Vienna, Liszt accepted Rosenthal as a pupil; but before joining the Liszt circle, the young virtuoso toured Poland and Romania. Rosenthal joined Liszt at Weimar in the summer of 1877 and spent two years in the enviable Liszt circle at both Weimar and Rome. In the fall of 1878 he was fortunate enough to be the only student in residence at the Villa d'Este in Tivoli, where he had daily instruction from Liszt. As Liszt's pupil, Rosenthal played concerts in Warsaw, St. Petersburg and Paris. Later, while a student at the University of Vienna, Rosenthal studied again with Liszt for three consecutive summers, from 1884 until Liszt's death in 1886, "profiting by his wonderful knowledge and advice." Asked in his later years if he remembered Liszt as a great teacher, Rosenthal replied, "Liszt was a great musician, a powerful musical personality. . . . When one was with Liszt one felt the power of his overwhelming personality . . . one was inspired to reach greater heights of interpretation and understanding. . . . He had great delicacy and, of course, tremendous power also." (*Etude*, March 1928)

The fact was that Rosenthal found Liszt's method of teaching far different from that of either Mikuli or Joseffy. Liszt never assigned music. "Each pupil would select what he wished to study, and then he would perfect it, quite alone, as though he were preparing for a concert. At lesson time each student would lay his notes on the piano; then Liszt would look them through and select the music as it pleased him best. He would hold up the notes, and the student who had brought them would announce himself and be invited to play. When he had finished, Liszt would comment on his performance, praising, suggesting, or advising." (Wollstein, "The Apprentice. . .")

In 1880 Rosenthal withdrew from concertizing in order to complete his academic studies. He studied philosophy and aesthetics at the University of Vienna and at the same time he conscientiously kept up with his piano practicing and music studies. When he resumed his concert career in 1886, he soon became known as a virtuoso "who played the instrument and its music as grandly as it ever had been played." Even the eminent, often severe, Vienna critic Eduard Hanslick acknowledged that, "Through many years of acquaintance with modern piano virtuosity, I have almost forgotten what it is to be astonished, but I found young Rosenthal's achievements indeed astonishing." (Han/Vie, see Bibliog.)

Rosenthal likewise astounded American audiences when he made his American debut (9 Nov 1888) at the Boston Music Hall and four days later played (13 Nov) at Steinway Hall in New York. It was his many brilliant concerts in America—at least a dozen tours, some very extensive—that brought Rosenthal international fame. His British debut came later—a performance (25 June 1895) of Liszt's Concerto in E-flat Major at London's St. James's Hall.

In 1922 Rosenthal married Hedwig Loewy Kanner, one of his pupils and later a renowned piano teacher. They remained in Vienna until the onslaught of the Nazi regime forced them to leave and thereafter lived in New York.

Rosenthal continued to concertize and began teaching. He eventually took many pupils, including Charles Rosen.

The aristocratic, cultivated and intelligent Rosenthal was also famous for his sharp tongue, flashing wit (startling and humorous but never malicious) and his physical prowess. Throughout his life he kept physically fit (he could stay at the piano 8 or 10 hours at a stretch!), in the early years with swimming, boxing, fencing and weight lifting, later with daily jujitsu exercises. Rosenthal was also one of the greatest pianists of all ages.

Moriz Rosenthal must have been an absolutely bedazzling pianist to inspire such rhapsodic superlatives: "the perfect pianist," "a magnificent pianist," "a superhuman pianist," "a godlike performer," "a piano magician." To Johann Strauss, Jr., Rosenthal was "the greatest of pianistic geniuses"; to Isaac Albéniz, he was "the greatest of all pianists." Karl Goldmark declared that Rosenthal had "no equal and no superior among pianists dead or alive."

Rosenthal's grand style—power, brilliance, gusto; a rich palette of colors; an intense tone; mighty chords and pealing octaves—was the keynote of his success, a success, as he always generously acknowledged, that he owed largely to his teachers. It is also interesting that whenever asked who his teachers were, Rosenthal would reply: "Mikuli, Joseffy and Liszt. . . . But please note this. I have learned all that I know about piano playing from the music of Frederic Chopin. . . . When you have the right enthusiasm for a piece of music by Chopin, and you get it into your fingers and into your heart and nail it down firmly in your mind, then you have learned more than any teacher can impart to you."

There is no doubt that Rosenthal had one of the greatest techniques of all time, a "supernatural perfection of technique" said to have a peculiar and stimulating brilliancy all its own. He had a prodigious left hand. He also had an uncanny skill for making every note clean and clear, even in the most rapid passages. Watching Rosenthal's hands (as he played the Chopin E Minor and the Liszt E-flat Major concertos) fascinated Sir Henry Wood, conductor of the famous London Promenade Concerts: "He held them in such a position that even his clear octaves *looked* as though he were striking chords; and yet nothing except the octaves sounded, for his playing was always crystal-clear." (Woo/My, see Bibliog.)

As if technique were not enough, Rosenthal was also endowed with absolute pitch and an incredible memory, one so reliable that he often went on concert tours without his scores. He had no special method for memorizing; after playing a work three or four times, he usually had it note-perfect. And he believed that "study outside the field of music is essential, that poetry, other arts, nature and literature, old and new, are indispensable in the development and employment of that fundamental ingredient of art, the imaginative faculty." (*MA*, 22 May 1926)

Contemporary writers described Rosenthal's repertoire, said to include some 600 works, as both tasteful and eclectic. His concert reviews show a decidedly traditional repertoire extending from Bach and Scarlatti to Chopin and Schumann; his programs indicate that he most often played works by Chopin,

Beethoven, Liszt, Schubert and Schumann. At times he programmed contemporary music, such as Debussy's *Reflets dans l'eau*, but in his later years Rosenthal
condemned what he considered the "extremists" of 20th-century music.

As with other outsize musical talents of the past, it is difficult now to
realize the immense response Rosenthal had from audiences some 60 or 70 years
ago. From the beginning to the end of his career, his mind-boggling technique
and sheer power dominated almost every review of his playing. The *New York
Times* reviews of Rosenthal's New York recitals in the decade following his New
York debut (13 Nov 1888) are in themselves fascinating. Although unsigned,
the perceptive and often acerbic style indicates that they were probably written by
William James Henderson, music editor of *The Times* from 1887 to 1902 and
one of America's most renowned critics. Henderson seems to have made up his
mind initially that an astounding technical virtuoso like Rosenthal (his European
fame had preceded him to America) could not also be a perceptive musician.
Henderson granted (1) that Rosenthal's piano playing brought audiences,
even orchestra members, to their feet with "tumultuous applause and loud
cheers"; and (2) that from the first, Rosenthal captured not only ordinary audiences but "all the cognoscenti," meaning other great musicians, managers, poets
and editors; and (3) that Rosenthal's technique was absolutely the greatest he had
ever heard. However, wrote Henderson, "if the cold and dispassionate truth must
be told Herr Rosenthal is not a great musician. . . . Notwithstanding the fact that
he is a notably fine legato player, with a delightful variety of tone color, it remains incontrovertible that he is not an interpreter . . . the spiritual quality
without which real piano exposition cannot exist is not found in his playing."
(*NYT*, 14 Nov 1888)
But the *New York Times* gave Rosenthal's recital on 4 December 1888
a rave review: "Under the hands of Mr. Rosenthal the tinsel of Liszt's music
[Hungarian Rhapsody No. 12] gleams with a lustre which ordinary players cannot impart to it. . . . Rosenthal galvanized it into the most overwhelming dance
of death that was ever heard. . . . What is left for one to say after last evening's
marvelous revelations in the Brahms Variations on a theme by Paganini! . . .
Rosenthal played them not only with absolute accuracy, but with the most
superb abandon, Titanic power, and an apparently foolhardy audacity in the
matter of tempo." And he played an early Beethoven Sonata "with an utter
absence of affectation. . . . It was a manly, straightforward, honest, and thoughtful interpretation, worthy of one who is not only a great pianist but a man of intelligence and general culture." (*NYT*, 5 Dec 1888)
When Rosenthal returned to New York for the 1898–99 season, the
New York Times critic again seesawed. On 19 November 1898 Rosenthal "gave
a remarkable exposition of piano playing and at times an equally wonderful
exposition of pounding." However, "he has never played with more clearness
and crispness as he did in some passages, nor with a warmer and mellower tone
than he did in others. . . . His reading of the Beethoven Sonata, op. 106, was
that of a clear-headed and earnest man, with a profound respect for the composer.
It was judicious and convincing without being at all exaggerated." (*NYT*, 20
Nov 1898)

Other critics unreservedly recognized Rosenthal as more than an electrifying virtuoso. At a Boston recital (8 Dec 1906) of works by Beethoven, Chopin, Schubert, Strauss and Henselt, Rosenthal's "masterly interpretative powers and phenomenal technical facilities excited equal admiration. . . . Throughout, Rosenthal was eloquent, with a varied and scrupulously adjusted eloquence. His analytic faculty designed and proportioned the Beethoven Sonata (op. 109) from the broadest contour to the smallest arabesque; it followed each large mood and each momentary fancy." (*MA*, 22 Dec 1906)

And this: "Although the name of Moriz Rosenthal is practically synonymous with almost supernatural perfection of technique . . . Rosenthal is a *musician* in the very first place, a technician in the second. He belongs to that narrow circle of interpretative artists who are magnetic to the extent of hypnotizing the public at will. . . . Like Paderewski, he is a scholar and a thinker of the profoundest order, one whose lofty mental accomplishments react powerfully and beneficially on his art." (*MA*, 12 Oct 1912)

Inevitably, there would be times when Rosenthal's thundering technique took over a performance. For example, one Herculean program (7 Nov 1906)— the Chopin Concerto in E Minor, the Brahms Paganini Variations and Liszt's Concerto in E Flat, performed with the New York Symphony Orchestra under Walter Damrosch—bedazzled the wildly applauding audience. But the sophisticated Richard Aldrich, Henderson's successor as music critic of the *New York Times*, disparaged the audience as one "not, on the whole, deeply versed in the higher things of music." Aldrich greatly admired Rosenthal's technique in the Chopin Concerto, but missed "the delicate and plangent note of poetry that is its greatest charm." In the Brahms, Rosenthal "did not approach the variations with the strong imaginative power that they demand." As for the Liszt Concerto, said Aldrich, "few make it so coruscate and triumphantly thunderous. A musical enjoyment it was not." (*NYT*, 8 Nov 1906)

Henderson and Aldrich were in the minority, and with the passing years more and more reviewers applauded Rosenthal for his masterly and poetic interpretations. On 11 February 1928 he played a Town Hall program of works by Beethoven, Chopin, Schubert, Liszt and Albéniz. "No one in our day has ever equalled him in sheer glittering virtuosity and the building of exciting climaxes in fervor and force. And his all-conquering execution never leaves the strictly musical line or forsakes the artistic duty of retaining quality and color in tone." (*NYA*, 12 Feb 1928) On 19 February 1928 this same program drew raves from all Chicago critics. For example, Rosenthal is "a heavenly mazurka [Chopin] player; one suspects him of having the soul of a dancer as an important part of his musical equipment." (*CT*, 20 Feb 1928)

Similar themes prevail in almost all the reviews. A London recital (27 Jan 1934) included works by Beethoven, Chopin and Szymanowski. "It was in the small things in the program, a couple of Mazurkas and one or two of the Etudes of Chopin, that he most clearly showed his unique quality. The form of these formal pieces was transcended, and they became little poems reflecting various moods, now wistful, now smiling, and always exquisite." (*TL*, 29 Jan 1934)

In his later years Rosenthal still possessed the magic with which he had charmed audiences for half a century. He was 74 when he played a recital (11 Nov 1937) at Town Hall made up largely of works by Liszt, Chopin and Schubert. "To hear a melody sung on the piano with the velvety smoothness, enchanting nuance and plasticity of phrase which issued forth from under Mr. Rosenthal's magic fingers in the [Chopin] prelude in F-sharp major, and on in-numerable other occasions during the afternoon, was to come in contact with a nearly lost art." (*NYT*, 12 Nov 1937)

Rosenthal celebrated the 50th anniversary of his American debut with a recital (13 Nov 1938) at Carnegie Hall played on a gilded Baldwin piano with matching bench, both especially built for the occasion. It was a taxing program (Beethoven, Schubert, Chopin, Liszt, Weber) for the 75-year-old pianist; yet, al-though age had made certain inroads upon his physical resources, "he was still 99.9 per cent the Rosenthal of old. His legato was a miracle of sinuousness. His octaves pealed. . . . The evening was again a revelation of the most prodi-gious technique developed in the span of the pianoforte and of a musicianship that went a great distance beyond breath-taking virtuosity." (Rosenfield)

Just a month before his 80th birthday, Rosenthal gave an all-Chopin recital (15 Nov 1941) at Town Hall, and played every piece flawlessly, without a memory slip. "It was a recital of serene, quiet playing, characterized by exquisite beauty of tone and startling clarity of all rapid passages. If there were none of the thundering octaves to learn the secret of which pupils used to come from the four corners of the earth, they were not missed. It is open to question whether any other living pianist could have given a Chopin program in such a way. Certainly none has, in a long time." (*MA*, 25 Nov 1941)

Moriz Rosenthal enjoyed a long, spectacular career. If a few critics believed that, like so many musicians accustomed to fervent applause, he continued to play when he should have retired, by far the majority of reviewers agreed that "until three years before his death Rosenthal could outplay any pianist one might recall, except the earlier Rosenthal." (*DMN*, 8 Sept 1946) Even when his heroic style of playing was no longer in vogue, audiences flocked to hear him. As one reviewer put it, "Time has not dimmed in the slightest Mr. Rosenthal's enthusiasm for his art, or his ability to provide interpretations of the most poetic and eloquent nature. . . . His playing was backed by an inner enthusiasm and a technical virtuosity quite uncanny for a performer in his 80th year." (*NYT,* 17 Nov 1941)

Rosenthal began making recordings comparatively late in life, begin-ning about 1924 with piano rolls for the Ampico reproducing piano. About 1927, at age 65, he began making discs, and from 1929 through 1931 he recorded principally for the *Odéon* and *Parlophone* labels. It seems incredible that of his HMV discs—more than 80 sides cut during eleven sessions (1934–37)—only six were ever published (at that time) in England and an additional eight titles released in America. A number of the master pressings have sur-vived, and they are available today.

Rosenthal's recordings were made when he was technically past his prime, but the beautiful tone and subtle phrasing of his later years can be heard.

"There is scarcely one of them that is not stamped with a musical personality strikingly different from any presented by the foremost pianists of today." In listening to Rosenthal play any of the Chopin Mazurkas, for example, "the poetry and distinction seem to belong to another day." (Sackville-West) That comment was made 30 years ago. Today, there is even a greater, more remarkable difference between the musical personality emerging on the Rosenthal recordings and that of any of the present generation of ranking pianists recording today.

The Chopin Etude, op. 10, no. 1, (see Discog.) reveals something of the fabulous Rosenthal technique. The harmonic progressions slip out of and back into the key of C major, drenched with pianistic color. The Chopin Mazurkas provide ample illustrations of Rosenthal's art: a homogeneity of touch, delicacy and precision in the melodic decorations, controlled *rubato*. The E Minor Concerto pinpoints Rosenthal as a pupil once removed of Chopin. The first movement is almost leisurely, the difficult passagework never hurried. The *rubato* in the deeply felt slow movement must be very close to the Chopin ideal whereby the basic pulse must never be lost sight of, however flexibly the rhythm is treated.

For pure enjoyment, we have some of Rosenthal's dazzling transcriptions. One of the first to recognize the virtuoso possibilities of the Johann Strauss waltzes, Rosenthal's paraphrases of these waltzes are among his most brilliant compositions. Few pianists (Shura Cherkassky and Earl Wild are exceptions) play or attempt to play anything like Rosenthal's version of Strauss's Blue Danube or his Viennese Carnival.

Those unaccustomed to late 19th-century performance practice may find some of Rosenthal's interpretations strange, even disturbing. The practice of asynchronism of the hands—the left slightly before the right—was characteristic of many pianists of the period. Rosenthal sometimes added his own bravura endings to other composer's works and was known to alter rhythm and indulge in other textual liberties. But this was his way of playing. Obviously most critics admired it, and the public loved it.

SELECTED REFERENCES

Anderson, H. L., and Patrick Saul. "A Moriz Rosenthal Discography." *Recorded Sound*, Summer 1962, pp. 217–220.

Asklund, Gunnar. "Eighty Years of Musical Triumph: A conference with Moriz Rosenthal." *Etude*, March 1928, pp. 629–630.

Barnett, Elise. "An Annotated Translation of Moriz Rosenthal's 'Franz Liszt, Memories and Reflections'." *Current Musicology*, 1972, pp. 29–37.

Biancolli, Louis. "Moriz Rosenthal, Last of the Pianistic Titans." *HiFi/Stereo Review*, Feb 1965, pp. 55–58.

Brower, Harriette. "The Training of a Virtuoso: An interview with Moriz Rosenthal." *Etude*, March 1928, pp. 189–190.

Crimp, Bryan. "*Dear Mr. Rosenthal*". . . ."*Dear Mr. Gaisberg*." An account of the making of Moriz Rosenthal's HMV recordings compiled from the correspondence of the pianist and his record producer, Fred Gaisberg. Horsham, West Sussex: Archive Piano Recordings, 1987.

Holcman, Jan. "Last of the Liszteans." *Saturday Review*, 28 Dec 1957, pp. 34, 43.
"King of the Piano Technicians." *Musical America*, 12 Oct 1912, p. 105.
Obituary. *New York Times*, 4 Sept 1946, p. 23. *The Times* (London), 5 Sept 1946, p. 6.
Potter, Warren. "Moriz Rosenthal Marks 80th Birthday." *Musical America*, Jan 1943, p. 34.
Rosenfield, John. "Passing of 'the World's Greatest Pianist'." *Dallas Morning News*, 8 Sept 1946, p. 14.
Rosenthal, Moriz. "The Genius of Chopin." *Etude*, Feb 1926, pp. 105–106.
———. "If Franz Liszt Should Come Back." *Etude*, April 1924, pp. 223–224.
———. "New Light On Some Masterpieces." *Musical Times*, 1 April 1923, pp. 237–241.
———. "A Radiance of Yesterday that Flashes Still." (written in commemoration of the 40th anniversary of Liszt's death). *Musical America*, 25 Sept 1926, p. 22.
Sackville-West, Edward. "Rosenthal." *Recorded Sound*, Summer 1962, pp. 214–216.
Wollstein, R. H. "The Apprentice Years of a Master: A Conference with Moriz Rosenthal." *Etude*, Nov 1938, pp. 707, 772.
———. "The 'Grand Manner' in Piano Playing: An interview with Moriz Rosenthal." *Etude*, Oct 1943, pp. 301–302.
See also Bibliography: Ald/Con; Bro/Mod; Coo/Gre; Dow/Oli; Kol/Que; Lah/Fam; Nie/Mei; Pay/Cel; Sch/Gre.

SELECTED REVIEWS

CT: 3 May 1926; 20 Feb 1928. *MA*: 24 Nov 1906; 22 Dec 1906; 9 March 1912; 3 April 1916; 18 Feb 1928; 25 Nov 1941. *MT*: 1 March 1921; 1 July 1926; March 1934. *NYA*: 5 April 1926; 12 Feb 1928. *NYT*: 14 Nov 1888; 21 Nov 1888; 5 Dec 1888; 6 April 1890; 20 Nov 1898; 9 Nov 1906; 15 Dec 1923; 16 Jan 1924; 7 March 1924; 30 March 1924; 28 Jan 1927; 8 April 1927; 5 Jan 1928; 12 Feb 1928; 30 Nov 1936; 12 Nov 1937; 14 Nov 1938; 17 Nov 1941. *TL*: 25 June 1895; 31 Oct 1895; 14 Nov 1895; 10 Dec 1895; 30 March 1898;10 June 1911; 29 Jan 1934.

SELECTED DISCOGRAPHY

The Ampico Recordings. Albéniz: Oriental. Bortkiewicz: Etude, op. 15, no. 8. Chopin: Etude, op. 25, no. 6; Waltz, op. 42. Chopin-Liszt: *Chant polonais* in G-flat Major, op. 74, no. 5. Mendelssohn: Songs without Words, op. 19, no. 1, op. 62, no. 30. Rosenthal: *Carnaval de Vienne*; *Papillons*. Rubinstein: Valse-Caprice. *L'Oiseau-Lyre* 414 098-1.
Moriz Rosenthal. Chopin: *Berceuse*, op. 57; *Chant polonais* (arr. Liszt); Concerto No. 1 in E Minor, op. 11; Etude in C Major, op. 10, no. 1; Etude in G-flat Major, op. 10, no. 5 (Black Keys); Mazurka, op. 24, no. 4; Mazurka in C-sharp Minor, op. 63, no. 3; Mazurka in G Major, op. 67, no.

1; Waltz in C-sharp Minor, op. 64, no. 2; Waltz in E Minor, op. posth. Strauss: *An der schönen blauen Donau* op. 314; Vienna Carnival. Pearl GEMM CD 9339. Weissman/SO.

Moriz Rosenthal: Vol. 2. Albéniz: *Triana*. Chopin: Mazurkas, op. 33, nos. 2 and 4; op. 50, no. 2; op. 63, nos. 1 and 3; op. 67, no. 1; Nocturnes, op. 9, no. 2; op. 27, no. 2; Preludes, op. 28, nos. 3, 6 and 7; Waltzes, op. 42; op. 64, no. 3. Chopin-Liszt: Maiden's Wish. Debussy: *Reflets dans l'eau.* Liadov: Prelude, op. 46, no. 1; *Tabatière à musique.* Liszt: *Liebestraum*, no. 3; Hungarian Rhapsody No. 2. Rosenthal: *Papillons.* Schubert/Liszt: *Soirée de Vienne*, no. 6. Pearl GEMM CD 9963.

Moritz Rosenthal: The Complete HMV Recordings 1934–37. Chopin: Etudes, op. 10, no. 5, op. 25, no. 2; *Nouvelle Etude* No. 3 in A-flat Major; Mazurkas, op. 24, no. 3, op. 33, nos. 2 and 4, op. 50, no. 2, op. 63, no. 1, op. 67, no. 1; Nocturnes, op. 9, no. 2, op. 27, no. 2; Preludes, op. 28, nos. 3, 6, 7, 13; Waltzes, op. 42, op. 64, no. 2. Chopin-Liszt-Rosenthal: *Chant polonais* No. 1 in G Major. Rosenthal: *Papillons.* Schubert: *Moment musical* no. 3 in F Minor, D. 780. Schubert-Liszt: *Soireé de Vienne* no. 6. Strauss-Rosenthal: New *Carnaval de Vienne.* CDAPR 7002.

Romantic Rarities, *Volume One. The Rare Chopin Recordings. Berceuse* in D-flat Major, op. 57; *Chant polonais* No. 6 (arr. Liszt); Etude in C Major, op. 10, no. 1; Etude in G-flat Major, op. 10, no. 5; Etude in A-flat Major, op. posth.; Mazurka in B-flat Minor, op. 24, no. 4; Mazurka in C-sharp Minor, op. 63, no. 3; Preludes, op. 28, no. 6 in B Minor, no. 7 in A Major, no. 11 in B Major, no. 23 in F Major; Waltz in A-flat Major, op. 42. Rosenthal: *Papillons*; Paraphrase on The Blue Danube (J. Strauss II). CDAPR 7013.

RUBINSTEIN, ARTUR: b. Lodz, Poland, 28 January 1887; d. Geneva, Switzerland, 20 December 1982.

> Arthur Rubinstein left a rich legacy of an art that can never die: it is so vibrant, so full of warmth and humanity; so aristocratic, so glorious. It is the stuff of Legend.
>
> Wilson Lyle (*The Music Review*, February 1986–87)

What a rare human being we have in Artur Rubinstein. He was a musical genius and, as he never tired of repeating, he was also "the happiest man he had ever met." Genius and joyfulness; it was a remarkable pairing of blessings, and it made Rubinstein one of the greatest pianists and one of the most *beloved* pianists of the 20th century. After a full eight decades of playing concerts, Artur (also Arthur or Arturo, depending on the country he was in) Rubinstein, at age 92, could still say that he was the happiest man he had ever met.

Rubinstein's very nature—he genuinely loved music and his fellow man—may have been the secret of his overwhelming success. Impresario Sol

Hurok, the pianist's longtime manager and friend, set Rubinstein apart from other artists because, said Hurok, "Rubinstein is one artist in music who, despite the strict demands of his art and the deep passion he accords it, is never limited to it. His world stretches out in all directions and his art feeds on that rich world. He is interested in life, in people, in food, cigars, painting, politics, literature, philosophy and conversation. . . . Sometimes I think that Artur Rubinstein is the last civilized man." (Program Biography, 1959)

Hurok's "last civilized man" began life as the youngest of seven children—number six had arrived eight years earlier—born to Isaak and Felicia (Heyman) Rubinstein. Neither side of his family, all Polish Jews who had prospered in Lodz's textile industry, had produced a professional musician, but at age three Rubinstein taught himself how to play the piano simply by sitting in on his sister's lessons. As he remembered it, even with his back to the instrument he could identify the notes of any chord played for him and in no time was able to play with one hand, then with both hands, any tune he heard.

No one in his bewildered family knew what to do about his amazing musical precocity. To their credit, they never exploited him as a child prodigy. At age four he was tested thoroughly by Joseph Joachim, director of the Berlin *Hochschule für Musik*. For example, Joachim played "many tricky chords" on the piano and made the little boy call out the notes; and at the end of the test Joachim hummed the second theme of Schubert's Unfinished Symphony and made Rubinstein play it back. He had to find the right harmonies, and later transpose the tune into another tonality. Impressed by the child's performance, Joachim advised the family not to force his development, to wait until he was six years old before placing him with a good teacher. When the time came, said Joachim, he would be pleased to supervise Rubinstein's studies.

In the meantime Rubinstein had some piano lessons with Adolf Prechner in Lodz, and at age seven made his first public appearance, on 14 December 1894, at a Lodz charity concert. At age eight he was taken to Warsaw, where he boarded with relatives and had some unsatisfactory piano lessons with Prof. Alexander Rózycki. Finally, at age 10 Rubinstein was taken once again to Joachim in Berlin, and this time Joachim offered to assume responsibility for his musical education and his schooling. Joachim even found four patrons to underwrite Rubinstein's studies, a necessity since his father's handloom factory in Lodz had gone bankrupt trying to compete with the large, modern textile factories.

Only 10 years old, Rubinstein had in effect reached the end of both his childhood and family life. For more than six years, until he was 17 years old, he lived in Berlin literally by himself, boarding in a pension, or with friends or relatives, and spending only brief interludes with his family. Joachim wasted no time in arranging private piano lessons with Heinrich Barth and lessons in theory, harmony and ensemble playing with Max Bruch and Robert Kahn at the Berlin *Hochschule für Musik*. Barth collected the money from the patrons and paid all expenses for Rubinstein's living, musical education and schooling.

He never attended the *Gymnasium* in Berlin. All his schooling came from daily lessons with Dr. Theodor Altmann, who prepared him in the studies required to pass the *Gymnasium's* yearly examinations. But Altmann gave him much more than that—"a constant joy in learning," as Rubinstein expressed it in his memoirs. "Instead of treating me with the customary dry discipline, he had a miraculous way of initiating me into the flowers of literature in many languages." Thanks to Altmann, by the time Rubinstein was 14 years old he was attending scholarly lectures and all kinds of theater, and he was avidly reading, in the original language, German, French, English, Russian and Polish literature.

At age 12 Rubinstein made his orchestral debut at Potsdam, playing Mozart's Concerto in A Major, K. 488, a rehearsal, actually, for his Berlin debut two weeks later, playing the same concerto with Joachim conducting the orchestra of the *Hochschule für Musik*. In December 1900 he played a program at the *Beethoven Saal*.

Barth was a good teacher in many respects, but his choice of repertoire disappointed Rubinstein. In their six years together Barth assigned very little Bach (just three preludes and fugues from the Well-Tempered Clavier, the Fantasia and Fugue in G Minor in the Liszt arrangement), very little Chopin and lots of the minor works of Mendelssohn, Schumann and Schubert. Otherwise, however, Rubinstein expanded his musical horizons by attending the wonderful concerts and operas offered in Berlin.

In 1902 he was a soloist with the Warsaw Symphony Orchestra, conducted by Emil Mlynarski, who 30 years later would become his father-in-law; and he also played concerts in Hamburg and Dresden. He spent the summer of 1903 with Paderewski at Morges, Switzerland, not having real lessons (Professor Barth, explained Rubinstein to Paderewski, would have his feelings hurt), but listening to Paderewski play, practicing on his own and sometimes playing for Paderewski. "I just played and he listened, and he would tell me little things," said Rubinstein. He went back to Berlin, Barth and his lessons but, increasingly disappointed, before the end of that year he broke with Barth and set off for Paris—his home base until World War II.

For the 17-year-old Rubinstein, now on his own and without funds from patrons, another era had begun—a decade of "always fighting for success, for money." Years later he would say that he had left Barth too early, that he should have had further advanced training under a good teacher. Still, Rubinstein matured rapidly. Experienced beyond his years and an exciting pianist to boot, he moved easily into the luxurious world of high society, where he was wined, dined and generously befriended. For many, many years he lived an odd life, at times struggling desperately to make ends meet, but often living splendidly as the guest of a grand household. For example, he spent the summer of 1904 with friends at Zakopane, a resort in the Tatra Mountains, devoting his days and nights to glittering social events and practicing the piano after the household had retired, usually from midnight until three or four in the morning.

Aware of his small and dated repertoire, in those two months at Zakopane Rubinstein worked on the music Barth had forbidden him to play all those years in Berlin: Brahms (Concerto No. 1), Beethoven (Concertos Nos. 3 and 4, the "*Appassionata*" Sonata), Chopin (Sonatas Nos. 2 and 3, two ballades, three scherzos, several preludes, six etudes, the Fantasy in F Minor, the Barcarolle, two polonaises), Schumann (*Carnaval*, Symphonic Etudes) and Liszt (Mephisto Waltz No. 1).

Rubinstein learned fast, really too fast. Music was part of him, as natural as breathing. His musical instincts, his unbelievable memory and his ability "to project the grand design of the music, to crystallize the ebb and flow of its inner voices," enabled him, after only a few readings, to have a work in hand. (*Time*, 25 Feb 1966) But, as he later frequently admitted, in his eagerness to acquire repertoire he never took the time to work out an interpretation and he skipped over details, especially technical problems, using a sustained pedal to cover up missing notes and masking difficult technical passages with bravura displays. And when he began giving concerts, he soon learned that a loud, smashing performance, even if totally devoid of musicianship, would always get bravos from the musically unaware segment of an audience. "I exploited this knowledge," Rubinstein wrote, "and for some time to come I was able to get away with murder, figuratively and musically." (Rub/MyY, see Bibliog.) He got away with it, he thought, because then, as always, he paid attention to the line, to the overall meaning of a work.

After a successful concert of his new repertoire for the summer colony at Zakopane, Rubinstein returned to Paris, where he had an audition with Gabriel Astruc, founder of the *Société Musicale*, and signed a contract guaranteeing him $100 a month for five years. Astruc would take 60 percent on concerts he arranged, 40 percent on other concerts; nevertheless, with the $100 each month and occasional money from giving piano lessons, Rubinstein began to feel financially more secure. He made his Paris debut in December 1904, playing the Chopin F-Minor Concerto and the Saint-Saëns G-Minor Concerto with the Lamoureux Orchestra, conducted by Camille Chevillard. Astruc also arranged other concerts in Paris and in Nice.

But Rubinstein's first American tour came about indirectly. A Boston critic who had heard Rubinstein play at Paderewski's villa in the summer of 1903 induced William Knabe of the Knabe Piano Company to sponsor a Rubinstein tour—40 concerts in three months, with Knabe paying all traveling expenses and Rubinstein paying his own living expenses. He would get $4,000, less Astruc's 40 percent. Thus he made his American debut at Carnegie Hall on 8 January 1906, playing the Saint-Saëns Concerto in G Minor with the Philadelphia Orchestra, Fritz Scheel conducting. The audience loved him, critics were divided. On 15 January his solo recital at the Casino Theatre received a more severe critical response.

Some writers suggest that Rubinstein was so disappointed with that first American tour that he stayed away from the United States for more than a decade. But, in the sum, those 1906 reviews show that while critics felt that his playing lacked breadth and symmetry, that he was too immature, too interested in showing off his technique, they also recognized his great talent and predicted a brilliant career. As for Rubinstein's not returning to America, no one, he said, offered him another contract.

Back in his beloved Paris, he played some professional concerts and frequently entertained at elegant parties and musicals. Giving occasional piano lessons added to his income, but more typical of his playboy lifestyle was his *Salome* "stunt," as he called it. "I made a good living [500 francs each time] in Paris in 1907 by playing the whole of Strauss's *Salome*, from memory, in the salons." Those remarkable performances may have been merely moneymaking stunts, as Rubinstein said, but he was always deadly serious about how much the pianist can learn about phrasing and legato by playing through reductions of operas. Decades later pianist Aldo Ciccolini told an interviewer that once when he and Rubinstein had dined with mutual friends, Rubinstein had played through a vocal reduction of the first act of *Otello*, and played so wonderfully that to Ciccolini it "sounded like the best of orchestras you can dream of." To that compliment, Rubinstein replied, "You have no idea of real phrasing if you have not played the love scene from the first act of Otello." (*MuM*, Jan/Feb 1984)

Anecdotes abound about Rubinstein's fabulous memory. As he played, he could mentally picture the music, even to turning the pages in his mind. Friends used to test his memory by calling out a title—not just from the piano literature, but excerpts from operas, symphonies, songs, popular music—to see if he could play it, and invariably he did. "Rubinstein," said conductor Edouard van Remoortel, "is the only pianist you could wake up at midnight and ask to play any of the 38 major piano concertos." (*Time*, 25 Feb 1966)

In 1907 Rubinstein spent some months in Poland, giving solo recitals and playing sonata recitals with the violinist Paul Kochanski. He also gave an immensely successful concert at the St. Petersburg Conservatory. Unfortunately, when he returned to Berlin in January 1908, he had no further engagements lined up. Out of money, in debt and worn out, Rubinstein tried to hang himself, but the belt (of his bathrobe) broke, a sign, he thought, that this was yet another turning point in his life. Grateful to be alive and his innate love of life restored, he returned to Warsaw and an intense musical life, enlarging his repertoire, playing many concerts throughout Poland and developing a fine trio with Paul and Eli Kochanski.

In 1909 Prince Ladislas Lubomirski gave Rubinstein $5,000 to underwrite a series of concerts, thus at the end of that year he played the Beethoven G Major and the Brahms B-flat Major concertos with the Berlin Philharmonic Orchestra, Gregor Fitelberg conducting. Critics generally liked his playing, but his old teacher Barth attended that concert and later wrote to say that while he had loved the way Rubinstein had played the beginning and the second movement of the Beethoven, the rest was "muddy." Barth admired Rubinstein's power and rhythmical energy in the Brahms, but warned him that he must pay more attention to details and use less pedal. Unquestionably the concerts subsidized by Prince Lubomirski—in L'vov, Kraków, Vienna, Rome, Berlin—did much to establish Rubinstein's career in Europe.

In the summer of 1910 Rubinstein, then 23 years old, impulsively entered the Anton Rubinstein Competition to be held in St. Petersburg. Friends had earlier urged him to compete, but Rubinstein had resisted: "I am not prepared for it. You know very well that I was never able to learn a piece up to the last finish—there is always a bit of improvisation left." (Rub/MyY, see Bibliog.) But then, only two weeks before the competition was to begin, a newspaper article revealed that the Tsar had refused the competition jury's request to allow Russian Jews to stay more than 24 hours in St. Petersburg, thus effectively eliminating them. Incensed and humiliated by that outrageous refusal,

Rubinstein determined to enter the competition—his first ever—in protest. As always, friends arranged all the formalities and details.

For his part, in just two weeks Rubinstein learned the required program, and at the competition his thrilling performance of the Rubinstein Concerto No. 4 in D Minor (first two movements) sent the audience wild, and even the jurors stood and applauded. Later his solo recital created an even more frenzied response. With everyone expecting Rubinstein to win, bedlam erupted when the jury announced that a German pianist named Alfred Hoehn had won the prize of two thousand rubles. The next announcement, that "a special first prize, a document of praise" was unanimously awarded to Artur Rubinstein, meant that Rubinstein actually shared the first prize with Hoehn, but was not to share in the money.

This nasty incident proved a stepping-stone in Rubinstein's career. Serge Koussevitzky, enraged by the injustice done to Rubinstein, offered compensation: a concert tour in Russia, including two performances at his symphony concerts in Moscow and St. Petersburg, and two thousand rubles as an advance on the tour.

Early in 1912 Rubinstein played Karol Szymanowski's Sonata No. 2 in Berlin, Leipzig and Vienna, and later that year he played six concerts in London: a sonata recital with Pablo Casals at Queen's Hall, two sonata recitals with Jacques Thibaud and three solo recitals. Inspired by an invitation to return to London in 1913, in just two weeks Rubinstein added considerably to his repertoire: two major Beethoven sonatas, Chopin's B-minor Sonata and some short pieces by Brahms and Schumann. He spent several months in England in 1913, giving concerts and enriching his musical experience playing chamber music with great musicians like Pablo Casals, Lionel Tertis and Jacques Thibaud.

At the start of World War I Rubinstein volunteered for the Polish army, but since he spoke German, Polish, Russian, French and English, he was put to work as a translator in Paris. An invitation to play a Beethoven concerto with the London Symphony Orchestra in January 1915 took him to England, where he gave more than 20 joint concerts with Eugene Ysaÿe and, very important to his emerging career, met Enrique Arbos, conductor of the Madrid Symphony Orchestra, who invited him to play the Brahms Concerto No. 1 in San Sebastian, Spain.

Spanish audiences so adored Rubinstein's improvised way of playing and his commanding personality that he returned to London with a contract to tour 20 Spanish cities, beginning in January 1916. And on a second Spanish tour in the fall of 1916 Rubinstein completed his conquest of Spain with three Madrid concerts, each of which included four of the 12 pieces of Albéniz' *Iberia*—his first public performances of Spanish music. During the 1916–17 season Rubinstein played more than 100 concerts in Spain alone. Spain became like a second homeland for him, and Spanish audiences idolized him until the day he died.

His Spanish triumphs led to further riotously successful concerts in South America, the first on 2 July 1917. In two seasons (1917–18, 1918–19) he played, mostly to sold-out houses, in Brazil, Argentina, Uruguay, Chile and Peru. And in 1919 Rubinstein tried for the second time to win American critics.

His six performances with the Boston Symphony Orchestra (in New York, Philadelphia, Baltimore, Washington, D.C., and Boston), two New York recitals and a sonata recital with Ysaÿe won critical approval and a contract for another American tour (15 concerts), beginning in January 1920. In the meantime he had an immense success in Mexico City—26 concerts in succession, four a week, to full houses.

Between the two world wars Rubinstein, still based in Paris, divided his time between giving concerts and enjoying life in the most elite social circles. He performed more and more concerts in Europe, especially in Poland and Russia, and expanded the range of his tours to include Turkey, Greece, Egypt, Israel and Scandinavia. Although he was now famous, he was not all that proud of his playing. At that stage of his career Rubinstein was, in his words, "an unfinished pianist who played with dash." And no wonder! It was a rare day that he was not out socializing at a luncheon, tea, dinner, the theater, the opera or an evening gala, sometimes more than one such event, which of course left little time for practicing and concert preparation.

In his memoirs Rubinstein confessed that in those days he prepared concerts using the large repertoire he had by then accumulated, but without feeling any need to improve his playing, simply relying entirely on his flair and technique, his immense memory and his trick of using certain surefire encores (Albéniz' *Navarra*, Falla's Ritual Fire Dance, for example) to capture his audiences. He never bothered about being faithful to the text or about technical mishaps, yet despite these flaws, Rubinstein held audiences. Why? Because, he said, every piece he played for the public he played with "a deep emotion and a deep love for it, and when (and this is a great gift from heaven) I am inspired, this emotion and love reaches the public." (Rub/MyM, see Bibliog.) Put another way, like his life, Rubinstein's music was "always about love, tempered with inspiration." (*RR*, Feb 1977)

At age 45 Rubinstein married (27 July 1932, in London) Aniela (Nela) Mlynarski, daughter of conductor Emil Mlynarski. Although she was 21 years his junior, they made a good marriage and raised four children. Until World War II they lived in Paris and also kept a flat in London for those months when he had to be there to make recordings (the first was made with HMV in 1927) and give concerts.

Rubinstein had become enormously successful, a pianist famous for the sheer brilliance of his attack, his immense technique, his passionate involvement in the music; and he had accomplished it all with little effort. But hearing the proofs of his first recordings made him painfully aware of the deficiencies in his playing. "There was a heavy price to pay for not being taught by a Leschetizky or, better still, a Busoni, after Barth," he wrote years later. "I was much too young to take my musical education into my own hands." (Rub/MyM, see Bibliog.) Appalled at what he heard on those early recordings, he realized that when playing in public his intense emotional involvement prevented him from listening to himself critically, and that he had to do something about it.

Even though he was 47 years old and an established celebrity, Rubinstein began a frank appraisal of his approach to music during summer vacation at St. Nicolas de Veroce in 1934. After his family went to bed, he retired to the stable, where he had an upright piano, and set to work, one by one, on the pieces of his repertoire, giving detailed attention to all the passages he had neglected for so many years. In the process he discovered the joy of finding new meanings in the works he performed. "I began practising as I had never done before. I enjoyed life more than ever, and I found that my natural vitality and gusto for living was reflected in the increasing range of my interpretations." (*MM*, June 1968) Critics, too, found a new refinement, depth and discipline in his playing. By the time Rubinstein reappeared at Carnegie Hall on 21 November 1937 (he had not played in America for 14 years), he was acclaimed as "a giant who had transformed his joie de vivre into the strongest alloy of his music." (*NYT*, 21 Dec 1982)

    In 1939 Hitler's spreading power forced the Rubinsteins out of Paris, leaving behind all their treasures and their house on the Avenue Foch, purchased only a year earlier. They lived for 13 years in the expensive Los Angeles suburbs. Rubinstein immediately adjusted to the Hollywood social life and before too long was earning huge sums of money playing for film soundtracks. In the fall of 1947 he returned to Europe for his first postwar concerts. He was 60 years old, but for three more decades he pursued a relentless schedule, extending his tours to cover the world (not including Germany, because of the treatment of the Jews) and usually playing more than 100 concerts a season.

    About 1953 the Rubinsteins left California for a Manhattan apartment, and in 1954 finally were able to recover their home in Paris. Although he had become an American citizen in 1946, made extensive tours of America year after year and maintained the New York apartment, obviously Paris was "home."

    Rubinstein's amazing energy and zest for living actually seemed to increase with age. On 29 October 1944 he played the Beethoven Concerto No. 3 with Toscanini and the NBC Orchestra at 5:30 P.M., and at 8:30 P.M. gave a solo recital at Carnegie Hall. During the 1955–56 season he undertook three massive cycles of works for piano and orchestra, in five concerts performing 17 orchestral compositions: all the Beethoven and Brahms concertos; concertos by Chopin, Mozart, Grieg, Tchaikovsky, Rachmaninoff, Liszt and Schumann; and works by Franck and Falla. He played this series in London and Paris during November 1955 and in New York's Carnegie Hall performed it in 13 days, beginning on 7 February 1956.

    In 1961, between 30 October and 10 December, Rubinstein gave a 10-recital series at Carnegie Hall, playing 90 compositions by 17 composers, ranging from Bach to Stravinsky. Critics called it a music marathon; Rubinstein called it a thank-you to New York for 25 years of enjoyment together. "I became more and more popular," he said, "not only as a pianist but as one who never cancels a concert." Loving every minute of it, even all the hard traveling, Rubinstein became one of the, if not *the* most popular, most celebrated, most respected, most recorded and highest paid classical musicians in the world.

    Shortly after starting a long tour in 1975, the 88-year-old Rubinstein discovered that he was unable to see clearly, but he continued the tour, playing concerts in the United States and Europe and making recordings in Israel and London. He was playing from memory. Although he could see things around him fairly well, he was unable to see straight ahead. He could no longer read, write or see the keyboard. The gracefully aging Rubinstein ended his glorious career with a recital at London's Wigmore Hall on 10 June 1976.

The honors bestowed on Rubinstein over the course of his long, illustrious career are just too numerous to mention in detail. He was a Commander of the French *Légion d'honneur*, Commander of the Order of Leopold II of Belgium, Commander of the Order of Chile, Grand Officer of Alfonso of Spain. The French government awarded him the Medal of Arts and Letters; the Royal Philharmonic Society of London awarded him its Gold Medal. Yale, Brown and Northwestern universities conferred honorary degrees upon him. In 1974 the Artur Rubinstein International Master Piano Competition was inaugurated in Tel Aviv, Israel. On 1 April 1976 President Ford presented him with the United States Medal of Freedom.

Rubinstein spent his last years completing his second book of memoirs. At age 95 he died peacefully in his sleep in Geneva, Switzerland, his love for humanity undiminished, his generous, gentlemanly spirit intact.

Early in his career Rubinstein gave piano lessons out of necessity, later taught only rarely. Occasionally he took on a promising pupil and said that in teaching them (explaining construction, climax, the composer's intentions), he learned more than from studying on his own.

One wonders what Rubinstein may have told students about practicing. He himself for years was absolutely indifferent to practicing, excusing himself on the grounds that he had a good memory and practiced mostly in his head. In truth, Rubinstein was afraid of working over a piece too much for fear that his playing of it would lose spontaneity. Generally he practiced about two hours (or less!) a day. Before a concert he would go over any passages that he thought might give him trouble, and on the day of a concert he would play through the entire program fast just to be sure he had it in his fingers. All his life he loved to *play* the piano; after an hour of practicing, he got tired.

Rubinstein amassed a huge repertoire and, due more to his astonishing memory than his practicing, he retained it. He defined the nucleus of his lifetime repertoire as consisting of works by Mozart, Beethoven, Schubert, Schumann, Brahms, Chopin and Liszt. In Paris between the two great wars Rubinstein played the new music of the modernists of the period (Debussy, Ravel, Milhaud, Prokofiev, Stravinsky, Albéniz, Granados, Falla, Villa-Lobos), but he adamantly rejected contemporary music. "Altogether I don't understand the modern music . . . so I hate it and I have no means of judging it." (Rosenwald)

A master pianist, Rubinstein played all compositions with "the same bigness, health and virility. . . . All have the big line, the subtle color, the majesty of utterance when Rubinstein plays them." (*NYT*, 29 Oct 1961) Above all, he is remembered as one of the greatest Chopinists of his time. That was not always true. Early in his career critics denounced his "revolutionary" Chopin interpretations for being too severe, too dry, too shallow and absolutely contrary to the traditional dreamy, precious way of playing Chopin. But Rubinstein persisted in playing "the real authentic Chopin," as he called it, and always credited Frederic Harmon, a young Polish composer, for dispelling "the Chopin myth," for freeing him of the "affected, forced tradition" prevalent when he was a boy in Poland.

After his own intensive study of Chopin, Rubinstein played Chopin's music "without sentimentality (sentiment, yes!), without affectation, without the swan dive into the keyboard with which pianists customarily alerted the audience to the fact that they were listening to the music of Chopin." (*Piano Teacher*, July/Aug 1960) And for the rest of his long career Rubinstein's profound, elegant and sane Chopin playing enthralled audiences—and critics.

Before a concert he always felt a nervous excitement, but never paralyzing stage fright, and the build-up of tension and concentration invariably disappeared just before he went onstage. Extravagantly gifted, he dared to leave a lot to the moment. He needed to take chances, to be surprised himself by what came out. "I want to enjoy it more than the audience," he would say. "That way the music can bloom anew."

That ever-present feeling of spontaneity and freshness helps to explain Rubinstein's charismatic communication with an audience—but only partly. A study of Rubinstein the pianist may turn up dozens of different attempts to describe his magic. Many attribute it to Rubinstein's undisguised joy in playing for his audience. Others say it was his powerful personality and the sense of grandeur and poetry that enveloped his playing. And there are those who feel that it was Rubinstein's elegant, golden sound—described by one critic as "one of the miracles of 20th-century pianism. He simply cannot produce an ugly, forced or jagged sound. . . . As soon as his fingers touch the keys . . . the penetrating tone rolls out and fills the house." (*NYT*, 21 Dec 1982)

Some observers attributed Rubinstein's tonal genius to his physique. He was fairly short, with a muscular torso, long arms, powerful biceps, hands that could easily span a twelfth and little fingers nearly as long as his index fingers. But even Rubinstein himself could not really explain his distinctive tone. As he told one interviewer, "You can use the pedal to hold the tone and somehow feel under the finger the length of the vibrations. And you can *feel* the pedal under your foot. It's at these points—the fingers and the feet—that the body relates to the instrument and through their agency translates thought into sound. It's purely technical, but you can't really explain it: it's like breathing." (Richardson)

The hundreds of glowing reviews inspired by Rubinstein's wondrous tone and his unique way of breathing new life into every work he played tend to render adverse criticism (that his playing was "lacking in profundity," that he lacked "musical intellect") unimportant. Simply put, Rubinstein was Rubinstein. "No pianist has put everything together the way Rubinstein has. Others may be superior in specific things, but Rubinstein is the complete pianist." (Schonberg, "The Rubinstein Touch. . .")

Critical assessments of Artur Rubinstein's playing make for interesting reading.

From 1906: "He has a crisp and brilliant touch, remarkable facility and fleetness of technique—though this is not altogether flawless. . . . There is little warmth or beauty in Mr. Rubinstein's tone, and little variety in his effects. All is meant for brilliancy and display; and in so far he is highly successful. It would be interesting to know whether he can express some of the deeper things there are in music of deeper import." (*NYT*, 9 Jan 1906)

From 1919: "One got the breadth, the finely sustained rhythmic line in the Beethoven sonata. It was . . . a reading in which the classic depth was preserved, though not to an extent that forced the romantic side of the work into the background. Those who admire tone color should have been present to observe Mr. Rubinstein's attainments in this respect. But the brilliance of style, the colossal and rightly employed technique, the fine modelling of phrase and the well-controlled interpretative taste were shown to fuller advantage in the four Debussy numbers and the two by Albéniz. Finer pianoforte playing than Mr. Rubinstein disclosed in Debussy's waltz *La plus que lente* would be difficult to imagine." (*The World*, 16 March 1919)

From 1934: "He is a pianist in whom every other pianist may delight, and in whose playing every musician will find, in certain works, great expressiveness. . . . His arm control is wonderful; his wrists are miraculous. But his fingers do not achieve the brilliance of a Horowitz; they are intent on establishing a depth and richness of tone. . . . Extraneous noises, such as that produced when the finger meets the key with any force, are as nearly as possible excluded in Rubinstein's playing; his fingers sometimes seem hardly to be working, because they are doing their work during key depression. His performance of Petrouchka was . . . almost as rich and varied as any orchestra could have obtained; it was delightful in its humour, irrepressible in its vigour, and full of understanding—more deeply expressive than any other remembered performance. The Chopin pieces were exquisite." (*MT*, Dec 1934)

From 1943: "There is probably no artist in the world who knows so much about pianistic tone color, or does so much with it. Add to this one other tremendous important characteristic of Rubinstein's Chopin playing—it is the music making of a man of deep intellectual perception. . . . Last of all there is the man's complete mastery of the technique of the piano. . . . Wherefore a sonata comes out of the piano perfect in proportion, intensely alive in line and build, equally intense in emotion and communication, and the last word in technical detail, finish and polish." (*SFC*, 10 May 1943)

From 1973: "What especially makes Rubinstein the man he is . . . is a supreme degree of intuitive musicianship . . . that is hard to define in precise, calculable terms, yet which remains a recognizable phenomenon present in all that he does. . . . What lent distinction to Rubinstein's performances . . . was their unfailing clarity . . . exemplary phrasing and limpid shaping of paragraphs, an incomparable feeling for nuance and style, faultless technique, a fine judgment of tempo. . . . If one wanted the nearest thing to traveling back in time to hear the composer [Chopin] playing himself with that magical touch . . . then one could do little better than hear Rubinstein play with that keyboard alchemy, the exact secret of which continues to remain elusive." (*RR*, Oct 1973)

From 1976—Artur Rubinstein's final public appearance, at the Wigmore Hall in London: "His recital contained a performance of Schumann's *Carnaval* that no one who was present will ever forget. It remains the greatest musical experience of my life, and during the interval of this recital I spoke briefly with Murray Perahia. . . . We were both amazed at what we had just heard, but Perahia's words made the most eloquent tribute. 'No matter how long I live, I will never be able to play *Carnaval* a tenth as well as that.' It was four months after Rubinstein's 89th birthday." (*Hi-Fi News & Record Review*, March 1983)

But the following appraisal, written in 1961, 15 years before Rubinstein's final appearance, may be the finest: "His playing reflects a culture, a joie de vivre, a sheer sanity, that must make him the despair of all possible competitors. This has nothing to do with the gorgeous sound he produces or the brilliant technique at his disposal. It is a question of bigness, directness and emotional clarity.

"He is a romantic pianist who consistently has avoided the showy elements of romanticism and has retained all that is good. He never breaks a line or a rhythm. . . . He has sentiment without sentimentality; brilliance without non-sensical virtuosity; logic without pedantry; tension without neurosis. . . .

"And even when he is a little off form, as can happen with anybody, and especially with a man of his age, he invariably goes directly to the musical heart of the matter. Even if he splattered the keyboard with wrong notes (and that has never happened) his conceptions would be absorbing, because he has something to say." (© *The New York Times Company*, 29 Oct 1961. Reprinted by permission.)

One of Rubinstein's great attributes was that he could turn his hand to just about any composer and emerge as an apparent specialist in that composer's music. This was true of his live performances and is doubly true of his great discography. That discography is staggering—over 80 entries in the current Schwan Artist Catalogue—and the quality is mind boggling, for while performances do vary, seldom could Rubinstein be accused of making a bad recording. (From 1958 through 1981, his recordings, solo and with orchestra, received 21 Grammys.) As Max Wilcox, his longtime record producer at RCA relates, "The important thing that distinguishes him was that he was able to disassociate himself from his ego while he was making records." (Montparker, "Max Wilcox") After each take, Rubinstein would listen carefully and objectively. If dissatisfied, he did it again—and again—until he was pleased with the results.

His first recordings were made in 1927. He had just given the first performance of John Ireland's Piano Concerto with Sir Henry Wood, when he was approached by Fred Gaisberg, producer for HMV (His Master's Voice), the British parent company of RCA Victor. The recording studio piano was not a concert grand but, as Rubinstein later wrote, when he tried it, "This Blüthner had the most beautiful singing tone I had ever found. Suddenly I became quite enthusiastic and decided to play my beloved *Barcarolle* of Chopin. The piano inspired me. I don't think I ever played better in my life." (Rub/MyM, see Bibliog.) Thus was Rubinstein "seduced" into a recording career. The Pearl CD (GEMM 9464) contains a number of recordings from this early period—youthful examples of Rubinstein, the young, spontaneous performer. While his later playing may show greater fidelity to the text, the phrasing here sounds completely natural and gives the impression that the pianist knew exactly where he was going.

Of course, the recordings made from live performances were not subject to the pianist's painstaking scrutiny, but any wrong notes, wayward phrases, etc., are amply compensated for by the excitement generated by the live audience. For instance, two of Rubinstein's favorite French works, the Saint-Saëns Concerto No. 2 and the Symphonic Variations of Franck, recorded at a live concert (14 April 1953) with Dimitri Mitropoulos and the New York Philharmonic-Symphony Orchestra, appear on a CD (see Discog.), together with the Schumann Concerto. The Franck is a poetic gem. "The marvelous spectrum of moods in this deeply expressive masterwork has been unerringly communicated by Rubinstein and Mitropoulos with absolute sovereignty." And the Saint-Saëns is magnificent. "Here there is a brilliance that can best be described as incandescent. . . . At the conclusion of the Scherzo spontaneous applause breaks out, and in the final few measures [of the Finale] occurs one of those tumultuous Rubinstein blazes of technique that must be heard to be believed." (*ARG*, July/Aug 1991)

His Brahms was consistently ideal, authoritative when called for, reflective when the music reflected the composer's lyrical simplicity. The CD of solo pieces (see Discog.) contains superb Brahms playing. The Sonata No. 3, recorded in 1959 when Rubinstein was in his seventies, "has a disarmingly youthful vigour, and although the all-important maestoso elements are impressively done, the work is allowed to reflect the hesitancy of the young Brahms, as well as his confidence." (*Gram*, Feb 1988) The Ballades, op. 10, recorded some 11 years later, are equally persuasive.

While perhaps not a Schnabel, Rubinstein knew his Beethoven and performed it well. He did not attempt to play everything, but his readings can compare with the finest anywhere. He recorded all five concertos, some of them several times. Concerto No. 3, made in 1944 with Toscanini and the NBC Symphony Orchestra, offers the fascinating example of the meeting of two strong minds. Toscanini, always the opinionated conductor, somehow came to terms with the consummate pianist for a performance with much vitality and character.

The impressive *Chopin Collection* (11 CDs) issued by RCA bodes to become a lasting and permanent legacy of Rubinstein's mastery in this repertoire. Rubinstein made several versions of many compositions and for the most part they are all fine. RCA has chosen in general the later recordings, when sound quality was the only basic difference. "What one has to marvel at first, in Rubinstein's Chopin is how simple it is, how robust. . . . Yet, Rubinstein's artistry is not of a sort likely to inspire frenzied adulation. There is little here that can be characterized by such adjectives as *heroic* or *profound*. What says it much better is, *natural*. And always that rounded, singing tone." (Glass)

Not too many pianists have cared to play, let alone record, all 51 Chopin Mazurkas. These Mazurkas are "so intricate in their variety of moods that the successful pianist has to be able to treat each one as a definite entity, contrasting the emotional content within the context of that particular piece." (*Gram*, Sept 1989) Rubinstein does this with his usual expertise, judging to perfection which details to bring out so as to give each piece a special character. The same authoritative treatment is heard in the Ballades and Scherzos.

Technique and superb musicianship meld to create some of the most memorable readings of these works that are available even at the present day. The Preludes date from 1946, when the pianist was in his late fifties. He only recorded them once, but this recording, even with the 78 rpm hiss and distortion, is one to be treasured. The other works—concertos, sonatas, waltzes, nocturnes, impromptus, etc.—found in the RCA *Chopin Collection* reaffirm that Artur Rubinstein was one of the pianistic giants of the 20th century.

SELECTED REFERENCES

Bernheimer, Martin. "Rubinstein: The Echoes Linger." *Los Angeles Times*, 29 Aug 1982, CAL, p. 54.

Cardus, Neville. "Artur Rubinstein." (An Appreciation) *Gramophone Record Review*, March 1957, pp. 344–345.

Cariaga, Daniel. "Remembering Rubinstein." *Performing Arts*, Jan 1987, pp. 43–49.

Chotzinoff, Samuel. "Artur Rubinstein." In *A Little Night Music*. New York: Harper & Row, 1964, pp. 119–136.

"A Conspiracy of Conscience." *Time*, 3 May 1963, pp. 41–42.

Elder, Dean. "Masters of the Past." *Clavier*, April 1990, pp. 36–37.

Glass, Herbert. "Rubinstein Centennial: A Personal Tribute." *Los Angeles Times*, 24 May 1987, CAL, pp. 44–45.

Henahan, Donal. "Rubinstein at 85: Still a Fresh Outlook." *New York Times*, 28 Jan 1972, p. 24.

———. "This ageless hero, Rubinstein." *New York Times Magazine*, 14 March 1976, pp. 19–20, 28–36.

Jepson, Barbara. "Artur Rubinstein: Portrait of an Artist." *Keyboard Classics*, Nov/Dec 1983, pp. 4–7.

Kammerer, Rafael. "King of his Realm: Rubinstein." *Musical America*, March 1962, pp. 8–9.

Longworth, R. C. "Rubinstein at 90: a master of music and life." *Chicago Tribune*, 23 Jan 1977, sec. 9, p. 15.

Lyle, Wilson. "Arthur Rubinstein (1887–1982): A Centenary Appreciation." *The Music Review*, Feb 1986-87, pp. 44–48.

Matthew-Walker, Robert. "Arthur Rubinstein (1886–1982)." *Hi-Fi News & Record Review*, March 1983, pp. 86–87.

———. "Arthur Rubinstein." (An assessment on the occasion of the Centenary of his birth, January 28.) *Music and Musicians*, Feb 1987, p. 22.

———. "Rubinstein." *Music and Musicians*, June 1984, p. 14.

Montparker, Carol. "John Rubinstein: Life with Father." *Clavier*, Jan 1987, pp. 12–17.

———. "Max Wilcox: Rubinstein's Recording Alter-Ego." *Clavier*, Jan 1987, pp. 18–19.

The New York Times Great Lives of the Twentieth Century, edited by Arthur Gelb, A. M. Rosenthal and Marvin Siegel. New York: Times Books, 1988, pp. 539-554. Five articles on Rubinstein taken from the *New York Times*.

Obituary. *Music and Musicians*, March 1983, p. 6. *New York Times*, 21 Dec 1982, sec. 1, p. 1, sec. 4, p. 22. *Times-Union* (Albany), 26 Dec 1982, sec. D, pp. 1, 7.

Orga, Ates. "The Art of Arthur Rubinstein and Chopin." *Records and Recording*, Oct 1973, pp. 24–27.

Richardson, Trevor. "Gifted for Life." *Records and Recording*, Oct 1973, pp. 20–24.

Rosenwald, Peter J. "Rubinstein at ninety." (interview) *Records and Recording*, Feb 1977, pp. 22–23.

Rubinstein, Artur. "Audiences I Have Known." *Etude*, Sept 1950, pp. 11, 49.

————. "How Can I Become a Pianist?" *Etude*, June 1948, pp. 343, 381.

————. *My Many Years*. New York: Alfred A. Knopf, 1980.

————. *My Young Years*. New York: Alfred A. Knopf, 1973.

————. "Problems of the Advanced Piano Student." *Etude*, June 1941, pp. 365, 424.

————. "Rubinstein on Chopin." *Piano Teacher*, July/Aug 1960, pp. 4–6.

Schonberg, Harold C. "A Natural, Born to Play the Piano." (An Appreciation) *New York Times,* 21 Dec 1982, sec. 4, p. 22.

————. "He Remains King." *New York Times*, 29 Oct 1961, sec. 2, p. 11.

————. "The Rubinstein Touch: Untouched at 75." *The Piano Teacher*, May/June 1964, pp. 2–6.

"That Civilized Man." *Time*, 17 April 1964, p. 110.

"The Undeniable Romantic." *Time*, 25 Feb 1966, pp. 84–88.

Wechsberg, Joseph. "Metamorphosis." *The New Yorker*, 1 Nov 1958, pp. 47–95.

See also Bibliography: Cha/Spe; Cur/Bio (1945, 1966); Eld/Pia; Ewe/Li; Ewe/Mu; Gav/Vin; Jac/Rev; Kai/Gre; Moh/My; New/Gro; Sal/Fam.

SELECTED REVIEWS

CE: 1 March 1919; 2 April 1976. *CSM*: 15 Jan 1969. *CT*: 23 March 1976. *LAT*: 11 Aug 1948; 9 May 1949; 1 Feb 1962; 21 March 1963; 6 March 1965; 4 March 1966; 14 March 1967; 12 March 1971. *MA*: 13 Jan 1906; 25 Nov 1940; Nov 1987. *MM*: July 1965 *MT*: 1 Dec 1920; 1 July 1927; 1 Jan 1932; Dec 1934; Jan 1959; Feb 1967; July 1968; July 1969; Jan 1970; Aug 1976. *NYA*: 16 March 1919. *NYS*: 21 Feb 1919. *NYT*: 9 Jan 1906; 16 Jan 1906; 21 Feb 1919; 16 March 1919; 31 Oct 1961; 8 Jan 1971. *ORE*: 15 Nov 1975. *OT*: 12 Nov 1975. *SFC*: 10 May 1943. *SFE*: 12 Nov 1975 *STL*: 6 June 1976. *TL*: 2 May 1912; 5 June 1912; 24 Nov 1926; 7 Nov 1933; 2 Nov 1934; 17 May 1961; 6 June 1961; 15 June 1963; 10 March 1975.

SELECTED DISCOGRAPHY

Arthur Rubinstein in Performance. Franck: Symphonic Variations (Mitropoulos/Phil-SO). Saint-Saëns: Concerto No. 2 in G Minor, op. 22 (Mitropoulos/Phil-SO). Schumann: Concerto in A Minor, op. 54 (Mehta/Montreal SO). Music and Arts CD-655.

Bach-Busoni: Chaconne. Franck: Prelude, Chorale and Fugue. Liszt: Sonata in B Minor. RCA 5678-2.

Beethoven: Concerto No. 1 in C Major, op. 15; Sonata in C-sharp Minor, op. 27, no. 2. RCA 5674-2. Leinsdorf/Boston SO.

Beethoven: Concerto No. 2 in B-flat Major, op. 19 (1987); Concerto No. 3 in C Minor, op. 37. RCA 5675-2. Leinsdorf/Boston SO.

Beethoven: Concerto No. 3 in C Minor, op. 37. RCA 60261-2. The CD also contains the Violin Concerto (with Heifetz), both conducted by Toscanini with the NBC Symphony Orchestra.

Beethoven: Concerto No. 4 in G Major, op. 58; Concerto No. 5 in E-flat Major, op. 73. RCA 5676-2. Leinsdorf/Boston SO.

Brahms: Ballades, op. 10; Intermezzo, op. 116, no. 6; Romance, op. 118, no. 5; Sonata in F Minor, op. 5. RCA 09026-61862-2.

Brahms: Concerto No. 1 in D Minor, op. 15. RCA 5668-2. Reiner/Chicago SO.

Brahms: Concerto No. 2 in B-flat Major, op. 83. RCA RK1243 (CD). Ormandy/PO.

The Chopin Collection. A magnificent set of 11 CDs comprising the bulk of Rubinstein's work in this repertoire. The collection includes 19 Nocturnes, 24 Preludes, 51 Mazurkas, 4 Ballades, 4 Scherzos, 7 Polonaises, 2 Sonatas, 1 Fantaisie, 2 Concertos, 14 Waltzes, 4 Impromptus, 1 Barcarolle, 1 Bolero, 1 *Berceuse*, 3 *Nouvelles Etudes*, 1 *Tarantelle*. RCA 60822-2.

Chopin: Concerto No. 1 in E Minor, op. 11. Schumann: Concerto in A Minor, op. 54. Caracciolo/*RAI-Napoli*. Virtuoso 2697102 (CD).

Chopin: Concerto No. 2 in F Minor, op. 21; Fantasia on Polish Airs, op. 13 (Ormandy/PO); *Andante spianato* and *Grande Polonaise brillante*, op. 22 (Wallenstein/Symphony of the Air). RCA 60404-2.

Chopin: Mazurkas. Musical Heritage Society MHS 522543L (2 CDs).

Chopin: Mazurkas (51); Polonaises (7); Scherzi (4); *Andante spianato* and *Grande Polonaise brillante*, op. 22; *Berceuse*, op. 57; Barcarolle, op. 60; Waltz, op. 34, no. 1. EMI 7-64697-2 (3 CDs).

Chopin: Mazurkas in D Major, op. 33, no. 2, B Major, op. 63, no. 1; Barcarolle in F-sharp Major, op. 60; *Berceuse* op. 57; Scherzos (4). Brahms: Capriccio in B Minor, op. 76, no. 2. Debussy: *La Cathédrale engloutie* (Preludes, Book I). Albéniz: *Navarra*. Granados: *La Maja y el ruiseñor* (*Goyescas*). Recorded 1927–1933. Pearl GEMM CD 9464.

Chopin: Nocturnes (19). RCA 5613 (2 CDs). Also MHS 523870T (2 CDs).

Grieg: Ballade, op. 24 (1953); Concerto in A Minor, op. 16); Lyric Pieces (10, 1953). RCA 09026-60897-2. Ormandy/PO.

The Last Recital for Israel. Beethoven: Sonata in F Minor, op. 57. Chopin: Etude, op. 10, no. 4; Etude, op. 25, no. 5; Nocturne, op. 15, no. 2; Polonaise, op. 53. Debussy: *La plus que lente*; *Prélude* (*Pour le piano*). Schumann: *Fantasiestücke*, op. 12. RCA 09026-61160-2.

Liszt: Consolation No. 3; *Funérailles*; Hungarian Rhapsody No. 12; *Liebestraum* No. 3; Mephisto Waltz No. 1; *Valse impromptu*; *Valse ou-*

bliée No. 1. A. Rubinstein: Barcarolle No. 3; Barcarolle No. 4; *Valse-caprice.* RCA 09026-61860-2.

Mozart: Concerto in G Major, K. 453 (Wallenstein/RCA Victor SO); Concerto in A Major, K. 488 (Golschmann/St. Louis SO). RCA 09026-61859-2.

Mozart: Concerto in D Minor, K. 466; Concerto in C Major, K. 467. Haydn: Andante and Variations in F Minor. RCA 7967-2. Wallenstein/RCA Victor SO., 1960.

Mozart: Concerto in A Major, K. 488; Concerto in C Minor, K. 491; Rondo in A Minor, K. 511. RCA 7968-2. Wallenstein/RCA Victor SO.

The Music of France. Chabrier: Scherzo-Valse. Debussy: *Hommage à Rameau; Jardins sous la pluie;* Minstrels; *La plus que lente; Poissons d'or; Reflets dans l'eau; La Soirée dans Grenade.* Fauré: Nocturne, op. 33, no. 3. Poulenc: Intermezzo 2; *Mouvements perpétuels.* Ravel: *Forlane; La Vallée des Cloches; Valses nobles et sentimentales.* RCA 61446 (CD).

The Music of Spain. Albéniz: *Cordoba; Evocacion; Navarra; Sevilla.* Falla: *Andaluza;* Dance of Terror; Miller's Dance; Nights in the Gardens of Spain; Ritual Fire Dance. Granados: The Maid and the Nightingale; Spanish Dance No. 5. Mompou: *Cancions y Danzas* 1 and 6. RCA 09026-61261 (CD).

Rachmaninoff: Concerto No. 2 in C Minor, op. 18; Rhapsody on a Theme of Paganini, op. 43. RCA RCD1-4934. Reiner/Chicago SO.

The Rubinstein Collection: Schumann and Liszt. Liszt: Concerto No. 1 in E-flat Major (Wallenstein/RCA Victor SO). Schumann: Concerto in A Minor, op. 54 (Giulini/Chicago SO); Novelettes, op. 21, nos. 1 and 2. MHS 512533H (CD).

Schumann: *Arabeske,* op. 18 (1969); Concerto in A Minor, op. 54 (Krips/RCA Victor SO., 1958); Symphonic Etudes, op. 13 (1961). RCA 09026-61444-2.

Schumann: *Carnaval,* op. 9; *Waldscenen,* op. 82, *Fantasiestücke,* op. 12; Romance, op. 28, no. 2. RCA 5667-2.

VIDEO

Arthur Rubinstein. Beethoven: Concerto No. 3 in C Minor, op. 37. Brahms: Concerto No. 1 in D Minor, op, 15. Bernard Haitink with the *Concertgebouw* Orchestra. London 071 209-3.

Artur Rubinstein. Chopin: Mazurka in C-sharp Minor; Nocturne in F-sharp Major; Polonaises in A Major, A-flat Major; Prelude in F-sharp Minor; Scherzo in C-sharp Minor; Waltz in C-sharp Minor. Liszt: Liebestraum. Mendelssohn: Spinning Song. With Heifetz and Piatigorsky: Mendelssohn: Trio in D Minor (movts. 1-3). Schubert: Trio in B-flat Major (1st movt.). Kultur V1102 (Black and White).

Artur Rubinstein: The Last Recital for Israel. Beethoven: Sonata in F Minor, op. 57. Chopin: Etudes, op. 10, no. 4 and op. 25, no. 5; Nocturne in C-sharp Minor, op. 15, no. 2; Polonaise, op. 53; Scherzo in C-sharp Minor, op. 39; Waltz in C-sharp Minor, op. 64, no. 2. Debussy: *Ondine; La plus que lente; Prélude (Pour le piano).* Mendelssohn: Spinning Song. Schumann: *Fantasiestücke,* op. 12. RCA Victor Red Seal 09026 61160-3.

Also available on CD (09026 61160-2) minus the Chopin Scherzo and Waltz, Debussy *Ondine* and Mendelssohn Spinning Song.

Rubinstein In Concert. Chopin: Concerto No. 2 in F Minor, op. 21. Grieg: Concerto in A Minor, op. 16. Saint-Saëns: Concerto No. 2 in G Minor, op. 22. Andre Previn with the London Symphony Orchestra. London 071 200-3.

Rubinstein Remembered. Narrated by John Rubinstein. Video Artists International, Inc. 69045.

S

SAUER, EMIL GEORG CONRAD VON: b. Hamburg, Germany, 8
October 1862; d. Vienna, Austria, 27 April 1942.

> Sauer is definitely the finest tone-artist amongst the great virtuoso pi-
> anists of our time . . . a profound thinker, a metaphysicist or intellec-
> tual of the piano he is not.
>
> Walter Niemann (*Meister des Klaviers*, 1921)

Emil Sauer was one virtuoso pianist who owed everything to his mother. Not a
child prodigy, he was in fact indifferent to music and already 12 years old before
he showed any signs of real talent for the piano. But Sauer's Scotch mother
Julia (Gordon) Sauer was a well-trained pianist and the daughter of a Scotch
painter; and it was his mother, wrote Sauer years later, who "kept faithfully peg-
ging away at me and insisted that because my grandfather had been a noted artist
and because she was devoted to music it must be in my blood." (*Etude*, Dec
1908)

Sauer's father, a merchant, preferred that his son would study law, but
his "musical mother" prevailed. She started Sauer on the piano when he was
five years old, and for several years (1869–71) she also had him study with her
own former teacher Ludwig Deppe, director of the Music Academy in Hamburg.
Between them, these two early teachers gave Sauer a rock-solid foundation. "My
mother instilled Deppe's ideas into me together with a very comprehensive training in the standard etudes and classics within my youthful technical grasp."
(*Etude*, Dec 1908)

About 1877 Sauer played for Anton Rubinstein, and played so well that Rubinstein recommended him to his brother Nicholas. Thus in 1879, having completed his academic studies in Hamburg, Sauer went to the Moscow Conservatory to study (on a scholarship) with Nicholas Rubinstein and was his student until Rubinstein's death two years later.

Sauer's very successful debut in Hamburg in 1881 resulted in offers to perform in other major German cities; but his first appearances (1883) in London were not as successful. As Sauer remembered it a quarter-century later, he played "at a few little concerts, but nobody took any notice of me, and I eked out an existence by giving lessons at five shillings per hour." (*MA*, 16 April 1910) He was rescued from this dismal London situation by a painter named Herkules Brabazon, who took Sauer to Spain where audiences responded warmly to his playing.

After Spain, Sauer played in Italy and also played for Princess Sayn-Wittgenstein, who gave him a letter of introduction to Liszt. Accepted as a pupil, Sauer spent two summers (1884, 1885) with the Liszt colony at Weimar. His article titled "Lessons with Franz Liszt" is "probably the sanest, best-balanced article ever written upon the historical gatherings at Weimar." (*Etude*, Dec 1910)

After his Berlin debut at the *Singakademie* on 13 January 1885, Sauer began regular tours of Europe, first in Russia, Denmark and Sweden. In Berlin in 1889 he gave premieres of Tchaikovsky's three piano concertos. (Tchaikovsky stayed at Sauer's home in Dresden while they prepared and re-hearsed, then he conducted all three concertos.) During the 1890s Sauer went from one intense concert tour (in 1891–92 he played 11 concerts in Vienna alone) to the next, touring from England to Russia and in between—Spain, Belgium, the Netherlands, Switzerland, Austria, Hungary, Bulgaria and Finland.

Sauer's first American tour, sponsored by piano manufacturer William Knabe, began with his New York debut at the Metropolitan Opera House on 10 January 1899. After appearances in Philadelphia, Boston, Washington, Baltimore, Chicago, Cincinnati, Minneapolis, Spokane and San Francisco, he ended with a Carnegie Hall recital on 24 May 1899. Since Sauer detested ocean voyages, he made just one other American tour—40 appearances in 1908.

Sauer simply had to have enormous reserves of energy to keep up the kind of strenuous concert schedule he followed for so many years. In 1910 he told a London interviewer that his schedule that season included 15 concerts in England, 6 in Paris, many in the French provinces and many in Spain, in all about 80 concerts. He remained active almost to the day of his death. In 1937 he was a judge at the Warsaw Chopin Competition and also gave three master classes on the music of Liszt at the *Salle Erard* in Paris. In 1938 he was one of the judges for the Queen Elisabeth Piano Competition in Brussels. And just two weeks before his death from a heart attack, at the age of 80, Sauer played the Schumann Concerto with the Vienna Philharmonic Orchestra, Hans Knappertsbusch conducting.

Sauer taught all through his career, both privately and, during three different periods, at the *Meisterschule für Klavierspiel* at the Vienna Conservatory.

He taught in the piano department from 1901 to 1907; was head of the Master School from 1915 to 1921; returned in 1931 and taught there until his death.

The works he composed, mostly piano music (two concertos, two sonatas, numerous concert studies), have rarely been played. However, he published a fine edition of the complete piano works of Brahms; and his autobiography *Meine Welt* is valuable for its self-analysis and its view of Sauer's world of music.

Sauer's first marriage, to Alice Elb in 1877, produced nine children. After her death he married Angelica Morales in 1939 and had two more children. Morales, one of his prize students, had started her lessons with Sauer when she was 10 years old; and in 1933 he arranged a series of recitals to introduce her to the European concert world. When they married, Angelica was 28 years old and Sauer was 77.

He was, said Sir Henry Wood, a charming personality who "could keep us in fits of laughter with his views on art and even politics and finance." In 1917 the Austrian government made Sauer a hereditary knight, which permitted him to use the prefix *von* before his family name. Sauer was also awarded the Commander's Cross of the Order of *Isabel la Católica*, Commander's Cross of the Italian Crown, the Commander's Cross of the Order of the Medjidie (Turkey), the Knight's Cross of the Austrian Order of Francis Joseph, the Commander's Cross and Medal for Art and Science from Bulgaria and the Great Golden Medal of King Ludwig of Bavaria.

Sauer was known as an excellent teacher—he taught for most of his life—and he wrote several articles on the subject for *Etude* magazine. The practical and personal advice given in his long, two-part essay titled "The Training of a Concert Pianist" is just as pertinent today as it was then. He advocated slow, systematic practice, but warned against "pounding away" at just one or two exercises. "If you are not interested in them, work with them until you become interested in them. They should be played with accents and in different rhythms." Sauer wanted his students to strive for clean playing, to develop finger strength and flexibility and to play naturally, without mannerisms or ostentation. And, apart from technical expertise, he wanted students to acquire absolute self-confidence and a pleasing stage personality.

Sauer suggested two hours of practice in the morning and another two hours later in the day. That was his own routine. As a mature pianist, he made up his own exercises by selecting difficult parts of famous pieces and practicing them repeatedly. The most important thing, for himself and for students, was, said Sauer, "concentration—absolute concentration—so that it is possible to learn as much in two hours as many would in two weeks. And let me say that if piano students worked their heads properly, and kept their thoughts under control, they would not need to work their fingers so much, and the result would be astonishing." (Whithorne)

As his practice methods indicate, Sauer was a methodical pianist. When studying a new composition, he first read it through carefully in order to understand the general concept and to make note of exceptionally difficult passages. Next he studied small sections at a time, paying particular attention to fingering. Once he had those difficult parts "in his fingers," he began working on matters of interpretation.

Sauer played a very conservative repertoire—mostly works by Beethoven, Schumann, Chopin, Schubert, Liszt, Brahms, Mendelssohn—and his writings prove that he had little sympathy for contemporary music: "The modern composer is a sort of musical mathematician and engineer, who, with great labor and a tremendous amount of calculation, builds an enormous edifice which, like an American skyscraper, attracts our attention and our wonder for the marvels of its construction and the wonderful precision with which every strain has been calculated and every inch of height and breadth proportioned. Compared to such works as these, to play Mendelssohn is like migrating from the American skyscraper I have used as a simile to a tiny cottage in the country, built in some peaceful spot amid exquisite scenery, where one can live in peace and quiet, fanned by warm breezes carrying with them the scent of a myriad bright flowers." (*MA*, 8 June 1907)

Sauer was a real virtuoso of the old school, a romantic player with the authentic "grand manner." His highly imaginative pianism was, as dozens of reviews expressed it, playing of "great individuality and charm" that delighted audiences everywhere. The renowned pedagogue Martin Krause (Claudio Arrau was his most famous pupil), who heard Liszt play in 1871, declared that Sauer was the true heir to Liszt, that he had more of the master's "charm and geniality than any other Liszt pupil." (Keh/Pia, see Bibliog.)

Clarity, freshness of delivery, beautifully finished interpretations and a phenomenal technique were Sauer's strong points. Critics repeatedly complimented his playing for its fiery virtuosity, its great elegance, the sprightly and infectious rhythms, delicate nuance and invariably good tone. Adverse critical comments dwelt on the point that Sauer's playing was neither profound nor poetic, that it lacked warmth and breadth.

"He plays at times like one possessed," wrote one of Sauer's contemporaries, "but his supreme taste and masterly control enable him to avoid excess and mere sensationalism. Exciting in a high degree is his building up of climaxes, but he never indulges in noise, nor in his wildest flights do we miss a noble self-restraint and repose. Technically we never heard a pianist better equipped." (Lah/Fam, see Bibliog.)

Sauer's first American appearance (10 Jan 1899), at the Metropolitan Opera House with the New York Philharmonic Society and conductor Emil Paur, drew a mixed response. The program opened with the Beethoven Concerto No. 5, closed with the Henselt Concerto in F Minor, op. 16, and in between Sauer played the Chopin A-flat Ballade and the Etude, op. 25, no. 11, the Bach-d'Albert Prelude and Fugue in D Minor and a Schumann *Nachtstück*. A detailed review included the following: "The salient characteristics of Mr. Sauer's performance of the Beethoven concerto were sobriety of color and continence of style. The pianist's range of tone-coloring as exhibited last night did not seem to be wide. He does not revel in the extremes of brilliancy or gloom; but his palette is rich in delicate half-tints. . . . Mr. Sauer did not play the Beethoven concerto with such breadth and dignity as some other artists have shown to this public. . . . In the Bach number the pianist put forth his strongest claim to a high place among players of the older works. . . . The clarity of its polyphonic utterance was beautiful, and the vigor of its style and the splendor of its tonal color left nothing to be desired. In this work, indeed, Mr. Sauer established his right to be called one of the most eminent pianists of the day. The Chopin ballade was too bare of high coloring, and its range of expression was held within too narrow limits. . . . Elegance is one of the most conspicuous features of this pianist's playing, and his performances have a fine finish in their technic that is altogether delightful." (*NYT*, 11 Jan 1899)

Sauer's London program of 20 March 1901 (a Schubert Sonata [B Major, D. 575], something he very seldom programmed, and also the Chopin Sonata in B Minor) "was interesting, and was well adapted for the display both of the celebrated pianist's wonderful technique and of his artistic powers." (*TL*, 21 March 1901) A week later his recital (27 March 1901) included Beethoven's *"Waldstein"* Sonata and the Schumann *Carnaval*, and in both works he played "the most brilliant and the most delicate passages with equal success. . . . Among his other performances must be noted the wonderfully delicate readings which he gave of Mendelssohn's Scherzo in E minor and of Chopin's Nocturne, op. 27, no. 2." (*TL*, 29 March 1901)

At a Carnegie Hall performance (5 Dec 1908) of the Schumann Concerto with the Boston Symphony Orchestra, Max Fiedler conducting, Sauer played "with much clarity and fleetness of finger, but he did not penetrate deeply into the tender poetry of either the first movement or the entrancing simplicity of the intermezzo. They were set forth in a clear and rather dry light. In the finale he gave a richer view of the musical content of the movement. There were a finely elastic spirit and a clear-cut rhythm in his playing, which sparkled with a delicate brilliancy." (*NYT*, 6 Dec 1908)

Sauer doted on long recital programs. On 14 March 1911 his Queen's Hall program consisted of the Beethoven Sonata, op. 110, Schumann's *Faschingsschwank aus Wien*, op. 26, and works by Schubert, Chopin, Rubinstein, Mendelssohn, Liszt and Sauer himself. "Perhaps the finest performance of the afternoon was the F Minor Scherzo of Mendelssohn. Here was a piece which might have been written for Sauer, so beautifully does it show forth all of his fine qualities. It was like a breath from fairyland under his wonderful fingers." Contrarily, "It may be captious to state that the 'Faschingsschwank' left much to be desired rhythmically and from the interpretive side, but certainly that was my impression. The rhythms were too distorted in the first section, while the tone was often cold and unsympathetic." (*MA*, 1 April 1911)

Exactly one year later (14 March 1912) Sauer's very successful recital in Glasgow, Scotland, was again dominated by Beethoven (Sonata in F Minor, op. 57) and Schumann (Fantasia in C Major, op. 17), and also included works by Chopin, Liszt, Sgambati and Sauer. He played the opening movement of the Beethoven "in his biggest manner and with a fine sense of its dramatic character. The Andante was delicately touched, and the finale had wonderful fire and brilliance. . . . Sauer always plays Schumann well, and last night he gave a great performance of the Fantasie—a performance full of poetry and with the intimate note that marks the real Schumann lover; one cannot recall a more masterly performance of the middle movement." (*GH*, 15 March 1912)

A review of Sauer's London recital (19 Jan 1924) at Wigmore Hall states that his playing of Beethoven's "*Appassionata*" lacked musical and emotional depths, but his performance of Mendelssohn's *Rondo capriccioso* was a marvel. "The quality of mind which M. Sauer here displayed has no one technical term; it was the quality of understanding the pianoforte in precisely the same way that Mendelssohn, when writing this admirable *Rondo*, understood it." (*MT*, 1 Feb 1924)

Sauer's recital on 10 October 1930 in Berlin's Philharmonic Hall marked the 50th anniversary of his formal debut in Hamburg at the age of 18. "The evening was an eloquent manifestation of the esteem in which this fine old master of the art of piano playing is held by his host of admirers and disciples, who came to render homage to a magnificent career and to wonder anew at the gigantic technic, the interpretative insight, the glowing temperament and the imposing power and authority which are still almost without counterpart among his confrères." (*MA*, 10 Nov 1930)

Considering the fact that Sauer made his first professional tour in 1882, it is astonishing to find him making recordings as late as 1941. The 10 compositions included in the 2-CD *Pupils of Liszt* album (see Discog.) date from 1925 (Chopin Waltz in E Minor, op. posth., Mendelssohn Scherzo in E Minor) through 1941 (Chopin Waltz in F Major, op. 34, no. 3, Liszt *Ricordanza*). This collection of works by Beethoven, Chopin, Mendelssohn, Liszt and Sauer provides good examples of Sauer at his best, playing in the "grand manner" for which he was famous.

Sauer, the only Liszt pupil to record both Liszt concertos, made those recordings when he was 76 years old. They have been reissued, together with five Liszt piano solos, on a single CD: "Sauer pursued a moderate artistic path typified by a deeply felt, lyrical, poetic approach to his repertoire. This is not to suggest that he lacked strength or virtuosity, but only that he chose not to emphasize these elements. . . . The solid, sober musical values inherent in the concertos are also very much evident in the five solo works. Sauer molds the melodic lines with a deep singing tone and is never in a hurry to reach his musical goals." (*ARG*, July/Aug 1990) Another reviewer enthusiastically recommends this "primary document. . . . Of the present performances, what may be said is that they are expansive, lovingly detailed without loss of cohesion, and—above all—unself-conscious." (*Fan*, July/Aug 1990)

And a final judgment, based on a comparison with recordings of the Liszt Concerto No. 1 by five other pianists: "While all the modern pianists make this concerto sound easy, Sauer makes it sound difficult because of sluggish tempos and wrong notes. However, if Sauer at age seventy-six cannot match the young pianists of today in matters of dexterity, they cannot match him in interpretive insight, sense of proportion and nobility of phrasing. . . . Sauer's recording is our link to the nineteenth century." (Yin)

SELECTED REFERENCES

"Emil Sauer Champions Simplicity." *Musical America*, 8 June 1907, p. 19.
"Emil Sauer's Advice To Students." *Musical America*, 17 Oct 1908, p. 6.
"Emil von Sauer." *Phonographianna*, Jan/Feb 1957, pp. 9–10.
Lipatti, Dinu. "Emil Sauer." In *Lipatti*, by Dragos Tanasescu and Grigore Bargauanu. London: Kahn & Averill, 1988, pp. 66–68.
Obituary. *Musical America*, May 1942, p. 26. *New York Times*, 30 April 1942, p. 19.
Renfroe, Anita Boyle. *Emil Von Sauer: A Catalogue of his Piano Works.* DMA Dissertation, Southern Baptist Theological Seminary, 1981.
Sauer, Emil. "Lessons With Franz Liszt." *Etude*, Dec 1910, pp. 721–722.
———. *Meine Welt. Bilder aus dem Geheimfache meiner Kunst und meines Lebens.* Stuttgart: Verlag von W. Spemann, 1901.
———. "Progress in Music Study." *Etude*, Jan 1914, pp. 13–14.
———. "The Training of a Concert Pianist." Part I. *Etude*, Dec 1908, p. 763.
———. "The Training of a Concert Pianist." Part II. *Etude*, Jan 1909, p. 23.
"Sauer's Success Secrets." *Musical America*, 24 Feb 1912, p. 37.
"Von Sauer Feted on Anniversary." *Musical America*, 10 Nov 1930, p. 8.
Whithorne, Emerson. "It's a Dog's Life, Says Emil Sauer." *Musical America*, 16 April 1910.
Yin, Chung-Sil. *Franz Liszt's Piano Concerto No. 1 in E-flat Major: A Comparison Of Recorded Performances Representing Different Schools of Piano Playing From Emil Von Sauer To Liu Shih-kun.* Thesis, Master of Arts, Dec 1982. California State University, Long Beach.
See also Bibliography: Ald/Con; Coo/GrP; Lah/Fam; New/Gro; Nie/Mei; Pay/Cel; Rat/Cle; Reu/Gre; Sal/Fam; Woo/My.

SELECTED REVIEWS

GH: 15 March 1912. *MA*: 1 April 1911. *MT*: 1 Feb 1924. *NYT*: 11 Jan 1899; 19 Jan 1899; 6 Dec 1908. *TL*: 11 May 1896; 18 May 1896; 21 March 1901; 29 March 1901; 10 Feb 1910; 15 March 1911; 10 May 1911; 13 March 1912; 21 March 1919.

SELECTED DISCOGRAPHY

The Compositions of Franz Liszt. *Auf Flügeln des Gesanges* (Mendelssohn-Liszt); *Mazeppa* (Transcendental Etude No. 4). From Welte Piano Rolls.
Emil von Sauer. Chopin: Etudes, op. 10, no. 3, op. 25, no. 7; Impromptu, op. 36; *Fantasie-Impromptu*, op. 66; Waltz, op. 42. Liszt: Consolation in D-flat Major; *Gnomenreigen*; *La Campanella; Valse oubliée no. 1*; *Ricordanza*. Beethoven-Rubinstein: Turkish March. Mendelssohn: Scherzo from "A Midsummer Night's Dream." Sauer: *Frisson de Feuilles*; *Galop de Concert*; *Konzert Polka*; *Spieluhr.* Gustafson Piano Library cassette GPL 166.
Emil von Sauer plays Liszt. Concerto No. 1 in E-flat Major; Concerto No. 2 in A Major; *Ricordanza;* Consolation in D-flat Major; *Valse oubliée no. 1*;

Gnomenreigen; La Campanella. Pearl GEMM CD 9403. Weingartner/
  Orch. du Conservatoire de Paris.
The Pupils of Liszt. Beethoven-Rubinstein: Turkish March. Chopin: Etude in
  C Minor, op. 25, no. 12; Waltzes in F Major, op. 34, no. 3, in A-flat
  Major, op. 42, in E minor, op. posth. Liszt: *Ricordanza.* Mendelssohn:
  Scherzo in E Minor, op. 16, no. 2; Mendelssohn-Sauer: Scherzo from "A
  Midsummer Night's Dream." Sauer: *Espenlaub*; Concert Polka. Pearl
  Gemm CDS 9972 (2 CDs). A different selection from that on the LP of the
  same title.
The Pupils of Liszt. Chopin: Etude in E Major, op. 10, no. 3; Waltz in A-flat
  Major, op. 42. Liszt: *Liebestraum no. 3*; *Ricordanza.* Pearl OPAL 824/5.
Welte-Mignon 1905. Chopin: Nocturne in D-flat Major, op. 27, no. 2.
  TELDEC CD 8.43930.

SCHIFF, ANDRÁS: b. 21 December 1953, Budapest, Hungary.

> He is entirely without the traditional pomposities associated with pi-
> anists. He strips everything away, and lets the music pass through him
> with absolute naturalness and no distortion. He is one of the few musi-
> cians whose goals are purely musical.
>   Steven Isserlis (*The Sunday Times* [London], 2 September 1990)

András Schiff possesses more than enough talent, technique and individuality to
achieve the kind of high-profile, high-profit success desired by so many modern
musicians; but Schiff stands apart in that his goals are indeed "purely musical."
Schiff performs because he loves to make music, so much so that he will forgo
a lucrative concerto engagement in favor of a more intimate—and for him far
more satisfying—chamber-music performance. Schiff is also unique in that he
finds musical inspiration in listening to historical recordings made by an older
generation of musicians—Alfred Cortot, Artur Schnabel, Pablo Casals, Joseph
Szigeti, Wilhelm Furtwängler, Adolf Busch—all of them, in his view, very
great, very personal artists not afraid to take risks in their playing. Like them,
Schiff gives the listener the impression that the music is being created as he performs it; however, behind his seeming improvisation there is an "ironclad discipline and intellectual integrity." (*NYP*, 18 Aug 1987)
        András Schiff was not a child prodigy, and his parents were only ama-
teur musicians—his father played violin, his mother the piano. Although Schiff
started piano lessons at the early age of five, he had a normal childhood. "I was
playing the piano and making music for fun, never practicing for more than half
an hour a day. I was playing football and all the usual things." (Greenfield) His
mother (his father, a physician, died when Schiff was about five) never pressured
him to practice or gave him any lessons. At age 12 Schiff himself realized that
he wanted to be a pianist, and after eight years of study with Elizabeth Kadass ("a

very good teacher," recalls Schiff), he enrolled at the Franz Liszt Academy, where he studied piano with Pál Kadosa and Ferenc Rados; chamber music with György Kurtág; and also had three hours a day of academic courses. The mature Schiff is grateful that his teachers were composers, thus lessons were never just piano playing but also discussions of style, taste and structure.

During the mid-1970s Schiff attended the summer master classes offered in London (from age 12 Schiff usually spent summers with London relatives) by George Malcolm, the renowned British harpsichordist, conductor and scholar. An expert on Bach's keyboard music, Malcolm doubtlessly encouraged young Schiff to give special attention to Bach. Schiff played Bach's Goldberg Variations as his graduation program at the Franz Liszt Academy in 1975. Meanwhile, in 1974 he placed fourth in the Tchaikovsky Competition in Moscow; and in 1975 earned a third place at the Leeds International Piano Competition.

However, he was not dependent on winning competitions to obtain playing engagements. To help start their careers, young Hungarian artists were given an opportunity to perform an hour program of works of their own choosing before a selected group of important critics, managers, teachers, sometimes even conductors. Schiff actually got his first professional engagement through television exposure (the finals of the Leeds Competition were widely televised) and through Charles Rosen, one of the judges at Leeds, who recommended Schiff to his own manager. Tours of Austria, Holland, Poland, Denmark, the USSR, Poland and Great Britain followed.

Schiff was in full command at his American debut (4 May 1978, Carnegie Hall), performing Bach's Concerto No. 1 in D Minor and Mozart's Concerto in E-flat Major, K. 449, with the Franz Liszt Chamber Orchestra of Budapest. "His fingers are remarkably deft and accurate. He played with very little pedal and perfect articulation, no matter how swift the ornaments. The fast movements had an energy, rhythmic élan and unflagging pace that made them exhilarating." His reading of the Mozart was "a quicksilver performance that gave the evening a special radiance." (*NYT*, 5 May 1978)

Extensive tours of Europe and the United States established Schiff as one of Hungary's leading young artists. Although he had a good life and a privileged position, he realized that to develop and improve he needed a broader outlook on the world, and in Hungary, small and then somewhat isolated, the possibilities for personal and artistic growth were limited. Seeking to further his career in the West, he moved to New York in 1979. Now recognized as one of today's finest pianists, Schiff usually plays about 90 concerts a year—in Europe, the United States, the Orient—and divides his time between New York, London (where he has always performed frequently) and Salzburg, where his wife, the violinist Yuuko Shiokawa, is a professor at the *Mozarteum*.

Not many star recitalists play chamber music, but András Schiff has a passion for playing with other instrumentalists and with singers; and he regularly sets aside a substantial amount of his performance time for chamber music—"there is a warmth in it that one cannot duplicate in anything else." Endowed with a fabulous memory, Schiff memorizes the full scores, thus always knows what the other players are doing. He had a valuable chamber-music experience during three summers (1978–80) at Marlboro with Rudolf Serkin and Mieczyslaw Horszowski. Schiff has performed with violinists Yuuko Shiokawa, Gidon Kremer and Sándor Végh, with oboist Heinz Holliger and with cellist Steven Isserlis. Among singers (playing with singers, says Schiff, is the way to learn about color and legato), he has appeared with tenor Peter Schreier, bass-baritone Robert Holl and sopranos Barbara Hendricks and Cecilia Bartoli. Schiff has also played with the Juilliard, Guarneri, Panocha and Takács string quartets. In 1988 he was artistic director of a Haydn chamber-music festival held at Wigmore Hall in London and later repeated in New York and Vienna. In 1989 he founded a small chamber-music festival in Mondsee, Austria, about 10 miles east of Salzburg, where each September musicians spend a week concentrating on just two composers. Schiff has also participated in mini-festivals, such as the Hohenems *Schubertiade* in Austria; the International Musicians' Seminar at Prussia Cove, Cornwall.

Among Schiff's varied pantheon of idols and influences, he especially admires Edwin Fischer and Alfred Cortot because, he says, "they were complete human beings, representing not just the piano, not just music, but the whole of European culture, cosmopolitan in the best sense." (*MA*, April 1984) He also acknowledges that he owes a great deal in all his music making to George Malcolm, "who knew how to put life into a musical text—how to use knowledge of musical history and how to compose ornamentation and phrasing." (Wigler) And the revolutionary Glenn Gould was also one of Schiff's early idols. "What I probably admired most about him was that he took risks. He never followed the well-trodden path. Too few musicians take risks these days." (*NYT*, 16 Oct 1983) Finally, Schiff's admiration for the late Mieczyslaw Horszowski ("a miracle," says Schiff, "he opened up a new world to me") is so great that he once canceled one of his own performances in order to hear Horszowski play. "If Mr. Horszowski gives a concert in Los Angeles," said Schiff in a 1987 interview, "I would get on a plane immediately to go hear him." (*NYT*, 15 Nov 1987)

András Schiff's broad repertoire ranges from the Baroque to the 20th century. He adores the music of Bach and dislikes the music of Liszt. As he has often said, "I value music where there is not one unnecessary note, like a Bach fugue. You really can't take anything out. I find that in Liszt you can take out half of the notes and you lose nothing. In fact, it probably sounds better." It may be that Schiff simply had an overdose of Liszt in Budapest, where, he says, "there is a big Liszt cult. . . . Everybody bangs Liszt day and night. . . . I feel no sympathy or affection for the music of Liszt." (Chism)

In Schiff's own words, his repertoire follows what he calls "the Bach line," meaning Bach (and to the side Scarlatti and Handel), Haydn, Mozart, Beethoven, Schubert, Mendelssohn, Schumann, Chopin, Brahms and, surprisingly, Max Reger. In recent years Schiff has been playing Reger's Variations on a Theme of J. S. Bach, "a fantastic piece." Schiff especially likes the music of his compatriot Bartók, and while Grieg and Debussy appear on his programs, he finds it difficult to identify with contemporary music, and will play only that which he really likes. In 1987 he learned all of Schoenberg's solo piano works, not, he says, a very successful venture ("I can't make heads or tails of it"), but he does better with the music of Alban Berg.

At one time Schiff played a great many concertos. For example, in the mid-1980s he toured extensively with 25 concertos (Mozart, Beethoven, Chopin, Brahms, Bartók). Since then Schiff has become increasingly disillusioned with the commercial aspects of concerto performances, where soloist and orchestra have too little time for rehearsing, where everything is geared according to expense. In recent years he has been concentrating more and more on cycles, preferring to make a carefully researched, in-depth statement of one composer at a time. In 1990–91 he gave eight all-Bach recitals at Wigmore Hall in London.

Above all, András Schiff is most famous for performing Bach works on the modern piano, playing them so well that most authorities now rank Schiff as the successor to the late Glenn Gould, also famous for playing Bach on the piano. The usually mild Schiff (like Claudio Arrau, another gentle pianist, Schiff hates things mechanical, avoids television and does not know how to drive a car) is very outspoken on the controversial subject of playing Bach on the piano versus playing Bach on so-called historically faithful instruments. In Schiff's plain language, playing Bach only on the harpsichord is ridiculous and dogmatic because we today cannot really know just how works were performed in the past. Schiff looks on the harpsichord as a mechanical, inexpressive tool, and reminds us that the clavichord cannot be heard in a modern concert hall. "I don't think the authentic people today are very authentic. They do everything right, but they never improvise or have any sense of liberty or freedom. There is no flexibility, they take repeats like photocopies of the first time, with the same *rubato* and phrasings. I just don't think authenticity exists. After all, there have to be two sides, authentic players and authentic audiences—and where are the audiences?" (*OV*, July 1985)

Schiff's Bach playing resembles Gould's "not only in its rhythmic control and alertness but also in its audacity with dynamics, tempo, rubato and decoration." (*MT*, April 1983) A Glenn Gould performance of Bach on the piano is, like his other playing, very articulated—staccato, marcato, nonlegato. Schiff uses the Gould attacks, but he believes that Bach on the piano should also include legato and not try to be an imitation of the harpsichord. Indeed, "he seems miraculously to translate Bach's musical language in terms of the modern grand piano. There is never the suggestion that he is imitating a harpsichord, yet he produces harpsichord effects." (*CST*, 1 Feb 1982)

Critics take sides on the issue of playing Bach on the piano. Some find it beguiling and beautiful, but those who adhere to the idea of historically faithful performances complain that Schiff's playing is marred by excessive *rubato*. To that, Schiff responds that Bach is the greatest Romantic and very emotional and should be played with freedom, and that his works contain a world of colors that can be re-created on the piano.

Schiff organizes demanding programs from his weighty repertoire. Each must have form and shape, and the works must be somehow connected, either in terms of history, tonality or form. When he is preparing, say, a Mozart composition, he will read about Mozart and listen to recordings of Mozart's other works—not just the piano works but quartets, quintets, especially the operas. If preparing a Schubert work, he invariably thinks of Lieder, so he studies German romantic poetry. His preparation does not usually include listening to other pianists' recordings of the works he has scheduled.

As for practicing, Schiff loves it and practices a great deal, sometimes as much as seven or eight hours at a time. His is not routine mechanical practicing. He reads scores, and he plays a lot of Bach, in whose music he finds all the important requisites for piano technique. "My day always starts with Bach. It's like a brainwashing every morning to play and work on three or four of the Preludes and Fugues from the Forty-Eight. Then I feel like a different person. For me Bach is the most essential composer. There is no great music after Bach which does not have its roots in Bach's polyphony. If you approach it from that point of view, it helps. Even Bartók is related to Bach." (*MA*, April 1984)

András Schiff's profound, natural musicianship may be his greatest asset. From a dozen years of reviews he emerges as one of the new-style pianists (Murray Perahia, Radu Lupu, Peter Serkin, among others) replacing the bedazzling technical wizards (Horowitz, Cherkassky, for example) of the preceding generation. Schiff, in his playing and in his choice of works to play, forgoes the Horowitz kind of flamboyance for the kind of simplicity he so admires in the playing of Horszowski. "For all his freewheeling rhetoric, his subjective nuancing, his sometimes controversial idiosyncrasies, everything about Schiff's procedure . . . is governed by a deep seriousness; by a probing, erudite intellect, and by a deeply musical impulse." (*MA*, April 1983)

To those critics who say that his playing lacks drama, Schiff replies that they may not understand subtlety and understatement. He prefers to suggest things to an audience, "not to force things down their throats. I give my audience credit for fantasy and imagination. I'm not interested in raping the music or the audience, and I get very angry when I listen to exhibitionistic performers. Instead of assaulting my audience I like to indicate the drama through sonority and the timing." (Dub/Ref, see Bibliog.)

Although he detests sentimentality, Schiff loves sentiment and feeling. "His pianism has been widely praised for its keen intellectual command and beautiful tonal surface within a poetic, sophisticated style." (Rhein) Critics have noted Schiff's occasional willingness to take rhythmic liberties, to apply a generous *rubato* to preclassic music, to bend the line for the sake of emotional expression.

Like his idols of the past, Schiff likes to take risks. Phrasing, he tells interviewers, is all-important. "The written note is not the be-all and end-all in 18th-century music. The pianist is almost a composer; that was expected in those days, and the 19th-century approach of being faithful to every note is silly." If taking risks means playing wrong notes, that too is not important to Schiff, who thinks that nowadays there is far too much emphasis on perfection. While he does not like to hear himself play wrong notes, when he listens to the old recordings of his musical heroes, he finds them so exciting that, he says, he never even thinks about the mistakes, never even hears them.

Schiff's performance (7 Oct 1984) of Bach's Well-Tempered Clavier, Book I, at Chicago's Orchestra Hall drew critical raves: "He keeps the music flowing, the rhythm firm, the contrapuntal lines well defined. There is no gratuitous infusion of accent and expression, and the dynamic range of the instrument is kept within the limits suggested by the style. . . . His playing is clear, clean, orderly and expressive in the highest sense that you are always more aware of what Bach is doing to the music than what Schiff is doing to Bach." (*CST*, 8 Oct 1984) Equally complimentary, another critic praised Schiff for his individuality and integrity, and opined that Schiff plays Bach so convincingly because he is a remarkable technician and "delivers the music without a trace of dry pedantry. He seems to have thought through every note Bach wrote in pianistic terms. . . . The clarity of his voicings, the beauty of his legato, the crispness of his articulations, the pliability of his rhythm, the subtlety of his dynamics, the rightness of his tempo choices—it was all there." (*CT*, 8 Oct 1984)

Schiff gave a compelling performance of Book II of the Well-Tempered Clavier at London's Wigmore Hall on 16 November 1985: "Consistently impressive throughout were his seemingly infallible sense of rhythm, his irreproachable tempi, and a fascinating variety of touch, accent and colour, deployed without a trace of affection, but invariably to clarify and illuminate the distinctive essence of each individual piece." (*DT*, 18 Nov 1985)

In 1985 Schiff gave a three-recital exploration of Bach's *Klavierübung* (the Goldberg Variations, Six Partitas, the French Overture, Italian Concerto and Four Duets) at the New York Metropolitan Museum of Art. "With a humanistic view of Bach, Schiff puts his prodigious technique and gorgeous sound in the service of the music. . . . The most immediately striking feature of Schiff's Bach, both on his London records and in person, is its beguiling surface beauty. No matter how complex the textures or how intricate the contrapuntal discourse may be, he never permits the slightest suggestion of a forced or unmusical sound. The ability to produce a piano tone characterized by such consistently deep-centered, warmly rounded solidity and clarity is one hallmark of a prodigious technique. It takes even greater discipline, control, and intelligence to put this gorgeous sound completely in the service of the music—not an end in itself, but the starting point to create absorbing Bach performances that draw upon the piano's most relevant coloristic, rhythmic, and articulative resources." (*New York Magazine*, 15 April 1985. Reprinted by permission.)

At the other end of the repertoire spectrum, there is Schiff's performance (3 Oct 1985) of Tchaikovsky's Piano Concerto No. 1 with Georg Solti and the Chicago Symphony Orchestra. "What made this exceptional was not the fire and brimstone of Schiff's grand virtuoso manner—though that is undeniably impressive—but the attention to small details of rhythm, accent and nuance. This may have been the most exciting performance of this music I have heard in some time. It certainly was the most accurate." (*CST*, 4 Oct 1985)

Schiff often programs Bartók's works. On 5 January 1982 he played Bartók's Piano Concerto No. 3 with the Philadelphia Orchestra, William Smith conducting. "It was clear last night that Schiff is a major talent. He handled the Bartók concerto with finesse and intense feeling combined. The three movements were polished and charged with the authentic Hungarian idiom. Schiff's use of octaves was refined and exciting, while his attention to rhythmic detail was exact and evocative." (*PEB*, 6 Jan 1982)

Schiff's performance of the overplayed Grieg Concerto at Chicago's Orchestra Hall on 20 May 1982 brought a freshness and poetry to the familiar piece. "His was not a view predicated on fiery bravura display. It was essentially a poetic, intimate statement, an interpretation that let the singing lines expand at a relatively unhurried pace, the soaring melodies take shape with purling delicacy. It was Grieg without Romantic indulgence masquerading as style. It was refreshing." (*CT*, 22 May 1982)

In 1993 Schiff gave a six-concert survey of those Schubert sonatas—18 of them—which the composer left in a more or less complete state. At the first recital (6 Jan 1993) of the London series, the major work was the Sonata in A Minor, D. 845. "Here, in music that ranges as wide as anything in the repertoire, Schiff needed to draw on every facet of his considerable art. He relished alike every turn of the imposing opening movement, the rich variations of the C major slow movement, and the fleet virtuosity, still of a spiritual rather than an exhibitionistic kind, demanded by the Rondo finale." (*TL*, 8 Jan 1993)

The most striking aspect of Schiff's playing is his obvious joy in what he does. This is particularly true with the music of Bach.

"Over the years," Schiff tells interviewers, "I've grown more accustomed to recordings. At the beginning I hated it because it was so clinical, so difficult to create an atmosphere." Recording has taught him to hear himself better, a big shock at first, but "it develops your self-control enormously." Schiff does not believe in splicing; he records in long, continuous takes and does any necessary cosmetic editing later.

His numerous Bach recordings draw the most critical attention (Grammys: Well-Tempered Clavier, 1986, 1987; English Suites, 1989). In his recording of the Six Partitas, it is "the pliancy, the lightness of touch, the variety of sound and phrasing that make this recording so evocative, creating an atmosphere of elegant tranquility." (*NYT*, 16 June 1985) Schiff's recording of the Goldberg Variations (*Ovation* magazine listed it as a "Recording of Distinction" and *Stereo Review* as a "Recording of Special Merit") has reaped a rich harvest of praise. "The recording is . . . genuine and unpretentious: an expansive, thoughtful, clarifying, yet utterly unselfconscious reading by a performer who is thoroughly inside the music." (*StR*, Jan 1984) Outstanding in this performance is the manner in which Schiff adds ornaments to the repeated sections. He merely does what he thinks is artistically correct, and the effect is thrilling. "Ornamentation is the style," he says, "and it's necessary. You have to think, for instance, of the ornate character of Baroque churches. If you play the music without ornamentation and the other stylistic devices, it's like showing a Baroque church without woodcarvings or paintings, just bare walls." (Kozinn, "Hungarian Virtuoso")

In the recordings of Bach's complete solo keyboard concertos, performed with the Chamber Orchestra of Europe, Schiff conducting from the keyboard (see Discog.), the sound is excellent and the performances superb, with the pianist showing great variety of touch and sensitivity to harmonic tension. For an example of the younger Schiff, the CD (Omega OCD 1014) consisting of three substantial Bach solo pieces is a gem. Recorded in Tokyo in 1978, it first appeared on the *Hungaroton* label (SLPX 12131), and it shows that even at age 25 Schiff was in full command of his art. "His playing of Bach is clear, unmannered, and irresistibly lively. . . . He is at his best in the joyous playing of the fast movements." (*Fan*, Sept/Oct 1991)

In 1970 he recorded the complete set of Mozart sonatas, now remastered to CD format. The competition—notably Barenboim and Uchida—offers a formidable challenge, but each of these individualistic artists has something valuable and different to express. In Schiff's recordings, some of the sonatas, i.e., the C Minor, K. 457 (with its Fantasy, K. 475), are delightful, others sound somewhat dry, with overemphasis on nonlegato playing.

As a set the sonatas, splendid as they are, in no wise compare to the masterly cycle of 21 Mozart concertos put on disc by Schiff and the *Camerata Academica* of the Salzburg *Mozarteum*, conducted by Sándor Végh. From a review covering Concertos K. 271 and K. 415: "At this point, it hardly seems necessary to indicate in so many words the excellences of this performing team, which achieves readings of such definite character that all but a few predecessors seem bland and routine by comparison." (*Fan*, Nov/Dec 1990) Remarks from another reviewer on K. 414 and K. 449 are similarly laudatory. "Schiff is superb. In both works, using almost no rubato and limiting his tonal range, he manages a rich expressivity achieved with pointed textural clarity and a highlighting of inner voices often smudged by other pianists." (*Fan*, May/June 1990)

Other noteworthy Schiff recordings include his two collections of Scarlatti sonatas, upon which he lavishes as much affection and care as he does on the music of Bach. And he reveals another completely different facet of his playing in the two Mendelssohn concertos and the collection of Songs Without Words (see Discog.), in which his exquisitely varied touch and precise articulation let Mendelssohn's romanticism speak for itself.

Schiff is presently engaged in recording a seven-CD cycle of Schubert sonatas for London (see Discog.). An opinion on one of these discs: "This Schubert cycle is beginning to look like one of the more encouraging achievements of our time. . . . Those who like their C minor Sonata [D. 958] bulging with Byronic sentiment or exploding with theatrical sparks will no doubt find Schiff's approach intolerably ascetic. For me, though, the absorption, the inner penetration of his playing here is worth the loss of a few histrionic thrills." (*Gram*, Oct 1994)

SELECTED REFERENCES

Cera, Stephen. "Looking to the mind of a virtuoso pianist." *Baltimore Sun*, 23 July 1984, sec. D, p. 1.

Chism, Olin. "His key to success." *Dallas Times Herald*, 6 March 1983, sec. J, p. 1.

Dyer, Richard. "The well-tempered pianist." *Boston Globe*, 11 Aug 1985, sec. A, pp. 1, 5.

Elder, Dean. "András Schiff." *Clavier*, Nov 1983, pp. 16–20.

Fleming, Shirley. "András Schiff." *Stereo Review*, July 1992, pp. 53–55.

Goldsmith, Harris. "A Young Hungarian Surpasses the Masters." *American Record Guide*, July/Aug 1993, pp. 21–22.

Greenfield, Edward. "András Schiff." *Musical America*, April 1984, pp. 4–5, 39.

Keller, James M. "The Outspoken András Schiff." (interview) *Piano Quarterly*, Winter 1991-92, pp. 22–27.

Kenyon, Nicholas. "Living in the past with Bach." *The Times* (London), 27 Oct 1984, p. 8.

Kimmelman, Michael. "András Schiff." *Ovation*, July 1985, pp. 11–13.

———. "A New Image for the Virtuoso." *New York Times*, 15 Nov 1987, sec. 2, p. 29.

Kozinn, Allan. "For this Pianist, Bach Is the Greatest Romantic of All." *New York Times*, 16 Oct 1983, sec. 2, p. 25.

———. "Hungarian Virtuoso András Schiff." *Keyboard*, Dec 1984, pp. 33–36.

Margles, Pamela. "Pianist András Schiff: Young and Distinctive." *Music Magazine*, May/June 1983, pp. 6–10.

Methuen-Campbell, James. "András Schiff." *Music and Musicians*, April 1985, pp. 9–10.

Oestreich, James R. "A pianist who swallows composers whole." *New York Times*, 7 March 1993, sec. 2, pp. 25–26.

Rhein, John von. "Well-tempered pianist." *Chicago Tribune*, 8 May 1988, sec. 13, p. 10.

Rosenberg, Donald. "Bartók's his hero, pianist admits." *Pittsburgh Press*, 28 Jan 1990, sec. G, pp. 1, 5.

Seckerson, Edward. "András Schiff." *Gramophone*, March 1989, pp. 1401–1402.

Smith, Harriet. "Far from the madding crowd." *Gramophone*, Oct 1994, pp. 22–23. Schiff discusses his ongoing Schubert sonata cycle.

Wigler, Stephen. "Schiff Proves Bach Is Beautiful on the Piano." *Baltimore Sun*, 22 Feb 1987, sec. D, pp. 1, 3.

See also Bibliography: Dub/Ref; IWWM.

SELECTED REVIEWS

BaS: 24 March 1986. *BG*: 16 Aug 1985. *CST*: 1 Feb 1982; 8 Oct 1984; 20 Feb 1989. *CT*: 22 May 1982; 8 Oct 1984; 4 Oct 1985. *DT*: 18 Nov 1985. *LAHE*: 2 March 1989. *LAT*: 31 July 1980; 2 March 1989; 10 Oct 1990. *LIN*: 4 Nov 1987. *MA*: April 1983 *MT*: April 1983. *NewY*: 15 April 1985. *NYP*: 18 Aug 1987. *NYT*: 5 May 1978; 22 Aug 1982; 3 March 1987; 19 March 1993; 12 April 1993. *PEB*: 6 Jan 1982. *PI*: 24 March 1993. *PP*: 2 Feb 1990. *SFC*: 18 Feb 1992. *S-L*: 18 Feb 1991. *STL*: 4 Nov 1984; 17 Jan 1993. *TL*: 22 Sept 1980; 5 Jan 1981; 16 Aug 1983; 19 June 1985; 15 Nov 1985; 8 Jan 1988; 8 Jan 1993; 7 March 1994. *WP*: 26 March 1984.

SELECTED DISCOGRAPHY

András Schiff plays Schumann. Arabeske, op. 18; *Humoreske*, op. 20; *Papillons*, op. 2. MHS 513658Z (CD).

Bach, J. S.: Chromatic Fantasy and Fugue, BWV 903; English Suite No. 4, BWV 809; Partita No. 5, BWV 829; Toccata in D Major, BWV 912. *Hungaroton* HCD-11690.

Bach, J. S.: Concertos (complete). London 425676-2 (2 CDs). Schiff/CO of Europe.

Bach, J. S.: English Suites (6). London 421640-2 (2 CDs).

Bach, J. S.: French Suites (6). London 433 313-2.

Bach, J. S.: Goldberg Variations. London 417116-2.

Bach, J. S.: Italian Concerto, BWV 831; French Suite No. 5, BWV 816; Partita in B Minor, BWV 971. Omega OCD 1014.

Bach, J. S.: Partitas (6). London 411732-2 (2 CDs).

Bach, J. S.: Well-Tempered Clavier, Book I. London 414388-2 (2 CDs).

Bach, J. S.: Well-Tempered Clavier, Book II. London 417236-2 (2 CDs).

Bartók: Dance Suite; Hungarian Peasant Songs; Romanian Folk Dances; 3 Rondos. Denon C37-7092 (CD).

Chopin: Concerto No. 2 in F Minor, op. 21. Schumann: Concerto in A Minor, op. 54. London 411942-2. Dorati/*Concertgebouw*.

Mendelssohn: Concerto No. 1 in G Minor, op. 25; Concerto No. 2 in D Minor, op. 40. London 414672-2, also MHS 513134A. Dutoit/Bavarian Radio SO.

Mendelssohn: Songs Without Words (selections). London 421119-2.

Mozart: Concerto in D Major, K. 175; Concerto in B-flat Major, K. 238; Rondo in D Major, K. 382. London 430 517-2. Végh/*Camerata Academica*.

Mozart: Concerto in E Major, K. 271; Concerto in C Major, K. 415. London 425466-2. Végh/*Camerata Academica*.

Mozart: Concerto in A Major, K. 414; Concerto in E-flat Major, K. 449. London 417886-2. Végh/*Camerata Academica*.

Mozart: Concerto: Concerto in G Major, K. 453; Concerto in B-flat Major, K. 456. London 414289-2. Also MHS 513156F. Végh/*Camerata Academica*.

Mozart: Concerto in F Major, K. 459; Concerto in B-flat Major, K. 595. London 421259-2. Also MHS 513157Z. Végh/*Camerata Academica*.

Mozart: Concerto in E-flat Major, K. 482; Concerto in A Major, K. 488. London 425855-2. Végh/*Camerata Academica*.

Mozart: Sonatas (17). London 430333-2 (5 CDs).

Scarlatti, D.: Sonatas (15). London 421369-2.

Scarlatti, D.: Sonatas (12). London 421422-2.

Schubert: Impromptus, D. 899; Impromptus, D. 935. *Hungaroton* SLPX 12130.

Schubert: Six *Deutsche Tänze*, D. 820; *Grazer Galopp*, D. 925; Impromptus, D. 899; Six *Moments musicaux*, D. 780; *Ungarische Melodie* in B Minor, D. 817. London 430 425-2.

Schubert: Sonatas, Vol. 1. Sonata in F-sharp Minor, D. 571; Sonata in C Major, D. 840; Sonata in A Minor, D. 845. London 440 305-2.

Schubert: Sonatas, Vol. 2. Sonata in E Minor, D. 566; Sonata in A Minor, D. 784; Sonata in D Major, D. 850. London 440 306-2.
Schubert: Sonatas, Vol. 3. Sonata in A-flat Major, D. 557; Sonata in B Major, D. 575; Sonata in G Major, D. 894. London 440 307-2.
Schubert: Sonatas, Vol. 4. Sonata in E-flat Major, D. 568; Sonata in C Minor, D. 958. London 440 308-2.
Schubert: Sonatas, Vol. 5. Sonata in A Minor, D. 537; Sonata in A Major, D. 959. London 440 309-2.

VIDEO

Bach: Goldberg Variations. Teldec Video 9031-73670-3.
Bartók: Concerto No. 3; Dance Suite; Concerto for Orchestra. PolyGram (London) Video 071 227-3. Solti/Chicago SO.
Schubert: Impromptus, D. 899; Impromptus, D. 935; *Moments musicaux*, D. 780. Teldec Video 9031-73664-3.

SCHNABEL, ARTUR: b. Lipnik, Austria, 17 April 1882; d. Axenstein, Switzerland, 15 August 1951.

> Schnabel was one of those rare artists who sets his own standards early in life and adheres to them faithfully no matter what happens. In his case, those standards, though not generally accepted at first, eventually prevailed. He was not a reformer so much as a crusader among pianists.
> Victor Chapin (*Giants of the Keyboard*)

It is precisely because of his lifelong allegiance to his personal musical convictions that Artur Schnabel stands apart among the great pianists of his day. In the midst of the freewheeling virtuosity and crowd-pleasing programs of his time, Schnabel dared to program only serious music written by the greatest composers (he never played showy pieces, so-called "light classics" or transcriptions), and respectfully adhered to the composer's score. "Schnabel's performances were considered revolutionary not only because they introduced great music to the public, but also because they made listeners feel that they were encountering the music directly, rather than through the mediating—sometimes intruding—presence of an interpreter." (Wigler)

Heredity seems not to account for Artur Schnabel's innate talent and musical taste. Neither of his parents—Isidor and Ernestine (Labin) Schnabel—was a musician, although his mother, like Schnabel, had absolute pitch. A few years after his birth, his parents moved from their tiny hamlet into nearby Bielitz, a step meant to improve the family's textile business. When an older sister began piano lessons with a Bielitz teacher named Minka Patzau, it was discovered that Schnabel, then age four, quickly learned to play the pieces assigned to his sister. He studied with Patzau for about two years; had a few lessons with two other Bielitz teachers; and at age six played for Hans Schmitt, a professor at the Vienna Conservatory.

At age seven, too young for the Conservatory, Schnabel began private lessons with Schmitt in Vienna, a happening that, in retrospect, marked the end of his childhood. Thereafter, heavy concentration on music and the gifted boy's rapidly developing maturity left little time for normal growing up. Years later, Schnabel recalled being taken to the opera as a very small boy in Vienna, but he had no recollection of childhood friends, of toys or even of much contact with other children. Since he was so young, his family moved to Vienna and cared for him until 1893, when their business required them to return to Bielitz. Thus Schnabel, from the young age of 11, lived on his own as a lodger with family friends until his parents were able to return in January 1897. Three generous patrons subsidized his eight years (1889–97) in Vienna—his living, music studies, even a tutor for academic studies.

Under Schmitt's guidance, at age nine Schnabel played the Mozart Concerto in D Minor, K. 466, at a private concert. About that same time he also auditioned for Theodor Leschetizky. Accepted as a pupil, he studied with Anna Essipoff, Leschetizky's wife and assistant, and with Malwine Brée, another assistant, before becoming a true Leschetizky student, meaning that he had private lessons and also attended the Wednesday night class held for all Leschetizky students. Through six years of these classes, Leschetizky called on Schnabel to perform at almost every session, thus giving him "an inestimable training in playing before people and, moreover, only musical people." Though Leschetizky was difficult, sometimes even cruel, Schnabel was forever grateful to him. He could not say exactly what he had learned, only that Leschetizky "succeeded in releasing all the vitality and élan and sense of beauty a student had in his nature, and would not tolerate any deviation or violation of what he felt to be truthfulness of expression." (Schnabel, *My Life and Music*)

Apparently Leschetizky quickly recognized Schnabel's unusual musical disposition, for out of the approximately 1,800 pupils Leschetizky taught in the course of half a century, Schnabel was one of only a small handful not required to study the repertoire popular at contemporary piano recitals. Early on, Leschetizky singled Schnabel out from the rest of the class when he said—and later often repeated—"You will never be a pianist; you are a musician." Schnabel never understood but was always thankful for that distinction, for it inspired Leschetizky to advise young Schnabel to look into some remarkable Schubert piano sonatas ("food for a musician," said Leschetizky) which nobody played and scarcely no one knew. Thus Schnabel came to know the Schubert sonatas when only a boy. "I loved them immediately, and my love has been growing ever since." (Schnabel, "Schubert Sonatas")

To ensure that his young pupil became a complete musician, Leschetizky arranged for him to study theory and composition with the scholarly Eusebius Mandyczewski, archivist of the Friends of Music (*Gesellschaft der Musikfreunde*), professor at the Vienna Conservatory and co-editor of scholarly editions (Brahms, Haydn, Schubert). His association with (in Schnabel's words) "this wonderful man," who gave him free rein among the musical manuscripts and historical treasures of the library, marked the start of Schnabel's lifelong process of exploring the great masterworks of music. The musical knowledge and values acquired from Mandyczewski and his library must also largely account for Schnabel's unshakeable confidence in his own lofty musical standards and monumental programs.

Schnabel played his official recital debut (12 Feb 1897) in Vienna's Bösendorfer Hall, and at about that time began teaching piano to supplement his income. (Leschetizky even sent pupils to him for advice.) He also began composing in his teens. Except for the periods 1905–14 and 1925–35, Schnabel composed throughout his life: solo piano works (never included on his own recital programs), a piano concerto, five string quartets, an orchestral rhapsody and three symphonies (see MGG in Bibliog. for complete list).

By the time he was 16 Schnabel had completed his music studies, and his subsidy had expired. Since Berlin offered better opportunities, he moved there in September 1898 and immediately made his Berlin debut (10 Oct 1898) at the *Bechsteinsaal* (the program included a Schubert sonata, most unusual for the time). To support himself, he gave piano lessons, played accompaniments for other musicians and accepted whatever performing engagements were offered. He made a tour of Norway with the German violinist Willy Burmester, and a tour of East Prussia, memorable because he met Therese Behr, a well-known Lieder singer and his future wife. In the autumn of 1899 Schnabel gave two more recitals at the *Bechsteinsaal*, presumably financed by friends, and on the whole "not only scored a resounding popular success, but earned the almost unanimous praise of the critics." (Saerchinger, *Artur Schnabel*)

Self-assured and independent, Schnabel always went his own way, and from the first his programs consisted only of works that he loved, works that presented a particular challenge or neglected works that he hoped to restore to the performing repertoire. Free for the first time in his life of both family and academic supervision, he spent much time, from the tender age of 17, in cafes and night haunts, and, as he later admitted, "continued to suffer from his own peculiar kind of indolence." He worked very little at the piano, slept late and generally wasted his time. Yet there is no doubt that Schnabel at the same time absorbed all the benefits to be gleaned from the many incredibly talented musicians (among them Eugen d'Albert, Ferruccio Busoni, Teresa Carreño, Frederic Lamond, Joseph Joachim, Felix Weingartner, Richard Strauss, Ossip Gabrilowitsch) in those days coming and going in Berlin. Moreover, with his easy entrée into Berlin's literary and artistic circles, Schnabel, like many gifted people, seems to have absorbed knowledge by a process of mental osmosis.

Schnabel's professional career moved slowly, but he grew to love Berlin—his home for 35 years and the city that brought him his first fame. On 30 November 1903 he made his debut with the Berlin Philharmonic Orchestra, conducted by Arthur Nikisch, playing the Brahms Concerto No. 2 in Hamburg. Schnabel's electrifying performance prompted Nikisch to engage him to play the same concerto with the *Gewandhaus* Orchestra in Leipzig and also to play the Brahms Concerto No. 2 with the BPO in Berlin. Buoyed with success, Schnabel made his London debut on 16 February 1904, playing the Brahms Concerto No. 2 with the Hallé Orchestra under Hans Richter, and his recital debut at Bechstein

Hall four days later. The London reviews ranged from good ("an artist of exceptional worth") to downright poor ("lack of breadth of interpretation, narrowness of phrasing"). Whether because of the uncertain response, or because he hated the cold, damp weather or for some other reason, Schnabel stayed away from England for 20 years. However, back in Berlin that same year (1904) the young pianist—he was only 22—had a resounding success performing the Beethoven E-flat Major Concerto ("Emperor") with Richard Strauss conducting the Berlin Philharmonic Orchestra.

After their marriage (June 1905), Schnabel and Therese Behr often performed together. For years their joint recitals marked the highlight of Berlin's musical season; in 1928 they presented an historic series of Schubert recitals in Berlin.

The Schnabel family (Karl Ulrich, born 1909, became a pianist; Stefan, born 1912, became an actor) stayed in Berlin right through the First World War. Schnabel and his wife both taught (their large apartment had two studios, each equipped with two grand pianos), and performed wherever the German authorities sent them. Those wartime German concerts produced little income, but Schnabel managed to earn hard currency playing in countries (Holland, Scandinavia, Switzerland) not involved in the war. After the war, he accepted a great many pupils from sound-currency countries and quickly resumed his concert tours.

By the time he made his first American tour (1921–22), Artur Schnabel had become a German celebrity (idolized by the German public, he drew packed houses whenever he played) and had toured extensively (Belgium, Switzerland, Sweden, Spain, Portugal, Russia). Consistently his performances reflected his personal and, for that time, most unusual convictions in matters of interpretation, programs and audiences. Despite the pleadings of American managers and press agents, Schnabel held firm to his beliefs, rejecting the idea that American audiences were less cultured than those abroad and refusing to change his programs to include any popular repertoire. No wonder, then, that the typically uncompromising program (only three large-scale works—the Schumann Fantasia, op. 17, the Schubert Sonata in B-flat Major, D. 960, and the Brahms Sonata in F Minor, op. 5) Schnabel played at his American debut recital (25 Dec 1921) at Carnegie Hall disappointed an audience accustomed to the prevailing flamboyance in virtuoso performances and infuriated certain critics, who disparaged "this German professor who tells us what we ought to like."

Response to his first American tour tempted Schnabel to give up the piano and devote all his time to composing, but friends persuaded him to try another American tour. That second tour (1922–23) consisted of about 30 concerts, including concerto performances with Willem Mengelberg and the New York Philharmonic Society, Walter Damrosch and the New York Symphony Orchestra and Bruno Walter and the Boston Symphony Orchestra. Schnabel may have felt that he was not fully appreciated in America. For some reason he stayed away from America until Koussevitzky invited him to play with the Boston Symphony Orchestra in 1930. But meanwhile all through the 1920s he played widely in Europe and made four tours of the Soviet Union.

He also, ending a 20-year absence, returned (April 1925) to England, where his name had long since been forgotten, to play two recitals in the small

Aeolian Hall. This time the British critics loved his "vivid and stimulating playing," and his splendid performances created a faithful British following. (In 1933 the University of Manchester awarded Schnabel an honorary doctorate of music.) And when he returned to America in 1930, Schnabel earned glowing reviews for his New York performances of the Brahms Concertos (No. 2 on 10 April; No. 1 on 12 April) with the Boston Symphony Orchestra, conducted by Serge Koussevitzky. Now at the peak of his powers and recognized internationally, he toured constantly, in the early 1930s expanding his itinerary to include Poland, Greece and the Middle East.

Schnabel first performed all 32 Beethoven sonatas in Berlin (seven consecutive Sunday recitals at the Berlin *Volksbühne*) in 1927, the centennial of Beethoven's death. His playing them from memory created a sensation; his interpretation enraptured critics and public alike. (Schnabel repeated this Beethoven cycle in London in 1932, in Berlin again in 1933 and in New York in 1936.) In February and March of 1928, the year of the Schubert centennial, Schnabel and his wife performed all the important Schubert piano works and song cycles in six recitals in Berlin. German audiences adored him. In 1933 all seven recitals of his Beethoven sonata cycle, this time played in the enormous hall of the Berlin *Philharmonie*, were sold out. These were the first concerts Schnabel allowed to be broadcast. As it happened, they were also the last performances he ever gave in Germany. After the fourth recital in the series, the Nazi regime informed him that "non-Aryan" music could no longer contaminate the German airwaves, therefore his last three Beethoven recitals would not be broadcast.

Indignant and fearful of the ominous events building in Nazi Germany, in May 1933 Schnabel and his family left Berlin to take up residence in Tremezzo, Italy. Although he continued to perform in other European cities (Vienna, Zurich, Florence, Warsaw) and in the Soviet Union (Leningrad and Moscow), from now on he played mostly in England and America. Without lowering his standards, he had won over both British and American audiences. Whether playing in large cities or small towns, Schnabel always presented heroic programs of the great piano masterpieces and never gave a single encore.

In 1939 the encroaching war once again uprooted the Schnabels. Following a tour of Australia (May–Aug), during which he gave 16 recitals (with five totally different programs) and played nine times with orchestra (performing 12 different concertos), Schnabel and his wife, realizing it would be unwise to return to their home in Tremezzo, went directly to New York, where he established residence (he became an American citizen in 1944) and resumed his three-pronged career of performing, teaching and composing. Engagements were few during wartime, and after the war he played less and less frequently, mostly in the United States, Great Britain, Holland, Belgium and Switzerland. At times failing health—heart problems and poor eyesight—caused him to cancel concerts and recording sessions. Schnabel played his final recital on 20 January 1951 at Hunter College. Performances and recording sessions planned for May in London had to be canceled. His wife took him to Switzerland to recuperate, and Schnabel died there on 15 August 1951.

If a pedagogue's skills can be measured by his students, Artur Schnabel gets a most excellent rating. The roster of his pupils includes such musical luminaries as Clifford Curzon, Lili Kraus, Rudolf Firkušný, Leon Fleisher, and André Watts. Schnabel began teaching in his early teens and taught all his life—hundreds of students, some of them for many years. Except for the six years (1924–30) he taught at the Berlin *Hochschule für Musik*, he had only private pupils. From 1933 until 1939 he held a summer class, usually 15 selected students, at Tremezzo, Italy. In New York from 1939, he taught privately and conducted summer master classes (1940–45) at the University of Michigan at Ann Arbor. Although Schnabel allowed an unlimited number of auditors to these classes (only six students admitted), he gave all his attention to the student performing and rarely addressed the audience.

To the despair of students and assistants alike, Schnabel never taught (just as he never played) the same piece in the same way, although his basic approach always remained the same. His teaching—aimed at making students think for themselves—revolved around interpretation, and he had a natural gift for finding remarkably graphic words (even in English, which he learned as an adult) to evoke the spirit or character of a musical composition. There are delightful examples of his ability to suggest images. For instance, with Beethoven's op. 110, starting at the end of the first fugue the student was to "shiver" at the G Minor harmony preceding the second *Arioso dolente*. This (in Schnabel's imagery) "sick aria" should sound "exhausting and gasping for life." Then, from the beginning of the second fugue (marked "gradually returning to life"), "the blood comes back, jubilant and happy, a paroxysm of gratitude and finally, ecstasy." (Goldberger, Part 2)

Like Schnabel the performer, Schnabel the teacher was more concerned with musical problems than technical difficulties. Any technical advice made during a lesson usually pertained to the use of the arm. He would say, "Up with the arm, not down with the fingers to bring out the inner voice. Use your arms! It's possible to play legato even in a leap of two octaves . . . if you use your arm." He advised students learning a new work to first immerse themselves in it as deeply as possible—to study it for a week, analyze it, sing it, think about it, try to write it out from memory—before ever attempting to play it.

Schnabel was also a meticulous editor, an articulate lecturer and a readable author. His edition of the Beethoven Sonatas (Memorial Edition, Simon and Schuster), which can compete with the finest available today, is an indispensable companion to his recorded sonatas. "He has not contented himself with correcting errors that appear in other editions, but has consulted the original manuscripts, early editions and the like. The result is an edition that is unrivaled, both for its authenticity and its suggestiveness." (Kramer)

César Saerchinger, Schnabel's biographer, describes Schnabel's three lectures—titled "Some Aspects of Music"—delivered at the University of Chicago in 1940 as "a dialectical tour de force in highly condensed thinking and vivid epigrammatic composition." (These lectures were published by the Princeton University Press in 1942 under the title *Music and the Line of Most Resistance*.) The 12 seminars Schnabel gave at the University of Chicago in 1945 were recorded by a stenographer and, with only glaring grammatical slips corrected, published as *My Life and Music*. These highly informative discourses are easy and relaxed, yet Schnabel never talked down to his audience.

"It is now difficult to remember what the piano repertoire was like before Schnabel. There was scarcely any Mozart or Haydn; Beethoven was usually represented by such famous sonatas as the 'Moonlight' or the 'Appassionata'; and except for pieces such as the Impromptus and the 'little' A-major Sonata, performances of Schubert were unheard of." (Wigler)

Early in his career Schnabel played a varied repertoire, including "enchanting" performances of Chopin (24 Preludes), Liszt (Sonata, Mephisto Waltz) and Tchaikovsky (Concerto No. 1). But gradually he gave up playing such works in public because he realized he was not learning anything new from this music, that it was impossible for him to re-create such works afresh every time he played them. Increasingly, he programmed music that he considered "to be better than it can be performed." Music had to present a continuing problem, or he lost interest.

Schnabel's mature repertoire consisted almost entirely of works by Mozart, Beethoven, Schubert, Schumann and Brahms. During the first 25 years of his career he performed with a great many orchestras, often playing the Brahms concertos. He was probably the first pianist to consistently play the Schubert sonatas in public, and he must be credited for reviving interest in these long-neglected works. Although for a time considered too different and too difficult, Schnabel's restricted repertoire and uncompromising programs ultimately attracted a large following and inspired later generations of pianists, notably Rudolf Serkin, Arrau, Solomon, Brendel, Pollini and Perahia.

How did Artur Schnabel achieve his musical goals? He was certainly not endowed with a natural technique, and he did not practice *per se*. Instead, he worked at the keyboard, constantly experimenting to find new ways—fingerings, physical gestures, phrasings—to bring out the subtle and beautiful nuances of articulation that he heard inwardly. And he never hesitated to try something unorthodox to achieve a particular effect.

That he had none of the flair and personal magnetism expected of piano virtuosos in his era never bothered Schnabel. Even more unusual, he showed no interest whatsoever in acquiring a dazzling technique. On the contrary, he despised keyboard gymnastics and all extravagant gestures. Serious, truthful interpretation always superseded pianistic brilliance. A purist, but not a literalist, Schnabel insisted on working from an accurate text, and tried to follow it faithfully. Unlike many pianists of his time, he rarely changed expression marks, dynamic marks, phrasing marks or tempo directions; and he never added notes. But he had the skill and common sense to make changes in a score if musical logic so dictated.

Structure, phrasing and spontaneity were his chief concerns. Inner voices and the bass line had to be given their exact values in the structure. Protesting against "the tyranny of the bar line," he conceived musical compositions as being made up of phrases, not just measures. He insisted that there were too many accents, especially accents placed indiscriminately on the first beat of every measure, and that a work could be organized in larger units by "passing" some first beats and landing more forcefully on others. Most of all, despite his intellectual approach and intense study, Schnabel desired a free, spontaneous (he used such words as "alive," "vital," "*con amore*") performance. To achieve that, he was willing to change his mind about a passage, even an entire work. More than that, he was willing to risk not playing perfectly in order to play beautifully.

Sir Clifford Curzon, a Schnabel pupil who became a great pianist, had a more intelligible, if less imaginative overview, of Schnabel's playing. Curzon lists tone, rhythm and poetic feeling as the distinguishing hallmarks of Schnabel's style. "First, his tone, which was quite unlike anyone else's, and which came from his power of individualising all the parts, all the voices, of every phrase, even to individualising each single note of every chord he played. Then there was his rhythm, which was equally characteristic. It was never produced by extraneous accents, but by the most careful placing of each sound; as he frequently put it to us: 'Rhythm is a matter of proportion and not of accent.' And, finally, there was the extraordinary poetic freedom of his playing. This he had a way of making clear to us, to his pupils, by inventing little sentences which he would sing to a given phrase. Not only to show the mood of the music, but also to show the actual stress of its syllables." (Curzon)

Some critics insisted that Schnabel was not really a virtuoso, that his technical deficiencies sometimes interfered with the music, that his playing was too cerebral, too austere, too analytical. Yet praise for Schnabel's playing overwhelms any complaints. Schnabel was a truly great pianist, unique because of his "immense seriousness, his refusal to play any but the very best music, the meticulous care he bestowed on small details, the impression he made that he was re-creating every bar of the music. . . . But the quality that most of all won him his unique position with knowledgeable pianists of his day was intellectual power. This enabled him so to grasp the form of a musical work . . . that he could convey it to the listener, seemingly without effort, while at the same time delighting him by the detailed beauty of the material that went to the building of the total structure." (Sackville-West)

When Schnabel made his American debut (25 Dec 1921) at Carnegie Hall, Deems Taylor, writing in the *New York World*, noted that he "produced the most arduous effect with that ease and dignity which are among the marked signs of a really great artist." Richard Aldrich's review included: "Mr. Schnabel was happiest in the forthright, vigorous music of Brahms, in which his natural calm, his affectionate care for each phrase, his reserve power in larger and leisurely climaxes displayed qualities of musicianship in harmony with his reputation for twenty-five years abroad. . . . His Schubert was a more curious if not so vital miniature, most attractive in its simpler scherzo, *vivace e con delicatezza*. His Schumann, hardly the romantic Robert of some tone-poets of the piano, was yet a scholarly and clarifying performance." (Ald/Con, see Bibliog.)

Three weeks later at Town Hall Schnabel played a typical long and serious all-Beethoven program—four sonatas and the 32 Variations in C Minor. The acknowledged Beethoven authority, Henry Krehbiel of *The Tribune* wrote:

"The tones of Beethoven, as played by Mr. Schnabel, detached themselves from the instrument and became embodied beauty, vitalized by feeling." But other criticisms so depressed Schnabel that he wanted to cancel his next recital. Urged on by his old friend Ossip Gabrilowitch, on 25 January 1922 Schnabel played what was, for him, a "popular" program: Chopin's Sonata in B-flat Minor, the Schubert Impromptus, D. 899, and the Weber Sonata in A-flat Major. Most of the major newspapers were silent; the *New York Herald* did comment that the pianist was a "piano interpreter of high rank."

A Schnabel recital (8 Feb 1929) at London's Queen's Hall tested "the endurance of the audience rather severely" in that it included the Beethoven Sonata in B-flat Major, op. 22, Schubert's Four Impromptus, D. 935, and concluded with Beethoven's monumental "Diabelli" Variations. "Mr. Schnabel's outstanding merit was that in spite of the disadvantages of length and in spite of the repellent form of the work (33 variations on a dead waltz tune) he kept his hearers entranced not by his own virtuosity, but the inexhaustible fertility of Beethoven's mind and art." (*TL*, 11 Feb 1929)

In 1930 Schnabel's performances at a New York Brahms Festival greatly enhanced his reputation in America. On 10 April he played the Brahms Concerto No. 2 and on 12 April the Brahms Concerto No. 1, both with the Boston Symphony Orchestra, conducted by Serge Koussevitzky. Schnabel's masterly playing of the Concerto No. 2 "showed him not only as a consummate musician and technician of his instrument, but as one who conceived the whole work from the symphonic standpoint and with the keenest appreciation and the most detailed knowledge of the orchestral score." (*NYT*, 11 April 1930)

When Schnabel played the Beethoven sonata cycle in New York in 1936, large audiences filled Carnegie Hall for each of the seven recitals, and reviewers wrote glowing notices. For example, "There was reason to marvel at the perfect proportion, the depth of thought and the genuineness of feeling that Mr. Schnabel conveyed. His is an art that recognizes at the same time the grand line and the most significant finish of detail. His interpretive purpose is true and unostentatious as is his manner on the platform. . . . The performance is complete concentration upon the music. . . . Everything is done with the minimum of effort and the maximum of result." (*NYT*, 16 Jan 1936)

In 1942 the New Friends of Music sponsored Schnabel's five all-Schubert recitals (played between 4 Jan and 1 Feb) at Town Hall. Since audiences of the time were not accustomed to hearing much Schubert piano music apart from the Impromptus and *Moments musicaux*, this was a novel and risky undertaking. The first recital (4 Jan 1942) included the Sonata in A Major, D. 664, and the Sonata in C Minor, D. 958. "The wistful, intimate nature of the sonata in A major was admirably captured, and the contrast between it and the nobler and more deeply poetic sonata in c minor sharply defined. In both works Mr. Schnabel's tempi were carefully chosen. His unremitting attention to detail never obscured the larger architectural patterning, and he managed to bring to these offerings the singing tone, in all gradations from pianissimo to forte, they require." (*NYT*, 5 Jan 1942)

In 1946, between 13 May and 31 May, Schnabel appeared six times at London's Albert Hall—three solo recitals and three appearances with the

Philharmonia Orchestra. These performances earned extraordinary kudos. "The source of many of Schnabel's most wonderful effects is almost sinister in its simplicity. He plays what is written. . . . Nevertheless, 'playing what is written' is only a part of Schnabel's greatness. There are many things which are inimitable. No one else in the world could play those trills in the second movement of op. 111 [Beethoven] as he does; nor those three pages of heavenly pianissimo. . . . One could go on forever enumerating these wonderful moments." (*MT*, June 1946)

Schnabel's playing of the Beethoven Sonatas ops. 13, 90, 53 and 101 at his very last recital (Hunter College, 20 Jan 1951) drew these astute comments: "On occasion the mechanism faltered but I shall never forget my overriding reaction to certain pages that came over the footlights with unforgettable conviction and authenticity. 'This,' I thought, 'must have been the way Beethoven conceived the music.' It was so right, so thoroughly appropriate in terms of sonority, character, pace and rhythm. One felt the essentials of the music; one shared in a revelation. And so it was with his greatest performances. It was this quality of inevitability, of extraordinary conviction that gripped us and relegated the technical flaws to the shadowy lanes of memory, where they belonged." (Freundlich)

Except for a few piano rolls, Schnabel made no recordings until he was fifty. That he even made these recordings is due in great part to Fred Gaisberg, who in 1931 finally persuaded the pianist to overcome his distrust of recording and who again, in the face of considerable opposition, agreed to Schnabel's terms—that he would record *all* the Beethoven sonatas and concertos, or nothing at all. The Beethoven sonatas were recorded between 1932 and 1935.

The Beethoven sonatas, the Beethoven concertos, the Schubert sonatas and the Mozart concertos comprise most of Schnabel's discography. The Beethoven sonatas have been available for some time on CD—EMI *Références*. Not everyone agrees with Schnabel's interpretations, and not every sonata is done to perfection. "But even when Schnabel's ideas may seem off-target they remain interesting and clearly the product of a probing interpretive artist whose grasp of structure, Classical style, and emotional content infuses these performances with tasteful nuances and cogent insights that remain extraordinary." (*Fan*, Sept/Oct 1990)

"Schnabel was almost ideologically committed to extreme tempos; something you might say Beethoven's music thrives on, always provided the interpreter can bring it off. By and large, Schnabel did. There are some famous gabbles in this sonata cycle, notably at the start of the *Hammerklavier*, with him going for broke and the metronome marking. . . . [Yet] they are virtuoso readings that demonstrate 'a blazing intensity of interpretative vision as well as a breathtaking manner of execution.' Even when a dazzlingly articulate reading like that of the *Waldstein* is home and dry and safely stowed, the abiding impression in its aftermath is one of Schnabel's astonishing physical and imaginative *daring*. . . . .At the other extreme, Schnabel is indubitably the master of the genuinely slow slow movement. . . . From the earliest sonatas to the final movement of Op. 111 . . . Schnabel is able to reconcile a calm and concentrated slowness with a breathing pulse and stirring inner life that is beyond the wit of most latter-day imitators." (*Gramophone*, July 1991. Reprinted by permission.)

Pearl Records, claiming that previous transfers have given a false picture of Schnabel's pianism, has issued yet another set of the complete Beethoven sonatas in five volumes (see Discog.), and these "minimalist, noisy transfers yield extraordinary fidelity to Schnabel's sound. We can now hear his refined tonal palette, wide dynamics and subtle pedalling." (*CP*, April 1995)

Schnabel was the first to record all five Beethoven concertos. Begun in 1932 and completed by 1935, all recordings were made with Malcolm Sargent conducting either the London Symphony Orchestra (Nos. 1 and 5) or the London Philharmonic Orchestra (Nos. 2, 3, 4). The sound cannot, of course, compare with that produced by our modern technology, but it is certainly acceptable. "As for the performances, they illustrate better than anything else in the catalogue the German pianist's probity, his identification with the music and his executive ability. . . . In these five concertos he is complete master of the situation. Has there ever been a stronger recorded performance of the 'Emperor' Concerto, with Schnabel outlining the contours in heroic strokes and singing the slow movement with a pure, seraphic tone?" (*NYT*, 1 May 1955)

There are five CDs (see Discog.) of Schubert performed by Schnabel, his wife Therese and their son Karl Ulrich. Each CD may be purchased separately, but the complete set is a must for the Schubert devotee. "Some interpreters add color and bring out voices to arrest audiences' attention; by comparison Schnabel's limpid tone and natural phrasing are as refreshing as a spring breeze. His natural approach lets the music speak for itself. . . . Artur Schnabel's art is subtle. The miracle is that he can spin out a short piece such as the Allegretto in C minor [D. 915], simple in terms of notes, and clothe it convincingly in depth and beauty. Never does he play an overly loud *forte*. His tempos in the Sonata in D [D. 850] can be spinningly *vivace*, with soft, fast, rippling fingerwork." (*CL*, May/June 1990)

An EMI CD (see Discog.) contains the complete Schubert Impromptus, D. 899 and D. 935. These were originally recorded on tape in 1950 when Schnabel was almost 70 years of age and approaching the end of his career. Most everyone who has heard these performances agrees that age and illness appear to have had no influence on the master pianist's command of the keyboard. "I think it would be difficult for a present-day pianist to play Schubert in such a manner as Schnabel plays him here. He shows a confident, open-hearted, generous response to the music, whose gentle rhythms and song-like melodies are presented to us in the most natural, uncomplicated fashion." (*Gram*, April 1989)

Schnabel recorded six Mozart piano concertos, including K. 365 in E-flat Major for two pianos, performed with Karl Ulrich Schnabel and the London Symphony Orchestra conducted by Sir Adrian Boult. The Mozart Concerto in F Major, K. 459, and the Concerto in C Major, K. 467, were both recorded with Malcolm Sargent and the London Symphony Orchestra. The ever-popular Concerto in D Minor, K. 466, and the Concerto in C Minor, K. 491, were recorded with Walter Susskind conducting the Philharmonia Orchestra. Finally, Schnabel recorded the Concerto in B-flat Major, K. 595, with Sir John Barbirolli and the London Symphony Orchestra. These concertos are available on both the

Arabesque (with two Mozart sonatas) and EMI labels (see Discog.). There are of course other recordings taken from live performances or radio broadcasts, but these "studio" versions remain glorious experiences—"remarkable documents of Schnabel's sensitivity to the music's wide emotional range and structural coherence." (*Fan*, May/June 1991)

Even though sometimes the pianist's phrasing and that of the orchestra are noticeably out of sync and Schnabel's choice of cadenzas is not entirely to everyone's liking, this is of little importance against his overall concept of Mozart. Looking more to the past than to the present, Schnabel "remained a Romanticist but 'a Romanticist with brains.' And that brain, more often than not, grasped all sorts of subtleties in these works that have eluded other performers: the wonderfully zany humor in the finale of K. 570; the 'comedy' that infuses so much of K. 459; the imperious grandeur of K. 467; the dramatic struggle suggested in the soloist's reiterated motif in the first-movement development of K. 466; and the prevailing contrast between sensual, ethereal delicacy on the one hand and bold passion on the other." (*Fan*, March/April 1989)

"Schnabel's magnificent artistry, his sublime command of sound in space, his elucidation of structure and meaning, quivering nuances, and wonderfully robust spirituality have been—and through recordings will remain—an inestimable treasure in the annals of musical interpretation. His provocative editions have given much food for thought and have sparked the inspirations of subsequent interpreters. For these gifts, he has won deserved immortality." (Goldsmith)

SELECTED REFERENCES

Bloesch, David. "Artur Schnabel: A Discography." *ARSC Journal*, Nov 1987, pp. 33–143.

Boyd, Mary Homan Boxall. "The Genius of Artur Schnabel." *Etude*, Feb 1952, pp. 17, 51.

Cardus, Neville. "Artur Schnabel." *Gramophone Record Review*, July 1958, pp. 736–737. Discography by Clough and Cuming.

———. "Schnabel." In Car/Ful (see Bibliog.), pp. 51–57.

Curzon, Clifford. "Artur Schnabel, Pianist and Teacher." (interview with Alan Blyth). *The Listener*, 25 April 1974, pp. 544–546.

Frank, Claude. "Schnabel's Edition of Beethoven Sonatas." *Piano Quarterly*, Winter 1973–74, pp. 23–27.

Freedman, Frederick. "Artur Schnabel: A Bibliography." *Piano Quarterly*, Winter 1973–74, pp. 51–52.

Freundlich, Irwin. "The Teaching of Artur Schnabel by Konrad Wolff." (Book Review) *Piano Quarterly*, Winter 1973-74, pp. 49-50.

Gerber, Leslie. "Artur Schnabel: A Discography." *Piano Quarterly*, Winter 1973–74, pp. 54–62.

Goldberger, David. "Artur Schnabel's Master Classes." (Part 1) *Piano Teacher*, March/April 1963, pp. 5–7.

———. "Artur Schnabel's Master Classes." (Part 2) *Piano Teacher*, May/June 1963, pp. 18–21.

Goldsmith, Harris. "Schnabel the pianist." *Musical Times*, June 1989, pp. 336–339.

Kramer, A. Walter. "Schnabel Edits Edition of Beethoven Sonatas." *Musical America*, 25 Jan 1936, p. 15.

Maier, Guy. "Some Highlights of Schnabel's Teaching." *Etude*, Feb 1952, pp. 9, 59.

Mann, Victor. "Artur Schnabel's Pioneer Venture of Yesteryear." *Music Magazine*, July/Aug 1982, pp. 21–23.

Obituary. *Musical Times*, Oct 1951, p. 472. *The Times* (London), 16 Aug 1951, p. 4.

Sackville-West, Edward. "Schnabel." *Recorded Sound*, June 1961, pp. 40–43.

Saerchinger, César. *Artur Schnabel*. London: Cassell & Company Ltd., 1957.

———. "Schnabel in Retrospect." *Saturday Review*, 29 Sept 1951, pp. 43–46.

Schnabel, Artur. "The Hand and the Keyboard." *Etude*, Feb 1922, p. 87. Also appears in Coo/Gre (see Bibliog.).

———. *Music and The Line of Most Resistance*. Princeton: Princeton University Press, 1942.

———. *My Life and Music*. New York: St. Martin's Press, 1961.

———. "The Qualities a Pianist Must Possess." *Etude*, Aug 1941, pp. 511, 571.

———. "Reflections on Music Teaching." *Etude*, Sept 1948, pp. 521–522.

———. "Schubert Sonatas." *New York Times*, 4 Jan 1942, sec. 9, p. 7.

Schnabel, Karl Ulrich. "My Father." (interview) *Piano Quarterly*, Winter 1973–74, pp. 10–18.

Webster, Beveridge. "Artur Schnabel—(A Memorandum at Random)." *Piano Quarterly*, Winter 1973–74, pp. 19–22, 65.

Wigler, Stephen. "Schnabel: First Modern Pianist." *Baltimore Sun*, 16 July 1989, sec. E, pp. 1, 3.

Wolff, Konrad. "Artur Schnabel." *Piano Quarterly*, Winter 1973–74, pp. 36–40.

———. *The Teaching of Artur Schnabel*. London: Faber and Faber, 1972.

See also Bibliography: Ald/Con; Bro/Mod; Car/Del; Car/Ful; Cha/Gia; Cha/Spe; Coo/Gre; Cur/Bio (1942); Dan/Con; Dow/Oli; Ewe/Li; Ewe/Mu; Gai/Mus; Gol/Jou; Hag/Dec; Hag/Mus; Hag/Thi; Kol/Que; MGG; New/Gro; Nie/Mei; Ran/Kon; Rub/MyM; Sal/Fam; Sch/Gre.

SELECTED REVIEWS

LAT: 18 March 1948. *MA*: 24 March 1923. *MT*: 1 June 1925; 1 Jan 1928; 1 Feb 1929; 1 Feb 1931; 1 March 1932; 1 Dec 1932; Dec 1934; Jan 1935; Feb 1939; June 1946. *NYT*: 15 Jan 1923; 11 April 1930; 13 April 1930; 22 May 1932; 9 Nov 1933; 16 Jan 1936; 23 Jan 1936; 30 Jan 1936; 6 Feb 1936; 13 Feb 1936; 20 Feb 1936; 27 Feb 1936; 13 March 1939; 5 Jan 1942; 12 Jan 1942; 2 Feb 1942; 23 March 1942; 13 Dec 1942; 14 Jan 1951. *TL*: 17 Feb 1904; 22 Feb 1904; 26 Jan 1926; 18 Nov 1927; 1 Feb

1928; 11 Feb 1929; 22 Jan 1930; 6 Feb 1934; 3 Feb 1937; 14 May 1946; 21 May 1946; 17 May 1947.

SELECTED DISCOGRAPHY

Artur Schnabel in Performance. Mozart: Concerto in A Major, K. 488 (Rodzinsky/Philharmonia, rec. 1946); Concerto in C Minor, K. 491 (Wallenstein/-Standard SO, rec. 1946). Music and Arts CD-632.

Artur Schnabel: Legendary Public Performances. Beethoven: Concerto No. 3 in C Minor, op. 37 (Szell/Phil-SO, 1945). Mozart: Concerto in E-flat Major, K. 482 (Walter/ Philadelphia SO, 1941). Music and Arts CD-681.

Artur Schnabel Plays Bach & Brahms (Vol. II). Bach: Toccata in C Minor, BWV 911; Toccata in D Major, BWV 912. Brahms: Concerto No. 1 in D Minor, op. 15. Pearl GEMM CD 9376. Szell/London SO.

Artur Schnabel plays Beethoven. Concerto No. 1 in C Major, op. 15 (Sargent/ London SO); Concerto No. 2 in B-flat Major, op. 19 (Sargent/London PO). Arabesque Z6549 (CD).

Artur Schnabel plays Beethoven. Concerto No. 3 in C Minor, op. 37; Concerto No. 4 in G Major, op. 58. Arabesque Z6550 (CD). Sargent/London PO.

Artur Schnabel plays Beethoven. Andante in F Major, op. 170; Concerto No. 5 in E-flat Major, op. 73; Polonaise in C Major, op. 89. Arabesque Z6551 (CD). Sargent/London SO.

Artur Schnabel plays Beethoven. "Diabelli Variations," op. 120. Pearl GEMM CD 9378.

Artur Schnabel plays Mozart. Concerto in D Minor, K. 466; Sonata in F Major, K. 533/ 494. Music and Art CD-750. Szell/Phil-SO.

Beethoven: The Complete Piano Sonatas. EMI *Références* CHS7 63765-2 (8 CDs).

Beethoven: Sonatas Vol. I. Sonatas, op. 2, nos 1-3, op. 7, op. 10, nos. 1-2, op. 49, nos. 1-2; Rondo WoO 49; *Rondo a capriccio*, op. 129. Pearl GEMM CD9083 (2 CDs). Remastered from earlier Schnabel discs.

Beethoven: Sonatas Vol. II. Sonatas, op. 13, op. 14, nos. 1-2, op. 22, op. 26, op. 27, no. 1. Pearl GEMM CD9099. Remastered from earlier Schnabel discs.

Beethoven: Sonatas Vol. III. Sonatas, op. 27, no. 2, op. 28, op. 31, nos. 1-3; Bagatelles, op. 33; Variations, op. 34. Pearl GEMM CDS9123 (2 CDs). Remastered from earlier Schnabel discs.

Beethoven: Sonatas Vol. IV. Sonatas, ops. 53, 54, 57, 78, 79, 81a, 90; Variations, op. 35. Pearl GEMM CDS9139 (2 CDs). Remastered from earlier Schnabel discs.

Beethoven: Sonatas Vol. V. Sonatas, ops. 101, 106, 109, 110, 111; Bagatelles, op. 126; Variations, op. 120. Pearl GEMM CDS9142 (2 CDs). Remastered from earlier Schnabel discs.

Mozart: Concerto in E-flat Major, K. 365 (with Karl Ulrich Schnabel); Concerto in F Major, K. 459; Concerto in D Minor, K. 466; Concerto in C Major, K. 467; Concerto in C Minor, K. 491; Concerto in B-flat Major, K. 595; Sonata in F Major, K. 332; Sonata in B-flat Major, K. 570; Rondo in A

Minor, K. 511. Arabesque Z6590/92 (3 CDs). Barbirolli, Boult, Sargent, Susskind/London, Philharmonia.
Mozart: Concertos Nos. 10, 19, 20, 21, 24, 27 (Same recordings as the above). EMI 7 63703-2 (3 CDs).
Schubert: Music for Piano Solo, for Four Hands, and Songs (Artur and Karl Ulrich Schnabel, pianists; Therese Behr Schnabel, alto). Arabesque Z 6571-75 (5 CDs).
Schubert: Piano Sonatas. Sonata in D Major, D. 850; Sonata in A Major, D. 959; Sonata in B-flat Major, D. 960; *Moments musicaux*, D. 780; March in E Major, D. 606. EMI *Références* CHS7 64259-2 (2 CDs).
Schubert: Piano Works. Impromptus, D. 899; Impromptus, D. 935; Allegretto, D. 915. EMI *Références* CDH7 61021-2.

SERKIN, PETER ADOLF: b. New York City, New York, 24 July 1947.

> There is no doubt that Serkin's extensive work on behalf of new music has contributed to the exploratory, recreative freshness of his interpretations of standard works—just as there is no question that Serkin's solid grounding in the classics guides him to what is significant in contemporary music.
>
> Richard Dyer (*Boston Sunday Globe*, 14 January 1990)

Any young pianist struggling for fame might justifiably imagine how easy it must have been for Peter Serkin, destined from birth to live a privileged musical life, to come by his distinguished concert career. In reality, however, Serkin made his career not because of, but almost in spite of, his musical lineage. And it was not by any means easy.

Peter Serkin's family produced world-class musicians. He is the son of Rudolf Serkin, the illustrious Austrian-born American pianist who died in 1991, and the grandson of Adolf Busch, the eminent violinist. And that is only Serkin's immediate heritage. What with musicians past and present (grandfather Busch had two renowned brothers—Fritz Busch, the noted conductor, and Hermann Busch, a well-known cellist; grandmother Busch was born a Grueter, also a family of musicians), not to mention assorted musical uncles and great-uncles, Peter Serkin's exceptionally musical family has a performing history reaching back into the last century. In the early 1950s family members Rudolf Serkin, Adolf Busch and Hermann Busch co-founded the prestigious Marlboro Music Festival in Vermont. Last but by no means least, Peter Serkin's mother Irene (Busch) Serkin, a fine violinist, often played in the Marlboro Festival Orchestra.

He was brought up in a household drenched in music. His mother started him on violin lessons at age three, guided his earliest musical training and, making a trio with Peter and his brother John, now a horn player, often made music at home. Living his childhood years on a quiet farm in Guilford, Vermont, with grandfather Busch nearby, Serkin had unusual opportunities to play music and to hear wonderful music. And when his father was home between tours, there was always the sound of the great Rudolf Serkin practicing. It is not surprising, then, that Peter Serkin was a musical prodigy; who can say where he got his musical independence.

Not satisfied with playing a basically monophonic instrument, he traded the violin for the piano. Years later Serkin would tell interviewers that he changed to the piano because he wanted "to add the harmonies and to get to know all kinds of music—not just piano solos, but chamber music, orchestral scores, and choral works too." He first studied piano with Blanche Moyse and Luis Battle and made rapid progress. A gifted sight reader, Serkin "played everything he could get his hands on in a house that must have contained most of the piano literature in print, and thousands of other scores." (Conroy) Serkin himself has often remarked that he rarely practiced scales, like most children beginning piano, but would sight-read orchestral scores, choral works and operas. That some of those works were modern must have amazed his elders. As he recalls, "I used to buy records and scores for Schoenberg's Quartets and some of the great classics by Stravinsky and Wolpe. I ate it up, even though sometimes this would be discouraged by people around me." (Reich)

Serkin was about nine years old when his family moved to Philadelphia to have more time with his father, since 1939 a member of the piano faculty at the Curtis Institute of Music. At age 11 Peter Serkin enrolled at Curtis, where he studied piano with Lee Luvisi (his father's assistant), with Mieczyslaw Horszowski and, from age 14 through 18, with his father. Despite close living, Serkin feels that he learned a lot from his father; but for encouragement and guidance he often turned to Horszowski, his mentor for life, and to Alexander Schneider, noted violinist and conductor. Serkin names Horszowski, Schneider, flutist Marcel Moyse and pianist Carl Ulrich Schnabel as the major influences on his musical development.

He made his public debut at the 1958 Marlboro Music Festival in Vermont, playing the Haydn Concerto in D Major, with Schneider conducting the Marlboro Chamber Orchestra. For his New York debut (29 Nov 1959), performed at the New School for Social Research in New York, the 12-year-old Serkin played the same Haydn Concerto with Schneider and his chamber orchestra. And at age 14 Serkin joined his father for a Carnegie Hall performance (22 May 1962) of Mozart's Concerto in E-flat Major for Two Pianos, K. 365, with the supportive Schneider conducting the Marlboro Festival Orchestra.

By the time he was 17, Serkin had graduated (1964) from Curtis and was touring in both the United States and Canada. Starting his career mostly in the best concert halls and with the best orchestras, he was immediately successful. For example, on 16 February 1965 he played the Mozart Concerto in F Major, K. 459, at Carnegie Hall with the Philadelphia Orchestra under Eugene Ormandy. He made his London recital debut (28 Feb 1965) at Wigmore Hall and his New York recital debut (27 March 1965) at the Metropolitan Museum of Art. Young Serkin also, with his mentor Alexander Schneider, made a recording of Schubert violin and piano sonatas for Vanguard Records, and he recorded the

Bach Goldberg Variations for RCA Victor. On the surface it appeared that Peter Serkin, having so easily gained so much so fast, would now become a carbon copy of his father—a conservative, eminently successful concert pianist. The truth is that, though he had good critical notices and more than enough engagements, Serkin was neither content nor at all sure of what he wanted. One thing he did know was that he hated the touring life.

If he seemed to be living in a pianist's paradise, it was one riddled with long-smouldering anxieties and pressures. For starters, being a child prodigy must have created some tensions. Then, because of his unusual family, when Serkin began concertizing, he had too much media attention, too easy access to engagements and always the annoyance of being compared with his celebrated father. Before long, stress affected both his nerves and his playing. Performing in public became so agonizing that his hands would shake uncontrollably right before a concert. The time came when, as he has often said, "music was on my back. I couldn't get away from it." All Peter Serkin could think of was getting completely away from music.

It may have been his unbearable nerves or his hatred of traveling or possibly critical disapproval of both his playing and his stage appearance that prompted Serkin into action. There was, for example, a lukewarm review of his performance (8 Feb 1967) of Beethoven's Variations on a Waltz by Diabelli, part of the prestigious Great Performers at Philharmonic Hall series. And critics complained about Serkin's informal concert appearance—a tuxedo, not the traditional white tie and tails, or a Nehru jacket or other exotic garb. For whatever reasons, in 1968 Serkin spent about half a year in Mexico away from the piano.

Once back home, he restricted himself to giving concerts only two or three months a year. It was not a good idea, for Peter Serkin seems to have an inborn need to make music, a need that playing only a few months out of the year could never fulfill. In 1970 he again took time off and, with his wife (married Wendy Spinner, a student at Marlboro College, in October 1968) spent several months traveling about in India, Tibet, Nepal, Thailand, Iran and Morocco. It is worth mentioning that Serkin recalls that even while away from the piano, away from all Western music, pieces he had not worked on for years "came bubbling up to the surface of my mind. . . . I could experience the whole piece, not having seen a piano for six months and not having heard Western music anyway for a long time. Somehow it's in me. It's in my head." (Stein)

His exposure to non-Western music and Oriental philosophies and religions would have lasting beneficial results. On returning home, Serkin went back to performing, but obviously playing in public still did not feel right. In the winter of 1971–72 he made another retreat to Mexico, this time with his wife and daughter (Karina, b. 1970). Spending several months literally isolated from the world of classical music and pianos, he may have felt that he had now truly quit the concert life; but Serkin came home from Mexico with an urgent desire to perform. (In 1973 he separated from his wife.)

Peter Serkin's story is complex. To begin with, as the son of a great pianist, he endured everlasting comparisons between *his* piano playing and that of his father. Then, having always been taught by conservative musicians, who prepared him for the traditional concert life, the youthful Serkin felt compelled to fulfill all expectations. What no one seems to have noticed is that he had always been absolutely fascinated by contemporary music. No wonder that this pianist, groomed for one world but destined for another, developed "unbearable" nerves.

At this stage, although still performing traditional repertoire—mostly the Bach Goldberg Variations, Beethoven's "Diabelli" Variations and many Mozart concertos—he was giving equal attention to works by 20th-century composers like Schoenberg, Webern, Berg, Stravinsky, Messiaen. Following his musical instincts and still wanting desperately to get away from performing solo, early in the 1970s Serkin began playing chamber music with clarinettist Richard Stoltzman, violinist Ida Kavafian and cellist Fred Sherry. That proved to be exactly the right move, for all his life Serkin had delighted in playing ensemble music. "His affinity for chamber music grows from his ability to listen, to pick up all the threads of the music and weave them into his own part, exploring and revealing new connections. . . . He has an incredible memory. When he comes to a rehearsal, he knows everybody's part and plays every piece, whether a Mozart trio or a Brahms concerto, with the same intensity." (Trustman)

Even more important, the ensemble—later named *Tashi* (a Tibetan word roughly translated as "good fortune")—satisfied Serkin's desire to perform contemporary music. On 18 March 1973 they made a sensational debut at New York's New School for Social Research with a performance of Olivier Messiaen's Quartet for the End of Time. Since compositions written for their instruments (piano, violin, cello, clarinet) are few (Serkin says they must have played the Messiaen Quartet at least 159 times!), they fleshed out their programs (a mix of traditional and contemporary music) by playing duos, trios, sometimes solo works. They invited guests to play in order to perform differently scored chamber pieces, and they also commissioned new works for themselves. Successful from the start, *Tashi* earned a reputation as superb interpreters of 20th-century music.

Exactly one month after the *Tashi* debut Serkin gave a solo performance (18 April 1973) at Alice Tully Hall, playing Olivier Messiaen's long (two-and-a-half hours) *Vingt regards sur l'Enfant Jésus*, a suite of pieces he had been working on for about four years and parts of which he had performed individually. This performance—he played it all from memory—earned ecstatic reviews; and he repeated it some 25 times in other cities. Composer Messiaen, having heard Serkin play the *Vingt regards* at Dartmouth, complimented him for showing respect for the score, then added, "but when you do not, it is even better."

Tashi seems to have been the antidote for Serkin's deep fear of playing solo performances. Once at the point of desperation about playing alone, he discovered that practicing with a group, performing together, even the daily routine of preparation and traveling, could be both restorative and uplifting. He played with *Tashi* for seven years, meanwhile also performing as soloist, and withdrew from the group in 1980. *Tashi*'s influence—on his repertoire and on his attitude toward performing—has endured. This time Peter Serkin approached his concert career refreshed, more at ease and on his own terms.

Serkin has served, or is currently serving, on the piano faculties of Mannes College of Music (appointed 1981), the Juilliard School (appointed 1987) and the Curtis Institute (appointed 1992). He also coaches chamber ensembles at the Tanglewood Music Center run by the Boston Symphony Orchestra in Lenox, Massachusetts. A much-respected teacher, Serkin is "gentle, demanding, perceptive, persistent. He doesn't get aggressive. He's not a know-it-all. He sits back, listens, waits for their reactions, is very encouraging. Then he'll say something like, 'I'm a little unhappy.' 'Really?' the students inquire. And Peter comes up with five or six brilliant ideas." (Tommasini, "The Key...")

Serkin personally is described as deeply serious, disarmingly gentle and friendly, full of avid curiosity, reflective, honest, shy. He and his family (married Regina Toughey, a professional photographer, in 1984, three children) live in New York. A man of diverse musical interests, he listens to jazz, rock and soul music, to native American Indian music, to Oriental musics. In August 1983 Serkin had the honor of being the first pianist to be awarded a major new international prize—the *Premio Accademia Musicale Chigiana Siena*—in recognition of outstanding artistic achievement.

Serkin's innovative programs have evolved into a mixture, not necessarily evenly balanced, of traditional works (Bach, Mozart, Beethoven, Brahms, Chopin, Ravel) and contemporary works (Stravinsky, Webern, Schoenberg, Messiaen, Wolpe, Takemitsu, Lieberson). To those who construe his dedication to modern music as a personal crusade to attract converts, Serkin replies that he is only playing the music he believes in. "Playing new music," he has said, "where there are no reference points other than one's personal experience with those notes, revitalizes one's outlook on how to play traditional repertoire."

He frequently commissions new works. During the 1989–90 season he made an 18-city tour, presenting a "celebration of the present," a program consisting only of 11 new works written by 10 composers, all commissioned by Serkin with funding from the National Endowment for the Arts, among other sources. "The Serkin Commissions," as they came to be called, were enormously successful. He also commissioned Peter Lieberson to compose a piano concerto for him and, despite protests from managers and orchestras, he has promoted performances of the Schoenberg Piano Concerto.

Whether working on old or new music, Serkin typically prepares a piece for a year or two before performing it in public. He has a tremendous technique, a rare sight-reading ability and a remarkable memory, any one of which skills might tempt a pianist to reduce preparation time; but Serkin, as always, thinks first of the music and the composer. His approach to any work, even those he has often played before, starts from ground zero, and essentially consists of an in-depth analysis of the work to discover the composer's motives and to solve any technical problems. Serkin also considers ear training an important factor.

He gives the closest attention to each note, "one might even say each *part* of a note, from attack to release. . . . This attention to sheer sound—to the way a note is articulated, the way it is perceived in the space of the hall, the way it is allowed to die away—makes listening to him a joy." (Pniewski) Which does not mean, however, that Serkin is literal-minded about notation. Aware that sometimes a composer's personal idiosyncrasies, say, a certain rhythmic sense, cannot really be notated exactly, Serkin "avails himself of choices and opinions, but he never allows himself to go far afield." (*LAT*, 7 Jan 1985)

Serkin's practicing, like his playing, is unusual. As a boy he preferred to read through scores (string quartets, oratorios, symphonies) instead of playing the scales and finger exercises approved by his family. As a young professional he did not practice much, and would even test himself by performing a piece in concert after only having read it through three or four times, just to see if he could pull it off. But the years with *Tashi*, musicians who insisted on having plenty of time to learn music leisurely, completely changed Serkin's attitude toward practicing. In a 1980 interview Serkin, then age 33, reported that he practiced a "different scale each day—this morning was F sharp major. I'll do some solfège, then scales and arpeggios, all in F sharp. I'll play a Bach invention, or a prelude, some Brahms and Chopin, and then I'll work on the music I'm performing this season." (*NYT*, 13 Jan 1980)

Peter Serkin may have been the cosseted heir of a musical dynasty, but he has reached the top of his profession through his own remarkable talent. He no longer has to coax concert managers into allowing him to program contemporary works. He decides what he wants to play, and he has developed a strong audience and critical following. As for the stress of solo performing, the desperate feelings have long since disappeared. Although he still gets nervous before a concert, he has learned to redirect that nervous energy into his performance. As his father once put it, "Peter was so full of tension when he played; I didn't realize that was his real gift."

An egoless performer with fearsome powers of concentration, Serkin has been criticized at times for being too intense, too austere, too analytical, too aloof; for playing so introspective that it is colorless; for playing so anti-Romantic that it lacks emotion. But such negative comments matter little when one reads an appraisal that seems to sum up how critics—and audiences—feel about his playing: "With the tradition in his bones, the talent in his fingers, the power in his head and—now—the song in his heart, Peter Serkin will give new life for new generations to whatever music commands his attention or strikes his fancy." (Mayer)

The most striking discovery one finds in the Peter Serkin reviews is how much critics respect his intensely thoughtful, intelligent musicianship. Of more than 100 reviews spanning over three decades (1959–93), most are complimentary. A virtuoso but never theatrical pianist, Serkin is acclaimed for his artistic integrity, highly individualized interpretations, diverse repertoire, exquisite taste and immaculate technique. His playing, as noted in these reviews, is sensitive, introspective, original, brilliant, elegant, lucid; and always at the service of the composer. As Serkin himself puts it, "I am always looking for the *music's* own voice, the composer's conception of his own piece, and always asking myself why the composer used these notes, voicings, registrations and why those dynamics, tempos, expression marks?"

At his first New York appearance, 29 November 1959 at the New School for Social Research, the 12-year-old Serkin "handled his instrument with assured mastery and showed a decided insight into the concerto's form, style and import." (*MA*, 15 Dec 1959)

For his formal New York recital debut (27 March 1965) at the Metropolitan Museum of Art, the 17-year-old Serkin chose a program that would have challenged even the most seasoned pianist: Schubert's Sonata in G Major, D. 894, *plus* the Bach Goldberg Variations. And he did very well. "In deeply felt musical and intellectual fashion, he made the program successful, all of it. With both towering works, he created complete structures, moving and interesting at all times. One was not aware of the high-powered pianism involved; it was hidden behind serious purpose." (*NYT*, 29 March 1965) Serkin had also played the Goldberg Variations at his London recital debut (28 Feb 1965) at Wigmore Hall. Wrote one reviewer: "One marvelled at the lucidity and nimbleness of Mr. Serkin's playing. . . . Imagination and stylistic consistency, not to mention technical control, almost made us forget the piano's limitations for the Variations, and the intimacy of No. 25 showed that he could also relax (if not yet smile) in his playing. All in all, an impressive first appearance." (*MM*, April 1965)

Serkin's performance (8 Feb 1967) of Beethoven's "Diabelli" Variations, op. 120, failed to impress one New York reviewer. Serkin's approach to the "Diabelli" was "serious, accurate and in its way musical. . . . But he, like most others [of his generation] could not get the essence of the music. One of Mr. Serkin's troubles was rhythmic. Surprisingly often he failed to establish the basic pulse of a variation. . . . The playing throughout was determined, a bit heavy, sometimes rather muddy. Through it all did come a strong musical mind, but a mind that is not yet ready for the 'Diabelli' Variations." (*NYT*, 9 Feb 1967)

During the 1973–74 season he gave around 35 concerts, including an impressive performance (18 April 1973, Alice Tully Hall) of the complete set of Messiaen's *Vingt regards sur l'Enfant Jésus*, a grueling series of 20 compositions lasting well over two hours. His first New York performance of the work in its entirety was "a remarkable experience. . . . He takes its difficulties in stride, so that they do not interfere with his concentration on its musical and emotional values. He is able to give the quiet exalted passages their feeling of radiant power, and his tone is of an exceptionally consistent beauty." (*NYT*, 21 April 1973)

It became increasingly obvious that Serkin intended to concentrate on quality of performance rather than accumulate a vast repertoire. Through the years he has often played Mozart with orchestras, but instead of playing *all* of the Mozart concertos Serkin has concentrated on six or seven, in particular those which he recorded with Alexander Schneider in the 1970s. On 7 May 1978 Serkin, with Schneider conducting the New York Philharmonic Orchestra, played the Concerto in E-flat Major, K. 482. "Mr. Serkin approached the concerto not as a virtuoso vehicle, but as a telescope through which he could look for the tone poetry that always lies beneath the courtly surface of Mozart's later works. . . . The entire performance had the transparency and texture of chamber music, and a seldom encountered give and take among the musicians." (*NYT*, 9 May 1978)

During the 1981–82 and 1984–85 seasons Serkin emerged as a convincing Beethovenist. His Palm Beach, Florida, performance (15 Nov 1981) of the Beethoven Sonata, op. 110, was "often a discovery even to ears long familiar with it. The stature of Serkin's performance, challenging to the point of the tragic, was Beethoven moving into his own ground." (*MH*, 18 Nov 1981) Glowing reviews followed his performance (9 Oct 1982) of ops. 90, 109 and 110 at London's Wigmore Hall. "Mr. Serkin's near reverence for the music's metaphysical dimensions was awe-inspiring." (*DT*, 12 Oct 1982) Also, "It was a deeply absorbing evening. . . . In close detail, Serkin's Beethoven is highly original and very much his own; yet in their striking fidelity to the composer's text, their close focus and quick, quirky excitement, the performances summoned the shade of no other artist more vividly than that of Glenn Gould." (*FT*, 11 Oct 1982)

In the 1990–91 concert season Serkin captivated audiences and critics with a typically unconventional program—three Brahms organ Choral Preludes (in transcription), the Beethoven Bagatelles, op. 126, a hybrid Mozart Sonata in F Major, K. 533/494 (its first two movements were added to a rondo Mozart had composed earlier) and the Chopin Bolero, op. 19, comprised the "standard" fare, to which were added three of the short commissioned works: Peter Lieberson's Breeze of Delight, Oliver Knussen's Variations and Alexander Goehr's In Real Time. Serkin played this program extensively, and the various reviews are worth comparing. From Cleveland: "To compositions representing the styles and ideas of three centuries, he brought beautiful tone, flawless technique and an intensity of purpose that focused exclusively on the music." (*CPD*, 8 Oct 1990). From San Francisco: "If there were awards for thoughtful programming, Serkin's . . . might take top prize. Olympian playing brought it to life." (*SFE*, 22 Jan 1991). From New York: "He showered his enthusiastic capacity audience . . . with the gold of immaculate pianism. . . . He made the piano grand and affecting, with rich sonorities. . . . Altogether, this was a musical event of intelligence and delight." (*MA*, July 1991)

Serkin's Bach recital of 12 October 1993 consisted of just two works—the Partita No. 6 in E Minor and the Goldberg Variations. "This was a stimulating evening of elevated musicmaking, one of those memorable occasions when a brilliant artist finds himself at the top of his form." In Serkin's reading of the Goldberg Variations, "detail was gently etched, never overly harsh or insistent. . . . There was a wonderfully modest lyricism about this performance that seemed to emanate from a spirit in repose." (*ARG*, Jan/Feb 1994)

Serkin's sometimes turbulent career has been, if nothing else, consistently interesting. "As Serkin discusses his life, you realize that his real mission has been to keep his connection to music as fresh and as real as it was when he was a child. To do so, he had to reject his musical heritage in order to reclaim it with his own brand of *Back to the Future* progress. Like many other self-serious '60s youths, he had to lose himself in order to find himself." (Tommasini, "The Key. . .") Indeed, in every respect Peter Serkin has found himself.

The 1974 LP album of six Mozart concertos with Peter Serkin as the soloist and Alexander Schneider conducting the English Chamber Orchestra won the *Deutsche Schallplaten* Prize in 1976, a Grammy nomination, and *Stereo Review's* designation as "one of the best recordings of the last 20 years." The LP album is no longer available but the concertos have been reissued on 3 CDs (see Discog.).

In his recording of Messiaen's *Vingt regards sur l'Enfant Jésus* for RCA (3-0789, no longer available), "Serkin plays the piece with high regard for its detail, but without substituting its detail for its scope. There is a compelling logic in the playing and a level of intensity that does not let a listener brush the music's surface." (*PI*, 10 Aug 1975) Still another important performance awaiting reissue is Serkin's reading of the Schoenberg Piano Concerto with the London Symphony Orchestra, Pierre Boulez conducting (Erato NUM 75256). "Peter Serkin in particular creates from bar one a seamless stream in which there is constantly shifting light, half-light and shadow. Rarely too can the Brahmsian overtones have registered so strongly." (*Hi-Fi News*, Oct 1986)

Serkin's Pro Arte CD of Beethoven's Variations in C Major on a Waltz by Diabelli, op. 120, is outstanding. "His approach is closer to Arrau's than to Richter's . . . but he is more straightforward overall and freer of what might be regarded as idiosyncrasy than either of his senior colleagues. The new recording is, in short, a sound, tasteful, eminently musical exposition of this unique work." (*StR*, Aug 1989)

Serkin's recording of Beethoven's "*Hammerklavier*" prompted one critic to note that he "favors whirlwind tempos that approximate Beethoven's metronome indications. But unlike Schnabel, who came to grief under such pressure, Serkin's mind and fingers are awesomely commensurate to demands. He commands lovely nuances but is never the sensualist; instead of robust weight, Serkin favors a kind of finely etched, blueprint clarity." (*OP*, Sept 1988)

Serkin recorded both Brahms concertos with Robert Shaw and the Atlanta Symphony Orchestra (see Discog.). The Concerto No. 1 in D Minor "is a monumental performance, one that achieves extraordinary levels of expression, particularly in the Adagio. . . . Here Peter Serkin, with sensitive support from Shaw, attains a rapt concentration that seems at intervals to hover in midair—to cast a spell that holds us in perfect equilibrium until the first affirmative notes of the Rondo summon us back to life and movement. It's really quite magical." (*OV*, July 1988)

One notable recording (Grammy, 1987) contains a sampling of the new and the not quite so new (Stravinsky, Wolpe, Lieberson), items from a highly successful recital given (31 Aug 1985) by Serkin at the 92nd Street Y. His performances of Wolpe's Passacaglia (1936) and Form IV (1979) are strikingly exciting. "His pacing [Passacaglia] and attention to the voicing of the complex contrapuntal fabric sustain growing suspense until it explodes in the prodigious climax for the coda." And in Lieberson's Bagatelles, perhaps inspired indirectly by the composer's association with Tibetan Buddhism, Serkin succeeds in "bringing forth an extraordinary variety of colors from the quieter dynamic ranges and so is able to realize this music with utmost sensitivity within the limitations of the modern grand piano." (*AmM*, Spring 1989)

Even in our sophisticated, supposedly unprejudiced society, it is rare that a large-scale work in contemporary idiom garners outright praise. But Peter Lieberson's Piano Concerto (commissioned by the Boston Symphony Orchestra for its centennial in 1981) has done just that. Serkin played the world premiere performance with Seiji Ozawa and the Boston Symphony Orchestra on 22 April 1983, and the same ensemble recorded the Concerto for New World Records (see Discog.). This is "a superb performance. . . . As for Mr. Serkin, he seems to me America's preeminent young pianist—his intelligence and perceptivity invariably take the listener directly to the heart of the music." (*NYT*, 22 April 1985)

SELECTED REFERENCES

Berger, Karen. "Peter Serkin: classical piano's 'enfant terrible' comes of age." *Keyboard*, Feb 1984, pp. 42–44, 48, 52, 56, 59.

Cariaga, Daniel. "Peter Serkin: Grace Under Pressure." *Los Angeles Times*, 6 Jan 1985, sec. 6, pp. 1, 8.

Chute, James. "Peter Serkin: He plays the piano, not the game." *Milwaukee Journal*, 3 March 1985, Entertainment, pp. 1, 3.

Coleman, Emily. "Typical, Untypical Teen-Ager." *New York Times*, 29 Jan 1967, sec. 2, pp. 13, 27.

Conroy, Frank. "The Serkin Touch." *Esquire*, Dec 1985, pp. 92–95, 98, 102.

Dyer, Richard. "Peter Serkin to open a bag of surprises." *Boston Globe*, 14 Jan 1990, sec. A, pp. 1, 11, 13.

Guregian, Elaine. "Cleveland, pianist old friends." *Beacon Journal*, 30 Sept 1990, sec. G, pp. 1, 5.

Henahan, Donal. "Peter Serkin—Who Is He Nowadays?" *New York Times*, 18 March 1973, sec. 2, pp. 1, 17.

Jepson, Barbara. "Making It New: Pianist Peter Serkin." *Wall Street Journal*, 3 Sept 1985, p. 22.

Kimmelman, Michael. "Peter Serkin." *Ovation*, Jan 1986, pp. 8–12.

McLellan, Joseph. "Serkin's All-New Sound." *Washington Post*, 17 Nov 1989, sec. D, pp. 1, 3.

Mayer, Martin. "Peter Serkin." *Musical America*, Jan 1985, pp. 4–5.

Montparker, Carol. "Peter Serkin: A Pianist for All Seasons." *Clavier*, Nov 1989, pp. 10–15, 48.

Pniewski, Tom. "The Serkins: Masters of Past and Present." *The World & I*, June 1987, pp. 224–226.

Reich, Howard. "Premier pieces." *Chicago Tribune*, 19 Nov 1989, sec. 13, p. 10.

Stein, Ruthe. "A Private Pianist Perks Up." *San Francisco Chronicle*, 22 Jan 1986, (People), pp. 17, 19.

Swed, Mark. "Peter Serkin Walks the High Wire." *Keynote*, Nov 1989, pp. 8–11.

Sweeney, Louise. "Serkin on 'Music's Own Voice'." *Christian Science Monitor*, 6 Feb 1989, p. 11.

Tommasini, Anthony. "The Key To Peter Serkin." *Boston Globe Magazine*, 16 Aug 1987, p. 14.
————. "Peter Serkin's two 'old friends'." *Boston Globe*, 30 Nov 1990, pp. 39–40.
Trustman, Deborah. "Peter Serkin: Playing in a New Key." *New York Times Magazine*, 13 Jan 1980, pp. 22–27, 61, 63, 74.
Valdes, Lesley. "A Concerted Performance." *Philadelphia Inquirer*, 7 Jan 1990, sec. E, pp. 1, 13–14.
Wiser, John D. "A Conversation with Peter Serkin." *Fanfare*, Sept/Oct 1984, pp. 151–155.
See also Bibliography: Cur/Bio (1986); Dub/Ref; Eld/Pia; Kol/Que; New/GrA; WWAM.

SELECTED REVIEWS

AJ: 7 April 1984. *ARG*: Jan/Feb 1994. *BE*: 19 Aug 1991; 18 July 1994. *BG*: 4 May 1982; 26 Feb 1985; 4 Dec 1987; 15 Jan 1990; 7 Dec 1990. *BH*: 14 Nov 1994. *CoP*: 17 Nov 1994. *CPD*: 7 May 1984; 8 Oct 1990. *CT*: 18 Aug 1986; 30 March 1987; 12 July 1993. *DT*: 12 Oct 1982; 2 April 1985. *FT*: 11 Oct 1982; 2 April 1985. *LAT*: 7 Jan 1985; 29 Jan 1987; 6 Feb 1988; 24 Jan 1991; 14 Jan 1995. *MA*: 15 Dec 1959; March 1990; July 1991. *MH*: 18 Nov 1981; 18 March 1986. *MM*: April 1965. *NW*: 1 March 1965. *NYP*: 21 April 1980. *NYT*: 30 Nov 1959; 17 Feb 1965; 29 March 1965; 15 Feb 1966; 9 Feb 1967; 5 May 1967; 21 April 1973; 22 Dec 1973; 9 May 1978; 18 Oct 1982; 2 Dec 1985; 5 April 1987; 13 Nov 1989; 29 March 1991; 23 Jan 1993; 16 April 1994. *PI*: 19 June 1990; 27 March 1991; 14 Nov 1994. *PP*: 1 Feb 1992. *SFC*: 12 April 1985; 4 Dec 1989; 23 Jan 1991. *SFE*: 22 Jan 1991. *WDT*: 23 March 1991. *WP*: 23 Feb 1985; 20 Feb 1989. *WSJ*: 1 Dec 1989.

SELECTED DISCOGRAPHY

Bach: Goldberg Variations; Italian Concerto. Pro Arte CD-331 (2 CDs).
Beethoven: Sonata in B-flat Major, op. 106 ("*Hammerklavier*"). Pro Arte CDD-270.
Beethoven: Variations in C Major on a Waltz by Diabelli, op. 120. Pro Arte CDD-447.
Berg: Chamber Concerto for Piano, Violin and 13 Wind Instruments (w/I. Stern). Sony Classical SK 45999 (CD). Abbado/London SO.
Brahms: Concerto No. 1 in D Minor, op. 15.   Pro Arte CDD-266. Shaw/Atlanta SO.
Brahms: Concerto No. 2 in B-flat Major, op. 83.   Pro Arte CDD-336. Shaw/Atlanta SO.
Chopin: *Andante spianato* and *Grande Polonaise*, op. 22; Ballade No. 3 in A-flat Major, op. 47; Impromptu No. 1 in A-flat Major, op. 47; Mazurkas, op. 59, nos. 1-3; Nocturne in E-flat Major, op. 55, no. 2. RCA (Red Seal) ARC1-4356.

Chopin: Ballade No. 4 in F Minor, op. 52; Fantasy in F Minor, op. 49; 4
    Mazurkas, op. 41; 3 Mazurkas, op. 63; Nocturne in B Major; Three
    Waltzes: E Minor, A Minor, F Major. Pro Arte CDD-246.
Lieberson: Bagatelles. Stravinsky: Serenade in A; Sonata for Piano. Wolpe:
    Form IV: Broken Sequences; Passacaglia; Pastorale. New World NW 344-
    2.
Lieberson: Piano Concerto. New World NW 325-2. Ozawa/Boston SO.
Mozart: Concerto in E-flat Major, K. 449; Concerto in B-flat Major, K. 450.
    RCA RCD1-1492. Schneider/English CO.
Mozart: Concerto in D Major, K. 451; Concerto in G Major, K. 453. RCA
    RCD1-1943. Schneider/English CO.
Mozart: Concerto in G Major, K. 453; Concerto in B-flat Major, K. 456. RCA
    60790-2. Schneider/English CO.
Mozart: Sonata in B-flat Major, K. 570; Sonata in D Major, K. 576; Rondos: D
    Major, K. 485 and A Minor, K. 511. Pro Arte CDD 247.
Schubert: Dances. Pro Arte CDD-358.

SERKIN, RUDOLF: b. Eger, Austria (now Cheb, Czechoslovakia), 28
    March 1903; d. Guilford, Vermont, 8 May 1991.

> Occasionally there comes into our midst an artist whose outlook is an
> all-embracing one, whose talents are fully developed, and whose sense
> of perspective is not bound by the limits of a musical period, a style, or
> even the repertoire confines of his own chosen instrument. Such an
> artist is Rudolf Serkin.
>
> Richard O'Harra (*Musical Courier*, May 1960)

Articles about Rudolf Serkin—there are not many interviews—invariably focus
on his unswerving devotion to the art of music. One of a rare kind, Serkin was
both a great pianist and a complete musician engrossed in all music. "Although
I am a pianist," he said, "the piano has always been less interesting to me than
the music."

His intensely musical life began with musical parents—Augusta
(Scharg) Serkin and Mordko Serkin, both of Russian ancestry. Mordko Serkin,
trained as a basso and a merchant only because of necessity, gave all his children
elementary lessons in violin and piano. The obviously gifted Rudolf learned his
notes before he learned his letters; at age four started piano lessons with a local
teacher; and within a year made his public debut playing a few pieces by Heller
and Schubert at a concert in Franzensbad. He made a tremendous impression and
might have become a public prodigy had not his father refused to exploit him.

At age nine Serkin played for the celebrated pianist Alfred Grünfeld,
who recommended lessons with Professor Richard Robert in Vienna, which
meant that for the next eight years Serkin studied with Robert and lived as a

boarder ("I was very lonely," he said in later years) in some Vienna household. At age 12 he made a successful debut in Vienna, playing the Mendelssohn Concerto in G Minor with the Vienna Symphony Orchestra, Oskar Nedbal conducting; and once again all proffered concert tours were rejected by his father. Serkin continued his piano studies with Robert, studied composition with Joseph Marx and, for about three years, with Arnold Schoenberg.

This early phase of Serkin's life, like all the rest of it, was wholly directed toward music. Although he never attended school, all his life Serkin read voraciously in literature, philosophy and the arts. He finished his music studies in 1920, began working by himself on developing a keyboard repertoire and, to support himself, gave music lessons and occasionally played concerts. He had hoped to study with Ferruccio Busoni but, after hearing Serkin play, Busoni told him he was too old to take lessons, that instead he must play many concerts.

That same year (1920) Serkin met the violinist Adolf Busch at an evening of music making organized by friends. Serkin was 17 and had just finished his studies; Busch was 30 and a teacher of violin at the Berlin *Hochschule für Musik*. Busch must have been terribly impressed with Serkin's playing, for he invited the teenager to tour with the Busch chamber players the following spring and in the meantime to come live with the Busch family in Berlin so that they could prepare for the upcoming concerts. Thus began a close association that lasted until Busch's death three decades later. Adolf Busch, now recognized as one of the great musicians of the century, proved to be the single greatest influence on Serkin's music making, his career, even his life. Serkin moved in with the Busch family in Berlin in 1920; in 1922 they went together to Darmstadt, Germany, and in 1927 moved together to Basel, Switzerland. In 1935 Serkin married Irene Busch, Adolf's only daughter and herself a gifted violinist. (Peter, the fourth of the six Serkin children, has become one of the outstanding pianists of his generation.)

Right from the start, Busch was a good influence. Serkin made his first Berlin appearance in 1920, playing the Brandenburg Concerto No. 5, with Busch conducting. The audience applauded so enthusiastically that Busch encouraged him to give an encore. Serkin asked what he should play; Busch jokingly suggested Bach's Goldberg Variations; and the innocent Serkin complied. As the story goes, when he finished 55 minutes later, only four people were left in the hall—Adolf Busch, Artur Schnabel, Alfred Einstein and Serkin!

Over the next decade Serkin gained invaluable experience and acquired an impressive, if not widespread, reputation touring in Europe with Adolf Busch and his chamber ensemble. Serkin played solo recitals, sonata recitals with Busch and also chamber music with the Busch Quartet. In 1933 he gave his first performance in the United States—a sonata recital with Busch at the Coolidge Festival in Washington, D.C. Three years later Serkin made his American concerto debut (20 Feb 1936), playing the Beethoven Concerto No. 4 and the Mozart Concerto in B-flat Major, K. 595, with the New York Philharmonic Society, Arturo Toscanini conducting. The following year Serkin made his New York recital debut (11 Jan 1937) at Carnegie Hall.

The threat of World War II made it expedient for the Busch and Serkin families (then living in Basel in adjoining houses connected by a shared library) to move to the United States in 1939. Serkin almost at once joined the piano faculty of the Curtis Institute of Music in Philadelphia and soon became head of the department. For about eight years Mrs. Serkin and the children lived in Guilford, Vermont, near her parents, and Serkin commuted between Guilford and Philadelphia. He was director of the Institute from 1968 to 1975.

The Marlboro Music School and Festival, one of Serkin's great achievements, took root in 1949 when the newly established Marlboro College in Vermont asked Adolf Busch to start a summer program on campus. In the summer of 1950 Busch, his brother Hermann, Marcel Moyse, Blanche Moyse, Louis Moyse and Rudolf Serkin tried an experimental program—not exactly a school but a community of musicians, professionals and students, who got together to talk about and especially to play the full repertoire of chamber music: classic and modern, instrumental and vocal.

The experiment proved successful, and in 1951 the founding group inaugurated the Marlboro Music School and Festival. Busch died the following year, and Serkin became artistic director. Under his guidance Marlboro developed into one of the most prestigious summer sessions in the world. Pianist Ruth Laredo recalls that one of the greatest things about Marlboro was Serkin's "special attitude about music-making. He made us feel that the performer can never do enough for the music." (Kozinn) For its part, Marlboro gave Serkin some of the happiest, most rewarding and most musical times of his life.

Marlboro and Curtis must have made enormous demands on Serkin's time and talents, but he never gave up playing concerts, typically less than 100 appearances a season. He toured annually in North America and Europe; made tours in South America, Iceland, India, Israel, Australia, New Zealand, the Far East and the Orient; and for many years he was a regular performer at Pablo Casal's festivals in Prades, Perpignan and Puerto Rico.

Serkin never officially retired, although in later life illness frequently forced him to cancel appearances. At his final New York recital, at Carnegie Hall on 8 April 1987, the 84-year-old Serkin received a glowing review (*NYT*, 9 April 1987) for his performance of Beethoven's last three sonatas. In 1988 his performances of the Beethoven Concerto No. 5 ("Emperor") with both the Chicago and Cleveland orchestras were the last he ever gave. Rudolf Serkin died of cancer on 8 May 1991.

His prodigious talents reaped honors, awards and degrees from around the world. In America alone Serkin received the Presidential Medal of Freedom in 1963; the Governor's Award of Excellence in the Arts (Vermont Council on the Arts) in 1967; the Fifth Annual Pennsylvania Award for excellence in the arts in 1971; the Art Alliance Medal (Philadelphia) in 1972; honorary membership in the New York Philharmonic in 1972 to commemorate Serkin's 100th performance with that orchestra; the National Medal of Art from President Reagan in 1988; and honorary doctorates from Harvard University, Williams College, Temple University, Oberlin College, University of Rochester, the Curtis Institute of Music.

However, for Rudolf Serkin, music meant far more than all the honors, far more than international fame as one of the greatest pianists (along with Arrau, Horowitz, Rubinstein) of his day. From start to finish, music shaped his life, and every single phase of that life—studying in Vienna, performing with the Busch ensemble in Europe, making a career in America—was completely dedicated to the service of music. Personally he was warm and affectionate, full of the joy of living and, considering his exalted reputation and busy life, amazingly sweet-tempered. A longtime colleague who knew Rudolf Serkin very well may have unknowingly provided an epitaph: "It's impossible to talk about anybody's being saintly in this age, but Serkin is." (*NYT*, 10 May 1991)

Among colleagues Serkin had a reputation for being one of the most knowledgeable of musicians. Moreover, he had a gift for explaining what he knew, and Serkin is remembered as one of the most respected, distinguished teachers of his time. Despite his busy life, he kindly tried to find time to listen to young musicians play. But in the early years the "saintly" Serkin could be very hard on students. Any kind of thoughtless, disrespectful or show-off playing transformed the usually jovial Serkin into a stern, even sarcastic, teacher. Age softened his hard attitude, and later students fared better, but, as an early student recalled, Serkin had "a talent for making me, and other students as well, feel extremely bad, to put it bluntly. I have discussed this with him since, and he felt that we absolutely needed this. He felt that we needed a rude awakening, that this was the only way to save us as artists." (Kuerti) But if Serkin was sometimes a hard master, he was always a great inspiration.

An article entitled "Strength of Finger, Strength of Thought" (*Etude* March 1941) is actually a detailed account of Serkin's ideas on teaching, on the piano and piano playing, technique and practicing, tone and interpretation. He was a great believer in scales ("the time honored system of scales. There is no detour around them!"), and he had a personal concept of technique: "Instead of developing a technic as such, and then trying to apply it first to Bach and then to Brahms, we would do better to develop a Bach technic from a careful study of Bach's works, adjusting our finger work to the demands of his thought and style. A Brahms technic should develop directly from the study of Brahms, and so on through the full list of composers." Finger facility and technique were not enough. A student also "had to develop his ear, his mind, his taste, his sense of style, to bring life to the meaning behind the printed notes."

Serkin may have been hard on some students; we know he was merciless with himself. Although absolutely a musical genius, he had neither a natural technique nor "a pianist's hands" (his were large with a wide spread between thick fingers). He never felt easy at the piano, and early reviewers made much of Serkin's nervous anguish as he bounced around on the piano bench, humming, grunting, groaning and pedal-stamping.

Such keyboard mannerisms had to be distracting, but one astute writer admitted that with Serkin's playing he had "often been missing the forest for the trees. Gradually, with eyes closed and ears open, I began to discern that Serkin played not only with his whole body but also with his whole soul. I began to perceive what music means to him. Finally, I became vividly aware of the sheer exaltation that music arouses in this man, and at last I realized that his muscular agitation reflects a compulsive bodily response to what he hears and feels within him and struggles physically to transmit." (Cha/Spe, see Bibliog.)

Serkin practiced endlessly. In the years at Curtis he practiced all morning until about one o'clock. Colleagues at Marlboro recall hearing Serkin practicing all day, sometimes nothing but scales (the whole day!), at other times practicing just pieces, without playing one scale. After he had mastered the technical problems in a composition, he would invent—and reinvent—devilishly difficult fingerings to keep his practicing from becoming routine and stale. (Even in recitals Serkin often changed fingerings on the spur of the moment to accommodate different pianos or acoustics.)

Hard work produced a secure, polished, often dazzling technique, but Serkin was an "artistic" rather than "heroic" virtuoso. A Vienna recital in late 1935 (Serkin was 32 years old) drew this comment: "Inasmuch as he has absolutely no fascinations of personality to exert, his triumphs are all the more a matter of sheer piano playing. . . . Enhanced, moreover, have become the unfaltering artistic rectitude of his performances, the sense of fanatic, aspiring, incorruptible zeal which informs them." (*NYT*, 16 Feb 1936)

How similar is that analysis to one taken from a review written 50 years later, when Serkin at age 83 played (15 Oct 1986) the Beethoven Concerto No. 5 with the Dallas Symphony Orchestra under Sergiu Comissiona: "Serkin has never made his way as a grand-style virtuoso or a delicate colorist. Energy and the impact of a tightly coiled spring have been more his trademarks. Musically, he remains an artist of enormous directness and simplicity." (*DMN*, 18 Oct 1986)

It is obvious, then, that to the end of his life Serkin remained faithful to his aesthetic and musical ideals. His very personal musical style (intense, dedicated, profound, exciting) stemmed from his rock-solid integrity, an ingrained sense of responsibility to the composer and his profound grasp of the overall design of a composition. His firm control of *rubato* and tempo gave his playing great unity, formal organization, line and thrust. His tone varied. He had a big sound, which in his excitable youth could turn percussive, shrill, even metallic, but the mature Serkin produced a "rich," "warm," "sonorous," "gorgeous," "firm," and "beautifully weighted" tone.

Rudolf Serkin was without question one of the most respected of all pianists, but not everyone could enjoy his playing. To begin with, his was not a style to accommodate audience-pleasing showpieces. And for some listeners his playing was too reserved, too controlled, too meticulous. But Serkin played with an incredible authority, sweep and thrilling rhythmic élan that overwhelmed audiences, not to mention critics and colleagues.

Serkin never compromised his lofty standards. He triumphed, said a long-ago critic, because of "the formidable quality of his musical intellect—and the exciting tensions that he manages to convey, as musical ideas, both subtle and adventurous, struggle to life on his keyboard." (*Time*, 10 Nov 1961) Three decades later Serkin, recognized as one of the great pianists of the century, was remembered as "a rare artist who combined a powerful intellect, conscience and humanity. . . . These qualities made his performances—above all of Beethoven—unequalled in vitality and revelatory properties." (*SFC*, 10 May 1991)

Although extremely knowledgeable about keyboard literature, Serkin played a limited solo repertoire, mostly the intellectually demanding works of the Austro-German composers (Bach, Beethoven, Brahms, Mozart, Schubert, Schumann), less frequently works by Bartók, Chopin, Mendelssohn, Reger. Serkin's concerto repertoire was also restricted—he played mostly Bach, Beethoven, Brahms, Mendelssohn, Mozart, Schumann, the Reger Concerto in F Minor. He also played some contemporary works: the Strauss *Burleske*, Prokofiev Concerto No. 4 and Bartók's Concerto No. 1. His interpretations of the classical literature are regarded as the last word in authenticity and faithfulness. Just about every recital included at least one Beethoven sonata; large-scale Brahms and Schumann works also figured prominently.

Serkin continually refined rather than enlarged his repertoire, but he knew the entire piano literature and other repertoires as well. He simply loved music, in fact, in 1960 he took a break from concertizing and from Curtis so that he could study several Bach cantatas and Haydn quartets; not that he would ever play them, but simply because "they are such beautiful music."

In 1931, before Serkin ever played in America, Herbert F. Peyser, foreign music correspondent of the *New York Times,* heard him in recital in Berlin and wrote a glowing review. "Before Mr. Serkin had played ten bars of the Haydn sonata music, I realized I was in the presence of something extraordinary. More than two hours later—the artist having, in the meantime, added to his program the Paganini-Liszt variations, the F sharp minor Polonaise of Chopin and that same master's 'Butterfly' étude and study in thirds—I reluctantly left the *Singakademie,* impressed as I have been by few pianists. I harbor the immutable conviction that under the name of Rudolf Serkin lives one of the most commanding pianists of the age." (*NYT*, 15 Feb 1931) Serkin was then 27 years old.

In 1932 Serkin played in Great Britain in the Busch chamber concerts and also gave two Wigmore Hall recitals. His recital of 23 February 1932 was "a magnificent exhibition of pianism. His playing is not without sensibility, but more prominent characteristics are musical insight, brilliant execution, and a robustly healthy style." (*TL*, 25 Feb 1932)

Serkin's New York orchestral debut on 20 February 1936 with the Philharmonic-Symphony Society was a smashing success, made even more rewarding by the applause of conductor Arturo Toscanini. Serkin's interpretation of Beethoven's Concerto No. 4 in G Major deserved "detailed mention. We have seldom heard a pianist's performance which so admirably combined the most penetrating analysis with artistic enthusiasm and warm feeling. Similarly, the technical performance was clean and precise, but also beautiful and of a poetic coloring." This critic dismissed the Mozart Concerto in B-flat Major, K. 595— "admirably interpreted" by Serkin—as "by no means one of Mozart's strongest concertos." (*NYT*, 21 Feb 1936)

A review of Serkin's first New York recital, at Carnegie Hall on 11 January 1937, is actually an essay on Serkin and his artistry. "Whether he is playing Beethoven or Reger or the calmer and lighter Mendelssohn, he appears to respond to every note with every fiber of his being. . . . It is selfless playing in the most literal sense, for one is never conscious of the prodigious technical equipment which forms its base or the erudition which gives it authenticity." (*NYP*, 12 Jan 1937)

Reviewers might disagree with what Serkin did, but they never questioned his musicianship and authority. On 28 January 1939 he played the mighty Brahms Concerto No. 1 in D Minor with the National Orchestral Association under Leon Barzin's direction. "Mr. Serkin's interpretation of it was deeply subjective throughout, but at the same time filled with power and energy where he felt decided contrasts were in order. There was not a dull moment in his performance, which was as perfect in its way as anything the artist has played in this city." (*NYT*, 29 Jan 1939)

A review of an early Hunter College recital (20 Oct 1956)—a program ranging from Bach and Mozart to Beethoven and Schumann—ranks Serkin as "one of today's masters." He played with considerable freedom: "Mr. Serkin, classic though his inclinations may be, has never hesitated to employ so-called 'romantic' techniques when he felt it suited the music. . . . In general, throughout the recital, the playing was . . . mature, beautifully finished, musicianly, with the ideas in strong profile." (*NYT*, 22 Oct 1956)

Most of the time Serkin played severe, uncompromising programs, like the one he played on 14 June 1971 at London's Royal Festival Hall—Beethoven Sonatas in G Major, op. 31, no. 1, and F Minor, op. 57, *and* the great Schubert Sonata in B-flat Major. No one complained. "Our misfortune that Serkin's visits to London are not more frequent is to some extent balanced by the fact that his rare appearances lodge in the memory, giving food for thought long after lesser recitals have passed into oblivion." (*MT*, Aug 1971)

Serkin disdained even the idea of "popular" programs, insisting that only music of the very highest quality (meaning Beethoven, Schubert, Brahms, particularly the large-scale works) deserved his fullest attention. At a London recital (3 Feb 1975) his performance of Beethoven's monumental "Diabelli" Variations, "a piece that takes possession of pianists who attempt to play it . . . had this compulsive quality: a severe, uncompromising reading. . . . He does not concern himself with superficies such as balance or euphony. The piano rarely sings, or even speaks sweetly, under his fingers. But everything it says is heavy with meaning, with dynamic energy, with intensity of feeling." (*TL*, 4 Feb 1975)

For Rudolf Serkin, the ideal recital program consisted of the last three sonatas of Beethoven. When he played that ideal program on 26 August 1982 in Los Angeles, an articulate critic wrote, "It is easier to describe what he does rather than how he does it. . . . He simply plays directly and naturally all that the composer has prescribed. But in this process of transcription, which never can be totally accomplished, the music takes on particles of the performer's knowledge, of his intelligence, his experience, his sympathies and, above all, his feeling and his emotional constitution. When all those things function maximally, we have the Serkin Beethoven that awed and elevated those who heard it." (*LAT*, 28 April 1982)

Serkin played the same three Beethoven sonatas at his last New York recital (8 April 1987), this time like "a diver who finds with experience that he can drop deeper and deeper, always finding new levels that would be inaccessible to the young, no matter how brave. At age 84, Mr. Serkin knows where the dangerous reefs and coral beds lie in these mighty works, and he does not so much avoid them as dare them to block his descent into the depths. . . . All in all, this recital found a great virtuoso and musician at the top of his game, playing with astonishing precision as well as the interpretative penetration he has accustomed us to expect from him." (© *The New York Times Company*, 9 April 1987. Reprinted by permission.)

Although in ill health, in 1988 Serkin played the Beethoven "Emperor" Concerto with both the Cleveland and Chicago orchestras. These were his final public appearances, and one Chicago review offers a particularly poignant testimonial: "Serkin has been preaching the gospel according to Beethoven to devout congregations of listeners for more than a half century, and this audience hung raptly on every word of the high priest's sermon. . . . Revered institutions have their privileges, after all. Long may this grand philosopher of the piano continue to instruct and enlighten us." (*CT*, 29 Sept 1988)

Serkin purportedly disliked recording and his performances vary artistically and technically. "Yet, at his best, his driving energy, his fierce intelligence, his quick mind, and (until comparatively recently) his unfailing lucidity of touch often produced recordings that do that rare thing: they transcend the medium." (*Gram*, July 1991)

His CBS recordings of both Brahms concertos (see Discog.) capture the musicianly communion between two great musicians, Rudolf Serkin and Eugene Ormandy. The two CDs offer many moments of pleasure, although Serkin's technique fails him at times and his phrasings, as one critic expressed it, "have more than their share of strangeness. The Schumann fillers display Serkin in much better form and the lovely *Introduction and Allegro appassionato* is a highlight." (*ARG*, Jan/Feb 1991) Most critics rate the Brahms recordings Serkin made in 1967 with Szell and the Cleveland Orchestra (see Discog.) as superb. In the Concerto No. 1 in D Minor, Serkin was "at the peak of his form, emotionally, intellectually, and technically. . . . There are miracles of dynamic shading yet dynamic changes that are elementally swift and steep. Above all, there is a revelatory way with rhythm, full of potency and drive in quicker music, and turning the more reflective passages into slow sustained acts of transcendental enquiry." (*Gramophone*, July 1991. Reprinted by permission.)

The term legendary, so often applied without much thought or discretion, honestly applies to several of Serkin's recorded performances—and particularly to his recording of the two Mendelssohn concertos (see Discog.), originally issued over 30 years ago. "With this around, no other recording of No. 2 is worth considering; and when you've listened to one or two other excellent firsts you still come back to this for excitement, emotion, balance, and charm that the others have only in part. Few records merit the term, but these are bests: they have never been surpassed." (*American Record Guide*, Jan/Feb 1992. Reprinted by permission.)

Given Serkin's devotion to Beethoven's music (almost every program during his entire career included at least one Beethoven sonata), it is surprising—

and disappointing—that he did not record the complete sonatas. He recorded sonatas from all periods, and was particularly well known for his recordings of the "*Pathéthique*," the "*Appassionata*," the "*Waldstein*" and the late sonatas. In October 1987, at the age of 84, Serkin recorded the last three Sonatas (ops. 109–111) in the Vienna *Konzerthaus* (see Discog.), a performance also captured on video cassette. "Although his stamina and the manipulative aspects of his technique are still in excellent order, one is conscious of more weight on the keys, generally, and the lack of sustained quiet playing tells against this record a little, perhaps most of all in the arioso of the last movement of Op. 110. . . . Notwithstanding the circumscribed dynamic range, there is plenty of colour and no lack of warmth. . . . In Op. 111 . . . Serkin shows how much is to be gained in coherence from interpreting the text as Beethoven marked it and by avoiding exaggeration." (*Gram*, Oct 1989)

Serkin recorded (1981–84) all five Beethoven concertos with Seiji Ozawa and the Boston Symphony Orchestra (Grammys, Nos. 3 and 4, 1982-83). Opinions vary, particularly since there are so many sets by other pianists—e.g., Barenboim, Ashkenazy, Brendel—for comparison. One admiring critic states unequivocally that Serkin's readings of the five concertos set a standard: "Serkin is in his greatest form, technically and interpretively. He takes slightly slower tempos for the last movements of the first and third concertos than are usual. However, at his tempos the rondo themes have individual character and charm instead of sounding rushed." (*CL*, Jan 1986) Others prefer the performances recorded from 1962 to 1966 with either Ormandy and the Philadelphia Orchestra or Bernstein and the New York Philharmonic Orchestra, feeling that, in those readings, "Serkin himself is in prime form and technically more assured. . . . The C major Concerto is given a vital, winning, almost neo-classical reading, whilst the G major effects an astonishing progress from dark to light; from a notably brooding first movement to a dazzling treatment of the finale's coda." (*Gram*, July 1991)

A recent catalogue lists 13 Mozart concertos recorded by Serkin. Most of his "classic" readings of the Mozart concerto repertoire were made with either George Szell and the Cleveland Orchestra, Eugene Ormandy and the Philadelphia Orchestra or Alexander Schneider conducting the Columbia Symphony Orchestra. In his later years he began recording a series of concertos with Claudio Abbado and the London Symphony Orchestra, and by most accounts, these are noticeably inferior to the earlier ones. Serkin was in his mid-seventies, he was not concertizing very much, his tonal attack had become more crisp, more harsh and more brittle. His musicianship was never in question and his technique holds up well for most of the time, but the fire and the latent passion are often not there.

Over the course of his career Serkin recorded many of the concertos in his repertoire twice, even three or four times, sometimes with the same orchestra and conductor, sometimes with a different ensemble. This makes for a confusing discography, but among the various performances now reissued on CD, high marks go to the album titled *Rudolf Serkin: The Legendary Concerto Recordings 1950–1956* (see Discog.). This collection contains some of his truly memorable interpretations. The Beethoven Concerto No. 5 (Ormandy/PO) is "better controlled and musically superior to earlier and later Serkin versions with the New York Philharmonic and far more vital than his most recent account with Seiji Ozawa and the Boston Symphony." The two Mozart concertos are splendid. Serkin's readings of K. 467 and K. 503 "feature an uncommon blend of freedom and discipline: here is a highly expressive rhythmic give and take, with dynamics pointedly inferred and shaded, yet never reaching beyond the bounds of what eighteenth-century style dictates. . . . On balance this [Brahms No. 2 in B-flat Major] is my favorite of Serkin's four commanding recordings of the Brahms. . . . The Strauss *Burleske* comprises a rousing, virtuosic account capturing all of the music's brash satiric humor." (*Fanfare*, Jan/Feb 1992. Reprinted by permission.)

Serkin made three different recordings of the Schumann Concerto in A Minor. The version listed in the above collection, dating from 1956, "may be a bit too efficient and businesslike for some tastes, and it is more aggressive than the Serkin-Ormandy edition of 1964. But the music can stand this approach, and careful listening reveals a number of subtle rhythmic adjustments that add dimension to the reading." (*Fan*, Jan/Feb 1992) The 1964 version is available for comparison (coupled with the Schumann Piano Quintet, op. 44) on CD, and one critic finds this version of the concerto "as possibly the finest of Serkin's three recordings. . . . There is glorious music-making here." (*Fan*, Sept/Oct 1988)

SELECTED REFERENCES

Banowetz, Joseph. "Arrau, Horowitz, Serkin: A Walk Among Giants." *Piano Quarterly*, Fall 1979, pp. 23–28.

"The Big Four." *Time*, 10 Nov 1961, pp. 58–60.

Cairns, David. "Keepers of the eternal flame." *Sunday Times* (London), 7 July 1991, sec. 5, p. 5. Arrau, Kempff, Serkin.

Frank, Claude. "Rudolf Serkin: Servant of Music." *Keynote*, March 1983, pp. 13–16.

Kolodin, Irving. "The Complete Musician." *Horizon*, Sept 1961, pp. 82–87.

Kozinn, Allan. "The Miracle of Marlboro: Rudolf Serkin's Musical Mecca." *Ovation*, June 1981, pp. 10–13, 20.

Kuerti, Anton. "Artists in Their Own Ways: Arthur Loesser and Rudolf Serkin." (interview with Jeffrey Wagner). *Clavier*, Nov 1987, pp. 10–13.

Layton, Robert. "The End of an Era." *Gramophone*, Aug 1991, pp. 50–51.

Levinger, Henry W. "Serkin: Devoted Classicist." *Musical Courier*, Nov 1954, p. 9.

Obituary. *New York Times*, 10 May 1991, sec. 4, p. 18. *San Francisco Chronicle*, 10 May 1991, sec. E, p. 4.

O'Harra, Richard. "Serkin: Some thoughts about Music." *Musical Courier*, May 1960, pp. 10–11.

Reich, Howard. "The modest maestro." *Chicago Tribune*, 9 Oct 1988, pp. 18, 20.

Rich, Alan. "A Musical 'Republic of Equals'." *New York Times*, 19 Aug 1962, sec. 10, p. 9.

Roddy, Joseph. "Rudolf Serkin." *High Fidelity*, July 1961, pp. 24–28, 82.

Schonberg, Harold C. "Forty Years In Pursuit Of an Ideal." *New York Times*, 25 Jan 1976, sec. 2, p. 19.

Serkin, Rudolf. "Strength of Fingers, Strength of Thought." (interview) *Etude*, March 1941, pp. 155, 196.

Silverman, Robert. "Serkin." (interview) *Piano Quarterly*, Winter 1977–78, pp. 3–6.

Ulrich, Allan. "Rudolf Serkin: Humanist, thinker, genius." *San Francisco Examiner*, 12 May 1991, sec. E, p. 5.

See also Bibliography: Cha/Spe; Cur/Bio (1940, 1990); Dow/Oli; Eld/Pia; Ewe/Li; Ewe/Mu; Jac/Rev; Kai/Gre; New/Gro; Ran/Kon; Rub/MyM; Sal/Fam; Sch/Fac; WWAM.

SELECTED REVIEWS

ABJ: 28 Sept 1984. *BG*: 10 Jan 1977; 25 Nov 1985; 6 April 1987. *CPD*: 27 Oct 1985. *CSM*: 12 Dec 1984. *CST*: 18 Dec 1978. *CT*: 29 Sept 1988. *DMN*: 18 Oct 1986. *LAT*: 18 March 1949; 10 Feb 1950; 25 Nov 1958; 21 Nov 1967; 19 Jan 1974; 28 April 1982; 14 March 1986. *MA*: 25 Dec 1941. *MiT*: 15 Dec 1980; 17 Dec 1981. *MT*: Aug 1971; July 1977. *NYP*: 12 Jan 1937; 10 June 1976. *NYT*: 15 Feb 1931; 16 Feb 1936; 21 Feb 1936; 12 Jan 1937; 1 Feb 1938; 29 Jan 1939; 2 Dec 1941; 27 March 1949; 8 Dec 1951; 22 Oct 1956; 6 April 1960; 3 Feb 1969; 6 Dec 1973; 30 Jan 1986; 9 April 1987. *SFE*: 30 April 1979. *SPPP*: 15 Dec 1980. *TL*: 25 Feb 1932; 4 March 1932; 4 Feb 1975. *WP*: 2 Dec 1985. *WS*: 9 Dec 1975; 24 Jan 1977.

SELECTED DISCOGRAPHY

Beethoven: Concertos (complete). Telarc CD-80061 (3 CDs). Ozawa/Boston SO.

Beethoven: Concerto No. 1 in C Major, op. 15; Sonata in E-flat Major, op. 81a. CBS Great Performances MYK 37807 (CD). Ormandy/PO.

Beethoven: Concerto No. 2 in B-flat Major, op. 19; Concerto No. 4 in G Major, op. 58. Telarc CD 80064. Ozawa/Boston SO.

Beethoven: Concerto No. 3 in C Minor, op. 37 (1964); Choral Fantasy, op. 80 (1962). CBS Great Performances MYK 38526 (CD). Bernstein/NYPO.

Beethoven: Concerto No. 4 in G Major, op. 58 (Ormandy/PO); Concerto No. 5 in E-flat Major, op. 73 (Bernstein/NYPO). CBS MK-42260 (CD).

Beethoven: Sonata in C Minor, op. 13(*Pathétique*); Sonata in C-sharp Minor, op. 27, no. 2 ("Moonlight"); Sonata in F Minor, op. 57("*Appassionata*"). CBS (Great Performances) MYK 37219 (CD).

Beethoven: Sonata in C Minor, op. 13; Sonata in B-flat Major, op. 106; Fantasy in G Minor, op. 77. Sony Classical 47666 (CD).

Beethoven: Sonata in E Major, op. 109; Sonata in A-flat Major, op. 110; Sonata in C Minor, op. 111. DG 427 498-2.

Beethoven: Sonatas in F Major, op. 10, no. 2; C Minor, op. 13; G Major, op. 31, no. 1; F Minor, op. 57. *Arkadia* 912 (CD).

Beethoven: Sonatas in A-flat Major, op. 26; E-flat Major, op. 27, no. 1; C
Major, op. 53; E-flat Major, op. 81a. *Arkadia* 911 (CD).

Beethoven: 32 Variations on a Waltz by Diabelli, op. 120; Bagatelles, op. 119.
Sony Masterworks Portrait CD 44837.

Brahms: Concerto No. 1 in D Minor, op. 15 (Szell/Cleveland SO). Strauss:
Burleske in D Minor (Ormandy/PO). CBS Masterworks CD 42261.

Brahms: Concerto No. 1 in D Minor, op. 15. Schumann: Introduction and
Concert Allegro. Sony Classical SBK 48166 (CD). Ormandy/PO.

Brahms: Concerto No. 2 in B-flat Major, op. 83; Piano Pieces, op. 119. CBS
Masterworks CD 42262. Szell/Cleveland SO.

Brahms: Concerto No. 2 in B-flat Major, op. 83. Schumann: Introduction and
Allegro Appassionata, op. 92. CBS Odyssey 46273 (CD). Ormandy/PO.

Mendelssohn: Concerto No. 1 in G Minor, op. 25; Concerto No. 2 in D Minor,
op. 40. Sony Classical SBK-46542 (CD). Ormandy/PO.

Mozart: Concerto in E-flat Major, K. 365 (Schneider/Marlboro FO, with Peter
Serkin); Concerto in A Major, K. 414 (Schneider/Columbia SO); Concerto
in E-flat Major, K. 449 (Schneider/Col. SO); Concerto in G Major, K. 453
(Schneider/Col. SO); Concerto in F Major, K. 459 (Szell/Col. SO);
Concerto in D Minor, K. 466 (Szell/Col. SO); Concerto in B-flat Major, K.
595 (Ormandy/PO); Rondo in D Major, K. 382; Rondo in A Minor, K.
511. Sony Classical (Legendary Interpreters) SM3K 47207 (3 CDs).

Mozart: Concerto in C Major, K. 467; Concerto in B-flat Major, K. 595. MHS
13047T. Abbado/London SO.

Prokofiev: Concerto No. 4, op. 53. Reger: Concerto in F Minor, op. 114.
Sony Classical Masterworks 46452 (CD). Ormandy/PO.

Reger: Variations and Fugue on a Theme by Johann Sebastian Bach, op. 81.
Haydn: Sonata in C Major, Hob. XVI:50. CBS Masterworks MK 39562
(CD).

Rudolf Serkin: The Legendary Concerto Recordings 1950–1956. Beethoven:
Concerto No. 5 in E-flat Major, op. 73 (Ormandy/PO). Brahms: Concerto
No. 2 in B-flat Major, op. 82 (Ormandy/PO). Mozart: Concerto in C
Major, K. 467 (Schneider/Columbia SO); Concerto in C Major, K. 503
(Szell/Col. SO). Schumann: Concerto in A Minor, op. 54 (Ormandy/PO).
Strauss: *Burleske* in D Minor (Ormandy/PO). Sony Classical SM3K 47269
(3 CDs).

Schumann: Concerto in A Minor, op. 54; Introduction and Allegro
Appassionata, op. 92. Sony SBK 46543 (CD). Ormandy/PO.

VIDEO

Beethoven: Sonata in E Major, op. 109; Sonata in A-flat Major, op. 110;
Sonata in C Minor, op. 111. DG 072-222-3.

SOLOMON (Solomon Cutner): b. London, England, 9 August 1902; d. London, 22 February 1988.

> Even if he called himself Mr. X there would be no doubt about his identification, for he is unquestionably one of the great artists of our time.
> Albert Goldberg (*Los Angeles Times*, 5 February 1951)

Solomon lived to be 85 years old, but audiences had not heard him play the piano, and most likely had not heard much about him, for three decades. Actually he had not been able to play the piano for 31 years, not since a massive stroke ended his flourishing career in 1956. Nevertheless, and despite the fact that until recently very little has been written about him, Solomon has held his reputation as "one of the great artists of our time." Now Bryan Crimp's authoritative, highly readable book *Solo: The Biography of Solomon* provides valuable new information, all thoroughly documented, about Solomon's life and career and also corrects earlier misinformation. The book is divided into three parts ("Prodigy fame and its aftermath," "The long journey to true recognition," "A secluded existence") and three appendices (Selected listing of appearances; Repertoire Listings; Discography).

Solomon Cutner took great pride in his richly mixed heritage: German-Jewish on the maternal side; Polish-Jewish on the paternal side; and himself a true Cockney, born in Spitalfields in London's East End. He was the seventh child born to Rose (Piser) Cutner and Harris Cutner, a master tailor who loved music. He was born Harris Schneiderman, but changed the family name to "Cutner," a clever reminder of his cloth-cutting trade and of "Cutnow," his home district in Poland.

Solomon's aptitude for the piano appeared early, and it must have delighted his music-loving father to hear his small son play little tunes (ranging from a Beethoven minuet to the popular songs of the day) on the family's old upright piano. Solomon began piano lessons with a local teacher at age five, made excellent progress and, just before he turned eight, played (his own arrangement of Tchaikovsky's "1812" Overture) for Mathilde Verne, a well-known London piano teacher who had studied six years with Clara Schumann and in 1909 founded the Mathilde Verne Pianoforte School in South Kensington, London.

Verne knew at once that in Solomon she had found a genuine musical prodigy, and she quickly took control. She signed a contract with Solomon's parents—not poor people, yet not prosperous enough to support an advanced musical education—and the terms of the agreement gave her full charge of Solomon, then eight years old, for five years. Besides musical training, Verne provided board, lodging (Solomon lived at her school), clothing and academic lessons, first at a convent school, from 1914 at the King Alfred School in Hampstead.

In her book titled *Chords of Remembrance*, Verne gives the impression that her only goal was to develop Solomon's budding musical talent; but Bryan Crimp's biography now makes it clear that Verne was a cruel, ambitious tyrant primarily concerned with exploiting Solomon to make money and to enhance her own reputation. The final word comes from Solomon himself. In 1915, when the contract expired, he adamantly refused to have any further association with Mathilde Verne. As an adult, he rarely mentioned her name, instead giving credit for his success to others, especially his father. And at age 70, Solomon finally admitted to an interviewer that his years with Verne had been "awful, terrible," that after the first year she had taught him very little.

That first year she gave him a lesson every day for nine months, then arranged his public debut—a performance (30 June 1911) with the Queen's Hall Orchestra, conducted by Dr. Theodor Müller-Reuter. To accommodate Solomon's small hands, Verne had a special piano (with very small keys and a device to enable him to use the pedals) sent from Blüthner in Germany. On the program she billed him simply as "Solomon—Aged 8 years," and "Solomon" he was for the rest of his career. Very few people ever knew that his last name was Cutner.

Verne had apparently arranged Solomon's debut not knowing that the London County Council would not permit children under the age of 10 to perform in public for a fee. She was counting on the proceeds but, rather than cancel the concert, she announced it as a benefit for the Children's Hospital. At the performance Solomon's natural charm and remarkable talent captivated the audience, but *The Times* (1 July 1911) reviewer, while granting that Solomon had unusual gifts and a delightful personality, reminded readers that he was too young to be so exploited.

Mathilde Verne had another viewpoint. Solomon's successful debut and the ensuing publicity added luster to her reputation as a piano teacher; they also brought new students to her school, and she was determined to keep his name before the public. Since he could not appear as a paid soloist, Verne pushed the London City Council and got permission for him to perform at charity concerts and, always with other performers, at semi-private events at her school and at the Thursday noontime concerts she presented at Aeolian Hall.

Verne even induced the family of one of her pupils to wangle a court appearance for Solomon. This so-called "command performance" took place on 22 March 1912 at Buckingham Palace before King George V, Queen Mary and other members of the royal family. Three months later, on 24 June 1912, Solomon gave a second performance at the Queen's Hall, this time with Sir Henry Wood conducting the Queen's Hall Orchestra. The nine-year-old Solomon played Beethoven's Concerto No. 3 and Liszt's Hungarian Fantasia, and once again drew a standing, cheering ovation.

Mathilde Verne obviously worked hard to keep Solomon before the public, which to a certain extent was good for his career. But Verne also worked the child too hard. She badgered him at lessons, made him learn long, strenuous concertos and scheduled far too many public appearances, especially after he reached the age of 10 and was no longer subject to the rules of the LCC. (See Bryan Crimp's biography, Appendix A1, for a selected listing of appearances.) Most damaging of all, Verne completely spoiled Solomon's childhood.

Sir Henry Wood was, if the term is appropriate, a bright spot in Solomon's unhappy childhood. After their first triumph together at the Queen's

Hall on 24 June 1912, Sir Henry repeatedly invited Solomon to play at his famous "Proms" concerts. In 1914 Solomon performed under Sir Henry Wood six times, playing the Beethoven Concertos Nos. 2 and 3, the Grieg Concerto, the Tchaikovsky Concerto No. 1 and the Liszt Hungarian Fantasia. In 1915 the two performed together at least 15 times; and in that year Solomon, still only 13 years old, repeated the three concertos and Liszt Fantasia from 1914 and, amazingly, also played Mendelssohn's *Rondo brilliant*, the Schumann Concerto, Stanford's Variations on "Down among the dead men," the Schubert-Liszt "Wanderer" Fantasy, the Brahms Concerto No. 1 and Liszt's Fantasia on Beethoven's "Ruins of Athens."

Only a genuine prodigy could play such a repertoire, and Sir Henry Wood confirms that Solomon played well: "The piano seemed too large for such a small person, but the music was never beyond his reach and his performance of the second of Beethoven's concertos was amazing. Even in those early days his classical feeling was already to the fore. . . . Solomon was a genius and his playing of the great B flat minor concerto of Tchaikovsky took us by storm." (Woo/My, see Bibliog.)

Verne lost control of her prodigy in mid-1915 when the contract with the Cutners finally expired, and Solomon absolutely refused to agree to another. Bitter and revengeful over their bad parting, Verne tried to destroy his career, but in 1916 Solomon performed almost 40 concerts—in cities (London, Liverpool, Edinburgh, Glasgow) and in the provinces. He was not yet 14 years old, but he was worn out from six years of playing before the public, angry at the thought of his lost childhood and uncertain of his future without a teacher to guide him.

Inevitably, stress and anxiety affected his playing. Critics noted that he had reached "the fate of the immature artist forced into untimely maturity," and detected "a certain lack of control in some of his interpretations." All Solomon could think of to do was withdraw for a time from the concert platform. At his "farewell recital" (5 June 1917) the public and press wished him well and looked forward to his return. Two years later the *Daily Telegraph* reported that the boy Solomon had suffered a nervous breakdown.

Solomon got through this painful period of his life with the help and advice of caring friends, especially Sir Henry Wood and John Russell, headmaster of the King Alfred School in Hampstead, London, where Solomon had been a pupil since 1914. Financial support came from a group of benefactors who set up a fund for his living expenses and further musical studies. Percy Colson, a longtime Solomon supporter, advised the fund on musical matters; and Colson's wife, a delightfully outgoing socialite, took on the task of showing Solomon the social side of life. To make up for the lack of friends and social graces in his isolated, work-centered childhood, Mrs. Colson saw to it that Solomon attended parties and met new people; and he was often a guest at the Colson villa in the south of France.

Mrs. Colson's kind lessons in living set in motion the gradual transformation of the lonely boy from Spitalfields (the last traces of his Cockney accent disappeared) into "a more balanced personality. In later life Solomon was equally at ease at an Embassy party or when chatting to the postman. Away from the piano he never thought of himself as being any different to the next man. . . . An innate warmth and unforced naturalness was part of his persona and it was soon to become a vital ingredient of his playing." (Crimp)

Loving care from friends and family restored Solomon's spiritual and mental health, and two remarkable teachers led him back to the piano. The first was a Lithuanian pianist named Simon Rumschisky, a onetime Leschetizky pupil who had been teaching in London since 1909. Rumschisky simply brushed aside all Solomon's years as a celebrated prodigy and made him start all over again with months and months of scale work. Rumschisky insisted on a fine sound for every single note played; not only that, he made Solomon *listen* to every note he played. Working nearly three years with Rumschisky restored Solomon's technique, control and confidence. In later years he would tell interviewers that Rumschisky had greatly influenced his career and his life.

But, still not certain that he was ready to return to concertizing, Solomon spent the next two years in Paris searching, as Bryan Crimp expresses it, "for what lay behind the music." He studied harmony and counterpoint with Marcel Dupré, at that time interim organist at Notre Dame Cathedral, and although he never played the organ, Solomon treasured the hours he spent in the organ loft listening to Dupré's marvelous improvisations. He also studied the piano in Paris, briefly with Alfred Cortot (their personalities clashed) before he found Lazare Lévy, an excellent, if strict, teacher who gave him "a free, spontaneous approach to interpretation, one that was always open to reconsideration and reassessment." (Crimp)

Four years after his "farewell recital" in London, Solomon, now an adult pianist (he was almost 19) returned to the concert platform with a recital (8 April 1921) at the *Salle des Agriculteurs* in Paris. That October he went over to England to give two recitals at Wigmore Hall, went back again in 1922 for another pair of recitals in the same hall, made a tour of Germany in 1923 and later that year returned permanently to Britain to start all over again as a mature pianist.

Solomon need never have worried about artistic success. As always, he charmed his audiences. Perhaps they sensed that to him every single audience mattered. "A concert in a small town in the midwestern United States or in Lancashire was every bit as important to him as an appearance in New York, Paris, Vienna or London, and caused him no less nervousness, no less arduous preparation. Like Paderewski, he had, sometimes, to be coaxed onto the platform." (Moo/Am, see Bibliog.)

Not only audiences, but increasingly reviewers recognized Solomon as one of the big pianists—an individual and compelling performer. "His secret lies in his rhythm, which gives irresistible momentum to his playing." (*TL*, 28 Jan 1924) There were not all that many performances in the early 1920s, but his reputation grew steadily.

Solomon's first performances in the United States—a debut recital at New York's Town Hall on 20 January 1926 and a second recital 10 days later— won over almost the entire body of New York's critics. It was a hectic period in his life. A letter (25 Jan 1926) written from New York at that time mentions: "I have been terribly busy for months and months, teaching on an average of six to seven hours a day; practising about the same amount, and between times dashing off to different places for concerts." (Alfieri)

The fact is that Solomon had to teach to survive, for despite his often stunning recitals, engagements were irregular. But he loved to teach, and students remembered him as a caring and attentive teacher (see Crimp, Chapter 14). His first rule, for himself as well as his students, was to be 100 percent faithful to the composer. Solomon, convinced that most pianists listen to their imaginations, not to what they are actually playing, would often interrupt a lesson to play exactly what the pupil had just played for him, proving to the astonished student that there had been no real correlation between what he had heard in his mind and what he had executed with his fingers.

It was absolutely essential, Solomon told students, for them to hear *every* note they played—a very difficult task because the mind wanders. In his own practicing—and he practiced faithfully—whenever he realized he had not consciously heard a measure, or a single note, he began again until he reached the end completely aware of every note he had played. Except for those days when he was rehearsing with an orchestra or on tour, Solomon usually practiced eight or nine hours a day.

In 1927 Gwendolyn Byrne began lessons with Solomon, and two years later they began living together, marriage at the time being out of the question (Gwendolyn Byrne was a gentile and a mixed marriage would have been unbearable for Solomon's orthodox Jewish family). However, their relationship lasted for 60 years (they married in 1970), until Solomon's death in 1988.

Gwendolyn Byrne also set up a teaching studio, and as Solomon's engagements increased, she acquired the students he was unable to accommodate. During the 1930s Solomon's growing popularity produced more and more concert engagements, his playing drew more and more plaudits and, said critics, he had become one of the greatest of living pianists. Near the end of that decade Solomon returned briefly to America to join Sir Adrian Boult in the premiere performance of Sir Arthur Bliss's Piano Concerto, commissioned by the British Council for British Week at the New York World's Fair. However, those in charge of the Fair canceled "all serious high grade music on the grounds that it would discourage public attendance," so Solomon played the premiere at Carnegie Hall on 10 June 1939.

During World War II he played recitals both overseas and all over Great Britain to entertain the troops and civilian war workers. (When not performing, he served as an air raid warden in his Kensington district, fighting fires and digging out bomb victims, completely ignoring his "pianist" hands.) In October 1943 Solomon gave 28 concerts in 25 days for the men and women serving in North Africa, Egypt, Palestine, Malta and Gibralter. Packed together like sardines in a tin, these audiences applauded his programs, usually a mix of the classics and modern piano works, with a kind of fervor he had never before experienced.

In the autumn of 1945 Solomon played for the British occupation forces in Germany and almost immediately thereafter began a two-month tour to perform for military personnel still stationed abroad (India, Burma, Singapore, Bangkok, Saigon). He traveled close to 40,000 miles and gave 36 recitals in 51 days, but he apparently enjoyed every minute. He even found the flying not only exhilarating but peaceful compared to London under the bombs. In 1946 Solomon was awarded the Order of Commander of the British Empire (C. B. E.) for his wartime services.

His reputation blossomed after the war. He toured throughout Great Britain and in Europe (Italy, Germany, France, Holland, Switzerland, Scandinavia) and often toured elsewhere: Australia, New Zealand, South Africa (1946); North America (1949–50, 1951–52, 1953, 1955); Central and South America (1953); Japan (1954).

Solomon always boasted an enormous working repertoire. However, as he passed from prodigy to mature adult, the contents changed noticeably. In his youth he performed works by composers (Colson, Evers, Parry, Stanford) barely recognizable today. As an adult, he concentrated on more "standard" compositions, in most cases considerably expanding his youthful repertoire. For example, as a youngster he played around three Beethoven sonatas, but during his adult career he played just about all 32. This same expansion applies to Brahms, Chopin, Mozart, Schubert and Schumann. New composers (Balakirev, Franck, Debussy, Ravel) enhanced the later programs. The Crimp biography (Appendix B) gives a comprehensive comparison of youthful and mature repertoires.

A massive stroke paralyzed Solomon's right hand and arm in December 1956. He never again played the piano, but he lived another 31 years. Nurtured by his wife and friends, he rarely succumbed to bitterness. "He showed tremendous courage in adversity and continued to listen to other people's concerts and opera." (Gwendolyn Cutner, letter to the authors, 29 June 1988). "I visit him," wrote Gerald Moore, "only to come away invigorated by his cheerfulness, his gentle courtesy, his absolute lack of bitterness." (Moo/Am, see Bibliog.)

Solomon, at age 19, began his first adult London recital (1 Oct 1921) with the Beethoven Sonata in E-flat Major, op. 31, no. 3, and "created the strongest impression, not by any display of the technical command which he quite clearly possessed, but by the thought which he gave to the music. It was the finest performance of that sonata which we have heard for a long time, fine in its distinction of phrase, its emphasis of important details, and the perception of the structure as a whole." (*TL*, 3 Oct 1921)

At his New York debut recital (20 Jan 1926) Solomon "had not traveled ten bars in Liszt's transcription of Bach's A minor organ fugue before it became clear that another pianistic star of the first magnitude had risen. . . . This Bach performance was one of the finest imaginable. It did not thunder in the index or amass tidal surges of tone in a futile effort to transform the piano into an organ, but within the limits of an uncommonly judicious dynamic scale it achieved its full scope and proportions." (*NYWT*, 21 Jan 1926)

Ten days later Solomon's second New York recital (30 Jan 1926) confirmed that his coming had enriched the season: "The eloquence and persuasion of his playing reside much less in any quality of searching emotion than in a captivating musicianship, a poised sensitiveness, and an inward grace, a classic purity of style, an extraordinary feeling for the beauty of sound and the symmetry of form." (*NYS*, 1 Feb 1926) On the other hand, a not so ecstatic critic agreed that Solomon was "a very good pianist," but still immature. "He gave the impression of being practical and matter-of-fact, of knowing his composers outwardly. But the spark of imagination was missing. Mr. Solomon is neither imaginative nor romantic, and this defect of his qualities could be felt in all he did." (*NYT*, 31 Jan 1926)

For the rest of his career Solomon's playing elicited warm, often glowing reviews. On 12 March 1927 he gave a brilliant and exhilarating performance of the Brahms-Handel Variations: "The athlete in him was inclined to tempt providence at times, and in matters of *tempo* he occasionally outran the tardiness of Brahms's sonorities. Through sheer musicianship, however, he is able to persuade, even when the risk seems foolhardy. The secret of it all is his unerring rhythmic sense." (*MT*, April 1927)

Before 1949 Solomon had given only three performances in America—two recitals in 1926 and the Bliss Concerto in 1939. World War II postponed his American career, but in 1949 it gathered astonishing momentum. His Carnegie Hall recital on 12 February 1949 overwhelmed reviewers. "Solomon has become an interpreter of the stripe called magisterial. . . . There was an impression, as he played, that Solomon was listening, even as the audience; that it was his pleasure to enjoy the rich, resonant tone he produced, and his challenge to make it the means of a vital, imaginative musical experience." (*NYS*, 14 Feb 1949)

Later that year cheers and raves hailed Solomon's Boston debut (13 Oct 1949). "The man has everything. He has a technique that is not surpassed by that of any virtuoso. Yet he is not a virtuoso player. He is a musician, an artist, a poet. . . . His Mozart [Sonata in B-flat, K. 333] is as near perfection as we are likely to hear in an imperfect world. . . . His treatment of the fugue [Brahms's Variations and Fugue, op. 24] was a model of clarity and proportion. . . . Debussy's musical pictures were exquisitely painted." (*CSM*, 14 Oct 1949) Booked immediately for a second Boston recital, Solomon played an all-Chopin program (6 Dec 1949) that was, said one reviewer, "the most compelling I have ever heard." (*CSM*, 7 Dec 1949)

Solomon was said to possess all the virtues of pianists of the Romantic school while avoiding all their excesses. His first Los Angeles recital (4 Feb 1951) drew this comment: "There is a constant glow of warmth and well-being to his playing but it never oversteps the bounds of good taste and superior musicianship. He has ample technique, but he is more poet than virtuoso, and if there are any limits to his thorough understanding of all musical styles, his comprehensive program failed to reveal them." (*LAT*, 5 Feb 1951)

On 14 February 1953 at Hunter College, Solomon gave his first New York recital of the season. "Whether Solomon played Mozart, Beethoven, Schumann or Chopin, one was constantly delighted by the artist's ability to produce a decidedly singing tone, a tone capable of a wide range of color and invariably of pleasing quality. Imaginative use of dynamics formed another important factor in the performances and helped to give all of them their undeniable charm and allure." (*NYT*, 16 Feb 1953)

Seven months before his devastating stroke, Solomon played (7 May 1956) the Brahms Concerto No. 1 at Festival Hall, with Rafael Kubelík and the

Vienna Philharmonic Orchestra—"a majestic and Jove-like exposition of that Olympian concerto. Mr. Solomon presents it in a huge span which he effortlessly fills, and the orchestra blazed away at those trills in the first movement to expand its power. The slow movement . . . was like a river with a smooth surface and an unhurrying current beneath. . . . Interpretation as demonstrated at this level by Mr. Kubelík, Mr. Solomon, and the Viennese players is seen as fundamentally the same art as composition—the art of creating music." (*TL*, 8 May 1956)

The reviews are nearly unanimous in that Solomon's interpretations were individual, rich in interesting detail, sharply contrasted in style; that he subordinated virtuosity to poetry; that his playing shone with elegance, clarity and brilliance. Above all, Solomon captivated his hearers with the quiet communication of his playing; his gorgeous, singing tone; his pellucid, aristocratic technique.

In 1929 Solomon's first recording sessions with the Columbia Graphophone Company produced two Liszt solo works (*La Leggierezza, Au bord d'une source*) and the Tchaikovsky Concerto No. 1 with the Hallé Orchestra, conducted by Sir Hamilton Harty. Many fine recordings followed (see Crimp biography, Appendix C); however, Solomon's debilitating stroke ended his plans to record the complete Beethoven sonata cycle. Only 17 sonatas were recorded. They were issued separately and also together as a boxed set. Many are no longer available, and one hopes that eventually all will be reissued. They are masterful interpretations from a master pianist.

A CD reissue of Beethoven's last six sonatas (see Discog.) is outstanding, with highest honors perhaps going to the Sonata in B-flat Major, op. 106. A 1988 survey of selected recordings of the "*Hammerklavier*," op. 106, gives Solomon's version very high marks: "His entire performance achieved that elusive balance between continuity and detail, between propulsion and revelation, which most of his predecessors seemed to have been striving for. In accuracy, clarity and physical power he has since been surpassed (though the shortcomings are only slight), in wholeness of artistic vision arguably not." (*Gram*, Oct 1988)

Solomon's dispassionate and fastidious architectural style was eminently suited to Beethoven and Brahms. His recordings of the five Beethoven concertos verify his musical integrity, superb technique and innate musicianship. There is no attempt to flaunt virtuosity or to overpower the composer. These are Solomon's elegant testimonials to his love for, and understanding of, Beethoven's masterpieces for piano and orchestra. And his recordings of the two Brahms Concertos (recently reissued on CD, see Discog.) with Rafael Kubelík (No. 1) and Issay Dobrowen (No. 2) conducting the Philharmonia Orchestra, stand as tributes to his mastery of the Brahms idiom.

His recordings of the Grieg and Schumann concertos, currently available on CD (see Discog.), are exquisite reminders that Solomon belongs to the immortals of 20th-century pianism. "The limpid delivery of both first movement main themes, beautifully exploiting the mellow, 'covered' tone of the 1950s Steinway, soon shows why his playing is held in such affection. His reposeful, yet strictly disciplined slow movements, his heart-warming response to the flute theme in Grieg's finale, his care for the musical flow throughout, are all things to cherish." (*Gram*, Nov 1989)

Solomon's robust, inventive reading of Sir Arthur Bliss's Concerto in B-flat Major with Sir Adrian Boult and the Liverpool Philharmonic Orchestra has been reissued together with two other highly expert Solomon performances—the Scriabin Concerto in F-sharp Minor, op. 20, and Liszt's Hungarian Fantasia, with Issay Dobrowen and Walter Susskind respectively conducting the Philharmonia Orchestra (see Discog.). The Bliss Concerto, performed by the pianist for whom it was written, still provides excitement. The Scriabin is "very much worth repeated listenings, and the popular Liszt showpiece is superb in every respect." (*Fan*, Jan/Feb 1992)

Solomon's complete Chopin recordings are available on a single CD (see Discog.). These are very special performances. "Less urbane than Rubinstein, less volatile than Cortot (certainly less neurotic than Horowitz), Solomon's Chopin is enviably sensitive and patrician. From him the *Etudes* are both bracing and interior, their pedagogical origins remembered yet transformed into the purest poetry. . . . Larger-scaled works, too, confirm Solomon's additional capacity to join apparently disparate elements into a seamless whole, one idea effortlessly and naturally generating the next." (Morrison)

In the spring of 1956 Solomon paid a rare visit to Germany—eight days during which he gave recitals in four cities, appeared with the Berlin Philharmonic Orchestra and recorded two recitals for Berlin radio. Now on CD (APR 7030), those broadcast recitals reveal Solomon at the very peak of his magnificent powers.

SELECTED REFERENCES

Alfieri, Bernard. "Solomon (1902–1988)." *Music and Musicians*, May 1988, pp. 18–19.

Crimp, Bryan. *Solo: The Biography of Solomon.* Northumberland: Appian Publications, 1994.

Holland, A. K. "Solomon: Prodigy and Genius." *The Canon*, Jan 1951, pp. 285–288.

Morrison, Bryce. "Chopin and Solomon." Liner notes, Testament SBT 1030 (CD).

Obituary. *Sunday Times* (London), 24 Feb 1988, p. 14. *New York Times*, 1 March 1988, sec. 4, p. 23.

"Pianist from Bow Bells." *Time*, 28 Feb 1949, pp. 48–49.

Plaistow, Stephen. "Solomon Mined." *Gramophone*, July 1993, p. 14. A discussion of Solomon's recordings that was originally published in August 1972.

Rogers, Harold. "British Pianist Discusses His Art." *Christian Science Monitor*, 13 Oct 1949, p. 5.

"Solomon, Pianist." *Newsweek*, 19 Nov 1951, pp. 98, 100.

Stern, Antony M. "London Kind to New Piano Prodigy." *Musical America*, 13 July 1912, p. 29.

Verne, Mathilde. *Chords of Remembrance*. London: Hutchinson & Co., 1936, pp. 98–104.

Wilde, David. "Solomon: An Appreciation." *Recorded Sound*, July 1982, pp. 1–4.

See also Bibliography: Bro/Mas; Dan/Con; Ham/Lis; Moo/Am; Ran/Kon; Rat/Cle; Rub/MyY; Sal/Fam; Sch/Gre; Woo/My.

SELECTED REVIEWS

CSM: 14 Oct 1949; 7 Dec 1949. *LAT*: 5 Feb 1951; 23 Jan 1952; 21 Jan 1953. *MT*: 1 April 1927; June 1934; Sept 1939. *NYT*: 21 Jan 1926; 31 Jan 1926; 11 June 1939; 13 Feb 1949; 6 Nov 1950; 5 Nov 1951; 16 Feb 1953. *SFC*: 5 Jan 1952; 12 Jan 1955. *TL*: 1 July 1911; 25 June 1912; 3 Oct 1921; 25 April 1927; 16 Oct 1928; 10 May 1948; 15 Oct 1948; 22 Oct 1948; 25 Oct 1954; 23 Jan 1956; 8 May 1956.

SELECTED DISCOGRAPHY

Beethoven: Concerto No. 2 in B-flat Major, op. 19. Brahms: Concerto No. 1 in D Minor, op. 15. MYTO MCD 89005. Cluytens, Jochum/Berlin PO.

Beethoven: Concerto No. 5 in E-flat Major, op. 73 ("Emperor"). Seraphim Cassette 4XG-60298. Menges/Philharmonia.

Beethoven: Sonata in C Minor, op. 13; Sonata in C-sharp Minor, op. 27, no. 2; Sonata in F Minor, op. 57. Seraphim Cassette 4XG-60286.

Beethoven: Sonata in E Minor, op. 90; Sonata in A Major, op. 101; Sonata in B-flat Major, op. 106; Sonata in E Major, op. 109; Sonata in A-flat Major, op. 110; Sonata in C Minor, op. 111. EMI Classics HB 64708 (2 CDs).

Bliss: Concerto in B-flat Major (Boult/Liverpool PO). Liszt: Fantasia on Hungarian Folk Themes (Susskind/Philharmonia); Scriabin: Concerto in F-sharp Minor, op. 20 (Dubrowen/Philharmonia). EMI ("Great Recordings of the Century") CDH7 63821-2.

Brahms: Concerto No. 1 in D Minor, op. 15; Variations and Fugue on a Theme by Handel, op. 24. Testament SBT1041 (CD). Kubelík/Philharmonia.

Brahms: Concerto No. 2 in B-flat Major, op. 83; Intermezzos, op. 117, no. 2, op. 119, no. 3; Rhapsody in G Minor, op. 79, no. 2. Testament SBT1042 (CD). Dobrowen/ Philharmonia.

The Complete Recordings of Chopin. Ballade No. 4 in F Minor, op. 52; *Berceuse*, op. 57; Etudes, op. 10, nos. 3, 8, 9, op. 25, nos. 1, 2, 3; Fantaisie in F Minor, op. 49; Mazurka in A Minor, op. 68, no. 2; Nocturnes, op. 9, op. 27; Polonaise in A Major, op. 40; Polonaise in A-flat Major, op. 53; Waltzes in A-flat Major, op. 42, E Minor, op. posth. Testament 1030 (CD).

Grieg: Concerto in A Minor, op. 16. Schumann: Concerto in A Minor, op. 54. EMI Eminence CD-EMX 2002. Menges/Philharmonia.

Mozart: Concerto in B-flat Major, K. 450; Concerto in A Major, K. 488; Concerto in C Minor, K. 491. EMI *Réferences* CDH7 63707-2. Menges/Philharmonia.

Solomon: The first HMV recordings: 1942–43. Brahms: Variations and Fugue on a Theme by Handel, op. 24. Chopin: *Berceuse*, op. 57; Etudes, op. 10, no. 9; op. 25, nos. 2 and 3; Nocturne in D-flat Major, op. 27, no. 2. Beethoven: "Archduke" Trio. APR 5503 (CD).

Solomon in Berlin. Bach: Italian Concerto. Beethoven: Sonata in C Major, op. 2, no. 3; Sonata in C-sharp Minor, op. 27, no. 2. Chopin: Fantasy in F Minor, op. 49; Nocturne in B-flat Minor, op. 9, no. 1; Scherzo in B-flat Minor, op. 31. Brahms: Intermezzo, op. 116, no. 4; Intermezzo, op. 118, no. 6; Rhapsody in B Minor, op. 79, no. 1. APR 7030 (CD).

Tchaikovsky: Concerto No. 1 in B-flat Minor, op. 23. Chopin: Etude in F Major, op. 10, no. 8; Etude in A-flat Major, op. 25, no. 1; Etude in F Major, op. 25, no. 3; Fantaisie in F Minor, op. 49; Polonaise in A Major, op. 40; Polonaise in A-flat Major, op. 53. Liszt: Hungarian Rhapsody No. 15; *Au bord d'une source.* Pearl GEMM CD 9478. Harty/Hallé Orchestra.

T

TURECK, ROSALYN: b. Chicago, Illinois, 14 December 1914.

> Only a great person can play Bach greatly. Rosalyn Tureck is just that: great in the subtlety of her understanding, in her will for knowledge, and in the ultimate simplicity of her art.
>
> Geoffrey Crankshaw (*Music and Musicians*, February 1958)

Mentioning Rosalyn Tureck's name almost immediately brings forth a spontaneous recognition response: "Oh, yes, the Bach specialist." Which is true, of course, and Tureck has had an enormously successful career playing only the music of Johann Sebastian Bach. But she studied a wide range of piano music, and for about 15 years performed both all-Bach programs and traditional piano recitals.

Even as a student Tureck played all-Bach recitals, and at age 22 gave a memorable series of all-Bach programs (Nov–Dec 1937) at Town Hall. Yet at a recital (3 Jan 1937) earlier that year she had played Bach, Beethoven and Brahms. Programs of the 1940s show the same diversity; for example, in 1945, a decade after graduating from Juilliard, Tureck played two conventional programs at Town Hall. The first recital (12 Jan 1945) had works by Graun, Scarlatti-Tureck, Bach, Chopin and Paganini-Liszt; the second, her tenth anniversary recital (12 Nov 1945) at Town Hall, had works by Bach, Mozart, Beethoven, Brahms and Copland.

By the early 1950s Tureck had become "the Bach specialist." Reviews over the next four decades show that she played almost exclusively the music of Bach until the early 1990s. For example, Tureck's program (14 Aug 1992) at the

Teatro Colón in Buenos Aires included the Mendelssohn Song Without Words, op. 19, no. 1, Schubert's *Moments musicaux*, D. 780, nos. 2 and 3, and the Brahms Variations and Fugue on a Theme by Handel, op. 24.

With Rosalyn Tureck, music is in the blood. Her parents Samuel and Monya (Lipson) Turk came to America in the early part of the century (upon arrival Turk became Tureck); her father was a Russian of Turkish descent, her mother was Russian, and for two centuries both families had produced an unbroken line of rabbis and cantors. Understandably, their three daughters all studied music.

Rosalyn Tureck was the prodigy, but never exploited. She has an extraordinary memory and absolute pitch, and by age four could play the pieces she heard her older sisters working on at their piano lessons. Of course, she also had piano lessons, and at age nine gave two recitals at the Lyon & Healy Hall in Chicago. The next year Tureck began lessons with Sophia Brilliant-Livin, once a teaching assistant to Anton Rubinstein, and she provided an unusually solid foundation in the classics. By age 12 Tureck had studied a formidable repertoire: a great number of Scarlatti's works, the early Haydn sonatas, some early Beethoven, all of Bach's Two- and Three-Part Inventions and several Bach Suites. In 1926, still only 11 years old, Tureck was soloist with the Chicago Symphony Orchestra, and in 1928 she won first prize in a Greater Chicago Piano Tournament.

At age 14 Tureck began lessons with Jan Chiapusso, a Dutch-Italian pianist and Bach scholar, and also began her first concentrated study of the music of Bach. At their first lesson—she had two each week—Chiapusso assigned Bach's Prelude and Fugue in C Major from the Well-Tempered Clavier (Book I) and some other pieces. At the next lesson two days later, Tureck played the Prelude and Fugue from memory. Chiapusso made no comment, merely assigned the second Prelude and Fugue. "Three or four days later," Mme. Tureck recalls, "I returned and handed him the music. He said, 'What's this, have you memorized this too?' I said 'yes,' and played it, and at that point, he said, 'Good God, girl, if you can do this, you should specialize in Bach.' So I did." (Kozinn)

Chiapusso and Tureck worked together on two courses of study (one concentrating on Bach's works, the other on standard repertoire) and on several instruments (clavichord, harpsichord, organ and piano). Because of Chiapusso, Tureck made a stunning impression at her piano audition (she was 16 years old) for admission to the Juilliard Graduate School in New York. The required pieces for entrance included a work of Bach, a Beethoven sonata, a Chopin piece and a piece of her own choice. Tureck arrived at her audition prepared to play the Bach-Busoni Chaconne, the Beethoven Sonata, op. 2, no. 2, Chopin's G Minor Ballade, the Paganini-Liszt *La Campanella* and so many Bach Preludes and Fugues (actually 16 of them) that Ernest Hutcheson, then president of Juilliard, read off her list to the faculty and judges and asked, "*Which* Prelude and Fugue would you like to hear?"

In 1931 Tureck received a four-year scholarship to Juilliard and was assigned to Olga Samaroff. At her first lesson she asked permission to learn the remaining Preludes and Fugues of the Well-Tempered Clavier. Working on three each week (and performing them, along with works from general repertoire, at

Samaroff's Saturday evening recitals), by the end of her first year at Juilliard, she had learned all 48! By the time another year had passed, she had learned, among other works, Bach's Goldberg Variations. Meanwhile she also kept adding to her 18th- and 19th-century repertoire and took classes in chamber music, theory and languages.

Tureck also won a scholarship to study electronic instruments with Leon Theremin. They had weekly lessons and lengthy practice sessions at his house on 59th Street, and Tureck learned to play Theremin's invention named the "Theremin" and also one of his electronic keyboard instruments. On 25 April 1930 the 15-year-old Tureck appeared for the first time at Carnegie Hall, not as a pianist but playing one of Theremin's instruments in his "recital of ether-wave and electrical music."

On 26 April 1935 Tureck won first place in the finals for piano in the National Federation of Music Clubs Competition and simultaneously received the Schubert Memorial Award, which guaranteed an appearance with the Philadelphia Orchestra. Thus, on 15 December 1936 she played the Brahms Concerto No. 2 in B-flat Major with the Philadelphia Orchestra, conducted by Eugene Ormandy. Meanwhile in 1935 she was "graduated with distinction" from Juilliard and made her piano recital debut on 18 October 1935 at Carnegie Hall, playing works by Bach, Chopin, Stravinsky, Albéniz, Ravel, Debussy and the Brahms-Handel Variations.

At her first all-Bach series—six weekly recitals (Nov–Dec 1937) at Town Hall—Tureck played the complete Well-Tempered Clavier, the Goldberg Variations, the Suites and Partitas and some miscellaneous works. In recognition of this remarkable achievement, she won the newly created (1938) Town Hall Young Artist Award—an award bestowed on the artist under 30 who, in the judgment of the Town Hall Music Committee, had given the most notable performance in Town Hall during the preceding season. Tureck's "prize" for this award was another Town Hall recital, at which she played a mixed program (11 Jan 1939) of Bach, Beethoven, Brahms, Sibelius, Debussy, Infante and the Strauss-Godowsky *"Fledermaus"* paraphrase.

For the next 15 years or so Tureck lived in New York, performing and teaching. She played regularly in New York and, after World War II, played all around the United States, still offering both traditional programs and all-Bach programs. On her first tour of Europe in 1947 she played all-Bach recitals in Copenhagen, Denmark; Stockholm, Sweden; and in England over the facilities of the BBC. And she played only Bach at her London recital debut, on 17 June 1953 at Wigmore Hall: four Preludes and Fugues from the WTC, the E-Minor Partita, the Capriccio On the Departure of a Beloved Brother, the Italian Concerto and three little minuets.

Her London recitals in the summer of 1953 (two more Bach recitals followed her debut) mark the beginning of a new life for Tureck. She returned to London the following year to play all the Bach concertos with the Boyd Neel Orchestra under Bryan Balkwill; and in 1955 her projected five-month tour of the British Isles and Scandinavia was so successful that she stayed abroad for three years, making her base in London. When she returned to the United States in early November 1958, she realized that she had only a limited popular following at home, that she would find her greatest fame abroad. Tureck bought a house in London and for many years spent as much time in England as she did in America, always playing, except on rare occasions, only the music of Bach. Concert managers may have worried about offering all-Bach recitals, but British audiences loved them. So did the British press.

During the 1954-55 season 25 of her recitals consisted of the Goldberg Variations, and for her first appearance at the Edinburgh Festival, she again performed those Variations, overwhelming her audience. "The encomiums she has received are not exaggerated," said a *Times* reviewer. "She plays the piano beautifully and Bach authentically. She demolishes our cherished purism and proves the piano a better instrument than a harpsichord, and better for Bach." (*TL*, 19 Oct 1954) From 1955 through 1960 Tureck played in London at least four times a year, nine times out of ten receiving rave reviews. Tureck seems to have attained the peak of her fame in Great Britain, but she returned often to the United States to give Town Hall recitals and make tours of America and Canada.

Sometimes Tureck conducts the Bach concertos from the keyboard. In 1958 she was the first woman to conduct the New York Philharmonic Orchestra, performing as both soloist and conductor in a series of three concerts covering all the Bach concertos for one clavier. Tureck organized her own ensemble in London. Known as the Tureck Bach Players, the group made its debut on 11 October 1959, with Tureck conducting six Bach concertos from the keyboard.

On 30 December 1973 she gave an amazing performance at Carnegie Hall, first playing the Goldberg Variations on the harpsichord and, after a 50-minute break, playing them again on the piano. To mark the 40th anniversary of her first all-Bach concerts in New York, she played a series of six Bach concerts at Carnegie Hall, beginning on 11 October 1977. And during the Bach tricentennial year (1984–85) she took part in a six-concert series at Carnegie Hall, playing two solo recitals and, in the other concerts, conducting the Tureck Bach Players from the keyboard.

Tureck, the esteemed Bach performer, and Tureck, Bach scholar and teacher, are equally formidable. She has held a series of prestigious teaching positions—at Mannes School of Music (1940–44), Juilliard (1944–46, 1947–1955), Washington University (1963–64), University of California at San Diego (1967–72), University of Maryland (1981–83), Princeton (1984), Yale (1991–92) and the University of Oxford (1974–75, 1984–88). She has also lectured on radio and television, and conducted master classes. That her way with words is as persuasive—and intriguing—as her way with the music of Bach was well in evidence at her master class at the University of California, Santa Barbara, on 29 May 1992. Tureck's humanistic approach, her insistence on a combination of intellect and emotion in performing Bach, substantiated her reputation as both Bach scholar and Bach player.

Tureck's three-volume work *Introduction to the Performance of Bach* has been translated into Japanese and Spanish, and she has recorded all the musical examples found in that series on one LP (see Discog.). Her edition of the Italian Concerto is a performance edition with text taken from Bach's own copy of the first printing. It is edited for harpsichord and for piano performance, with critical notes on original textual sources and stylistic historical performance practices.

Tureck has also published many essays on teaching and performing. In "Learning to Understand Bach" (*Etude,* Oct 1947), she states that, "The ultimate goal of Bach study is to recognize the several lines and to treat them *simultaneously* as both independent melodies *and* closely interwoven parts of a unified whole. . . . In my own teaching, I begin to build this polyphonic sense by asking the student to learn, by memory, the first of the 'Two-Part Inventions,' exactly as it is written. . . . When the student has learned the individual lines separately and in combination, I ask him to transpose them into all keys."

In "Learning to *Learn* Bach," another *Etude* article (May/June 1956), Tureck explains that to play Bach the student needs to develop "(1) a finger technique which is much more complete than that which is generally acquired today. One of the most important factors is the strength and true independence of each finger; (2) a good, dependable *legato*; (3) a technique for changing fingers. . . (4) a wide variety of *staccato*; and (5) a swift foot for pedalling."

Rosalyn Tureck has received four honorary doctorates from American institutions and in 1977 one from the University of Oxford. In 1975 she became an Honorary Life Fellow, St. Hilda's College, University of Oxford. In May of 1979 she received the Officer's Cross of the Order of Merit from the Federal Republic of Germany for her work dedicated to Bach and his music.

For 40 years Rosalyn Tureck has performed the music of Bach almost exclusively, which makes it easy to forget that during the first years of her career she also played standard solo repertoire (Scarlatti, Beethoven, Mendelssohn, Schubert, Chopin, Brahms and others); concertos by Rachmaninoff, Tchaikovsky, Brahms, Beethoven and Mozart; and a surprising number of contemporary works. For example, Tureck gave the premiere performances of piano concertos by William Schuman and Vittorio Giannini; she has also played Aaron Copland's Piano Sonata and Wallingford Riegger's Concerto for Piano and Winds; and David Diamond composed his prodigious 30-minute Sonata especially for her.

But Tureck, now in her eighties, will be remembered as the consummate Bach specialist. The essence of her study, preparation, approach and style all are grounded in the works of that master. She begins her preparation by studying relevant manuscripts, scholarly editions from the Bach *Gesellschaft*, contemporary manuals of performance practice, especially those dealing with ornamentation, and modern writings on all these various subjects. Structure in all its musical forms—harmonic, contrapuntal, rhythmic, fugal—is the foundation of her approach. In her words, "It is the behavior of the structure that contains the integrity of the music and orders the relationships within the structure."

Tureck's highly personal interpretations reflect her profound studies and scholarship; more than that, they mirror her attitude "to life, to art as a symbol of life, and to Bach as the archetype of that symbol." (Crankshaw) And for the most part throughout her career critics have consistently approved of her approach ("a completely harmonious interplay between intellect and imagination") and her playing (unhurried, deliberately articulated, generously ornamented).

When at age 22 Tureck played a series of six Bach recitals within the space of seven weeks (8 Nov–28 Dec), her prodigious memory and challenging playing stunned New York critics. "A few more performances like that," wrote a reviewer after the first program, "and Miss Tureck will have gone far toward impressing upon the local consciousness the fact that Bach is not only interesting, but positively exciting." (*NYT*, 9 Nov 1937) And after the third recital in the series, this from a different critic: "Miss Tureck established herself not only as mistress of her piano in its mechanical aspects, but as the medium of musical expressiveness." (*NYT*, 25 Nov 1937)

For her tenth anniversary recital at Town Hall (12 Nov 1945) Tureck played a mostly traditional program of Bach, Mozart, Beethoven and Brahms. In the Bach (two Preludes and Fugues) her phrasing "seemed willful, and she often arrived at the end of a melodic line with an exaggerated crescendo or equally exaggerated decrescendo for which no musical reason existed." And in Beethoven's "*Appassionata*" Sonata, "she banged and thumped in an attempt to produce a tone that might have come easily and smoothly from a muscular man." However, Tureck played the Copland Sonata, the one modern composition on her program, and the Brahms-Handel Variations "in excellent style . . . proof that she is, when the music in hand fits her special abilities and personality, one of the most valuable pianists about." (*NYT*, 13 Nov 1945)

Tureck's London debut recital at Wigmore Hall (17 June 1953) was an all-Bach program. One enthusiastic critic concluded that it was Tureck's immersion in the style of the early eighteenth century that gave her readings authenticity and distinction: "Without ever raising her voice unnecessarily she sustained a high degree of tension as with perfect clarity of texture, rhythmic composure, and careful choice of staccato or slurred treatment for every individual note she laid bare the contrapuntal cunning of this composer's part-writing." (*TL*, 22 June 1953)

On 20 October 1957 Tureck played the Goldberg Variations at London's Royal Festival Hall. "Miss Tureck's incredible variety of touch, buoyant sense of rhythm and expressive phrasing made nonsense of the purist view that a harpsichord is essential to recapture the true Bach idiom. She is able at will to evoke the timbres of harpsichord, clavichord or even *Lautencembalo*, and her rhythmic impetus enables the purest counterpoint to emerge as a lively vehicle of musical expression. Her approach is the reverse of 'sewing-machine Bach,' yet its emotional inflexions are scrupulously in keeping with the period style and her ornamentation is meticulous." (*Musical Times*, Dec 1957. Reprinted by permission.)

Year after year Tureck's Bach playing has garnered tributes. "She is always correct, but she is never academic. Her stylistic comprehension is unquestionable, and while she does not exclude individuality from her interpretations her taste is always of the purest quality." (*LAT*, 30 Jan 1966) And this: "The pianist's all-Bach program [30 Jan 1966], including fully four encores, sent students away inspired (or defeated), teachers mumbling to themselves and plain old music lovers enriched by a performance that could not today be surpassed." (*SFC*, 1 Feb 1966)

But Tureck's approach to Bach on the piano (her concept of interpretation, her ornamentation) does not please every Bach enthusiast. A London

Festival Hall recital (17 March 1967) produced this comment: "She played true to form: iron discipline, immaculate control. If at the end she had decided to start all over again, it would surely have been exactly the same. . . . What I miss in her Bach playing is any sense that music-making can embrace such things as whim or sudden poetic impulse. Her manner is carried to its illogical conclusion when she plays repeats as carbon copies." (*MT*, May 1967)

And Tureck's program (30 Dec 1973) of the Goldberg Variations on the harpsichord *and* on the piano during one afternoon elicited this: "In Miss Tureck's approach to her formidable task, there was occasionally something more scholastic than scholarly. I should have relished a flash of the sudden insight and infectious joy that fill the recorded performances of the work by Landowska on the harpsichord and Glenn Gould on the piano—however perverse and willful these great artists may show themselves elsewhere. In Freudian terms, the superego was too evidently in control in much that Miss Tureck did. Her performance was intense and majestic and refined; but something of the life and humanity of Bach's music had evaporated." (*NY*, 14 Jan 1974)

Tureck's program at an all-Bach recital (22 Jan 1980) in Miami, Florida, included five Preludes and Fugues, the Chromatic Fantasy and Fugue, the Fantasy in C Minor and the Partita No. 2 in C Minor. "How did she play them? It all depends, no doubt, on how you like your Bach, for unquestionably, Tureck likes it her way. Which means Bach particularly successful in slow movements, where her delicate touch and tone are persuasive, but less felicitous when that tone turns hard and ugly in rigid attack. . . . Whatever Tureck does comes out of deep personal conviction, and a good deal of the time she is convincing." (*MH*, 23 Jan 1980)

In her performance (21 Oct 1990) of the Goldberg Variations at the New York Temple Emanu-El, "Miss Tureck's long experience with and intense feeling for this music was everywhere apparent, especially in her knowing and easy handling of ornamentation. But her technique seems slightly problematic at this stage in her career, and to judge from glaring wrong notes at the end of the 16th Variation and the beginning of the 23rd, so does her concentration." (*NYT*, 25 Oct 1990)

She continues to perform Bach in Europe and Britain. In Florence, Italy, the 78-year-old Tureck's performance of the Goldberg Variations was praised as "a superhuman tour de force." (*La Repubblica*, 26 Jan 1993) From Munich: "She has earned and retains the title of 'High Priestess of Bach'." (*Allgemeine Zeitung*, 2 Dec 1993) And after a Wigmore Hall recital: "Her confidence in every detail, her unfailing clarity, and the sheer force of her concentration made for a compelling musical journey." (*IND*, 28 May 1993)

Tureck's recital (14 Aug 1992) at the Teatro Colón in Buenos Aires included some of the music from her "pre-Bach" days: the Brahms-Handel Variations, some Mendelssohn and Schubert and, wonder of wonders, a Bach transcription, the mighty violin Chaconne as conceived for keyboard by Ferruccio Busoni. "Music's high priestess has been revisiting areas of the repertoire which she discarded for many years, finding once again a richness and magic in diversity." (*Gram*, Aug 1993) A video and CD were made from this recital.

Many of Tureck's numerous LP discs have disappeared from the catalogues, including her piano recordings of Bach's Well-Tempered Clavier, made
for Decca in the 1960s. Each of these musically and historically important albums contains eight Preludes and Fugues, and each is supplied with explanatory
notes by Tureck herself. Another important LP, *An Introduction to Bach* (see
Discog.), was compiled as both a collection of representative compositions and
as a teaching aid; it contains the complete set of compositions which appear in
Tureck's *Introduction to the Performance of Bach*.

Between 1979 and 1984 Tureck played a series of five Bach recitals at
the home of her friend William F. Buckley, Jr. They were recorded and eventually appeared on four CDs (see Discog.), with explanatory notes by Tureck. For
those who enjoy Bach on the piano, these albums present the essence of Tureck's
artistry—mature, thoughtful interpretations by a pianist who has lived with this
music for many years. An objective critique of the first CD to appear—the
Goldberg Variations, BWV 988—has this to say: "Half a century of scholarship
and interpretive refinement have resulted in a *Goldberg* set that doesn't always
sing and very rarely soars, but always engages the imagination. Repeated listenings reveal all manner of delicate (or explosive) touches that lesser pianists will
wish they'd thought of. If you make it through the opening *Aria*, taken at a really ponderous pace, you'll discover that her choice of tempo had nothing to do
with energy conservation or concealment of technical lapses. In fact she dazzles
whenever it suits her design. If her rhythmic elasticity and wide-ranging dynamics seem anachronistic at times, her musical conscience keeps her firmly rooted
in the spirit of the Baroque." (*Fanfare*, Sept/Oct 1989. Reprinted by permission.)

The second CD issued contains three Partitas, BWV 825, 826 and 830.
One brief, succinct appraisal reads, "Put simply, this is as fine a set of piano
performances of these three partitas as you are likely to hear. We were impressed
with the *Goldberg Variations* but this recital is, if anything, even more remarkable; transcendent playing, perfectly conceived, and rendered with consummate
artistry. . . . A record reviewer runs out of ways to praise exalted interpretations,
so I will not try. This is one." (*American Record Guide*, May/June 1990.
Reprinted by permission.) On the other hand, we have these comments from another reviewer, a Bach purist: "To compensate for the wrong sonority of the
modern piano, Tureck attempts to create the illusion of its keyboard antecedent
[harpsichord] by using Baroque affect: her touch is basically light; her articulation crisp and *senza pedale*; the timbre she elicits is pingy." But, he grants that
"Tureck is an intelligent musician, one whose virtuosity and technical mastery
of these devilishly difficult works allow her to think on her feet, as it were, and
to make interpretive choices *in medias res*. Even more impressive, she has
achieved nearly note-perfect accounts performing live in a single-take—a well-
nigh miraculous feat." (*Fan*, March/April 1990)

VAIA has initiated (1994) a series collectively titled *The Rosalyn
Tureck Collection*, a reissue of Tureck's most memorable early performances.
The first CD—*Rosalyn Tureck: The Young Firebrand* (see Discog.)—includes
items from recitals played in 1939, 1945 and 1974. The second CD—*Rosalyn
Tureck: The Young Visionary*—comes from a live 1948 all-Bach recital.

SELECTED REFERENCES

Ampolsk, Alan G. "An Interview with Rosalyn Tureck." *The Piano Quarterly*, Fall 1988, pp. 18–25.

Bach, Johann Sebastian. *Concerto in the Italian Style*, edited for harpsichord and piano by Rosalyn Tureck. New York: G. Schirmer, 1983.

Buckley, William F., Jr. "A Week" (Journal), Part II." *New Yorker*, 28 Aug 1971, pp. 42–43.

Cowan, Robert. "Off the Stage." *Gramophone*, Aug 1993, p. 10.

Crankshaw, Geoffrey. "What Tureck Thinks on Bach." *Music and Musicians*, Feb 1958, pp. 16–17.

Distler, Jed. "On The Record: A Tour-de-Force Career." *Keyboard Classics*, March/April 1995, pp. 60, 63.

Doerschuk, Bob. "The Importance Of Bach In The Modern World." (interviews with Keith Jarrett, Rosalyn Tureck, Philip Glass and Joshua Rifkin). *Keyboard*, March, 1985, pp. 44–45, 49–52, 57–58.

Downes, Edward. "Bach Pianist: Rosalyn Tureck Returns After Success Abroad." *New York Times*, 9 Nov 1958, sec. 2, p. 9.

Elder, Dean. "Bach Talk with Rosalyn Tureck." *Clavier*, Jan 1979, pp. 18–23.

"Harpsichord v. Piano in Playing the Classics." *The Times* (London), 21 Feb 1958, p. 3.

Kozinn, Allan. "Rosalyn Tureck's 40-Year Search for Bach." *New York Times*, 9 Oct 1977, sec. 2, pp. 19, 38.

"Pianist Abroad." *Time*, 29 July 1957, p. 68.

Reich, Howard. "Rosalyn Tureck reprising her career." *Chicago Tribune*, 18 Jan 1990, sec. 5, p. 8.

"Rosalyn Tureck." *New Yorker*, 10 Oct 1977, ("Talk of the Town") pp. 36–38.

Rothstein, Edward. "Which Instruments Are Best for Bach?" *New York Times*, 18 March 1984, p. 21.

"Secure in the Universe." *Time*, 3 Jan 1964, p. 67. Bach, Gould, Tureck.

Tureck, Rosalyn. "Artist's Life." *Keynote*, Jan 1985, p. 31.

————. "Bach on the Piano? Why Not? After All, He Was a Piano Salesman." *High Fidelity*, Oct 1977, pp. 91–93.

————. "Bach Performance in the Modern Concert Hall." *The Concert Goer's Annual No. 1*. London: John Calder, 1957, pp. 113–123.

————. "How I Play Bach." (interview with Teri Towe). *American Record Guide*, July/Aug 1980, pp. 6–10, 56–59.

————. *An Introduction to the Performance of Bach*. Oxford: Oxford University Press, 1960, 3 volumes.

————. "Learning to *Learn* Bach." (interview) *Etude*, May-June 1956, pp. 13–14, 48.

————. "Learning to Understand Bach." (interview with Rose Heylbut). *Etude*, Oct 1947, pp. 549, 586.

————. "My Electric Side." *Keyboard Classics*, May/June, 1986, pp. 6–7.

"The Well-Tempered Clavierist." *The Times* (London), 27 Jan 1958, p. 11.

See also Bibliography: Car/Del; Cur/Bio (1959); Doe/Tra; Dub/Ref; Eld/Pia; Ewe/Li; Ewe/Mu; Mac/Gre; New/Gro; Sal/Fam.

SELECTED REVIEWS

ALJ: 10 Feb 1983. *LAT*: 25 April 1949; 30 Jan 1966; 20 Feb 1968; 2 March
    1970; 2 March 1979. *MA*: 25 Oct 1935; 25 Nov 1937; 10 Dec 1937; 25
    Dec 1937; 25 Jan 1939. *MH*: 23 Jan 1980; 4 Feb 1986. *MT*: Dec 1957;
    May 1967. *NY*: 14 Jan 1974. *NYHT*: 16 Dec 1936. *NYP*: 12 Oct 1977;
    14 June 1979. *NYT*: 19 Oct 1935; 16 Dec 1936; 4 Jan 1937; 9 Nov 1937;
    18 Nov 1937; 25 Nov 1937; 2 Dec 1937; 9 Dec 1937; 29 Dec 1937; 12 Jan
    1939; 13 Jan 1945; 13 Nov 1945; 18 Nov 1948; 12 Nov 1953; 7 Dec
    1958; 9 July 1968; 2 Dec 1969; 1 Jan 1974; 23 March 1984; 25 Oct 1990.
    PJ: 22 Jan 1978 *SFC*: 1 Feb 1966. *SLGD*: 2 Nov 1981. *TL*: 22 June
    1953; 6 July 1953; 10 Oct 1955; 29 Jan 1956; 30 Jan 1957; 9 Feb 1959; 9
    May 1960; 1 April 1963; 12 May 1964; 18 March 1967; 30 Sept 1972; 12
    May 1977; 18 Aug 1980. *WP*: 16 Feb 1994.

SELECTED DISCOGRAPHY

Bach: Goldberg Variations. VAIA 1029 (CD). Originally released on Albany
    (Troy 007).
Bach: Three Partitas (Nos. 1, 2, 6). VAIA 1040 (CD). Originally released on
    Albany (Troy 008).
Bach: Well-Tempered Clavier. Preludes and Fugues Nos. 1–8 from Book 1.
    Decca DL 710120.
Bach: Well-Tempered Clavier. Preludes and Fugues Nos. 9–16 from Book 1.
    Decca DL 710121.
An Introduction to Bach . CBS Masterworks IM 37275.
Rosalyn Tureck Plays Bach: The Great Solo Works. Vol. 1. Adagio in G
    Major; Aria and Ten Variations in the Italian Style; Capriccio on the
    Departure of a Beloved Brother; Chromatic Fantasy and Fugue; Fantasia in
    C Minor; Prelude and Fugue in B-flat Major (WTC II); Toccata, Adagio, and
    Fugue in D. VAIA 1041. Originally released on Albany (Troy 010).
Rosalyn Tureck Plays Bach: The Great Solo Works, Vol. 2. English Suite No.
    3 in G Minor, BWV 808; Italian Concerto, BWV 971; Preludes and Fugues
    in C Major and C Minor (WTC I); Preludes and Fugues in C-sharp Major
    and G Major (WTC II); Sonata in D Minor, BWV 964. VAIA 1051.
    Originally released on Albany (Troy 009).
Rosalyn Tureck: A Tribute to a Keyboard Legend. Bach: *Allegro* (Sonata in D
    Minor, BWV 964); Gigue (English Suite No. 3, BWV 808); Gigue (Partita
    No. 1, BWV 825); Italian Concerto, BWV 971; Musette in D Major; Partita
    No. 2, BWV 826; Prelude and Fugue in B-flat Major, BWV 866; Variations
    28 and 29 (Goldberg Variations, BWV 988). Mendelssohn-Hutcheson:
    Scherzo ("A Midsummer Night's Dream"). Paganini-Liszt: Etudes Nos. 1,
    2, 6. Schubert: *Moments musicaux*, D. 780, no. 2. VAIA 1086.
Rosalyn Tureck: The Young Firebrand. Brahms: Variations and Fugue on a
    Theme by Handel, op. 24. Debussy: *La Danse de Puck*; *La Soirée dans
    Grenade*. Graun: Gigue. Mendelssohn-Hutcheson: Scherzo from "A

Midsummer Night's Dream." Paganini-Liszt: *Six Grand Etudes*. Paradies: Toccata in A. A. Scarlatti: Aria; Minuetto. VAIA 1058 (CD). Live performances from 1939, 1945, 1974.

Rosalyn Tureck: The Young Visionary. Bach: Six Preludes, BWV 933-938; English Suite No. 3 in G Minor, BWV 808; Three Preludes and Fugues, BWV 855, 880, 849; Sonata in D Minor, BWV 964. VAIA 1085 (CD) Live all-Bach recital from 1948.

VIDEO

Rosalyn Tureck Live at the Teatro Colón. Bach: Adagio in G Major; Chromatic Fantasy and Fugue. Bach-Busoni: Chaconne in D Minor. Brahms: Variations and Fugue on a Theme by Handel, op. 24. Mendelssohn: Sweet Remembrances. Schubert: *Moments musicaux*, D. 780, nos. 2 and 3. VAI 69081 (also on CD VAIA 1024-2). Taped on 14 August 1992.

𝒰

UCHIDA, MITSUKO: b. 20 December 1948, Tokyo, Japan.

> The process of hopefully evolving into a performer of some sort of stature or consequence is so consuming. . . . Is music your life's blood or not? . . . If not then you have to do something else, and live a life less full of savage demands and sacrifices.
>
> Mitsuko Uchida (*Music and Musicians*, November 1985)

Despite those "savage demands and sacrifices," music remains Mitsuko Uchida's greatest love, an elemental force that rules and nourishes the very fiber of her existence. She had her first private piano lesson at age three, which seems remarkably premature, but very likely playing the piano came naturally to Uchida. When her kindergarten class took part in a study on muscle development in children—each child being tested to see how well he or she could operate a hand-held counting device—the five-year-old Mitsuko proved to have the fastest reflexes and the most coordinated fingers. By age 12 she had developed into an exceptional music student. Just a few weeks after her twelfth birthday her life changed dramatically, all because her father, a member of Japan's diplomatic corps, was assigned to Vienna. The Uchida family left Tokyo in January 1961, and for Mitsuko, the youngest of the three children, it was literally a final parting with her homeland. "I'm Japanese," she told an interviewer in 1985, "but I no longer belong there."

She was shy, just barely 12 and spoke no German, but within a matter of weeks she was enrolled in the Vienna Academy of Music. Looking back, Uchida believes that her playing would be very different had she remained in

Japan, where children, typically obedient and hard-working, usually learn to play Western instruments very well mechanically but are rarely exposed to a Western musical tradition. Unlike people steeped in music—for example, the Italians who live daily with opera, and the British with their enduring choirs—the Japanese approach music as another mechanical function at which to excel. Analyzing the music or simply playing for the sheer joy of playing rarely enters into it. Moving from that kind of a musical environment, the only one Uchida had ever known, into that of Vienna, which to her seemed nothing but tradition, forever changed her world. Although she hated the restrictions (Beethoven had to be played like this, Schubert like that), in Vienna she learned about the sensuous side of music and the benefits of being analytical.

Uchida began studies with Richard Hauser at the Vienna Academy of Music in 1961 and graduated in 1968. In 1969 she won the International Beethoven Competition, held in Vienna. In 1970 she studied for a short time with Stefan Askenase in Bonn, working on some Chopin, and that same year she placed second in the Chopin Competition in Warsaw. In 1971 Wilhelm Kempff invited her to Positano, Italy, to participate in his summer course—two weeks spent going through the five Beethoven concertos and the 32 sonatas. Her brief coaching sessions with Kempff and Askenase are often mentioned but, says Uchida, "Richard Hauser was my only teacher, really."

In 1972 she left Vienna for London, hoping that in that cosmopolitan musical city she could (1) rid herself of the effects of both the conservative conformity of Japan and the stifling traditionalism of Vienna, and (2) review all that she had learned, and from it work out her own way of playing. On her own, she learned a great deal about music by listening to great performers like Szigeti, Casals, Furtwängler, Cortot, Edwin Fischer, Enesco and especially Fritz Busch. Uchida believes that listening to Busch's legendary Glyndebourne opera recordings, made in the 1930s, is what really opened her eyes to Mozart's greatness and gave her the courage to play Mozart the way she wanted to.

In 1975 Uchida won the Leeds Competition in England. Nevertheless, she built her career slowly and carefully. She has attracted a large following because of the way she plays, not by high-powered publicity. Her stunning, critically acclaimed performances of the Mozart sonatas in London in 1982 brought her international prominence. Requests for her to play flowed in, and Philips signed her to record all the sonatas and other important Mozart works. During the 1985–86 season she played a Mozart concerto marathon (10 concertos in nine months, 5 Oct 1985–3 June 1986), performing as soloist and conducting the English Chamber Orchestra from the keyboard. (Uchida likes to direct from the keyboard because "to play and direct gets rid of that one-eighth of a gap; you can control every detail.") Orchestra and soloist repeated the cycle in Tokyo the following season. Ever since these highly praised performances, Uchida has been known as a Mozart specialist, considered by some to be the finest, most passionate Mozart pianist living.

She prefers not to think about the large repertoire she played as a very young pianist, adding works too quickly, without taking the time to learn and relearn them. However, the experience of playing them helped immensely in getting a lot of problems out of her system. Her greatest love has always been for the Viennese classics—Mozart, Haydn, Beethoven, Schubert. Chopin, Schumann, Debussy and the second Viennese school (Schoenberg, Webern, Berg) and Bartók are also favorites. She feels basically uneasy about playing Liszt, thinks that Brahms, Prokofiev and Rachmaninoff are presently not for her. She plays Bach privately, beginning each day with a Prelude and Fugue as a sort of cleansing or revitalizing process. But as she told an interviewer in 1984, "Mozart has been important to me, always, yes, and Schubert." (*Hi-Fi News & Record Review*, Aug 1984))

Uchida plays only about 50 concerts a season and does not follow a pattern of repeated tours. She has toured extensively in Great Britain, the United States, Europe, Japan and the Far East. She made her New York debut (26 July 1985) playing the Mozart C Major Concerto, K. 467, with the Mostly Mozart Festival Orchestra, conducted by David Zinman, and made her New York recital debut (15 Feb 1987) at Lincoln Center on the Great Performers Series.

Mitsuko Uchida seems to love the piano as much as she loves music. She loves the physical action of actually playing the piano, to the point that she even loves to practice. Such total involvement with music has inevitably influenced her personal life. Uchida has always been a loner, never a joiner, and still is. Records and books are her closest friends. When not concertizing or involved in preparation, she reads (in Japanese, German, English) a great deal, especially biographies relevant to her music. During the concert season she reads less germane subjects (mostly history and musicology, but also bridge hands and grammar books), reading that keeps her mind active without being emotionally stimulating. Uchida also enjoys knitting and tapestry work. An avid cyclist, she rides her bicycle everywhere, but not on rehearsal or performing days because, as she says, she is "too nervous to be safe on the bike." On holidays she often cycles through the French countryside.

Mitsuko Uchida, the least showy of musicians, is a meticulous, intelligent, sensitive and exciting pianist. Above all, the listener senses the zest, the sheer joy in her playing. "Whether Ms. Uchida performs Mozart, Chopin, Schoenberg or Debussy, the results are the same—playing that is never eccentric yet also is unmistakably her own; playing that relishes the sensation of the moment but that also is entirely considered." (Swed)

Uchida is indeed an individualist at the keyboard. There are some listeners who relish her every note and every phrase. But there also those who confess to perplexity. "Hers is a curious style," wrote one reviewer. "Sometimes she is almost brusque in her refusal to taper phrase-endings and 'shape' lines." (*NYT*, 29 July 1985) On the other hand, another critic writes: "What Miss Uchida substitutes for cantabile is an intense understanding of how the music is made: the exact point at which to mark a climax, the way a phrase rises towards its answer, the precise function of just one note in a theme. She does not sing the music; she exists in it." (*TL*, 7 Oct 1985)

Uchida's opening concert of her nine-month Mozart concerto cycle in London drew this comment: "Mitsuko Uchida is a deeply thoughtful, unflashy Mozart pianist, playing right into the notes, never forcing the tone but letting it create its own luminosity, setting speeds which give the phrases time to speak."

(*STL*, 13 Oct 1985) A different critic, reviewing another concert in the same cycle, wrote, "No one plays Mozart more delicately or neatly than Mitsuko Uchida. . . . However, delicacy and refinement cannot by themselves reveal the heart of those concertos. Just as Uchida's natural touch seems to eliminate the piano's harsher overtones, so her interpretations also seem to filter out much of the music's drama and wit." (*TL*, 1 Nov 1985)

Reviews for these performances of the entire Mozart solo concertos were consistently good, if often tempered with reservations. For example, this comment on her eighth concert: "Mitsuko Uchida's way with the piano concertos of Mozart is undeniably alluring. She has almost impeccable control over the weight she places upon each note, while her sense of phrase and form is wonderfully intuitive. . . . And yet is there not something slightly worrying about the delicacy of her playing? . . . There were occasions . . . when a little more tang would have been welcome." (*TL*, 27 March 1986)

Uchida's performances have met with dazzling success in the United States. At a Dallas, Texas, recital (16 Feb 1988), "The surprises came quickly. First, the amplitude and muscle of her sound. Secondly, the wonder of how so girded a sound could be made so expressively flexible. Part of the answer is in Uchida's ability to find those proportions for a phrase, a crescendo or a tempo that give the internal musical elements of a composition dimension and perspective." (*DMN*, 18 Feb 1988) And this critique of an all-Mozart recital (14 Jan 1989) at New York's Metropolitan Museum: "Miss Uchida's Mozart is unlike anyone else's: it is not a Romanticized approach; yet she uses the modern piano's steely power when she needs it. Nor is it a fully Classicist, early-instrument view, although she often plays with a nimbleness that suggests a fortepiano texture." (*NYT*, 18 Jan 1989)

Like Lili Kraus, Uchida has become known, whether intentionally or not, as a specialist in Mozart. However, she often programs works by Chopin and Debussy. Her recital (15 Feb 1987) at New York's Alice Tully Hall included the Chopin Sonata No. 3 in B Minor, op. 58, which was, from all reports, a glorious performance. "I cannot recall ever hearing such a spirited, affirmative, beautifully conceived performance of this wonderful work before," wrote one reviewer. "In her care for musical purpose and fine shading of each phrase, her wonderful pointing of rhythm, her easily flowing legato and her understanding of balance and dynamic perspective, she is a true artist." (*NYT*, 17 Feb 1987)

A Pasadena recital (18 Feb 1988) included five of the Debussy Etudes, beautifully played. "She is not exactly a wide-ranging colorist, and there is more variety in her intimate playing than in her bravura. . . . She could display the stated technical problem [in the Etudes] as if each were a specialty and at the same time she controlled the shifting harmonic basis with a sharp ear for balance and color." (*LAT*, 20 Feb 1988)

One of Uchida's recital programs for the 1992–93 season featured music by Beethoven (Sonata in E Minor, op. 90), Schubert (Sonata in G Major, D. 894), Schumann (*Carnaval*) and Webern (Variations, op. 27). When she played the program on 4 December 1992 at Washington's Kennedy Center, reaction was mixed. One reviewer, disappointed with the Beethoven, wrote: "The first movement was too vigorously played and the lilting grace of the Rondo suffered from a surfeit of speed and sound. Robert Schumann's long and brilliant 'Carnaval' suite fared somewhat better but not uniformly so . . . the opening *'Préambule'* was rushed as was the 'Chopin' nocturnal sketch while forte passages especially in the concluding *'Marche'* were percussive and harsh. The second half was sheer delight. Following Anton Webern's 'Variations' (Op. 27), in which she excelled in the interplay of sounds and silences and in the contrasts of the percussive with subtle nuance, Uchida made the piano sing in Schubert's G Major Sonata." (*WP*, 7 Dec 1992)

"Sometimes, very rarely, one comes away from a recital thinking how perfectly right it all was. Not necessarily how sublime or how cerebral, or what extraordinary skills were displayed, but simply how *right*. Mitsuko Uchida's concert . . . was one of those occasions." The 1993 London recital (Wigmore Hall) that evoked such enthusiasm was somewhat unusual. After Haydn's Sonata in D Major, Hob. XVI:37, where Uchida "revelled in his daring," she played the completed movements of Schubert's magnificent C major "Reliquie" Sonata, D. 840, and here her playing showed "an open, entirely natural response to the breadth of Schubert's vision and to the harmonic diversions and gestural extravagances which nevertheless fit perfectly into these richly orchestrated patterns." After intermission, she played Schumann's *Kreisleriana*, with its "different challenges. . . . But again, Uchida was well up to the task, intelligently balancing the poetical and the passionate, preserving a sense of immediacy, and never making an ugly sound in what was another deeply satisfying performance." (*TL*, 18 Sept 1993)

The release of the Concerto No. 17 in G Major, K. 453, completes Uchida's project of recording Mozart's original solo concertos with the English Chamber Orchestra, Jeffrey Tate conducting (Grammy, K.450, K.451, 1991). Each presently available cycle of concertos is remarkable in its own way and Uchida, with her individuality and splendid musicianship, will join an illustrious roster of notable interpreters (Anda, Kraus, Barenboim). A review of two CDs, one containing Concertos K. 415/387b and K. 449 (Philips 422359), the other Concertos K. 456 and K. 459 (Philips 422348), is typical of many critiques: "She provides exquisitely crafted performances of all four concertos, each phrase lovingly played, each note infused with life-giving energy. Her tone is a marvel. If she has been accused of being too reticent in her Mozart playing, I attribute this to a most subtle means of expression." (*ARG*, July/Aug 1990)

And this reaction to Uchida's recordings of Concertos K. 491 and K. 503 (Philips 422331): "She can etch a flourish in bright, ringing tone, then in an instant transform her sound into something mellow so a melody can exude warmth. . . . And where other pianists find only a barrage of sixteenth notes, Uchida reveals something with color and shape." (*OrS*, 24 Dec 1989)

Uchida has also recorded most of Mozart's solo keyboard works. One CD combines recitals given in Tokyo during May 1991 (see Discog.). There are four sonatas plus other works and, as one reviewer puts it, "Much of this music has already been studio recorded by her, and these performances reveal a distinct and different beauty. As ever, with Uchida, there is the sheer pleasure of hearing the fingers' apparently direct contact with the vibrating strings as she coaxes the listener to experience the 'inscape' of a particular melody or harmonic transition. In live performance, though, there is a sense of her recreating an improvisation of the mind, not just of the fingers." (*Gram*, April 1993)

Of Uchida's recording of the Debussy Etudes (Grammy, 1990, see Discog.), one critic writes, "Uchida's recording is unobtrusively fine. . . . It is as fine a recording as these pieces have had." (*ARG*, Jan/Feb 1991) Another reviewer agrees: "She has made a dazzling recording of these forbidding, truly avant-garde works, with their foreshadowings even of polytonality. In doing so, she has revealed a new and unexpected facet of her formidable talent." (*MA*, Nov 1990)

SELECTED REFERENCES

Ames, Katrine. "Zen and the Art of the Piano." *Newsweek*, 26 March 1990, p. 57.
Catalano, Peter. "Mitsuko Uchida: You Can't Live Twice." *Schwann Opus*, Fall 1994, pp. 6–12.
Davis, Peter G. "Mozart Over Easy." *New York*, 22 April 1991, pp. 79–80.
Elder, Dean. "Mitsuko Uchida: One of a Kind." *Clavier*, Oct 1990, pp. 10–14.
———. "Mitsuko Uchida Plays Debussy." *Clavier*, Dec 1991, pp. 32–34, 45. An in-depth review of Uchida's Debussy video.
Humphreys, Ivor. "Like-Minded Mozart." *Gramophone*, Aug 1987, p. 263.
———. "Mitsuko Uchida." *Gramophone*, Feb 1989, p. 1275.
———. "Mitsuko Uchida." *Hi-Fi News & Record Review*, Aug 1984, pp. 72–73.
Kupferberg, Herbert. "Mitsuko Uchida." *Stereo Review*, July 1990, pp. 63–65.
"Making a direct approach to Mozart." *Sunday Times* (London), 13 Oct 1985, p. 41.
Morrison, Bryce. "Mitsuko Uchida." (interview) *Music and Musicians*, Nov 1985, pp. 5–6.
Specter, Michael. "Classical Soul Music." *Washington Post*, 3 April 1991, sec. C, pp. 1, 11.
Swed, Mark. "Music: Pianist Mitsuko Uchida." *Wall Street Journal*, 14 March 1990, sec. A, p. 16.
Waleson, Heidi. "A Pianist Who Does Just As She Likes." *New York Times*, 16 Oct 1988, sec. 2, p. 27.
Wigler, Stephen. "Sought-after pianist puts head and heart into Mozart's works." *Baltimore Sun*, 23 Feb 1992, sec. H, p. 1.
See also Bibliography: IWWM; WWAM.

SELECTED REVIEWS

CPD: 1 Feb 1987. *CT*: 5 March 1990. *DFP*: 6 Dec 1992. *DMN*: 18 Feb 1988. *DT*: 2 March 1985. *FT*: 1 March 1985. *LADN*: 17 Dec 1992. *LAHE*: 24 Nov 1986. *LAT*: 24 April 1985; 20 Feb 1988. *MT*: May 1983. *NY*: 2 March 1987. *NYT*: 29 July 1985; 3 April 1986; 17 Feb 1987; 23 Feb 1988; 22 Oct 1988; 18 Jan 1989; 9 April 1991. *OrS*: 6 May

1990. *PI*: 8 March 1990; 21 March 1991; 2 Nov 1991. *SFE*: 4 Aug 1988. *SMU*: 26 Aug 1991. *TL*: 19 July 1983; 16 May 1984; 7 Oct, 13 Oct, 1 Nov, 25 Nov, 16 Dec, 17 Feb, 11 March, 27 March, 21 April, 5 June 1985–86 (Mozart cycle); 7 Feb 1990; 18 Sept 1993. *WP*: 4 April 1991; 7 Dec 1992. *WT*: 5 April 1991.

SELECTED DISCOGRAPHY

Chopin: Sonata No. 2 in B-flat Minor, op. 35; Sonata No. 3 in B Minor, op. 58. Philips 420949-2.
Debussy: Etudes. Philips 422412-2.
Mitsuko Uchida Live In Concert. Mozart: Adagio in B Minor, K. 540; Fantasia in D Minor, K. 397; Fantasia in C Minor, K. 475; Rondo in A Minor, K. 511; Sonata in C Minor, K. 457; Sonata in F Major, K. 533; Sonata in C Major, K. 545; Sonata in D Major, K. 576; Variations on "Unser dummer Pöbel meint," K. 455. Philips 432 989-2 (2 CDs). Recorded in Tokyo in 1991.
Mozart: Concertos for Piano and Orchestra. Philips 9-438207-2 (9 CDs). Tate/English CO.
Mozart: Concerto in D Minor, K. 466; Concerto in A Major, K. 488. Philips 434 164-2. Tate/English CO.
Mozart: Sonatas (complete). Philips 6-422115-2.
Schumann: *Carnaval*, op. 9; *Kreisleriana*. Philips 442 777-2.

VIDEO

The Debussy Etudes (performed and discussed [in German with English subtitles] by Mitsuko Uchida). Philips 070 227-3.
Mozart on Tour, Vol. 4. Concerto in E-flat Major, K. 271 (with Jeffrey Tate and the Salzburg *Mozarteum* Orchestra). Philips 070 241-3. (Also Dezsö Ranki)

V

VIÑES, RICARDO: b. Lérida, Spain, 5 February 1875; d. Barcelona, Spain, 29 April 1943.

> Who would have ventured [at the turn of the century] to present to the public the works of Debussy or Ravel and incurred the risk of compromising his career in the attempt? . . . One must recall the hisses that greeted Viñes when he interpreted, for the first time, Maurice Ravel's *Miroirs*.
>
> G. Jean-Aubry (French Music of Today)

It seems highly possible that Ricardo Viñes, a pianist with a spectacular technique, phenomenal memory and prodigious repertoire, would have had a brilliant virtuoso career had he not ardently and actively promoted modern music. In the early decades of this century, Viñes stood as the sole defender of the new French, Spanish and Russian piano music, especially the innovative, controversial piano works of Debussy and Ravel. Despite an indifferent, sometimes hostile public, Viñes waged a lifelong crusade for contemporary music, repeatedly playing new music which no other pianist would even think of performing.

He gave the first performances of almost all of the piano works of Debussy and Ravel and a good many of those written by Séverac, Fauré and Satie. He also introduced piano pieces composed by his compatriots Granados, Falla and Albéniz; and after discovering Russian music in 1897, Viñes gave the first performances outside Russia of piano compositions by Balakirev, Glazunov, Rimsky-Korsakov, Mussorgsky and Prokofiev, music then hardly known beyond the Russian frontiers. (Years later the critic M. D. Calvocoressi said that by 1903 he had acquired an extensive knowledge of these modern Russian composers, and admitted that he owed much of that knowledge to "Ricardo Viñes, who was playing quantities of new music which no other pianist dreamt of touching.") While living in South America during the 1930s, Viñes introduced piano works by young Latin American composers such as Humberto Allende, Juan José Castro and Alberto Williams. And he was still supporting younger composers as late as 1936 and 1937, when he played new piano compositions by Olivier Messiaen and Daniel Lesur. (For a selective list of Viñes's first performances, see Brody: "Viñes in Paris.")

"This unselfish devotion won him many kudos, but he also had to pay the penalty of it. People grew accustomed to think of him only as an interpreter of new music, and lost sight of the tremendous amount of splendid work he put into his playing of the classics. He never could resist a request to play a new work; and the tradition was established, as a matter of course, that he was always available when wanted. . . . He has done far more for others than for himself." (Calvocoressi)

The late Elaine Brody's comprehensive study of Viñes and his era (Bro/Par, see Bibliog.) convinced her that Viñes had definitely influenced certain composers of his time. She concluded that both Ravel and Debussy had deliberately composed piano works with Viñes's extraordinary technique in mind, and that Viñes, by influencing *their* compositional style, had also influenced the style of some of their contemporaries. Some of these early 20th-century composers believed that having Viñes introduce a work guaranteed its success, and several gratefully dedicated piano pieces to him, notably Ravel (*Oiseaux tristes*), Falla (*Noches en los jardines de España*) and Debussy (*Poissons d'or*). However, the full measure of the debt modern music, musicians and composers owe to Ricardo Viñes has been largely forgotten.

Born in Lérida, Spain, Viñes began solfège at age five and piano lessons at six, both with Joaquín Terraza, the local organist and music teacher. At age 10 Viñes began piano study with Juan Bautista Pujol at the Barcelona Conservatory, and two years later he received a first prize in piano. When his mother asked Isaac Albéniz, then age 27 and an experienced concert pianist, to hear the 12-year-old Viñes play, Albéniz recommended further study at the Paris Conservatory. Thus on 13 October 1887, Viñes and his mother arrived in Paris (his father and two brothers followed a few weeks later); and except for concert tours, a hiatus during World War I and a stay in South America, Ricardo Viñes spent the rest of his life in the French capital. The family of five eked out a bare living from Viñes's small scholarships (granted by Barcelona and Lérida) and occasional jobs they found through the well-established Spanish emigré community. Viñes himself began working at age 13, playing the piano at private soirees for about 20 francs ($4.00 U.S.) an evening. As he gained experience and a reputation, he increased his fees, and by 1895 was earning 200 francs per event. An expert sight reader, he later found work as an accompanist and as a rehearsal pianist.

On 7 November 1887 Viñes was admitted to the Paris Conservatory as an auditor (the foreign student quota had been filled) to Charles de Bériot's piano class for superior students. Within a week he began private lessons with de

Bériot, but had to wait until 4 November 1889 to enroll as a regular Conservatory student. He studied piano with de Bériot, chamber music with Benjamin Godard and harmony with Albert Lavignac. In July 1894 he won first prize (a Pleyel grand piano) in the Conservatory competition. Viñes greatly admired de Bériot. He spent many evenings with the de Bériot family, sometimes trying out new music, and sometimes honing his sight-reading skills with the help of flash cards, each one bearing a different rhythmic configuration. (De Bériot believed that once a student could quickly translate the configurations into sound, he would have no trouble sight-reading.) Viñes studied with de Bériot for several years, and their close friendship continued until de Bériot's death in 1914.

By January 1895 Viñes felt secure enough financially to refuse a position (de Bériot had recommended him) at the Budapest Academy at 6,000 francs a year. By that time he was earning more money and also had further support from a patron who gave him 1,000 francs and gave his family 2,500 francs. By then a true Parisian, Viñes hated the thought of living elsewhere. He made his professional debut (21 Feb 1895) in Paris before a crowded house at the *Salle Pleyel*, playing a very long (2 1/2 hours) and very successful program. Since his father, who had returned to Spain, managed to get him a deferment from Spanish military service, he was free to begin his concert career.

Ricardo Viñes seemed to belong in Paris. The city gave him both fame and respect. He was called upon to judge competitions; he served on the admissions board at the Paris Conservatory; and in 1911 he was sent by the *Société Musicale Indépendente* to the Berlin *Hochschule* to promote interest in French music. Viñes played countless recitals in Paris, including a memorable four-piano concert at the *Salle d'Horticulture* with Alfred Cortot, Edouard Risler and Blanche Selva. From about 1908 he played literally hundreds of concerts in Europe and South America. At one London performance (28 Jan 1926) he played the Mozart Concerto in C Minor, K. 491, and Vincent d'Indy's Symphony on a French Mountain Air with the Royal Philharmonic Orchestra, conducted by Rhené-Baton. Viñes never performed in North America.

Viñes began taking pupils at age 15 and taught for most of his life. On Albéniz's recommendation, in 1900 he was hired to teach a weekly class for superior students at the *Schola Cantorum*. His most famous pupil was Francis Poulenc. Viñes encouraged Poulenc to compose, introduced him to other musicians and composers and arranged for him to study composition with Satie. An appreciative Poulenc later said of Viñes, "I owe him everything," and always kept a picture of Viñes on his piano. (Jewett)

Viñes waited out the First World War at Bagnères-de-Bigorre in southwestern France, close to the Spanish border. During the 1920s he made two tours of South America, and then lived there between 1930 and 1935. Upon his return to Paris, Viñes gave a smashing homecoming concert, but thereafter his career slowly declined. Possibly his compulsive gambling (he had a lifelong obsession with numbers) caused him to deteriorate. What bookings he found were at shamefully low fees. He made his final appearance, not in his beloved Paris but in Barcelona at the *Palau de Música* (19 Feb 1943). Alone and destitute, Ricardo Viñes died in a Barcelona hospital (29 April 1943) and was buried at Lérida.

Viñes precociously began a Journal at age 12 when he left Barcelona for Paris, and he kept it quite faithfully from 1887 to 1916. Most important are his personal notes on some of the early 20th century's most famous composers (Falla, Granados, Satie, Poulenc, Fauré), especially Ravel and Debussy, with whom Viñes at various times had almost daily contact. On the practical side, his Journal offers a wealth of information about social life, performance practice, audience behavior, programming and much more. The complete Journal was never published. Excerpts appeared in the *Revue internationale de musique française* (June 1980).

This detailed, informative diary reflects its author. Although Viñes had very little formal schooling, he was endowed with an insatiable intellectual curiosity and a remarkable memory. He spent hours prowling the Paris quayside stalls searching for bargains in music and books; he taught himself several languages; he wrote well and was an erudite music critic. His circle of friends—musicians, writers, poets, painters, dancers and philosophers—often met to recite, talk and hear the new music, usually played by Viñes or by Viñes and Maurice Ravel playing four hands at one piano. "Viñes, alert and cheerful, ever on the track of new music and new ideas, as keen on literature and painting as on his own art, was, whenever he turned up, the life and soul of our meetings. We loved his childlike ingenuity as much as we admired his playing and appreciated the colossal amount and rare quality of his disinterested work as a pioneer." (Calvocoressi)

Ravel—Viñes called him Mauricio—was one of his best boyhood friends. They met in Paris (22 Nov 1988) when both were 13, brought together because Ravel's Basque mother had quickly sought out the company of the Spanish-speaking Mme. Viñes. Ravel and Viñes liked one another immediately, and for more than two decades their lives and careers were closely intermingled. For years they met almost daily, spending hours together at the piano practicing, trying out new chords and sight-reading; or at *Maison Pleyel* rehearsing on two pianos. They went to concerts, operas, plays and picture galleries, as often as possible with free tickets. They took long walks together, played games in the evenings and avidly exchanged books and music. For example, in his Journal (9 Jan 1897) Viñes tells that he lent his copy of Debussy's *Rêverie* to Ravel and also his copy of Louis (Aloysius) Bertrand's poems *Gaspard de la nuit*. As Elaine Brody concluded, it was Viñes who introduced Ravel to these poems. Later on Ravel helped Viñes plan his recital programs, and by 1896 Ravel was constantly bringing his new piano compositions to Viñes. Viñes would play the new work, and the two would discuss it. Viñes's Journal (29 Jan 1898) states that "Ravel brought me his *Menuet antique* today. He says he likes the way I play it and he's going to dedicate it to me. He's surprised that I intend to perform it next week." (Brody)

Viñes had an equally important friendship with Claude Debussy, although they did not meet as schoolboys, Debussy being 13 years older. About six years before Viñes actually met Debussy, he wrote in his Journal (10 Dec 1895) that he was learning Debussy's *Rêverie*. And when Viñes first heard the *Prélude à l'après-midi d'un faune* at a Colonne Concert (22 Jan 1897), he noted in his Journal that it was the most beautiful thing he had heard in his life. An ecstatic admirer of all Debussy's music, Viñes played it for himself and took every opportunity to hear it, always noting in the Journal how "marvelous" or "divine" it was. After Debussy and Viñes finally met (30 Nov 1901), Viñes became Debussy's special pianist and favorite interpreter. For years Viñes visited Debussy regularly to try out new piano pieces or some other piano works the composer had started years before but had been "too lazy," as he said, to finish. Viñes would play these pieces over and over for Debussy. He also played them for their mutual friends, and ultimately introduced them to the public. Between 1902 and 1918 Viñes played 13 first performances of Debussy piano works.

About 70 years ago G. Jean-Aubry noted that Viñes was not simply an interpreter but truly an inspiration and a collaborator, a statement now supported by the late Elaine Brody's thorough research. Present and future music historians must be indebted to her for documenting Ricardo Viñes's important contribution to the development of early 20th-century piano music.

Viñes had an enormous repertoire, thanks to his incredible memory. Although he played a great deal of modern music, he never abandoned the classics, which he played, said critics of his time, like a grand artist. In Viñes's day a Paris recital typically consisted of about a dozen pieces, half of them virtuoso dazzlers. Transcriptions and arrangements were very popular, and one or two sonata movements (not necessarily the complete sonata) were always included. Viñes's programs had better balance. He played complete works; sometimes organized his programs along national or historical lines; and often alternated programs, one of traditional works with one of modern works. During the 1920s and 1930s, he sometimes played recitals featuring works dedicated to him. Later he often joined his friend Calvocoressi in giving lecture-recitals, the critic commenting on the music, usually French or Russian, while Viñes demonstrated at the piano.

"Ricardo Viñes played simply, with his heart, with his hands, the most eloquent that a pianist ever had." (Fontbernat) That playing won critical and public approval despite Viñes's sometimes stubborn insistence on programming newly composed works. "As early as 1894, critics spoke of Viñes's solid yet supple technique, marvelous octaves, variety of pianistic color, dazzling trills, all handled with unforgettable delicacy and perfect style. After each concert, reviews mentioned that he was repeatedly recalled to the platform by enthusiastic audiences. In 1895, his irreproachable style, his warmth and his extraordinary use of the pedal were already mentioned." (Brody) Indeed, it was Francis Poulenc's opinion that "no one could teach the art of using the pedals, an essential feature of modern piano music, better than Viñes." (New/Gro, see Bibliog.)

The poet Léon-Paul Fargue has provided an aesthetic description of Viñes's playing. "He knew how to impart to the sonorities and language of the piano a personal thrust, a kind of legible and fluid strength. . . . He added to his playing something which was no longer playing, which transcended the keys and offered itself as a direct contact of his heart with ours. . . . He had passion, authority, precision, the versatility of celebrated pianists, but he surpassed them by an enchanting personal distinction." (Fargue)

Viñes made few recordings. Playing for an audience truly inspired him, but he disliked the recording studio, fearing that it could only result in an artificial, lifeless performance. His 78 rpm records, apparently recorded in 1930 and again in 1936, are available on an LP (1983) pressing and, for the most part, on a CD reissue (see Discog.). Most are Spanish pieces (Albéniz, Falla, Turina, Blancafort) vibrating with the essence of Spanish rhythm, in turn nonchalant, incisive or fantastic. From these brief characteristic sketches Viñes has created miniature tone pictures, musical evocations of Spain, with its vitality, its sadness and its joys.

The Scarlatti Sonata in D Major, K. 29, perhaps overinterpreted for modern taste, still impresses with the evenness of touch, the clarity and, above all, the avoidance of exaggerated tempos—one of Viñes's greatest assets. The Brahms arrangement of a Gluck gavotte shows yet another side of Viñes's artistry. The melody sings with controlled lyricism sustained by an artfully articulated accompaniment. Perhaps the gems of the brief collection are Debussy's *Poissons d'or* from *Images,* Book II (Side 2, band 1, instead of band 2 on the LP recording) and *La Soirée dans Grenade*. Viñes's playing is remarkable: "Possessed of a dazzingly brilliant, seemingly effortless technique, his performances demonstrate an enormous range of color and an awesome mastery of pedaling. His sound is clear and bright, yet never hard. The playing is flexible, expressive and elegant. Although there is no stiffness or rigidity, Viñes's firm rhythmic control keeps any rubato from ever destroying the musical line and overall formal structure. Never is there a trace of cloying sentimentality or mock overstatement." (Banowetz)

Other composers in the album—Borodin, Troiani and Lopez-Buchargo—are treated with the same devotion, skill and musicianship. The brief collection stands as a monument to the memory of this unselfish pianist who steadfastly promoted the cause of contemporary music.

SELECTED REFERENCES

Banowetz, Joseph. "Reflections on Playing Debussy." *Piano Quarterly*, Fall 1982, pp. 42–46.

Brody, Elaine. "Viñes in Paris: New Light on Twentieth-Century Performance Practice." In *A Musical Offering: Essays in Honor of Martin Bernstein.* New York: Pendragon Press, 1977, pp. 45–62.

Calvocoressi, M. D. *Music and Ballet: The Recollections of M. D. Calvocoressi.* London: Faber and Faber, 1934.

Collet, Henri. *L'Essor de la musique espagnole au vingtième siècle.* Paris: Editions Max Eschig, 1919.

"Dossier: Le Journal inédit de Ricardo Viñes." *Revue internationale de musique française*, No. 2, June 1980.

Fargue, Léon-Paul. "*Un héros de la musique: Ricardo Viñes.*" In *Portraits de famille. Souvenirs.* Paris: J. B. Janin, 1947, pp. 221–229.

Fontbernat, Joseph. "Ricardo Viñes." *Guide du Concert*, 10 May 1957, p. 1045.

Jean-Aubry, G. *French Music of Today.* Trans. Edwin Evans, preface by Gabriel Fauré. London: Kegan Paul, Trench, Trubner & Co., Ltd., 1919.

Jewett, Diana. "Francis Poulenc: The Man and the Composer." *Piano Quarterly*, Summer 1984, p. 41.

Sitton, Michael. "Ravel, Viñes and *Gaspard de la nuit.*" *Clavier*, April 1990, pp. 14–16.

See also Bibliography: Bro/Par; Cal/MG; Ewe/Li; New/Gro.

SELECTED DISCOGRAPHY

Ricardo Viñes Recital. Albéniz: Granada (*Serenata*); *Torre bermeja* (*Piezas características*, op. 92, no. 12); *Tango en La mineur*, op. 164; *Sérénade espagnole*, op. 181; *Orientale* (*Cantos de España*, op. 232); *Seguidillas* (*Cantos de España*, op. 232). Blancafort: *Le Parc d'Attractions* (*L'Orgue du Carroussel*; *Polka de l'Équilibriste*). Borodin: *Scherzo en La bémol majeur* (*Extrait de la Petite Suite*). Debussy: *La Soirée dans Grenade* (*Extrait des Estampes*); *Poissons d'or* (*Extrait du 2e Livre des Images*). Falla: *Danse de la Frayeur et Récit du Pêcheur* (*Extrait de l'Amour Sorcier*). Gluck (Arrangement Brahms): *Gavotte d'Iphigénie en Aulide*. Lopez-Buchardo: *Baïlecito*. Scarlatti: *Sonata en Ré majeur*, K. 29. Troiani: *Milonga*. Turina: *Miramar* (*Contes d'Espagne* no. 3); *Dans les Jardins de Murcia* (*Contes d'Espagne* no. 4). Pathé Marconi EMI 1731791.

Ricardo Viñes and Francis Planté. Opal CD 9857. The same as the above LP, with two omissions (Granada [Albéniz]); *Danse de la Frayeur et Récit du Pêcheur* [Falla] and one addition (*Tonadas Chilenas* [Allende]).

$\mathcal{W}$

WATTS, ANDRÉ: b. Nuremberg, Germany, 20 June 1946.

> He has a decided charisma that comes right over the footlights. This cannot be taught. The great pianists are born with it—an ability to communicate, an ability to impress one's personality on the music.
> Harold C. Schonberg (*New York Times*, 16 January 1969)

A quarter of a century after Mr. Schonberg made that statement, André Watts is still a great communicator. Years of performances confirm that he is a pianist born with innate facility and musicality, which makes it all the more interesting to learn that Watt's talent emerged naturally in the course of his general cultural education, and that neither his parents (Watts is the only child born to Sergeant Herman Watts, an African-American soldier stationed in Germany, and Maria Alexandra [Gusmits] Watts, a refugee Hungarian) nor anyone else deliberately schooled him to be a musical prodigy. "My mother really didn't want me to be a musician; that wasn't her aim. She wanted me to be a surgeon. That was respectable. But she said she wanted me to be musically educated. That was civilized." (Zailian)

Watts started on the violin at about age six, but soon changed to piano lessons, taught by his mother. He was about eight at the time his father, transferred home to America, settled the family in Philadelphia. Watts enrolled at the Philadelphia Musical Academy (now the Philadelphia College for the Performing Arts), where he studied principally with Genia Robinor and Doris Bowden, and made such remarkable progress that at age nine he was selected from a field of 40 contestants to play Haydn's D Major Concerto at one of the children's concerts presented by the Philadelphia Orchestra. At age 11 Watts played the Mendelssohn Concerto No. 1 in G Minor with that same orchestra at a summer performance at Robin Hood Dell; and at age 14 he played César Franck's Symphonic Variations at one of the orchestra's regular subscription concerts.

In December 1962 Watts's dazzling playing at an audition for the Young People's Concerts of the New York Philharmonic Orchestra led to a second audition, this time with Leonard Bernstein present. The astonished Bernstein ("I flipped," he said) immediately engaged Watts to play at the next Young People's Concert (12 Jan 1963); and Watts, only age 16, gave such a stunning performance of the Liszt Concerto No. 1 in E-flat Major that three days later a telecast of that concert drew an avalanche of mail from all over the country.

Watts's next performance, totally unplanned, proved to be the event that launched his career. On very short notice, an indisposed Glenn Gould canceled two concerts with the NYPO, and Bernstein called upon the young, unknown Watts as replacement. Short on repertoire, Watts again played the Liszt Concerto No. 1, giving a virtuosic, charismatic performance (31 Jan 1963) that elicited 15 minutes of applause and cheers from both audience and orchestra members. André Watts was, in every sense of the term, an overnight sensation. Bombarded with offers to perform, he might have played dozens of concerts that first year; but fortunately he had an intelligent mother to protect both his youth and his musical precocity.

Separated from her husband about the time Watts was 11 years old, and eventually divorced, Mrs. Watts had sole charge of her son's upbringing. Refusing most of the proferred engagements, she signed a contract with Columbia Artists Management that guaranteed her son $10,000 a year plus all concert expenses. The first year under contract he played only about six concerts, the next year about 12, then 15, a number that doubled for the 1966–67 season. His mother may have been his sharpest critic and a strict taskmaster when it came to his music, but she was not, says Watts, "the usual pushy stage mother," and she did all she could to compensate for what had to be an isolated, somewhat restricted childhood and youth.

Still a schoolboy when he played with Bernstein, Watts finished his final two years of high school with an eight-month accelerated course, and planned to continue his musical training at the Curtis Institute of Music right there in Philadelphia. But Curtis rejected his application on the grounds that he was "not Curtis material." Years later Watts recalled that members of the examining panel had intimated that "he had some talent and was a nice kid, but that the Curtis was for people who were going to make it as professional musicians. . . . It did not deter me because I didn't quite believe it. I knew I could play better than many of the people who went there." (Dawson)

Considering André Watts's remarkable career, it seems safe to assume that he has never regretted not being admitted to Curtis. Instead, at age 19 he began lessons with Leon Fleisher at the Peabody Conservatory in Baltimore. (Peabody records show Watts was registered from 1965 through 1970 and awarded his Artist Diploma in 1972.) His five or six years with Fleisher, the only teacher the adult Watts ever had, completed his formal musical training. Fleisher was obviously good for him ("Psychologically he was terrific," says

Watts, "and I owe him a lot."); and whenever Watts talks about his career, he invariably mentions how grateful he is for what he learned from Fleisher. Almost every Watts interview and article contains some quotes about Fleisher.

For Years Watts had been following a strict regime of practice and preparation and had already experienced the pressures of performing before the public. When he began lessons with Fleisher, his main problem was nervousness, not technique. Fleisher's more musical, not so rigid approach was just what Watts needed. And his advice that Watts did not have to practice all the time was, said Watts, "very freeing. It enhanced the creativity, made me breathe more. And therefore the music could breathe." (Levine)

Fleisher shared with Watts his own concert experiences and his practical knowledge of concertizing. More important, he was sensitive enough to be reassuring and supportive when Watts was preparing for a concert, saving criticism for other sessions. Quick to praise him, Fleisher was also quick to let him know when he played, says Watts, "like an imbecile." Watts still considers Leon Fleisher to be a great teacher. "Whenever I teach a class, I invariably bring up things I learned from him. He is responsible for so many of the things I do and the feelings I have about music. My senses were ignited by Leon." (Dawson)

There never has been any doubt about Watts's success. He started at the top and, being a tremendous audience-pleaser, he has stayed at the top. Since his smashing first appearance in 1963 with Bernstein, he has been one of the busiest pianists of his generation. Playing mostly in the United States, Europe, India, Russia, Japan and South America, he is normally on the road from nine to 10 months a year and makes from 90 to 100 (at one time an incredible 150) appearances. In 1978 he was largely responsible for organizing "A Celebration of Schubert," a tour (8 months, 24 cities, 44 concerts) of all-Schubert programs (solo, chamber, Lieder) commemorating the 150th anniversary of Schubert's death. Watts played solo recitals and also duo performances with violinist Charles Treger, cellist Denis Brott and baritone Bernard Krupsen. On 13 January 1988 he celebrated the 25th anniversary of his New York debut recital by performing three concertos (Liszt No. 1, Beethoven No. 2, Rachmaninoff No. 2) with the New York Philharmonic Orchestra, conducted by Zubin Mehta.

Being in such great demand has had its price. Inevitably, his was a restricted, disciplined kind of childhood and youth. Studies with Fleisher, courses at the Peabody Institute, daily piano practice (about 6 hours), ever increasing concert appearances, all left little time for social activities. Still, the mature André Watts depicted in myriad articles and interviews is (choosing from a wide selection) extremely sociable, articulate, intelligent, sophisticated, witty, gregarious, animated, good-humored, candid, direct, generous; a wonderful conversationalist; a man of integrity, broad culture and remarkable self-discipline. Observing Mr. Watts conducting a long, informative and delightful master class (28 April 1993) at the University of California at Santa Barbara confirmed much of the above.

He teaches master classes as his schedule permits, perhaps because he feels that teaching enriches a performer. "As a teacher I'm not in the business of just being critical. When I ask a student why he or she plays a phrase a certain way, it is out of genuine curiosity. Also, it is a learning experience for me to hear myself articulate the things I take for granted as a performer." (Edmonds)

In 1972, at age 26, André Watts became the youngest person in 200 years to receive an honorary doctorate from Yale University. Other honors include degrees from Miami University in Ohio, Albright College and the distinguished alumni award from Peabody Institute. In 1994 Watts was awarded an honorary doctorate from The Julliard School.

Since the mid-1970s he has lived on a secluded estate in Rockland County, New York; he also keeps an apartment in New York City. Away from his music, he reads, listens to recordings, plays chess, poker, perhaps tennis. The *bon vivant* André Watts also loves gourmet meals and good cigars.

Critics may complain that Watts plays only a limited Romantic repertoire, yet most will grant that within his chosen limits he frequently offers his audience "a typically Wattsian knuckle-cracker" program. For example, the first half of a 1977 recital was made up of a Schubert Impromptu and the 50-minute Schubert Sonata in D Major, D. 850; the second half consisted of Chopin's G Minor Ballade, Debussy's Children's Corner and Liszt's Don Juan Fantasy. "As encores, he unwound everyone with Liszt's *En Rêve* and then wound them back up again with Beethoven's *Chorus of Dervishes*. 'A really marvelous program,' Watts says, 'but it's the kind of recital where they come and carry you offstage on a stretcher'." (Andrews)

As to the charge that his repertoire is limited, he replies that no matter how many times he may have played a work, he still must keep working on it. "These works are better than any performer can make of them, so it's never-ending," says Watts. "You always find new things, or even with the things you already know, it becomes difficult to put them together successfully. I mean, it can be a very successful concert but in a private sense of success, that's something else." (*NAO*, 19 Feb 1989)

Ticking off names of composers found in a large collection of Watts reviews establishes that all through his career he has concentrated on works by Scarlatti, Mozart, Haydn, Beethoven, Schubert, Liszt, Chopin, Brahms, Debussy, Ravel and Rachmaninoff. Not many contemporary composers appear there, simply because Watts has little feeling for 20th-century music; and, as he says, "I won't play anything that I don't know fully, admire unqualifiedly and believe in wholeheartedly." Watts, who will at the last minute remove a work from an already announced program if he feels that he is not wholly prepared to play it, has consistently followed those criteria.

Watts has a prodigious technique. Although endowed with an innate facility and large hands capable of spanning a twelfth, he has never counted solely on those gifts. Behind his dazzling technical displays lay years of steady, persistent practice: about six hours a day, usually three hours at a sitting interrupted by brief breaks during which he walks about, smoking a cigar and still practicing mentally. Since his own busy concert schedule allows few opportunities to hear other pianists in live performance, he listens to recordings of works he is preparing. For him, it is most helpful, not harmful.

André Watts wants his playing to be fluid, electric and alive. It is all of that. Reviews and interviews (there must be hundreds, beginning in 1963, the year he rocketed into the concert world, and continuing right up to 1995) depict an exciting pianist, a big Romantic pianist with a grand style, a powerful technique and, most of all, charisma. Call it what you will, critics never tire of expounding on the personal kind of excitement—infectious, joyous, emotional—that Watts generates at the piano. And audiences obviously love his playing. He often plays to a packed house, even overflowing onto the stage and into the orchestra pit. For one thing, Watts creates excitement because, like that older generation of Romantic pianists he so admires, he is not afraid to take chances, not afraid of missing a note here and there. "I don't believe hitting the right notes makes you a good pianist," Watts tells interviewers. "If I know I can get the effect I want and miss a few notes along the way, I'll go for the effect."

Beyond that, Watts's enormous drawing power must emanate from his own great love for music—and for the piano. "I'm totally freaked out on music," he says. "At a performance, I open up my chest and put my guts out on the piano and let the public see what I'm really made of. No one will ever get to know me better than by listening to me play." (Andrews) He is most contented and happy when he is playing, and if away from the piano for any length of time, he gets restless.

André Watts has given hundreds of performances. Acquiring reviews of his playing is easy; however, the reviews are so numerous and so varied that making an overall assessment of how he plays becomes far more difficult. Possessed with the bravura flair and assured technique required for playing Liszt, he remains one of his generation's most convincing Liszt performers. He usually gets very good notices for his Ravel performances, not quite as uniformly good for his Beethoven. Watts is no stranger to adverse criticism. Some critics find that he often gets carried away by his emotions and, in truth, excitability has at times been one of the most controversial aspects of his playing. Other critics contend that by staying with his limited repertoire, he has not lived up to the potential hinted at earlier in his career. And some complain of his mannerisms, the way he swoops low over the keyboard, arms flailing; the way he hums aloud. As with all concert performers, Watts comes off a nearly perfect pianist in some reviews, and as a less than satisfying pianist in others.

In view of the fact that the way Watts plays the romantic works of Liszt and Rachmaninoff usually delights reviewers, possibly comparing critiques of some of his other performances (Mozart, Schubert, Brahms) at different stages of his career will better reveal his musical style and development.

For example, a review of a youthful Watts performing (7 March 1968) the Mozart Concerto in D Major, K. 491, with Zubin Mehta conducting the Los Angeles Philharmonic Orchestra, reports that he seemed "uncomfortable in the delicate idiom." In the first two movements "the line refused to flow with consistency of articulation, the playing was patchy, the stylistic perspective unclear." (*LAT*, 9 March 1968) Some 10 years later his Los Angeles performance (5 Nov 1979) of Mozart's Rondo in A Minor, K. 511, showed "some pliable phrasing, a singing tone and an interpretation sympathetic to the melancholic undercurrent that gives the work its profile. Missing were a degree of crispness and a basically Classic attitude." (*LAT*, 7 Nov 1979)

Watts's New York performance (11 Aug 1987) of the Mozart Concerto in C Minor, K. 491, with George Cleve conducting the Mostly Mozart Festival Orchestra, earned deserved praise: "Mr. Watts has a Mozart style that works, musically. . . . On its own terms, and especially in this concerto, it makes sense. Mr. Watts knows how to shape a Mozartean phrase and accent a Mozartean run; he hints at a more thunderous pianistic power just beneath the surface, but he doesn't overburden the idiom." (*NYT*, 13 Aug 1987)

Watts's Mozart kept on improving. When he played (26 June 1991) the Concerto in E-flat Major, K. 271, in Washington, D.C., with the Mostly Mozart Festival Orchestra under Gerard Schwarz, "Perfect trills grew into glorious phrases, bringing out the inner voices in the music with surprising candor. This was not a particularly polite reading: With so many dainty keyboard purists becoming popular these days, it was a welcome gift to hear such full-blooded virtuosity in this Mozart concerto." (*WT*, 28 June 1991)

Watts usually earns good notices for his Brahms playing. A review of an early performance (18 Jan 1968) of the Brahms Concerto No. 2 in B-flat Major with Leonard Bernstein and the New York Philharmonic Orchestra reads: "Technique goes hand in hand with music. . . . There were subtle ritards, dynamic contrasts, rubatos, and all these were aimed at an emotional heightening of the music. . . . The big point was that these expressive devices did not sound calculated as Mr. Watts used them. They were natural, a part of his normal musical thinking, and they made the Brahms sound much more pianistic than usual." (*NYT*, 19 Jan 1968)

Two decades later a London performance (18 Nov 1988) of that same concerto with the Hallé Orchestra, Stanislaw Skrowaczewski conducting, was striking from the start because of the easy power of Watts's playing. "He never for a moment had to bang the keys to convey the epic strength of Brahms's crowded piano writing; its lyricism was allowed to expand naturally without technical problems ever being allowed to intrude. Big-boned as his performance was, he was able to scale his tone down without losing intensity in the hushed pianissimos of the Andante, before the finale brought an ideal sparkle and lightness, surprising when until then weight of expression had been Watts's watchword." (© *The Guardian*, 21 Nov 1988. Reprinted by permission.)

The Watts reviews show that his interpretations have been controversial. Playing only Schubert works on the first half of a San Francisco program (26 July 1976), Watts's readings were "pianistically impressive but not musically convincing. . . . In a word, his interpretations were watery. The music slipped through the fingers. . . . It wanted concern for detail, and while Watts encompassed it all, the finer elements were all fluent, as if enameled over. . . . Perhaps for Schubert, total pianistic command can tempt a pianist too far." (*SFC*, 28 July 1976) And in Washington, D.C., his performance (5 March 1977) of Schubert's Sonata in G Major, D. 894, was still uneven. "The large sections must balance; otherwise, a certain amount of boredom soon sets in. That's what happened. It had its moments of sheer loveliness, but, by and large,

Watts's reading could not stand up against those of pianists such as Brendel and Badura-Skoda." (*WS*, 7 March 1977)

But Watts's Los Angeles performance (18 April 1977) of this same Schubert Sonata (D. 894) was "a miracle. This was lieder singing on the piano. . . . It was a matter of total involvement, emotionally and pianistically. The poignant melodies sang with an inexhaustible variety of nuance, the dramatic accents were like stabs of pain. But there was charm, too, in the rippling passage work, in the subtle Viennese lilt of the rhythm. It was unalloyed Schubert, but it also was personal and intimate—a gigantic step forward for Watts." (*LAT*, 20 April 1977) And much more recently we have a Dallas, Texas, review subtitled "The pianist climbs to the highest level with his Schubert." In Watts's performance (4 Dec 1990) of Schubert's Fantasy in C Major ("Wanderer"), "there were brilliant, agile octaves, dazzling cascades of arpeggios, thundering chords; and, if my ears can be trusted, not a note out of place. . . . I basked in this magnificent technical mechanism at work and sat awestruck at the excitement of the ideas and the security with which they were being expressed." (*DMN*, 6 Dec 1990)

There are not too many examples of devastatingly bad reviews. A Philadelphia critic first complained about Watts's "extraordinarily narrow and unadventurous" program (12 Nov 1989), then reported that Watts's interpretation of Chopin's B-Minor Sonata "came out all surface and effect: heavy of accent and flourish, but weak of pulse and incompletely coherent—at times even sloppy." Watts did better with the Rachmaninoff Variations on a Theme of Corelli, yet went "almost out of control wherever there was an opportunity for pianistic display." (*PI*, 13 Nov 1989)

Dozens of excellent reviews counterbalance the poor notices. From a review of a Dallas recital (2 Oct 1989): "He was not in immaculate form, but his wrong notes are more interesting than the right ones from most pianists. . . . He is a virtuoso in the grand sense of the word, one who brings great fantasy, line and depth to the music he plays. He possesses a remarkable feeling for the proportions and sonorities of music, and if there is a better and more complete American pianist about, he has escaped my attention." (*DMN*, 4 Oct 1989)

And there is this glowing summation of Watts's playing from an enthralled London critic who heard him play the Brahms Concerto No. 2 with Simon Rattle and the City of Birmingham Symphony Orchestra on 19 February 1987. "This wonderful American pianist possesses a charismatic force and presence, a combination of electrifying bravura and a listening tonal resource that can make even the most hardened listener—particularly pianists—gasp in awe and envy. He is a born performer elucidating the text with a mischievous, improvisatory freedom that nonchalantly scorns convention, is worlds apart from academic notions of correctness expressed in . . . bleak, unvaried sonority." (*MM*, June 1987)

Watts's discography is surprisingly small, seemingly through no lack of desire on his part. He prefers live recordings and disapproves of extensive splicing, a procedure not uncommon in recording procedure. "I particularly dislike splicing that creates fraud. I'm not bothered by fixing one or two wrong notes, but to splice to the point where the recording is made by the editing rather than by the performer is wrong. It then becomes a record of the work of the engineer in the studio rather than of the artist." (Edmonds)

When Watts's contract with CBS was up for renewal, he chose instead to go with Sony. There were extenuating circumstances. At least one Columbia executive expressed the thought "that Watts somehow comes through less excitingly on records than in the concert hall." Watts, on his part, wanted to record live performances, which CBS was loathe to do.

His recorded recital of Schubert's works (see Discog.) faces serious competition with the recordings of other Schubert stylists—Kempff, Richter, Brendel and others. Watts fares best in lyrically romantic movements, for example, the slow movements of the Sonata in A Major (D. 664) and the Wanderer Fantasy. However, "the sonata opening movement is uncommitted and needs something more, while the *Wanderer* opening needs a grab-you-in-the-throat quality." (*ARG*, May/June 1993)

Watts's two Liszt albums were his first in a decade (see Discog.). Originally issued on LP in 1986, they substantiate his talent for that composer's keyboard music. His readings are outstanding. In the Sonata in B Minor, Watts "gets inside the music better than anyone after Arrau. He has more tonal warmth than anyone since Arrau. He makes the piano sing. . . . *Un Sospiro* really sighs here. . . . The Hungarian Rhapsody [No. 13] is not one of the most-played ones, and Watts is quite thrilling." (*ARG*, Jan/Feb 1993) And from another critic: "Though some listeners will prefer a more explicitly personal approach to these Liszt works, the performances are highly satisfactory all the same, and André Watts's playing has never sounded so good on record." (*HF*, Dec 1986)

His recording of three Beethoven Sonatas (see Discog.) is sure to elicit comparisons with the literally dozens of other interpretations available. For one reviewer, "These thoughtful and serious performances, played with conviction and commanding technique, give much pleasure even as they leave room for further depth and authority. . . . In the Sonata in E-flat, op. 27, no. 1, Watts's suave, poised performance catches the transitional classico-romantic mood . . . [and he] finds a comfortable middle ground between form and fantasy in the 'Moonlight' Sonata as well." Watts's "passionate and purposeful performance [of the "*Appassionata*," op. 57], combines eloquence and grace with the romantic temperament." (*Fan*, March/April 1988) However, in true fashion, another listener finds more to criticize, feeling that in the op. 27, no. 1, Watts's "artistry encompasses everything except charm and a melodic, singing quality. . . . Watts should rethink his tonal balance in bringing out melody." The "*Appassionata*" was finely achieved, but the "Moonlight" Sonata is less successful: "The introductory bars . . . present a mood; but when the soprano melody enters, Watts whispers it so softly that there is no theme." (*CL*, Nov 1989)

Watts has recorded both Chopin concertos and a recital of solo pieces (see Discog.). The latter has one ballade, one sonata and a group of nocturnes and etudes. Two starkly opposing reviews of the solo disc are food for thought—and totally confusing! One critic finds the Etude, op. 25, no. 1 "stiff and uninteresting," parts of the Sonata in B-flat Minor "snarling and vehement," and the Ballade in G Minor "shallow and ordinary." (*ARG*, Nov/Dec 1992) For another reviewer this very same CD is "a release that enhances the composer's discography as significantly as it does Watts's own." In the B-flat Minor Sonata, "Watts does honor to Chopin and to himself by focusing on musical substance rather than accumulated layers of romantic patina. . . . The overall feeling of solidity and substance throughout this wonderful hour is enhanced by a sonic focus almost as unusual in a Chopin recording as the kind of performance Watts gives us; nothing gossamer or unmoored here, but real flesh-and-blood sound." (*StR*, Oct 1992)

One of Watts's most successful recordings is a CD made from a live recital (6 April 1988) at Carnegie Hall (see Discog.). It contains "a quite glorious account of the Mozart F major Sonata and some treasurable playing in the other works as well." The Haydn Sonata in C Major, Hob. XVI:48, "admittedly takes a while to relax, but when it does relax, there is a delightful fluency to the phrasing and exquisite gradation in the tone. . . . There are bones one might wish to pick with the Schubert [Sonata in D Major, D. 784]. The tempestuous undertones of the first movement come prematurely to the surface and the delay for each turning figure in the *andante* becomes predictable. For me these are forgivable concomitants of the live performance situation, especially so when the understanding of Schubert's harmonic direction is so acute." (*Gram*, June 1989)

SELECTED REFERENCES

Adamo, Mark. "Watt's incidental achievement." *Washington Post*, 16 April 1993, sec. B, pp. 1, 5.

Alexander, Victor. "André Watts: The High Voltage Pianist." *FM Guide*, June 1968, pp. 4–8.

Andrews, Peter. "Totally Freaked Out on Music." *Horizon*, Dec 1977, pp. 10–16.

Bredemann, Dan, with Gloria Ackerman. "The Point Is To Make Music." (interview) *Piano Quarterly*, Spring 1973, pp. 12–15.

"Classical Music Prodigy Turns 40." *Ebony*, April 1987, pp. 44–46, 50.

Conaway, James. "I'm Doing All Right, I'm Never Good Enough, But I'm Not Standing Still." *New York Times Magazine*, 19 Sept 1971, pp. 14–17, 22–24.

Dawson, Jack. "Concert pianist André Watts: an international success." *Baltimore Sun*, 14 Feb 1984, sec. C, p. 1.

Edmonds, Arlene Hamilton. "The Romantic Bent of André Watts." *Music Magazine*, Sept/Oct 1985, pp. 16–18.

Gaines, James R. "André Watts." *People*, 26 June 1978, pp. 48–50, 55.

Henahan, Donal. "Watts Emerging As Major Pianist." *New York Times*, 25 Jan 1968, p. 32.

Hertelendy, Paul. "Star pianist strikes candid chords." *San Jose Mercury*, 28 May 1981.

Isacoff, Stuart, and Charles Passy. "A 25th Anniversary Celebration." *Keyboard Classics*, Jan/Feb 1988, pp. 4–5.

Kozinn, Allan. "André Watts." *Contemporary Keyboard*, May 1981, pp. 34–48, 66.

Kupferberg, Herbert. "André Watts." *Ovation*, June 1980, pp. 10, 30–31.

Levine, Joe. "My Lunch with André." *Johns Hopkins Magazine*, Oct 1990, pp. 17–28.
Mach, Elyse. "André Watts: The Early Years." *Clavier*, Oct 1989, pp. 10–14.
Massaquoi, Hans J. "André Watts." *Ebony*, May 1969, pp. 91, 94, 96, 98.
Montparker, Carol. "André Watts Celebrates 25th Anniversary of Debut." *Clavier*, March 1988, p. 8.
Morrison, Bryce. "André Watts." *Music and Musicians*, Feb 1987, pp. 32–33.
Nagy, Christine A. "Aristocrat of Virtuosos: André Watts." *Clavier*, Dec 1979, pp. 12–19.
O'Connor, John J. "Piano Rarity: André Watts' Success." *Wall Street Journal*, 26 Nov 1968, p. 20.
Russell, Frank. "André Watts Interview." *Piano Quarterly*, Fall 1966, pp. 17–20.
Zailian, Marian. "A Genius Who Eschews the Title of Prodigy." *San Francisco Chronicle*, 4 Sept 1983, pp. 17–18.
See also Bibliography: Cur/Bio (1968); Dub/Ref; Ewe/Mu; Jac/Rev; Kol/Que; Mac/Gre; New/GrA; Noy/Pia.

SELECTED REVIEWS

BG: 19 Oct 1987; 18 July 1994. *CE*: 9 June 1990. *CPD*: 11 Oct 1988; 15 April 1991. *CST*: 1 May 1989; 6 April 1992. *CT*: 2 Dec 1985; 8 Oct 1987; 25 July 1993; 11 April 1995. *DMN*: 4 Oct 1989; 6 Dec 1990. *GM*: 21 Nov 1988. *IS*: 27 Oct 1980. *LAT*: 31 Aug 1963; 9 March 1968; 13 May 1969; 20 April 1977; 7 Nov 1979; 12 May 1981; 22 March 1988; 29 April 1993; 6 Aug 1994. *MiT*: 22 Jan 1993. *MM*: June 1987. *NAO*: 28 Feb 1989. *NewY*: 19 Oct 1992. *NY*: 5 Nov 1966. *NYT*: 2 Feb 1963; 10 July 1963; 27 Oct 1966; 19 Jan 1968; 16 Jan 1969; 9 March 1970; 26 Feb 1971; 24 Feb 1985; 13 Aug 1987; 15 Jan 1988; 5 Oct 1992; 9 May 1994. *PEB*: 5 Feb 1975. *PI* : 13 Nov 1989. *PP*: 13 May 1979. *SFC*: 28 July 1976; 10 Feb 1978; 2 April 1992. *SFE*: 19 April 1990. *SJM*: 17 July 1991; 31 Jan 1992. *S-L*: 8 May 1978; 8 Jan 1990. *TL*: 13 June 1966; 5 Nov 1969; 11 Feb 1977; 24 June 1986; 12 Nov 1993. *WP*: 6 April 1992; 12 April 1993; 29 Jan 1994. *WS*: 7 March 1977. *WT*: 28 June 1991; 11 April 1993.

SELECTED DISCOGRAPHY

André Watts at Carnegie Hall. Haydn: Sonata in C Major, Hob. XVI:48. Mozart: Sonata in F Major, K. 332. Schubert: Sonata in A Minor, D. 784. Brahms: *Klavierstücke*, op. 119. EMI Classics CDM 64598-2.
André Watts plays Liszt, Album 1. Six Grand Etudes after Paganini; Hungarian Rhapsody No. 13 in A Minor; *Les Jeux d'eau à la Villa d'Este*; *Au Lac de Wallenstadt*; *Il Penseroso*. Angel CDC 7 47380-2.
André Watts plays Liszt, Album 2. *Bagatelle ohne Tonart*; *En Rêve*; *Nuages gris*; *Schlaflos*; Sonata in B Minor; *Un Sospiro*; Transcendental Etude No. 10; *Valse oubliée*. Angel CDC-47381.

Beethoven: Sonata in E-flat Major, op. 27, no. 1; Sonata in C-sharp Minor, op. 27, no. 2; Sonata in F Minor, op. 57. EMI Classics CDM-64600 (CD).

Chopin: Concerto No. 1 in E Minor, op. 11; Concerto No. 2 in F Minor, op. 21. Sony Classical SBK 46336. Schippers/NYPO.

The Chopin Recital. Ballade in G Minor, op. 23; Etudes, op. 10, nos. 9 and 12; op. 25, nos. 1 and 7; Nocturnes, op. 27, no. 1; op. 48, no. 1; Sonata in B-flat Minor, op. 35. EMI 54151 (CD).

Liszt: Concerto No. 1 in E-flat Major. Sony Classical SMK 47571 (CD). Bernstein/NYPO. The Royal Edition (No. 43 of 100).

The Schubert Recital. Impromptu in B-flat Major, D. 935, no. 1; *Klavierstück*, D. 946; Sonata in A Major, D. 664; "Wanderer" Fantasy, D. 760. EMI CDC 54153.

VIDEO

André Watts in Concert. Beethoven: Sonata in C-sharp Minor, op. 27, no. 2. Chopin: Etudes, op. 25, nos. 1 and 12; Sonata No. 2 in B-flat Minor, op. 35. Debussy: *La plus que lente*; *Danse*; *L'Isle joyeuse.* Gershwin: Three Preludes. Liszt: Transcendental Etude No. 10. MacDowell: *Moto perpetuo.* Scarlatti: Sonata in A Major, K. 345; Sonata in D Minor, K. 422. Bel Canto 12708. Taped live from a "Great Performers At Lincoln Center" recital on 20 February 1985.

WEISSENBERG, ALEXIS SIGISMUND: b. Sofia, Bulgaria, 26 July 1929.

> Alexis Weissenberg has been as liberated in his life and career as in his dynamic, idiosyncratic performances.
>
> *Current Biography* (1978)

Liberated! Idiosyncratic! How perfectly both suit Alexis Weissenberg's uncommon career and his stubbornly individual way of playing the piano. An only child, he was raised by his mother after his parents Paul and Lillian (Piha) Weissenberg divorced. His mother, a pianist, often took him to concerts; and she may have started his piano lessons as early as age three, for Weissenberg remembers playing a little by age four and not finding it difficult. At age five he began composition and piano lessons with the Bulgarian composer-pianist Pantcho Vladigerov in Sofia. Three years later he gave his first public concert.

In 1944, having spent nine months in a prison camp, Weissenberg and his mother escaped into Turkey and made their way to Palestine (now Israel). Living in Tel Aviv, he studied piano with Leo Kestenberg, gave a recital, played often with the Palestine Symphony Orchestra and made a tour of South Africa. After the war, the 17-year-old Weissenberg traveled alone to the United States, fortified with letters of introduction to Artur Schnabel and Vladimir Horowitz. He approached only Schnabel, who reportedly told him that he had "nothing to learn, but something to develop."

Weissenberg studied piano with Olga Samaroff at Juilliard and had some lessons with Artur Schnabel and Wanda Landowska. According to Juilliard records, "Sigi" (his youthful nickname) Weissenberg enrolled in the diploma piano course for the academic year 1947–48 and formally withdrew on 3 April 1948. According to contemporary newspaper reports, his professional career began almost immediately. As winner of a youth contest sponsored by the Philadelphia Orchestra, he performed (12 Nov 1947) the Rachmaninoff Concerto No. 3 in D Minor, op. 30, with that orchestra, conducted by Eugene Ormandy. He also won the eighth annual Edgar M. Leventritt Award, and consequently played (28 Feb 1948) the Chopin Concerto in E Minor with the New York Philharmonic-Symphony Orchestra, conducted by George Szell. His career launched, Weissenberg toured intensely that year (more than 50 appearances, including 25 with orchestra) in Mexico, Central America and South America; and he made his American recital debut on 6 October 1948 at Town Hall.

Eight years on the concert circuit ended with a disillusioned Weissenberg facing the fact that his career had stalled. Invitations to play in the important cities and with major orchestras had dwindled, and for the most part he was endlessly repeating the same program at community concerts in backwater towns. Although he blamed poor management, there had also been poor reviews. There never was any doubt that Weissenberg has a marvelous technique. It was his ideas about interpretation that "could leave one stunned. There was so much pulling-about, so much distortion of phrase, that one felt like screaming. So much talent, such a waste!" (*NYT*, 4 Dec 1970) In 1955 Weissenberg discussed his unhappy situation with some well-known conductors (Ormandy, Szell, Steinberg, Bernstein), but nothing came of it. And when he threatened to stop playing unless he had better engagements, his manager told him there would be no problem replacing him.

It was then that Weissenberg gave up the concert stage, and early in 1957 he left for Europe. He had a small family allowance to live on and made additional income designing Christmas cards. (A talented artist, Weissenberg is well known for his comical caricatures of famous artists and musicians.) He spent most of this sabbatical in Paris, thinking over "things I had done well, things I could do so much better, and things I would never do again." (Hemmings) He played a small number of concerts each year, but mostly occupied his time analyzing scores, reading about music and musicians, studying literature and philosophy and reappraising his musical attitudes. A naturalized French citizen, he still makes his home in Paris.

Weissenberg gradually returned to the international concert stage, billed now as Alexis Weissenberg, no longer "Sigi." He gave a concert in Paris; there is a record of a recital he played in Florence, Italy, on 20 February 1965; in 1966 Swedish television filmed his performance of Stravinsky's Three Movements from Petroushka. And Herbert von Karajan's invitation to play the Tchaikovsky Concerto No. 1 in B-flat Minor—at the opening concert of the Berlin Philharmonic Orchestra's 1966–67 season—opened the door to a second virtuoso career. Engaged as replacement when Arturo Benedetti Michelangeli canceled some appearances with the New York Philharmonic Orchestra, Weissenberg's "triumphal" performance (16 Feb 1967) of the Rachmaninoff Concerto No. 3 in D Minor, with Alfred Wallenstein conducting, reestablished his name in America. He usually plays from 80 to 90 performances a season and has had great success in Europe (France, Holland, Belgium, Austria, Switzerland, Poland, Hungary), the United States and Japan.

A very private man, Weissenberg discloses only bare essentials concerning his personal life, his daughters and the son born of a longtime second relationship. Urbane, intelligent and analytical, he is fluent in several languages and has wide-ranging interests. A born mimic, he creates devastatingly exaggerated impressions of friends and colleagues. He enjoys playing jazz because the fantastic harmonic possibilities fascinate him. Although he says he loves teaching and will hear aspiring young artists play, he does not teach, except for master classes, because he believes that it is impossible to be both a concert performer and a teacher.

Alexis Weissenberg, say some writers, has an eclectic repertoire ranging from Bach to Bartók, from Brahms to Stravinsky. Yet he is often accused of playing the same works over and over again. A batch of Weissenberg programs dating from the late 1940s into the 1990s shows that works by Bach and Rachmaninoff clearly predominate; that he plays a good deal of Schumann and Chopin; and that he also plays, less frequently but in more or less equal portions, works by Haydn, Liszt, Franck, Debussy, Ravel, Brahms and Stravinsky.

Weissenberg defends his repeatedly programming the same works on the grounds that there are some works an artist loves so dearly he is compelled to play them all his life, and that after many interpretative transitions these works become a definitive part of his imagination. "A great musician," says Weissenberg, "is a re-creator who takes a composer's effort and gives it new life with each performance." (*GRP*, 8 Feb 1975)

The prodigally gifted Weissenberg seems to require only about two-and-a-half hours of daily practice, and it is largely a matter of concentration. He first studies a new score away from the piano, assimilating it thoroughly before beginning the technical work at the keyboard. He prepares every work he performs, whether a three-minute piece or a 50-minute concerto, so that it is completely in his mind as a logical, unified whole. As he puts it, "Before an artist can walk out on the platform to perform it, he must have such an intimate idea of the piece's architecture that he can feel the space between the very first note and the last one." (Kozinn, "Outspoken Piano Virtuoso")

Critical reviews covering each decade of Weissenberg's nearly half-century of public performance corroborate his highly personal views on how to play the piano. In support of those views, Weissenberg argues that if music is not to remain in a museum, an interpreter must speak in a language that today's people understand, that just as the modern actor no longer performs in the old-fashioned style of the 1920s, the pianist must likewise develop a modern language and style. It baffles him that the public accepts contemporary changes in art, literature and drama, yet expects to hear the same musical interpretations it has heard for decades.

The Weissenberg reviews also prove, incontestably, that because of his convictions, "controversy seems to hound his every appearance." (Gruen) And it is true that the way Weissenberg plays the piano has always drawn a strong reaction. Critics unstintingly praise his technique ("stunning," "amazing," "unequaled,"); but right from the start of his career, reviewers have also consistently criticized Weissenberg for frequently playing too fast, sometimes overpedaling and, most noticeably, for his lack of interpretative skills. Those who dislike his playing employ these words (all found in the reviews): "enigmatic," "quirky," "wrong-headed," "distorted," "austere," "cold," "calculated," "uneven," "relentless," "unemotional." Some even go so far as to complain about Weissenberg's stage presence. Unsmiling and restrained, he sits like a statue, say his detractors, and they find it not only unfriendly but disturbing.

Positive criticism, equally consistent throughout his career, singles out Weissenberg's natural affinity for his instrument and his musical originality, a subject apparently often occupying the thoughts of this pianist. For example, "I don't think there is anything duller than careful playing. You've got to take risks to be original." (Cur/Bio, 1978, see Bibliog.) And this: "The first thing I expect of an artist is originality—a viewpoint from a totally different angle." Indeed, "original" is one of the most visible adjectives—along with "exciting," "powerful," "stimulating"—spotted in the Weissenberg reviews. A concise evaluation of Weissenberg's playing reads: "No other pianist so consistently challenges me to think through and reevaluate familiar repertory. My feelings about the music might in the end differ from his, but every Weissenberg recital is made memorable by the intellectual demands it makes." (Jenkins)

Whatever the response to his playing, Weissenberg, ever faithful to his convictions, has never really changed his approach to playing the piano. Now and again, especially immediately after his long sabbatical, a critic detected a new direction in Weissenberg's playing. For example, a review of a New York recital (2 Dec 1970) states that the way he played the slow movement of the Chopin B Minor Sonata revealed "a degree of poetry and tonal nuance that showed the direction in which he is heading. Here, for once, imagination was coupled to Mr. Weissenberg's infinite pianistic resource." (NYT, 4 Dec 1970)

But essentially almost all of the reviews, in any decade, invariably offer a mixed appraisal, mixed in the sense that Weissenberg is on the one hand lauded for his great individuality, taste, intelligence and, in almost every instance, for his phenomenal technical facility; and, on the other hand, he is invariably scolded because his playing is cold and without interpretative depth. Mixed reviews prevail, and there are more blistering critical assaults on Weissenberg's playing than there are all-out rave reviews, all of which makes a general assessment of his playing difficult to achieve. Excerpts from the above-mentioned reviews may help to decide exactly how Alexis Weissenberg ranks among modern pianists.

A review of his first American recital (6 Oct 1948), played at Town Hall when he was only 19 years old, looks like a model for many to come. His dazzling technique and incredibly fast playing grabbed the headlines. And, "the young man immediately and consistently displayed a sensitivity for textures, which he projected through a dynamic range from thundering fortissimo to the sweetest of whispers. . . . One's reservations mostly concern Mr. Weissenberg's introspective passages." (*NYT*, 7 Oct 1948)

Lukewarm criticism reemerged in a review of Weissenberg's first New York recital (1 Nov 1967) after his 10-year sabbatical. "He still plays the piano as if he had been born for that alone. . . . He is primarily a romanticist, who deals very personally with the music at hand. . . . [After] a virtuoso performance of Bach's Chromatic Fantasy and Fugue, full of dashing brilliance and rich sonorities, he turned to . . . Schumann's Fantasy. The pianist's playing of the opening movement went quite beautifully, despite some unorthodox and not always persuasive shifts in tempo. . . . When Mr. Weissenberg turned to five Chopin nocturnes after the intermission he was at his best. These relatively short, moody pieces . . . afforded some extraordinarily poetic playing. . . . The pianist ended the recital with Stravinsky's 'Petruchka'. . . . Mr. Weissenberg did not care how many wrong notes he hit, but the performance was hair-raising for its sheer animal excitement and physical dexterity." (© *The New York Times Company*, 2 Nov 1967. Reprinted by permission.)

At his first Los Angeles recital (8 April 1973), Weissenberg's massive technical equipment overwhelmed one reviewer. Nevertheless, he was "never once moved nor stirred. . . . It is unarguable that Weissenberg is a formidable technician. . . . But all the furioso generally fails to generate the expected excitement, possibly because he is a dead-pan type of performer who takes everything so easily." (*LAT*, 10 April 1973)

In Minneapolis (18 Nov 1975), "though his approach was certainly questionable . . . Weissenberg made an impressive essay of the Bach Goldberg Variations. It was impressive in being yet another display of Weissenberg's extraordinary technique and accuracy. . . . However, the performance was also austere, humorless, overly rhetorical and, for the most part, lacking variety as to dynamics and touch." (*MiT*, 20 Nov 1975)

Reviewers sympathetic to Weissenberg's approach to the piano give him very high marks. For example, his performance (26 Feb 1976) of the Brahms Concerto in B-flat Major with the Baltimore Symphony Orchestra, conducted by Lawrence Foster, revealed a master pianist of magnificently controlled temperament, "a musician whose interpretive vistas are exalted. . . . Everything is clear and lucid; everything seems articulated to perfection. . . . There is a provocative grandeur in his playing. It is certainly expressive . . . without the slightest hint of sentimentality. It seems calculated, yet it is never impersonal. Weissenberg is an artist of individuality." (*BaS*, 27 Feb 1976)

And there is this rave review of a Los Angeles recital (26 Nov 1977), written by a critic delighted because of the size, beauty and pungency of the sound Weissenberg produced at the instrument. He played Harold Bauer's seldom-heard transcription of César Franck's Prelude, Fugue and Variation in B minor, "to stunning effect." In the Schumann *Davidsbündlertänze*, he "defined every whim, colored every mood, and integrated all the disparate parts. . . . The group of Chopin Nocturnes . . . showed the controversial side of this pianist's nature: They emerged highly individual, unorthodox, even willful. Yet they engaged the interest in every moment." (*LAT*, 29 Nov 1977)

A review of a Carnegie Hall recital (23 Feb 1988) begins, "Alexis Weissenberg is a continuing enigma. Few pianists can play with his staggering facility, but even fewer give such maddeningly uneven performances on a regular basis. . . . The low point was reached in a hurried and shallow reading of Chopin's Sonata in B minor, which Mr. Weissenberg seemed eager to be done with." And in his reading of Ravel's *Valses nobles et sentimentales*, the pianist gave "a performance that did not waltz, gave little hint of nobility and conveyed as much sentiment as a sausage machine." (*NYT*, 26 Feb 1988)

Even more recent—and much more typical—is this critique of Weissenberg's performance (22 April 1991) of the Beethoven Concerto No. 4 with the Seattle Symphony Orchestra, Gerard Schwarz conducting. "What an elegant pianist he is. Weissenberg's playing can sound subtle and velvety or crisp and incisive, and he tosses off long chromatic-scale passages of perfect clarity and evenness. What you don't get is a sense of any passionate response to the music; this is playing that engages the intellect and the senses, but rarely the heart." (*ST*, 23 April 1991)

Weissenberg's somewhat extensive discography has been subjected to the same conflicting appraisals. It should be noted that of the Weissenberg recordings listed in the 1991–92 Schwann Artist Issue, fully one-third are missing from the Spring 1995 issue of Schwann.

A CD collection of 15 Scarlatti sonatas (see Discog.) is outstanding. "Alexis Weissenberg made his reputation on repertory powerhouses, in which his combination of warmth and digital prowess served him well. How interesting to find that Scarlatti's delicacy is also within his grasp, and that he gives an aura of strength to the music that few others impart." (*OV*, March 1987).

The Chopin Sonatas Nos. 2 and 3, originally recorded in the mid-1970s, show Weissenberg "more at home in the tense, almost brutal playing that characterizes the first and last movements of both sonatas, than in the lyrical sections and movements. . . . The Third Sonata begins too swiftly. . . . It ends in a mighty swirl that is thrilling." (*Fan*, March/April 1990)

Weissenberg's 1977 recordings of all five Beethoven concertos with Herbert von Karajan and the Berlin Philharmonic Orchestra have been reissued on CD. Weissenberg plays "with his usual precision and with an even-handed control that shows off sparkling passage-work. But if he never sounds hurried or forced, neither does he sound personal, except for his consistently brilliant tone." (*OV*, April 1989) Another reviewer finds that in Concerto No. 1 and Concerto No. 2, the "slow movements are better than quick ones, and the Second Concerto better than the First, but one can't help feeling that the performers have set out to be interpretatively different in this music in a way that has not had especially fruitful results." (*Gram*, Sept 1988)

Weissenberg's recording of a Bach program (the Italian Concerto and Partitas Nos. 4 and 6) is a definite choice of one critic who compares the pianist's readings with those of Glenn Gould: "Both are among the greatest re-creative keyboard artists of our age. In their distinctive ways, both know few equals and no superiors. Mere interpretations come and go; but this level of re-creation is rare in any musical age, golden or otherwise." (*ARG*, July/Aug 1991) However, at least two critics disagree with this appraisal. One believes that the *Italian Concerto* brings out the worst in Weissenberg: "It is possible that some-one, somewhere, has galloped through the outer movements faster, but I have not heard them. . . . The cantilena of the *Andante* enters like an impatient post-man's knock on the door, and unfolds in a manner worthy of an impassioned op-eratic aria." (*Gram*, April 1990) The other unenthusiastic reviewer admires Weissenberg's clean fingerwork, but adds: "It is often washed with pedal, which results in a most curious Bach sound. The first movement of the *Italian Con-certo* . . . is played entirely within a *mezzo-forte* to *forte* dynamic. The second movement is loaded with crescendos and dimenuendos, yet the sound is nearly always percussive." (*Fan*, Sept/Oct 1991)

Some of Weissenberg's best playing is found in his *Ermitage* recital al-bum (see Discog.), but unfortunately the sound quality is poor, the material hav-ing been recorded carelessly from live concerts. The performances are excellent. "His Bach is beautifully proportioned and clearly played. . . . He is on his best behavior in the Chopin pieces, too, playing with an unassuming poetry which is not always characteristic of his work with that composer. The Brahms seems to be a heroic performance, but it is really done in by the poor sound." (*Fan*, Nov/Dec 1990)

The CD reissue of Weissenberg's recording of the Rachmaninoff Preludes, originally made in 1968–69, gets a rave notice: "He storms through the most difficult of these Preludes with power and finesse reminiscent of Rachmaninov himself, or of Richter." (*Fan*, May/June 1991)

Weissenberg's Debussy album—*Suite bergamasque*, *Estampes*, *L'Isle joyeuse*—reveals him as "a superb pianist, with a huge technique and great con-trol over tone color and pedaling. . . . At first, Weissenberg's playing seems rav-ishingly beautiful. Slowly, one gets the feeling that the effective coloristic tricks he is playing are designed more to draw attention to his talents, rather than to Debussy's music. What is missing is a firm rhythmic framework to underlay the 'Impressionistic' surface effects; eventually his performances dull the senses." (*OV*, Feb 1987)

There are other collections that deserve serious consideration and objec-tive listening: the Chopin Nocturnes (2 CDs), the Schumann Album for the Young and a coupling of Franck's Symphony in D Minor with his Symphonic Variations (see Discog.). These delightful Variations are romantically projected and stand as one of Weissenberg's most successful performances on disc.

SELECTED REFERENCES

Berger, Karen. "Alexis Weissenberg: Indefatigable Musician." *Clavier*, Oct 1982, pp. 14–18.

Gruen, John. "A Pianist Confronts the 'Blue Light' in Himself." *New York Times*, 9 Jan 1983, pp. 19, 23.

Hemming, Roy. "Alexis Weissenberg." *Stereo Review*, April 1974, pp. 75–76.

Holcman, Jan. "The Tangled Talents of Sigi Weissenberg." *Saturday Review*, 24 Sept 1960, pp. 48–49, 62–63.
Isacoff, Stuart. "Alexis Weissenberg Sounds Off." *Keyboard Classics*, March/April 1984, pp. 9–12.
Jacobson, Bernard. "Pianist's Progress." *Records and Recording*, Feb 1979, pp. 39–40.
Jenkins, Speight. "Alexis Weissenberg: The Controversial Pianist on Critics, Competitions & Conductors." *Ovation*, June 1981, pp. 14–17.
Kozinn, Allan. "Alexis Weissenberg: Outspoken Piano Virtuoso." *Contemporary Keyboard*, March 1981, pp. 22–32, 66.
————. "A Talk with . . . Alexis Weissenberg." Carnegie Hall program, Nov 1982, pp. 12, 15.
Schonberg, Harold. "Living Dangerously." *Newsweek*, 7 Nov 1977, pp. 103–104.
Weissenberg, Alexis. "Thoughts on Life, Music, and Classical Piano." (interview) *Contemporary Keyboard*, July–Aug 1976, pp. 14, 27–38.
See also Bibliography: Cur/Bio (1978); Dub/Ref; Ewe/Mu; IWWM; Jac/Rev; New/Gro; Sal/Fam; WWAM.

SELECTED REVIEWS

BaS: 27 Feb 1976; 12 Oct 1979; 23 Oct 1980. *BG*: 25 Feb 1978. *CST*: 15 Nov 1971. *CT*: 20 March 1972; 1 Aug 1974; 16 Feb 1982. *GRP*: 8 Feb 1975. *LAT*: 10 April 1973; 16 March 1976; 29 Nov 1977; 27 Feb 1982; 21 Jan 1983. *MA*: April 1957. *MH*: 2 March 1976. *MiT*: 20 Nov 1975. *NYT*: 1 March 1948; 7 Oct 1948; 19 Oct 1949; 30 Jan 1951;17 Feb 1967; 2 Nov 1967; 5 Feb 1970; 4 Dec 1970; 5 March 1973; 21 Feb 1977; 26 Oct 1977; 3 March 1980; 10 Nov 1983; 5 Nov 1985; 26 Feb 1988. *ORE*: 22 Feb 1986. *ST*: 23 April 1991. *TL*: 14 Jan 1977. *WP*: 18 Oct 1977.

SELECTED DISCOGRAPHY

Alexis Weissenberg Recital. Bach: Partita No. 4 in D Major, BWV 828. Brahms: Rhapsody in G Minor, op. 79, no. 2. Chopin: Etude in C-sharp Minor, op. 25, no. 7; Nocturnes in B Major, op. 9, no. 3, F-sharp Minor, op. 15, no. 2; D-flat Major, op. 27, no. 2, C Minor, op. 48, no. 1; C-sharp Minor, op. posth. *Ermitage* ERM 102 (CD).
Bach: Italian Concerto, BWV 971; Partita No. 4 in D Major, BWV 828; Partita No. 6 in E Minor, BWV 830. DG 423 592-2.
Bartók: Concerto No. 2 (Ormandy/PO, 1969). Rachmaninoff: Concerto No. 3 in D Minor, op. 30 (Prêtre/Chicago SO, 1967). RCA Victor 09026-61396-2.
Beethoven: Concertos (5); Bagatelle in A Minor; *Rondo a capriccio*, op. 129; Rondo in C Major, op. 51, no. 1; Variations on an Original Theme in C Minor. EMI CDM 69334/36 (3 CDs). Karajan/Berlin PO.
Brahms: Concerto No. 1 in D Minor, op. 15. Liszt: *Les Preludes*. Angel CDD-63899. Muti/Phil. Orch.

Chopin: Nocturnes, vol. 1(10); Mazurkas, op. 17, no. 4, op. 50, no. 3, op. 56, no. 3. EMI Studio CDM 7 69694-2.

Chopin: Nocturnes, vol. 2 (11). EMI Studio CDM 7 69695-2.

Chopin: Sonata No. 2 in B-flat Minor, op. 35; Sonata No. 3 in B Minor, op. 56; Polonaise-Fantasy in A-flat Major, op. 61. EMI Studio CDM 7 63158-2.

Debussy: Children's Corner; *Estampes*; *Etude No. XI pour les Arpèges composés*; *La Fille aux cheveux de lin*; *L'Isle joyeuse*; *La plus que lente*; *Suite bergamasque*. DG 415 510-2.

Franck: Symphonic Variations. Symphony in D Minor. EMI CDM-64747. Karajan/ Berlin PO.

Rachmaninoff: Preludes (complete). RCA Victor 60568-2.

Scarlatti: Sonatas in B Minor, K. 87; A Minor, K. 109; E-flat Major, K. 193; F Minor, K. 481; F Minor, K. 184; C-sharp Minor, K. 247; G Minor, K. 450; E Major, K. 20; E Major, K. 531; C Major, K. 132; E Minor, K. 233; F Major, K. 107; G Major, K. 13; G Minor, K. 8; B-flat Major, K. 544. DG 415 511-2.

Schumann: Album for the Young, op. 68. EMI Studio CDM 7 63049-2.

VIDEO

Rachmaninoff: Concerto No. 2 in C Minor, op. 18. *Deutsche Grammophon* Video 072 204-3. Karajan/Berlin PO.

Tchaikovsky: Concerto No. 1 in B-flat Minor, op. 23: Symphony No. 6 in B Minor, op. 74. *Deutsche Grammophon* Video 072 241-3. Karajan/Berlin PO.

WILD, EARL: b. Pittsburgh, Pennsylvania, 26 November 1915.

> He stands as a consummate professional in an era when polished craftsmanship is vanishing.
>
> Julian H. Kreeger (*Clavier*, March 1981)

Earl Wild has been a hardworking, no-nonsense professional for a very long time. He is American born and American trained, and most certainly America's "Great Depression" determined the course of his musical career. Were it not for that Depression, the exceptionally gifted Wild most likely would have begun a concert career while still in his teens. That was not to be. He celebrated his 14th birthday a month after the American stock market crashed in October 1929. As the Depression worsened steadily, everybody was looking for work, including young Wild, who, his parents having separated, now had to help support his mother. Only 15 years old, he was extremely lucky in finding intermittent musical jobs at radio station KDKA in Pittsburgh—a contact that would ultimately lead to his spending 30 years as a staff pianist, going from KDKA to NBC, from there to ABC.

And all through his years in radio and television, Wild also managed to give concerts, increasingly so during the 1950s and 1960s. As fate would have it, he acquired his initial fame as a concert pianist playing Gershwin's Rhapsody in Blue, causing critics to classify him as a performer of "light" music; and for years that label plus the stigma of working in commercial music cast a shadow on all Wild's successes in concerts. In 1968 he finally left studio work to concertize and teach. Ironically, a quarter-century later the controversial Wild, having outlived all his American pianist contemporaries, is now, say a good many critics, "the dean of American music."

It appears that no one else in his family was at all musical. Royland Wild, his father, worked for the Pittsburgh Steel Company; his mother Lillian kept house and cared for the four children. The Wilds did own an upright piano and an old Edison phonograph, on which they sometimes played opera overtures; and their son, only age four, amazed them ("I must have been like someone from another planet," says Wild) with his ability to pick out on the piano, playing the right notes and in the correct rhythm, the melodies he heard on the phonograph. Credit his parents for being sufficiently cognizant of his gifts to arrange piano lessons. His first teacher quickly discovered that Wild could improvise and that he had absolute pitch.

At age six he was admitted to the Pittsburgh Musical Institute, a public-school program enabling artistically gifted children to study with the music faculty of the Carnegie Institute of Technology (now Carnegie Mellon University). Wild first studied with Alice Walker, a teacher he remembers with much respect; and from age 12 until he graduated from the Institute in 1934, he was trained by Selmar Jansen, a German pianist who had studied with Eugen d'Albert and Xavier Scharwenka, both pupils of Liszt. A strict and passionate disciplinarian, Jansen would instantly dismiss the unprepared pupil, but those who practiced had his full attention.

Lessons, studies and so much practicing left Wild little free time. Indeed, all through school he kept up a round of musical activities. He tried his hand at various instruments—flute, cello, double bass, for example. Every week he rehearsed with the high-school orchestra, the Institute orchestra, the downtown YMCA orchestra and the Carnegie Tech orchestra. He also made arrangements for piano and small orchestra, which he would take around to KDKA, the local radio station, "because it was a way in. I got my first job at 13. Whenever the station needed something fancy, they would ask me to play it." (Rubin) Wild worked intermittently at KDKA, either as soloist or accompanist, until 1934, the year he graduated from the Pittsburgh Musical Institute. By the time he reached age 14, he had also played (glockenspiel, celesta) with the Pittsburgh Symphony Orchestra; and from age 17 to 21 he was the pianist for that orchestra, working under such renowned guest conductors as Otto Klemperer and Fritz Reiner.

Such varied accomplishments prove that even as a youngster Wild must have been an exceptional pianist. Not only that, he had studied good music from the age of four. It seems strange, in retrospect, that no one either in his family or in the musical world encouraged him to become a concert pianist. Wild himself may have thought about it, but he had his mother to support; and prosperity was a long time in returning to America. Exchanging his steady salary at the studio for the uncertain income of a concert career would have been a risk.

In 1934 he went to New York (partly aided by a prize from the Pittsburgh Arts Society for a song he had composed) to study ("not long but intensely") with the eminent Dutch pianist Egon Petri, a pupil of Busoni. He also had occasional lessons with Paul Doguereau, a student of Ravel. Under the care of these two "giants," as Wild calls them, he advanced rapidly. He has never forgotten that both teachers played the piano, even the most tremendous crescendos and diminuendos, in a quiet manner, very likely the same manner we see in Wild today.

Thanks to Selmer Jansen, Wild had developed a fast, accurate technique before he went to study with Petri, but he played with a high-finger articulation that produced a clear but thin, brittle tone lacking texture. After listening to Wild play a difficult piece, Petri (who had an exceptional talent for mimicking the style of other pianists) announced that he would show Wild what he sounded like. Petri reproduced Wild's sound to perfection—an absolute revelation to Wild—and showed him how he could begin to change it. "It took two weeks— that's all," Wild says, "to see what he meant and to start to feel differently about the technique and the flexibility and whatnot." (Kipnis)

Wild regularly brings up the fact that his general approach to pianism was also largely molded by Petri's personal attitude toward the great composers (only human beings, after all) and their masterworks (not to be treated as sacrosanct). If Petri is responsible for Wild's old-fashioned attitude toward textural accuracy, he is also responsible for giving Wild the mental strength to cope with the endless difficulties inevitable in a concert career and "the courage to pass through life unscathed by the barrage of trendy criticism." (Liner Notes, Chesky CD 32, see Discog.)

Apart from his teachers, Wild considers Josef Hofmann's interpretations, "always delivered with great logic and beauty," as "the biggest influence on my attitude towards gaining a fluid and flexible technique." (Harrison) He also admires the playing of Josef Lhévinne, Walter Gieseking and Artur Schnabel.

Though living in New York, Wild held on to his pianist job with the Pittsburgh Symphony until 1936. In 1937 he began working at the National Broadcasting Company, doing, as he had at KDKA, all kinds of musical odd jobs, from making arrangements for the radio program "Colonel Stoopnagle and Bud" to performing with Walter Damrosch and the NBC Symphony Orchestra. There was always variety. One week Wild was assigned to play the celesta in "The Dance of the Sugarplum Fairy" with Damrosch and the NBC Symphony Orchestra; two weeks later he again played the celesta, this time in *Iberia*, with Toscanini conducting. Sometimes he played concertos with the NBC Symphony, at other times he played solo works on various programs; or played accompaniments for famous musicians, such as Mischa Elman; and he also performed a great deal of chamber music at NBC, including the American premiere of the Shostakovich Trio in E Minor. He even at times played what he calls "boom-cha-cha, boom-cha-cha" accompaniment for operettas—not, he says, as easy as it sounds.

Wild counts his years (1937–45, but on leave for Navy duty 1942–44) as staff pianist at NBC among the most important of his life—a rich experience rarely available to concert pianists. To be working with master musicians, especially the perfectionist Toscanini, was, says Wild, "like going to a great music school and getting paid at the same time." He liked the wonderful, terrifying Toscanini, conductor of the NBC Symphony Orchestra, and Toscanini left his imprint on the young Wild. "There is within Wild an artist of uncompromising principles shaped by a lofty role model—Toscanini." (Reich, "Showman Wild . . .")

During World War II Wild served as a musician first class in the Navy. Stationed in Washington, D.C., he once again found himself performing a variety of musical jobs. He played fourth flute in the Navy Band; piano recitals at the White House; and frequently accompanied First Lady Eleanor Roosevelt on her many speaking engagements, his duty being to play the national anthem prior to her speech. He also played more than 20 piano concertos with the Navy Symphony Orchestra and sometimes, on special leave, performed at civilian concerts.

One of those civilian concerts definitely influenced Wild's career. It was Toscanini's first all-American music program (1 Nov 1942), and he asked Wild, only a few months in the Navy, to play Gershwin's Rhapsody in Blue with the NBC Symphony Orchestra. This enormously successful concert (Benny Goodman played solo clarinet) brought Wild national recognition. At the same time, however, it marked him as a Gershwin specialist for years to come, even though the "Rhapsody," which he had learned expressly for Toscanini's concert, happened to be the only Gershwin piece he knew. In demand to play Gershwin, he quickly added other Gershwin works to his repertoire, including the Concerto in F, and in the following years played Gershwin's music all over America. The downside of this instant recognition was that Wild, already dismissed by "serious" musicians and critics as a studio pianist, now suffered further discrimination as a purveyor of lightweight music.

Discharged from the Navy in 1944, Wild left NBC in 1946 to join the newly formed American Broadcasting Company, and his 22 years (1946–68) there proved another invaluable, all-encompassing musical experience. At one end of the musical spectrum, Wild for four years (1954–57) composed some highly successful musical parodies, notably burlesques of Italian opera, for comedian Sid Caesar's radio program. Working with the comedy writers (a now famous array of names including Mel Brooks, Carl Reiner, Neil Simon, Paddy Chayefsky), Wild improvised at the piano and later orchestrated the music for use on the show. At the other far end of the musical spectrum, Wild played "a wealth of chamber music" on ABC's weekly FM broadcasts. In addition, he was called upon to compose both serious and light music.

"I wasted a lot of time in those years making a living," says Wild, "but I still practiced every day. I would find a studio when I had a few hours off, and I'd work on new pieces, building a repertoire." (Robinson) Reviews show that he was also performing concerts—from 5 to 15 a season—throughout his years

at ABC. In those early years, the ever self-critical Wild often played his programs for Helen Barere, wife of pianist Simon Barere and herself a pianist, and
had great faith in her critiques. He gave his first New York recital on 30 October
1944, playing works by Haydn, Schumann, Medtner and Rachmaninoff; and he
continued to tour regularly, if not as frequently as a full-time concert artist.

Wild finally resigned (1968) his position at ABC in order to devote
himself to concertizing and teaching. Since that time he has played all over the
world (North and South America, Mexico, the Far East, Australia, New Zealand,
Europe), and now has behind him a long, colorful, immensely rewarding and,
putting aside what some critics may say, an enormously successful concert career. And he has acquired his fame making less than 40 appearances a year, because, says the plain-spoken Wild, "playing a hundred or more concerts a season
is crazy."

Concert pianist or staff pianist, Wild has always been a versatile musician—pianist, teacher, composer, conductor. During the 1960–61 season of the
Santa Fe Opera he conducted the first seven performances of *La Traviata* and also
four performances of *Gianni Schichi* (on a double bill with Igor Stravinsky conducting his *Oedipus Rex*). A composer since his teens, Wild's works range from
highly entertaining piano transcriptions of Gershwin songs to large-scale heroic
oratorios.

He is also a longtime teacher, having held positions at the Eastman
School of Music (1964), Pennsylvania State University (1964–65), Manhattan
School of Music (1982–83), Beijing Central Conservatory of Music (1983),
Toho-Gakuen Conservatory, Tokyo (1985) and The Juilliard School (1977–85).
Since 1986 he has been Artist-in-Residence at the School of Music at Ohio State
University at Columbus, where he typically takes about seven students, gives
four lectures per year and has the freedom to come and go as his performing
schedule demands.

Wild vehemently decries the goal of many new-generation precision
musicians, technically brilliant but emotionally bereft. "The beauty has been
bred out of them," Wild asserts, "by musicologists who never stop counting the
note values and rest stops long enough to hear the music." (Bosworth) "What's
important," Wild tells his students, "is to get away from the dreadful 20th century teaching methods and all the 19th century baloney. I don't talk *forte* or *piano*, I talk warmer or cooler. I don't talk crescendo or they get there too fast. I
tell them they must control emotions without thinking dynamics or tempo.
And I talk about pedal a lot, because pedal technique is terribly neglected."
(Redmond, "A truly . . .")

He tries to get students to develop a more beautiful, firm sound, along
with a feeling of structure, technical security, line and mood and a constant feeling of creation. He makes them study the music thoroughly before trying to interpret it; in other words, to have the piece in the hands before starting to think
emotionally. "Think beauty," he tells students. "As soon as you learn the
piece, stop counting. Start to think the spirit of the thing. If you feel something, do it instead of going along like a good little pupil." (Bosworth)

Like his own teacher Petri, Wild warns his students about making excessive movements at the keyboard. "If you move too much it destroys the

communication between the brain and the finger tips. You end up being a mime of the music." (Robinson) He also cautions students against singing along as one plays in the mistaken belief it will help to achieve a singing tone or legato. If the pianist sings along as he plays, says Wild, "careful listening is lost and a false security supplants what should be intense concentration on the production of tone. . . . The pianist's ear should be placed in the end of the fingers, not in the vocal chords." (Silverman)

By request, Wild has performed at the White House for six consecutive American presidents, from Herbert Hoover to Lyndon Johnson. He served as artistic director (1979–81) of the Concert Soloists of Wolf Trap (Vienna, Virginia), a resident chamber ensemble (piano, violin, cello, flute, harp, guitar) composed of seasoned performers and some of the most talented of the younger generations of musicians. In 1986 Wild received the Liszt Medal from the People's Republic of Hungary. That same year a documentary titled "Earl Wild: Wild about Liszt," filmed at Wynyard, the Marquess of Londonderry's estate in northern England, received the British Petroleum Award for best musical documentary.

Every interviewer makes much of Wild's wit, intelligence and humor, particularly his colorful, usually controversial, opinions on colleagues, composers, customs and critics. He is celebrated for his impeccable, piercing (but never mean) imitations of famous pianists at the piano. Not only that, Wild has an enormous repertoire of anecdotes, and "would make a formidable standup comedian if he were not a formidable sitdown pianist." (S-L, 20 June 1978) Underneath this marvelously colorful Earl Wild, interviewers find a wholly confident musician secure of himself and his place in history.

Earl Wild believes—an interesting concept—that "there is no difference between technique and music. In order to project music, you must have ability. So I never separate the two." (Rubin) That may come easily to Wild because, as many knowledgeable colleagues and critics agree, he possesses one of the great piano techniques of the 20th century. He is "a master of every variety of sonority from a whispered pianissimo to a majestic, but never hard or forced, fortissimo. Even the biggest chords have every note within them exquisitely clear and balanced, unlike many other pianists who play them as undifferentiated block harmony." (Fagan) Even in his late seventies, there are few who can match Wild's wondrous technique.

Reading about Wild—and there is much to absorb—one gets the feeling that he was born with a veritable cornucopia of musical assets. Besides that great technique, he has an amazing skill for taking musical dictation that enables him to immediately write down any music he hears. He is an incredible sight reader, has a natural talent for improvising and, not least, a very attractive physical stage presence.

Not relying on his innate gifts, he prepares his programs thoroughly. He practices, has always practiced, a great deal—five or six hours at home, two to three hours on tour—believing that technique has to be exercised every day "because it slips out of the fingers all too easily." Wild uses a kind of lay-away process to prepare his repertoire, that is, he studies a new work for a while, puts it aside for six or eight weeks, and returns to it with a new perspective. When he has a program ready, he will test himself with three or four home perform-ances for friends, usually 10 or 15 at a time. Although thoroughly prepared, he can still get nervous before a concert.

Wild's extensive, eclectic repertoire proves his catholic tastes in music; and it suggests that he has the ability to play any kind of music he chooses. It includes Classic, Romantic and contemporary music, fewer of the classical mas-terworks, perhaps, than that of any other pianist of his quality; and only con-temporary works that he really likes. In 1949 Wild played the world premiere of Paul Creston's Piano Concerto in Paris; on that same visit he performed Morton Gould's Concertino and Samuel Barber's Excursions on *Radio française*. In 1970 he played Marvin David Levy's Concerto, a work Wild commissioned, with Sir Georg Solti and the Chicago Symphony Orchestra. But Wild hates atonal music and dismisses the decades of the serialists as "a terrible period."

Most of the time Earl Wild plays Romantic music and is best known for his interpretations of Liszt, Rachmaninoff, Chopin and Gershwin. Playing Liszt for more than 60 years, he has made a special impact with his monumental Liszt programs. One such program, played (3 Jan 1961) in New York in honor of the 150th anniversary of Liszt's birth, included (on just the last half of the program!) the Sonata in B Minor, the Mephisto Polka and the Hungarian Rhapsody No. 4. In 1986, the centennial of Liszt's death, Wild gave a series of three recitals (Liszt the Poet, Liszt the Transcriber, Liszt the Virtuoso) at Carnegie Hall on 12, 19 and 26 February and later played them in other American cities and in England.

Many Wild programs are awesome. For example, in London he played (25 Sept 1980) not one but three "of the heavyweights which most piano recitals would include as their high point—Franck's Prelude, Chorale and Fugue, Schumann's Symphonic Studies, Ravel's *Gaspard de la nuit*, along with a Mozart sonata and, at the end, two Wagner transcriptions: Moskowski's of Isolde's *Liebestod* and Brassin's of 'The Ride of the Valkyries'." (Maycock)

It is true that Wild likes to program the showy kinds of pieces most other "serious" pianists would not touch (and many of whom could not play). And he has been criticized for his choice of repertoire. However, it is also true that Wild, an artist of great musical integrity and with a fine classical training has consistently held to a standard of excellence seldom encountered today. Without compromising his high standards, he tries to make music both mean-ingful and enjoyable for his audiences.

Much of the controversy over Wild's repertoire arises from his passion for transcriptions. He plays them a lot, confident that most of his admirers agree with him that this music is just plain fun to hear. He has even dared to play a program ("The Art of Transcription," 1 Nov 1981) consisting of nothing but transcriptions. Wild dares such programs because "he actually plays the piano incomparably better than all but a handful of today's virtuosos," and he succeeds because of "the elegance, charm, virtuosity and sheer charisma of his playing." (Fagan)

Even a critic very obviously not counting himself among those readily able to accept transcriptions ("this kind of musical processing") had to admit that at that Carnegie Hall performance (1 Nov 1981) "Mr. Wild's power and control were sensational and his five-finger technique in the Rimsky-Korsakov-Rachmaninoff 'The Flight of the Bumble Bee' was enough to make any piano student weep with frustration and envy." (*NYT*, 3 Nov 1981)

Earl Wild is an arch Romantic. His musical approach is a matter of fierce personal conviction, and any critic accusing him of having an "old-fash-ioned" approach gets a fast, sharp response. The piano recital is now in the dol-drums, according to Wild, because "certain artists haven't learned a new piece in years and years. The average audience, who are the people who *made* piano recitals, stay away now because they're not up to hearing three sonatas by one composer on a single program. They need some entertainment—the joy of pi-ano." (Reich, "Showman Wild. . .")

Wild's approach is well-rounded and takes into consideration not just the musical score but also the ideas, religion, art and literature of the era during which the music was composed. He strongly believes that music is meant to be uplifting and that so-called "profound" music all too often becomes dull. If the word "frivolous" comes to mind, it will disappear when confronted by the "sheer content of his programmes, and certainly by noting his manner of playing, which is direct and unmannered, technically of extreme sophistication but never showy or demonstrative against the spirit of the music. The point is his capac-ity for taking pleasure from serious music-making." (Maycock)

Not too long ago an interviewer accurately summed up Earl Wild as probably the greatest virtuoso pianist born and trained in America. "His musical credentials are impeccable. . . . But he has had constantly to battle prejudices against native musicians, particularly outspoken ones whose interests were wide-ranging. . . . Pianists who couldn't begin to play Wild's repertoire condescend to him because he chooses not to play theirs." (Dyer)

Prejudices die hard. And they have affected Earl Wild's reputation in se-rious music circles, but never his success with audiences. From the start of his concert career to the present, reviewers mention wildly enthusiastic audiences and, despite any prejudices, often describe Wild's playing as "patrician" and de-scribe Wild as a "musician of refined taste and of aristocratic inclinations." All the same, he has had an uphill battle obliterating the "commercial pianist" label and, perhaps more difficult, overcoming criticism of his repertoire and musical approach.

Prejudice and cynical comments appear insignificant against the many rave reviews Wild has accumulated throughout his long career. For example, "With a technique that has always rivaled Horowitz's, a strong interpretive point of view that—despite its development over the years—remains instantly recog-nizable, and a repertoire that makes most other pianists seem narrow-minded, Earl Wild stands among the greatest modern pianists, and arguably as the most distinguished American-born keyboard artist alive." (*Fan*, June 1989)

And this: "Earl Wild . . . is essentially Earl Wild. There is an underly-ing Americanism implied in his performances. Although there are huge effects, tempestuous crescendos subsiding into gentle lyricism, underneath it all he plays with a sort of good humor. It's all fun. . . . Wild has a rare pianism, a gift that is seldom found, even in this age of technical prowess. . . . Somehow, he has been able to tune in to the North American identity, which is rare in the classical idiom." (*The News*, Mexico City, 9 Jan 1991)

It is hard to find a review that does not rhapsodize over Wild's phenomenal technique. Most also agree that he is more than a technician. His performance (25 Oct 1957) of seven Liszt Transcendental Etudes and the Ravel *Gaspard de la nuit* was brilliant, particularly the Ravel. Wild's "articulation, together with the coloristic resource he maintained, made this 'Gaspard' not only a technical tour de force, but, in addition, a subtle interpretation that mirrored the shifting hues of the piece. . . . Mr. Wild gave it a performance that will live long in the memory." (*NYT*, 26 Oct 1957)

An all-Liszt program in Washington, D.C. (21 March 1971) earned these comments: "He is a true super-virtuoso, one of those rare players whose facility is of such a degree that no piece written can completely take up the slack. . . . As his recital Saturday confirmed, he is an interpreter of the first rank, one who, for example, not only fully appreciated the heroic, histrionic and dreamy sides of Liszt, but who also deeply comprehends the satanic streak that is at the heart of Liszt's genius." (*WP*, 22 March 1971)

At an all-Chopin recital (9 April 1991) at Ohio State University, Wild "set aside flamboyance for poetry . . . a sweet respite from 19th century extravagance, if not harsh 20th century realities. . . . I have heard Earl Wild play more spectacular works, music with more dazzle and bravura, literature that overwhelms by its sheer density and scope. I have never heard him play more beautifully than last night." (*CD*, 10 April 1991)

What of Wild's more unorthodox programs? His "Art of the Transcription" recital (1 April 1982) at London's Wigmore Hall met with amazement and enthusiasm. "The cheers rang to the rafters . . . as Earl Wild concluded what was surely one of the most stunning piano recitals in the entire history of the Wigmore Hall. And as seemingly millions of notes sparkled and cascaded from his extraordinary fingers, Mr. Wild gave new meaning to virtuosity." (*DT*, 3 April 1982)

Several weeks before his 77th birthday, Wild gave a Carnegie Hall recital (30 Oct 1992) that many a much younger pianist would have been horrified to undertake. The program's first half was all Rachmaninoff: the Corelli Variations, op. 42, Wild's own transcription of the Vocalise, op. 34, no. 14, and the gigantic Sonata No. 2 in B Minor, op. 36. Following the intermission he played all twelve Chopin Etudes, op. 25, and the Scherzo in B Minor, op. 20! "This has been a career devoted not to music that springs from piano playing but to music that is about piano playing. And so on Friday, music and technique mingled, almost indistinguishable from each other. One of the few musicians who actually perform the Etudes . . . to his enormous credit Mr. Wild played [them] for their musical content." (*NYT*, 3 Nov 1992)

Earl Wild has produced a staggering quantity of recordings: more than 31 piano concertos, 14 chamber works and some 400 solo piano pieces. Since making his first disc in 1934 for RCA, he has recorded with 20 different record labels, including CBS, Chesky, dell'Arte, EMI, Nonesuch, Stradavari and Vanguard.

Wild treats recording as just that—a recording. He disparages the idea that editing interrupts the flow of the music, fragments the piece, etc. In the studio he plays the pieces straight through two or three times so as to get a feeling of continuity. He listens to every take, and makes additional takes of tedious or technically difficult passages. These he listens to again very carefully at home before the edited tape is made.

He may be best known for his Liszt recordings, especially the three recitals commemorating the centenary of the death of Liszt, recorded by Wild before he performed them in public. The three double CDs (*Liszt the Virtuoso, Liszt the Transcriber, Liszt the Poet*, see Discog.) have received fine, even extravagant reviews, some of them from Wild's most severe critics. A feature article in the *New York Times* (10 April 1988) noted: "We have here a huge harvest of Liszt's piano music played by a terrific virtuoso who is also a stylist. . . . Mr. Wild can match fingers with any pianist alive. . . . Technique as demonstrated by Mr. Wild means a union of finger, foot and ear. . . . He is awfully good. When he plays such pieces as the E flat 'Paganini' Etude, it is not only supervirtuosity but also sheer pianist elegance." And this: "In these sweeping [Liszt] performances Mr. Wild maintains his pre-eminence in the field, blending scholarship and showmanship to achieve power without bombast. Moreover, Mr. Wild's lyricism is not merely a matter of touch but of infinitesimal gradations of tempo rubato that impart a remarkable flexibility to the musical statement." (*WSJ*, 1 Dec 1986)

Wild's recently recorded Chopin Etudes show that at age 77 he still possessed a technique and musicianship surpassing that of many pianists half his age. "His playing still sparks and flashes with much of his old fire, and yet it is his sheer musical quality that strikes one at every turn." (*Gram*, March 1993) An earlier CD of Chopin (Ballades and Scherzos, see Discog.), released by Chesky in honor of Wild's 75th birthday, received equally fine reviews. "Wild's technique still must be the envy of pianists everywhere: Every note is in place, not a passage is smudged or obscured by the sustaining pedal. If you're new to this repertoire, this will serve as a perfect introduction, for he makes the shape of the pieces vividly clear. If you're a Wild devotee, you'll be delighted anew with the vigor and depth of his art." (*CT*, 13 Jan 1991) Another appraisal voices similar sentiments: "All the qualities that have distinguished Wild's pianism over the years are brought to bear on the eight masterpieces recorded here: tonal and technical refinement, an unerring sense of dramatic continuity, impressive reserves of power, the thoughtful searching for significant detail, and a rhythmic and dynamic flexibility that always enhances Chopin's designs." (*ARG*, March/April 1991)

There are other fine albums: Wild's piano transcriptions of Gershwin songs, The Art of the Transcription, two Beethoven sonatas, a CD of Medtner's piano music and, most recently, Wild's own delightful Variations on an American Theme coupled with the Gershwin Concerto in F (see Discog.). All have one thing in common—pianism that will enchant the listener.

SELECTED REFERENCES

"Babes in Cheskyland." *The Absolute Sound*, May 1992, pp. 119–123. An in-depth review of five Wild CDs.

Bosworth, Adrienne. "Learning from a master at OSU." *Columbus Monthly*, Jan 1987.

Cariaga, Daniel. "Earl Wild: Bemused Pianist has Serious Side." *Los Angeles Times*, 13 Sept 1985, sec. VI, p. 13.

Dyer, Richard. "Candid Notes from Earl Wild." *The Boston Globe*, 26 Aug 1989, pp. 20, 24.

Elder, Dean. "Earl Wild: In the Rachmaninoff Tradition." *Clavier*, Feb 1986, pp. 6–16.

Fagan, Keith. "Romance." *Classic CD*, Nov 1990, pp. 64–65.

Finn, Robert. "Wild settles down as a full-time pianist." *Cleveland Plain Dealer*, 25 Aug 1977, sec. C, p. 12.

Harrison, Max. "Earl Wild." *Musical Opinion*, Nov 1990, pp. 374–375.

Kammerer, Rafael. "Earl Wild." *Musical America*, 15 Dec 1957, pp. 8, 26–27.

Kipnis, Igor. "Blood in the Notes." (interview) *Stereophile*, June 1989, pp. 168–183.

Kozinn, Allan. "Earl Wild." *Keyboard*, Dec 1986, pp. 52–56, 61–64.

Kreeger, Julian H. "Earl Wild: The Complete Pianist." *Clavier*, March 1981, pp. 18–19.

Maycock, Robert. "Spirit of delight." *Classical Music*, 13 Sept 1980, p. 7.

Morrison, Bryce. "Earl Wild." (interview) *Music and Musicians*, Sept 1980, pp. 11–12.

Rabinowitz, Peter J. "Pianist without Piety: A Conversation with Earl Wild." *Fanfare*, June 1989, pp. 396–401.

Redmond, Michael. "A truly 'Wild' occasion at Carnegie Hall." *Newark Star-Ledger*, 25 Nov 1990.

———. "Unbridled virtuosity, still." *Sunday Star-Ledger* (Newark), 25 Oct 1992, sec. 4, pp. 1, 20.

Reich, Howard. "Showman Wild delights in confounding the longhairs." *Chicago Tribune*, 9 Feb 1986, p. 13.

———. "Wild isn't Liszt-less." *Chicago Tribune*, 3 Jan 1988, sec. 13, p. 8.

Robinson, Harlow. "Earl Wild." *High Fidelity/Musical America*, Feb 1986, *MA*, pp. 4–5, 40.

Rubin, Stephen E. "For Earl Wild, Music Shouldn't Sound Difficult." *New York Times*, 14 Nov 1976, sec. 2, pp. 19, 22.

Scherer, Barrymore L. "A Novel Way of Looking at Liszt." *New York Times*, 9 Feb 1986, sec. 2, pp. 25–26.

Schonberg, Harold C. "Earl Wild's 'Defiantly Kitsch' Celebration." *New York Times*, 25 Oct 1981, pp. 21, 24.

———. "Earl Wild Harvests a Cornucopia of Liszt." *New York Times*, 10 April 1988, sec. 8, p. 37.

Sheridan, Margaret. "Tuned To Perfection." *Asia Magazine*, 11–13 May 1990, p. 50.

Silverman, Robert J. "Earl Wild: Pianist-Teacher." *Piano Quarterly*, Fall 1985, pp. 45–48.
Wild, Earl. "If You Heard What I Heard!" *High Fidelity/Musical America*, Feb 1986, *MA*, pp. 6–8, 16–17.
Wolfberg, June. "Wild About Liszt." *Keyboard Classics*, March/April 1986, pp. 8–9, 44.
See also Bibliography: Cur/Bio (1988); Dub/Ref; IWWM; New/GrA; Tho/Mus; WWAM.

SELECTED REVIEWS

BG: 29 April 1986; 14 May 1986. *BH*: 6 March 1956. *CD*: 10 April 1991 *CPD*: 8 Aug 1975. *CST*: 10 Oct 1979; 13 March 1989. *CT*: 9 Oct 1979. *DMR*: 27 Sept 1992; 24 Jan 1993. *DT*: 11 June 1973; 3 April 1982; 4 Aug 1986. *GM*: 16 July 1986. *Gram*: Feb 1991. *LAT*: 15 Aug 1966; 23 Dec 1968; 18 Sept 1972; 15 Jan 1976; 19 Dec 1977; 21 May 1986; 24 Aug 1991. *MH*: 27 April 1981. *MM*: Summer 1986. *MT*: Nov 1980; March 1984. *NYT*: 2 Nov 1942; 31 Oct 1944; 6 Jan 1954; 26 Oct 1957; 19 Dec 1968; 18 March 1972; 18 March 1975; 3 Nov 1981; 28 Nov 1990; 3 Nov 1992; 1 Nov 1994. *SCMP*: 17 March 1990; 20 March 1990. *S-L*: 28 Nov 1990. *SPPP*: 27 Jan 1986. *STL*: 17 June 1973. *TL*: 20 April 1993. *V-P*: 11 Feb 1980. *WP*: 10 Dec 1952; 22 March 1971. *WS*: 22 March 1971.

SELECTED DISCOGRAPHY

The Art of the Transcription. Bach-Tausig: Toccata and Fugue in D Minor. Chopin-Liszt: *Trois Chants Polonais*. Gluck-Sgambati: *Mélodie d'Orfée*. Kreisler-Rachmaninov: *Liebesleid*. Mendelssohn-Rachmaninov: Scherzo from "A Midsummer Night's Dream." Rameau-Godowsky: *Trois Pièces*. Rimsky-Korsakov-Rachmaninov: The Flight of the Bumblebee. Rossini-Thalberg: *Grand Fantaisie sur l'opéra Semiramide*. Strauss-Schulz-Evler: Concert Arabesques on themes of "The Beautiful Blue Danube." Tchaikovsky-Wild: *Pas de Quatre sur Lac des Cygnes*. Wagner-Moszkowski: *Isoldens Tod*. *Audiofon* CD72008-2 (2 CDs).
Beethoven: Sonata in C Minor, op. 13 ("*Pathétique*"); Sonata in C-sharp Minor, op. 27, no. 2 ("Moonlight"); Sonata in B-flat Major, op. 106 ("*Hammerklavier*"). Chesky CD120.
Brahms: Ballades, op. 10; Variations on a theme by Paganini, op. 35. Liszt: Paganini Etude No. 2 in E-flat Major. Vanguard Classics OVC 4034 (CD).
Chopin: The Complete Etudes. Chesky CD77.
Chopin: Concerto No. 1 in E Minor, op. 11 (Sargent/RPO). Fauré: Ballade, op. 19 (Gerhardt/National PO). Liszt: Concerto No. 1 in E-flat Major (Sargent/RPO). Chesky CD93.
Chopin: Four Ballades; Four Scherzos. Chesky CD44.
Earl Wild plays Schumann. Aufschwung, op. 12, no. 2; *Papillons*, op. 2; Romance, op. 28, no. 2; Sonata No. 1 in F-sharp Minor, op. 11; *Vogel als Prophet*, op. 82, no. 7. *dell'Arte* DBS 7005 (CD).

Gershwin Transcriptions. Fantasy on Porgy and Bess; Improvisation in the form of a Theme and Three Variations on "Someone To Watch Over Me"; Seven Virtuoso Etudes: "Embraceable you"; "Fascinatin' Rhythm"; "I Got Rhythm"; "Liza"; "The Man I Love"; "Oh, Lady, Be Good"; "Somebody Loves Me." Chesky CD32.

Grieg: Concerto in A Minor, op. 16. Liszt: Hungarian Fantasy. Saint-Saëns: Concerto No. 2 in G Minor, op. 22. Chesky CD50. Leibowitz/Royal PO.

Liszt: The Poet. Ballade No. 2; Consolation No. 3; Dante Sonata; *Funérailles*; *Les jeux d'eau a la Villa d'Este*; *Liebesträume* No. 2 and No. 3; Mephisto Polka; Mephisto Waltz No. 1; 3 *Sonetti del Petrarca*; *Valse oubliée* No. 1. Etcetera KCT-2012 (2 CDs).

Liszt: The Transcriber. Bach-Liszt: Fantasia and Fugue in G Minor. Beethoven-Liszt: Symphony No. 1 in C Major, op. 21. Chopin-Liszt: *Mes joies.* Liszt-Liszt: *Die Lorelei.* Paganini-Liszt: Etude No. 2 ("*La Capricciosa*"); Etude No. 3 ("*La Campanella*"); Etude No. 5 ("*La Chasse*"). Schubert-Liszt: *Du bist die Ruh*; *Soirées de Vienne* No. 7. Schumann-Liszt: *Frühlingsnacht*; *Widmung.* Weber-Liszt: Overture to *Der Freischütz.* Wagner-Liszt: Spinning Song (The Flying Dutchman). Verdi-Liszt: *Rigoletto* Paraphrase. Etcetera KCT-2011.

Liszt: The Virtuoso. 4 *Etudes de Concert;* 5 *Etudes transcendantes;* 3 Hungarian Rhapsodies; Polonaise No. 2; Sonata in B Minor. Etcetera KCT-2010 (2 CDs).

MacDowell: Concerto No. 2 in D Minor, op. 23 (Freccia/RCA Victor SO). Rachmaninov: Concerto No. 3 in D Minor, op. 30 (Horenstein/RPO). Chesky CD76.

Medtner: Second Improvisation, op. 47; *Sonate-Idylle*, op. 56; *Vergessene Weisen*, op. 39. Chesky AD1 (CD).

Rachmaninoff: The Four Piano Concertos; Rhapsody on a Theme of Paganini, op. 43. Chandos 2-8521/22 (2 CDs). Horenstein/Royal PO.

Rachmaninoff: Preludes, op. 23; Preludes, op. 32, nos. 1–8; Sonata No. 2 in B-flat Minor, op. 36. Chesky CD 114.

Rachmaninoff: Variations on a Theme of Chopin, op. 22; Variations on a Theme of Corelli, op. 42. Song transcriptions: Do Not Grieve, op. 14, no. 8; Floods of Spring, op. 14, no. 11; In the Silent Night, op. 4, no. 3; Vocalise, op. 34, no. 14. Chesky CD58.

Showpieces for Piano. Godowsky: Symphonic Metamorphosis on Themes from Johann Strauss "Kunstlerleben." Herz: Variations on "Non più Mesta" from Rossini's *La Cenerentola.* Liszt: *Réminiscences de Don Juan*; *Réminiscences de Robert le Diable* (*Valse infernale*). Thalberg: *Don Pasquale* Fantasy, op. 67. Vanguard VCD-72010.

Wild: Variations on an American Theme for Piano and Orchestra ("Doo-Dah"). Gershwin: Concerto in F. Chesky CD 98. Giunta/Des Moines SO.

Z

ZIMERMAN, KRYSTIAN: b. Zabrze, Poland, 5 December 1956.

> I started to play at age five and to perform at six. And it was always fun. I couldn't wait to get on stage and to play for people.
>   Krystian Zimerman (*Keyboard Classics*, Sept/Oct 1987)

Although nearly 20 years traveling the professional concert circuit, Krystian Zimerman still loves to play for people; and sincerely believes that he does his best playing up on the stage before an audience—his "sounding board." Somehow he senses a rapport, somehow picks up a feedback from an audience. Whatever it is, it can inspire him to do things in the concert hall that, he says, he could never do at home, and often it helps him in creating an interpretation. Long hours of study and practice prepare him so that he knows exactly how he will play every note; yet when he actually begins playing the work for an audience, "inspiration comes and the spaces in between the notes fill out with music and that creates the emotion, the atmosphere. No two performances are the same because this never happens twice in the same way." (Marsh)

For example, Zimerman himself was astounded at the sound of his ("white-hot, sensationalist") playing on the tape of his Chopin Competition performance (1975), but soon realized that the audience had inspired his playing, had even made him dare to do things he would not normally risk. And for his part, Zimerman always tries to give back to his audiences something beyond just playing the right notes, meaning the kind of playing that will induce feelings— joy, sadness, nostalgia, excitement, anything that will touch their emotions.

One wonders if this intangible link Zimerman has with the audience took root in his childhood. His father, a professional pianist before going into business, occasionally played piano in restaurants. Sometimes so did young Zimerman, entertaining with pieces by Art Tatum and Erroll Garner, and that experience, he says, was "a good school for getting the feeling of an audience, for making them listen to you; they don't listen." (Dyer)

Zimerman had his first piano lessons from his father, and at age seven began studying with Andrzeij Jasinski, only 25 years old at the time and taking his first pupils. Jasinski, in fact, has been his one and only teacher, beginning with private lessons and continuing all through Zimerman's years at the conservatory at Katowice. Young and inexperienced, Jasinski more or less improvised at the lessons, figuring out as he went along what was right for his young charge and what was not. Zimerman gave his first recital at age six, and occasionally performed on radio programs, but he was never treated as a child prodigy. He cannot remember whether he was a good or poor child pianist; but how interesting that he does remember being mesmerized by the stage. "I'm a needy person," he says, "I need communication to exist." (Monson)

Postwar Poland's stark living conditions naturally affected his childhood and youth. With few commercial toys available, the piano became everything. For a small boy it was a huge, fantastic toy ("a big black horse to ride on," "a place to sleep under"); later on, having the piano more than compensated for not having a television set. Zimerman was further fortunate in that his father and Jasinski provided him with books and took him to what was available in the way of movies, theater and concerts. Sometimes Jasinski would take his pupils on holidays, where they would go fishing and talk about music. "Jasinski was one of the greatest teachers in the world," said Zimerman (then age 30 and a famous pianist), "and we still talk often on the phone about the music I'm playing." (Robinson)

In October 1975 Zimerman entered the ninth International Chopin Competition. Although the youngest among 118 competitors from 30 countries, he won first prize. Even under the stress of competition, he seemed to find great enjoyment in playing for the audience. It helps immeasurably, of course, that he never gets stagefright, as many performers do. His training and attitude were well in evidence at that Chopin Competition. Calm and collected, he was obviously enjoying himself. "I remember wondering," a jury member later recalled, "whether he could maintain such a standard, his virtuosity was so crystalline, his musical vitality alternately raffish and intense and, as he threw caution to the wind, he prompted scenes of enthusiasm seldom seen at any competition." (Morrison) Perhaps more telling, another juror later told Zimerman that most of the competitors were obviously nervous, and the judges suffered for them. "Then you came onstage, and it was obvious you were having fun." (Isacoff)

Winning the Chopin Competition generated an unexpected bonus—an invitation from Artur Rubinstein to visit him at his home in Paris. For about a week in 1976 Zimerman was able to observe Rubinstein up close—how he worked, his general attitude toward giving concerts and, most inspiring for Zimerman, his joy in playing for people. Best of all, Zimerman played for Rubinstein, who gave him advice on music. "My greatest love will always be for Artur Rubinstein who I visited many times, particularly during his final years. Above all Rubinstein taught me that art is a mirror of your feelings, your very soul." (Morrison) That 1976 visit, still one of the high points of his life, has had a long-lasting effect on Zimerman and his playing.

Winning the Chopin Competition also opened doors to playing in the best concert halls and with the best orchestras; but Zimerman, only age 19 and lacking concert experience, felt unsure of what direction he should take—to plunge immediately into a learn-as-you-go concert career or continue with his musical training and education. He wisely chose a slow path, and gradually gained concert experience by accepting a small number of quality engagements, such as appearing with the Berlin Philharmonic Orchestra and the *Concert-gebouw* Orchestra. Since that gentle beginning, Zimerman has essentially dictated the terms of his career, an untypical career in that this modest pianist does not, as he repeatedly tells interviewers, want his career to get "too big." Though much sought after for performances, he has consistently resisted "the temptations of exploitative superstardom . . . in order to burnish and refine his musical gift on his own terms." (*CSM*, 25 Aug 1987)

Zimerman does seem to have an inborn awareness of a musician's need for growth and change. After only four years of giving concerts, in 1980 he stopped accepting bookings, moved to London and treated himself to a 14-month sabbatical. He worked on his English, studied scores, enlarged his repertoire, went to plays and concerts and read a great deal. He did not play a single concert, prompting the media to hint that he had developed problems. On the contrary, the benefits of this rejuvenation period, taken at such a young age (Zimerman was only 25) have been obvious. His career has moved steadily forward, at his pace, and could have gone faster were it not for his commitment to slow growth. He is in great demand in Europe, Japan and the United States, at major festivals and with leading conductors and orchestras.

Growing up in Poland at a time when limited resources made acquiring most kinds of knowledge a struggle may explain Zimerman's unquenchable desire for knowledge. Intelligent, inquiring and endowed with an ability to absorb learning, he speaks several languages and insatiably pursues (with the aid of more than 20 magazine subscriptions) a wide variety of subjects, including psychology, medicine, electronics, architecture, art, philosophy and pianos.

Zimerman and his wife Maya were schoolmates all through music school, and she always traveled with him before they had a family. They keep an apartment in Paris; a country retreat outside of Basel, Switzerland, a quiet, private spot where he has few interruptions and gets most of his work done; and they have a rented flat in Warsaw. (An ardent Pole, he has retained his Polish citizenship.) He limits his concert touring to about eight months (50 or 60 appearances) a season, and as much as possible arranges his schedule so that he is not away from home more than 10 days at a time. Zimerman hates airplanes, but must fly for concerts abroad; for his European concerts, he takes the train or drives his car. Music he loves; and it has brought him fame. His great love for his family and his passionate zest for people make him an unusually contented virtuoso.

With Zimerman, quality always comes first. Indeed, perusing his file of interviews, articles and reviews makes one think that "Zimerman" is synonymous with "quality"—a word that stands out in all the writings. For instance, "the quality of his playing had to come before the size of his career." (Dyer) And, "his career is solidly founded on the quality of his playing." (Marsh)

Zimerman is a self-effacing performer, always serving the music and the composer, never promoting himself as a pianist. Earnestly self-critical, he tries to record every rehearsal and performance (as of 1987 he had amassed almost 700 tapes from 15 years of concerts). He listens to each tape (bar by bar), comparing his playing with other taped performances of the same works and always, he says, trying to listen as someone else would listen and marking down all the improvements he would like to make.

In a typical season Zimerman offers two or three new recital programs, two concertos and some chamber music. He expands his repertoire slowly, at his own pace, each year learning new works, of which less than half will appear on that season's programs. He plays only music that he feels strongly about, works he feels he can really share with people. And if he suddenly realizes that he cannot say something with a work, he will take it off the program, sometimes even at the last minute.

After the Chopin Competition, nearly every booking required him to play Chopin's music, and for about two years he did play just that. Realizing, however, the precariousness of a reputation based solely on the compositions of one composer, he gradually branched out. Now his largely Romantic repertoire centers on the works of Chopin, Liszt, Brahms and Beethoven. He also plays Bach, Mozart, Schubert, Debussy and others; and frequently adds to his programs works written by Polish composers, from Karol Szymanowski to Witold Lutoslawski.

For Zimerman, the secret of musical structure lies in making it clear *musically*, which means, he says, that if a piece starts in a certain way, it must unfold and end in keeping with what came before. The theme played in the exposition should sound different in the recapitulation, because of all that has taken place in the development. Zimerman is so acutely aware of this sense of musical structure that he has been able to detect the cut on an edited tape of his playing, not that he could *hear* the cut, but because *musically* he knew it had been made.

There has been much discussion about Zimerman's "sound," but in truth, as he himself insists, there is no "Zimerman sound." He never wants the listener to be able to recognize him in the first few minutes of playing, for that would mean that he plays all composers alike. He believes that each composer requires particular skills and particular sounds (his Mozart playing, for example, must sound totally different from his Brahms playing); and to achieve this, before attempting to play a work on the keyboard—and bearing in mind its composer—Zimerman attempts to "imagine the sound" he wants to create for that particular work. He has been doing this for a long time. "I never practiced scales in school. . . . My technical practice is in trying to find that right sound." (Isacoff) And it would seem that his method has been successful. "When he

plays Schumann, the piano becomes crazed; with Liszt, drama becomes reality."
(Kevorkian)

Zimerman himself gives the best explanation of what he tries to accomplish in a concert. "I always try to play music, not notes," he tells interviewers, "and I'm not afraid of striking some wrong notes here and there. Spontaneity is much more important than routine accuracy." Indeed, Zimerman's spontaneity—sometimes called "freshness," "vitality," "verve"—gets much attention from reviewers. His musical imagination, deep musicality, poetic ardor; his fine sense of color and nuance; his phenomenal technique and disciplined musicianship—all get equal billing.

Above all, says Zimerman, he wants "to share whatever emotions a composer has put into the notes. It's as if each composer wrote a beautiful book, and I'm reading it to the audience." (Jepson)

Critical opinion shows more or less similar views of Zimerman's playing. Very early in his career—he was only 22 years old—a London critic wrote: "Soft tone colors, whether in cantilena or bravura, are his specialty. . . . Gentle, unhurried, highly controlled pianism was the chief quality of his reading." (*TL*, 18 Jan 1978) At age 36 he possessed a "deep-forged, stupendous technique . . . [an] intensely musical mind and heart, and a poetic and fiery temperament. . . . A very wide palette of dynamic gradation in piano tone makes his playing constantly expressive and fascinating—its technical finish can be compared to an exquisitely cut diamond." (*ARG*, Sept/Oct 1992)

Negative critiques accuse Zimerman of contortionism and small-scale playing. If some critics also "quarrel with some nuance of his interpretation, they never accuse him of sacrificing a composer's intention in order to stamp a piece with his own imprint, as many young musicians do." (*CSM*, 25 Aug 1987)

His first London recital (6 Nov 1977)—thrilling for its "technical marvels" and even more impressive for the "unaffected poise, the naturalness, indeed the inevitability of the interpretation"—consisted of just three sonatas: Chopin's Sonata No. 3 in B Minor, Beethoven's "*Pathétique*" Sonata and the Brahms F-sharp Minor Sonata. Expectedly, Zimerman was at his best with the Chopin. "Many artists have to grow old to find this kind of simplicity. Melody was intimately expressive, yet it seemed to flow of its own accord. . . . Mr. Zimerman could have been Chopin himself, playing in his room to close personal friends." (*TL*, 7 Nov 1977)

At his first North American appearance (25 Oct 1978), performing in Minneapolis with the Minnesota Orchestra, conducted by Stanislaw Skrowaczewski, Zimerman's patrician playing of the Chopin Concerto No. 1 in E Minor reminded one critic of the work of the late Dinu Lipatti. "Zimerman has an extraordinary ability to color a line or a phrase at the lower end of the dynamic spectrum and to vary the dynamics just slightly. He doesn't indulge in a great deal of fancy rubato, however; if a phrase is stretched, it's done delicately." (*MiT*, 27 Oct 1978)

Zimerman's Los Angeles performance (12 Nov 1978) of Chopin's Concerto No. 2 in F Minor and also the *Andante spianato* and *Grande Polonaise*,

op. 22, with the Los Angeles Philharmonic Orchestra under Carlo Giulini, "re-called Josef Hofmann in his prime, with none of Hofmann's frequent willfulness.
. . . Zimerman is plainly a Romantic pianist of a sort rarely encountered in these literal times. . . . The smoothness and fluency of the Zimerman technique is phenomenal. His playing is small in scale, but within its natural limits it is microscopically varied in nuance and color. . . . He makes the piano sing ar-dently, and he sustains arabesques with breathtaking lightness and ease." (*LAT*, 15 Nov 1978)

At his "sensational" first appearance (14 March 1985) with the Cleve-land Orchestra, Charles Dutoit conducting, Zimerman played the Beethoven Con-certo No. 4 with "a gentleness and fluency that served this score superbly. He connected the cascading figurations and shimmering scales in seamless fashion. Yet, while Zimerman's touch could achieve the ethereal, it also could roar mightily. The first movement cadenza's flying arpeggios emerged with startling drama, and then Zimerman suddenly dropped to a hush, holding us rapt." (*ABJ*, 15 March 1985)

More recently, his London performance (27 June 1992) of the Beetho-ven Concerto No. 3 with the Philharmonia Orchestra, Christoph von Dohnányi conducting, was "playing of pellucid textures, classical proportions and bright, distilled expression. Shot through with stinging chords and octaves, it could turn from exquisitely tailored *pianissimi* to moments of near aggression as speeds accelerated and passagework snapped into place." (*TL*, 30 June 1992)

A London critic hearing Zimerman's recital of 8 November 1978 praised and condemned in about equal proportion. "The steady pulse in the first of Schubert's Four Impromptus (D. 935) was almost mesmerizingly regular, but within this there were fine gradations of shading and a prodigious dynamic range.
. . . Zimerman's technical prowess was particularly evident in Chopin's Fantaisie in F Minor, op. 49, where the control was masterly and the passagework fault-less. [However] sections that should have been breathtaking were not; there was no sense of risk. . . . In the Nocturne in E Minor, op. 72, the touch was ex-tremely beautiful and every line was exquisitely shaped. It never sounded laboured; Zimerman possesses an uncanny deftness and persuasiveness. But this very facility lent an air of detachment, as if he were not playing from within the piece, but commenting on it." Finally, Zimerman's performance of Liszt's B Minor Sonata was "a display of consummate technical skill, of knowledge and ability acquired before the performance, not of power and momentum created dur-ing it." (*Musical Times*, Jan 1988. Reprinted by permission.)

A "daring, original" Boston program (16 March 1990) began with two Liszt pieces (*La lugubre Gondola* and *Nuages gris*), continued with three Debussy Preludes), the Liszt B Minor Sonata and the Brahms Sonata No. 2 in F-sharp Minor. "He must have one of the biggest sounds around. . . . Yet his tone is clarion and never harsh, and his range of color and dynamics is astonishing; his control of voices and his luminous pianissimo passagework are marvels. Zimerman's approach to the Liszt Sonata was go-for-broke big in gesture and in-tention from start to finish. . . . All the ideas, the shaping of the lines, the heav-ings of sound and the utterly incredible tempos he took during those pages of arm-blurring octaves were grand-scaled. . . . This is probably what it was like to hear Liszt play his sonata." (© Antony Tommasini, *The Boston Globe*, 17 March 1990. Reprinted by permission.)

At a London recital (4 April 1993) consisting of just three works, Zimerman's masterly performances left one critic wondering which to admire most: "Was it his hazy evocation of Debussy's atmospheric *Estampes*? Or the subtle blend of poetry and brilliance in Chopin's Sonata No. 3 in B minor? Or perhaps the rapt introspection of Schubert's last great Sonata in B flat, D. 960?" (*TL*, 6 April 1993)

Krystian Zimerman, an exclusive *Deutsche Grammophon* artist since 1980, has made a goodly number of recordings, even though he really does not like making records. In 1991 he made five recordings, a record in itself for him, and, he says, "too many." The problem goes back to that old familiar theme: Zimerman needs an audience present for a sounding-board, and seemingly dreads playing by himself in the recording studio. As he has often said, "I try to record live, in concert, whenever possible. I need an audience for every phrase, every note." Before ever recording a work, Zimerman will play it extensively in concerts until he knows it intimately.

His recording of the Chopin Waltzes (see Discog.) "is arguably the finest version . . . to have appeared since Lipatti's." (Pen/Gui, 1984, see Bibliog.) His interpretations of the two Chopin concertos, recorded with Carlo Giulini and the Los Angeles Philharmonic Orchestra, are both masterful readings, and "there's plenty in these youthful Zimerman reissues to explain why he won the 1975 Chopin contest when still in his teens." (*Gram*, Sept 1986)

Zimerman recorded the two Liszt concertos and the *Totentanz* with Seiji Ozawa and the Boston Symphony Orchestra (see Discog.). For one reviewer, this is "playing in the grand manner. . . . Not only do lyrical sections sing with subtlety, the big passages also are shapely. . . . In the gorgeously grisly *Totentanz*, both music and playing should make your hair stand on end." (*Gram*, Nov 1988) Several years after recording the concertos, Zimerman made an album of Liszt piano works, including the ubiquitous Sonata in B Minor; and his version of this overplayed and often poorly played work presents a new approach and a new atmosphere that are truly refreshing. Reviews are excellent: "Zimerman brings to bear a combination of ardour, forcefulness, drive and sheer technical grasp which are tremendously exciting and for which I can think of no direct rival. . . . For me Zimerman's dramatic timing . . . is wonderful, and the sternness which regulates the emotional pressure is close to my ideal for the whole of the long *allegro energico*. This is playing in the grand manner." (*Gram*, Oct 1991) "Zimerman's recording," wrote another critic, "probably comes closer to perfection in this work than any performance of it I have heard." (*ARG*, Sept/Oct 1992)

Zimerman's collaboration with Leonard Bernstein produced some incredibly beautiful music making. In 1984, together with the Vienna Philharmonic Orchestra, they recorded (CD and Video) the Brahms Concerto No. 1 in D Minor, op. 15, and the following year the Concerto No. 2 in B-flat Major, op. 83. In April 1987 *Ovation* listed the latter as a "Recording of Distinction": "The opening moments of this performance—with the horn call sounding so spacious, expansive and utterly lofty—promise greatness. And, for the most part, the rest of the recording delivers just that. . . . Here they [Zimerman and Bernstein] have a rare unanimity, which along with the musicians' deep and noble musical insights puts this recording up there with the best ever made of the work. . . . More than any other recording I can think of, this one brings out the organic sense of give-and-take in the music. Nearly every *accelerando* is balanced by a *ritardando*. Tension is balanced by repose; despair gives way to hope; angst coexists with serenity." (Stearns)

Another Bernstein-Zimerman project—recording live (2 sets of concerts) all five Beethoven piano concertos with the Vienna Philharmonic Orchestra—was never completed. The problem was one of time—and timing. The two weeks booked with the VPO proved inadequate. Zimerman found that "for a live recording, on disc and video, I would have had to play three concertos in one evening. The pieces are very different, I was changing the instrument between them and finally I decided that it was better to play the Third and Fourth Concertos in the first week, and the Fifth in the second." (Duchen) Unfortunately conductor, soloist and orchestra were unable to fix a date to record the remaining two concertos within the near future; and Leonard Bernstein died a year after they recorded the first group of concertos.

Zimerman and his producer agreed that Zimerman would record the Beethoven Concertos Nos. 1 and 2, conducting from the keyboard. The recordings of all five concertos are thus available, and general consensus is that the Bernstein-Zimerman combination is superior. "Zimerman himself directs the early C major and B flat Concertos, which become rather characterless when the by-play of soloist and orchestra is channelled through a single authority. . . . Zimerman seems most at home in the monumental and heroic account of the *Emperor* Concerto that Bernstein maps out for him." (*Gram*, Nov 1992)

Not all of the Zimerman recordings have won critical approbation. A review of his recording of Schubert Impromptus acknowledges that Zimerman is in his element with the technical brilliance required, but also notes that "he favors a rather hard, glittery sound which, in *forte* passages, can sound very hammered." For this critic, Zimerman's playing is often marred by exaggeration: fussy *rubatos*, long pauses between phrases, "ridiculous" tempo changes. (*Fan*, Sept/Oct 1992)

However, Zimerman's performances on disc of the Debussy Preludes (Books 1 and 2) set a standard that will be difficult to match. For one reviewer, "such sensitively conceived and wonderfully executed Debussy playing stands, at the very least, on a level with a classic recording such as Gieseking's." (*Gram*, March 1994) Zimerman's Debussy Preludes received the 1994 *Gramophone* Award for Record of the Year in the instrumental category.

SELECTED REFERENCES

Duchen, Jessica. "In Tempo." *Gramophone*, Nov 1992, p. 12.
Dyer, Richard. "Quality Comes First for Pianist Zimerman." *Boston Globe*, 8
    March 1985, sec. 3, p. 39.

Ericson, Raymond. "Music Notes: From Poland." *New York Times*, 28 Oct 1979, sec. 2, pp. 21, 27.

Isacoff, Stuart. "Krystian Zimerman: The Art of Communicating." *Keyboard Classics*, Sept/Oct 1987, pp. 4–6.

James, Jamie. "Krystian Zimerman." *Stereo Review*, March 1993, p. 104.

Jepson, Barbara. "In Concert: Pianist Krystian Zimerman." *Wall Street Journal*, 13 April 1987, p. 21.

Kevorkian, Kyle. "Krystian Zimerman: Intimate Connections with Romantic Piano." *Keyboard*, Dec 1987, pp. 50–56, 161.

Manuel, Bruce. "Young pianist takes stardom at his own pace." *Christian Science Monitor*, 25 Aug 1987, pp. 1, 28.

Marsh, Robert C. "Talent is key for Polish pianist." *Chicago Sun-Times*, 29 May 1988, "Arts & Show," p. 2.

Methuen-Campbell, James. "Profile of a Pianist." *Records and Recording*, May 1979, pp. 14–16.

Monson, Karen. "Krystian Zimerman: A Compelling Communicator." *Ovation*, April 1987, pp. 12–18.

Montparker, Carol. "Krystian Zimerman." *Clavier*, April 1988, pp. 10–14.

Morrison, Bryce. "Sheep May Safely Graze." *Gramophone*, May 1991, pp. 1997–1998.

Reich, Howard. "One note no more." *Chicago Tribune*, 3 June 1988, sec. 5, p. 3.

Robinson, Harlow. "Krystian Zimerman." *Musical America*, May 1987, pp. 13–15.

Stearns, David Patrick. "Zimerman and Bernstein: A Glowing Brahms." *Ovation*. April 1987, p. 32.

See also Bibliography: Sch/Gre; WWAM.

SELECTED REVIEWS

ABJ: 15 March 1985. *BG*: 17 March 1990. *CPD*: 14 Oct 1986. *CST*: 29 May 1988; 6 June 1988. *CT*: 6 June 1988. *FT*: 10 Nov 1987. *LAHE*: 27 Aug 1982; 22 Aug 1987. *LAT*: 11 Nov 1978; 15 Nov 1978; 27 Aug 1982; 4 Sept 1982; 4 April 1985; 27 Aug 1987; 28 Aug 1987; 20 April 1995. *MiT*: 27 Oct 1978. *MM*: July 1978. *MT*: Jan 1988. *NY*: 24 Dec 1979. *NYT*: 2 Nov 1979; 3 May 1987; 3 Dec 1988; 29 March 1990; 12 May 1992; 29 April 1993. *PP*: 26 April 1991. *S-L*: 29 Oct 1979. *STL*: 12 March 1977; 13 Nov 1977. *TL*: 22 March 1977; 7 Nov 1977; 18 Jan 1978; 6 March 1978; 9 June 1981; 30 June 1992; 6 April 1993. *WP*: 4 May 1992.

SELECTED DISCOGRAPHY

Beethoven: Concertos for Piano and Orchestra (5). *Deutsche Grammophon* DG 435 467-2 (3 CDs). Nos. 1–2: Zimerman/Vienna PO; Nos. 3–5: Bernstein/Vienna PO.

Brahms: Concerto No. 1 in D Minor, op. 15. DG 413472-2. Bernstein/ Vienna PO.

Brahms: Concerto No. 2 in B-flat Major, op. 83. DG 415359-2. Bernstein/ Vienna PO.

Chopin: Ballades (4); Barcarolle, op. 60; Fantasie in F Minor, op. 49. DG 423090-2.

Chopin: Concerto No. 1 in E Minor, op. 11; *Andante spianato* and *Grande Polonaise*, op. 22. DG 419054-2. Kondrashin/*Concertgebouw*.

Chopin: Concerto No. 1 in E Minor, op. 11; Concerto No. 2 in F Minor, op. 21. Deutsche Grammophon DG 415970-2. (Giulini/LAPO).

Chopin Recital: *Andante spianato* and *Grande Polonaise*, op. 22; Ballade in G Minor, op. 23; Fantasie in F Minor, op. 49; Mazurkas, op. 24, nos. 1–2, 4; Waltz in A-flat Major, op. 34, no. 1. DG 431 579-2.

Debussy: Preludes, Books I and 2. DG 435 773-2 (2 CDs).

Grieg: Concerto in A Minor, op. 16. Schumann: Concerto in A Minor, op. 54. DG 439015-2. Karajan/Berlin PO.

International Chopin Piano Competitions, Vol. 4 (1975). Chopin: Ballade in F Minor, op. 52; Etudes, op. 10, nos. 7–8, op. 25, no. 4; *Grande Valse brillante*, op. 34, no. 1; Four Preludes, op. 28, nos. 16–19; Scherzo in E Major, op. 54. Muza PNCD 004.

Liszt: Concerto No. 1 in E-flat Major; Concerto No. 2 in A Major; *Totentanz.* DG 423 571-2. Ozawa/BSO.

Liszt: *Funérailles*; *La lugubre gondola*; *la notte*; *Nuages gris*; Sonata in B Minor. DG 431 780-2.

Lutoslawski: Concerto for Piano and Orchestra; Chain 3; Novelette. DG 431 664-2. Lutoslawski/BBC SO.

Stravinsky: *Les Noces.* DG 423 251-2. With pianists Martha Argerich, Cyprien Katsaris and Homero Francesch, Leonard Bernstein conducting.

VIDEO

Beethoven: Concerto No. 3 in C Minor, op. 37; Concerto No. 4 in G Major, op. 58. DG 072 279-3. Bernstein/Vienna PO.

Beethoven: Concerto No. 5 in E-flat Major, op. 73. DG 072 286-3. Bernstein/Vienna PO.

Brahms: Concerto No. 1 in D Minor, op. 15; Concerto No. 2 in B-flat Major, op. 83. DG 072 207-3. Zimerman/Vienna PO.

Krystian Zimerman Plays Chopin and Schubert. Chopin: Ballades (4); Barcarolle in F-sharp Major, op. 60; Fantasie in F Minor, op. 49; Nocturne in F-sharp Major, op. 15, no. 2; Scherzo in B-flat Minor, op. 31. Schubert: Impromptus, D. 899. DG 072 218-3.

Index_____

Boldface entries represent featured pianists

About the Authors

JOHN GILLESPIE is Professor Emeritus, University of California, Santa Barbara, Music Department, where he taught courses in keyboard literature and American music. He is the Series Editor for Greenwood's Bio-Critical Sourcebooks on Musical Performance.

ANNA GILLESPIE and JOHN GILLESPIE have collaborated on and coauthored several books and anthologies.

ISBN 0-313-29696-0

90000>

EAN

9 780313 296963

HARDCOVER BAR CODE